THE PERFECT SAT Tutorial

STUDENT VERSION

BY ERIK KLASS

The Test Prep Experts

Edition 2.0, April 2020

Written by Star Tutors LLC
Copyright © 2020 Star Tutors LLC
All right reserved.
ISBN-13: 9798638471149

Printed in the United States of America.

A NOTE FROM THE AUTHOR

Dear Student,

Congratulations! You now have the most complete and effective SAT tutorial available: *The Perfect SAT Tutorial*. I know, because I have read just about every other tutorial on the market, and unlike many of the techniques found in other tutorials, the methods taught here are easy to learn, clearly presented, and proven to work. At Star Tutors, we have tested and perfected every technique in this tutorial. I know they work because I have been watching them work for years.

But this tutorial does not work magic. You must be prepared to work hard, complete your homework assignments, and diligently study the methods and examples. I can't predict how high your score will go. That is up to you. What I can guarantee is that this tutorial will provide you with the tools and information you need to succeed on nearly every problem on the SAT. With practice and effort, you should walk into the testing room prepared and confident.

Study with discipline and diligence as you set your pace toward the college of your dreams.

Best of luck!

Erik Klass and Star Tutors

INTRODUCTION

THE PERFECT SAT TUTORIAL

This tutorial provides you with the techniques you need to excel on the SAT. These techniques will be displayed using clear example problems, and you will have opportunities to practice and master the techniques on literally hundreds of practice problems.

THE OFFICIAL SAT* STUDY GUIDE

You may have noticed that there are no practice tests in this tutorial. At Star Tutors, we believe that students will benefit from taking *real* SATs, not ones made up by a test-prep company.

! **In order for this tutorial to be most effective, you should purchase *The Official SAT Study Guide* by The College Board.**

This is the best official source of *real* SAT tests and problems. (*Note: SAT is a registered trademark of the College Board, which was not involved in the production of and does not endorse this book.)

So why do you need *The Perfect SAT Tutorial*? Why not just buy the College Board book? The College Board book is an excellent source of SAT problems and tests but not a great source of SAT *techniques*. That's where we come in—we provide the techniques, and you can practice and perfect them on real SAT tests. *The Perfect SAT Tutorial* contains references to every single question in the College Board book. You will see these on the following pages.

PRACTICE TESTS

There are currently 8 tests in the College Board book, and an additional two tests (Tests 2 and 4) available online. We will use Tests 7–10 for *timed* practice tests (Tests 2–6 are optional). The tests will give you the practice and experience you will need before tackling the real test on "game day." We'll cover test-taking in detail soon.

PRACTICE PROBLEMS

In addition to the homework problems, worksheets, and practice passages in this tutorial, we will use Test 1 in the College Board book for extra practice. You'll see these assignments as you work through the tutorial.

DISCLAIMER

This tutorial is the most accurate and up-to-date SAT guide that we know of, at the time of this writing. But the SAT has been known to make small changes to the test's format and content from time to time, often with little or no warning. We recommend that you check the College Board's website to see if there have been any recent changes since the publication of this tutorial.

PROGRAMS

We have prepared three general SAT programs that you may follow as you work your way through the tutorial. The hours below are estimates of *actual tutoring times* (including learning techniques, reviewing homework, taking quizzes, and completing lesson problems). **The hours do *not* include time for completing homework and taking practice tests.** To determine the program that is right for you, consider the following: (1) the time you have before you plan to take the SAT and (2) your desired level of mastery.

Throughout the tutorial, you will notice notes **in bold** for each of the programs, such as when to take or correct practice tests. Details for each program are found on the following pages (Tutoring Schedules).

20-HOUR PROGRAM

Our shortest standard program should take about 20 hours of lesson time. Rest assured that the 20-hour program still covers many of the important SAT topics.

30-HOUR PROGRAM

For most students, we recommend the 30-hour program. This program covers nearly all of the questions you will find on the SAT. This is our most popular program at Star Tutors.

40-HOUR PROGRAM

If you are looking for the highest score possible and if time permits, look at every topic in the tutorial, as covered by the 40-hour program. Students with high starting scores should definitely consider this program (although these students will probably choose to skip easier lessons).

TUTORING SCHEDULES

As you may have noticed in the Table of Contents, *The Perfect SAT Tutorial* is divided into three main parts: Reading, Writing & Language, and Math. You should *not* work straight through this tutorial. The Tutoring Schedules on the following pages will give you an idea of how to plan your work.

TIMES

Take a look at one of the schedules. You can see that each lesson is scheduled for *two hours*. As described before, these hours are estimates of *actual lesson time* (including learning techniques, reviewing homework, taking quizzes, and completing lesson problems). The hours do *not* include time for completing homework and taking practice tests. For most students, completing one or perhaps two lessons per week is a realistic pace. Obviously, consider your final test date as you plan your lessons.

For each lesson, the schedule gives time breakdowns for each part of the curriculum (Reading, Writing & Language, and Math); see the number in parentheses following each list of lessons. These time estimates also include time that you might spend going over the previous lesson's homework.

Students have different strengths and weaknesses and work at different paces, so treat the schedules as general guides. Don't worry if your actual times don't match the times on the schedules. You may choose to spend extra time on more difficult topics or skip entire sections that you are already comfortable with.

HOMEWORK

As you work your way through the tutorial, you will notice assignments labeled with a homework symbol (see below). The following schedules will include *additional* homework assignments: see the homework (HW) row following each lesson. All homework assignments (those labeled with the symbol below and those on the schedules) should be completed *between* lessons—we recommend you "step away" from the material before completing these assignments.

20-HOUR SCHEDULE

Hrs.	Reading	Writing & Language	Math
1/2	□ Introduction (0.25)	□ Introduction □ Verb Tense □ Subject-Verb Agreement (0.75)	□ Introduction □ Calculators □ No-Calculator Section □ Basic Concepts (1.00)
	□ Go over "Taking the Practice Tests" in the Introduction.		
HW	□ **Take Test 10***	□ **Take Test 10***	□ **Take Test 10*** □ Basic Concepts Worksheet
3/4	□ Strategies (0.50)	□ Pronouns □ Apostrophes & Confused Words (0.50)	□ Percent □ Proportions □ Ratios (1.00)
HW		□ Study for Grammar Quiz 1 (sections 1–4)	
5/6	□ Direct & Citing-Textual-Evidence (CTE) Questions (0.50)	□ Take Grammar Quiz 1 □ Vocabulary & Idioms □ Concision & Redundancies □ Parallelism (0.50)	□ Exponents □ Tables & Graphs □ Probability (1.00)
	□ Go over "Correcting the Practice Tests" in the Introduction.		
HW	□ Correct Test 10: Direct Questions†	□ Study for Grammar Quiz 2 (sections 5–7)	□ Arithmetic Worksheet 1 □ Correct Test 10: Arithmetic†
7/8	□ Extended Reasoning & Purpose Questions (1.00)	□ Take Grammar Quiz 2 □ Punctuation (0.50)	□ Basic Functions □ Growth & Decay Functions (0.50)
HW	□ Correct Test 10: Ext.-Reasoning & Purpose Questions† □ Passage I		□ Functions Worksheet □ Correct Test 10: Functions†
9/10	□ Words-in-Context Questions (0.50)	□ Fragments □ Run-ons (0.25)	□ Basic Algebra □ Algebraic Word Problems (1.25)
HW	□ Passage II		
11/12	□ Main Idea Questions (0.50)	□ Misplaced Words □ Combining Sentences (0.25)	□ The Pick Tricks □ Linear Equations (1.25)
HW	□ Correct Test 10: WIC & Main Idea Questions† □ Passage III	□ Study for Sentence Structure Quiz	
13/14	□ Comparison Questions (0.50)	□ Take Sentence Structure Quiz □ Grammar & Sentence Structure Guidelines □ Grammar & Sentence Structure Passage ("The Same Old Story") (0.50)	□ Systems of Equations □ Factoring □ Working with Polynomials (1.00)
HW	□ Passage IV	□ Grammar & Sentence Structure Passage ("Alien Invasion")	□ Algebra Worksheet 1 □ Correct Test 10: Algebra†

* Practice Tests are found in *The Official SAT Study Guide*.

† Test correction instructions are found in the "Practice & Corrections" sections at the end of relevant chapters. Actual questions, as well as correction hints, are found in the Techniques section at the end of the tutorial. Make sure to refer to this section. All work should be done in *The Official SAT Study Guide*. These assignments are "open book."

Continued →

20-HOUR SCHEDULE (continued)

Hrs.	Reading	Writing & Language	Math
15/16	□ Informational Graphics Questions (0.50)	□ Go over homework. (0.25)	□ Polynomial Division □ Common Denominators (1.25)
HW	□ Correct Test 10: Comparison and Informational Graphics Questions† □ Passage V	□ Correct Test 10: Grammar & Sentence Structure†	□ Algebra Worksheet 2 □ Advanced Algebra Worksheet 1 □ Correct Test 10: Advanced Algebra† □ Test 1 Practice Problems: {Arithmetic, Functions, Algebra, Advanced Algebra}†
17/18	□ Go over homework and review. (0.50)	□ Go over homework and review. (0.25)	□ Go over homework and review. □ Graphs of Functions (1.25)
HW	□ **Take Test 9***	□ **Take Test 9***	□ **Take Test 9***
19/20	□ Review Test 9	□ Review Test 9	□ Review Test 9

*/† See first page of Schedule

30-HOUR SCHEDULE

Hrs.	Reading	Writing & Language	Math
1/2	□ Introduction (0.25)	□ Introduction □ Verb Tense □ Subject-Verb Agreement (0.75)	□ Introduction □ Calculators □ No-Calculator Section □ Basic Concepts (1.00)
	□ Go over "Taking the Practice Tests" in the Introduction.		
HW	□ **Take Test 10***	□ **Take Test 10***	□ **Take Test 10*** □ **Basic Concepts Worksheet**
3/4	□ Strategies (0.50)	□ Pronouns □ Apostrophes & Confused Words (0.50)	□ Percent □ Proportions □ Ratios (1.00)
HW		□ Study for Grammar Quiz 1 (sections 1–4)	
5/6	□ Direct & Citing-Textual- Evidence (CTE) Questions (0.50)	□ Take Grammar Quiz 1 □ Vocabulary & Idioms □ Concision & Redundancies □ Parallelism (0.50)	□ Exponents □ Tables & Graphs □ Probability (1.00)
	□ Go over "Correcting the Practice Tests" in the Introduction.		
HW	□ Correct Test 10: Direct Questions†	□ Study for Grammar Quiz 2 (sections 5–7)	□ Arithmetic Worksheet 1 □ Correct Test 10: Arithmetic†
7/8	□ Extended Reasoning & Purpose Questions (1.00)	□ Take Grammar Quiz 2 □ Punctuation (0.50)	□ Basic Functions □ Growth & Decay Functions (0.50)
HW	□ Correct Test 10: Ext.-Reasoning & Purpose Questions† □ Passage I		□ Functions Worksheet □ Correct Test 10: Functions†
9/10	□ Words-in-Context Questions (0.50)	□ Fragments □ Run-ons (0.25)	□ Basic Algebra □ Algebraic Word Problems (1.25)
HW	□ Passage II		
11/12	□ Main Idea Questions (0.50)	□ Misplaced Words □ Combining Sentences (0.25)	□ The Pick Tricks □ Linear Equations (1.25)
HW	□ Correct Test 10: WIC & Main Idea Questions† □ Passage III	□ Study for Sentence Structure Quiz	
13/14	□ Comparison Questions (0.50)	□ Take Sentence Structure Quiz □ Grammar & Sentence Structure Guidelines □ Grammar & Sentence Structure Passage ("The Same Old Story") (0.50)	□ Systems of Equations □ Factoring □ Working with Polynomials (1.00)
HW	□ Passage IV	□ Grammar & Sentence Structure Passage ("Alien Invasion")	□ Algebra Worksheet 1 □ Correct Test 10: Algebra†

* Practice Tests are found in ***The Official SAT Study Guide***.

† Test correction instructions are found in the "Practice & Corrections" sections at the end of relevant chapters. Actual questions, as well as correction hints, are found in the Techniques section at the end of the tutorial. Make sure to refer to this section. All work should be done in *The Official SAT Study Guide*. These assignments are "open book."

Continued →

30-HOUR SCHEDULE (continued)

Hrs.	Reading	Writing & Language	Math
15/16	□ Informational Graphics Questions (0.50)	□ Go over homework. (0.25)	□ Polynomial Division □ Common Denominators (1.25)
HW	□ Correct Test 10: Comparison and Informational Graphics Questions† □ Passage V	□ Correct Test 10: Grammar & Sentence Structure†	□ Algebra Worksheet 2 □ Advanced Algebra Worksheet 1 □ Correct Test 10: Advanced Algebra† □ Test 1 Practice Problems: {Arithmetic, Functions, Algebra, Advanced Algebra}†
17/18	□ Go over homework and review. (0.50)	□ Go over homework and review. (0.25)	□ Go over homework and review. □ Graphs of Functions (1.25)
HW	□ Take Test 9*	□ Take Test 9*	□ Take Test 9*
19/20	□ Tone Questions (0.25)	□ Main Ideas (0.50)	□ More Graphs of Functions □ Area & Perimeter (1.25)
HW	□ Passage VI □ Correct Test 9: Up through Informational Graphics Questions†		□ Graphs of Functions Worksheet □ Correct Test 10: Graphs of Functions† □ Correct Test 9: {Arithmetic, Functions}†
21/22	□ Go over homework. (0.50)	□ Transitions □ Organization (0.25)	□ Triangles □ Angles □ More Circles (1.25)
HW	□ Test 1: Passage I*	□ Correct Test 9: Grammar & Sentence Structure†	□ Correct Test 9: {Algebra, Advanced Algebra, Graphs of Functions}†
23/24	□ Structure & Relationship Questions (0.50)	□ Answer the Question □ Style □ Main Ideas & Organization Passage ("The Cat Who Lived and Died") (0.50)	□ Solids & Volume □ Coordinates □ One-Dimensional Lines (1.00)
HW	□ Correct Tests 2 & 3: Tone, Structure & Relationship Questions† □ Passage VII	□ Main Ideas & Organization Passage ("A Prickly Subject")	□ Geometry Worksheet 1 □ Correct Test 10: Geometry†
25/26	□ Difficult Passages (0.50)	□ Go over homework. (0.25)	□ Means, Medians & Modes □ Statistics □ Studies (1.25)
HW	□ Passage VIII	□ Correct Tests 2 & 3: Main Ideas & Organization†	□ Geometry Worksheet 2 □ Correct Test 9: Geometry† □ Test 1 Practice Problems: {Graphs of Functions, Geometry}† □ Arithmetic Worksheet 2 □ Algebra Worksheet 3
27/28	□ Go over homework and review. (0.25)	□ Go over homework and review. (0.50)	□ Go over homework and review. (1.25)
HW	□ Take Test 8*	□ Take Test 8*	□ Take Test 8*
29/30	□ Review Test 8	□ Review Test 8	□ Review Test 8

*/† See first page of Schedule

40-HOUR SCHEDULE

Hrs.	Reading	Writing & Language	Math
1/2	□ Introduction (0.25)	□ Introduction □ Verb Tense □ Subject-Verb Agreement (0.75)	□ Introduction □ Calculators □ No-Calculator Section □ Basic Concepts (1.00)
	□ Go over "Taking the Practice Tests" in the Introduction.		
HW	□ Take Test 10*	□ Take Test 10*	□ Take Test 10* □ Basic Concepts Worksheet
3/4	□ Strategies (0.50)	□ Pronouns □ Apostrophes & Confused Words (0.50)	□ Percent □ Proportions □ Ratios (1.00)
HW		□ Study for Grammar Quiz 1 (sections 1–4)	
5/6	□ Direct & Citing-Textual-Evidence (CTE) Questions (0.50)	□ Take Grammar Quiz 1 □ Vocabulary & Idioms □ Concision & Redundancies □ Parallelism (0.50)	□ Exponents □ Tables & Graphs □ Probability (1.00)
	□ Go over "Correcting the Practice Tests" in the Introduction.		
HW	□ Correct Test 10: Direct Questions†	□ Study for Grammar Quiz 2 (sections 5–7)	□ Arithmetic Worksheet 1 □ Correct Test 10: Arithmetic†
7/8	□ Extended Reasoning & Purpose Questions (1.00)	□ Take Grammar Quiz 2 □ Punctuation (0.50)	□ Basic Functions □ Growth & Decay Functions (0.50)
HW	□ Correct Test 10: Ext.-Reasoning & Purpose Questions† □ Passage I		□ Functions Worksheet □ Correct Test 10: Functions†
9/10	□ Words-in-Context Questions (0.50)	□ Fragments □ Run-ons (0.25)	□ Basic Algebra □ Algebraic Word Problems (1.25)
HW	□ Passage II		
11/12	□ Main Idea Questions (0.50)	□ Misplaced Words □ Combining Sentences (0.25)	□ The Pick Tricks □ Linear Equations (1.25)
HW	□ Correct Test 10: WIC & Main Idea Questions† □ Passage III	□ Study for Sentence Structure Quiz	
13/14	□ Comparison Questions (0.50)	□ Take Sentence Structure Quiz □ Grammar & Sentence Structure Guidelines □ Grammar & Sentence Structure Passage ("The Same Old Story") (0.50)	□ Systems of Equations □ Factoring □ Working with Polynomials (1.00)
HW	□ Passage IV	□ Grammar & Sentence Structure Passage ("Alien Invasion")	□ Algebra Worksheet 1 □ Correct Test 10: Algebra†

* Practice Tests are found in ***The Official SAT Study Guide***.

† Test correction instructions are found in the "Practice & Corrections" sections at the end of relevant chapters. Actual questions, as well as correction hints, are found in the Techniques section at the end of the tutorial. Make sure to refer to this section. All work should be done in *The Official SAT Study Guide*. These assignments are "open book."

Continued →

40-HOUR SCHEDULE (continued)

Hrs.	Reading	Writing & Language	Math
15/16	□ Informational Graphics Questions (0.50)	□ Go over homework. (0.25)	□ Polynomial Division □ Common Denominators (1.25)
HW	□ Correct Test 10: Comparison and Informational Graphics Questions† □ Passage V	□ Correct Test 10: Grammar & Sentence Structure†	□ Algebra Worksheet 2 □ Advanced Algebra Worksheet 1 □ Correct Test 10: Advanced Algebra† □ Test 1 Practice Problems: {Arithmetic, Functions, Algebra, Advanced Algebra}†
17/18	□ Go over homework and review. (0.50)	□ Go over homework and review. (0.25)	□ Go over homework and review. □ Graphs of Functions (1.25)
HW	□ Take Test 9*	□ Take Test 9*	□ Take Test 9*
19/20	□ Tone Questions (0.25)	□ Main Ideas (0.50)	□ More Graphs of Functions □ Area & Perimeter (1.25)
HW	□ Passage VI □ Correct Test 9: Up through Informational Graphics Questions†		□ Graphs of Functions Worksheet □ Correct Test 10: Graphs of Functions† □ Correct Test 9: {Arithmetic, Functions}†
21/22	□ Go over homework. (0.50)	□ Transitions □ Organization (0.25)	□ Triangles □ Angles □ More Circles (1.25)
HW	□ Test 1: Passage I*	□ Correct Test 9: Grammar & Sentence Structure†	□ Correct Test 9: {Algebra, Advanced Algebra, Graphs of Functions}†
23/24	□ Structure & Relationship Questions (0.50)	□ Answer the Question □ Style □ Main Ideas & Organization Passage ("The Cat Who Lived and Died") (0.50)	□ Solids & Volume □ Coordinates □ One-Dimensional Lines (1.00)
HW	□ Correct Tests 2 & 3: Tone, Structure & Relationship Questions† □ Passage VII	□ Main Ideas & Organization Passage ("A Prickly Subject")	□ Geometry Worksheet 1 □ Correct Test 10: Geometry†
25/26	□ Difficult Passages (0.50)	□ Go over homework. (0.25)	□ Means, Medians & Modes □ Statistics □ Studies (1.25)
HW	□ Passage VIII	□ Correct Tests 2 & 3: Main Ideas & Organization†	□ Geometry Worksheet 2 □ Correct Test 9: Geometry† □ Test 1 Practice Problems: {Graphs of Functions, Geometry}† □ Arithmetic Worksheet 2 □ Algebra Worksheet 3
27/28	□ Go over homework and review. (0.25)	□ Go over homework and review. (0.50)	□ Go over homework and review. (1.25)
HW	□ Take Test 8*	□ Take Test 8*	□ Take Test 8*

*/† See first page of Schedule

Continued →

40-HOUR SCHEDULE (continued)

Hrs.	Reading	Writing & Language	Math
29/30	(0.00)	Back to Grammar Chapter: □ Comparisons □ Illogical Comparisons □ Noun Agreement □ Paired Conjunctions □ More Confused Words □ Adjectives & Adverbs (0.50)	□ Basic Trigonometry □ More Trigonometry (1.50)
HW	□ Correct Test 8: all questions†	□ Correct Test 8: Main Ideas & Organization† □ Study for Grammar Quiz 3 (sections 8–10)	□ Correct Test 8: {Arithmetic, Functions}†
31/32	□ Go over homework. (0.50)	□ Take Grammar Quiz 3 (0.50)	□ Complex Numbers □ Parabolas □ Mixtures (1.00)
HW	□ Test 1: Passage II*	□ Correct Test 8: Grammar and Sentence Structure† □ Study for Grammar Quiz 4 (sections 1–10)	□ Correct Test 8: {Algebra, Advanced Algebra, Graphs of Functions, Geometry}† □ Odds & Ends Worksheet 1
33/34	□ Go over homework. (0.25)	□ Take Grammar Quiz 4 (0.50)	□ Go over homework. (1.25)
HW	□ Test 1: Passage III*	□ Test 1: Passage I* □ Test 1: Passage II*	□ Odds & Ends Worksheet 2 □ Test 1 Practice Problems: Odds & Ends† □ Correct Tests 2–4: Odds & Ends†
35/36	□ Go over homework. (0.25)	□ Go over homework. (0.50)	□ Go over homework. (1.25)
HW	□ Test 1: Passage IV* □ Test 1: Passage V*	□ Test 1: Passage III* □ Test 1: Passage IV*	□ Complete the Review Worksheet for Chapters I–VII (found after the Odds & Ends worksheets)
37/38	□ Go over homework and review. (0.50)	□ Go over homework and review. (0.50)	□ Go over homework and review. (1.00)
HW	□ Take Test 7*	□ Take Test 7*	□ Take Test 7*
39/40	□ Review Test 7	□ Review Test 7	□ Review Test 7

*/† See first page of Schedule

TAKING THE PRACTICE TESTS

Practice tests are found in *The Official SAT Study Guide*. Each test is really four (or five) tests in one: Reading, Writing & Language, Math (no calculator), Math (calculator), and the Essay (optional); the tests will always be in this order. **Make sure to time yourself when you take these tests.** Use the following schedule:

- **Reading Test: 65 minutes**
   —10-minute break—
- **Writing & Language Test: 35 minutes**
- **Math Test (no calculator): 25 minutes**
   —5-minute break—
- **Math Test (calculator): 55 minutes**
   —2-minute break—
- **Essay (optional): 50 minutes**

You should leave yourself about **3 hours and 15 minutes** to take the Reading, Writing & Language, and Math tests (or **a little over 4 hours** if you plan to also complete the Essay).

! **To closely simulate the actual test-taking experience, we recommend that you take each test in *one sitting* and use the full amount of time available for each individual test.** This will help you prepare for the actual test day, when you may spend over 4 hours completing the test.

Show all work in *The Official SAT Study Guide*. For practice, cut out and use the answer sheets and lined essay pages provided for each test in the book. **Do not look back to the tutorial while taking the practice tests.**

GUESSING ON THE SAT

You no longer lose points for guessing on the SAT. This means that when you're done with each individual test, you should have filled in a bubble for every question, even if you had to guess. For this reason, you need to create a strategy for answering the questions. You have two options:

1. **Skip questions:** As you work your way through a test, skip a question that gives you trouble (and leave the corresponding answer blank on your answer sheet). Circle the problem number on your *answer sheet* so you can easily find it later (make sure to erase any circles before finishing the test). But here's the catch: you must diligently watch the clock so that, worst-case scenario, you have about 30 seconds left at the end of the test to guess on any questions that you skipped. Of course, you will hopefully have more time than that so you can go back and actually *look* at some of

these questions, but *at the very least* you need to scribble in your favorite letters before you run out of time.

2. **Guess as you go:** If you're not sure about a problem when you get to it, take a guess, fill in the answer on your answer sheet, and move on. Again, circle the question number. If you have time at the end of the test, quickly flip through your test booklet and revisit any of the questions you guessed on. The advantage to this technique is that you don't have to worry about guessing at the end of the test if you run out of time (because you've been filling in answers all along). The disadvantage is that, if you do have time to go back to some of these questions, you might spend a little extra time erasing each guessed answer that you decide to change.

We recommend the first option above, but both are fine. Decide which one you prefer, and stick with it. You might experiment on the practice tests to see which strategy you're more comfortable with. Just make sure you have a plan in place before you take the real SAT.

PROCESS OF ELIMINATION

Process of elimination (POE) is an important, all-around strategy on the SAT. This means physically crossing off the letter in your test booklet when you're "very sure" that an answer choice is wrong. A process of elimination will not only help you focus on the answer choices that may be correct (by eliminating the ones that are *not* correct), but this process will also sometimes lead you to the correct answer simply by removing the three *incorrect* answers. You will undoubtedly identify the correct answer immediately on some questions, without having to scrutinize the other answer choices. This is great. But often, you should aggressively eliminate answer choices to help zero in on correct answers.

If you're having trouble finishing sections of the SAT in time, or if you'd simply like to confirm your pace while taking the test, the following timing plan will help.

TIMING

Not all students need to worry about timing. Many students have no trouble finishing the test in time. But many students run out of time. If this is you, read on. . . .

Because the criteria for ordering the questions varies on each test (Reading, Writing & Language, Math), the timing strategies will also vary. For example, when you are completing the Reading and Writing & Language sections (with questions that are *not* arranged in order of difficulty), it is important to try to get to the end of the test—the last questions may be easy. On the other hand, when you are completing a Math section (with questions that *are* arranged in order of difficulty), it is important to spend time on the questions that you can answer correctly, even if that means leaving some of the harder questions blank at the end of the section.

Before we get into specific strategies, note the times for each test on the SAT. You do not need to memorize these times—they are found on the first page of each individual test. The break times are given by the College Board, but they may vary, depending on the proctor:

- **Reading Test: 65 minutes**
  —10-minute break—
- **Writing & Language Test: 35 minutes**
- **Math Test (no calculator): 25 minutes**
  —5-minute break—
- **Math Test (calculator): 55 minutes**
  —2-minute break—
- **Essay (optional): 50 minutes**

SILENT STOPWATCH

The timing strategies below require you to use a stopwatch. Your stopwatch must not make beeping noises, and it must be a *wrist* watch (no "separate timers" —College Board). Check out: www.silentstopwatch.com. Make sure you practice with your watch so you are comfortable using it before you take a real SAT.

DEADLINES

Deadlines will help you avoid falling behind as you take each test. They give you an idea of when you need to finish up one passage (or math sub-section) and move on to the next one. This way, you won't fall behind as you work your way through the test. We'll discuss deadlines for each separate test below.

Note that deadlines should be used *in addition* to watching the overall time. A good proctor should tell you when the test will be finished, and will give you warnings as you near the end of a test.

As you practice using the following deadlines, feel free to use a cheat sheet. But eventually, of course, you should have the deadlines memorized (there are only 5 of them). We recommend making flashcards for each test. Drill yourself frequently so there's no hesitation on "game day."

READING DEADLINES

The Reading test includes 5 passages, each with 10 or 11 questions. Thus, there are two possible times for the passages, as shown below. After you start your watch for a passage, quickly count the number of questions so you know how long you have. (Do NOT count the questions and *then* start your watch; always start your watch immediately at the beginning of the passage.) Here are the times:

- **10-question passage = 12 minutes, 30 seconds (12:30)**
- **11-question passage = 13 minutes, 30 seconds (13:30)**

Note that these are *estimates*. On an actual test, you'll probably take a little longer than the times above on some harder passages, and you'll likely finish easier passages a little faster. But these values give you a good approximation of your allowable time. If you're taking much longer on passages, you'll need to pick up the pace.

Also, the times above give you 30 seconds of extra time for the entire Reading test. This should make up for any time you spend stopping, resetting, and starting your stopwatch. **But you should still practice with your watch to make sure you can reset it quickly between passages. You should only be adding a couple seconds each time.**

WRITING & LANGUAGE DEADLINE

The Writing & Language test (35 minutes) includes 4 passages, each with 11 questions. The deadline for each passage is below:

- **Each passage = 8 minutes, 30 seconds (8:30)**

The above time gives you an extra minute to finish the test, which, as above, should give you plenty of time to reset your watch between passages.

MATH DEADLINES

Remember, there are two Math sections: a no-calculator one (20 questions in 25 minutes) and a calculator one (38 questions in 55 minutes). The two sections are each divided into two sub-sections: a **multiple choice section** and a **grid-in section**. Since the beginning of the grid-in section often includes some easier questions, you definitely want to get there with enough time. Thus, we'll apply deadlines to the multiple-choice sections of each Math test. In other words, you should finish the multiple choice sections (the first 15 questions of Section 3 and the first 30 questions of Section 4) in the times given below:

- **§3: No-calculator multiple choice = 18 minutes, 30 seconds (18:30)**
- **§4: Calculator multiple choice = 43 minutes, 30 seconds (43:30)**

GETTING FASTER

Not all students will be able to answer every question and meet the deadlines above. You will get faster as you learn techniques and complete practice problems, but even if you're not able to get to every question, you still must be able to follow the deadlines. The trick is to skip the harder questions. This way, if you do run out of time for a passage or section, the questions you did not get to were probably hard ones. You're in charge of which questions you choose to answer—not the SAT.

❗ If you can't meet the deadlines, start skipping harder questions.

WHICH QUESTIONS DO I SKIP?

Below is a quick overview of questions that may be harder than average. These are good ones to skip on your first pass through any passage or math section. We'll get into more detail for each individual test in the Introductions of the Reading, Writing & Language, and Math parts of the tutorial.

READING

If you're having trouble meeting Reading deadlines, start skipping Extended Reasoning, Purpose, and Main Idea questions (these questions are described later). You might also skip additional questions on passages you find difficult. Don't let the time you spend on harder passages eat into the time you have for easier passages, where you'll get most of your points.

WRITING & LANGUAGE

If you have trouble finishing this test, consider skipping Main Idea and Organization questions (Chapter V, in the Writing & Language part of this tutorial). Most students find the Grammar (Chapter II) and Sentence Structure (Chapter III) questions easier, especially after going through the tutorial. Again, these questions will be described later. Make sure you can quickly identify them.

MATH

Most students will want to skip long word problems, especially ones that show up later in the test. You should also consider skipping questions that test material you're not comfortable with (yet). For example, if you haven't covered trigonometry, you might skip any trig problems. In general, don't let yourself get bogged down on difficult problems. Keep moving. And remember, each sub-section generally gets harder as you go, so, the further into the test you get, the more questions you'll probably skip. Finally, you can always go back and look at skipped questions if you finish a sub-section early.

■

The above material is an overview of our timing strategies. Review the Timing sections in the introduction of each part of the tutorial for more details. Make sure you practice the timing strategies whenever you complete practice passages or practice tests. You should be ready to comfortably put them to work for you when you take the real SAT.

EXTENDED TIME (× 1.5)

If you have extended time ("accommodations"), your approach will be similar to that described above, but of course all of your times will be different. Below are the times for each test. They are found by multiplying the given time (on the first page of each section) by 1.5 and, if necessary, rounding up to the nearest minute. The College Board is vague about breaks, but we expect *at least* a 5-minute break between each section. As always, however, prepare for the unexpected. We've heard stories of shorter, longer, and fewer breaks. For instance, don't be surprised if the proctor decides to skip the break between the two math sections. We've also heard of breaks in the *middle* of longer sections, such as Reading.

- **Reading Test: 98 minutes**
- **Writing & Language Test: 53 minutes**
- **Math Test (no calculator): 38 minutes**
- **Math Test (calculator): 83 minutes**
- **Essay (optional): 75 minutes**

As with regular time, you will use *deadlines* to stay on track (review deadlines above). Below are the deadlines for each test:

READING DEADLINES

- **10-question passage = 18 minutes, 30 seconds (18:30)**
- **11-question passage = 20 minutes, 30 seconds (20:30)**

The times above give you 2 minutes and 30 seconds of extra time for the entire test.

WRITING & LANGUAGE DEADLINE

- **Each passage = 13 minutes (13:00)**

The above time will give you a full extra minute to finish the test.

MATH DEADLINES

- **No-calculator multiple choice = 28 minutes, 30 seconds (28:30)**
- **Calculator multiple choice = 65 minutes, 30 seconds (65:30)**

SCORING THE PRACTICE TESTS

To score a practice test you must find a *raw score*, which is just the sum of all the questions you get correct on a given test, and then convert the raw score to a *scaled score*. Details on how to do this are found in *The Official SAT Study Guide* and at sat.org/scoring. We recommend you turn to the official book for more information on scoring the tests. Here are the scores we think are most important:

- Reading and Writing = 200 to 800

- Reading sub score = 10 to 40
- Writing & Language sub score = 10 to 40
- Math = 200 to 800
- Total Score = 400 to 1600

The College Board will also give you a national percentile, which will help you interpret your scores by comparing them to other test takers.

CORRECTING PRACTICE TESTS

Of course, when you've taken and scored a test, the next step is to correct it. Learning from your mistakes is one of the most important ways to improve your scores. But it is important that you correct your tests in the right way and at the right time.

USE STAR TUTORS TECHNIQUES

The key to correcting missed questions is to use the techniques taught in this tutorial. Tackling a problem that you missed while using the same approach that you used the first time doesn't usually make a lot of sense. Rather, try to determine which technique applies to a missed problem, review that technique as necessary, and try the problem again. But how do you know what techniques to use? This is something you'll cover as you work through the curriculum, but if, for a particular problem, you're not sure about what technique to use, we strongly recommend that you turn to the Techniques chapter at the end of this tutorial. Techniques, and often hints, for every single question in the College Board book are included.

! Use the Techniques chapter at the end of this tutorial while correcting practice tests.

WHEN TO CORRECT? AND WHICH QUESTIONS?

Obviously, you don't want to correct questions until you've covered the techniques that apply to those questions. Thus, pay close attention to the Tutoring Schedules (previous pages). These schedules will tell you exactly when to tackle various questions as you finish relevant chapters in the tutorial.

Since questions of different types are scattered throughout each practice test, you'll have to refer to the Techniques chapter at the end of this tutorial to know which ones to correct. For each test, the questions are categorized by type and/or chapter. For example, when it's time to correct Arithmetic questions for a Math test, go to the appropriate test, and look at the list of Arithmetic questions for that test. Similarly, when it's time to correct Extended Reasoning questions for a Reading test, find the list of Extended Reasoning questions for the appropriate test. You'll see more details on correcting practice tests later.

FLASH CARDS

There are many opportunities throughout this tutorial to create flashcards. Many of the important and more specific items that should be memorized are indicated with a flashcard symbol:

FLASH
CARDS

There are different ways to create flashcards, but, in general, there should be some form of a question on the front of the card and the answer on the back. Create flashcards for any items that you are worried you may forget before taking the test. And, of course, don't forget to study them frequently.

ANSWERS & SOLUTIONS

To keep the size of this tutorial to a minimum, we no longer include printed answers and solutions. Answers to all questions can be found at https://www.startutors.net/sat-answers. The page numbers of the online tutorial match the page numbers of this tutorial, so to find the correct answer for a question, simply go to the correct page.

/ Answers and solutions to all questions in this tutorial can be found at https://www.startutors.net/sat-answers.

THE FIRST ASSIGNMENT

OK—it's time to get started. Before completing any of the lessons in this tutorial, we recommend that you take a practice test in *The Official SAT Study Guide*. This will give you an idea of your starting score and will perhaps allow you to create a sensible program that focuses on your weaknesses. As you make your way through the tutorial and cover relevant topics, you will frequently go back and make corrections to this practice test.

Note the symbol to the left below. We'll use this symbol throughout the tutorial for all practice test assignments.

 All Programs: Take Test 10 in *The Official SAT Study Guide*. Review "Taking Practice Tests" in this introduction. (Remember, we'll be saving Test 1 for practice problems.)

PART 1

READING

I
READING INTRODUCTION

The Reading section is divided into four chapters:

   I.   Introduction

   II. Reading Strategies

   III. Question Types

   IV. Practice & Corrections

TYPES OF QUESTIONS

The questions on the Reading Test are multiple choice, with four answer choices each.

TEST LAYOUT

The Reading Test includes:

- 52 questions
- 4 single passages and 1 double passage
- 10–11 questions per passage
- A total test time of 65 minutes

TYPES OF PASSAGES

The test includes passages that test the following subjects:

- Literature: 1 passage per test (usually the first passage)
- History/Social Studies: 2 passages per test
- Science: 2 passages per test

Each type of passage has some specific features worth being familiar with. Read over the following information for homework:

LITERATURE

Literature passages are taken from novels or short stories. Things are not always as they seem in these passages. The following literary tools are ones authors use to say one thing but mean something else. You don't need to memorize the names of these tools, but be comfortable with how they work:

- **imagery** - Refers to words that trigger mental pictures (images) in the reader's mind of any of the five senses. Writer's use imagery to create moods that go beyond the simple definitions of the words. "They arrive at dawn in their geography of hats. A dark field of figures, stalks in motion, bending towards the docklands." —Colum McCann

- **irony** - A figure of speech in which the intended meaning of the words is different from the actual meaning. Guy Montag, the protagonist of Ray Bradbury's *Fahrenheit 451*, a man who starts fires, is ironically called a "fireman." Irony also may describe an outcome contrary to what might have been expected, such as a traffic cop losing his job because of unpaid parking tickets.

- **metaphor** - A statement where one thing is something else, when in fact, literally, it is not. "[A] mind that is free from passion is a very citadel." —Marcus Aurelius

- **personification** - The attribution of human characteristics to animals or inanimate objects. "Only the champion daisy trees were serene. After all, they were part of a rain forest already two thousand years old and scheduled for eternity, so they ignored the men and continued to rock the diamondbacks that slept in their arms. It took the river to persuade them that indeed the world was altered." —Toni Morrison

- **satire** - A literary tool designed to expose human follies and vices. In *Gulliver's Travels* by Jonathan Swift, the author introduces two fictional political parties, which are distinguished by the relative high or low boot heels of each party's members. Swift is satirizing the trivial differences and minor disputes between the two English political parties of his time.

- **simile** - A figure of speech in which two unlike things are compared. A simile displays an *alikeness* between two things, using the words "like" or "as." "Elderly American ladies leaning on their canes listed toward me like towers of Pisa." —Vladimir Nabokov

- **symbolism** - A literary tool in which one thing may be understood as something else, usually something bigger or more significant. The most obvious symbol in *Lord of the Flies*, by William Golding, is the conch shell. The conch shell, used to summon the boys to meetings and keep order during those meetings, represents order and civilization. By the end of the novel, the shell is destroyed, symbolically reflecting the demise of civilized instincts for most of the boys on the island.

- **understatement** - To say something is less important or less significant than it really is. "I have to have this operation. It isn't very serious. I have this tiny little tumor on the brain." —J.D. Salinger

Tones and emotions are particularly important in Literature passages. How does the author feel about the characters? How do the characters feel about the other characters in the passage? How do these emotions create mood in the passage? What does dialog reveal about a character?

SOCIAL STUDIES/HISTORY

Social studies passages discuss such varied topics as economics, civil rights, urbanization, and government. Be prepared to see dates, events, and names of people, places, and concepts. These passages may include "U.S. founding document" texts or similar historical articles; often, the language of these older texts will sound antiquated and thus may be difficult for some students. Social studies passages often include *informational graphics* (charts and graphs).

SCIENCE

All branches of science are fair game with science passages. These passages are often difficult to read because of technical-sounding language and concepts. You will very likely read about some scientific topic that you're not familiar with. And you can expect to see unfamiliar words. But don't worry about it! Stay aggressive. Because the questions are often based on concrete details in the passage, these questions may be easier than those of other types of passages. You might find the reading a challenge, but that doesn't mean the questions will be—and you score points answering *questions*, not reading passages. These passages, unsurprisingly, often include informational graphics.

■

TIMING

ORDER OF DIFFICULTY

The Reading test is NOT arranged in order of difficulty. In other words, later questions, or later passages, may be easier than earlier ones. Thus, it is essential that you get to the last question of the last passage. On the Math test, running out of time is sometimes OK, because the questions at the end of a section are usually difficult. But on the Reading test, you must strive to get your eyeballs on every question.

SKIPPING QUESTIONS

But looking at every question does not mean spending *time* on every question. As you work your way through the test, you might need to leave some questions blank. We recommend circling the number of a skipped question on your answer sheet so you can come back to it if you have time. Obviously, the questions you skip should be ones you find difficult. At the end of the test, start going back to the skipped questions. Sometimes returning to a question—or a passage—after some time away from it will help you. You might look at the question in a different way, or feel better about the passage after having answered other questions. But if you're still unsure, take a guess and move on.

GUESSING

You don't lose points for wrong answers on the SAT, so before your time is up, make sure to guess on any unanswered questions. This should take less than a minute. Watch the clock so you don't run out of time.

GETTING FASTER

It's important to carefully time yourself when you take the practice SATs in the College Board book. If you have trouble getting to the last question, follow the guidelines below:

- **Skip harder questions**. As mentioned above, work on identifying and skipping harder questions. As you'll learn in the following chapters, easier questions tend to be supported by clear and direct context in the passage. Harder questions tend to require "extended reasoning" or determining the author's *purpose*. We'll cover these types of questions soon.

- **Skip more questions on difficult passages**: Some students have a tendency to spend too much time on difficult passages and then run out of time on easier passages. Remember, every question is worth the same, so get your points where you can. Don't let hard passages drag on too long.

- **Read quickly**: You might not understand every word, or grasp main ideas, but you need to find a good reading pace that guarantees you'll have time to answer the questions. You score points answering *questions*, not reading passages.
- **Look for "time savers"**: Time savers are questions that you may be able to answer quickly, in just a few seconds. There are two types:
  - **Direct hits**: Sometimes, you'll spot an answer choice that sounds perfect. This could be a *direct hit*. Go for it and move on; don't worry about reading the other answer choices. This can be a good way to save time. **Caution:** Make sure you don't fall into traps. For example, you may think you've spotted a direct hit because the answer choice contains words from the passage, but the answer choice might be an *eye catcher*. If you find that you miss a number of your direct hits, you'll have to be more careful, and perhaps review the other answer choices.
  - **Memory questions**: You will soon learn that the answers come from information in the passage. And you will usually want to go back to the passage to find your answers. But sometimes you'll read a question and have a pretty good idea of the answer without having to go back and review the passage. If you can answer a few questions from *memory*, you'll save some time. **Caution:** If you miss memory questions, then the time savings didn't do you much good. Through practice, you'll get better at *retaining* information while you read. This may take a while, so if you don't answer many questions from memory at first, that's OK. It's something to work toward.

SKIP THE PASSAGE (GO STRAIGHT TO THE QUESTIONS)

As you'll learn in the next chapter, we generally recommend reading the passage *first* and then moving on to the questions. However, if you have ongoing difficulty finishing the Reading Test in time, you may try going straight to the questions. You'll probably have to skip a number of the more difficult questions, but this approach allows you to get to the easier questions, especially ones that have clear line numbers and test one small part of the passage. In any case, but we recommend first trying the recommended approach, as discussed in the next chapter. Skip the passage only if scores have plateaued and you're still not getting to the last several questions of the test.

TIMING PRACTICE

You will frequently work on a single passage as you work your way through this tutorial. When doing so, use the following time estimates:

- **10-question passage**: 12 minutes, 30 seconds (12:30)
- **11-question passage**: 13 minutes, 30 seconds (13:30)

Remember, these are *estimates*. On an actual test, you'll probably take a little longer than the times above on some harder passages, and you'll likely finish easier passages a little faster. But these values give you a good approximation of your allowable time. If you're taking much longer on practice passages, you'll probably need to pick up the pace.

If you have trouble finishing the test in time, review Timing in the Introduction of this tutorial for more details about our timing strategy.

VOCABULARY

Unlike past versions of the SAT, "difficult" vocabulary is not directly tested. This is not to say that you won't come across words you don't know as you read the passages. But for most students, spending a ton of time learning vocabulary words, and perhaps word parts (prefixes, suffixes, and root words), is not the best use of time. Even when you do come across an unfamiliar word, you can often use context to figure it out.

Of course, vocabulary that is easy for some students may be difficult for others (hence, the quotes above). If you do find that you frequently struggle with words in the passages or the questions, you might want to supplement the material in this tutorial with some focused vocabulary study. There are several books available. Just make sure they focus on the new SAT (2016 or later).

But, again, vocabulary is not a huge part of the SAT anymore. Rest assured that the material in this tutorial should adequately prepare most students for the test.

II
READING STRATEGIES

The act of actually *reading* the passages is, of course, one of the most important parts of the test. In this chapter we'll give you some tips on what to do while you're reading the passage. Your skill as a reader will improve by following these tips.

1. THE PASSAGE

READ THE INTRODUCTION (IF THERE IS ONE)

Each passage will include some brief text preceding the main body of the passage. There are two things to look for before moving on to the main text:

- **Title**: Read the title of the book or article from which the passage is excerpted. This may give you a clue about the passage's main idea (especially for social science, history, and science passages).
- **Brief introduction**: Some passages may have a short sentence or two following the copyright information. This introductory information is usually essential for you to understand the context of the passage, so read it carefully.

READ THE PASSAGE

After reading the introduction, read the passage—and when we say read, we mean *read*. For most students, we do not recommend skimming or skipping the passage.

/ Do *not* read the questions first. Here's why:

1. Reading the passage is the best way to understand its *main idea*, *purpose*, and *tone*. Some of the harder questions will test these topics.
2. For most students, there is enough time to read the passage and *then* answer most if not all of the questions.
3. Not all questions provide line numbers. Some will require you to remember something from the passage, or at least have an idea of where to look. This knowledge comes from *reading*.
4. Some educators recommend looking at the questions first, and then reading the passage. But this approach typically distracts the student from understanding the passage, making the reading less effective.

THE EXCEPTION

As stated before, if you're not able to get to the end of the test, or if you're missing most of the broader questions (those that test main ideas, purpose, or tone), you might try skipping the passage entirely and going straight to the questions. See the Timing section in the previous chapter for more details.

WHAT TO DO WHILE YOU'RE READING

As you read, you should plan to mark up the passage. This will help you identify main ideas and tone and quickly find information when necessary.

LOOK FOR TONE WORDS

Tone words are words that convey *feeling*, sometimes positive and sometimes negative. Some examples of tone words are: *stubborn*, *envious*, *irritated*, *pleased*, and *groundbreaking*. Tone words help you identify the attitude of the author or a character in the passage.

Darkly underline tone words as you read.

CONTRAST SIGNALS

A great way to determine the author's tone is to look for *contrast signals*. Contrast signals are words that signal a change in the flow of a sentence. Examples:

although	even so	instead of	rather than
but	however	nevertheless	still
despite	in contrast	on the contrary	yet
even though	in spite of	on the other hand	

What's the big deal with contrast signals? The information that comes *after* contrast signals is often something the author feels is important. For example, would you say the following sentence is more positive or more negative?

> The candidate's poll numbers have been slipping, but she performed well in yesterday's debate.

The fact that the candidate performed well in the debate, which follows the contrast signal ("but"), suggests that the author is feeling somewhat positive about her chances. Sure, the candidate's poll numbers have been slipping, *but* perhaps things are about to change.

How about this sentence—more positive or more negative?

> The candidate performed well in yesterday's debate, but her poll numbers have been slipping.

Now things sound gloomier. Maybe the candidate's performance in the debate isn't making much of a difference. The voters don't seem to care.

While the words are the same in both sentences, those that follow the contrast signal make a big difference in the sentence's overall tone.

Draw a **box** around contrast signals as you read.

Let's try an example. Darkly underline tone words and draw a box around contrast signals in the following paragraph, and then try the example question:

> ... The result of this diligent attention to detail may be well and good, but even the most accomplished editor has the tendency to lose the forest for the trees, as the saying goes. Yes, of course one must take care, cross his *t*'s and dot his *i*'s. Let us not forget, however, *why* we do this—to bring about art from a tangle of letters and words.

(EX) According to the passage, the author expresses which of the following attitudes?

A) Many editors today have become lax about crossing *t*'s and dotting *i*'s.

B) Editors must do more than simply concern themselves with the details of writing.

C) Editors must learn that creating artistic work is the sole domain of the writer.

D) The best editors excel at looking at details and identifying mistakes in writing.

FOCUS ON THE EASY STUFF

Don't worry about the hard stuff. Focus on the easy stuff. Every test will likely offer even the best readers with some challenging reading. The trick is to focus on the parts of these harder passages that you *do* understand. Don't get discouraged. Don't give up. Even if you finish a passage and only understood half of it (or less), that's better than giving up entirely.

> **Underline** the easy stuff while you read, particularly on harder passages. Search out clear statements that help you understand the passage.

Underline *the easy stuff* in the following paragraph, and then try the example question:

> One must wield his mighty sword against the manifest bureaucracy surrounding him, the sweeping malfeasance of our day. Do not bridle. Do not defer. But no shining shank or cutlass will do. No. Rather, put your pen to paper, and write, with anger, yes, and with resolve. Write.

(EX) One of the main points that the author seeks to make in the passage is that:

A) when writing fails, one must turn to violent activism.
B) the best writers hold their emotions in check when writing.
C) the pen is mightier than the sword.
D) any means of action is better than doing nothing when faced with injustice.

MAIN IDEAS

Passages often have one question that directly asks about the passage's main idea, so it's a good idea to consider the main idea while you read. If you identify a sentence or two that you believe may reflect the main idea—anything that you think is particularly important—put an asterisk (★) in the margin to the left of the sentence. This may help you find important information when you get to a main idea question.

FIRST AND LAST PARAGRAPHS

To identify main ideas, pay close attention to the first and especially the last paragraphs. (If the paragraphs are long, focus on the first couple sentences of the first paragraph and the last couple sentences of the last paragraph.) Often, just reading a few sentences will give you a good sense of the passage's main idea.

Indicate potential main ideas with an asterisk (✶) in the margin.

CIRCLE IDENTIFIERS

About 80% of the questions on the SAT Reading Test include line numbers, mention a specific paragraph, or refer to informational graphics. Most of the remaining questions test main ideas or passage structure. In other words, you probably won't spend a ton of time looking for information in the passage. The questions tell you where to look.

However, you still might want to circle some important words as you read. We'll call these words *identifiers*. These words might help you identify the main topic of a paragraph or quickly find a difficult or technical word. They also may help you process what you're reading, which will help you retain information and better understand the passage. Identifiers are almost always *nouns* that stand out for a particular part of the passage. The following guidelines will help you find identifiers:

- **Proper nouns**: The best identifiers are proper nouns, such as the name of a city, organization, book, movie, or person (just circle last names). These words will be *capitalized*.
- **Titles**: Identifiers may be the specific title or designation of a concepts or idea, such as *pharming* or *demographic immersion*. These identifiers are often *not* capitalized.
- **Other nouns**: You can also circle other nouns, usually technical words, such as *antithrombin* or *oligarchy*.

WORDS OF CAUTION

- Do not circle **numbers** or **dates**. These are great identifiers, but they are fairly easy to spot without being circled.
- Do not circle words that show up too frequently, perhaps more than three or four times in a passage. For example, the word *biplane* is likely <u>not</u> a good identifier for a passage on *biplanes* because the word is probably used throughout the passage. Similarly, *George Washington* is <u>not</u> a good identifier for a passage that focuses on *George Washington* (but *John Adams* might be).

Don't get carried away with identifiers. If you've worked through our ACT curriculum, you know that identifiers are extremely important for that test; there's often no other easy way to find information in the passage. On the SAT, however, you usually won't need them. Use them as a way to keep track of important words and concepts as you read. And of course, if they come in handy while looking for information, great.

Circle identifiers as you read the passage.

■

Below is a summary of what to mark up while you read a passage:

- Darkly underline tone words
- Box contrast signals
- Underline the easy stuff (especially main ideas)
- Indicate main ideas with an asterisk
- Circle identifiers

You will have plenty of opportunities to practice these markups on the following pages and on homework passages.

2. CONTEXT

ANSWER QUESTIONS USING CONTEXT

Context – the parts before or after a statement that can influence its meaning.

Answering questions using context is analogous to figuring out the meaning of an unknown word by using the context of the sentence in which the word is found. You must answer questions *contextually*, using the information in the passage. This simple-sounding rule is perhaps the most important one found in this tutorial:

 Make sure your answer to any question is clearly stated or supported by context.

ANSWER QUESTIONS BEFORE LOOKING AT THE ANSWER CHOICES

This is one of the best ways to answer questions contextually. This approach will force you to use the information in the passage to find your answer, and it will eliminate the temptation of picking answer choices that sound correct *out* of context.

> When the question tells you where to look, usually with given line numbers, answer the question *before* looking at the answer choices.

THE EXCEPTION: BROAD OR GENERAL QUESTIONS

When the question is broad or if it covers a large part of the passage (such as a main idea question), you might have to look at the answer choices first and *then* use the context of the passage. See the following figure:

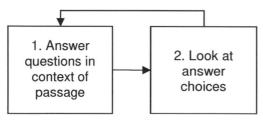

Questions with line
numbers or identifiers

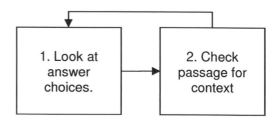

Broad questions and
most main idea questions

Remember, regardless of whether you look at the answer choices before or after answering the question, you will still answer *all* questions using the context of the passage.

USE BRACKETS TO KEEP TRACK OF WHAT TO REREAD

If the question gives line numbers, draw a *bracket* to the left of the passage to keep track of what to reread. This is faster than underlining and won't interfere with the underlines you may have already drawn.

But keep in mind: you should be prepared to read several lines above and/or below the given line numbers to find your answer. If the specified lines are near the beginning of a paragraph, go back and start reading from the paragraph's first sentence. If the lines are near the end of a paragraph, you might read to the end of that paragraph. In short:

/ **The correct answer is often <u>not</u> found in the lines specified in the question.**

3. ANSWERING THE QUESTIONS

READ THE QUESTIONS CAREFULLY

There are three main reasons why it is important to carefully read a given question before trying to answer it:

1. Often one or two answer choices are absolutely true according to the *passage* yet don't properly answer the *question*.
2. Words in the question may help identify its *type* (as listed below). Different types of questions will be answered in different ways.
3. The question may give clues (identifiers) that will help you know where to look in the passage to find your answer. (Of course, usually these "clues" are line numbers or the mention of a paragraph.)

TYPES OF QUESTIONS

The SAT uses several different types of questions on the Reading Test. The list below is roughly in order of most common to least:

- Direct
- Citing Textual Evidence (CTE)
- Extended reasoning
- Purpose
- Words in Context (WIC)
- Main Idea
- Comparison
- Informational Graphics (IG)
- Tone
- Structure
- Relationship

We'll get into each of these question types in the next chapter.

ANSWER CHOICES

ELIMINATING ANSWER CHOICES

Eliminating answer choices that you know are incorrect, particularly when you don't spot the correct answer right away, is an essential technique on the Reading Test. We call this "Process of Elimination" (POE). Usually, anywhere from one to three answer choices can be eliminated using context. The following elimination methods, listed roughly in order of importance, will be covered on the following pages:

- Eye Catchers
- Not Mentioned
- False
- Every Word Counts
- Too Strong
- Tone

When we introduce an elimination method, you'll see the following symbol:

CAMOUFLAGED ANSWER CHOICES

The SAT likes to *camouflage* the correct answers with words that are different from, and often more *difficult* than, the words used in the passage. For lack of understanding, students are often tempted to eliminate these answer choices.

! **Just because the words in an answer choice are different from those in the passage, don't assume the answer choice is wrong. It may be *camouflaged*.**

III
QUESTION TYPES

This chapter will get into the different types of questions that show up on the test. Different types of questions should be approached in different ways. Understanding and practicing these different strategies is one of the keys to success on the Reading Test. We'll also cover methods for eliminating answer choices in this chapter.

1. DIRECT AND CITING-TEXTUAL-EVIDENCE (CTE) QUESTIONS

Now it's time to answer some questions. We'll use the abridged passages on the following pages to introduce each type of question. **Note that real SAT passages will be longer, and will have 10 or 11 questions each.** We'll see plenty of these in the homework assignments and practice tests.

Remember, we'll be using *context* as we answer the questions, often by answering questions *before* looking at the answer choices (review the Context section of Chapter II if necessary).

Don't forget to mark up these passages while you read them:

- Darkly underline tone words
- Box contrast signals
- Underline the easy stuff (especially main ideas)
- Indicate main ideas with an asterisk
- Circle identifiers

DIRECT QUESTIONS

Direct questions ask you to find information that is *explicitly stated* in the text. This doesn't mean these questions will necessarily be easy—the context may be difficult to understand, or the answer choices may be camouflaged—but these questions are usually easier than those that require you to *infer* something from the passage, such as Extended reasoning questions (to be discussed soon).

 Direct questions are probably easier to identify by *default*. Most of the other question types have clear keywords, such as "central idea" (Main Idea question) or "implies" (Extended reasoning question). If a question does not seem to fit into another category, it's probably a Direct question.

This passage is adapted from Hugh Johnson, *The World of Trees*. ©2010 by University of California Press.

Darwin could have been more specific. Not of all landscapes, but of most, he could have said: "trees form the chief embellishment." Of all plants they are the most prominent and the most permanent, the ones that set the scene and dictate the
Line atmosphere. Trees define the character of a landscape, proclaim its climate, divulge
5 the properties of its soil—even confirm the preoccupation of its people.

I wrote the first edition of this book 37 years ago, in the excitement of discovering for the first time the beauty and diversity there is in trees, and dismay at seeing the principal and biggest trees around me suddenly dying. In 1973 Dutch elm disease had just arrived. Within five years it had destroyed the landscape where I had come to live,
10 in the east of England.

I remember a before-and-after sequence of two photographs in *Time* magazine. Before: main street in some New England town; all harmony; comely cream clapboard dappled with light from the crowns of an avenue of tremendous elms. After: the elms gone; comeliness has become nakedness. What was all proportion and peace is
15 desolate.

It was partly in impotent protest that I started this book. What, I asked, can we do and what should we plant to restore the serenity we had lost? Over time the question has answered itself: in East Anglia oaks, ashes, and willows now fill many of the spaces and delineate the devastated skyline. But as soon as I started to investigate, to
20 visit botanical gardens and get lost in forests, above all simply to look around me with an inquiring mind, I discovered a variety of beauty and meaning I had never suspected.

First, make sure you marked up the passage appropriately:

- Did you underline tone words? Some examples include "excitement" (line 6), "beauty" (lines 7 and 21), "dismay" (line 7), and "devastated" (line 19) (there are several others).

- Did you draw a box around the important contrast signal ("But") in line 19?

- Did you circle some identifiers? Proper nouns, such as "Darwin," "Dutch elm disease," "England," "*Time* magazine," and "East Anglia" are the most obvious identifiers.

Start getting into the habit of quickly and efficiently marking up passages as you read. Make sure you practice this now, so that it becomes second nature when you start taking practice tests.

Let's try a Direct question. This one's fairly straightforward, just to get us started:

(EX) 1. In the first paragraph (lines 1–5), the author indicates that the preoccupation of a landscape's inhabitants may be

A line number is given, so go back and take a quick look at context. Remember, it's usually a good idea to check context *before* looking at the answer choices. What does the author say about "the preoccupation of a landscape's inhabitants"?

Now let's check the answer choices:

A) determined by the region's climate and soil properties.
B) associated with the scientific study of plants and trees.
C) influenced by the sudden destruction of trees due to disease.
D) verified by the types of trees found in the region.

Let's look at a common method for eliminating answer choices:

⊘ WATCH OUT FOR EYE CATCHERS

Eye catchers are words or phrases that come directly from the passage but are not part of the correct answer. Students tend to be attracted to answer choices with eye catchers because they recognize these words or phrases from the passage. But, as discussed in the last chapter, correct answers will often *not* be written with the exact words of the passage (they may be *camouflaged*, as we saw in the question above). Before you select an answer choice with an eye catcher, be absolutely sure it answers the question correctly.

Go back to Question 1. Do you see the eye catchers in the incorrect answer choices?

Here's another Direct question:

(EX) 2.   The aspect of trees that the author finds most impressive is their

The challenge to this question is finding the appropriate context in the passage (note that the question does not provide line numbers). But do you remember the contrast signal that you boxed in line 19 ("But")? What follows is often important. Try to answer the question using this context (don't look at the answer choices yet).

Can you identify the answer that best reflects this statement?

A) resilience
B) mystery
C) size
D) diversity

CITING-TEXTUAL-EVIDENCE (CTE) QUESTIONS

Citing-Textual-Evidence, or CTE, questions frequently follow Direct questions, especially Direct questions that don't provide line numbers. These questions ask you to identify support (context) in the passage for your answer to the question that comes before it. There are a few things to keep in mind on CTE questions:

- **You already did the work!** If you were proactive on the question that preceded the CTE question, you probably already have the correct answer. Students who diligently use context will usually find CTE questions relatively easy. In essence, you did the work before you got to the question.

- **Go back to the drawing board**: If none of the answer choices support your answer to the previous question, you probably missed the previous question. Double check your answer.

- **Look ahead**: Always be looking ahead for CTE questions. If you're having trouble finding context for the question that precedes the CTE question, especially if there are no line numbers provided in the question, look at the answer choices of the following CTE question. One of these answer choices, of course, will lead you to the correct answer of the previous question.

CTE questions are generally worded as follows: "Which choice provides the best evidence for the answer to the previous question?" You can also look at the answer choices, which display line numbers followed by parenthetical quotes from the passage.

Here's a Citing-Textual-Evidence question, based on the previous question.

(EX) 3. Which choice provides the best evidence for the answer to the previous question?

    A) Lines 1–2 ("Darwin . . . embellishment'")
    B) Lines 6–7 ("I . . . trees")
    C) Lines 14–15 ("What . . . desolate")
    D) Lines 21 ("I discovered . . . suspected")

STAND-ALONE CTE QUESTIONS

While most CTE questions refer to the previous question, some will simply ask which answer choice best supports a statement or claim given *in the question itself*. These are often easier because you won't have to worry about answering any previous questions correctly. But there aren't many of these, perhaps just a couple per test. A common mistake is to skip the question, assuming, by glancing at the answer choices, that it's a previous-question one, so make sure you watch out for these stand-alone CTE questions.

 Stand-alone CTE questions start like regular CTE questions: "Which choice provides the best evidence for the . . ." But read the rest of the question carefully. A claim or statement will be given that you need to find support for. **Note that stand-alone CTE questions, at a glance, are typically longer than regular CTE questions.**

(EX) 4. Which choice provides the best evidence for the claim that when one type of tree is destroyed by a disease, other types of trees may take its place?

    A) Lines 8–10 ("In 1973 . . . England")
    B) Lines 12–14 ("Before . . . nakedness")
    C) Lines 17–18 ("Over . . . itself")
    D) Lines 18–19 ("in East Anglia . . . skyline")

As stated earlier, Direct questions are not necessarily easy. If the context is difficult, the question might be difficult:

(EX) 5.   According to the passage, when the author started writing his book, he was

Once again, try to answer the question, using context, before you look at the answer choices. Hint: If you can't quickly find the appropriate context, always check to see if the next question is a CTE one. In this case, it is! (We may have expected this, since this question provides no line numbers.)

If you're comfortable with the vocabulary here, the answer is straightforward. Otherwise, the answer may be difficult to find. Can you spot it?

   A)   concerned that his book will not find a large readership.
   B)   doubtful of his ability to effect real change with his writing.
   C)   confident that his book will answer the questions related to the destruction of trees.
   D)   encouraged by changes that he sees in botanical gardens and forests.

⊘ ELIMINATE ANSWER CHOICES THAT ARE NOT MENTIONED

This is probably the most commonly used elimination technique. Especially look for **specific references** in the answer choices that are not mentioned in the passage (answer choices that are vague or broad are more difficult to eliminate using this technique).

Look back to Question 5. Do you see an answer choice that can be eliminated using the Not Mentioned technique? In addition, can you eliminate any answers with obvious eye catchers?

(EX) 6. Which choice provides the best evidence for the answer to the previous question?

   A) Lines 6–7 ("I . . . trees")
   B) Lines 9–10 ("Within . . . England")
   C) Lines 16 ("It . . book")
   D) Lines 17–18 ("Over . . . itself")

■

CORRECTIONS: DIRECT QUESTIONS

Now's a good time to go back to Practice Test 10 (which you should have completed already) and correct all missed Direct questions and associated Citing-Textual-Evidence questions. See Section 9 (Reading: Practice & Corrections) on page 116 for more details about correcting practice tests. The actual questions to correct for each test, as well as line numbers and other hints, are found in the Techniques section at the end of this tutorial.

2. EXTENDED REASONING AND PURPOSE QUESTIONS

EXTENDED REASONING QUESTIONS

Extended reasoning questions require you to go *beyond* the text to find the answers. This doesn't mean that you'll be making things up—you still must use context:

/ Even when you must "extend your reasoning" beyond the text, the answers, as always, must be supported by the passage.

While answering these questions, always check for additional context in the passage that may support your answer, and be prepared to occasionally use *logic*.

MINIMIZE YOUR "EXTENDED REASONING"

The challenge to Extended reasoning questions usually depends on how far your reasoning must be extended. In other words, how clearly does the passage support the correct answer? How much do you have to "read into it"? A good rule of thumb:

/ Go with the answer choice that requires the least amount of extended reasoning.

Also, don't be surprised if some questions that sound like Extended reasoning questions (because of keywords in the question such as *implies* or *suggests*) are actually Direct questions, with clear and explicit supportive context. Don't make questions harder than they need to be. If an answer choice is clearly supported by context, go for it.

Extended reasoning questions usually include words such as:
- implies
- infer (for example: "it can reasonably be inferred")
- most (for example: "most likely" or "most strongly")
- suggests
- apparently
- seems

Below are some very short "passages" and examples that will help you get the feel for these types of questions:

Writing my first screenplay was not something I considered trying alone. Late at night, when my characters fell flat, I'd read a few words of *Casablanca*. When my action felt forced, I'd read from *Jaws*. When I needed mystery, just a few lines from *Chinatown* would do. And dialogue? I'd turn to my old worn and dog-eared copy of *Annie Hall*.

(EX) 1. Which of the following statements is most likely true according to the passage?

A) The narrator collaborated with other writers while writing his screenplay.
B) There is wide acceptance among screenwriters about which screenplays are the most influential.
C) The narrator frequently found inspiration from other screenplays.
D) The narrator based different scenes of his first screenplay on similar scenes from other well-known screenplays.

"Harry," said Basil Hallward, looking him straight in the face, "every portrait that is painted with feeling is a portrait of the artist, not the sitter. The sitter is merely the accident, the occasion. It is not he who is revealed by the painter; it is rather the painter who, on the coloured canvas, reveals himself." (Oscar Wilde, *The Picture of Dorian Gray*)

(EX) 2. Which choice best describes the statements of Hallward in the passage?

A) The best painters are more interested in self-portraits than in portraits of other sitters.
B) The painter's character is revealed in the painting, regardless of the subject.
C) Painters consciously use their subjects to reveal their own appearances.
D) Painters must carefully look for sitters who reflect their own beliefs.

To go into solitude, a man needs to retire as much from his chamber as from society. I am not solitary whilst I read and write, though nobody is with me. (Ralph Waldo Emerson, "Nature")

(EX) 3. What does the author imply about "solitude"?

A) Only when one is completely alone does one experience solitude.
B) People often feel solitude even among company.
C) To find solitude, one must leave familiar comforts.
D) The type of books people read can determine their level of solitude.

I crossed into the Eastern time zone and then over the Blue River, which was a brown creek. Blue, Green, Red: yes—yet who ever heard of a Brown River? For some reason, the farther west the river and the scarcer the water, the more honest the names become: Stinking Water Branch, Dead Horse Fork, Cutthroat Gulch, Damnation Creek. (William Least Heat Moon, *Blue Highways*)

(EX) 4. Based on the information in the passage, it can reasonably be inferred that some people

    A) name a place before they have actually seen it.
    B) use names to discourage people from visiting certain places.
    C) become more honest as they move farther west.
    D) consider the name of a place more important than the place itself.

PURPOSE QUESTIONS

Purpose questions ask *why* an author made a particular decision with his or her writing. Some Purpose questions are clearly supported by the text (similar to Direct questions), but most of them will require you to extend your reasoning (Extended reasoning questions). Put yourself in the author's shoes (or, perhaps, a character's shoes). What is the author's central point or claim? What is the author trying to accomplish? It's important to consider authorial *intent* as you tackle Purpose questions.

To identify Purpose questions, look for the phrases below. Note that all of these include the word "to"; it's a small word, but it will help you identify these questions.
- purpose is to
- in order to
- serves to
- primarily to
- to indicate that
- to highlight
- functions mainly to
- main purpose of the . . . is to

Below are a few examples of Purpose questions:

First ascertain the facts, said the positivists, then draw your conclusions from them. In Great Britain, this view of history fitted in perfectly with the empiricist tradition which was the dominant strain in British philosophy from Locke to Bertrand Russell. (Edward Hallett Carr, *What is History?*)

(EX) 1. The author refers to "Locke" and "Bertrand Russel" in order to

A) highlight the differences between British philosophers and positivists.
B) indicate his own philosophical influences concerning the empiricist tradition.
C) support the idea that conclusions should always be drawn from facts.
D) emphasize the enduring appeal of a certain way of interpreting history.

It is not the philosopher's job to investigate particular moral issues, such as the issue of whether (or when) abortion is justified. Philosophers are not ministers or guidance counselors, it is said, and philosophers have no greater expertise in these matters than anyone else. This attitude, however, has recently begun to lose its influence. More and more work is now being done in which the techniques of philosophical analysis are used in the treatment of substantive issues. (adapted from James Rachels, *Moral Problems*)

(EX) 2. The author includes the words "it is said" in line 3 to indicate that

A) the role of philosophers in society is generally understood to not include the analysis of particular moral issues.
B) some people confuse the roles of philosophers with those of ministers and guidance counselors.
C) the views of some people regarding the role of philosophers may be different from the author's own views.
D) the job of being a philosopher is more similar to other jobs than some people realize.

Until now, only a handful of American cities and states have experimented with voucher programs. Around 500,000 of the country's 56 million schoolchildren use voucher-type programs to attend private or parochial schools. The results have been spotty. In the 1990s studies of small voucher programs in New York City, Washington, D.C., and Dayton, Ohio, found no demonstrable academic improvement among children using vouchers and high rates of churn—many students who used vouchers dropped out or transferred schools, making evaluation impossible. (Peg Tyre, "A Matter of Choice," *Scientific American*)

(EX) 3. The most likely purpose of the clause following the dash in line 6 ("many . . . schools") is to

    A) acknowledge a fault in the research.
    B) clarify an abstract concept.
    C) explain a term.
    D) support a hypothesis.

PURPOSE QUESTIONS FOR PARAGRAPHS

Many Purpose questions ask about a paragraph or even the entire passage. We'll discuss Purpose questions for the whole passage in the Main Idea lesson (coming soon). Purpose questions for paragraphs require you to have a sense of the main idea of the paragraph. Once again, consider the author's intent. What role does a paragraph serve in the larger essay? Here's an example, based on the paragraph above (of course, you can answer this one without reading the rest of the passage):

(EX) 4. The main purpose of the paragraph is to make the claim that "voucher-type programs"

    A) have been largely overrated by their proponents.
    B) are difficult to study but probably ineffective in raising academic achievement.
    C) are definitely counterproductive to efforts for improving education.
    D) are growing in popularity despite the lack of sufficient evidence of their efficacy.

There are two simple yet deeply rooted structures that form the foundation of special relativity. One concerns properties of light; we shall discuss this more fully in the next section. The other is more abstract. It is concerned not with any specific physical law but rather with *all* physical laws, and is known as the *principle of relativity*. The principle of relativity rests on a simple fact: Whenever we discuss speed or velocity, we must specify precisely who or what is doing the measuring. (adapted from Brian Greene, *The Elegant Universe*)

. . .

(EX) 5. The paragraph above serves mainly to

    A) discuss the similarities of the two elements that make up special relativity.
    B) outline the properties that form the foundation of special relativity.
    C) contrast special relativity with the principle of relativity.
    D) introduce one of the structures that form the foundation of special relativity.

■

Read the following passage. Don't forget to mark up the passage while you read.

Questions 1–6 are based on the following passage.

This passage is adapted from Stephen W. Hawking, *A Brief History of Time*. ©1988 by Bantam Books.

A well-known scientist (some say it was Bertrand Russell) once gave a public lecture on astronomy. He described how the earth orbits around the sun and how the sun, in turn, orbits around the center of a vast collection of stars called our galaxy. At
Line the end of the lecture, a little old lady at the back of the room got up and said: "What
5 you have told us is rubbish. The world is really a flat plate supported on the back of a giant tortoise." The scientist gave a superior smile before replying, "What is the tortoise standing on?" "You're very clever, young man, very clever," said the old lady. "But it's turtles all the way down!"
    Most people would find the picture of our universe as an infinite tower of tortoises
10 rather ridiculous, but why do we think we know better? What do we know about the universe, and how do we know it? Where did the universe come from, and where is it going? Did the universe have a beginning, and if so, what happened *before* then? What is the nature of time? Will it ever come to an end? Can we go back in time? Recent breakthroughs in physics, made possible in part by fantastic new technologies,
15 suggest answers to some of these longstanding questions. Someday these answers may seem as obvious to us as the earth orbiting the sun – or perhaps as ridiculous as a tower of tortoises. Only time (whatever that may be) will tell.

Let's take a moment and make sure you're marking up the passage effectively:

- **Tone words** (darkly underlined): well-known (line 1), rubbish (line 5), superior smile (line 6), ridiculous (lines 10 and 16)

- **Contrast signals** (boxed): But (line 8), but (line 10)

- Possible **Identifiers** (circled): Russell, lecture, astronomy, earth, sun, galaxy, old lady, tortoise, time, breakthroughs, physics, technologies

Hopefully you had a number of the above words marked accordingly. If not, you might want to go back and review the Passage section in Chapter II. Now, on to the questions . . .

Let's start with an Extended reasoning question. Always try to go back to the passage before looking at the answer choices. You might not have a perfect answer in mind on these questions, but make sure you are comfortable with the context.

(EX) 1. As used in line 1, the parenthetical phrase "(some say it was Bertrand Russell)" implies that

A) the description of the lecture on astronomy described in the passage is no longer considered accurate.
B) Bertrand Russell was not well-known before giving a public astronomy lecture.
C) the author is not sure about the actual identity of the well-known scientist.
D) the author does not believe that the lecturer could have been a scientist as well-known as Bertrand Russell.

Here's another Extended reasoning question:

(EX) 2. The phrase "as obvious to us as the earth orbiting the sun" (line 16) suggests that

A) answers to most questions in physics are already apparent.
B) the physics surrounding the motion of the earth has always been well understood.
C) some questions in physics are easier to answer than others.
D) the basic motions of the objects in our solar system are familiar and predictable.

Here's a Purpose question:

(EX) 3.   The author refers to the scientist's "superior smile" (line 6) primarily to suggest that

First, note the word "to" in the question, an easy way to identify Purpose questions. Also note how similar these Purpose questions can be to Extended reasoning questions, as made clear by the word "suggest." Think about the author's reasons for mentioning the scientist's "superior smile." What quality of the scientist is the author trying to convey? Let's try to use context before looking at the answer choices.

Can you find the correct answer?
A)   the scientist believes he has cleverly found a flaw in the lady's theory.
B)   the scientist considers the woman's ideas counterintuitive to real scientific discourse.
C)   the scientist is genuinely interested in the woman's claim.
D)   the scientist's social standing is much higher than the woman's.

⊘ ELIMINATE ANSWER CHOICES THAT ARE FALSE

The SAT sometimes includes answer choices that are just plain *false*. Of course, make sure to eliminate these answer choices.

Look back to Question 3 above. Do you see an answer choice that can be eliminated because it is false?

Here's another Purpose question. Again, note the word "to" in the question:

EX 4.   The author most likely mentions the "infinite tower of tortoises" (line 9) in order to

As usual, let's explore context before looking at the answer choices. Make sure to consider the text that follows the quote in the question, and look out for important contrast signals, such as "but."

Can you find the answer?

      A) reveal a false impression of the nature of the universe.
      B) examine recent changes in humans' knowledge of the cosmos.
      C) display the humorous notions of some non-scientists about astronomy.
      D) emphasize how little about the universe we actually know.

Here's a Purpose question that focuses on the function of *paragraphs*. We'll cover these types of questions in more detail in the Structure questions section.

(EX) 5. Which of the following statements best describes the way the two paragraphs function in the passage?

Take a quick glance at the answer choices below. Note that each one contains two parts. Before answering, here's a new elimination technique:

⊘ ELIMINATE DOUBLE ANSWERS ONE PART AT A TIME

On double answer questions, try eliminating one part at a time. If you can eliminate any *half* of an answer choice (particularly the *easier* half), you can eliminate the whole thing.

Purpose questions sometimes have broad answer choices. Which one do you think best describes the organization of the passage? If you don't spot the correct answer, use POE (remember, this means Process of Elimination). We recommend you start with the first part of each answer choice:

A) The first paragraph provides a humorous anecdote and the second paragraph introduces a subject.
B) The first paragraph recounts a personal story and the second paragraph provides a general overview of a subject.
C) The first paragraph describes a contentious conversation and the second paragraph details resulting actions.
D) The first paragraph gives a historical overview of a topic and the second paragraph summarizes the topic's current state.

Ø EVERY WORD COUNTS

The SAT will sometimes include an answer choice that is *perfect*, except for just one or two words. Don't fall for this trap. The first part of answer choice B above is correct, except for one word: "personal." Every word counts!

Let's try one more Purpose question for the previous passage. Note that the answer choices are doubles. Try eliminating one part at a time.

(EX) 6. The main purpose of the second paragraph (lines 9–17) is to present

    A) a scientific study and its ramifications.
    B) a statement followed by ironic questions.
    C) questions followed by speculation.
    D) questions followed by possible answers.

■

CORRECTIONS: EXTENDED REASONING AND PURPOSE QUESTIONS

Go back to Practice Test 10 and correct all missed Extended reasoning and Purpose questions (and any associated Citing-Textual-Evidence questions). See Section 9 (Reading: Practice & Corrections) on page 116 for more details about correcting practice tests. The actual questions to correct for each test, as well as line numbers and other hints, are found in the Techniques section at the end of this tutorial.

PRACTICE PASSAGE

The following passage and questions test Direct, Citing-Textual-Evidence, Extended reasoning, and Purpose questions. To approximate your timing, see if you can finish this 11-question passage in **13 minutes, 30 seconds** (see the introduction for more on timing).

REVIEW

Now might be a good time to review the techniques you've learned so far.

- Make sure you're effectively marking up the passage while you read.
- Make sure you're using **context** while answering the questions (see the Context section). Are you answering most questions before looking at the answer choices?
- Review the question types and elimination techniques that we've covered so far (see the previous two sections).

Practice Passage I

Questions 1–11 are based on the following passage.

This passage is adapted from Eudora Welty, "June Recital." ©1949 Harcourt, Brace.

Loch was in a tempest with his mother. She would keep him in bed and make him take Cocoa-Quinine all summer, if she had her way. He yelled and let her wait holding
5 the brimming spoon, his eyes taking in the whole ironclad pattern, the checkerboard of her apron—until he gave out of breath, and took the swallow. His mother laid her hand on his pompadour cap, wobbled his scalp
10 instead of kissing him, and went off to her nap.

"Louella!" he called faintly, hoping she would come upstairs and he could devil her into running to Loomis's and buying him an
15 ice cream cone out of her pocket, but he heard her righteously bang a pot to him in the kitchen. At last he sighed, stretched his toes—so clean he despised the very sight of his feet—and brought himself up on his
20 elbow to the window.

Next door was the vacant house.

His family would all be glad if it burned down; he wrapped it with the summer's love. Beyond the hackberry leaves of their
25 own tree and the cedar row and the spready yard over there, it stretched its weathered side. He let his eyes rest or go flickering along it, as over something very well known indeed. Its left-alone contour,
30 its careless stretching away into that deep backyard he knew by heart. The house's side was like a person's, if a person or giant would lie sleeping there, always sleeping.
35 A red and bottle-shaped chimney held up all. The roof spread falling to the front, the porch came around the side leaning on the curve, where it hung with bannisters gone, like a cliff in a serial at the Bijou.
40 Instead of cowboys in danger, Miss Jefferson Moody's chickens wandered over there from across the way, flapped over the edge, and found the shade cooler, the dust fluffier to sit in, and the worms thicker
45 under that blackening floor. In the side of the house were six windows, two upstairs and four down, and back of the chimney a small stair window shaped like a keyhole— one made never to open; they had one like
50 it. There were green shades rolled up to various levels, but not curtains. A table showed in the dining room, but no chairs. The parlor window was in the shadow of the porch and of thin, vibrant bamboo
55 leaves, clear and dark as a pool he knew in the river. There was a piano in the parlor. In addition there were little fancy chairs, like Sunday School chairs or children's drug store chairs, turned this way and that,
60 and the first strong person trying to sit down would break them one after the other. Instead of a door into the hall there was a curtain; it was made of beads. With no air the curtain hung still as a wall and yet you
65 could see through it, if anybody should pass the door.

In that window across from his window, in the back upper room, a bed faced his. The foot was gone, and a mattress had
70 partly slid down but was holding on. A shadow from a tree, a branch and its leaves, slowly traveled over the hills and hollows of the mattress.

In the front room there, the window was
75 dazzling in afternoon; it was raised. Except for one tall post with a hat on it, that bed was out of sight. It was true, there was one person in the house—Loch would recall him sooner or later—but it was only Mr.
80 Holifield. He was the night watchman down at the gin, he always slept all day. A framed picture could be seen hanging on the wall, just askew enough so that it looked straightened every now and then.
85 Sometimes the glass in the picture reflected the light outdoors and the flight of birds between branches of trees, and while it reflected, Mr. Holifield was having a dream.

1. The passage indicates that Loch's family

   A) does not share Loch's appreciation of the vacant house.
   B) is familiar with the vacant house's shabby details.
   C) considers the vacant house similar in many ways to their own house.
   D) have made plans to have the vacant house demolished.

2. Which choice provides the best evidence of the answer to the previous question?

   A) Lines 22–23 ("His . . . down")
   B) Line 24–27 ("Beyond . . . side")
   C) Line 27–29 ("He let . . . indeed")
   D) Line 45–50 ("In . . . like it")

3. The passage suggests that Loch knows that the "stair window" (line 48) does not open because

   A) the window is in the shape of a keyhole.
   B) he has never seen the window open.
   C) he is familiar with the stair window in his own home.
   D) it is common knowledge that stair windows never open.

4. The author most likely uses words like "careless stretching" (line 30), "spread falling" (line 36), "came around" (line 37), and "leaning" (line 37) in order to

   A) make clear Loch desires to enter the vacant house.
   B) give the vacant house qualities usually associated with something living.
   C) emphasize Loch's familiarity with the house.
   D) highlight the rundown nature of the vacant house's appearance.

Continued →

5. The passage indicates that Loch's description of Mr. Holifield is based on

   A) Loch's recollection of seeing Mr. Holifield in the past.
   B) Loch's observation of Mr. Holifield sleeping on the bed in the back upper room.
   C) a reflection of Mr. Holifield in the framed picture on the wall.
   D) a dream that Loch had about a made-up character.

6. Which choice provides the best evidence of the answer to the previous question?

   A) Lines 70–73 ("A shadow . . . mattress")
   B) Lines 74–75("In . . . raised")
   C) Lines 77–80 ("It was . . . Holifield")
   D) Lines 85–89 ("Sometimes . . . dream")

7. The fourth paragraph (lines 22–34) serves mainly to

   A) point out Loch's family's desire to see the vacant house burn down.
   B) make clear that the vacant house is next door to Loch's house.
   C) describe Loch's close association with the vacant house.
   D) highlight Loch's dread of the vacant house.

8. Based on the passage, the statement that describes Loch's feet as "so clean that he despised the very sight of" them (lines 18–19), implies that

   A) Loch had a strong disapproval of cleanliness of any kind.
   B) Loch was frequently restricted by his mother in different ways.
   C) Loch wished that he had a different body than his own.
   D) Loch would rather stay in bed than go outside.

Continued →

9. In the passage, Loch considers the most essential structural part of the vacant house to be

   A) the roof.
   B) the porch.
   C) the chimney.
   D) the side.

10. Which choice provides the best evidence of the answer to the previous question?

    A) Lines 31–34 ("The house's . . . sleeping")
    B) Lines 35–36 ("A red . . . all")
    C) Line 36 ("The roof . . . front")
    D) Lines 37–39 ("the porch . . . Bijou")

11. Which choice provides the best evidence that Loch observes the house for many hours at a time?

    A) Lines 53–56 ("The parlor . . . river")
    B) Lines 63–66 ("With . . . door")
    C) Lines 70–73 ("A shadow . . . mattress")
    D) Lines 80–81 ("He . . . day")

■

3. WORDS-IN-CONTEXT (WIC) QUESTIONS

Words-in-Context (WIC) questions ask you to define a word or group of words. You will often have to determine the right "flavor" of a word. For example, consider the differences between the words *alone*, *solitary*, and *abandoned*. The intensity of aloneness increases with each choice, and you might have to decide which one best captures the mood or tone of the passage. There are two steps to these problems:

1. **Define the original word.** Read the sentence from the passage that contains the word or phrase in question, and define the word or phrase **using context**. Even if you know (or think you know) what the word means, use *context*, not the dictionary in your head. Sometimes it's helpful to pretend you've never seen the word before, thus *forcing* you to use context.

   Make sure to use context as you define the word. These questions usually deal with words that have several meanings, and the correct answer is almost *never* the most common of these definitions (so you must use context).

2. **Choose an answer and check.** Choose the answer that is closest to your definition. Substitute your answer for the original word, and read the original sentence. The correct answer should sound correct.

If you don't spot the correct answer, or if the context is difficult and you have trouble defining the word before looking at the answer choices, consider the following:

- **Awkwardness**: Try plugging the answer choices into the passage (in place of the word in question). When you read the passage with the answer choices plugged in, incorrect answer choices will often sound awkward or obviously wrong.
- **Tone**: If you know the word is, for example, *negative*, eliminate any *positive* words.
- **Difficult Answer Choices**: It's OK to pick a difficult word as your answer, even if you don't know what the word means. Process of Elimination (POE) is encouraged on WIC questions. If you know the other words don't work perfectly, go with the remaining answer choice.
- **Word Familiarity**: If you're familiar with the word in question, consider possible definitions, especially if the context is difficult. This can help if you've narrowed it down to a couple answer choices that both seem to work.

Words-in-Context questions will typically ask what a word "most nearly means."

The following passage emphasizes Words-in-Context questions:

Questions 1–8 are based on the following passage.

This passage is adapted from *The Federalist Papers*, a collection of articles and essays originally published in 1787–88, and written by Alexander Hamilton, James Madison, and John Jay. The excerpt below is from "Federalist No. 14," written by Madison.

We have seen the necessity of the Union, as our bulwark against foreign danger, as the conservator of peace among ourselves, as the guardian of our commerce and other common interests, as the only substitute for those military establishments which
Line have subverted the liberties of the Old World, and as the proper antidote for the
5 diseases of faction, which have proved fatal to other popular governments, and of which alarming symptoms have been betrayed by our own. All that remains, within this branch of our inquiries, is to take notice of an objection that may be drawn from the great extent of country which the Union embraces. A few observations on this subject will be the more proper, as it is perceived that the adversaries of the new Constitution
10 are availing themselves of the prevailing prejudice with regard to the practicable sphere of republican administration, in order to supply, by imaginary difficulties, the want of those solid objections which they endeavor in vain to find.
    The error which limits republican government to a narrow district has been unfolded and refuted in preceding papers. I remark here only that it seems to owe its rise and
15 prevalence chiefly to the confounding of a republic with a democracy, applying to the former reasonings drawn from the nature of the latter. The true distinction between these forms was also adverted to on a former occasion. It is, that in a democracy, the people meet and exercise the government in person; in a republic, they assemble and administer it by their representatives and agents. A democracy, consequently, will be
20 confined to a small spot. A republic may be extended over a large region.

Now let's tackle a number of Words-in-Context (WIC) questions for this passage.

(EX) 1. As used in line 2, the word "guardian" most nearly means

Go back to the passage and consider context. See if you can come up with a definition for the word in question.

Now let's look at the answer choices. Which one is closest to your contextual answer?

    A) caregiver.
    B) parent.
    C) protector.
    D) originator.

(EX) 2. As used in line 16, the word "distinction" most nearly means

Review the context before checking the answer choices. Once again, try to define the word.

Now let's look at the answer choices. Which one is closest to your contextual answer?

    A) discrimination.
    B) difference.
    C) eminence.
    D) exception.

Now let's try some harder WIC questions:

(EX) 3. As used in line 8, the word "embraces" most nearly means

Review the context before checking the answer choices.

Now let's look at the answer choices. Which one is closest to your contextual answer?
- A) spans.
- B) clinches.
- C) accepts.
- D) snuggles.

(EX) 4. As used in line 4, the word "subverted" most nearly means

Once again, go back to the passage and consider context.

Now let's look at the answer choices. Which one is closest to your contextual answer?
- A) invalidated
- B) depressed
- C) eroded
- D) concluded

Many students find these last two WIC questions especially difficult:

(EX) 5.   As used in line 10, "availing themselves of" most nearly means

Now, in this phrase, we are faced with a difficult word. Usually the SAT tests relatively common words, but you may occasionally see a harder one. Going back to the passage is essential. Try to define the phrase, especially the word "availing," using context.

Now, to the answer choices:
- A) benefiting from.
- B) working against.
- C) answering for.
- D) dismissing.

(EX) 6.   As used in line 6, the word "betrayed" most nearly means

Once again, review the context before checking the answer choices.

Here are the answer choices. Does context lead you to the correct answer?
- A) deceived.
- B) seduced.
- C) revealed.
- D) abandoned.

The following questions review past question types. By now you are hopefully getting comfortable identifying question types. You should also have a sense of when to look back to the passage for context *before* looking at the answer choices (that is, usually). For the following questions, the answer choices will immediately follow the questions (which of course is how the questions look on the SAT). Just remember that for most questions, you should look for context *before* looking at the answer choices. Don't let the placement of the answer choices tempt you to peek.

(EX) 7. Madison claims that the "error" mentioned in line 13 is due to the fact that some people

    A) tend to form factions that are often fatal to popular governments.
    B) fail to distinguish between a democracy and a republic.
    C) celebrate the idea of people exercising government in person.
    D) overlook the fact that a popular government can be confined to a small region.

(EX) 8. Madison uses the words "in vain" (line 12) to emphasize that those who object to the new American Constitution will

    A) eventually come together to distinguish between a democracy and a republic.
    B) ultimately fail in their efforts to find genuine evidence to support their cause.
    C) surrender to the obvious benefits of a republic to a democracy.
    D) argue against the idea of governing over a large region.

PRACTICE PASSAGE

The following passage and questions test the question types we've learned so far. This is a 10-question passage, so give yourself 12 minutes and 30 seconds to complete it.

REVIEW

- Marking up the passage effectively.
- Direct and Citing-Textual-Evidence questions (Section 1)
- Extended Reasoning and Purpose questions (Section 2)
- Words-in-Context questions (Section 3)

Practice Passage II

Questions 1–10 are based on the following passage.

This passage is adapted from Alan Weisman, "The World Without Us." ©2007 by Thomas Dunne Books.

One June morning in 2004, Ana María Santi sat against a post beneath a large palm-thatched canopy, frowning as she watched a gathering of her people in
5 Mazáraka, their hamlet on the Río Conambu, an Ecuadoran tributary of the upper Amazon. Except for Ana María's hair, still thick and black after seven decades, everything about her recalled a
10 dried legume pod. Her gray eyes resembled two pale fish trapped in the dark eddies of her face. In a patois of Quichua and a nearly vanished language, Zápara, she scolded her nieces and
15 granddaughters. An hour past dawn, they and everyone in the village except Ana María were already drunk.

The occasion was a *minga*, the Amazonian equivalent of a barn raising.
20 Forty barefoot Zápara Indians, several in face paint, sat jammed in a circle on log benches. To prime the men for going out to slash and burn the forest to clear a new cassava patch for Ana María's brother,
25 they were drinking *chicha*—gallons of it. Even the children slurped ceramic bowls full of the milky, sour beer brewed from cassava pulp. Two girls with grass braided in their hair passed among the throng,
30 refilling *chicha* bowls and serving dishes of catfish gruel. To the elders and guests, they offered hunks of boiled meat, dark as chocolate. But Ana María Santi, the oldest person present, wasn't having any.
35 Although the rest of the human race was already hurtling into a new millennium, the Zápara had barely entered the Stone Age. Like the spider monkeys from whom they believe themselves descended, the
40 Zápara essentially still inhabit trees, lashing palm trunks together with *bejuco* vines to support roofs woven of palm fronds. Until cassava arrived, palm hearts were their main vegetable. For protein they netted fish
45 and hunted tapirs, peccaries, wood-quail, and curassows with bamboo darts and blowguns.

They still do, but there is little game left. When Ana María's grandparents were
50 young, she says, the forest easily fed them, even though the Zápara were then one of the largest tribes of the Amazon, with some 200,000 members living in villages along all the neighboring rivers. Then something
55 happened far away, and nothing in their world—or anybody's—was ever the same.

What happened was that Henry Ford figured out how to mass-produce automobiles. The demand for inflatable
60 tubes and tires soon found ambitious Europeans heading up every navigable Amazonian stream, claiming land with rubber trees and seizing laborers to tap them.
65 By the 1920s, rubber plantations in Southeast Asia had undermined the market for wild South American latex. The few hundred Zápara who had managed to hide during the rubber genocide stayed hidden.
70 Ecuador's Zápara were officially considered extinct. Then, in 1999, after Peru and Ecuador resolved a long border dispute, a Peruvian Zápara shaman was found walking in the Ecuadoran jungle. He
75 had come, he said, to finally meet his relatives.

The rediscovered Ecuadoran Zápara became an anthropological cause célèbre. The government recognized their territorial
80 rights, albeit to only a shred of their ancestral land, and UNESCO bestowed a grant to revive their culture and save their language. By then, only four members of the tribe still spoke it, Ana María Santi
85 among them. The forest they once knew was mostly gone: from the occupying Quichua they had learned to fell trees with steel machetes and burn the stumps to plant cassava. After a single harvest, each
90 plot had to be fallowed for years; in every direction, the towering forest canopy had been replaced by spindly, second-growth shoots of laurel, magnolia, and *copa* palm. Cassava was now their mainstay,
95 consumed all day in the form of *chicha*. The Zápara had survived into the 21st century, but they had entered it tipsy, and stayed that way.

They still hunted, but men now walked
100 for days without finding tapirs or even quail.

They had resorted to shooting spider monkeys, whose flesh was formerly taboo.

"When we're down to eating our ancestors," Ana María asked, "what is left?"

1. The main purpose of the passage is to

   A) examine the unique practices of an ancient society.
   B) consider the consequences of a world economy.
   C) highlight the decline of a group of people.
   D) discuss the generational differences in a tribal culture.

2. As used in line 97, "tipsy" most nearly means

   A) imbalanced.
   B) intoxicated.
   C) askew.
   D) unprepared.

3. Which choice best supports the idea that outsiders often determine a region's value by the region's abundance or quality of natural resources?

   A) Lines 57–59 ("What . . . automobiles")
   B) Lines 65–67 ("By the . . . latex")
   C) Lines 71–74 ("Then . . . jungle")
   D) Lines 77–78 ("The rediscovered . . . célèbre")

4. According the passage, which of the following is a likely reason why the Zápara formerly considered the flesh of spider monkeys "taboo" (line 102)?

   A) Spider monkeys, like the Zápara, live in trees.
   B) Spider monkeys are now considered an endangered species.
   C) The meat of spider monkeys does not provide as much protein as other foods commonly eaten by the Zápara.
   D) The Zápara believe that spider monkeys are distant relatives.

Continued →

5. As used in line 82, "grant" most nearly means

   A) sum of money
   B) tract of land
   C) privilege
   D) ownership

6. The main purpose of the third paragraph (lines 35–47) is to emphasize that

   A) the Zápara took advantage of the foods that were available to them.
   B) the Zápara were mostly extinct by the early nineteenth century.
   C) the lifestyle of the Zápara reflected those of ancient societies.
   D) other nations sought the natural resources that were available to the Zápara.

7. The passage indicates which of the following about the Zápara's consumption of cassava?

   A) Cassava plants were not the first source of vegetable for the Zápara.
   B) Cassava plants are used exclusively for their pulp in the form of *chicha*.
   C) Cassava was once plentiful but has now been replaced with non-native plants.
   D) The Zápara consume cassava only as a source of protein.

8. Which choice provides the best evidence for the answer to the previous question?

   A) Lines 26–28 ("Even . . . pulp")
   B) Lines 42–44 ("Until . . . vegetable")
   C) Lines 44–47 ("For protein . . . blowguns")
   D) Lines 85–89 ("The forest . . . cassava")

Continued →

9. The author uses the phrase
"anthropological cause célèbre" (line 78)
in order to suggest that

   A) National and international concern for
      Zápara culture is a relatively recent
      phenomenon.
   B) The Zápara now flourish after
      recovering from near extinction.
   C) The Zápara landscape became prized
      for its natural resources.
   D) The loss of the Zápara culture means
      that its history must be carefully
      preserved.

10. As used in line 22, "prime" most nearly
means

    A) prepare
    B) supply
    C) cover
    D) harvest

■

4. MAIN IDEA QUESTIONS

Main Idea questions ask about central ideas of the text. For example:

- What is the passage about?
- How would you summarize the passage?
- What is the principle argument expressed in the passage?
- What is the passage's point of view?

When you recognize a Main Idea question, watch out for answer choices that are absolutely *true*, according to the passage, but don't reflect the passage's main idea. Often, two or more answer choices will be supported by context, but only one will best capture the passage's main idea.

 Main Idea questions usually include phrases such as:
- main idea
- main point
- central idea
- central claim
- central problem
- summary
- point of view

PROCESS OF ELIMINATION (POE)

Sometimes, the correct answer to a Main Idea question is difficult to spot. Other types of questions usually refer to specific places in a passage, so you'll often find correct answers right away. The correct answer to a Main Idea question, however, will usually be based on a broader section of the passage, if not the *entire* passage, so the answer may be less obvious. Thus, we often recommend POE on these types of questions.

PURPOSE QUESTIONS AND MAIN IDEA QUESTIONS

Purpose questions (see Section 2) are often similar to Main Idea questions. Both questions typically require you to understand the author's main point and grasp the larger ideas of a passage. The difference is that Purpose questions specifically ask you about *why* an author makes a certain literary decision. Main Idea questions more generally ask about *what's going on*. But typically, if you have a sense of the *why*, you'll also have a sense of the *what*.

MAIN IDEA QUESTIONS FOR *PART* OF A PASSAGE

Main Idea questions don't always focus on the entire passage. They may ask about just a *section* of a passage, such as a paragraph or even a single sentence. As usual, we will focus on context for these questions.

Read the following passage. As always, don't forget to mark up the passage while you read:

Questions 1–3 are based on the following passage.

This passage is adapted from Johann Hari, *Chasing the Scream*. ©2015 by Bloomsbury Publishing.

I had been taught how to respond—by my government, and by my culture—when you find yourself in this situation. It is with a war. We all know the script: it is etched onto your subconscious, like the correct direction to look when you cross the street.
Line Treat drug users and addicts as criminals. Repress them. Shame them. Coerce them
5 into stopping. This is the prevailing view in almost every country in the world. For years, I had been publicly arguing against this strategy. I wrote newspaper articles and appeared on television to argue that punishing and shaming drug users only makes them worse—and creates a blizzard of other problems for the society. I argued instead for a second strategy—legalize drugs stage by stage, and use the money we currently
10 spend on punishing addicts to fund compassionate care instead.
But as I stared at these people I loved through my own drugged glaze, a small part of me wondered if I really meant what I had been saying. The voices in my mind were like a howling drill sergeant in an old Vietnam War movie, shrieking abuse at the recruits. You are an idiot to do this. This is shameful. You are a fool for not stopping.
15 Somebody should prevent you. You should be punished.
So even as I criticized the drug war with my words, I was often waging it in my head. I can't say I was evenly divided—my rational mind always favored reform—but this internal conflict wouldn't stop.

Let's try a Main Idea question for *part* of the passage:

(EX) 1.   Which choice best describes the central claim of the first paragraph?

See the words "central claim" in the question? Hence, it's a Main Idea question. You probably don't want to take the time to read the whole paragraph again, but go back and give it a skim. Did you note any of its most important points (with underlines or asterisks)? It's usually smart to have some idea of what you're looking for before checking the answer choices:

A)   The criminalization of drug use helps addicts eventually stop using drugs.
B)   No single approach to dealing with drug use works for all people.
C)   Government and culture often determine how one feels about solving social problems.
D)   The prevailing approaches to dealing with drug use create more problems than they solve.

MAIN IDEA QUESTIONS FOR THE WHOLE PASSAGE

Often, after reading a passage, you will have a feel for the passage's main idea. You may have also indicated some of the passage's main ideas with an asterisk (★) in the margin, as described in the Passage section.

FIRST AND LAST PARAGRAPHS

If you're not sure about a passage's main idea, remember to focus on the first and last paragraphs. If the paragraphs are long, focus on the first couple sentences of the first paragraph and the last couple sentences of the last paragraph:

/ **To quickly find a passage's main idea, look at the *first* and *last* paragraphs.**

NOT TOO BROAD, AND NOT TOO NARROW

Main-Idea-of-Passage questions often have answer choices that are too broad or too narrow:

1.   **Too Broad**: These answer choices will usually fail to mention the specific person or topic discussed in the passage.

2.   **Too Narrow**: These answer choices will usually only reflect *part* of the passage.

Here's a Main Idea question for the whole passage:

(EX) 2.   Which choice best describes the central claim of the passage?

You might quickly skim the last paragraph. Keep its main points in mind as you look at the answer choices:

A) The act of using drugs must be criticized with words, even as activists show compassion for drug users.
B) Punishing drug users has never been effective in the fight against drug abuse.
C) Drug use should immediately be legalized so that money can be used on care rather than criminalization.
D) Treating drug users as criminals is embedded in our culture but is not the best approach for solving the problems of drug abuse.

⊘ ELIMINATE ANSWER CHOICES THAT ARE TOO STRONG

Answer choices that are too strong may take one of two forms:

EXTREME WORDS

The first type uses extreme words such as *always*, *only*, *never*, *without exception*, *completely*, or *perfectly*. These answer choices are usually incorrect.

EXAGGERATIONS

The second type uses words that go *too far* in describing someone or something. An author may be *disappointed* but not *devastated*. She may be *upset* but not *furious*. She may be *surprised* but not *shocked*. Watch out for answer choices that seem to overly exaggerate the attitude of an author or character in a passage—the SAT may be trying to trick you.

Look back to the previous answer choices. Do you see an answer choice that is Too Strong?

Here's another Main Idea question:

(EX) 3.   Which choice best summarizes the passage?

   A)   An advocate for changes in drug-abuse laws first introduces his position on the issue and then acknowledges his own internal ambivalence.
   B)   A defender of drug use first gives an overview of the issue and then makes clear his personal opinion.
   C)   A recovering drug user first introduces the topic of drug abuse and then recounts his own experiences.
   D)   A social scientist evenhandedly discusses the ways in which drug users can be treated.

Here's one more short passage that we'll use to introduce Main Idea questions:

Questions 1–5 are based on the following passage.

This passage is adapted from Simon Winchester, *The Professor and the Madman*. ©2005 by HarperCollins Publishers.

At the railway station a polished landau and a liveried coachman were waiting, and with James Murray aboard they clip-clopped back through the lanes of rural Berkshire. After twenty minutes or so the carriage turned up a long drive lined with tall poplars,
Line   drawing up eventually outside a huge and rather forbidding red-brick mansion. A
5   solemn servant showed the lexicographer upstairs, and into a book-lined study, where behind an immense mahogany desk stood a man of undoubted importance. Dr. Murray bowed gravely, and launched into the brief speech of greeting that he had so long rehearsed:
"A very good afternoon to you, sir. I am Dr. James Murray of the London
10   Philological Society, and Editor of the Oxford English Dictionary. It is indeed an honor and a pleasure to at long last make your acquaintance—for you must be, kind sir, my most assiduous helpmeet, Dr. W.C. Minor?"
There was a brief pause, a momentary air of mutual embarrassment. A clock ticked loudly. There were muffled footsteps in the hall. A distant clank of keys. And
15   then the man behind the desk cleared his throat, and he spoke:
"I regret, kind sir, that I am not. It is not at all as you suppose. I am in fact the Governor of the Broadmoor Criminal Lunatic Asylum. Dr. Minor is most certainly here. But he is an inmate. He has been a patient here for more than twenty years. He is our longest-staying resident."

Here's a Main Idea question:

(EX) 1. Which of the following best describes the interaction between Mr. Murray and the Governor of the asylum?

   A) They are embarrassed to be meeting after such a long time.
   B) They are pleased to finally be meeting each other.
   C) They speak to each other with polite formality.
   D) They speak to each other courteously but suspiciously.

Here's another main idea question for the whole passage:

(EX) 2. Which choice best summarizes the events in the passage?

What is the passage's main idea? Don't forget to focus on the last paragraph. Here are the answer choices:

- A) Two old acquaintances meet in embarrassing circumstances.
- B) One man discovers the true identity of another man.
- C) Two adversaries discuss the possibility of reconciliation.
- D) One man humorously recounts a case of mistaken identity.

Did you notice that the answer choices for Question 3 were *broad*? You might have expected to see something about "Dr. James Murray" or "Dr. W.C. Minor," but instead the answer choices mention such vagaries as "old acquaintances" and a "man." Most SAT questions have specific answer choices, but don't be surprised to see some with answer choices that are broad.

BACK TO THE DRAWING BOARD

Sometimes, especially as you begin getting comfortable answering questions using context, your contextual answer does not lead you to the correct answer. Don't be afraid to go *back to the drawing board*: return to the passage and reconsider the context, or attempt POE. The point is, as you may have seen with the question above, you may not always spot the correct answer on your first try.

Also, if you're eliminating answer choices, don't go with the the fourth (remaining) answer choice simply because you've eliminated the other three. Read all answer choices carefully when using POE.

The next three questions review past question types:

(EX) 3. As used in line 7, "gravely" most nearly means

   A) seriously.
   B) critically.
   C) sadly.
   D) importantly.

(EX) 4. According to the passage, Dr. Murray views Dr. W.C. Minor as a

   A) psychotic inmate.
   B) important leader.
   C) helpful associate.
   D) solemn rival.

5. Which choice provides the best evidence for the answer to the previous question?

    A) Lines 6–8 ("Dr. Murray . . . rehearsed")
    B) Lines 10–12 ("It is . . . Dr. W.C. Minor")
    C) Line 16 ("I regret . . . suppose")
    D) Lines 18–19 ("But he . . . resident")

■

CORRECTIONS: MAIN IDEA AND WORDS-IN-CONTEXT (WIC) QUESTIONS

Go back to Practice Test 10 and correct all missed Main Idea and WIC questions (and any associated Citing-Textual-Evidence questions). See Section 9 (Reading: Practice & Corrections) on page 116 for more details about correcting practice tests. The actual questions to correct for each test, as well as line numbers and other hints, are found in the Techniques section at the end of this tutorial.

PRACTICE PASSAGE

The following passage and questions test the question types we've learned so far. This is an 11-question passage, so give yourself 13 minutes and 30 seconds to complete it. This passage emphasizes Main Idea questions, but make sure to review the sections you've already covered:

REVIEW

- Marking up the passage effectively.
- Direct and Citing-Textual-Evidence questions (Section 1)
- Extended Reasoning and Purpose questions (Section 2)
- Words-in-Context questions (Section 3)

Questions 1–11 are based on the following passage.

This passage is adapted from Alexis de Tocqueville, *Democracy in America*, originally published in 1835.

The American legislators had a difficult task to fulfill in wishing to create an executive authority dependent upon the majority yet strong enough to act
5 independently and without restraint within its own sphere.

It was essential to the maintenance of the republican form of government that the representative of executive power should
10 be subject to the will of the nation.

The President is an elective magistrate. His honor, his property, his freedom, his life are a permanent pledge to the people of the good use he will make of his power. In
15 exercising this power, he is, moreover, not completely independent: the Senate supervises him in his foreign policy and also in his appointments to office. As a consequence of this, he can neither corrupt
20 nor be corrupted.

The legislators of the Union acknowledged that the executive power could not worthily or usefully accomplish its task unless they managed to give it more
25 stability and strength than had been granted in the separate states.

The President was appointed for four years and could be reelected. With time before him, he had the courage to work for
30 the public good and the means to do so.

The President became the sole representative of executive power in the Union. Care was taken not to subject his will to that of a council, a dangerous
35 measure which weakens the actions of the government and diminishes its responsibilities. The Senate has the right to annul certain of the President's acts but it cannot in any way force him to act nor can
40 it share the executive power with him.

The action of the legislature over the executive power can be direct and I have just shown that Americans had taken measures to prevent that; but it can also be
45 indirect.

The power of the two houses to deprive any public official of his salary takes away some of that official's independence. Since they have control over all law-making, the
50 fear exists that they can gradually remove that share of power which the constitution had vested in his hands.

This dependency of the executive power remains one of the inherent defects
55 of republican constitutions. Americans have been unable to eliminate the tendency legislative assemblies have to take possession of government but they have reduced its irresistibility.

60 The President's salary is fixed on his assumption of office for the whole duration of his tenure. In addition, the President has a suspensive veto which enables him to halt the passage of laws which might
65 destroy that share of independence granted to him by the constitution. However, there could only be an unequal contest between the President and the legislature since the latter can always, by
70 persisting with its plans, overcome the resistance facing it. But at least the suspensive veto forces it to retreat and to reconsider the question at hand. At which point, it can settle the matter only by a two-
75 thirds majority. Moreover, the veto is a sort of appeal to the people. The executive power which, without such a guarantee, could have been secretly oppressed, can plead its case and convey its arguments.
80 But if the legislature persists with its plans, surely it can always overcome the resistance it confronts? To which I reply that there is in the constitution of all nations, whatever its complexion, a point at
85 which the legislator is bound to have recourse to the good sense and virtue of the citizens. This point is nearer and more obvious in republics, more remote and more carefully concealed in monarchies;
90 but it is always there somewhere. No country exists where the law can anticipate everything or institutions take the place of reason and custom.

1. The central problem that de Tocqueville describes in the passage has to do with

    A) the ineffectiveness of the American President.
    B) the failure of American democracy compared to other types of governments.
    C) the American President's tendency to seek control of the legislature.
    D) the limits of power of the American executive authority.

2. What can reasonably be inferred from the passage about the power entrusted to the executive power by "the separate states" (line 26)?

    A) The states recognized that a powerful executive could more capably protect states' rights.
    B) The states did not give enough power to the executive branch to allow it to function effectively.
    C) The states elected legislators who sought to eliminate the executive from the American government.
    D) The states believed that executive power could only be effective if it went unchecked by legislators.

3. As used in line 35, "measure" most nearly means

    A) standard of judgement
    B) course of action
    C) unit of size
    D) moderate amount

Continued →

4. According to the passage, Americans have addressed the tendency legislative assemblies have to become too powerful by

    A) giving more power to the executive authority than to the legislative assemblies.
    B) ensuring that the executive power is independent of the legislative assemblies.
    C) making legislative possession of government more difficult and less enticing.
    D) providing the executive with an opportunity to change the constitution.

5. Which choice provides the best evidence for the answer to the previous question?

    A) Lines 48–52 ("Since . . . hands")
    B) Lines 53–55 ("This dependency . . . constitutions")
    C) Lines 55–59 ("Americans . . . irresistibility")
    D) Lines 67–71 ("However . . . it")

6. Which choice best describes the central idea of the sixth paragraph (lines 31–40)?

    A) The existence of a legislative council dangerously weakens the effective strength of a democracy.
    B) The Senate cannot take direct action against the President's executive power.
    C) The Senate may inherit some of the responsibilities of the executive branch in certain situations.
    D) The Senate may remove the President from office in certain situations.

7. As used in line 60, "fixed" most nearly means

    A) set
    B) attached
    C) put in order
    D) directed

Continued →

8. According to the passage, the President may choose to use a "suspensive veto" (line 63) in order to

   A) bring a legislative issue to the attention of the people.
   B) permanently halt a passage of laws set forth by the legislature.
   C) give the President more time to consider a legislative issue.
   D) present an issue to the people for a popular vote.

9. Which choice provides the best evidence for the answer to the previous question?

   A) Lines 62–66 ("In addition . . . constitution")
   B) Lines 66–71 ("However . . . it")
   C) Line 71–73 ("But at . . . hand")
   D) Lined 75–76 ("Moreover . . . people")

10. The central idea of the tenth paragraph (lines 60–93) is that a country's legislature

   A) must be checked by the morals and good sense of the country's citizens.
   B) can only be controlled by the President's suspensive veto.
   C) will eventually overpower the executive power.
   D) must come up with laws that anticipate the needs of the country's people.

11. Which choice provides the best evidence for the answer to the previous question?

   A) Lines 62–66 ("In addition . . . constitution")
   B) Lines 80–82 ("But if . . . confronts")
   C) Lines 82–87 ("To which . . . citizens")
   D) Lines 87–89 ("This point . . . monarchies")

■

5. COMPARISON QUESTIONS (DOUBLE PASSAGES)

Comparison questions ask you to compare two relatively short passages. Usually these questions focus on *contrasts*, but some questions ask you to find *similarities* in two otherwise different points of view. Every test will have one double passage.

DOUBLE PASSAGES: ORDER

Double passages will be followed by 10 or 11 questions divided into 3 sets: one set for Passage 1, one set for Passage 2, and one set for both passages. The questions should be in the order of the two passages, and the wording of each question should make clear what passage is being tested (either by mentioning line numbers or referring specifically to "Passage 1" or "Passage 2"). For these double passages, go in the following order:

1. Read Passage 1 and answer the questions for this passage only.
2. Read Passage 2 and answer the questions for this passage only.
3. Finally, move on to the questions for both passages (where you'll see the Comparison questions). Usually there will be 4–6 Comparison questions.

! **Do not read Passage 2 until you have answered the questions for Passage 1.**

FOCUS ON THE CORRECT PASSAGE

When you get to the Comparison questions, the first step is to underline (in the question) which passage to focus on. You will likely see information from *both* passages in the answer choices, so be careful. For example, in the question below, which passage should you focus on?

> In the response to the claims made in lines 2–3 of Passage 1, the author of Passage 2 would most likely assert that . . .

Hopefully you underlined *Passage 2*. Yes, of course you must consider the "claims" made in Passage 1, but you should focus on the *opinion* of the Passage 2 author.

Comparison questions mention *both* passages (and, often, the authors of the passages) in the question. For example:
- Unlike Passage 1, Passage 2 . . .
- The author of Passage 1 would most likely respond to the author of Passage 2 . . .
- Which statement characterizes the differences between the authors of Passage 1 and Passage 2 . . .
- Which choice best states the relationship between the two passages?
- Both passages . . .

While typically, as explained above, you will read one passage and then answer questions for that one passage, before moving on to the next passage, the questions that follow the passage below are Comparison questions, so go ahead and read *both* passages now. (In other words, pretend that you already answered the questions related to each individual passage.)

Questions 1–5 are based on the following passages.

Passage 1 is adapted from Ronald T. Takaki, *Violence in the Black Imagination: Essays and Documents*. ©1972 G. P. Putman's Sons. Passage 2 is adapted from Jon Sterngass, *Frederick Douglass*. ©2009 Chelsea House Publishers.

Passage 1

Violence against the oppressor was a question Frederick Douglass faced with profound ambivalence. Committed to Garrisonian abolitionism during the 1840's, Douglass sincerely hoped the abolitionist movement could successfully appeal to
Line men's sense of right and emancipation could be achieved nonviolently. As a moral
5 suasionist, Douglass denounced Henry Highland Garnet's bold address to the slaves advocating a war to the knife against the slaveholding class. "There was," Douglass protested, "too much physical force both in the address and remarks of Garnet." But at the same time Douglass believed slave violence against the master class could have crucial psychological and political meaning for the wretched, for the oppressed. The
10 ambivalence Douglass felt toward violence was very personal: It was deeply rooted in his years of childhood and early manhood, in his relationships with gentlewomen like his slaveholding mistress Sophia Auld, and in his racial ties to both white and black.

Passage 2

Douglass had never been a real pacifist, even when he followed Garrison. Douglass took pride in having fought Edward Covey. He doubted the effectiveness of
15 Garrison's tactic of "moral persuasion" as a weapon for slaves. Douglass' arguments against violence were usually practical: The white masters had the guns, and the black slaves who fought against them would be killed. He wrote, "I never see much use in fighting, unless there is a reasonable probability of whipping somebody."

Let's try some Comparison questions for the passage above:

(EX) 1. On which of the following points would the authors of both passages most likely agree?

This question is broad, so let's look at the answer choices. Since you're looking for an answer that is true for both passages, eliminate answer choices that are true for only one of the passages.

A) Frederick Douglass fought for emancipation using William Lloyd Garrison's tactic of "moral persuasion."
B) Frederick Douglass considered violence a viable tool for emancipation in some instances.
C) Frederick Douglass always thought that emancipation could be achieved nonviolently.
D) Frederick Douglass was steadfast in his ideas about violence and emancipation.

Try the following Comparison question. Underline the author (or passage) that you should focus on:

(EX) 2. How would the author of Passage 1 most likely respond to the the claim made in line 13, Passage 2 ("Douglass . . . pacifist")?

The answer will reflect the opinions of the author of Passage 1, but first go back to Passage 2 and make sure you understand the claim made in line 13. How would the author of Passage 1 respond to this claim?

Now look at the answer choices. Do you see one that expresses the main idea of Passage 1?

A) Douglass's views on violence were complex and multifaceted.
B) Garrison and Douglass both considered violence a last resort in the battle for emancipation.
C) Douglass always disagreed with Garrison's views as an abolitionist.
D) Douglass dismissed violence as an ineffective means to achieve an end.

Citing-Textual-Evidence (CTE) questions often show up with Comparison questions. Here's one based on the previous question:

EX 3. Which choice provides the best evidence for the answer to the previous question?

A) Lines 1–2 ("Violence . . . ambivalence")
B) Lines 2–4 ("Committed . . nonviolently")
C) Lines 4–6 ("As a moral . . . class")
D) Lines 7–9 ("But at . . . oppressed")

Here's another Comparison question:

EX 4. Which of the following aspects of Frederick Douglass is addressed in Passage 1 but not in Passage 2?

The answer to this question will reflect the context of Passage 1 (again, don't forget to focus on the correct passage when answering these Comparison questions). The question is broad, so we must consider the answer choices before checking context. Eliminate answer choices that are either addressed in Passage 2 or not addressed in either passage:

A) Douglass's opinions about Garrison's principles of abolition
B) Douglass's reasons for his stance against violence
C) Douglass's race
D) The specific steps that Douglass felt should be taken before violence was acceptable

Most double passages will have one Comparison question that asks about the "relationship between the passages." These are similar to Main Idea questions. More than one answer choice might be true, at least to some degree, but only one will "best" answer the question.

(EX) 5. Which statement best describes the relationship between the passages?

    A) Passage 2 elaborates on an argument made in Passage 1.
    B) Passage 2 strongly challenges the point of view in Passage 1.
    C) Passage 2 provides further evidence to support a point made in Passage 1.
    D) Passage 2 questions a theory presented in Passage 1.

■

PRACTICE PASSAGE

The following passage and questions test the question types we've learned so far. This is an 11-question passage, so give yourself 13 minutes and 30 seconds to complete it.

REVIEW

- Marking up the passage effectively.
- Direct and Citing-Textual-Evidence questions (Section 1)
- Extended Reasoning and Purpose questions (Section 2)
- Words-in-Context questions (Section 3)
- Main Ideas (Section 4)
- How to approach double passages (one passage at a time) (Section 5)
- Comparisons Questions (Section 5)

Practice Passage IV

Questions 1–11 are based on the following passages.

Passage 1 is adapted from Garett Jones, *Hive Mind*. ©2016 by Stanford University Press. Passage 2 is adapted from Stephanie Solomon, *Stakeholders or Experts?* ©2009 by Palgrave Macmillan. An *epistocracy* is a system of government in which the votes of citizens with a particular knowledge or ability are given more weight than the votes of other citizens.

Passage 1

Yale's Dan Kahan and his coauthors gave people two kinds of tables to read. One group saw a table providing data about gun violence, and another group saw
5 data on skin rashes. The researchers asked respondents whether the data in the table backed the theories that (in the first case) gun control laws reduce violence and (in the second case) a particular cream
10 helped cure the rash.

Here's the trick: the data were all made up. As part of the experiment, Kahan asked people what political party they belonged to and how partisan they were. Also, there
15 were two sets of gun data given out randomly to different participants, one of which made it look like gun control cut crime rates while the other made it look like gun control raised crime rates; they did the
20 same scrambling with the rash data. The test subjects also took a short IQ-type test, a test of numerical skill. What did Kahan and coauthors find? Perhaps naturally, they found that Democrats were more likely to
25 say the gun data supported gun control regardless of which data they were given and Republicans fell victim to the opposite bias. As the saying goes, where you stand depends on where you sit. But Kahan's
30 study went further. He checked to see whether people who did well on the IQ-type test were more likely to get at the truth in both the skin rash case and the gun control case. And, no surprise, people who were
35 better at math were usually more likely to get to the truth.

That's not the end of the story, though. In the gun control case, greater numeracy predicted greater disagreement between
40 Democrats and Republicans. So if the data said that gun control worked, high-scoring Republicans were only a little more likely than low-scoring Republicans to read the table correctly, but high-scoring Democrats
45 were much more likely than low-scoring Democrats to realize that the news favored their team. The lesson: the well-informed disagree more than the poorly informed. More math skill means more knowledge,
50 and more knowledge might mean more disagreement, not more harmony.

But there's another lesson to draw from Kahan's study: overall, people with higher IQ type scores were more likely to read the
55 graph correctly, even when it was news they didn't want to see. And when it was news they wanted to see, the high scorers in both parties were likely to get the right answer. So overall, people with higher IQ-
60 type scores were more likely to get to the objective truth in studies at Yale, and perhaps they get closer to the objective truth in the real world as well. Yes, you're more likely to see the light if it's light you
65 want to see. But you're also more likely to see the light if you do better on a cognitive skill test.

Passage 2

There are many reasons to desire that our political systems are democracies and
70 not epistocracies. The social organization in a democracy is organized around the principle that the procedure ought to be fair in that each citizen gets one voice and one vote. Famously, John Stuart Mill argued for
75 a hybrid democratic/epistocratic system of weighted voting, where more votes are given to the better educated. He based this assertion on the somewhat intuitive, if politically incorrect, notion that superior
80 wisdom justifies superior political authority. He also argued that giving more votes to the educated minority is the only way to prevent political decisions from consistently reflecting the unreasoned views of the
85 majority, who by their sheer numbers would not be required to convince anyone of their views.

The argument against a political epistocracy is that the educated portion of
90 a population may correspond to a population that also has features that make it less worthy to rule, such as race, class, or gender biases, and that there is no systematic way to prevent this. Another,

95 more obvious problem with an epistocracy is that many political decisions regard beliefs about priorities of life, such as what should be taught in schools, or whether health care should be universally
100 accessible. In the domain of science, questions of which research questions to prioritize and fund and how to disseminate and apply research findings in society also reflect social priorities and values that are
105 indeterminable by specialist expertise. It is unclear how specialized training in a specific area, either within science or outside of it, has any direct bearing on the right one has to determine these issues.

1. The central claim of Passage 1 is that compared to people with lower IQs, people with higher IQs

    A) rarely make mistakes in interpreting information.
    B) tend to agree with one another, regardless of their political beliefs.
    C) are more likely to find objective truth in the real world.
    D) are incapable of speaking for the majority of the population.

2. In line 20, "scrambling" most nearly means

    A) obscuring
    B) confusing
    C) mixing
    D) randomizing

3. The author refers to the saying in lines 28–29 ("where . . . sit") in order to

    A) show that peoples' beliefs are profoundly impacted by exposure to new information.
    B) illustrate that peoples' beliefs are often at odds with their actions.
    C) signal that biases in data have no effect on how people identify the truth.
    D) emphasize that peoples' beliefs are usually hard to influence.

Continued →

4. Based on Passage 1, the author implies which of the following about the "IQ-type test" discussed in line 21?

   A) An IQ-type test is not necessarily a good measure of a person's intelligence.
   B) The test subjects' IQ-type test scores were dependent on their political views.
   C) A good IQ-type test should measure a person's proficiency in math.
   D) The IQ-type test directly measured the test taker's ability to determine what is true and what is fiction.

5. In the first paragraph of Passage 2 (lines 68–87), the author considers the views of John Stuart Mill as

   A) unfamiliar but worthy of further study among political scientists.
   B) apparently logical but objectionable upon closer examination.
   C) flawed but ultimately desirable if enacted as a hybrid democratic/epistocratic system.
   D) effective in preventing political decisions from always reflecting the uneducated minority.

6. In lines 98–99, the author of Passage 2 mentions schools and health care primarily to

   A) emphasize the need for unanimity when making decisions about typical social issues.
   B) provide examples of issues that should not be determined by well-educated experts alone.
   C) highlight the need for scientific expertise when making decisions about universal issues.
   D) support the claim that people must become better educated to more effectively make political decisions.

Continued →

7. In line 100, "domain" most nearly means

   A) set
   B) territory
   C) dominion
   D) realm

8. Which choice best describes the relationship of the two passages?

   A) Passage 2 offers an alternate solution to the problems of democracies discussed in Passage 1.
   B) Passage 2 challenges the primary deduction made in Passage 1.
   C) Passage 2 expands on one of the main points made in Passage 1.
   D) Passage 2 questions the accuracy of the evidence discussed in Passage 1.

9. Which choice provides the best evidence that the author of Passage 1 would agree to some extent with the views of John Stuart Mill in lines 74–87, Passage 2?

   A) Lines 30–34 ("He . . . case")
   B) Lined 47–48 ("The lesson . . . informed")
   C) Lines 59–63 ("So overall . . . well")
   D) Lines 63–65 ("Yes . . . see")

10. The author of Passage 2 would most likely respond to the claims made about people with high IQs in lines 59–63, Passage 1, by claiming that high IQ

   A) does not properly measure race, class, or gender biases.
   B) is impossible to measure objectively.
   C) fails to determine the special experts in a society.
   D) is not a good criterion for determining who gets to vote on political issues.

11. Which choice provides the best evidence for the answer to the previous question?

   A) Lines 68–70 ("There . . . epistocracies")
   B) Lines 77–80 ("He based. . . authority")
   C) Lines 81–87 ("He also . . . views")
   D) Lines 105–109 ("It is . . . issues")

■

6. INFORMATIONAL GRAPHICS QUESTIONS

Informational Graphics (IG) questions test information found in tables, graphs, and other figures. These figures relate to information in the passage, although most IG questions can be answered using the figure alone.

Each test will likely have 5–6 IG questions. The figures will show up on one of the history/social studies passages and one of the science passages.

 Informational Graphics (IG) questions are easy to identify. Just look for questions that mention a "figure," "chart," "table," etc. These questions show up at the end of a passage with figures.

FIGURES

The most common figures you'll see include line graphs, bar graphs, pie graphs, and tables. You can review these figures in the Tables & Graphs lesson in the Math part of this tutorial (Arithmetic chapter). Additionally, you may see more challenging figures, such as histograms or scatterplots. These figures are covered in Math's Statistics lesson (Odds & Ends chapter). Many students find the figures on the Reading test relatively straightforward—they're generally not as hard as the figures on the Math test—but if you often struggle understanding them, review (or cover) the related Math sections.

TYPES OF IG QUESTIONS

There are three basic types of IG questions:

- Direct questions: Information is found *directly* in the figure.
- Extended reasoning questions: You must interpret information found in the figure.
- Make Connection questions: You must make connections between the figure and the text.

We'll cover each type below.

DIRECT QUESTIONS

Direct questions can—and, importantly, *should*—be answered using information in the given figure. Do not be distracted by what you have read in the passage. Unless the question makes clear that you should make a connection with the text, Direct questions should be answered using only the figure.

/ Do not look back to the passage's *text* when answering Direct IG questions.

Here are some examples:

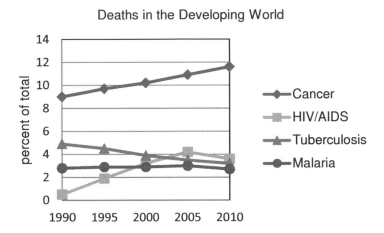

Deaths in the Developing World

(EX) 1. Data in the graph indicate that which of following diseases showed an increase in percent of total deaths in the developing world after 2005?

As with most questions, try to answer the question before looking at the answer choices. Can you identify the disease whose percent *increases* after 2005? Here are the answer choices:

A) Cancer
B) HIV/AIDS
C) Tuberculosis
D) Malaria

Some Direct questions ask about which claim or statement is supported by the figure:

(EX) 2. Which claim about deaths in the developing world is supported by the graph?

   A) In 2010, more people in developing countries died from cancer than any other cause.
   B) In 2010, more people in developing countries died from cancer than from HIV/AIDS, tuberculous, and malaria combined.
   C) In 2010, combined deaths from cancer, HIV/AIDS, tuberculous, and malaria made up the majority of all deaths in developing countries.
   D) In 2010, more people in developing countries died from HIV/AIDS than from tuberculous and malaria combined.

EXTENDED REASONING QUESTIONS

You may occasionally have to extend your reasoning on IG questions. In other words, you'll have to use information in the figure to make an inference. As with Extended reasoning questions for the text, always extend your reasoning *as little as possible*. Your answer should be clearly, if not directly, supported by the text. Here's an example based on the previous figure.

(EX) 3. Data in the graph suggest which of the following about HIV/AIDS in developing countries?

   A) Methods for combating HIV/AIDS became most effective after 2005 but declined by 2010.
   B) Methods for combating HIV/AIDS became most effective after 2005 and continued to improve by 2010.
   C) Methods for combating HIV/AIDS were not utilized until after 2005 but before 2010.
   D) Methods for combating HIV/AIDS were not utilized until 2010.

MAKE-CONNECTIONS QUESTIONS

The most difficult IG questions will require you to make connections with the text. They are easy to identify:

 IG questions that require you to make connections with the text will include words such as "the author" or "the passage." (If you do not see these obvious references, assume the question does NOT require connecting with the text.)

Read the following short passage, followed by informational graphics:

Questions 1–3 are based on the following passage.

Passage 1 is adapted from Daphne Bavelier and C. Shawn Green, "The Brain Boosting Power of Video Games." ©2016 Scientific American.

The stereotype of the avid player of Call of Duty and other action games is of someone who is impulsive and easily distracted. Our studies contradict this outdated preconception. Much of our research has focused on how action games affect a
Line player's attention—the mental processes that lead to finding relevant information in
5 one's environment. Studies of attention have been carried out ever since psychology emerged as a social science in the 19th century. Call of Duty and Medal of Honor have now become tools in research facilities because of their ability to enhance attention. A player must shift between a state of mental focus while monitoring the game scene for potential enemies, switching purposely between what psychologists call focused and
10 distributed attention.
To show a true cause-and-effect relation, scientists recruit a group of individuals who rarely play video games, and this larger group is randomly split into two. One group plays an action game, whereas a control group immerses itself in a social game or another non-action game. Groups trained on action games show consistently larger
15 gains in cognition than control groups.

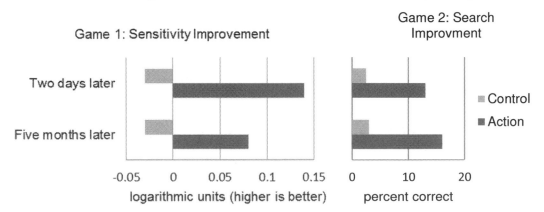

Relative Sensitivity Improvement and Search Improvement
for Players of Action Games and Non-Action Games (Control)

Here's how to tackle these problems

1. After reading the question, take a look at the figure, or at least the *part* of the figure mentioned in the question. Make sure you understand what is being presented.

2. Try eliminating answer choices that are *not* supported by the figure. (Note: At this point we have *not* gone back to the passage's text.)

3. Finally, if necessary, go back to the passage and make your connections. You may have to skim to find your information. Sometimes looking for keywords in the figure (that may show up in the text) will help.

Let's try some example questions:

(EX) 1. What concept is supported by the passage and by the information in the graphs?

   A) People who play action games show increased short- and long-term cognition because they must shift between focused and distributed attention.
   B) People who play action games show greater short-term improvement than long-term improvement in sensitivity cognition.
   C) People who play non-action games display greater short- and long-term cognitive improvement than people who don't play non-action games.
   D) People who play action games display greater short- and long-term cognitive improvement than people who don't play action games.

(EX) 2. Do the data in the graphs support the author's claim that people who frequently play action games are often stereotyped as impulsive and easily distracted?

   A) Yes, because the data reveal evidence that people who play action games have below average attention spans.
   B) Yes, because the data show that playing action games improves qualities related to impulsiveness and distraction.
   C) No, because the data do not reveal societal ideas about people who play action games.
   D) No, because the data do not quantifiably measure qualities that may be related to impulsiveness or distraction.

Here's another IG question that requires making a connection. It is similar to a Citing-Textual-Evidence (CTE) question:

(EX) 3. Based on the graphs, does playing an action game improve the player's attention, and which statement made by the authors is most consistent with the data?

  A) Yes; "Much . . . environment" (lines 3–5)
  B) Yes; "Call . . . attention" (lines 6–7)
  C) No; "To show . . . two" (lines 11–12)
  D) No; "One group . . . game" (lines 12–14)

■

CORRECTIONS: COMPARISON AND INFORMATIONAL GRAPHICS (IG) QUESTIONS

Go back to Practice Test 10 and correct all missed Comparison and IG questions (and any associated Citing-Textual-Evidence questions). See Section 9 (Reading: Practice & Corrections) on page 116 for more details about correcting practice tests. The actual questions to correct for each test, as well as line numbers and other hints, are found in the Techniques section at the end of this tutorial.

PRACTICE PASSAGE

The following passage and questions test the question types we've learned so far. This is an 11-question passage, so give yourself 13 minutes and 30 seconds to complete it.

REVIEW

- Marking up the passage effectively.
- Direct and Citing-Textual-Evidence questions (Section 1)
- Extended Reasoning and Purpose questions (Section 2)
- Words-in-Context questions (Section 3)
- Informational Graphics questions (Section 6)

Practice Passage V

Questions 1–11 are based on the following passage and supplementary material.

This passage is adapted from Daniel Kahneman, *Thinking, Fast and Slow*. ©2011 by Farrar, Straus and Giroux.

Regression to the mean was discovered and named late in the nineteenth century by Sir Francis Galton, a half cousin of Charles Darwin and a
5 renowned polymath. You can sense the thrill of discovery in an article he published in 1886 under the title "Regression towards Mediocrity in Hereditary Stature," which reports measurements of size in
10 successive generations of seeds and in comparisons of the height of children to the height of their parents. He writes about his studies of seeds:

They yielded results that seemed
15 very noteworthy, and I used them as the basis of a lecture before the Royal Institution on February 9th, 1877. It appeared from these experiments that the offspring did not tend to resemble
20 their parent seeds in size, but to be always more mediocre than they—to be smaller than the parents, if the parents were large; to be larger than the parents, if the parents were very
25 small . . . The experiments showed further that the mean filial regression towards mediocrity was directly proportional to the parental deviation from it.

30 A few years ago, John Brockman, who edits the online magazine *Edge*, asked a number of scientists to report their "favorite equation." These were my offerings:

success = talent + luck

35 great success = a little more talent + a lot of luck

The unsurprising idea that luck often contributes to success has surprising consequences when we apply it to the first
40 two days of a high-level golf tournament. To keep things simple, assume that on both days the average score of the competitors was at par 72. We focus on a player who did very well on the first day,
45 closing with a score of 66. What can we learn from that excellent score? An immediate inference is that the golfer is more talented than the average participant in the tournament. The formula for success
50 suggests that another inference is equally justified: the golfer who did so well on day 1 probably enjoyed better-than-average luck on that day. If you accept that talent and luck both contribute to success, the
55 conclusion that the successful golfer was lucky is as warranted as the conclusion that he is talented. By the same token, if you focus on a player who scored 5 over par on that day, you have reason to infer both that
60 he is rather weak and had a bad day. Uncertain though they are, the following inferences from the score on day 1 are plausible and will be correct more often than they are wrong.

65 above-average score on day 1 = above-average talent + lucky on day 1

and

below-average score on day 1 = below-average talent + unlucky on day 1

70 Now, suppose you know a golfer's score on day 1 and are asked to predict his score on day 2. You expect the golfer to retain the same level of talent on the second day, so your best guesses will be
75 "above average" for the first player and "below average" for the second player. Luck, of course, is a different matter. Since you have no way of predicting the golfers' luck on the second (or any) day, your best
80 guess must be that it will be average, neither good nor bad. This means that in the absence of any other information, your best guess about the players' score on day 2 should not be a repeat of their
85 performance on day 1. This is the most you can say:

- The golfer who did well on day 1 is likely to be successful on day 2 as well, but less than on the first,
90 because the unusual luck he probably enjoyed on day 1 is unlikely to hold.
- The golfer who did poorly on day 1 will probably be below average on
95 day 2, but will improve, because

his probable streak of bad luck is not likely to continue.

This is why the pattern is called regression to the mean. The more extreme *100* the original score, the more regression we expect, because an extremely good score suggests a very lucky day.

Scores for 8 Golfers

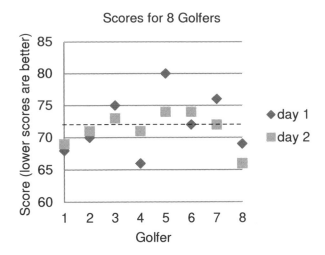

The dotted line displays the average score over the two days.

1. The author refers to and quotes Sir Francis Galton (lines 1–29) in order to

    A) introduce an argument against the idea of regression to the mean.
    B) provide a historical introduction to the idea of regression to the mean.
    C) highlight how little is still understood about the topic of regression to the mean.
    D) support the notion that the science behind regression to the mean was once unpopular but is now widely understood.

Continued →

2. As it is used in line 21, "mediocre" most nearly means

   A) ordinary
   B) small
   C) inadequate
   D) inferior

3. The passage suggests that most people predict an athlete's future performance based primarily on

   A) well-known equations of chance.
   B) both the athlete's apparent talent and his or her apparent luck.
   C) the athlete's apparent luck.
   D) the athlete's apparent talent.

4. According to the passage, concluding that a golfer who scored better-than-average was lucky

   A) makes as much sense as concluding that the golfer was talented.
   B) ignores the golfer's obvious talent.
   C) is one of several ways to predict the golfer's future performance.
   D) will probably lead to incorrect predictions of future performance.

5. Which choice provides the best evidence for the answer to the previous question?

   A) Lines 53–57 ("If you . . . talented")
   B) Lines 72–76 ("You expect . . . player")
   C) Lines 77–81 ("Since . . . bad")
   D) Lines 81–85 ("This . . . day 1")

Continued →

6. The passage indicates that if a golfer plays poorly on day 1, his score on day 2 will probably be

   A) better than average.
   B) better than his score on day 1, but worse than average.
   C) worse than his score on day 1.
   D) equal to his score on day 1.

7. Which choice provides the best evidence for the answer to the previous question?

   A) Lines 87–92 ("The golfer . . . hold")
   B) Lines 93–97 ("The golfer . . . continue")
   C) Lines 98–99 ("This . . . mean")
   D) Lines 99–102 ("The more . . . day")

8. Based on the data in the graph, how many, if any, of the golfers scored better than average on day 1 and worse than average on day 2?

   A) 0
   B) 1
   C) 2
   D) 3

9. Based on the data in the graph, which golfer's score improved the most from day 1 to day 2?

   A) Golfer 4
   B) Golfer 5
   C) Golfer 7
   D) Golfer 8

10. The author of the passage would likely explain the change in golfer 5's score from day 1 to day 2 as

   A) a sign that the golfer was especially unlucky on day 2.
   B) a sign that the golfer was especially lucky on day 2.
   C) relatively unlikely, because it does not agree with the regression to the mean.
   D) entirely expected, as described by the idea of regression to the mean.

Continued →

11. Overall, do the data in the graph display a regression to the mean, as discussed by the author of the passage?

   A) Yes, because, for most of the golfers, the further that a golfer's day 1 score was from the average score, the greater his day 2 score reverted back to the average score.
   B) Yes, because, for most of the golfers, the closer that a golfer's day 1 score was to the average score, the greater his day 2 score moved away from the average score.
   C) No, because half of the golfers improved their scores on day 2.
   D) No, because only one of the golfers had an average score on day 2.

■

 All Programs: After reviewing the tutorial up to here, and completing all correction assignments, take Practice Test 9 in *The Official SAT Study Guide*.

7. TONE QUESTIONS

Tone is defined as a quality, feeling, or attitude expressed by a person, usually in speaking or in writing. Tone questions often refer to the author of a passage, but they may also ask about characters in a passage, particularly those in prose fiction passages.

A good way to recognize Tone questions is to glance at the answer choices. They will usually contain *tone words*. As described in the Passage section, tone words are words that convey positive or negative *feelings*.

Also, the questions themselves usually contain one of the following words or phrases:
- tone
- attitude
- characterized as
- viewed as

⊘ ELIMINATE ANSWER CHOICES THAT CONTRADICT TONE

Since the answer-choice vocabulary is sometimes challenging on Tone questions, you might not spot the correct answer right away, but hopefully you can eliminate incorrect answers. Often one or more answer choices can be eliminated simply because they contradict tone (often the author's tone).

Make sure to look for, and darkly underline, tone words (see the Passage section) as you read the following passage.

Questions 1–4 are based on the following passages.

This passage is adapted from Charles Frazier, *Cold Mountain*. ©1998 by Atlantic Monthly Press.

At the first gesture of morning, flies began stirring. Inman's eyes and the long wound at his neck drew them, and the sound of their wings and the touch of their feet were soon more potent than a yardful of roosters in rousing a man to wake. So he
Line   came to yet one more day in the hospital ward. He flapped the flies away with his
5   hands and looked across the foot of his bed to an open triple-hung window. Ordinarily he could see to the red road and the oak tree and the low brick wall. And beyond them to a sweep of fields and flat piney woods that stretched to the western horizon. The view was a long one for the flatlands, the hospital having been built on the only swell within eyeshot. But it was too early yet for a vista. The window might as well have
10   been painted grey.
Had it not been too dim, Inman would have read to pass the time until breakfast, for the book he was reading had the effect of settling his mind. But he had burned up the last of his own candles reading to bring sleep the night before, and lamp oil was too scarce to be striking the hospital's lights for mere diversion. So he rose and
15   dressed and sat in a ladderback chair, putting the gloomy room of beds and their broken occupants behind him. He flapped again at the flies and looked out the window at the first smear of foggy dawn and waited for the world to begin shaping up outside.
The window was tall as a door, and he had imagined many times that it would open onto some other place and let him walk through and be there.

Let's try some questions that test tone:

(EX) 1.   That passage indicates that the hospital staff would most likely view the act of reading as

The word "view" in the question tells us that this is probably a Tone question. You might also glance at the answer choices below. Let's first try answering the question using context.

Here are the answer choices:

A) an insignificant distraction.
B) an enriching endeavor.
C) a calming amusement.
D) a harmful procrastination.

(EX) 2.   Inman's attitude toward the other occupants (line 16) in the hospital ward is best
          described as one of

We know this is a Tone question because of the word "attitude." Again, let's first try answering
the question using context.

Here are the answer choices:

    A) dread.
    B) ambivalence.
    C) detachment.
    D) arrogance.

(EX) 3.   In the last paragraph (lines 18–19), Inman's tone is best described as

First, consider context.

Now let's look at the answer choices. If the answer choice vocabulary is difficult for you, try
POE:

    A) introspective.
    B) wistful.
    C) resolute.
    D) resigned.

Here's one more question for this passage. This one reviews Words-in-Context questions. These questions sometimes also test tone:

(EX) 4.   As used in line 1, "gesture" most nearly means

Using context, how would you define the word "gesture"?

Here are the answer choices. If you don't spot the correct answer, use POE:

- A) cheerless expression.
- B) faint movement.
- C) subtle hint.
- D) bitter reminder.

■

Here's one more passage that we'll use to cover Tone questions. Note how on nonfiction passages (this is a social science one) Tone questions focus more on the *author*. Don't forget to underline tone words while you read:

Questions 1–3 are based on the following passages.

This passage is adapted from Jerry Mander, *Four Arguments for the Elimination of Television.* ©1978 by Morrow.

The first really shocking burst of figures appeared in newspapers in the early 1970s.

It was reported that in the generation since 1945, 99 percent of the homes in the
Line country had acquired at least one television set. On an average evening, more than 80
5 million people would be watching television. Thirty million of these would be watching the same program. In special instances, 100 million people would be watching the same program at the same time.

The average household had the set going more than six hours a day. If there was a child, the average was more than eight hours. The average person was watching for
10 nearly four hours daily. And so, allowing eight hours for sleep and eight hours for work, roughly half of the adult nonsleeping, nonworking time was spent watching television. Considering that these were average figures, they meant that half of the people in this country were watching television even more than that.

As these numbers sank in, I realized that there had been a strange change in the
15 way people received information, and even more in the way they were experiencing and understanding the world. In one generation, out of hundreds of thousands in human evolution, America had become the first culture to have substituted secondary, mediated versions of experience for direct experience of the world. Interpretations and representations of the world were being accepted as experience, and the difference
20 between the two was obscure to most of us.

(EX) 1. Over the course of the author's research into television, the author apparently had a shift in attitude from

Note the keyword "attitude" in the question. How does the author feel at the beginning of the passage? How does the author's tone change in the last paragraph ("As these numbers sank in . . .")? Go back to the passage, and make sure to look for tone words.

Do you see the correct answer below? Watch out for answer choices that are too strong (common on Tone questions):

    A) amazement to concern.
    B) surprise to curiosity.
    C) complacency to despair.
    D) apprehension to contentment.

(EX) 2. The author would most likely characterize the way people were "experiencing and understanding the world" (lines 15–16) as

Go back to the passage. How would you describe the author's tone in this paragraph? Do you see any other context that might come in handy?

Once again, the answers are "double answers":

    A) rapidly-changing and long-lasting.
    B) expected and disastrous.
    C) sudden and unfortunate.
    D) familiar and welcome.

Let's try one more Tone question:

(EX) 3.   Regarding a culture's "direct experience" (line 18) of the world, the author
          expresses which of the following attitudes?

What is the author's attitude toward "direct experience of the world" (line 18)?

Note that the answer-choice vocabulary may not be easy for you. As we said earlier,

vocabulary can be one of the challenges of Tone questions. If you don't spot the correct

answer, use POE:

     A)   Sorrow
     B)   Indifference
     C)   Resentment
     D)   Esteem

                                        ∎

PRACTICE PASSAGE

The following passage and questions test the question types we've learned so far. This is an
11-question passage, so give yourself 13 minutes and 30 seconds to complete it. This passage
emphasizes Tone questions so make sure to review this section. Additionally, make sure to
underline tone words as you read.

Practice Passage VI

Questions 1–11 are based on the following passage.

This passage is adapted from James Joyce, "Araby," originally published in 1905.

North Richmond Street, being blind, was a quiet street except at the hour when the Christian Brothers' School set the boys free. An uninhabited house of two stories
5 stood at the blind end, detached from its neighbors in a square ground. The other houses of the street, conscious of decent lives within them, gazed at one another with brown imperturbable faces.
10 The former tenant of our house, a priest, had died in the back drawing-room. Air, musty from having been long enclosed, hung in all the rooms, and the waste room behind the kitchen was littered with old
15 useless papers. Among these I found a few paper-covered books, the pages of which were curled and damp: *The Abbot*, by Walter Scott, *The Devout Communicant*, and *The Memoirs of Vidocq*. I liked the last
20 best because its leaves were yellow. The wild garden behind the house contained a central apple-tree and a few straggling bushes, under one of which I found the late tenant's rusty bicycle-pump. He had been a
25 very charitable priest; in his will he had left all his money to institutions and the furniture of his house to his sister.
When the short days of winter came, dusk fell before we had well eaten our
30 dinners. When we met in the street the houses had grown somber. The space of sky above us was the color of ever-changing violet and towards it the lamps of the street lifted their feeble lanterns. The
35 cold air stung us and we played till our bodies glowed. Our shouts echoed in the silent street. The career of our play brought us through the dark muddy lanes behind the houses, where we ran the gauntlet of
40 the rough tribes from the cottages, to the back doors of the dark dripping gardens where odors arose from the ashpits, to the dark odorous stables where a coachman smoothed and combed the horse or shook
45 music from the buckled harness. When we returned to the street, light from the kitchen windows had filled the areas. If my uncle was seen turning the corner, we hid in the shadow until we had seen him safely
50 housed. Or if Mangan's sister came out on the doorstep to call her brother in to his tea, we watched her from our shadow peer up and down the street. We waited to see whether she would remain or go in and, if
55 she remained, we left our shadow and walked up to Mangan's steps resignedly. She was waiting for us, her figure defined by the light from the half-opened door. Her brother always teased her before he
60 obeyed, and I stood by the railings looking at her. Her dress swung as she moved her body, and the soft rope of her hair tossed from side to side.
Every morning I lay on the floor in the
65 front parlor watching her door. The blind was pulled down to within an inch of the sash so that I could not be seen. When she came out on the doorstep my heart leaped. I ran to the hall, seized my books and
70 followed her. I kept her brown figure always in my eye and, when we came near the point at which our ways diverged, I quickened my pace and passed her. This happened morning after morning. I had
75 never spoken to her, except for a few casual words, and yet her name was like a summons to all my foolish blood.
Her image accompanied me even in places the most hostile to romance. On
80 Saturday evenings when my aunt went marketing I had to go to carry some of the parcels. We walked through the flaring streets, jostled by drunken men and bar-gaining women, amid the curses of
85 labourers, the shrill litanies of shop-boys who stood on guard by the barrels of pigs' cheeks, the nasal chanting of street-singers, who sang a *come-all-you* about O'Donovan Rossa, or a ballad about the
90 troubles in our native land. These noises converged in a single sensation of life for me: I imagined that I bore my chalice safely through a throng of foes. Her name sprang to my lips at moments in strange prayers
95 and praises which I myself did not under-stand. My eyes were often full of tears (I could not tell why) and at times a flood from my heart seemed to pour itself out into my bosom. I thought little of the future. I did not
100 know whether I would ever speak to her or not or, if I spoke to her, how I could tell her of my confused adoration. But my body was like a harp and her words and

gestures were like fingers running upon the
105 wires.

1. The author of the passage suggests which
   of the following about the "other houses"
   (lines 6–7)?

   A) They are uninhabited during the days.
   B) They appear similar to the
      uninhabited house at the blind end.
   C) They architecturally clash with one
      another.
   D) They reflect the demeanor of their
      occupants.

2. In line 13, "hung" most nearly means

   A) swung.
   B) lingered.
   C) dangled.
   D) inclined.

3. The narrator views the priest described in
   the second paragraph (lines 10–27) as

   A) kindly.
   B) altruistic.
   C) neighborly.
   D) sociable.

4. As presented in the passage, the narrator
   and his companions are best described as

   A) unruly and somber.
   B) rebellious and foolish.
   C) secretive and infatuated.
   D) boisterous and collaborative.

Continued →

5. Which choice provides the best evidence for the answer to the previous question?

    A) Lines 30–31 ("When . . . somber")
    B) Lines 36–45 ("Our shouts . . . harness")
    C) Lines 47–50 ("If my . . . housed")
    D) Lines 74–77 ("I had . . . blood")

6. In line 34, "feeble" most nearly means

    A) poorly constructed.
    B) intellectually deficient.
    C) incompetent.
    D) ineffective.

7. Mangan's attitude toward his sister could best be described as

    A) outwardly disobedient.
    B) reluctantly obedient.
    C) quietly affectionate.
    D) good-naturedly mocking.

8. The sentence in lines 61–63 ("Her dress . . . side") mainly serves to

    A) contrast the narrator's image of Mangan's sister from that of Mangan himself.
    B) emphasize the narrators dislike of Mangan's sister's authoritarian nature.
    C) show the difficulty of seeing Mangan's sister clearly in the shadows.
    D) present a description of Mangan's sister as viewed by the characters in the story.

Continued →

9. When the narrator followed Mangan's sister, he sought to

   A) follow her to her destination.
   B) speak to her before their paths separated.
   C) call to her so he could reveal his feelings for her.
   D) keep her in view but avoid conversing with her.

10. Which choice best describes the narrator's characterization of Mangan's sister?

    A) Appealing but condescending
    B) Beautiful but foolish
    C) Desirable but unattainable
    D) Silent but stern

11. Which choice provides the best evidence for the answer to the previous question?

    A) Lines 53–56 ("We waited . . . resignedly")
    B) Lines 64–65 ("Every . . . door")
    C) Lines 67–68 ("When she . . . leaped")
    D) Lines 74–77 ("I had . . . blood")

■

8. ODDS & ENDS

STRUCTURE QUESTIONS

Structure questions ask about the way a passage's paragraphs, or ideas *within* a paragraph, fit together. They may ask about a passage's overall structure, or how a passage shifts focus from one idea to the next. These questions usually require you to have a sense of main ideas within a passage, particularly how these ideas change.

As you read a passage, look for obvious changes in structure. These changes may occur at the beginnings of paragraphs. But focus may shift within a paragraph as well. You should already be looking for, and boxing, contrast signals, which often indicate a shift in the passage. Other shifts or structural changes may be signaled by whole sentences, especially topic sentences. Be on the lookout for these shifts as you read.

To identify Structure questions, look for any of the following phrases or questions:
- Over the course of the passage, the focus shifts from . . .
- Which choice describes the development of the passage?
- Which choice describes the sequence of events in the passage?
- How does a paragraph function within the passage?

RELATIONSHIP QUESTIONS

We've already discussed how different *passages* relate to each other (Comparison questions). Now we'll discuss how different parts of the *same* passage relate to each other. We'll call these questions *Relationship* questions. Some of these questions will test the relationship of parts of a passage, such as paragraphs. Others will test your understanding of how different ideas or viewpoints relate. Always go back and consider main ideas as you answer these questions.

To identify Relationship questions, you may see the word *relationship* or *relate* in the question. Also looks for words such as *compare* or *contrast*.

■

Structure and Relationship questions sometimes overlap. As you might imagine, a question that asks about the relationship of two paragraphs is also asking about the structure of the passage. In these cases, we'll typically refer to the questions as *Relationship* questions.

Here is a sample passage that tests Structure and Relationship questions. As usual, try to answer each question using context before looking at the answer choices. Even if line numbers are not given, it's usually a good idea to have an idea of what you're looking for before you start checking the answer choices.

Questions 1–5 are based on the following passage.

This passage is adapted from Niccolò Machiavelli, *The Prince*, first published in 1532. The work was composed for princes as a practical guide for ruling.

And here comes in the question whether it is better to be loved rather than feared, or feared rather than loved. It might perhaps be answered that we should wish to be both; but since love and fear can hardly exist together, if we must choose between
Line them, it is far safer to be feared than loved. For of men it may generally be affirmed,
5   that they are thankless, fickle, false, studious to avoid danger, greedy of gain, devoted to you while you are able to confer benefits upon them, and ready, while danger is distant, to shed their blood, and sacrifice their property, their lives, and their children for you; but in the hour of need they turn against you. The Prince, therefore, who without otherwise securing himself builds wholly on their professions is undone. For the
10 friendships which we buy with a price, and do not gain by greatness and nobility of character, though they be fairly earned are not made good, but fail us when we have occasion to use them.
Moreover, men are less careful how they offend him who makes himself loved than him who makes himself feared. For love is held by the tie of obligation, which, because
15 men are a sorry breed, is broken on every whisper of private interest; but fear is bound by the apprehension of punishment which never relaxes its grasp.
Nevertheless a Prince should inspire fear in such a fashion that if he does not win love he may escape hate. For a man may very well be feared and yet not hated, and this will be the case so long as he does not meddle with the property or with the women
20 of his citizens and subjects.

(EX) 1. During the course of the first paragraph, the author's focus shifts from

A) an investigation into whether princes should be loved or feared to the differences between men who love their rulers and those who fear them.
B) a discussion of the differences between love and fear to a discussion of their similarities.
C) the assertion that a prince must be both loved and feared to an admission that these sentiments cannot exist together.
D) the assertion that a prince should be feared to the consequences of a prince relying on men who love him.

(EX) 2. The relationship between a prince and the men described in the first paragraph (lines 1–13) is primarily determined by the prince's ability to

   A) earn his subjects' love and devotion.
   B) earn both his subjects' love and their fear.
   C) benefit his subjects.
   D) strike fear in his subjects.

(EX) 3. The second paragraph (lines 13–16) is primarily concerned with establishing a contrast between

   A) men who love their rulers and those who feel an obligation to them.
   B) men who fear punishment and those who do not.
   C) men who love their rulers and those who fear them.
   D) men who fear their rulers and those who hate them.

(EX) 4. Over the course of the passage, the main focus of the narrative shifts from

A) an overview of a problem to examples of ways to solve the problem.
B) a discussion of the similarities between two emotions to a discussion of their differences.
C) a recommended position on an issue to necessary limits on this position.
D) a solution to a problem to steps that can be taken to realize this solution.

(EX) 5. In the last paragraph (lines 17–20), the author primarily distinguishes between

A) citizens and subjects.
B) property and wealth.
C) fear and love.
D) fear and hatred.

■

CORRECTIONS: TONE, STRUCTURE, AND RELATIONSHIP QUESTIONS

Go back to Practice Test 10 and correct all missed Tone, Structure, and Relationship questions (and any associated Citing-Textual-Evidence questions). See Section 9 (Reading: Practice & Corrections) on page 116 for more details about correcting practice tests. The actual questions to correct for each test, as well as line numbers and other hints, are found in the Techniques section at the end of this tutorial.

At this point, you've probably completed Practice Test 9. See the Tutoring Schedule in this tutorial's Introduction for additional correction assignments.

PRACTICE PASSAGE

The following passage is an 11-question passage, so give yourself 13 minutes and 30 seconds to complete it. This passage emphasizes Structure and Relationship questions.

Questions 1–11 are based on the following passage.

This passage is adapted from Stephani Sutherland, "Itch: How It Arises Is Only Now Becoming Clear." ©2016 by Scientific American.

The best-known form of itch erupts when the body reacts to a simple mosquito bite. After the pest extracts its meal, it leaves behind chemicals and proteins that
5 our immune system recognizes as foreign and so mounts a reaction at the bite site. Immune cells in the skin release cytokines, tiny chemical messengers that escalate the response. The first inkling of itch is felt on
10 the skin—just enough to cause scratching. That, in turn, damages the protective outer layer of the epidermis. Immune cells then release a surge of histamine, a major itch-inducing chemical, along with other itch-
15 inducing substances called pruritogens. Histamine activates its receptors found on the fine endings of sensory nerves in the skin, triggering the familiar sensation of itch. Or does it? Histamine is turning out to
20 be less important to itch than researchers have long believed.

Until just a decade ago, histamine receptors remained the only known itch detectors, and so antihistamine medicines
25 today are still the go-to treatment for itch. But researchers have long suspected that chemicals other than histamine must trigger other kinds of itch—mainly because antihistamines do not aid many patients. To
30 find new itch receptors, scientists followed the trail of obscure substances known to trigger itch without involving histamine.

The first discovery was cowhage, a plant used as an ingredient in itching
35 powders sold in novelty shops. Back in the 1950s, the late Walter Shelley, a pioneer in itch research, speculated that cowhage's itch factor was a protein-cutting enzyme, a protease he named mucunain. In 2008 that
40 hunch was finally confirmed when Ethan Lerner, a dermatologist and itch researcher at Massachusetts General Hospital, found that mucunain activates a receptor found in skin and nerve cells: protease-activated
45 receptor 2 (PAR2). Certain proteases—including mucunain—can snip off a tiny piece of the PAR2 protein, which activates the receptor. That discovery led to a new

appreciation that proteases and the peptide
50 fragments they produce are key mediators of itch, at PAR2 and other receptors. Proteases are ubiquitous, including in insect saliva and bacterial secretions, perhaps explaining why bug bites and
55 infections can be so itchy.

The second clue to finding new itch receptors came from chloroquine, a medicine meant to protect people from malaria. In an ironic twist, the drug
60 prevents the disease but causes itching. The side effect, which is not alleviated by antihistamines, causes many at-risk Africans to refuse chloroquine, although it has made the drug a valuable tool for
65 investigators to study itch. One of them was Xinzhong Dong, then working in the laboratory of David Anderson at the California Institute of Technology. In 2001 Dong discovered a family of receptors,
70 activated by unknown chemicals, called Mrgprs (Mas-related G-protein-coupled receptors). Some of the Mrgprs were found only in sensory neurons, suggesting they detected external stimuli, but what kind
75 remained a mystery.

Dong applied chloroquine to cells containing Mrgprs to test whether the Mrgprs might qualify as undiscovered itch receptors. In research reported in 2009,
80 Dong—now at Johns Hopkins University—and Anderson created transgenic mice that lacked one of the Mrgprs found in sensory cells, a receptor designated MrgprA3. "Normal mice showed a robust scratching
85 response to chloroquine treatment," Dong says, but the transgenic mice lacking MrgprA3 did not. "Without MrgprA3, the animals just don't feel the itch. That was our breakthrough point," Dong says.
90 Thanks to the two quirky chemicals, researchers discovered some of the first new itch sensors since the histamine receptors were described in the latter half of the 20th century. "But the point was not
95 to find the receptor for chloroquine or cowhage; the point really is to find out what activates these nonhistamine itch neurons in chronic itch conditions," says Diana Bautista, an itch researcher at the
100 University of California, Berkeley. Researchers now want to identify those substances. "There are probably a small

number of molecules in the skin that turn
on Mrgprs, and finding them will lead to
105 very good drug targets and therapies,"
Lerner says.

1. During the course of the first paragraph,
    the focus shifts from

    A) a discussion of a well-known source
        of itching to an introduction of lesser-
        known sources.
    B) a description of the itching process to
        an introduction of the chemicals that
        suppress itching.
    C) a claim about the source of itching to
        a questioning of that claim.
    D) a disclosure of a discovery to a
        rejection of the importance of this
        discovery.

2. According to the description of a mosquito
    bite in lines 1–19 ("The best-known . . .
    sensation of itch"), which of the following
    describes the relationship between a
    mosquito bite and histamine?

    A) A mosquito bite releases histamine
        into a body's skin cells.
    B) A body releases histamine to help
        offset the itching caused by a
        mosquito bite.
    C) A mosquito feeds on histamine from
        the skin during a mosquito bite.
    D) A mosquito bite starts a chain reaction
        that results in the body's release of
        histamine.

3. Based on the passage, the statement
    "antihistamine medicines today are still
    the go-to treatment for itch" (lines 24–25)
    implies that today's itch medicines

    A) are never effective in combatting
        itching.
    B) are generally effective in combatting
        itching.
    C) have not kept pace with recent
        discoveries about the causes of
        itching.
    D) are considerably more effective than
        were itch medicines in the past.

Continued →

4. As used in line 37, "speculated" most nearly means

A) declared
B) risked
C) affirmed
D) guessed

5. According to the third paragraph (lines 33–55), which of the following describes the relationship between cowhage and mucunain?

A) Mucunain is an enzyme found in cowhage.
B) Mucunain is a protein found in cowhage.
C) Mucunain suppresses the itches caused by cowhage.
D) Cowhage suppresses the itches caused by mucunain.

6. The author's use of the word "clue" (line 56) serves to

A) question the likelihood of finding new itch receptors in the near future.
B) highlight the exceptional knowledge required by scientists in the search for new itch receptors.
C) support the idea that evidence for new itch receptors was apparent and informative.
D) emphasize that new itch receptors were discovered gradually and with some difficulty.

7. Based on the passage, which of the following best describes the relationship, if any, between chloroquine and itching?

A) Chloroquine is a side-effect of malaria and not related to itching.
B) Chloroquine was supposed to protect people from itching.
C) Chloroquine is a direct cause of itching.
D) Itching causes the body to release chloroquine.

Continued →

8. Which choice provides the best evidence for the answer to the previous question?

   A) Lines 56–59 ("The second . . . malaria")
   B) Lines 59–60 ("In a . . . itching")
   C) Lines 76–79 ("Dong . . . receptors")
   D) Lines 79–83 ("In research . . . MrgprA3")

9. Based on the passage, which choice best describes the relationship between Shelley's and Lerner's research?

   A) Lerner's research contradicts Shelley's.
   B) Lerner's research revises Shelley's.
   C) Lerner's research is unrelated to Shelley's.
   D) Lerner's research validates Shelley's.

10. In the fifth paragraph (lines 76–89), some of the mice in Dong's and Anderson's study did not itch because these mice

    A) lacked one of the Mrgprs found in sensory neurons.
    B) possessed Mrgprs in their sensory neurons.
    C) received a treatment of chloroquine.
    D) did not receive a treatment of chloroquine.

11. Which choice best reflects the developmental pattern of the passage?

    A) Established beliefs are questioned, new findings are discussed, and future research is proposed.
    B) Past discoveries are challenged, and new discoveries lead to new solutions to a problem.
    C) A problem is discussed, and solutions to this problem are introduced.
    D) Surprising discoveries give rise to a new set of questions.

■

DIFFICULT PASSAGES

Many SATs will include at least one especially difficult passage. As you work on these passages, remember to . . .

FOCUS ON THE EASY STUFF

If the passage is hard to understand or phrases or whole sentences confuse you, focus on the parts you *do* understand. Don't get discouraged. Read through the passage, underline parts that are clear to you and that you think are important, and focus on the easy stuff. Many of the questions, perhaps most of them, will focus on the parts of the passage that you *do* understand.

STAY OPEN-MINDED

This is an important tip, especially on difficult passages. As you know by now, for most questions we recommend you try answering the question using context *before* looking at the answer choices. But what happens if you go back to the passage and simply don't understand the relevant context? You shouldn't necessarily give up on the question. Start looking at the answer choices, and stay *open-minded*. If an answer choice is supported by context, even if it answers the question in a way you hadn't anticipated, it's probably the correct answer.

Many students will find the following passage difficult. Remember, just get through it. Focus on the easy stuff, and be ready to search for context when you get to the questions.

Questions 1–5 are based on the following passage.

This passage is adapted from Wallace Stegner, *Beyond the Hundredth Meridian.* ©1992 by Houghton Mifflin Co.

The tourist and the nature lover occupied a good large corner of Clarence Edward Dutton. He never quite made up his mind whether he was literary traveler or sober scientific analyst: the temptations were essentially equal. He escaped his dilemma by
Line being both, and in his reports a rich and embroidered nineteenth-century traveler's
5 prose flows around bastions of geological fact as some of the lava coulees on the Uinkaret flow around gables of sedimentary strata. The literary tendency is progressive; it is apparent in *The Geology of the High Plateaus of Utah* (1880) and dominant in *The Tertiary History of the Grand Canyon* (1882). With hardly an apology, Dutton forsook the "sever ascetic style" of science when he came to deal with the
10 Grand Canyon. The Grand Canyon was beyond the reach of superlatives, it compelled effusion of a kind. The result is a scientific monograph of great geological importance which contains whole chapters as ebullient as the writing of John Muir, and deviates constantly into speculations so far from geological that they sound more like Ruskin than Lyell.

(EX) 1. The primary purpose of the passage is to

A) point out the differences in two works of scientific writing.
B) caution against combining literary and scientific writing styles.
C) discuss the dualistic nature of a scientist's writing.
D) examine the background and success of a scientist.

This is a Purpose question. If you grasped the main purpose of the passage while you were reading, you probably identified the correct answer. If not, then read through the answer choices and decide which one is best supported by the passage. As stated at the beginning of this section, you may have to be open-minded while reading the answer choices (especially if you weren't comfortable with the context).

(EX) 2. As used in line 2, "sober" most nearly means

A) grave.
B) not intoxicated.
C) quiet.
D) dispassionate.

(EX) 3. The author presents Dutton's decision to write in a literary manner between 1880 and 1882 as something that

A) expanded markedly.
B) became apparent for the first time.
C) grew inconsistently.
D) had wide-ranging influence.

(EX) 4. The author's attitude toward Dutton's writing about the Grand Canyon is best described as one of

A) condescension.
B) indifference.
C) ambiguity.
D) understanding.

(EX) 5. The author most likely mentions Muir and Ruskin in order to

    A) give examples of writers who influenced the work of Dutton.
    B) compare Dutton to scientists known more for their informative scientific writing.
    C) argue that Dutton's writing is more like that of literary writers than science writers.
    D) provide well-known authors whose styles of writing are similar to that of Dutton.

■

PRACTICE PASSAGE

The following passage is a 11-question passage, so give yourself 13 minutes and 30 seconds to complete it. Many students find this passage difficult. As you read, you don't have to understand all of it, or even much of it. Just get through it. You don't earn points for reading the passage—only answering the questions. While you're reading, remember to search out the "easy stuff." When you get to the questions, try to tackle the easier-looking ones with confidence. Don't forget, it's good practice to skip harder questions (especially on harder passages), and come back to them if you have time (review "Skipping Questions" in the Reading introduction, under "Timing").

Practice Passage VIII

Questions 1–10 are based on the following passage.

This passage is adapted from Denise Scott Brown, "Learning from Pop." ©1984 by Harper and Row. Pop art is an American art movement from the 1950s and 1960s in which everyday objects of American life were used as subject matter.

Sensitivity to needs is a first reason for going to the existing city. Once there, the first lesson for architects is the pluralism of need. No builder-developer in his right
5 mind would announce: I am building for Man. He is building for a market, for a group of people defined by income range, age, family composition, and life style. Levittowns, Leisureworlds, Georgian-styled
10 town houses grow from someone's estimation of the needs of the groups who will be their markets. The city can be seen as the built artifacts of a set of subcultures. At the moment, those subcultures which
15 willingly resort to architects are few.

Of course learning from what's there is subject to the caveats and limitations of all behaviorisitic analysis—one is surveying behavior which is constrained, it is not what
20 people might do in other conditions. The poor do not willingly live in tenements and maybe the middle classes don't willingly live in Levittowns; perhaps the Georgian-styling is less pertinent to the townhouse
25 resident than is the rent. In times of housing shortage this is a particularly forceful argument against architectural behaviorism since people can't vote against a particular offering by staying
30 away if there is no alternative. To counteract this danger one must search for comparison environments where for some reason the constraints do not hold. There are environments which suggest what
35 economically constrained group's taste might be if they were less constrained. They are the nouveau rich environments: Hollywood for a former era, Las Vegas for today, and homes of film stars, sportsmen

40 and other groups where upward mobility may resemble vertical takeoff, yet where maintenance of previous value systems is encouraged.

Another source is physical
45 backgrounds in the mass media, movies, soap operas, pickle and furniture ads. Here the aim is not to sell houses but something else, and the background represents someone's (Madison Avenue's?) idea of
50 what pickle buyers or soap opera watchers want in a house. Now the Madison Avenue observer's view may be as biased as the architect's, and it should be studied in the light of what it is trying to sell—must pickle
55 architecture look homey like my house or elegant like yours if it is to sell me pickles? But at least it's another bias, an alternative to the architectural navel contemplation we do so often for research, i.e., ask: What did
60 Le Corbusier do? Both Madison Avenue and the builder, although they can tell us little of the needs of the poor, cover a broader range of the population and pass a stiffer market test than does the architect in
65 urban renewal or public housing, and if we learn no more from these sources than that architecture must differ for different groups, that is a great deal. But an alternative to both is to examine what people do to
70 buildings—in Levittowns, Society Hills, gray areas and slums—once they are in them. Here costs and availability are less constraining forces since the enterprise is smaller. Also, changes tend often to be
75 symbolic rather than structural, and aspirations can perhaps be more easily inferred from symbols than from structures.

Attention to built sources for information on need does not imply that
80 asking people what they want is not extremely necessary as well. This is an important topic, as is the relation between the two types of survey, asking and looking; but it is not the subject of this
85 enquiry, which is on what can be learned from the artifacts of pop culture.

1. The passage is primarily concerned with

   A) explaining the differences among different subcultures.
   B) identifying traditional strategies for identifying peoples' needs.
   C) describing the advantages of a particular way of learning about the needs of different groups.
   D) contrasting the work of architects with that of other professions.

2. As used in line 6, "market" most nearly refers to

   A) a place where food is sold.
   B) people with similar social and economic interests.
   C) a field of trade or business.
   D) a group of architects with similar tastes.

3. According to the author, which of the following is a reason for why "behavioristic analysis" (line 18) is of limited value?

   A) When people have multiple options, their decisions become random.
   B) Most groups would prefer to live in parts of a city they cannot afford.
   C) A group of people should not be analyzed using its individual members.
   D) People's behavior is often limited by their circumstances.

4. The author's use of the words "vertical takeoff" (line 41) mainly serves to

   A) illustrate the close connection between social mobility and value systems.
   B) emphasize the rapid change in some people's economic status.
   C) highlight the recent transformations of some cities.
   D) provide a contrast to the gradual nature of environmental change.

Continued →

5. As presented in the passage, Le Corbusier is best described as

A) an architect noted for his elegant designs.
B) an architect who offers an alternative viewpoint to traditional architectural theory.
C) an architect whose work other architects frequently turn to while researching.
D) an architect who paid little attention to the social needs of his clients.

6. The author states that no builder-developer admits to "building for Man" (lines 5–6) in order to emphasize that:

A) architects build for subgroups within the greater population.
B) some builder-developers use terms that are now considered antiquated.
C) architects must find ways to design buildings that appeal to most people.
D) builder-developers usually keep their methodologies secret.

7. One central claim of the third paragraph (lines 44–77) is that architects should

A) create physical backgrounds rather than entire houses.
B) focus less on building houses and more on selling them.
C) consider traditional solutions to design considerations.
D) study how people alter the places in which they live.

8. Which choice provides the best evidence for the answer to the previous question?

A) Lines 44–46 ("Another . . . ads")
B) Lines 46–51 ("Here . . . house")
C) Lines 57–60 ("But at . . . do?")
D) Lines 68–71 ("But . . . them")

Continued →

9. The main purpose of the fourth paragraph (lines 78–86) is to

A) shift the essay to a new subject of inquiry.
B) emphasize the relation between two types of survey.
C) summarize the points made elsewhere in the passage.
D) qualify the author's belief in the importance of a particular source of information.

10. As used in line 64, "stiffer" most nearly means

A) more solid
B) more stringent
C) more formal
D) more extreme

11. It can reasonably be inferred from the passage that "Levittowns, Leisureworlds, [and] Georgian-styled town houses" (lines 9–10) are examples of

A) places of leisure and escape from cities.
B) styles of architecture which make up most cities.
C) places frequently desired by the rich.
D) places each inhabited by a different type of subgroup.

■

30- and 40-hour programs: After reviewing all topics, take Practice Test 8 in *The Official SAT Study Guide.*

9. READING: PRACTICE & CORRECTIONS

PRACTICE PROBLEMS

For extra practice beyond the passages in this tutorial, complete passages from Test 1 of the *The Official SAT Study Guide*. Make sure you time yourself on each passage:

- **10-question passage**: 12 minutes, 30 seconds (12:30)
- **11-question passage**: 13 minutes, 30 seconds (13:30)

Here are the passages for Test 1. You can check them off as you complete them:

- ☐ Passage I
- ☐ Passage II
- ☐ Passage III
- ☐ Passage IV
- ☐ Passage V

See the Tutoring Schedules section in this tutorial's Introduction for more on when to tackle these passages for different programs.

TEST CORRECTIONS

After completing and grading each practice test, you should correct Reading questions that you missed or guessed on. Below are the three steps to correcting practice tests:

1. Turn to the Techniques section at the end of this tutorial and circle the Reading questions that you missed or guessed on for each test. Focus on the types of questions that you have covered. For example, don't correct Tone questions until you've covered Tone questions in the tutorial. (See the Tutoring Schedules in the Introduction.)

2. Correct the problems in *The Official SAT Study Guide*. As you correct the problems, go back to the tutorial and review the question types. The idea is to (1) identify question types that have given you trouble, (2) go back to the tutorial so you can review and strengthen approaches to these questions, and (3) apply these approaches to the specific problems on which you struggled.

3. If you have trouble finding or understanding context, refer to the line numbers and hints given in the Techniques chapter. This is an important part of correcting the tests.

READ

Perhaps the best way to raise your Reading Test scores is to read as much as possible.
Read material that is hard to understand at first. Choose a variety of reading materials, such as
novels, newspapers, and even poetry. While the techniques and strategies taught in this tutorial
are certainly helpful and will begin to compensate for less-than-great reading skills, no
instruction can completely take the place of a solid reading background. For this reason,
reading is a significant part of improving your Reading scores.

PART **2**

WRITING AND LANGUAGE

I
WRITING AND LANGUAGE INTRODUCTION

The Writing and Language section is divided into five chapters:

I. Introduction

II. Grammar

III. Sentence Structure

IV. Grammar and Sentence Structure Guidelines

V. Main Ideas and Organization

TYPES OF QUESTIONS

All questions on the Writing and Language Test are multiple choice, with four answer choices. The questions fall into one of three general categories:

1. Grammar: These questions test basic grammar, including topics such as subject-verb agreement and the correct use of apostrophes.

2. Sentence Structure: These questions test topics associated with entire sentences, including punctuation, run-ons, and fragments.

3. Main Ideas and Organization: These questions go beyond simple grammar topics associated with words or sentences. They often require comprehension of an entire paragraph or the passage as a whole. The also test the logical flow of ideas.

TEST LAYOUT

The Writing and Language Test includes:

- Four passages (11 questions each)
- A total of 44 multiple-choice questions
- A total test time of 35 minutes

A GENERAL APPROACH

Before moving on, take a moment now to open up the SAT book and see what these questions look like. Read the directions (this should be the only time you have to do this).

ANSWER QUESTIONS *WHILE* YOU READ THE PASSAGES

Unlike the SAT Reading Test, where all of the questions for a passage *follow* the passage, the questions on the Writing and Language Test show up *next* to the passage. You can, and should, answer them while you're reading the passage.

EXCEPTIONS

Be aware. Sometimes you have to read *beyond* the point where a question shows up before you can answer the question. You might have to consider the main idea of a paragraph, or the best way to transition to the next paragraph. We'll get more into this in Chapter V.

TIMING

ORDER OF DIFFICULTY

Like the Reading Test, the Writing and Language Test is NOT arranged in order of difficulty. In other words, later questions, or later passages, may be easier than earlier ones. Thus, it is essential that you get to the last question of the last passage.

SKIPPING QUESTIONS

If you have trouble finishing the test, consider skipping some of the more difficult questions. For most students, the most difficult questions, and thus the most time consuming, are Main Idea and Organization questions (Chapter V). Until you're fast enough to get to the last question on the test, consider skipping these questions. We'll get into how to identify these questions in Chapter V. We recommend circling the number of a skipped question on your answer sheet so you can come back to it if you have time.

GUESSING

You don't lose points for wrong answers on the SAT, so before your time is up, make sure to guess on any unanswered questions. This should take less than a minute. Watch the clock so you don't run out of time.

TIMING PRACTICE

If you're practicing on a single passage, use the following time estimate:

- **11-questions**: 8 minutes and 30 seconds (8:30)

Remember, this is just an estimate. On an actual test, you'll probably spend a little longer on some harder passages, and you'll likely finish easier passages faster. But this estimate gives you a good approximation of your allowable time. If you're taking much longer on practice passages, you'll probably need to pick up the pace.

If you have trouble finishing the test in time, review Timing in the Introduction of this tutorial for a detailed timing strategy.

TECHNIQUE IDENTIFICATION

Often, there are clues that will help you figure out what technique is being tested by a specific question. Throughout the tutorial, look for the magnifying glass for information about identifying techniques:

INFORMATIONAL GRAPHICS

Each Writing and Language test will have 1–2 questions that test *informational graphics*: tables and graphs. These questions typically don't have much to do with "writing and language" (go figure), so we're not going to cover them in this section. We'll cover informational graphics questions on the Reading Test section in this tutorial.

When you correct the practice tests or complete practice problems from *The Official SAT Study Guide*, we'll assign Informational Graphics questions along with the Main Ideas and Organization questions.

II
GRAMMAR

This chapter covers one of the most important parts of the Writing and Language Test: *grammar*. These grammar topics will also help you in your writing, so keep them in mind as you prepare for the SAT Essay.

1. VERB TENSE

The tense of a verb describes *when* a verb "happens." If events occur at the same time, the verb tenses must be the same. If events occur at different times, the verb tenses should reflect the order of these events.

VERB-TENSE TERMINOLOGY

Verb – The part of speech that expresses existence, action, or occurrence in a sentence.

TENSE

While there are many different tenses, it is helpful to be familiar with the five most important verb tenses found on the SAT. Since you will not be tested on their official names (such as *past perfect*), we will refer to them by the *times* that they occur, as shown on the time-line below:

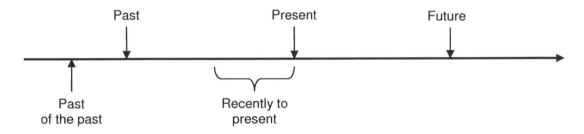

First, let's look at the easy ones. You are probably comfortable with these already.

Present: Today, I *study* with my tutor for the SAT.

Past: Yesterday, I *studied* for several hours for the SAT.

Future: Tomorrow, I *will study* several more hours for the SAT.

Now, for the harder ones—from now on, we'll call these the *"other" verb tenses*:

Past of the past: This tense always uses the word ***had***. For example:

> Before Aimee took the SAT last year, she *had studied* for several months. (The studying took place *before* Aimee took the SAT; hence, the *past of the past*).

Recently to present: This tense uses the word **has** for *he, she, it*, or any *singular* thing performing the action and **have** for *I, we, they, you*, or any *plural* thing performing the action.

> I *have studied* for the SAT for what seems like an eternity. (This has been going on for a while, and it sounds like it still is.)

TO SUMMARIZE

Past-of-the-past tense → use the word **had**

Recently-to-present tense → use the word **has** or **have**

TO BE

The verb *to be* is an irregular verb. Most of its forms don't even resemble the word itself. Luckily, your ear will probably pick up on correct and incorrect uses. You are probably already comfortable with the following:

> Yesterday, I *was* sick.
> Today, I *am* feeling great.
> They *were* the best in the class last year, but now they *are* struggling.
> She has *been* here for hours.

-ING WORDS

Words in the *-ing* form can be used to express continuous action. **However, a word in the *-ing* form—on its own—does not function as a verb.** For example:

> Incorrect: John *running* to the store.

Doesn't sound good, right? To correctly use an *-ing* word as part of a verb phrase, you must use a *to be* verb. The following are some examples:

> Past: Yesterday, we *were emptying* out the cupboard.
> Present: Today, John *is running* to the store while we finish the work.
> Recently-to-present: John *has been working* as a handyman this summer.
> Past-of-the-past: John *had been working* two jobs before he had enough money to buy the bike.

IRREGULAR VERBS

Irregular verbs may behave in unpredictable ways. For example:

present: Today, I *lie* on my bed.

past: Last night, I *lay* on my bed.

past of the past: Before I woke up this morning, I had *lain* on my bed.

recently to present: I have *lain* on my bed all morning.

As you can see, things can get a little tricky. The good news, however, is that the SAT does not put too much emphasis on these irregular verbs. But they *may* occasionally show up, so if your ear tells you that the form of a verb sounds "funny," you may have found one of these irregular verb errors.

VERB TENSE ON THE SAT

Verb tense questions on the SAT almost always ask you to recognize the tense set somewhere else in the passage—usually in the previous sentence or earlier in the sentence in question—and match the underlined verb to the previous verb. In the following problems, make sure you focus on the verbs that are not underlined (and are thus correct).

> To identify verb tense questions, look for questions with answer choices that contain the same verbs in different tenses—for example *look, looked, has looked, will look*, etc.

VERB TENSE LESSON PROBLEMS

Built at the turn of the century, the mansion displaying some of the oldest styles of architecture seen in the region today.

1. A) NO CHANGE
   B) will have displayed
   C) displayed
   D) displays

The scientists were sure they had uncovered an ancient human skeleton, but they **2** had not been sure of its origin.

2. A) NO CHANGE
   B) are not sure
   C) will not have been sure
   D) were not sure

Continued →

Since last night, Paul **3** worked on his history paper, and he will probably still be working on it until tonight.

3. A) NO CHANGE
   B) works
   C) will work
   D) has been working

Patrick learned to swim before he could walk, competed in his first swimming contest before he started kindergarten, and **4** winning his first race when he was five years old.

4. A) NO CHANGE
   B) won
   C) wins
   D) will win

Taking the time up front to properly plan the project will ensure success. Jumping right in with no planning, however, **5** leads to failure.

5. A) NO CHANGE
   B) will have lead
   C) lead
   D) will lead

Early in the morning, the majestic sun peeks over the distant hillside. Long shadows **1** stretched out over the yellow fields.

1. A) NO CHANGE
   B) stretch
   C) will stretch
   D) stretching

Before I finish my research paper, I **2** have read three books on the subject.

2. A) NO CHANGE
   B) will have read
   C) read
   D) had read

The teacher looked back fondly on the days when students **3** come to class free of cell phone distractions.

3. A) NO CHANGE
   B) came
   C) will have come
   D) could have come

Continued →

Before the rocket was launched, Ken **4** <u>written</u> dozens of articles about its expected path.

4. A) NO CHANGE
    B) had written
    C) had wrote
    D) will write

Cobwebs fell from the ceiling of the haunted mansion as Jason carefully **5** <u>crept</u> inside.

5. A) NO CHANGE
    B) will creep
    C) creeps
    D) has crept

2. SUBJECT-VERB AGREEMENT

Subjects must always agree with their respective verbs in number. In other words, if the subject is *singular* then the verb must be *singular*, and if the subject is *plural* then the verb must be *plural*.

There are two challenges to this topic. The first one is identifying the subject and its verb in the sentence. The second one is deciding whether the subject is singular or plural.

SUBJECT-VERB-AGREEMENT TERMINOLOGY

Subject – consists of a noun, noun phrase, or noun substitute which often refers to the person, place, or thing performing the action or being in the state expressed by the rest of the sentence.

Preposition – A word that locates things in *time, place,* or *movement.* ⎤
Prepositional Phrase – A preposition followed by a noun or pronoun. ⎦ See examples below.

Modifying Phrase – We'll get more into modifying phrases later. For now, you should know that a modifying phrase is part of a sentence that can be removed without greatly altering the grammatical correctness of the sentence. A modifying phrase is separated from the rest of the sentence with commas. This makes it easy to spot.

PREPOSITIONS

Since removing *prepositional phrases* will help you find subjects and verbs, first let's look at a lesson on prepositions. If a word sounds correct in *either one* (not necessarily both) of the following sentences, the word is probably a preposition. Memorize these sentences.

The professor walked _____ the desk. (good for *place* or *movement* prepositions: ex. *into*)

The professor talked _____ the class. (good for *time* prepositions: ex. *after*)

Here are some examples of prepositions. Try them out in one or both of the sentences above.

about	beside	in front of	through
across	between	into	throughout
after	by	like	to
against	concerning	next to	toward
around	during	**of***	under
at	except	off	until
before	for	on	upon
behind	in	past	without
beneath			

/ *The word "of" is probably the most common preposition.**

IDENTIFYING THE SUBJECT AND THE VERB

BAREBONES SENTENCES

The SAT loves to trick you by putting prepositional phrases or modifying phrases between the subject and its verb, but the subject is never part of these phrases. So:

/ Get rid of prepositional and modifying phrases when looking for the subject of a sentence.

After these phrases are removed, you will be left with the "barebones sentence." For example:

> The number of calories recommended for the average person by the Food and Drug Administration, according to a report last year, depend on the age and size of the individual.

First, remove the modifying phrase: "according to a report last year." Notice the commas on either side of the phrase. Next, remove the prepositional phrases (prepositions are in bold below). You should be left with the following sentence. The subject (and verb) become much easier to see.

> The number **of** calories recommended **for** the average person **by** the Food and Drug Administration, according **to** a report last year, depend **on** the age and size **of** the individual.

> The number recommended depend.

The subject is *number* and the verb is *depend*. (Note: "recommended" is an adjective. It is describing the noun "number." The "number" certainly did not recommend anything.) Since *number* is singular and *depend* is plural, the subject and verb do not agree (more on the number of a verb soon). The correct sentence should read:

> The *number* of calories recommended for the average person by the Food and Drug Administration, according to a report last year, *depends* on the age and size of the individual.

VERBS BEFORE SUBJECTS

Sometimes, the verb comes *before* the subject. When you spot a verb, ask yourself what or who is "performing" the verb, and be prepared to look beyond the verb in the sentence. Look for the word "there," especially at the beginning of a sentence:

There remain questions about the cause of the fire.

Remain is the verb and *questions* is the subject.

Never before has Bill been so successful.

Has is the verb and *Bill* is the subject.

IDENTIFYING THE NUMBER OF THE VERB

Verbs behave in strange ways, as we've already seen in the previous section. In general, the rules that define the number of a verb are the opposite of those for nouns. When a verb is singular, it generally has an *s* at the end:

He eats by himself.

When a verb is plural, it generally does not have an *s* at the end.

They eat together.

If you're ever in doubt, just try out the verb in question with *it* or *they*, and trust your ear.

IDENTIFYING THE NUMBER OF THE SUBJECT

A NOSE SUBJECTS

! **The most commonly missed subjects can be remembered using the acronym: *A NOSE*. These are all *singular* in number:**

    A   anybody, anyone
    N   nobody, no one, neither, none
    O   one
    S   somebody, someone
    E   everybody, everyone, either, each, every

Again, these subjects are all *singular*.

COLLECTIVE NOUNS

Collective nouns are almost always *singular* on the SAT, even though they may seem plural. If you can add an *s* to a collective noun to make it plural (for example: *group* → *groups*), then you know that without the *s*, it is singular:

number	audience	team	city, state, or country
amount	group	company or corporation	staff or department

SUBJECTS WITH "AND" OR "OR"

Make sure you are comfortable with the following rules:

AND

Linking two subjects with *and* creates a *plural* subject. For example:

> **Elizabeth *and* Jasmine** are going to drink coffee. (*plural*)

OR

Linking two subjects with *or* will make the linked subject *singular* if the word closest to the verb (usually the last word) is singular and *plural* if the word closest to the verb is plural. For example:

> Elizabeth or **Jasmine** *is* going to pay for the coffee. (*singular*)
>
> Andy *or* **the girls** *are* going to the museum. (*plural*)
>
> The girls or **Andy** *is* going to the museum. (*singular*)
>
> There *is* **one can** of soup *or* bagels in the pantry. (*singular*)
>
> There *are* **bagels** or one can of soup in the pantry. (*plural*)

■

The following steps outline the method for working with subject-verb agreement errors:

1. Identify the subject and its verb. Find the "barebones sentence," if necessary.
2. Determine the number of the subject (singular or plural).
3. Make sure the number of the verb matches the number of the subject.

 Subject-Verb Agreement questions will usually have answer choices that have the same verbs in singular and plural forms (ex: *take* and *takes*, or *has taken* and *have taken*).

SUBJECT-VERB AGREEMENT LESSON PROBLEMS

Each member of the group of scholars **1** has taken a number of courses at the university.

1. A) NO CHANGE
   B) have
   C) are going to have
   D) having

Ryan or Mike, no matter what you may have heard, **2** are going to be at the dance.

2. A) NO CHANGE
   B) have been going to
   C) is going to be at
   D) have been at

The team of representatives, many from as far away as China and India, **3** assembles in the banquet room.

3. A) NO CHANGE
   B) assemble
   C) are assembled
   D) are in assembly

One of the students **4** is going to the city finals for his or her success in the spelling bee.

4. A) NO CHANGE
   B) are going to the city finals for his or her
   C) is going to the city finals for their
   D) have gone to the city finals for their

I counted numerous boats at the docks, but there **5** was not as many boats as the year before.

5. A) NO CHANGE
   B) were not
   C) will not have been
   D) is not

Either football or basketball **1** are my favorite sport.

1. A) NO CHANGE
   B) are my favorite sports
   C) have been my favorite sport
   D) is my favorite sport

Continued →

Everyone on the team, even the goalies, **2** have been in great shape.

2. A) NO CHANGE
   B) are
   C) is
   D) are going to be

The hiking trails, just one small part of the park's many offerings, **3** giving visitors opportunities to exercise away from traffic.

3. A) NO CHANGE
   B) give
   C) has given
   D) gives

A good recipe, combined with the diligence to follow it closely, often **4** lead even the worst cook to culinary success.

4. A) NO CHANGE
   B) leads
   C) have lead
   D) have been leading

The feeling I got after listening to the lecture about the city's traffic jams **5** were that nothing is going to be done about them anytime soon.

5. A) NO CHANGE
   B) is that
   C) was that
   D) are that

3. PRONOUNS

PRONOUN TERMINOLOGY

Pronoun – A word that generally stands for or refers to a noun or nouns whose identity is made clear earlier in the text.

PRONOUN CASE

CASES OF PRONOUNS

The two general *cases* of pronouns are *subject* pronouns and *object* pronouns. Subject pronouns perform the actions in the sentence. Object pronouns are the recipients of the actions. If you are ever unsure of the case of a pronoun, plug the pronoun into a simple *performer-recipient* sentence and trust your ear, for example:

_He_ threw the ball to _her_.

He is performing the action and *her* is receiving the action. Thus, *he* is a subject pronoun and *her* is an object pronoun.

Subject pronouns		Object pronouns
I	→	*me*
he	→	*him*
she	→	*her*
they	→	*them*
we	→	*us*
it	→	*it*
who	→	*whom*
you	→	*you*

The following rules will help you choose the correct case for a pronoun.

PRONOUNS AND PREPOSITIONS

/ Use *object* pronouns when the pronoun shows up in a phrase with a preposition:

...between *you* and *me*...

...to Sherry and *her*...

...among *us* students...

...from *him* and *her*...

A PRONOUN LINKED WITH A NOUN

When a pronoun is side-by-side with a noun (*we* seniors, *us* students), **eliminate the noun to determine which type of pronoun to use.** For example:

(*We, Us*) seniors decided to take the day off.

We is the correct pronoun since *us* is clearly incorrect when *seniors* is removed.

The award was presented to (*we, us*) students.

Us is the correct pronoun since *we* is clearly incorrect when *students* is removed.

This approach can also help you when a pronoun is part of a linked subject or object. For example:

Toby and me decided to take the day off.

Remove the noun (*Toby*) and you will "hear" the error in the sentence.

Me decided to take the day off.

The pronoun should be in the subject case. The correct sentence reads:

Toby and *I* decided to take the day off.

WHO VERSUS *WHOM*

Recall that *who* is the subject pronoun and *whom* is the object pronoun. Make sure you don't "hypercorrect" by blindly changing *who* to *whom*. Some students think *whom* sounds smarter; it's only smarter when used correctly. Here are some examples:

My mom, *who* has the day off, is going to the store. [Here *who* refers to the subject of the sentence: *mom*.]
With *whom* are you speaking? [Note the conjunction: *with*. Technically, "*Whom* are you speaking with?" is also correct, but you probably won't see that tested.]
I am speaking to the telephone repair man, about *whom* I'm sure you've heard a lot. [Or: . . . *whom* I'm sure you've heard a lot about.]
Bob gave the gift to Sadie, *who* ended up giving it to Rachael. [Here *who* refers to Sadie, as a subject, giving the gift to Rachael.]

THAT VERSUS *WHICH*

While *who* or *whom* refers to people, as described above, *that* and *which* are pronouns that refer to groups or things. There is often confusion about whether to use *that* or *which*. There are distinct differences between the two.

THAT

That is used as a pronoun to introduce essential information that you absolutely need to understand what particular thing is being referred to. This information is typically called *restrictive*. **Restrictive clauses don't have commas**, because commas usually present added, but nonessential, information. For example:

> Heather likes bananas *that* are still green.

Out of all the types of bananas in the world, Heather likes the particular ones that are still green. Since the information *are still green* is essential to understand what kind of bananas Heather likes, use *that*. In addition, since this information could not be removed without greatly altering the sentence, do not use a comma.

WHICH

Which is used as a pronoun to introduce nonessential, added information, which may be helpful but is not totally necessary to understand what particular thing is being referred to. This information is typically called *nonrestrictive*. **Nonrestrictive clauses usually have commas**, suggesting that the information is nonessential. For example:

> Heather likes bananas, which are high in potassium.

The fact that bananas are high in potassium is added information that isn't essential to understand what kind of bananas Heather likes (since all bananas are high in potassium). ***Which* is usually preceded by a comma because it introduces information that could be removed without drastically changing the desired meaning of the sentence.**

■

 To identify pronoun case errors, look for questions with answer choices that have the same pronouns in different cases. (ex: *he* and *him*)

PRONOUN AGREEMENT

NUMBER AGREEMENT

In a sentence, the pronoun must agree in number with the noun or nouns it is replacing.

Everyone who plays an instrument knows *they* must practice for hours every day to master the craft.

This sentence sounds fine, right? But it is incorrect. The pronoun *they* is referring to the noun *everyone*, the subject of the sentence, which is singular. Therefore, *they* should be replaced with a singular pronoun.

Everyone who plays an instrument knows *he or she* must practice for hours every day to master the craft.

PRONOUN AGREEMENT

If pronouns are referring to the same thing in a sentence, make sure they are the same pronoun type. Watch out for illogical changes to the pronouns as a sentence develops.

When *one* prepares for a concert, *you* should visualize a standing ovation at the end.

Both pronouns should be *one* or *you*, such as:

When *one* prepares for a concert, *one* should visualize a standing ovation at the end.

■

The following steps will help you work with pronoun-agreement errors:
1. Identify the pronoun in the sentence.
2. Identify the noun that the pronoun is referring to. Usually the noun will precede the pronoun in the sentence.
3. Make sure the pronoun and the noun agree in number.

 To identify pronoun agreement errors, look for questions with answer choices that contain plural *and* singular pronouns.

PRONOUN AMBIGUITY

Pronouns must clearly refer to the noun or nouns—called *antecedents*—they replace. For example:

> The early marching music of New Orleans was probably the earliest form of jazz, and *they* used musical elements from both the African and European continents.

In the sentence, *they* is an ambiguous pronoun because there are no groups mentioned in the sentence to which *they* logically refers. The sentence could be corrected by either adding a group of people to the first part of the sentence or replacing *they* appropriately:

> The *musicians* of early marching music in New Orleans were probably playing the earliest form of jazz, and *they* used musical elements from both the African and European continents.

> Or:
> The early marching music of New Orleans was probably the earliest form of jazz, and *the musicians* used musical elements from both the African and European continents.

Another ambiguous pronoun problem occurs when it is unclear what noun is being referred to in the sentence. For example:

> Thomas told Jason that *he* was responsible for studying the origins of jazz for their report on American music.

It may sound strange, but for the sentence to be totally clear and unambiguous, it should read:

> Thomas told Jason that *Jason* (or *Thomas*) was responsible for studying the origins of jazz for their report on American music.

Here's one more example:

> A progressive movement toward electric instrumentation and freeform song structures became a kind of musical rebellion in the '60s. One musician who helped develop *this* was Miles Davis.

The pronoun *this* could refer to the "progressive movement," "electric instrumentation and freeform song structures," or "musical rebellion." Here's are some possible corrections:

. . . One musician who helped develop *this movement* was Miles Davis.

. . . One musician who helped develop *this new style of playing* was Miles Davis.

 To identify pronoun ambiguity errors, look for answer choices that include simple pronouns (such as *they, it, these, them*, etc.), and at least one answer choice that provides additional (clarifying) information (compare *this* to *this movement* above).

PRONOUN LESSON PROBLEMS

I will play the song for Dorothy and **1** he.

1. A) NO CHANGE
   B) him
   C) himself
   D) he, who listens

The speaker, about **2** whomever we had been talking for weeks, spoke with grace and eloquence.

2. A) NO CHANGE
   B) who
   C) whom
   D) DELETE the underlined portion

The after school programs have given the students something to do with **3** everyone's free time.

3. A) NO CHANGE
   B) their
   C) his or her
   D) one's

Nobody I know who has gone to the water park thinks **4** they will go again.

4. A) NO CHANGE
   B) he or she
   C) he or she, by themselves,
   D) all of them

The company was given financial support until **5** they pulled out of debt.

5. A) NO CHANGE
   B) they pulled themselves
   C) it pulled itself
   D) the staff pulled themselves

In 1963, Civil Rights leaders allowed children to march with the other protesters on the streets of Birmingham, Alabama. When **1** the children were seen on television being blasted by fire hoses and attacked by police dogs, much of the nation was outraged.

1. A) NO CHANGE
    B) they were
    C) it was
    D) he or she was

Waiting for over an hour, we wondered what **2** had happened to she and Daniel.

2. A) NO CHANGE
    B) had happened to her
    C) happened to she
    D) happens to her

Anyone starting ninth grade knows that **3** they were thrown from the frying pan into the fire.

3. A) NO CHANGE
    B) they have been
    C) they will be
    D) he or she has been

When you stand near the conductor, **4** anyone must be careful not to get hit by his baton.

4. A) NO CHANGE
    B) you
    C) one
    D) the audience members

The Polish accordion tradition known as *polka* has a recognizable rhythmic pattern because of **5** their consistent use of a triplet meter.

5. A) NO CHANGE
    B) the pattern's
    C) their pattern's
    D) the tradition's pattern's

4. APOSTROPHES & CONFUSED WORDS

Sometimes students confuse words that have similar *appearance* or *sound*. For example, you may come across words such as *principal* and *principle* (a *principal* works at your school—he's your "pal"—get it?; a *principle* is a rule or standard), or *stationary* and *stationery* (*stationary* means standing still; *stationery* goes in an *envelope*—see the *e*?). There are hundreds of other confused words, but luckily most of the confused words tested on the SAT concern the more manageable subject of possessive pronouns and apostrophes (').

Apostrophes have two general uses:

1. To indicate that letters have been removed from a word—this is called a *contraction*. For example, *they're* is a contraction of *they are* (note the missing *a*).
2. To show possession. For example, this is *Kathleen's* book. (The book belongs to Kathleen.)

CONTRACTIONS AND POSSESSIVE PRONOUNS

The most commonly tested confused words are contractions and possessive pronouns that sound alike. For example,

This is *there* cooler, so please put it over *they're*. *Their* going to be here soon.

If you read the sentence out loud, it sounds fine. But do you see the three errors? The following words may sound alike, but they have different uses: *their*, a possessive pronoun, describes something that *they* possess (in this case, a cooler); *there* indicates a place; and *they're* is a contraction for *they are*. The following corrects the sentence:

This is *their* cooler, so please put it over *there*. *They're* going to be here soon.

Here are a few other commonly-confused words involving contractions:

your/you're
The word *your* is used as a possessive for *you* (This is *your* book). The word *you're* is a contraction of *you* and *are* (*You're* going to have to study hard to raise your score).

its/it's/its'

This one can be tricky. The word *its* is a possessive of *it* (*Its* windows are dirty). The word *it's* is a contraction of *it* and *is* (*It's* a lovely day to clean the windows). Finally, *its'*, always incorrect, is not a word at all.

There are dozens of other contractions that might show up, but they typically fall into one of two categories. Either the apostrophe replaces the *o* in *not* (*can't* = can not, *wouldn't* = would not) or the apostrophe replaces the beginning of a *to-be verb* (*I'm* = I am, *he'd* = he would, *you'll* = you will). Note that the contraction of *will not* is *won't*, an unexpected change in spelling.

APOSTROPHES USED FOR POSSESSIVES

Apostrophes are often used to indicate that something or someone *possesses* something else. For example:

This is Jeff's car. (The car belongs to Jeff.)

There are three general rules to remember when turning a noun into a possessive:

1. If the word is singular, add *'s*. (Most grammarians, including the SAT test writers, require the *'s* even if the word already ends with an *s*; see the second example below.):
   Jeff → Jeff's car
   moss → the moss's growth
2. If the word is plural and ends with an *s*, add an apostrophe to the end of the word:
   girls → the girls' room
   the Smiths → the Smiths' house
3. If the word is plural and does *not* end with an *s*, add *'s* to the end of the word:
   children → the children's hospital (not *childrens'*)
   men → the men's room (not *mens'*)

POSSESSIVE PRONOUN

Possessive pronouns do *not* use apostrophes, even if they end with an *s*:

your = possessive of *you*
their = possessive of *they*
my = possessive of *I*
his = possessive of *he*
its = possessive of *it*
whose = possessive of *who*

The possessive pronoun may change if it comes at the end of a phrase. Trust your ear:

The bike is *yours*, but the skateboard is *mine*.

APPROACH TO APOSTROPHES ON THE SAT

The SAT often mixes contractions and possessives on the same question, so the first step is to decide which is appropriate. Here's a good test: **first check for a contraction.** If, after expanding the word, the sentence sounds correct, then the contraction is correct. For example:

The day's beautiful at this time—don't you think?

Expand the contraction, and you have:

The *day is* beautiful at this time—don't you think?

This sounds fine. The word is a contraction and the apostrophe is used correctly. Here's another example:

My *friend's* are going to be here soon. → My *friend is* are going to be here soon.

Clearly this is incorrect. Either the word *friend's* is a possessive or (as is the case here) the apostrophe should be removed: My *friends* are going to be here soon.

■

> To identify **apostrophe errors**, look for answer choices that contain variations in apostrophes for the same word (*aardvark's*, *aardvarks'*). Also, look for possessive pronouns and pronoun contractions (e.g. *your*, *you're*, *yours*).
>
> To identify **confused words** errors, look for answer choices with words that look similar (e.g. *principle*, *principal*).

APOSTROPHES & CONFUSED WORDS LESSON PROBLEMS

The <u>ancient shells shape</u> tells scientists much about the shape of the organism that inhabited it.

1. A) NO CHANGE
   B) ancient shells' shape
   C) ancient shell's shape
   D) ancient's shell's shape

Continued →

Nicholson Baker's first book, *The Mezzanine*, with **2** its copious digressions and footnotes, influenced many writers to come.

2. A) NO CHANGE
   B) it's
   C) its'
   D) their

Poison oak is difficult to identify because **3** its propensity to imitate the appearance of nearby plants.

3. A) NO CHANGE
   B) of its
   C) it's
   D) of it's

Since the members of the science team will work along the coast, **4** they're going to focus their report on beach erosion.

4. A) NO CHANGE
   B) their going
   C) theirs is one
   D) there will be

Small print on the labels of containers is more likely to **5** elude then attract the attention of consumers.

5. A) NO CHANGE
   B) elude than
   C) allude then
   D) allude than

1 It's in your best interest to keep your hands inside the vehicle during the tour.

1. A) NO CHANGE
   B) Its in your best interest
   C) Its' in your best interest
   D) It's your best interest

Only a few of the **2** country's regions are named using the native language.

2. A) NO CHANGE
   B) countries' regions'
   C) country's region's
   D) countries regions

3 Your going to regret staying up late because classes start an hour earlier tomorrow.

3. A) NO CHANGE
   B) You will
   C) Your
   D) You're going

Continued →

4 Giraffes long necks allow them to reach tree leaves and other foods that most other animals cannot.

4. A) NO CHANGE
   B) Giraffe's long necks
   C) Giraffes' long neck's
   D) Giraffes' long necks

Having explained his position carefully to the other group members, Franklin found it difficult to **5** accept there confusion.

5. A) NO CHANGE
   B) except there
   C) accept their
   D) except their

Before taking the following quiz, study sections 1–4. If you're working with a tutor, you will take the quiz during the next lesson. If you're working on your own, take the quiz after reviewing, and do *not* look back to the lessons. After grading, review any topics you struggled on. The quiz is untimed.

GRAMMAR QUIZ 1 (SECTIONS 1–4)

Played in a 1989 chess tournament in Belgrade, the longest game in history **1** ends in a 269-move draw.

1. A) NO CHANGE
   B) had ended
   C) will have ended
   D) ended

2 Its hot enough today to fry an egg on the sidewalk.

2. A) NO CHANGE
   B) Its hotter
   C) Its' hot enough
   D) It's hot enough

We wanted to give the package to **3** she and Marcus, but they had already left town.

3. A) NO CHANGE
   B) her
   C) herself
   D) hers

Continued →

The small specks at the edge of the photograph [4] were caused by a mistake during development, not one during the shoot.

4. A) NO CHANGE
    B) was
    C) is
    D) has been

He reads actively, but when he has to talk in front of a group, he [5] spoke like someone unfamiliar with the standard rules of grammar.

5. A) NO CHANGE
    B) speaks
    C) had spoken
    D) has spoken

[6] A puppy's first steps occur three to four weeks after birth, far earlier than a baby's first steps.

6. A) NO CHANGE
    B) A puppy's first step's
    C) A puppies' first steps
    D) A puppies first steps

Their aggressive and inappropriate actions make it clear [7] that theirs little hope of compromise.

7. A) NO CHANGE
    B) that theirs is
    C) that there's
    D) that they're is

The country was largely ignored until [8] they decided to build long-range weapons.

8. A) NO CHANGE
    B) they had decided
    C) it was decided
    D) it decided

The number of times that I have had to reprimand my employees for wasting time playing on their computers [9] approach the hundreds.

9. A) NO CHANGE
    B) have approached
    C) will have been approaching
    D) is approaching

The book discusses not only how the ancient city's inhabitants grew their crops but also how they [10] had hunted for game.

10. A) NO CHANGE
    B) hunt
    C) hunted
    D) hunting

5. VOCABULARY & IDIOMS

VOCABULARY

The SAT may test your *vocabulary* on the Writing and Language Test, but you won't be tested on difficult words such as *pulchritudinous* or *tergiversate*. Rather, you'll be tested on the appropriate use of relatively familiar words, typically words with similar meanings. For example:

When the blow fish senses danger, it brings in water to make its entire body *multiply*.

The word *multiply* means to increase in number. It is not the correct word for this context. You could correct the sentence with words such as *expand*, *enlarge*, *grow*, etc.:

When the blow fish senses danger, it brings in water to make its entire body *expand*.

Other vocabulary questions may test words that simply go together, based on common usage. For example:

Colleges often look for students who have *defeated* some sort of adversity.

Usage dictates that people *overcome* adversity. They don't *defeat* it, or *bury* it, or *overthrow* it. Again, these words are close, but not correct.

Colleges often look for students who have *overcome* some sort of adversity.

TRY YOUR OWN WORD FIRST

Similar to Words-in-Context questions on the Reading test, you might try coming up with your own word, based on context, before looking at the answer choices. Sometimes reading the answer choices first will confuse your inner ear. For example, in the example above, you may have naturally put the words *overcome* and *adversity* together—it's a relatively common phrase—and you would have spotted the correct answer on a multiple-choice question right away.

TRUST YOUR EAR

Your sense of what's "correct" and "incorrect" is largely a reflection of your experience reading and listening to correct grammar. (Of course, reading and listening to *incorrect* grammar can often work against you.) A good approach to these questions involves taking the key words (such as "overcome adversity") out of context, and trusting your ear. If an answer choice sounds strange or ungrammatical, it's probably wrong. Go with the answer choice that sounds the most usual.

❗ Read vocabulary questions out of context, and trust your ear.

> 🔍 To identify vocabulary questions, look for answer choices that contain different words with similar meanings, as in the examples above.

IDIOMS

Idioms are expressions based on the manner or style of a language. Rules for idioms are less predictable and consistent (and, thus, more difficult to remember) than most of the other grammar rules in this tutorial. The good news is that many of the idiom errors will simply sound wrong to your ear.

Most idiom mistakes on the SAT have to do with an incorrect *preposition* following an adjective or verb. For example:

We only wanted to look at the paintings; we were *indifferent **of*** the sculpture exhibit.

Idiom dictates that, in general, the preposition *to* (not *of*) should be used after *indifferent.* There is no real way to predict this rule—the choice seems arbitrary. This is why these idiom rules can be difficult. You must either memorize from a long list of rules or (hopefully) rely on your ear. The correct sentence should read:

We only wanted to look at the paintings; we were *indifferent **to*** the sculpture exhibit.

Here is another common mistake:

The oil paintings don't look *different **than*** the acrylic ones.

But one thing differs *from* another; it doesn't differ *than* another. Thus, idiom usually dictates that the preposition *from* should follow *different*:

The oil paintings don't look *different **from*** the acrylic ones.

SAME WORD, DIFFERENT PREPOSITIONS

Complicating matters, sometimes the same word can take different prepositions depending on the context. For example:

> We *agreed* ***to*** go to the museum together, but we could not *agree* ***on*** how to get there. I hope you *agree* ***with*** me that walking is out of the question.

Fortunately, most of these rules will sound natural to your ear. For example, you probably would never say: we could not *agree* ***to*** how to get there. It just sounds wrong.

WHICH

Writers sometimes want to avoid ending a sentence with a preposition. The result is often more formal or scholarly sounding. However, the wrong preposition is sometimes used. For example:

> One of my favorite paintings is Monet's *Wheatstacks (End of Summer)*, *over which* a simple painting of haystacks comes alive with color.

Is *over* the correct preposition? The haystacks do not come alive *over* the painting; they come alive *in* the painting:

> One of my favorite paintings is Monet's *Wheatstacks (End of Summer)*, *in which* a simple painting of haystacks comes alive with color.

LEARNING IDIOMS

The best way to learn idioms is by hearing (or reading) correct idioms. Simply put, this is how we all learn to speak correctly. In other words, there's no real trick or shortcut to learning idioms. That's the bad news. The good news is that many students will already "hear" the idiom errors that show up on the test. And for those who struggle with these idiom rules, keep in mind that any one test will probably include only one or two idiom questions—they are not a huge part of the SAT.

 To identify prepositional idiom errors, look for questions with answer choices that contain a variety of *prepositions* (e.g., *of, with, over, to,* etc.). If necessary, review prepositions in the Subject-Verb Agreement lesson.

■

VOCABULARY & IDIOMS LESSON PROBLEMS

After years of struggle, the country of Kosovo is finally **1** <u>independent by</u> Serbia.

1. A) NO CHANGE
    B) independent with
    C) independent of
    D) having independence from

If you expect to play in the game, you must **2** <u>abide by</u> the coach's rules.

2. A) NO CHANGE
    B) abide to
    C) abide from
    D) be abiding with

After observing the enemy's impenetrable defenses, the scout **3** <u>dismissed</u> a message of concern to the general.

3. A) NO CHANGE
    B) shipped
    C) granted
    D) dispatched

Little did Jonathan know that when he **4** <u>uncovered</u> his secret, a hidden microphone recorded every word.

4. A) NO CHANGE
    B) broadcasted
    C) disclosed
    D) exhibited

After such a **5** <u>rugged</u> ride, the passengers clapped and cheered when the plane successfully landed.

5. A) NO CHANGE
    B) bumpy
    C) blustery
    D) inclement

My uncle, who has three advanced college degrees, is always happy to sit down with us and **1** <u>impart</u> his wisdom.

1. A) NO CHANGE
    B) transmit
    C) disclose
    D) relinquish

After just a few hours working in the **2** <u>sweltering</u> kitchen, Wallace was ready to quit his new job as a fry cook.

2. A) NO CHANGE
    B) blistering
    C) heated
    D) feverish

Continued →

Some assume that screenwriting is a solitary endeavor, but many of the best screenwriters frequently **3** collude.

I understood the material when I read the math book but **4** was confused of my teacher's lengthy and boring lectures.

The author, Sir Arthur Conan Doyle, is **5** famous for his Sherlock Holmes mystery novels.

3. A) NO CHANGE
   B) participate.
   C) collaborate.
   D) tie in.

4. A) NO CHANGE
   B) had confusion for
   C) was confused by
   D) was confused with

5. A) NO CHANGE
   B) famous in
   C) famous by
   D) famous of

6. CONCISION & REDUNDANCIES

CONCISION

Concision comes from the word *concise*, which means *brief*, or *using few words*. Good writing is usually as concise and clear as possible, with no needless words. Besides being grammatically correct, the correct answers on the Writing and Language Test are usually the clearest and often the shortest of the answer choices. For example:

> Whoever comes up with the *plan that is the best* will get a bonus.
> Whoever comes up with the *plan to be considered the best* will get a bonus.
> Whoever comes up with the *plan that is better than the others* will get a bonus.

Notice how the following sentence concisely says the same thing as the relatively wordy sentences above.

> Whoever comes up with the *best plan* will get a bonus.

REDUNDANCIES

One of the most egregious examples of wordy writing involves the use of *redundancies*. A redundancy is a needless repetition of a word or idea. For example:

> That school's water polo team is favored to *repeat* and *duplicate* its championship of last year.

Of course, to *repeat* and to *duplicate* mean about the same thing. Eliminate one of them to correct the sentence:

> That school's water polo team is favored to *repeat* its championship of last year.

SHORT ANSWERS

! **The correct answer on concision and redundancy questions, not surprisingly, will almost always be the shortest one (since the redundancies are removed).**

This is an important tip because these questions often have considerable variation in the lengths of the answer choices.

CONCISION & REDUNDANCIES LESSON PROBLEMS

The company is able to stay on top of the tech world because of its emphasis on **1** new innovations.

1. A) NO CHANGE
   B) the newness of its
   C) new and current
   D) DELETE the underlined portion.

The judge was forced to **2** free the man and let him go after the judge determined that the evidence had been tampered with.

2. A) NO CHANGE
   B) free the man
   C) let the now free man go
   D) free and liberate the man

Ilene has more experience, better references, and a stronger resume; **3** simply put, she's the best candidate for the job.

3. A) NO CHANGE
   B) to put it in a simple way
   C) putting it simply
   D) in a more simply-put way

Because the conference room is flooded, we'll have to have the community meeting **4** later, at a future date.

4. A) NO CHANGE
   B) later, in a while
   C) at a future date
   D) at a later, future date

You have to score at least 90 points **1** or more on the company's written test to be considered for the job.

1. A) NO CHANGE
   B) but no less than that
   C) and no less than that
   D) DELETE the underlined portion.

Continued →

In the last sentence of the book, the author **2** concluded by hinting that everything had been a dream.

2. A) NO CHANGE
    B) concluded and hinted
    C) finished writing by hinting
    D) hinted

The new Corvette is not only one of the fastest American-made production cars, but I think it's also one of the best-looking cars on the road **3** too.

3. A) NO CHANGE
    B) as well.
    C) additionally.
    D) DELETE the underlined portion, and end the sentence with a period.

Before Sir Edmund Hillary conquered Mount Everest in 1953, many agreed that its steep and treacherous slopes **4** were insurmountable and would never be climbed.

4. A) NO CHANGE
    B) were insurmountably unclimbable
    C) were insurmountable
    D) could not be mounted by climbing

Orhan has been writing his report all weekend, but the work that **5** remains is daunting.

5. A) NO CHANGE
    B) still remains is daunting.
    C) remains is of a daunting nature.
    D) remains incomplete is daunting to him.

7. PARALLELISM

When you are expressing two or more ideas or actions, they should be *parallel* in form. In other words, they should be constructed in the same way. For example:

> An excellent employee is open to new ideas, responsive to company needs, and he complies with the company rules of business.

Notice the three phrases that describe the employee:
1. ...open to new ideas... (*adjective-prepositional phrase*)
2. ...responsive to company needs... (*adjective-prepositional phrase*)
3. ...he complies with the company rules of business. (*pronoun-verb-prepositional phrase*)

The first two phrases are similar. In each, an *adjective* ("open" and "responsive") is followed by a *prepositional phrase* ("to new ideas" and "to company needs"). In the third phrase, the structure is different. A *pronoun* is followed by a *verb* is followed by a *prepositional phrase* ("with the company rules of business"). The sentence is not parallel in construction.

To correct the sentence, replace "he complies" with the appropriate adjective ("compliant") to match the first two phrases. The words "compliant with" are parallel to "open to" and "responsive to," and the correct sentence reads:

> An excellent employee is *open to* new ideas, *responsive to* company needs, and *compliant with* the company rules of business.

Sometimes it's helpful to add a temporary colon so you can easily see where the series of items begins. Note the subtle differences in the two examples below (both are correct, although the first is more concise):

> An excellent employee is: open to new ideas, responsive to company needs, and compliant with the company rules of business.

> An excellent employee: is open to new ideas, is responsive to company needs, and is compliant with the company rules of business.

On the SAT, parallelism questions often test the parallelism of *verbs*, so watch out for changing verb forms. Also, look for the following:
1. A series of two or more actions or items
2. Lists, especially when there are distracting phrases thrown in between the items
3. Comparisons (because they always include at least two items)

PARALLELISM LESSON PROBLEMS

Ted would prefer **1** to watch grass grow to finishing his homework.

1. A) NO CHANGE
   B) watching grass grow to finishing
   C) to watch grass grow than finishing
   D) watching grass grow than to finish, on time,

While Nick hides in the basement, Louie **2** is looking in the attic.

2. A) NO CHANGE
   B) has looked
   C) looks
   D) looked

For most great artists, creative freedom is more important than **3** financially comfortable.

3. A) NO CHANGE
   B) being financially comfortable
   C) financial comfort
   D) having a comfortable finance

According to recent studies, when students get enough sleep, they are healthier, **4** happier, and more alert.

4. A) NO CHANGE
   B) happier, and alert.
   C) happier, and they are more alert.
   D) happy, and alert.

The coach preaches the idea that all of his players, no matter their current skills, can learn the intricacies of the game and **1** they can become great athletes.

1. A) NO CHANGE
   B) become
   C) so they can become
   D) becoming

Continued →

Jess **2** likes taking the bus more than driving her car because she can read, sleep, or talk to interesting new people.

For most great artists, **3** being creatively free is more important than being financially comfortable.

Many new homeowners are surprised by how much money they spend on closing costs, property taxes, and **4** insurance for the home.

2. A) NO CHANGE
    B) likes to have taken
    C) liked to take
    D) likes to take

3. A) NO CHANGE
    B) creative freedom
    C) having the freedom to create
    D) freedom to create

4. A) NO CHANGE
    B) insuring the home.
    C) matters of home insurance.
    D) home insurance.

Before taking the following quiz, study sections 5–7. If you're working with a tutor, you will take the quiz during the next lesson. If you're working on your own, take the quiz after reviewing, and do *not* look back to the lessons. After grading, review any topics you struggled on. The quiz is untimed.

GRAMMAR QUIZ 2 (SECTIONS 5–7)

1 <u>Enjoying</u> time with family and friends is more important than working all day and night.

1. A) NO CHANGE
   B) The enjoyment of
   C) To enjoy
   D) Taking enjoyment from

Karoline Mariechen Meyer broke the world's record by holding her breath for **2** <u>18 minutes and 33 seconds—nearly 20 minutes</u>.

2. A) NO CHANGE
   B) 18 minutes and 33 seconds, or nearly 20 minutes
   C) 18 minutes and 33 seconds
   D) less than 20 minutes—18 minutes and 33 seconds

Mrs. Reynolds makes her calculus class so competive that if you want to do well, you must be prepared to **3** <u>overmatch</u> your other classmates.

3. A) NO CHANGE
   B) domineer
   C) outwork
   D) dictate

Despite any scientific consensus on the issue, many people avoid **4** <u>foods that have been genetically modified</u> because they assume that they are not safe to eat.

4. A) NO CHANGE
   B) foods modified in a genetic way
   C) genetically modified foods
   D) foods in which genetic modifications have been made

As a reader, she **5** <u>has an ability for making</u> even the most mundane prose come alive.

5. A) NO CHANGE
   B) has an ability to make
   C) has an ability of making
   D) has an ability with making

Continued →

He was not only kind to his own children but also **6** showed kindness to the children of others.

6. A) NO CHANGE
   B) kind
   C) kindly
   D) had kindness

Since Ron has not saved up enough money to buy the bike, he must **7** uphold working two jobs for the rest of the summer.

7. A) NO CHANGE
   B) continue
   C) sustain
   D) promote

The sight of the movie's star actor on the red carpet **8** excited and invigorated the huge crowd.

8. A) NO CHANGE
   B) excited the huge crowd.
   C) excited the huge and massive crowd.
   D) excited the now invigorated, huge crowd.

■

20- and 30-hour programs: At this point, skip ahead to the Sentence Structure chapter (page 179). If you have time at the end of the program, we recommend you go back and cover the remaining Grammar topics on the following pages.

8. COMPARISONS

THE *NUMBER* OF A COMPARISON

The *number* of a comparison refers to the number of items being compared. There are grammatical differences between comparing two things and comparing three or more things.

When comparing **two** things, you will use the *-er* form of an adjective (words such as happi*er* or strong*er*) or the word *more* prior to an adjective (such as *more* beautiful). You will also often use the word *than* for these comparisons (not *then*, a common mistake).

Jason is *better than* I am at shooting with his left hand. (two people)

When comparing **three or more** things, you will use the *-est* form of an adjective (happi*est* or strong*est*) or the word *most* prior to an adjective (such as *most* beautiful). For example:

Jason is the *best* player on the team at shooting with his left hand. (three or more people)

DOUBLE COMPARISONS

Make sure to never create a *double comparison* by putting words like *more* or *most* in the same phrase with words in the *-er* or *-est* form. For example, avoid:

more friendlier, most friendliest

TRICKY COMPARISON WORDS

The table below shows some of the tricky comparison words. If you already hear these correctly, don't worry about memorizing them.

adjective	two things	three or more things
good	better	best
well	better	best
bad	worse	worst
little	less	least
much	more	most
many	more	most

The SAT may try to use *more* or *most* when one of the *tricky* comparison words should be used. For example:

Jason's game went from bad to more bad because of his injury.

The words "more bad" are not grammatically correct. They should be replaced with the word *worse*.

Jason's game went from bad to *worse* because of his injury.

These errors are essentially double comparisons, as described above.

■

> To identify comparison errors, look for questions with answer choices that contain the words *more* and *most* or have the same words in the *-er* and *-est* forms.

COMPARISONS LESSON PROBLEMS

An oil candle is both brighter and **1** more longer-burning than a conventional wax candle.

1. A) NO CHANGE
   B) longer-burning
   C) far more longer-burning
   D) long-burning

On our track team, Evan may have long legs, but he is definitely not the **2** faster of the group.

2. A) NO CHANGE
   B) fastest of the group
   C) most fastest of the group
   D) group's faster runner

Since he spends all day and night studying, Brian, not surprisingly, is the **3** most intelligent student in the class.

3. A) NO CHANGE
   B) more intelligent
   C) more than intelligent
   D) more than anyone else, intelligent

1 Amanda is definitely the more outspoken of the twins.

1. A) NO CHANGE
   B) Amanda is definitely the most outspoken of the twins
   C) Of the twins, Amanda is definitely the most outspoken
   D) More than the other of the twins, Amanda is definitely outspoken

When deciding whether to take the high road or the low road, the **2** best choice is often elusive.

2. A) NO CHANGE
   B) most best
   C) more better
   D) better

I would be **3** more than happier to take you and your friends to the airport.

3. A) NO CHANGE
   B) the most happiest
   C) more than happy
   D) a quality greater than happiest

9. ILLOGICAL COMPARISONS

These types of problems don't show up frequently on the SAT, but the rule is good to know. The saying goes that *you can't compare apples to oranges*. For example:

> The science department's projects are much more interesting than the English department this year.

The sentence is incorrect because the science department's *projects* are being compared to the English *department*. The correct sentence should read:

> The science department's projects are much more interesting than the English department's *projects* this year.

You don't always have to restate the noun being compared, as above. Using an *apostrophe-s* (*'s*) or the word *that* (singular) or *those* (plural) is usually acceptable.

> The science department's projects are much more interesting than the English department*'s* this year.

> The science department's projects are much more interesting than *those* of the English department this year.

■

When you spot a comparison, ask yourself: what items are being compared? You might want to underline the two items. **Always compare "apples to apples."**

To identify illogical comparison errors, look for questions with underlined comparisons. The answer choices will contain various comparing options; however, looking for the comparison in the passage is probably the best way to identify these types of questions.

ILLOGICAL COMPARISONS LESSON PROBLEMS

Our school's students are much stronger in math and science **1** than the average school.

1. A) NO CHANGE
    B) than the average school is in math and science.
    C) than the average school's students.
    D) than the students at the average school.

The history of Hawaii, **2** like other Pacific islands, is primarily concerned with the ocean.

2. A) NO CHANGE
    B) similar to other Pacific islands
    C) like that of other Pacific islands
    D) in comparison to other Pacific islands

A recent study suggests that eating fish twice a week is healthier **1** than eating other meats.

1. A) NO CHANGE
    B) than other meats.
    C) than other meats twice a week.
    D) than other meats are.

Daniel's score on this test, after diligent study and practice, is much better than **2** his last test.

2. A) NO CHANGE
    B) his score on his last test.
    C) the test he took last.
    D) that test that he took last.

Like John James Audubon, **3** Henry David Thoreau's writing captures the magic of nature in prose.

3. A) NO CHANGE
    B) that of Henry David Thoreau
    C) also Henry David Thoreau
    D) Henry David Thoreau

People who travel by subway may not arrive to their destinations faster **4** than cars, but they're often more refreshed and relaxed.

4. A) NO CHANGE
    B) then cars
    C) than do cars
    D) than those who travel by car

10. GRAMMAR ODDS AND ENDS

The following grammar rules do not often show up on the SAT, but they are good rules to know. If you have time, look them over.

NOUN AGREEMENT

Nouns must agree in number (plural or singular) with the number of the noun or nouns they are referring to. For example:

Dave and Scott are looking for *a girlfriend*.

Obviously, Dave and Scott are not looking for one girlfriend. *Girlfriend* must be plural so it agrees with the plural subject of the sentence. The correct sentence should read:

Dave and Scott are looking for *girlfriends*.

 To identify noun agreement errors, look for questions with answer choices that contain the same common noun in plural and singular forms.

NOUN AGREEMENT LESSON PROBLEMS

1 Once considered a place to meet people and drink coffee, bookstores are now generally used just to buy books.

1. A) NO CHANGE
   B) Considered then a place
   C) Once it was considered a place
   D) Once considered places

To become **2** a better reader, students are urged to read everything they can get their hands on, including newspapers and magazines.

2. A) NO CHANGE
   B) better readers
   C) the best reader
   D) a reader better than before

The cookies all come **1** <u>in an individual box</u>, so you should have no trouble separating the chocolate chunk ones from the peanut toffee ones.

1. A) NO CHANGE
   B) in a different box
   C) in different boxes
   D) in different and distinct boxes

2 <u>The vibraphone, melodic and percussive instruments</u> used mostly in jazz, can be played with two or four mallets.

2. A) NO CHANGE
   B) Vibraphones, a melodic and percussive instrument
   C) The vibraphone, at once melodic and percussive instruments
   D) The vibraphone, a melodic and percussive instrument

PAIRED CONJUNCTIONS

These conjunctions or phrases, which always come in pairs, are also called *correlative* conjunctions. Make flash cards for the ones you don't know.

both . . . and: Keep this construction concise and simple (with *and*):

> Correct: *Both* the lions *and* the tigers were putting on a show at the zoo.
> Incorrect: *Both* the lions *and also* the tigers were putting on a show at the zoo.
> Incorrect (usually): *Both* the lions *as well as* the tigers were putting on a show at the zoo.

not only . . . but also: Synonyms of *also*, such as *too* or *as well*, are also fine:

> Correct: The new electric car is *not only* more efficient than a gasoline-powered car *but also* much quieter.
> Correct: The new electric car is *not only* more efficient than a gasoline-powered car *but* much quieter, *too* (or: . . . much quieter, *as well*).
> Incorrect (usually): The new electric car is *not only* more efficient than a gasoline-powered car *but* much quieter.

not . . . but: Avoid *also* when there is no *only* following *not*:

> Correct: The movie is *not* light-hearted or trivial *but* dark and disturbing in the ways it portrays drug-use.
>
> Incorrect: The movie is *not* light-hearted or trivial *but also* dark and disturbing in the ways it portrays drug-use.

either . . . or: Some students "hyper-correct" the *either-or* construction with *nor*:

> Correct: You can be *either* for him *or* against him; there is no in between.
>
> Incorrect: You can be *either* for him *nor* against him; there is no in between.

neither . . . nor: The correct use of *nor* is with *neither*.

> Correct: He is *neither* as large *nor* as strong as his father, but he is much faster.
>
> Incorrect: He is *neither* as large *or* as strong as his father, but he is much faster.

whether . . . or: Avoid *or not* after *whether* when both options are given (first example below):

> Correct: *Whether* you go to a good university *or* straight to the work force is up to you.
>
> Correct: *Whether or not* you go to a good university is up to you.
>
> Incorrect: *Whether or not* you go to a good university *or* straight to the work force is up to you.

as . . . as: In a comparison, one *as* should always be followed by a second one:

> Correct: Amy was not *as* scholastic *as* her older sister, but she was much more sociable.
>
> Incorrect: Amy was not *as* scholastic *compared to* (or *with*) her older sister, but she was much more sociable.
>
> Incorrect (needlessly wordy): Amy was not *as* scholastic *as compared to* (or *with*) her older sister, but she was much more sociable.
>
> Incorrect: Amy was not *as* scholastic *in comparison to* (or *with*) her older sister, but she was much more sociable.

not so much . . . as: This one is rarely tested, but it's worth memorizing, just in case:

> Correct: It is *not so much* the sound of the breaking waves *as* the smell of the sea that characterizes my beach house.
>
> Incorrect: It is *not so much* the sound of the breaking waves *but* the smell of the sea that characterizes my beach house.

so . . . that: This is a common cause-and-effect pair:

> Correct: It is *so* hot today *that* I'm afraid to go outside.
>
> Incorrect: It is *so* hot today *and* I'm afraid to go outside.

 To identify paired-conjunction errors, look for the *first* part of each pair in the passage (the second part will often be incorrect or missing altogether).

PAIRED CONJUNCTIONS LESSON PROBLEMS

The new documentary is not only an important educational film **1** <u>and</u> a pleasurable viewing experience.

1. A) NO CHANGE
   B) but it is
   C) but also
   D) but

Both the pencil **2** <u>or</u> the pen are mightier than the sword.

2. A) NO CHANGE
   B) and
   C) and also
   D) and, too,

After reviewing paired conjunctions, try the problems below. Do NOT look back to the lesson while completing the assignment.

1 <u>Neither your muddy shoes or</u> your rain soaked jacket will be allowed in this house.

1. A) NO CHANGE
   B) Neither your muddy shoes nor
   C) Either your muddy shoes nor
   D) Neither your muddy shoes and also not

Frank, while frightening in his own ways, was not as gruesome or as sinister **2** <u>compared to</u> Drake.

2. A) NO CHANGE
   B) as
   C) as compared to
   D) when compared to

I can tell that you are angry not so much by your choice of words **3** <u>but by</u> the tone of your voice.

3. A) NO CHANGE
   B) but because of
   C) as by
   D) but from

MORE CONFUSED WORDS

We already saw how words such as *their*, *there*, and *they're* can be confused because of the similar look and sound of the words (see the Apostrophes & Confused Words section). Other words may be confused because of similar *meanings*. For example:

> You can only pay here if you have ten items or less.

Believe it or not, this sentence is incorrect. *Less* should be used when referring to things that cannot be counted, like mashed potatoes or water. *Fewer* should be used in place of *less* when the items can be counted:

> You can only pay here if you have ten items or *fewer*.

The following words are a few of the most commonly confused:

between/among

Between is usually used for two items or people; *among* is used for more than two.

> Just *between* you and me, I don't think the money was distributed properly *among* all the players at the poker table.

each other/one another

Each other refers to two; *one another* refers to more than two.

> While the happy couple kissed *each other* in the darkened room, the people still at the party wished *one another* a happy New Year.

fewer/less

Fewer is for things that can be counted; *less* is for things that cannot be counted.

> I would like *fewer* peas and *less* mashed potatoes.

into/in

Into refers to the motion of going from outside to inside; *in* means within.

> After jumping *into* the lake, you will be *in* over your head.

like/as

Like means of the same form, appearance, or kind; *as* means to the same degree or in the same manner. *Like* is not an acceptable substitute for *as*, *as if*, or *as though*. A good rule of thumb is to replace *like* with *as*, *as if*, or *as though*. If the sentence sounds OK, stick with the *as* construction. Otherwise, *like* is correct. Try circling the correct choice below:

> Adam fouls frequently, just (**as** or **like**?) Andrew does.
> The dog scratched on the door (**as if** or **like**?) it wanted to come in.
> Nick is (**as** or **like**?) his brother in many ways.

(The correct answers are *as*, *as if*, and *like*.)

many/much

Like *fewer* and *less*, *many* is for things that can be counted; *much* is for things that cannot be counted.

> I don't have *much* patience left—I don't know how *many* more arguments I can handle.

number/amount

Number is for things that can be counted; *amount* is for things that cannot be counted.

> Bill had a *number* of hundred-dollar bills in his wallet—the *amount* of money stolen is just a guess.

 To identify confused words questions, look for questions with answer choices that contain different words with similar meanings (not unlike Vocabulary questions). Of course, you should also look for the specific words listed above.

Try the following homework problems *after* you have reviewed the lesson material. Do NOT look back to the lesson while completing the problems:

The company's surplus was divided evenly **1** between all twenty hardworking employees.

1. A) NO CHANGE
   B) through
   C) around
   D) among

After Matt **2** walked in the theater, his eyes took several minutes to adjust to the dark.

2. A) NO CHANGE
   B) walked into the theater
   C) was walking in the theater
   D) walking inside the theater

Spooked by the moonless dark night and the eerily silent alley, we ran **3** like if we were being chased by a mob of zombies.

3. A) NO CHANGE
   B) like
   C) as if
   D) as

The members of the internet company had been a bit premature in **4** congratulating one another since just a few months later their company was nothing more than unpaid bills and worthless stock.

4. A) NO CHANGE
   B) congratulating each other
   C) their congratulating of each other
   D) congratulations for one another

ADJECTIVES & ADVERBS

TERMINOLOGY

Adjective – a word that describes or modifies a person or thing in a sentence (such as *blue*, *old*, *calm*, or *happy*).

Adverb – a word that modifies a verb, adjective, or other adverb in a sentence (such as *quickly*, *happily*, or *stubbornly*). Adverbs describe *how* something happens.

ADJECTIVE AND ADVERB ERRORS

Adjectives only modify *nouns*. On the SAT, adjective and adverb errors occur when an adjective is used incorrectly in place of an adverb, or vice versa. As you read the example below, first identify the adjective or adverb. If you spot an adjective, remember that it must describe a noun. If you can't identify the noun that the adjective should modify, the adjective is incorrect; replace it with an adverb.

> I was surprised how quick she walked to the store.

The adjective is "quick." Ask yourself: what is "quick" modifying? Since it's describing "*how*…she walked," it should be an adverb:

> I was surprised how *quickly* she walked to the store.

GOOD VERSUS *WELL* AND *BAD* VERSUS *BADLY*

The words *good* and *bad* are adjectives, and the words *well* and *badly* are adverbs. Following the rules above, if a noun is being modified, use *good* or *bad*, and if a verb is being modified, use *well* or *badly*. For example:

> He performed *well* on the test. (*Well* describes how he *performed*.)
> He received a *good* score on the test. (*Good* modifies the noun *score*.)

When dealing with any of the five senses, there is an exception to these rules. Use the word *good* or *bad* to modify verbs. For example:

> After sketching with a new type of charcoal, the drawing looks *good* (not *well*).
> The burnt bread made dinner smell *bad* (not *badly*).

■

To identify adjective and adverb errors, look for questions with answer choices that contain words in adjective AND adverb forms. You might also see similar words as nouns or comparison words in the answer choices. For example, if you see the words *happy* (adjective), *happily* (adverb), *happiness* (noun), and/or *happier* (comparison) in the answer choices, the question is probably testing adjectives and

ADJECTIVES & ADVERBS LESSON PROBLEMS

No matter **1** how careful tax returns are checked, there is always a good chance of mistakes.

1. A) NO CHANGE
   B) how much care
   C) the more care
   D) how carefully

Trying to find the source of the rumor, Elijah **2** moved rapid from one group to another.

2. A) NO CHANGE
   B) moved rapidly
   C) moved more rapid
   D) moved with rapidness

The speaker once again showed her skills with one of her **1** typical brilliant dissertations.

1. A) NO CHANGE
   B) typically brilliant
   C) typically brilliantly
   D) typical, brilliant

She received accolades for doing a **2** really good job on the science project.

2. A) NO CHANGE
   B) real good job
   C) a job as well as possible
   D) job that is well

Before taking the following quiz, study sections 8–10. If you're working with a tutor, you will take the quiz during the next lesson. If you're working on your own, take the quiz after reviewing, and do not look back to the lessons. After grading, review any topics you struggled on. The quiz is untimed.

GRAMMAR QUIZ 3 (SECTIONS 8–10)

Martin and Sid have similar running styles, but Sid is definitely **1** the fastest of the two.

1. A) NO CHANGE
   B) the faster
   C) fastest
   D) the most faster

Jason's backpack is as **2** large, if not larger than, mine.

2. A) NO CHANGE
   B) large as, if not larger
   C) large as mine, if not larger
   D) large, or larger

Woodrow's bone marrow transplant will be different from **3** the past in that a revolutionary new type of catheter will be used.

3. A) NO CHANGE
   B) patients from the past
   C) past transplants
   D) those ones of past times

Probably the best known of the species that Charles Darwin studied are now called "Darwin's finches," **4** birds also known as Galapagos finches.

4. A) NO CHANGE
   B) a bird also known as the Galapagos finch.
   C) also known as the Galapagos finch.
   D) birds also known as the Galapagos finch.

After last summer's brushfire, it seems to me that there are **5** less fireworks this year.

5. A) NO CHANGE
   B) lesser
   C) fewer than last year's
   D) fewer

Before taking the following quiz, study sections 1–10. If you're working with a tutor, you will take the quiz during the next lesson. If you're working on your own, take the quiz after reviewing, and do not look back to the lessons. After grading, review any topics you struggled on. The quiz is untimed.

GRAMMAR QUIZ 4 (SECTIONS 1–10)

Elephants, **1** a surprisingly fast creature, have been known to run forty miles per hour.

1. A) NO CHANGE
   B) surprisingly fast creatures, have
   C) a surprisingly fast creature, has
   D) a surprisingly fast creature that has

I almost fell asleep as the raft floated **2** lazy in the still waters.

2. A) NO CHANGE
   B) lazily
   C) lazier
   D) laziness

There are **3** not as much people on the beach each year because of the erosion caused by the high surf.

3. A) NO CHANGE
   B) lesser
   C) less
   D) fewer

Because she was having such a great time, the little girl **4** was opposed of leaving the theme park early.

4. A) NO CHANGE
   B) was opposed from
   C) was opposed to
   D) had opposition for

After analyzing the evidence and writing the research paper about the health risks of living near a cellular tower, researchers knew **5** it would cause an uproar.

5. A) NO CHANGE
   B) the results would
   C) they would
   D) this would

Continued →

Each of the three witnesses **6** were wary of testifying against the frightening gang leader.

6. A) NO CHANGE
   B) were warily
   C) was wary
   D) have been wary

The Grapes of Wrath, by John Steinbeck, tells the story of the **7** Joad family's migration west.

7. A) NO CHANGE
   B) Joad's family's
   C) Joad families
   D) Joad's families

It is a **8** usual custom at our family gatherings to toss the ball around a little after dinner, even though we are usually too full to run.

8. A) NO CHANGE
   B) usual and regular
   C) routine
   D) DELETE the underlined portion.

He is ambivalent about his favorite team going to the finals, both happy about the chance to win it all **9** but sad about the fact that he can't afford tickets.

9. A) NO CHANGE
   B) and
   C) but also
   D) combined with

Because he **10** hit so many game winning shots, he was considered last season's best closer.

10. A) NO CHANGE
    B) hits
    C) has been hitting
    D) will hit

Those **11** citizens which refuse to vote should be the last to complain about the government.

11. A) NO CHANGE
    B) citizens, whom
    C) citizens whom
    D) citizens who

Last year's company party, which was catered by the best cook in town, was much better than **12** this year.

12. A) NO CHANGE
    B) this year's party.
    C) the one of this year.
    D) that of this year.

Continued →

If you develop good study habits in high school, college will likely be easier for you **13** than its often portrayed.

13. A) NO CHANGE
    B) then it's
    C) than it's
    D) then its'

The company had to pay thousands of dollars to clean up the mess, but the ripple effect of the company's transgressions **14** are incalculable.

14. A) NO CHANGE
    B) is
    C) will have been
    D) were

After hiring a new public relations manager, the museum has seen a definite **15** upswing in charitable donations.

15. A) NO CHANGE
    B) expansion
    C) hike
    D) development

III

SENTENCE STRUCTURE

This chapter gets into the important topic of *sentence structure*. We'll learn how sentences are constructed and how to use punctuation to effectively separate different parts of sentences.

1. PUNCTUATION

Punctuation includes the use of commas, semicolons, periods, dashes, and colons. First, let's cover some basic terminology:

SENTENCE BUILDING BLOCKS

Sentences are generally made up of up to three distinct parts: *independent clauses*, *dependent clauses*, and *phrases*.

   Clause – a sequence of words that contains a subject and its verb

   Independent clause – a clause that can stand on its own and make sense

   Dependent clause – a clause that cannot stand on its own because it *depends* on the rest of the sentence to make sense

Let's look at an example to illustrate these parts.

   As he looked up at the blimp, William tripped on the curb.

In the example above, *William tripped on the curb* is the *independent clause*, and *As he looked up at the blimp* is the *dependent clause*.

   Phrase – a sequence of two or more words that does not contain a subject and a finite (non-*ing*) verb. We can refer to any group of words that is not a clause as a *phrase*.

By changing the first part of the sentence slightly, we can turn the dependent clause into a *phrase*. The *-ing* form of a verb is a common way to do this.

   Looking up at the blimp, William tripped on the curb.

Because there is no subject in the first part of the sentence, *Looking up at the blimp* is a phrase, modifying *William*.

Sentences must have at least one independent clause. Good writers will add different combinations of dependent clauses and phrases to these independent clauses to make interesting-sounding sentences.

COMMAS

Many comma problems on the SAT involve the use of a comma when one is *not* needed. So let's learn about the *correct* uses of commas—once you are familiar with these correct uses, you'll be ready to identify the *unnecessary* uses found on the SAT.

SEPARATING DEPENDENT CLAUSES FROM INDEPENDENT CLAUSES

Commas must be used to separate a dependent clause from a following independent clause of a sentence. For example:

As he looked down at his untied shoe, Gregg missed the UFO that flew over his head.

dependent clause   independent clause

When a dependent clause comes *after* an independent clause, the comma is unnecessary. Notice that there is no need to *pause* between the clauses in this situation, which is a good reminder that the comma is not needed. For example:

Gregg missed the UFO flying over his head as he looked down at his untied shoe.

independent clause   dependent clause

OR

Gregg missed the UFO because he was looking down at his untied shoe.

independent clause   dependent clause

SEPARATING MODIFYING PHRASES FROM INDEPENDENT CLAUSES

Commas must be used to separate modifying phrases from the independent clause of a sentence. This topic was introduced in the Subject-Verb lesson.

Looking down at his untied shoe, Gregg missed the UFO that flew over his head.

modifying phrase   independent clause

! **If a modifying phrase shows up in the middle of a clause, there should usually be commas on either side of the phrase.** This correctly suggests that the phrase could be removed and the sentence would still make sense. Try this in the following example:

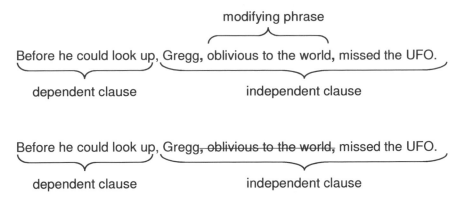

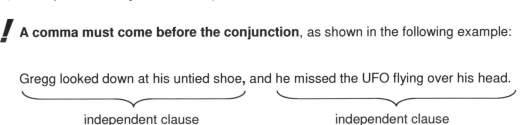

THE ONE-COMMA RULE

You might have two, or even more, commas between the subject and the verb of a sentence, as seen above ("Gregg" is the subject and "missed" is the verb), but you will never have *exactly one* comma between the subject and the verb. This rule will allow you to eliminate many answer choices on punctuation questions:

! **There will never be <u>exactly one</u> comma between a subject and a verb.**

Incorrect: Gregg oblivious to the world, missed the UFO.
Incorrect: Gregg, oblivious to the world missed the UFO.
Correct: Gregg, oblivious to the world, missed the UFO.

SEPARATING TWO INDEPENDENT CLAUSES

Some sentences will have two independent clauses separated by a conjunction, such as *and*, *or*, or *but* (more on conjunctions later).

! **A comma must come before the conjunction**, as shown in the following example:

Gregg looked down at his untied shoe, and he missed the UFO flying over his head.

independent clause · · · · · · · · · · · · independent clause

ONE INDEPENDENT CLAUSE WITH TWO ACTIONS

Make sure there are indeed two distinct independent clauses. The following example does not need a comma because the sentence has only one independent clause containing two actions.

Gregg looked down at his untied shoe and missed the UFO flying over his head.

ADJECTIVES

COMMAS BETWEEN ADJECTIVES

Sometimes, a noun will be modified by more than one adjective:

Gregg watched the *bright spinning* UFO.

The easiest way to determine whether you should use a comma between adjectives is to see if the word *and* could fit between them. If so, you'll need the comma:

Gregg watched the bright *and* spinning UFO.

This works, so the correct sentence should include a comma:

Gregg watched the bright, spinning UFO.

Here's another example:

Gregg plans to describe what he's seen in a serious 5,000-word essay.

Since we wouldn't say "serious *and* 5,000-word essay," the correct sentence, as shown, should not have a comma.

NOUNS AS ADJECTIVES

Some students might identify a noun at the beginning of a sentence as the subject of the sentence, when in fact it functions as an adjective, modifying the actual subject. In the example below, the commas suggest that "teacher" is the subject and that "Mr. Fermi" is a modifying phrase (two commas) and could be deleted:

Astronomy teacher, Mr. Fermi, looks forward to reading Gregg's essay.

But remove "Mr. Fermi" and listen to the new sentence:

Astronomy teacher, ~~Mr. Fermi,~~ looks forward to reading Gregg's essay.

Clearly, "Mr. Fermi" cannot be removed. He is the subject of the sentence, and "Astronomy teacher" functions as an adjectival phrase. The correct sentence has no commas:

Astronomy teacher Mr. Fermi looks forward to reading Gregg's essay.

A REMINDER

Always test comma-bound phrases by removing them from the sentence. If the new sentence still makes sense, the commas are probably fine. If not, the commas are incorrect.

LISTS

You probably already know that commas are used to separate items in a list.

Gregg will bring a camera, binoculars, a notebook, and a pencil to the park.

The comma before the *and* is optional, but the SAT will typically include it. Make sure you don't add a needless comma after the last item ("a pencil"):

Gregg will bring a camera, binoculars, a notebook, and a pencil, to the park. [remove the comma after "pencil"]

THE "WHEN IN DOUBT" COMMA RULE

The SAT often places commas in places where they are unneeded. Here's a little rhyme:

When in doubt, keep the comma out.

We talked earlier about *pausing* when you see a comma while reading. But you should also do the opposite and try *not* pausing when a no-comma answer is an option. If you don't "hear" a problem, then the no-comma answer is probably correct. For example, should we place a comma after *as* in the example below? (Make sure you read without pausing at this point.)

no pause!
⇩

There are important steps one should take before buying a new car, such as reviewing safety ratings, considering resale values, and looking into published reliability reports.

We're not saying the sentence sounds terrible if you *do* pause after *as*, but if the sentence sounds OK *without* pausing, take your chances with the no-comma choice. *When in doubt, keep the comma out.* Indeed, no comma is needed after *as* above.

OTHER PUNCTUATION

SEMICOLONS

Semicolons (;) are similar to periods; the sentences that they separate, however, must be closely related. **Semicolons are used to separate complete sentences**. The following example illustrates the correct use of a semicolon:

Gregg looked down at his untied shoe; he missed the UFO flying over his head.

    independent clause   independent clause

(Sometimes semicolons separate items in a list, when those items already contain commas, but this use is uncommon on the SAT.)

COLONS

Colons (:) are used to indicate that what follows is an elaboration, summation, or list of what precedes. For example:

Gregg made a list of what he should have ready for the next time a UFO appears: a camera, binoculars, a notebook, and a pencil.

When Gregg told his friends that there had been a UFO sighting, you could describe their reaction in a word: incredulous.

/ **Colons generally show up after _independent clauses_**, as in the examples above, but some students assume they work before any list. For example:

Incorrect: The list Gregg made for the next time a UFO appears included: a camera, binoculars, a notebook, and a pencil.

Correct: The list Gregg made for the next time a UFO appears included four items: a camera, binoculars, a notebook, and a pencil.
OR
Correct: The list Gregg made for the next time a UFO appears included a camera, binoculars, a notebook, and a pencil.

LONG DASHES

Long dashes (—), also called *em dashes*, are used to note an abrupt break or pause in a sentence or to begin and end a separate phrase or clause. You could think of them as "big" commas. Unless the break is clearly unneeded—you should use the pause idea discussed earlier—it's hard to get dashes wrong.

> Gregg decided he would study UFOs for the rest of his life—that he might need to eventually make a living someday did not concern him.

Note that long dashes don't have to come in pairs (see example above), but when they separate a phrase or clause *within* a sentence, you must use two dashes:

> His parents—his mom studied botany and his dad was an electrical engineer—both hoped that Gregg's interest was just a passing phase.

■

> To identify questions that test punctuation, look for questions with answer choices that contain changes in punctuation, particularly a variety of comma placements. Watch out for problems that correct one comma error but introduce another.

PUNCTUATION LESSON PROBLEMS

1 After spending, several years trying to grow a garden Linda decided she'd rather just buy her produce from the store.

1. A) NO CHANGE
   B) After spending several years trying to grow a garden,
   C) After spending, several years trying to grow a garden,
   D) After spending several years trying to grow a garden

2 Daniel not a large man by any means somehow seems to dominate our basketball games.

2. A) NO CHANGE
   B) Daniel, not a large man by any means
   C) Daniel not a large man by any means,
   D) Daniel, not a large man by any means,

Continued →

You should watch the **3** road but you should also occasionally, check your mirrors.

3. A) NO CHANGE
   B) road; but you should also occasionally,
   C) road, but you should also occasionally
   D) road, but you should also occasionally,

She skated with amazing **4** skill, and finesse as though she had wings on her back.

4. A) NO CHANGE
   B) skill, and finesse,
   C) skill and finesse;
   D) skill and finesse

The weather may seem nice now. In just a few **5** weeks, however, the ground will be covered with snow.

5. A) NO CHANGE
   B) weeks, however the ground
   C) weeks however, the ground,
   D) weeks however the ground

The professor offered a number of reasons for the low voter **6** turnout, such as, a lack of understanding of how politics work and a pronounced disillusionment in the role of government in general.

6. A) NO CHANGE
   B) turnout, such as:
   C) turnout such as
   D) turnout, such as

1 Tommy, friendly as always offered to assist the confused tourist.

1. A) NO CHANGE
   B) Tommy, friendly as always,
   C) Tommy friendly as always,
   D) Tommy friendly as always

Continued →

2 Skipping through the sprinklers and rolling through the grass, Katie became a wet and grassy mess.

2. A) NO CHANGE
   B) Skipping through the sprinklers and rolling through the grass
   C) Skipping through the sprinklers, and rolling through the grass
   D) Skipping through the sprinklers, and rolling through the grass,

Even though many **3** voters apparently unaware of the country's many problems, are happy with the incumbent, I feel that we are ready for a new leader.

3. A) NO CHANGE
   B) voters, apparently unaware of the country's many problems,
   C) voters, apparently unaware of the country's many problems
   D) voters apparently unaware of the country's many problems

George rocked the **4** boat many people fell out.

4. A) NO CHANGE
   B) boat, many
   C) boat; many
   D) boat in that many

Pete's **5** Bistro, the busiest and noisiest restaurant on the street, caters to a motley crew of tourists and locals.

5. A) NO CHANGE
   B) Bistro, the busiest, and noisiest
   C) Bistro, the busiest, and noisiest,
   D) Bistro, the busiest and noisiest,

6 Astronaut, Scott Kelly now officially holds the record for the longest consecutive time in space by an American.

6. A) NO CHANGE
   B) Astronaut Scott Kelly now
   C) Astronaut, Scott Kelly, now
   D) Astronaut: Scott Kelly now,

Some educators think that computer coding— the mysterious language that makes our computers and phones **7** work should be taught to students starting in elementary school.

7. A) NO CHANGE
   B) work,
   C) work—
   D) work:

2. FRAGMENTS

Several types of fragments show up on the SAT. You can identify them by looking for the specific parts described below.

DEPENDENT CLAUSE

First, let's define the word *conjunction*:

Conjunction – A word that links the parts of a sentence together.

There are several different types of conjunctions (we'll learn about others soon). One kind, called a **subordinate conjunction** (don't worry about memorizing the name), turns an independent clause into a dependent clause when placed in front of the independent clause. Remember that a dependent clause, on its own, is not a complete sentence—it's a fragment.

after	even though	though
although	if	unless
as	if only	until
as if	in order that	when
as long as	now that	whenever
as though	once	where
because	rather than	whereas
before	since	wherever
even if	so that	while

When you spot one of these words at the beginning of a sentence, look out for a fragment. For example:

Fragment: *As* the forest fire burned, bellowing smoke high into the air in huge spiraling spumes of blackness.

The sentence lacks an independent clause. Note that if the word "As" were removed, the sentence would be an independent clause.

-ING WORD USED AS A VERB

As taught in the Verb Tense lesson, a word in the *-ing* form—on its own—does not function as a verb. When the subject of a sentence lacks a verb, the sentence is a fragment. For example:

Fragment: The firefighters, many from hundreds of miles away, *preparing* to fight the fire.

The subject "firefighters" lacks a verb. You could fix this sentence by adding "are" or "were" in front of "preparing."

PRONOUN PHRASE

Watch out for phrases that begin with pronouns such as *that*, *which*, *who*, or *whom*. Especially watch out for *that*; the others are easier to identify because they will usually be preceded by a comma. The following are all fragments because the subjects ("fire," "fire," and "residents") lack verbs:

Fragment: The fire *that* burned over 1,000 acres last summer.

Fragment: The forest fire, *which* was likely started when someone threw a cigarette from his car.

Fragment: The residents, *who* lived in the small mountain town all their lives.

THAT CLAUSE

Sometimes the word *that* indicates a clause within a clause. This so-called *"that" clause* must have its own subject and verb. For example:

Fragment: The newspaper reporter said *that* residents returning to their homes.

The subject of the "that" clause ("residents") lacks a verb.

While less common, *question* words such as *why*, *where*, *who*, *what*, *how*, etc. can also create their own clauses, so watch out for them.

MODIFYING PHRASE

The SAT will often use long modifying phrases to disguise fragments. Try removing modifying phrases to find the barebones sentence.

Fragment: The fire captain, one of the most experienced firefighters in the county and not surprisingly the first on the scene.

The subject "captain" lacks a verb.

SEMICOLON

Watch out for fragments when two clauses are separated by a semicolon. As taught in the Punctuation section, a semicolon (like a period) separates two *independent clauses*.

Fragment: Jerry is a veteran firefighter; having worked his way up to captain.

Fragment: Many unpredictable factors must be considered when fighting a fire; changes in the weather and the direction and velocity of the wind perhaps the most significant.

The second phrase in each of the previous examples is a fragment. Both semicolons should be commas.

■

> A fragment usually contains one of the following:
> 1. Dependent clause (look for a subordinate conjunction)
> 2. *-ING* word used as a verb
> 3. Pronoun phrase
> 4. "That" clause
> 5. Modifying phrase
> 6. Semicolon

FRAGMENTS LESSON PROBLEMS

Bertrand Russell's **1** *The Problems of Philosophy, often* one of the first books assigned in introductory Philosophy courses because of its ability to make the abstruse comprehendible.

1. A) NO CHANGE
    B) *The Problems of Philosophy*, is often
    C) *The Problems of Philosophy* is often
    D) *The Problems of Philosophy*, often being

2 After the committee released its findings on the widespread use of cell phones, scientists warned that there may be a link between cell-phone use and brain tumors.

2. A) NO CHANGE
    B) The committee released
    C) The committee releasing
    D) After the committee releasing

Although better known as a movie star, Austrian actress **3** Hedy Lamarr, who became a pioneer in the field of wireless communications following her emigration to the United States.

3. A) NO CHANGE
    B) Hedy Lamarr
    C) Hedy Lamarr who
    D) Hedy Lamarr; who

Continued →

When choosing a health insurance <u>4 company;</u> <u>choose</u> carefully.

4. A) NO CHANGE
   B) company. Choose
   C) company, choose
   D) company, and you should choose

The <u>5 sculptor, carefully shaping</u> with his hands, transformed clay into art.

5. A) NO CHANGE
   B) sculptor carefully shaping
   C) sculptor carefully shaped
   D) sculptor, who carefully shaping

Jerry said that climbing <u>1 trees, an activity not</u> for everyone because of its inherent risks.

1. A) NO CHANGE
   B) trees is not an activity
   C) trees, an activity that is not
   D) trees, not an activity

Most <u>2 people showing</u> little concern for agriculture and farming, even though these fields were keys to the rise of human civilization.

2. A) NO CHANGE
   B) people show
   C) people, who show
   D) people, showing

The so-called wind car, possibly the first automobile, which used a machine similar to a windmill to drive gears, which in turn drove the <u>3 wheels, designed</u> by da Vigevano in 1335.

3. A) NO CHANGE
   B) wheels, was designed
   C) wheels; it was designed
   D) wheels. The car was designed

When turning <u>4 right, make</u> sure to look over your right shoulder for pedestrians and bikers.

4. A) NO CHANGE
   B) right; make
   C) right; you should make
   D) right; it is a good idea to make

Continued →

Most of the overnight campers know **5** <u>that the</u> <u>ghost stories being</u> told to scare them from leaving their bunks in the middle of the night.

5. A) NO CHANGE
    B) that the ghost stories are being
    C) that the ghost stories, which are being
    D) that the ghost stories

3. RUN-ONS

FANBOYS CONJUNCTIONS

Most run-on errors on the SAT involve a *compound sentence*, which is just two independent clauses linked with a conjunction called a FANBOYS, or *coordinating*, conjunction (once again, you don't have to memorize the official name). These are the seven FANBOYS conjunctions:

for, and, nor, but, or, yet, so

To help remember these conjunctions, use the acronym **FANBOYS**: **F**or-**A**nd-**N**or-**B**ut-**O**r-**Y**et-**S**o. You might also notice that each conjunction is either two or three letters long. (Many other conjunctions are longer.)

The FANBOYS conjunctions, listed above, are the only conjunctions that can link two independent clauses. As explained in the Punctuation section, when they link independent clauses, they should be preceded with a comma. For example:

In his books and essays, Thoreau challenged the traditional ideas of society**, and** he was thus both criticized and praised by his readers.

RUN-ONS ON THE SAT

From the Punctuation section, we know that two independent clauses must be separated by (1) a comma *and* a FANBOYS conjunction or (2) a semicolon—otherwise, the sentence is a run-on. On the SAT, there are three common types of run-on sentences related to this rule:

COMMA BUT NO CONJUNCTION

The first one, called a *comma splice*, involves two independent clauses separated by a comma but lacking a conjunction. For example:

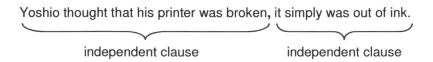

Yoshio thought that his printer was broken**,** it simply was out of ink.

independent clause   independent clause

To correct this run-on, simply add an appropriate conjunction:

Yoshio thought that his printer was broken, *but* it simply was out of ink.

CONJUNCTION BUT NO COMMA

The second type of run-on also has two independent clauses. This one correctly includes a conjunction but is lacking a comma before the conjunction. For example:

Yoshio thought that his printer was broken and this was because the page came out white.

independent clause   independent clause

Since the second part of the sentence is an independent clause, a comma must come before the conjunction. The correct sentence should read:

Yoshio thought that his printer was broken, and this was because the page came out white.

A more eloquent and succinct way to correct the error is to turn the second clause into a dependent clause or modifying phrase. The SAT may correct run-ons in this way:

Yoshio thought that his printer was broken because the page came out white.
Or:
Because the page came out white, Yoshio thought that his printer was broken.

NO COMMA, NO CONJUNCTION

Some compound sentences lack the comma *and* the FANBOYS conjunction. For example:

The page came out white Yoshio, thus, thought that his printer was broken.

You can add a comma and an appropriate FANBOYS conjunction—such as "and" or "so"—after the word "white," or just add a semicolon:

The page came out white; Yoshio, thus, thought that his printer was broken.

NON-*FANBOYS* TRANSITION WORDS

Watch out for transition words between independent clauses that are *not* FANBOYS conjunctions. These sentences may sound fine but are often considered run-ons. For example:

I practiced for hours while I taped myself, *then* I listened back to see how I sounded.

This sentence is a run-on. Use a FANBOYS conjunction, such as *and*, to correct the error. A good test is to notice that the word *then* could be moved around within the sentence (a FANBOYS conjunction is generally "stuck" between the clauses):

> I practiced for hours while I taped myself, *and then* I listened back to see how I sounded.
> I practiced for hours while I taped myself, *and* I *then* listened back to see how I sounded.
> I practiced for hours while I taped myself, *and* I listened back *then* to see how I sounded.

Here are some other transition words commonly used (incorrectly) to link independent clauses. This list will hopefully give you an idea of what to look for:

even so	in fact	on the other hand
furthermore	in other words	similarly
however	moreover	therefore
in addition	nevertheless	thus

■

> To identify run-on errors, look for questions with answer choices that contain various ways to connect independent clauses, including commas, conjunctions, periods, and semicolons.

RUN-ONS LESSON PROBLEMS

Most people rarely get to see the sunrise they are asleep that early in the morning.

1. A) NO CHANGE
    B) sunrise and they
    C) sunrise because they
    D) sunrise, and because they

 Kevin had run slowly at first, he then accelerated quickly to avoid the pursuing tacklers, who, to the delight of the crowd, fell harmlessly at Kevin's feet.

2. A) NO CHANGE
    B) Kevin had run slowly at first; he
    C) While Kevin had run slowly at first; he
    D) Kevin had run slowly at first he

Continued →

Many health experts agree that young people are not active **3** enough, this inactivity is likely a result of the temptations of such sedentary activities as watching television or working on the internet.

3. A) NO CHANGE
    B) enough this
    C) enough. This
    D) enough and this

Many people now watch more shows on their computers than on actual **4** televisions, and I wonder if the end of the television is near.

4. Which of following alternatives to the underlined portion would NOT be acceptable?

    A) televisions, leading me to wonder
    B) televisions I wonder
    C) televisions. I wonder
    D) televisions, which makes me wonder

At the end of the last day of school, the students **5** celebrated; however, the teachers, with stacks of ungraded tests on their desks, had much work ahead.

5. A) NO CHANGE
    B) celebrated, however,
    C) celebrated, however
    D) celebrated however

Playing a sport and learning an instrument offer good analogies for effective **1** studying, because these activities involve considerable practice to master, one can see the obvious benefits of hard work and persistence.

1. A) NO CHANGE
    B) studying because
    C) studying; because
    D) studying, and this is because

Continued →

The book was written without regard to punctuation or **2** paragraphs this unconformity made it difficult to understand.

2. A) NO CHANGE
   B) paragraphs, this unconformity
   C) paragraphs, an unconformity that
   D) paragraphs and this unconformity

He spoke with his **3** hands, but his voice was silent.

3. A) NO CHANGE
   B) hands but his voice
   C) hands, his voice
   D) hands his voice

He worked tirelessly to finish the experiment on the health benefits of soy **4** beans because the health conference was only a few weeks away.

4. A) NO CHANGE
   B) beans, the health conference was
   C) beans, the health conference being
   D) beans. The health conference being

The book *Dune*, by Frank Herbert, is the world's best-selling science fiction novel and has won both the Nebula and Hugo **5** Awards, in other words, it's a sci-fi classic.

5. A) NO CHANGE
   B) Awards, in other words
   C) Awards, in other words;
   D) Awards; in other words,

4. MISPLACED WORDS

MOVING WORDS TO AVOID AMBIGUITY

Sometimes the order of the words in a sentence creates an ambiguity. Look at the following example:

There was a scratch on the new wood table right in the center.

This sentence literally suggests that the wood table is "in the center." Likely, this is not the intended meaning. Move the related words together in the sentence to remove the error, as in the corrected version below:

There was a scratch *right in the center* of the new wood table.

Here is another example:

The ice cream competition will be the largest ever with ice-cream samples from over 100 contestants kept in a large freezer.

Our hearts go out to those poor contestants in the freezer. The following sentences remove the ambiguity:

The ice cream competition will be the largest ever with over 100 contestants. The ice-cream samples will be kept in a large freezer.

MOVING WORDS TO AVOID AWKWARDNESS

Sometimes the order of the words just plain sounds wrong:

Computer Aided Design offers at the same time opportunities to be artistic and technical.

Perhaps the meaning is clear, but the sentence doesn't sound great, does it? The following corrects the awkwardness:

Computer Aided Design offers opportunities to be artistic and technical *at the same time*.

IMPROPER MODIFIERS

As we've seen in the previous sections, dependent clauses and phrases can act as modifiers for a noun or nouns in the sentence. On the SAT, *improper modifiers* (sometimes called *danglers*), which are usually at the beginning of a sentence, appear to modify an illogical noun because of this noun's closeness to the modifying phrase. **You must make sure that the noun meant to be modified is as close as possible to the modifying phrase.** For example:

With power and skill, the volleyball was spiked over the net by Jill.

The modifying phrase in this sentence is *With power and skill*. It is obviously meant to modify *Jill*, but it seems to modify *the volleyball*. The sentence's intended meaning may be obvious, but the sentence should be corrected to read:

With power and skill, Jill spiked the volleyball over the net.

Sometimes modifying phrases show up at the ends of sentences. These are usually correct, even though the noun they modify is at the beginning. Here are two examples:

Jill spiked the volleyball over the net *with power and skill*.
Jill spiked the volleyball over the net, *hitting it with all her strength*.

Again, these are both correct.

■

 Look for questions with answer choices that rewrite a large portion of the sentence, often an entire clause. As you might imagine, words or phrases are repositioned in these answer choices.

APPROACH TO MISPLACED WORDS QUESTIONS

Even though you may use the answer choices to *identify* a misplaced word problem (as described above), try to answer these misplaced words questions without scrutinizing the answer choices right away. Just use the passage. This *aggressive* approach will often help you because the answer choices on Misplaced Words questions can be wordy and confusing.

MISPLACED WORDS LESSON PROBLEMS

Corporations are more **1** likely to hire college graduates with advanced degrees than smaller companies.

1. A) NO CHANGE
    B) likely to hire, as opposed to smaller companies, college graduates with advanced degrees
    C) likely to hire than smaller companies college graduates with advanced degrees
    D) likely than smaller companies to hire college graduates with advanced degrees

After sneaking out the window to play games with his friends, **2** his parents were the last people Sean expected to run into at the arcade.

2. A) NO CHANGE
    B) Sean least expected to run into his parents at the arcade
    C) running into his parents was the last thing Sean expected at the arcade
    D) his parents, at the arcade, were the last people Sean expected to run into

After sleeping through the entire semester, **3** a shock was receiving the A to Chrissie.

3. A) NO CHANGE
    B) receiving an A was a shock to Chrissie
    C) Chrissie was shocked that she received an A
    D) Chrissie's A was a shock to her

1 The writer discussed the negative impact of graffiti in the last chapter of his book.

1. A) NO CHANGE
   B) The writer, in the last chapter, discussed the negative impact of graffiti in his book.
   C) In the last chapter of his book, the writer discussed the negative impact of graffiti.
   D) The writer discussed the negative impact, in the last chapter of his book, of graffiti.

After hearing the CD of the live performance, **2** our disappointment in missing the show was unbearable.

2. A) NO CHANGE
   B) our disappointment in having missed the show was unbearable
   C) we were, because of having missed the show, unbearably disappointed
   D) we were unbearably disappointed about missing the show

The new navigation **3** system, when a button is pressed, will speak directions to the driver, on the steering wheel.

3. A) NO CHANGE
   B) system will speak directions, when a button is pressed on the steering wheel to the driver
   C) system will speak directions to the driver when a button is pressed on the steering wheel
   D) system, will speak directions to the driver, when a button is pressed on the steering wheel

With strength and endurance not found among any of the other **4** competitors, Greg Lemond's victory was an amazing one once again.

4. A) NO CHANGE
   B) competitors, Greg Lemond rode to an amazing victory once again
   C) competitors, to an amazing victory once again Greg Lemond rode
   D) competitors, as Greg Lemond rode to an amazing victory once again

5. COMBINING SENTENCES

Combining sentences tests all of the rules taught in this chapter. Always check punctuation, make sure your answer choice doesn't contain fragments or run-ons, and watch out for misplaced words, especially misplaced modifiers. Here are a few additional things to think about when combining sentences:

CONCISION

More than half the time, the shortest answer is the best answer. If you don't recognize any obvious errors in the shortest sentence, go for it.

/ The correct answer when combining sentences is usually the shortest answer choice.

CLAUSES AND PHRASES

When combining sentences, the best answer is often the one with the fewest clauses and phrases. Sometimes this is easy to check just by counting punctuation marks (commas, semicolons, long dashes, etc.). This is a rough way to check, but it's pretty easy.

/ Correct answers often have the fewest punctuation marks.

For example, let's combine the following sentence:

> Using high-octane gasoline usually does not improve a car's performance. Many drivers, however, continue to waste their money on expensive gasoline.

Which sentence sounds better?

> Using high-octane gasoline, while many drivers continue to waste their money on expensive gasoline, usually does not improve a car's performance. [two commas]
> OR?
> While many drivers continue to waste their money on expensive gasoline, using high-octane gasoline usually does not improve a car's performance. [one comma]

Count the punctuation. The extra comma in the first example is a clue that the better answer is the second one.

INDEPENDENT CLAUSES

Since you'll be combining two sentences, each typically with one independent clause, the correct answer will *usually* not maintain these two original independent clauses. One will probably be changed into a modifying phrase or dependent clause. For example, let's combine the following sentences:

Many drivers waste their money on high-octane gasoline. They are susceptible to deceptive advertising at their gas stations.

The examples below maintain the two independent clauses and, while grammatically correct, would likely *not* be the best sentence combination:

Many drivers waste their money on high-octane gasoline, **and** they are susceptible to deceptive advertising at their gas stations.

Many drivers waste their money on high-octane gasoline; they are susceptible to deceptive advertising at their gas stations.

Here's how you might see these sentences correctly combined:

Susceptible to deceptive advertising at their gas stations, many drivers waste their money on high-octane gasoline.

Note: We have occasionally seen exceptions to this rule, but unless you can easily eliminate the other three choices, stay away from choices that maintain the two original independent clauses.

AVOID AWKWARD PHRASE INTERRUPTIONS

When possible, try to avoid breaking up phrases, especially phrases that sound unified or cohesive when uninterrupted. These phrases often include prepositional phrases. Which example below sounds better?

While many drivers continue, on high-octane gasoline, to waste their money . . .
OR?
While many drivers continue to waste their money on high-octane gasoline . . .

Clearly, the second example is better. Again, counting punctuation may help.

PASSIVE VOICE

We'll get into the passive voice in the next chapter, but here's a quick example:

Active voice: Cindy took the test.

Passive voice: The test was taken by Cindy.

Hopefully the difference is clear. When possible, make sure the performer of the action (for example, *Cindy* above) is the subject of the sentence.

■

> To identify combining-sentences questions, look for questions that either ask you to "combine sentences at the underlined portion" or "combine the underlined sentences."

COMBINING SENTENCES LESSON PROBLEMS

Lori answered the questions quickly and **1** accurately. She earned the admiration of the interviewer.

1. Which choice most effectively combines the sentences at the underlined portion?

   A) accurately, earning did she
   B) accurately, earning
   C) accurately, and she also earned
   D) accurately; therefore earning

The school's running back had his worst game of the **2** season. This was because he was playing with a sprained ankle.

2. Which choice most effectively combines the sentences at the underlined portion?

   A) season because
   B) season, and the reason was because
   C) season; because
   D) season, which is because

Continued →

3 Wikipedia was once scoffed by higher education. Now professors are having their graduate students write their own Wiki entries.

3. Which choice most effectively combines the underlined sentences?

A) Professors, who once scoffed at Wikipedia, are now having their graduate students write their own Wiki entries.
B) Professors once scoffed at Wikipedia, but now graduate students are having their own Wiki entries assigned by them.
C) Wikipedia, once scoffed by higher education, is now having the graduate students of professors write their own Wiki entries for it.
D) Wikipedia was once scoffed by higher education, but now Wiki entries are being written by the graduate students of professors.

The Russian Cyrillic alphabet contains 33 **1** letters. They include 20 consonant, 10 vowels, a semi-consonant/semi-vowel, and 2 other signs that help with pronunciation.

1. Which choice most effectively combines the sentences at the underlined portion?

A) letters, and these letters include
B) letters; which include
C) letters, including:
D) letters, including

Continued →

2 Moviegoers are already confronted with high ticket prices, annoying "texters," and inconvenient parking. It's no surprise that many of them are choosing to watch movies at home.

2. Which choice most effectively combines the underlined sentences?

   A) It's no surprise that many moviegoers are choosing to watch movies at home, and they are already confronted with high ticket prices, annoying "texters," and inconvenient parking.
   B) High ticket prices, annoying "texters," and inconvenient parking are why it is no surprise that many moviegoers are choosing to watch movies at home.
   C) Not surprisingly, many moviegoers are already confronted with high ticket prices, annoying "texters," and inconvenient parking, and they are choosing to watch movies at home.
   D) Not surprisingly, many moviegoers, already confronted with high ticket prices, annoying "texters," and inconvenient parking, are choosing to watch movies at home.

3 Taking public transportation provides benefits besides reducing traffic and decreasing pollution. It also allows passengers to read or catch up on work while commuting.

3. Which choice most effectively combines the underlined sentences?

   A) Besides reducing traffic, taking public transportation allows passengers to read or catch up on work while commuting and decreasing pollution.
   B) Taking public transportation, providing benefits besides reducing traffic and decreasing pollution, allows passengers to read or catch up on work while commuting.
   C) Taking public transportation allows passengers to read or catch up while commuting on work, providing benefits besides reducing traffic and decreasing pollution.
   D) Besides reducing traffic and decreasing pollution, taking public transportation allows passengers to read or catch up on work while commuting.

Study the material in the Sentence Structure chapter before taking the following quiz. If you're working with a tutor, you will take the quiz during the next lesson. If you're working on your own, take the quiz after reviewing, and do not look back to the lessons. After grading, review any topics you struggled on. The quiz is untimed.

SENTENCE-STRUCTURE QUIZ

New high-definition **1** <u>televisions that</u> have resolutions far superior to those of the past.

1. A) NO CHANGE
   B) televisions
   C) televisions, that
   D) televisions, which

The **2** <u>MSPCA or Massachusetts</u> Society for the Prevention of Cruelty to Animals, is a national and international leader in the protection of animals.

2. A) NO CHANGE
   B) MSPCA Massachusetts
   C) MSPCA—Massachusetts
   D) MSPCA, or Massachusetts

One reason to keep your house **3** <u>clean, is that</u> a tidy environment leads to a relaxed mind.

3. A) NO CHANGE
   B) clean is: that
   C) clean is, that,
   D) clean is that

When you **4** <u>eat too much ice cream, as the child learned the hard way</u>, you might get a stomachache.

4. A) NO CHANGE
   B) eat too much, as the child learned the hard way, ice cream
   C) eat too much ice cream, as learned the hard way by the child
   D) eat, as the child learned the hard way, too much ice cream

5 <u>Now that you understand</u> the basics of electricity, particularly the dangers involved when you are working with bare wires.

5. A) NO CHANGE
   B) Now you understand
   C) Now that you have an understanding of
   D) Now you understand that

Continued →

Considered an expert in her field, the
6 <u>doctor's research papers</u> were widely read
and studied.

I walked **7** <u>slowly, away from the bear</u> as
though there was nothing out of the ordinary.

One of the best ways to keep your house
8 <u>tidy, donating,</u> which not only minimizes your
"stuff" but also is good for your community.

The storm hit last **9** <u>night, and the</u> electricity
was out for over eight hours.

The lawyer **10** <u>working tirelessly to</u> give her
client a decent chance in court, even though the
evidence strongly suggests guilt.

He thought the math class would be **11** <u>easy,
then</u> his class started working on limits.

6. A) NO CHANGE
    B) doctor wrote research papers that
    C) doctor's papers of research
    D) research papers of the doctor

7. A) NO CHANGE
    B) slowly away, from the bear,
    C) slowly, away from the bear,
    D) slowly away from the bear

8. A) NO CHANGE
    B) tidy, which is donating
    C) tidy, by donating
    D) tidy is by donating

9. A) NO CHANGE
    B) night and the
    C) night, the
    D) night; with the

10. A) NO CHANGE
    B) works tirelessly to
    C) had been working with tirelessness
        to
    D) tirelessly work and

11. A) NO CHANGE
    B) easy then
    C) easy but then
    D) easy, but then

Continued →

The **12** owner of the business or, as he likes to call himself, the boss, rules with an iron fist.

12. A) NO CHANGE
    B) owner of the business, or, as he likes to call himself, the boss,
    C) owner, of the business, or as he likes to call himself the boss,
    D) owner of the business or as he likes to call himself the boss,

John F. Kennedy defeated Richard Nixon in the 1960 presidential election popular vote by 0.1 **13** percent. This was the closest outcome in U.S. history.

13. Which choice most effectively combines the sentences at the underlined portion?

    A) percent, this being the closest
    B) percent, and this was the closest
    C) percent, the closest
    D) percent: which was the closest

IV
GRAMMAR & SENTENCE STRUCTURE GUIDELINES

This chapter covers a few additional guidelines that will help you tackle questions that test Grammar and Sentence Structure (as covered in Chapters II and III).

GRAMMAR AND SENTENCE STRUCTURE QUESTIONS ID

First, make sure you can identify these types of questions on the test:

 Unlike questions that test Main Ideas and Organization (to be discussed in Chapter V), **Grammar and Sentence Structure questions usually do not have a written question**—the question is *implied.* In other words, you will only see the answer choices. See the examples below.

GRAMMAR QUESTION

1. **A.** NO CHANGE
   B. are
   C. is
   D. has been

SENTENCE STRUCTURE QUESTION

2. A) NO CHANGE
   B) sunrise and they
   C) sunrise because they
   D) sunrise, and because they

AN EXCEPTION (COMBINING SENTENCES)

3. Which choice most effectively combines the sentences at the underlined portion?

   A) letters, and these letters include
   B) letters; which include
   C) letters, including:
   D) letters, including

MAIN IDEA AND ORGANIZATION QUESTIONS ID

Again, we'll cover Main Ideas and Organization questions in the next chapter. Here's how to identify them:

 Main Ideas and Organization questions typically have a *written* question. The question is *not* implied. See the examples below.

MAIN IDEA QUESTION

4. Given that all of following sentences are true, which one would most effectively conclude the paragraph?

   A) Michael Douglas certainly has been in a lot of movies.
   B) It is no surprise that an actor with this many awards is so highly respected.
   C) Actors come and go, but Michael Douglas is here for the long haul.
   D) Michael Douglas is certainly more than just an actor.

ORGANIZATION QUESTION

5. To make this paragraph most logical, Sentence 3 should be placed

   A) where it is now.
   B) before Sentence 1.
   C) after Sentence 1.
   D) after Sentence 4.

AN EXCEPTION (TRANSITION QUESTIONS)

Transition questions fall under the category of Main Ideas, but they typically do not include a written question. Note the obvious transition words in the answer choices in the example below:

6. A) NO CHANGE
   B) Nevertheless, it seemed
   C) On the other hand, it seemed
   D) In any case, it seemed

■

The guidelines taught in this chapter typically apply to Grammar and Sentence Structure questions—*not* to Main Idea and Organization questions—so make sure you know what kind of question you're working on before applying these tips.

1. AVOID WORDY ANSWER CHOICES

As mentioned in the Concision & Redundancies lesson (Chapter II), good writing is usually as concise and clear as possible, with no needless words. Correct answers to Grammar and Sentence Structure questions are usually the shortest answer choice available, and rarely the longest one. In fact . . .

> The shortest answer choice on Grammar and Sentence Structure questions is correct **greater than 50% of the time**!
> AND
> The longest answer choice is *in*correct **greater than 90% of the time**!
> AND
> When two answer choices are clearly longer than the other two choices, the answer will probably be one of the shorter answers (greater than 90%).

! **In other words, stay away from long answer choices, and when in doubt, guess shorter answers.**

DON'T FORGET THE **NO CHANGE** ANSWER CHOICE

The answer choice labeled NO CHANGE (A) refers, of course, to the words in the passage. These words won't be reprinted above the other answer choices—making their lengths hard to compare to the lengths of the other answer choices—so don't forget to look back to the passage. This NO CHANGE answer choice may very well be the shortest answer choice, but you won't know unless you remember to look.

T.S. Eliot was awarded the Nobel Prize in Literature in 1948 **1** by the consideration of his contributions to poetry and playwriting.

1. A) NO CHANGE
   B) for
   C) owing to
   D) due to the fact of

CLOSE ENOUGH TO CALL A TIE

Sometimes the differences in lengths of the answer choices are subtle—perhaps a couple letters or one word. Don't worry about wordiness for these answer choices. For example, the verb *is* is shorter than the verb *are*, but that's obviously not enough of a reason to select the former (*is*) as your correct answer. Look for answer choices that have more significant variations in length.

VERB PHRASES

Even answers with verbs and verb phrases seem to follow these rules. When the answer choices contain words such as *walked*, *has walked*, *had walked*, *will walk*, etc., the correct answer will be the simple verb (*walked*) nearly 90% of the time.

Stravinsky's ballet *The Rite of Spring* was an avant-garde orchestral concert that nearly **2** had caused a riot in the audience when it was first performed in 1913.

2. A) NO CHANGE
   B) has caused
   C) causes
   D) caused

A COMMON EXCEPTION: PRONOUN AMBIGUITY

When a question is testing Pronoun Ambiguity, the correct answer is often the one that removes the ambiguity by restating an important noun. This correct answer, thus, is often one of the longer choices, so don't apply the rules above on these questions.

While most competitors just lifted weights, and some lightly scrimmaged against other players, Marley swam each morning, ran hills each afternoon, and biked for miles every week. **3** This was why he outclassed his tired opponents at the ends of matches.

3. A) NO CHANGE
   B) It was
   C) These were
   D) This conditioning was

2. AVOID -ING WORDS

Answer choices that use words in the -ing form are usually incorrect. Words in the -ing form often create fragments or other awkwardness. As taught in the Verb Tense lesson, it is important to remember that a single word (on its own) in the -ing form does not function as an active verb:

> Fragment: John *running* to the store. ✗
> Correct: John *has been running* to the store. ✓

Be especially wary of the words *being* and *having*, which are almost always wrong. Let's look at an example:

The professor argued that although many universities have excelled at training future scientists, **1** the failure is in their not educating humanities majors in the methods of scientific thought.

1. A) NO CHANGE
    B) they have failed to educate
    C) the failure they have is in their not educating
    D) having failed to educate

EXCEPTIONS

GRAMMATICALLY CORRECT USES

The -ing form of a word is not *necessarily* incorrect, as seen in some of the grammar lessons. Thus, you should be able to recognize -ing words that *are* used correctly. As covered in the Grammar chapter, there are two common grammatically-correct uses of -ing words:

1. Recall that an -ing verb phrase can be used to express continuous action over a period of time, for example:

    Bob *has been working* at the mini-mart since he was in high school.
    Bob *is* certainly *gaining* the respect of his boss.

2. Modifying phrases often contain -ing words, as displayed in the Punctuation section. For example:

Using both hands, Bob has become the fastest bagger in the store.

Having the most experience, Bob is certain to become the store manager before long.

PARALLELISM

If you have to maintain parallel construction with *-ing* words that are not underlined (which means they must be correct), then an *-ing* word will be part of the correct answer.

For many a great artist, **2** being free to innovate is more important than being well paid.

2. A) NO CHANGE
    B) having freedom of innovation is more important
    C) there is more importance in the freedom to innovate
    D) to have the freedom to innovate is more important

-*ING* IN EVERY ANSWER CHOICE

Obviously, when there is an *-ing* word in every answer choice, one of them must be correct. You should still probably avoid answer choices that have more *-ing* words than the others or ones that contain *being* or *having*.

HARMLESS -*ING* WORDS

-*ING* words that function as simple nouns are usually OK. For example:

When the *going* gets tough, the tough go *fishing*.

There's really no better way to write this sentence. The good news is that when *-ing* words are used as simple nouns, they're usually found in every answer choice.

SUMMARY

Answer choices with *-ing* words are *usually* incorrect. But make sure you understand the few exceptions described above.

3. AVOID THE PASSIVE VOICE

The passive voice means that the performer of the action in the sentence is *not* the subject of the sentence. For example:

The books were carefully arranged on the shelf by Dan, a self-proclaimed neat-freak.

The subject of this sentence is *books*, but the books are obviously not performing the action of *arranging—Dan* is. This sentence is in the *passive voice*. To rewrite the sentence in the *active voice*, make *Dan* the subject of the sentence:

Dan, a self-proclaimed neat-freak, carefully arranged the books on the shelf.

Look to eliminate answer choices in the passive voice in the following example:

1 Dan arranged the books on the shelf, he proceeded to proclaim himself a neat-freak.

1. A) NO CHANGE
   B) The books, which were arranged on the shelf by Dan, who
   C) The books were first arranged on the shelf by Dan, who then
   D) After arranging the books on the shelf, Dan

4. AVOID NEW MISTAKES

READ TO THE ENDS OF ANSWER CHOICES

Let's say you're reading a passage on the Writing and Language Test and you identify a grammar error in an underlined portion of a sentence. When you look at the answer choices, you might pick the first one that corrects the error. But you must make sure that you don't end up selecting an answer choice that introduces a *new* error. How do you avoid these careless mistakes? By being careful! Make sure you read the whole answer choice before picking it, or look at the other answer choices to see if any of them also correct the original error.

His article in the school newspaper **1** <u>challenged, the student body to stop</u> blaming teachers and start becoming accountable for the widespread low test scores.

1. A) NO CHANGE
   B) challenged the student body to: stop
   C) challenged the student body to stop
   D) challenging the student body in stopping

READ TO THE ENDS OF SENTENCES

Similar mistakes occur when students don't read an entire sentence, especially when the underlined portion shows up early in the sentence. Some questions, especially ones that test sentence structure, require you to read all the way to the period. Generally, it's a good idea to get to the end of a sentence before choosing an answer choice.

While some scholars see a correlation between the rise of social media and the decline of printed books, **2** <u>others</u> think that the decline has more to do with increased internet gaming, the reality is that, for whatever reason, people are reading fewer and fewer physical books.

2. A) NO CHANGE
   B) and others
   C) however, others
   D) even so, others

5. NO CHANGE

The NO CHANGE answer choice (A) is the correct answer as often as each of the other answer choices (about one-fourth of the time). Some students have a tendency to find an error in the sentence at all costs, but often the sentence is correct as written. The SAT folks generally won't try to trick you on these—if the sentence sounds correct as written, don't be afraid to select NO CHANGE.

1 <u>Most experts considered</u> Michael Phelps to be the greatest swimmer ever after he won eight gold medals in the 2008 Beijing Olympics.

1. A) NO CHANGE
    B) Almost all experts considered
    C) Absolutely many experts considered
    D) Experts, but not all, considered

5. THINK "TECHNIQUE-LY"

Throughout the Grammar and Sentence Structure chapters, you saw information about identifying techniques as they are tested on the test. This information was always indicated with a magnifying glass:

It's essential that you consider techniques (think "technique-ly") while answering Grammar and Sentence Structure questions. Knowing what technique is being tested may change how you approach a problem and will reduce the tendency you may have of over-trusting your ear.

Here's some technique ID practice. Most techniques can be identified by looking at the answer choices. Try matching the following techniques to the answer choices (each is used once): Verb Tense, Subject-Verb Agreement, Pronoun Agreement, Pronoun Case, Apostrophes & Confused Words, Vocabulary, Idioms, Redundancies, Punctuation.

A) NO CHANGE	A) NO CHANGE	A) NO CHANGE
B) pledge	B) had left	B) their position
C) promise	C) left	C) his or her position
D) vow	D) leave	D) its position

1. _____   2. _____   3. _____

A) NO CHANGE	A) NO CHANGE	A) NO CHANGE
B) of	B) work tirelessly	B) theirs
C) from	C) works tirelessly	C) their's
D) about	D) working tirelessly	D) there's

4. _____   5. _____   6. _____

A) NO CHANGE	A) NO CHANGE	A) NO CHANGE
B) heading and leading	B) in the same way, such as	B) who
C) heading, and also leading	C) in the same way: such as	C) whom
D) heading	D) in the same way, such as:	D) them

7. _____   8. _____   9. _____

6. GRAMMAR & SENTENCE STRUCTURE: SUMMARY

As stated before, to do well on Grammar and Sentence Structure questions, you must understand the material taught in Chapters II and III. If you are comfortable with the additional guidelines below, you'll be ready to master these questions:

1. Avoid Wordy Answer Choices.
2. Avoid -*ING* Words.
3. Avoid the Passive Voice.
4. Avoid New Mistakes.
5. The NO CHANGE answer choice (A) is correct about as often as the other answer choices.
6. Think "technique-ly." Always consider techniques while answering questions, and don't over-rely on your ear.

7. *GRAMMAR AND SENTENCE STRUCTURE: PRACTICE & CORRECTIONS*

PRACTICE PROBLEMS

After reviewing the guidelines on the previous pages, tackle the lesson and homework problems on the following pages. Note that, unlike the passages on the SAT, these passages only test material taught in the Grammar and Sentence Structure chapters:

- ☐ Lesson Passage: "The Same Old Story"
- ☐ Homework Passage: "Alien Invasion"

In addition to these passages, you will eventually tackle practice passages from Test 1 in *The Official SAT Study Guide*. These will be assigned after you complete the Main Ideas and Organization chapter. See the Tutoring Schedules for more details (Introduction).

TEST CORRECTIONS

After completing and grading each practice test, you should correct Grammar and Sentence Structure questions that you missed or guessed on. Below are the three steps to correcting practice tests:

1. Turn to the Techniques section at the end of this tutorial and circle the Grammar and Sentence Structure questions that you missed or guessed on for each test.
2. Correct the problems in *The Official SAT Study Guide*. As you correct the problems, go back to the tutorial and review the techniques. The idea is to (1) identify techniques that have given you trouble, (2) go back to the tutorial so you can review and strengthen these techniques, and (3) apply these techniques to the specific problems on which you struggled.
3. If you have trouble identifying the best technique to use on a problem, refer to the Techniques chapter. This is an important part of correcting the tests.

LESSON PRACTICE PASSAGE

The following lesson passage only tests material taught in the Grammar and Sentence Structure chapters. The passage begins on the next page.

Questions 1–11 are based on the following passage.

The Same Old Story

George Smith—a leading archaeologist, historian, and linguist of his day—did not actually *find* his greatest **1** discovery, his claim to fame was that he *deciphered* it. It was a Mesopotamian tablet that had been collecting dust at the British Museum. In 1872, Smith **2** captured his fame by translating the tablet into English. He read his translation before the Society of Biblical Archaeology, **3** this was for an audience that included the Prime Minister of Britain. In a quiet and steady voice, **4** Smith told a story of a great flood, one that had remarkable similarities to the one recounted in the Bible.

Continued →

1. A) NO CHANGE
   B) discovery, and his
   C) discovery, but which his
   D) discovery; his

2. A) NO CHANGE
   B) produced
   C) achieved
   D) completed

3. A) NO CHANGE
   B) which was
   C) that was
   D) DELETE the underlined portion

4. A) NO CHANGE
   B) the story of the great flood was told by Smith,
   C) the great flood story, as told by Smith,
   D) Smith's story of the great flood was

The tablet Smith translated was called "The Flood Tablet," but it has since become known as Tablet XI of the Gilgamesh Epic. This epic, composed of tablets and fragments from numerous sources, **5** describes how the gods sent a flood to Earth to destroy the population of humans. One man, named Utnapishtim, **6** whom had been **7** forewarned in advance about the flood, built a ship for himself and his family. Of course, he saved room for plants and animals of every kind. After the flood, Utnapishtim **8** released the animals and, after some consultation among the gods, settled down on a **9** mountain. Here he and his wife enjoyed immortality.

The story was **10** familiar: but no one expected to find it on an ancient stone tablet. One can only imagine George **11** Smiths amazement as he deciphered these words for the first time.

5. A) NO CHANGE
   B) describe
   C) have described
   D) describing

6. A) NO CHANGE
   B) whom has
   C) who has
   D) who had

7. A) NO CHANGE
   B) forewarned
   C) forewarned before
   D) forewarned beforehand

8. A) NO CHANGE
   B) releases
   C) has released
   D) had been releasing

9. Which choice most effectively combines the two sentences at the underlined portion?
   A) mountain, and enjoying with his wife
   B) mountain, where he and his wife enjoyed
   C) mountain, and this is where he and his wife enjoyed
   D) mountain, and he and his wife enjoying

10. A) NO CHANGE
    B) familiar, but
    C) familiar, but:
    D) familiar, but,

11. A) NO CHANGE
    B) Smiths's
    C) Smiths'
    D) Smith's

The following homework passage only tests material taught in the Grammar and Sentence Structure chapters:

Questions 1–11 are based on the following passage.

Alien Invasion!

A few days ago, my science teacher, Mrs. Higgins, brought in a movie. Of course, **1** my classmates and me were expecting the **2** typical, dull, documentary on biology, but this was different. Mrs. Higgins popped in the disc and then, before pressing the play button, held the DVD case up so the class could see the **3** title; *Alien,* by Ridley Scott, the classic 1979 science-fiction horror movie. After warning the class that some of us might want to cover our eyes, she played a scene in which one of the baby aliens bursts through the chest of its human **4** host. However, that wasn't the worst part. After she stopped the movie and turned on the lights, she explained that certain wasps— right here on Earth—reproduce in much the same way.

Continued →

1. A) NO CHANGE
    B) my classmates and I
    C) us classmates and me
    D) we classmates and I

2. A) NO CHANGE
    B) typical dull documentary
    C) typical, dull documentary
    D) typical, dull documentary,

3. A) NO CHANGE
    B) title: *Alien,*
    C) title. *Alien,*
    D) title, *Alien,*

4. A) NO CHANGE
    B) host however
    C) host, however
    D) host, however,

These wasps are called parasitoid wasps. After the *Alien* scene, Mrs. Higgins showed us a video of one species of these wasps infecting a caterpillar. In an act called "ovipositing," the wasp sneaks up behind the caterpillar and, with a needle-like organ at the **5** wasps' abdomen, stabs the to-be host and injects its eggs. **6** Eventually, the eggs hatch within the caterpillar's body. The wasp larvae feed on the poor caterpillar's insides until the time comes to burst their way out.

Gruesome? Indeed. But if that's not bad enough, a few of the wasp larvae stay behind in the still-living caterpillar and **7** essentially take over its body. The caterpillar stops eating and becomes a protector for the released larvae, using its body like a tent to protect its ex-hosts and even **8** swung its head from side to side. Finally, the remaining wasps emerge from the caterpillar's body, and the caterpillar dies.

Continued →

5. A) NO CHANGE
   B) wasps abdomen, stabs
   C) wasp's abdomen, stabs
   D) wasp's abdomen, stabbing

6. Which choice best combines the underlined sentences?
   A) Eventually, the eggs hatch within the caterpillar's body, where the wasp larvae feed on the poor caterpillar's insides until the time comes to burst their way out.
   B) Eventually, the wasp larvae feed on the poor caterpillar's insides after the eggs hatch within the caterpillar's body, until the time comes to burst their way out.
   C) Eventually, within the caterpillar's body, the eggs hatch, and the poor caterpillar's insides are fed on by the wasp larvae until the time comes to burst their way out.
   D) Eventually, the eggs hatch and the wasp larvae feed on the poor caterpillar's insides within the caterpillar's body, until the time comes to burst their way out.

7. A) NO CHANGE
   B) originally
   C) approximately
   D) factually

8. A) NO CHANGE
   B) swinging
   C) swings
   D) had swung

You may think that parasitoid wasps are as bad **9** as a movie monster, but the surprising truth is that they **10** are quite actually useful. Because each species of wasp is specific to **11** there host, the wasps help in the battle against insect pests. Scientists, in an effort to control these pests, have actually introduced thousands of parasitoid wasps into ecosystems around the world. These efforts might be good for farmers, not to mention horror-movie buffs, but I suspect the caterpillars aren't too thrilled.

9. A) NO CHANGE
   B) as movie monsters,
   C) as are movie monsters,
   D) compared to movie monsters,

10. A) NO CHANGE
    B) were actually quite
    C) are being quite
    D) are actually quite

11. A) NO CHANGE
    B) their
    C) it's
    D) its

■

 All Programs: After correcting Practice Test 10 and reviewing the Grammar and Sentence Structure chapters, take Practice Test 9 in *The Official SAT Study Guide.*

V

MAIN IDEAS AND ORGANIZATION

This chapter focuses on main ideas, organization, and style. These questions—which usually make up from 10 to 16 questions per test (about a fourth of the questions)—tend to be more difficult than the questions discussed in Chapters II–IV. While the grammar techniques may come in handy, the questions discussed in this chapter, for the most part, do *not* rely on grammar knowledge. This chapter will discuss general techniques that will help you tackle Main Ideas and Organization questions.

IDENTIFYING MAIN IDEAS AND ORGANIZATION QUESTIONS

 These questions, unlike grammar questions, *usually* have a written question next to the question number. In addition, the answer choices tend to be longer than those on grammar questions.

If necessary, see page 212 for more on identifying Main Ideas and Organization questions.

■

A passage on "Snooker" is found on the following page. Don't read it yet. The questions and related lessons will be discussed on the pages following the passage.

1. MAIN IDEAS

A main idea is the central point or message of an essay, paragraph, or even a sentence.

MAIN IDEA OF A PARAGRAPH

While you read the essay, think about the main idea of each paragraph. Most paragraphs have a topic sentence, usually the *first* sentence, which can help you identify the paragraph's main idea. But remember that these essays are in need of revision and may lack clear and effective topic sentences. Therefore, you will likely have to look at details within the paragraph as well.

FIND KEYWORDS

You should usually be able to write down the main idea of a paragraph in just a few words. These words, we'll call them *keywords*, will help you when you look at the answer choices. Read Paragraph 1 below. Think about keywords while you read (we'll get to the questions soon):

Snooker: Yesterday and Today

—1—

Snooker, a table sport where each opponent uses a cue to hit colored balls into table pockets, has been around for over a hundred years. If you've watched a game of pool or Billiards, then you might be more familiar with Snooker than you think. **1** The game likely originated in India in the late 1800's when British Army officers made variations to traditional Billiards. The word *snooker* was a slang military term for an inexperienced military man. It is claimed that Colonel Sir Neville Chamberlain was playing this new game when his opponent failed to "pot" **2** —or sink—a ball. Chamberlain called his opponent a "snooker." The sport soon took this as its name.

What's the first word that comes to mind? (This should be straightforward. Write your first keyword below before moving on.)

First keyword for Paragraph 1 =

_____

Now that you have the first keyword ("Snooker"), let's dig a little deeper. What word best captures how the paragraph focuses on Snooker?

Second keyword for Paragraph 1 =

_____

So, based on these two keywords ("Snooker" and "originated"), the main idea of Paragraph 1 must have something to do with the **origin** of **Snooker**.

Now let's get into the types of Main Idea questions.

MAIN IDEA QUESTIONS

There are four kinds of Main Idea questions:

- Additions/Changes
- Deletions
- Topic/Transition Sentences
- Passage

ADDITIONS/CHANGES

These questions usually ask if you should add a given sentence to the essay. Sometimes, however, you'll be given the option to *change* a sentence in the essay. In both cases, you must consider the main idea of the relevant part of the essay.

 Most Additions/Changes questions have the following wording: "At this point, the writer is considering adding the following sentence. . . . Should the writer make this addition here?" Other questions may simply ask which choice provides the most relevant information or details.

YES/NO QUESTIONS

These questions usually have two "Yes" answers and two "No" answers (should the statement be added or not?). Try answering the yes/no question first, before looking at the rest of the answer choices. This will usually allow you to eliminate half of the answer choices.

OFF-TOPIC AND REDUNDANT ANSWER CHOICES

Pay close attention to what follows the "Yes" and the "No." The second parts of the answer choices might force you to rethink your original yes/no answer. Watch out for information that is off topic, but also look for redundant choices, ones that repeat information already found in the essay.

! **Don't be afraid to change your yes/no answer if the second parts of both remaining answer choices sound incorrect.**

Now, let's look at Question 1. The paragraph is copied below:

Snooker: Yesterday and Today

—1—

Snooker, a table sport where each opponent uses a cue to hit colored balls into table pockets, has been around for over a hundred years. If you've watched a game of pool or Billiards, then you might be more familiar with Snooker than you think. **1** The game likely originated in India in the late 1800's when British Army officers made variations to traditional Billiards. The word *snooker* was a slang military term for an inexperienced military man. It is claimed that Colonel Sir Neville Chamberlain was playing this new game when his opponent failed to "pot" **2** —or sink—a ball. Chamberlain called his opponent a "snooker." The sport soon took this as its name.

(EX) 1. At this point, the writer is considering adding the following sentence:

Billiards involves more colored balls than does Snooker.

Should the writer make this addition here?

Before we look at the answer choices, let's first decide whether the answer is *yes* or *no*. Review the first paragraph above. Do you think the sentence in question ties into the main idea of the paragraph (circle one below)?

YES or NO?

Now, let's look at the answer choices. We can eliminate A and B (the two "Yes" choices). Let's focus on C and D. Which answer choice is better? Consider the main idea of the paragraph.

A) Yes, because it gives the reader a better idea of the differences between Billiards and Snooker.
B) Yes, because it allows the reader to visualize Billiards.
C) No, because it doesn't help expand the historical background of Snooker.
D) No, because this paragraph is discussing table sports in general, not *specific* table sports.

ELIMINATE FALSE ANSWER CHOICES

Main Idea questions often have *false* answer choices. Look at the second parts (after the Yes/No) of the answer choices for Question 1. Do you see one that is definitely false?

Do you see a false answer choice for Question 1? Focus on what follows the Yes/No.

DELETIONS

These questions ask if the writer should delete a phrase or sentence from an essay. You must consider the main idea of the relevant part of the essay. Is the sentence (or underlined portion) adding appropriate details, or is it adding needless details that don't benefit the essay? Is it adding support or explanation? Providing a transition to a new topic? Presenting a contrast or comparison? Does the sentence stay on topic? Is it redundant? These are the kinds of questions you should ask yourself as you tackle Deletions questions.

As with Additions questions, pay attention to the second parts of answer choices. They may force you to reconsider your first inclination (to keep or to delete).

 Deletions questions typically ask if a sentence, or portion of a sentence, should be kept or deleted.

Now, let's look at Question 2 (next page). Again, the paragraph is copied below:

Snooker: Yesterday and Today

—1—

Snooker, a table sport where each opponent uses a cue to hit colored balls into table pockets, has been around for over a hundred years. If you've watched a game of pool or Billiards, then you might be more familiar with Snooker than you think. **1** The game likely originated in India in the late 1800's when British Army officers made variations to traditional Billiards. The word *snooker* was a slang military term for an inexperienced military man. It is claimed that Colonel Sir Neville Chamberlain was playing this new game when his opponent failed to "pot" **2** —or sink—a ball. Chamberlain called his opponent a "snooker." The sport soon took this as its name.

(EX) 2. The writer is considering deleting the underlined phrase from the sentence. Should the phrase be kept or deleted?

   A) Kept, because it provides supporting evidence of the challenge of a sport.

   B) Kept, because it provides a detail that clarifies a term in the sentence.

   C) Deleted, because it blurs the paragraph's main focus with a loosely related detail.

   D) Deleted, because it repeats information that has been provided earlier in the sentence.

TOPIC/TRANSITION SENTENCES

A *topic* sentence, which is usually found at the beginning of a paragraph, introduces the main idea (the *topic*) of the paragraph; it may also transition from the previous paragraph. A *transition* sentence leads the reader from one idea to the next, either between paragraphs or within a paragraph. Both types of sentences are similar in that they act as bridges between ideas in an essay. Once again, analyzing the main ideas and looking for keywords will help you solve these questions.

 Here are some typical topic/transition-sentence questions:
- "Which choice would most effectively introduce the topic of this paragraph?"
- "Which choice provides the best opening to this paragraph?"
- "Which choice provides the most effective transition to the next paragraph?"
- "Which choice provides the most effective transition to the next sentence?"

Also, any question that asks about the **first sentence of a paragraph** is probably testing topic sentences.

Read Paragraph 2 now. Don't answer any questions yet. When you're done reading, think about keywords for the paragraph. Can you come up with two or three of them?

—2—

3 The history of Snooker is filled with exciting matches and skilled players. The goal of Snooker is to score more points than the opponent. The game includes 15 red balls, one white ball, or cue ball, and six balls of different colors. Points are scored by potting balls. But the hard part is that the balls must be potted in a predetermined order. If you miss a shot on the desired ball, then your turn is done and the next player takes over. **4** Imagine the challenge of having to hit one specific ball with all of the other balls scattered around.

Keywords for Paragraph 2 =

_____

_____

Now, look at Question 3. Since the question asks about the first sentence of the paragraph, it's no surprise that it's testing the topic sentence. Make sure to read the question carefully. The question specifies that you must not only focus on Paragraph 2 but also Paragraph 1.

(EX) 3. Which choice best connects the sentence with the previous paragraph?

   A) NO CHANGE
   B) Billiards and Snooker are not the only games played with cues and balls.
   C) Snooker may have gotten its name from an unskilled player, but the game is not easy.
   D) Every game must have a means to determine winning from losing.

To answer Question 4, we'll have to read the first couple sentences of Paragraph 3:

—3—

Of the many great Snooker players,
Stephen Hendry stands out. Born on January
13, 1969 in Scotland, Hendry became the
youngest player to become a Snooker World
Champion—at the age of 21. . . .

It sounds like the paragraph is going to discuss one of the "great Snooker players": Stephen Hendry. Now, let's tackle Question 4 (go back to Paragraph 2). Once again, note that the question is asking you to consider the main ideas of Paragraph 2 *and* Paragraph 3:

(EX) 4. The writer wants to link the second paragraph with the ideas that follow. Which choice best accomplishes this goal?

   A) NO CHANGE
   B) No wonder Snooker players are considered so skilled.
   C) Tournaments are where Snooker players can show their stuff.
   D) So many balls; so little time.

Now, let's finish reading Paragraph 3. What are the keywords for this paragraph?

—3—

Of the many great Snooker players,
Stephen Hendry stands out. Born on January
13, 1969 in Scotland, Hendry became the
youngest player to become a Snooker World
Champion—at the age of 21. He went on to win
six more World Championships, and he was
Snooker's number one player for eight
consecutive years, between 1990 and 1998.
Hendry's skill as a player lead to amazing riches
and fame for him, and helped popularize the
sport of Snooker around the world. **5** <u>However,</u>
<u>you may not have heard of it.</u>

Keywords for Paragraph 3 =

_____

_____

PASSAGE QUESTIONS

Some essays will have a question that relates to the main idea of the entire passage.

 Look for a mention of the "passage as a whole" or the "entire passage."

The best way to tackle these questions is to think about the main idea of each paragraph. Let's do this with the practice essay:

- Paragraph 1 has to do with the **origin** of **Snooker**.
- Paragraph 2 has to do with **how to play** the **challenging** game of **Snooker**.
- Paragraph 3 has to do with the **Stephen Hendry** and how he helped **popularize** the sport of **Snooker**.

If you were to summarize the essay, you might say that it offers a general overview of the sport of Snooker, from its origins to its current popularity.

TOO BROAD OR TOO NARROW

Watch out for answer choices that are *too broad*. For example, the main idea of the whole essay has something to do with Snooker, not table sports in general. A choice that only refers to table sports would be incorrect. But also watch out for answer choices that are *too narrow*. For example, this essay briefly discusses how Snooker is played, but this is not the main idea of the whole essay.

TITLES

The title of the essay will often help you determine its main idea. This essay is titled "Snooker: Yesterday and Today." See if this helps you answer Question 5.

(EX) 5. The writer wants a conclusion that is consistent with the essay as a whole. Which choice best accomplishes this goal?
- A) NO CHANGE
- B) It's hard to imagine that Snooker, a sport with such humble beginnings, could become what it is today.
- C) The possibility of fame is real indeed.
- D) Snooker may be difficult, but that shouldn't stop you from giving it a shot.

■

MAIN IDEAS SUMMARY

To summarize, when you tackle main idea questions:
- For each paragraph, look for keywords that capture main ideas.
- Answer yes/no questions before looking (in detail) at the answer choices.
- When adding or deleting information, watch out for answer choices that are off topic or redundant.
- Watch out for, and eliminate, false answer choices.
- Make sure a topic sentence reflects the main idea of its paragraph.
- Make sure a transition sentence leads clearly from the main idea of one paragraph or sentence to that of the next one.
- Make sure the answers to Passage questions aren't too broad or too narrow, and remember to check the essay's title.

2. TRANSITIONS

CONJUNCTIONS AS TRANSITIONS

As we've already learned, conjunctions are words that connect phrases or sentences together. They transition from one thought or idea to another. These conjunctions can be broken into three main types:

CONTRAST TRANSITIONS

although	even so	instead of	rather than
but	however	nevertheless	still
conversely	in contrast	on the contrary	while
despite	in spite of	on the other hand	yet
even though			

SUPPORT TRANSITIONS

additionally	for example	in addition	moreover
also	for instance	in fact	similarly
and	furthermore	likewise	(colon) :
besides			

CAUSE & EFFECT TRANSITIONS

accordingly	for	since	therefore
because	hence	so	thus
consequently	in order to	so... that	when... then

To identify transition questions, look for questions with answer choices that contain various transitions, as shown above. Note that transition questions often look like innocent grammar questions, but they *do* require you to go beyond basic grammar and understand main ideas in the passages.

TRANSITIONS AND MAIN IDEAS

To choose a correct transition, you need to recognize the main idea of where you *were* and the main idea of where you're *going.* Whether you're dealing with phrases, sentences, or whole paragraphs, understanding main ideas is the key.

IGNORE THE UNDERLINED TRANSITION WORD

! **Don't let the underlined word influence your choice. Remember, it will be wrong 75% of the time. Ignore it, and just focus on the main ideas of the passage.** Here's an example:

1 <u>Since</u> it may take a long time to understand all of the intricacies of Snooker, you can enjoy watching the sport today if you just understand the basic rules.

1. A) NO CHANGE
    B) Because
    C) When
    D) While

Forget about the underlined word, and just focus on the two parts of the sentence. What kind of transition are you looking for?

Type of transition:

_____

Now, take a look at the answer choices. What's the best answer?

Answer Questions 1 now.

ELIMINATE SYNONYMS

Often, there will be at least two transitions in the answer choices that are synonyms. These are generally incorrect (we obviously can't have more than one correct answer). In the example above, *since*, *because*, and sometimes *when* (as in *when . . . then*) are all cause & effect transitions. Not surprisingly, none of them is correct.

ILLOGICAL TRANSITIONS

Transitions may be used in illogical ways. For example:

You can easily follow the Snooker action *so that* you understand the basic rules.

Do you see the error? *Following the Snooker action* does not allow you to *understand the basic rules*. Rather, *understanding the basic rules* allows you to *follow the Snooker action*. The direction of causation is wrong. Replace *so that* with a logical word, such as *because*, *since*, *now that*, or *if*:

You can easily follow the Snooker action *because* you understand the basic rules.

Here's another example:

I practiced Snooker for hours every day, *and* I still struggled during the match.

The conjunction *and* is not the best choice here. Can you think of a more logical transition word? The following sentence reflects the desired contrast:

I practiced Snooker for hours every day, *but* I still struggled during the match.

Let's try an SAT example:
Michael drove as fast as he could, **2** but he arrived in plenty of time to see the start of the match.

2. A) NO CHANGE
   B) so
   C) for
   D) yet

Do you see the logical transition?

Answer Questions 2 now.

SOMETIMES, NO TRANSITION IS BEST

Don't assume that you *must* use a transition. If the flow sounds awkward with a transition, or if none of the transitions seems to work, look for the answer choice that does *not* have a transition. For example:

I wanted to learn how to play Snooker. **3** It seemed the best place to start was learning how to break.

3. A) NO CHANGE
   B) Nevertheless, it seemed
   C) On the other hand, it seemed
   D) In any case, it seemed

Consider the main idea of each sentence and answer Question 3 now.

CAUSE & EFFECT TRANSITIONS TRUMP SUPPORT ONES

If you've narrowed down the answer choices to a cause & effect transition and a support transition—and if both seem to work—go with the cause & effect transition. Here's an example:

Playing Snooker well involves both hand-eye coordination and knowledge of the game. **4** <u>Similarly,</u> improvement is a matter of physical and mental practice.

4. A) NO CHANGE
   B) Hence,
   C) However,
   D) Regardless,

SPECIAL SUPPORT TRANSITIONS

Sometimes a transition will be the right type (contrast, support, or cause & effect), but it will not work in the specific context of the essay. There are several support transitions, in particular, that have special uses. Here are a few examples:

First, second...

Stay consistent with numerical transitions. If you don't see a *first*, don't use a *second*. Also, you should usually stay consistent with how the number is expressed: *first*, *second*, *third*..., *number one*, *number two*, *number three*..., and so on.

For example / for instance

For example and *for instance* are support transitions, but make sure there is indeed an example following the transition.

In summary

Make sure what follows "in summary" is an actual summary. There should not be any new information presented.

In addition

Make sure additional information is included and not just an elaboration of the previous topic.

Finally

Make sure *finally* precedes the last of several items. It should, not surprisingly, generally show up near the end of an essay when used correctly.

3. ORGANIZATION

Some questions ask you to change the organization of an essay. Usually this involves changing the placement of a sentence or adding a sentence somewhere in a given paragraph. You might also be asked to reposition an entire paragraph, but these questions are less common.

 Before you even get to an Organization question, you'll see that sentences in the paragraph are labeled [1], [2], [3], etc.

When you get to the actual question, you'll see that the answer choices typically give you placement options for a sentence within a paragraph. You may be moving an existing sentence (one already part of the paragraph) or a sentence given in the question.

FIRST STEPS

Organization questions tend to show up at the ends of paragraphs that have numbered sentences, but there are some important steps you should take before you get to them.

CIRCLE THE SENTENCE NUMBER THAT MIGHT BE MOVED

When you get to a paragraph with numbered sentences, as described above, you can be almost positive that an organization question is on the way. Before starting the paragraph, skip to the organization question (typically the last question for that paragraph) and take note of the sentence number in question (if there is one). Then circle the number of the sentence in the passage. This way, you'll know which sentence has a questionable placement (and you'll know that the other sentences are correct).

SKIP THE SENTENCE IN QUESTION

The sentence whose number you circled is probably misplaced (75% of the time), so skip it. When it's time to answer the organization question, you should use the other sentences to get a feel for the intended flow of ideas within the paragraph.

Do *not* read the sentence in question while reading the paragraph.

READ FOR AWKWARDNESS

As you read the paragraph, you may notice a sentence that feels abrupt, either because the flow of ideas is awkward or something is mentioned that should have been more formally or explicitly introduced. If this sentence is *not* the one you circled, then you'll probably move the circled sentence *before* the awkward sentence. Mark this point in the passage.

LOOK FOR CLUES

When you finally get to the organization question, you may already have an idea of where to move the sentence, as described above. If not, you'll look for *clues*. These clues will be words that suggest something must come before. They may either be in the sentence that you're moving, or in the passage: check sentences before and after potential points of placement.

The clearest clues are usually *pronouns*, words such as *he*, *they*, *his*, *their*, *its, these*, and so on. In the sentence that comes *before* the sentence in question, you'll probably notice the noun or nouns that the pronoun refers to:

[1] The first World Championship was organized by Englishman **Joe Davis**. [2] **His** efforts moved the game from a pastime to a professional sport.

[1] **New companies are becoming Snooker sponsors** all the time, and the game is showing **huge growth** in the Far East and China. [2] **These** are all signs that the future of Snooker is bright.

In both examples above, the clue words "His" and "These" reveal the order of the sentences.

Here's another example. Let's say the first sentence of a paragraph is:

This ranking system for Snooker may be confusing, but most agree that it's fair.

The clue words are "This ranking system." The preceding sentence (perhaps the last sentence of the preceding paragraph) probably has something to do with this ranking system.

Always look for clue words when you're dealing with organization questions.

The following Organization question is based on the paragraph below. Before reading the paragraph, circle the sentence in question:

[1] The Snooker World Championship, the most important event in Snooker, takes place annually in Sheffield, England. [2] It is televised throughout the United Kingdom, Europe, and the Far East. [3] He or she walks away with status, fame, and riches. [4] The prize money is impressive—over $500,000 goes to the winner.

1

1. To make this paragraph most logical, Sentence 3 should be placed

A) where it is now.
B) before Sentence 1.
C) after Sentence 1.
D) after Sentence 4.

Question 1 focuses on Sentence 3. Look for clue words in Sentence 3.

Clue word(s) for Sentence 3 =

_____

Considering these clue words ("He or she"), what's the best place for Sentence 3?

Answer Question 1 now.

MAIN IDEAS AND TRANSITIONS

Besides clue words, you might have to consider main ideas and transitions. Make sure ideas flow sensibly from one to the next, and look for any transition words in the sentence you're moving. Look at the following example, which relates to the paragraph on the Snooker World Championship above.

Question 2 asks about the previous passage as a whole.

2. The writer wants to add the following sentence to the paragraph.

> The event is held at the Crucible Theater, which seats fewer than 1,000 people, but that doesn't mean there aren't a lot of viewers.

The best placement for the sentence is immediately

A) before Sentence 1.
B) after Sentence 1.
C) after Sentence 2.
D) after Sentence 3.

First, look for clue words in the new sentence. You might not see anything obvious (no pronouns, for example). At least, from the words "The event," you know that the Championship has already been introduced (eliminate A). This is a useful rule:

/ The definite article "the" often means that the noun that follows was already introduced in the essay.

Think about the main idea of the sentence. It's talking about *where* the event is held, and it's also talking about the fact that there are a lot of *viewers*. Now look back to the essay and try answering the question.

Answer Question 2 now.

CHECK YOUR ANSWERS

With Organization questions, check your answers. Quickly read the part of the essay that you reorganized, making sure that the sentence order sounds sensible and fluid. If you hear obvious awkwardness with your answer, then you should take a look at the other choices.

WHOLE PARAGRAPHS

Organization questions that relate to whole paragraphs come in two varieties:

1. You'll be asked to move an entire paragraph.
2. You'll be asked to choose the best paragraph to move a given sentence. The sentence will probably be placed at the *beginning* of the paragraph.

As you're reading a passage, sometimes you'll have a feeling that a paragraph is misplaced, even before you get to the organization question. Here's a clue: If the paragraphs are labeled with numbers (for example: "—1—"), there's a good chance you might see a paragraph organization question. (If not, then you probably won't.)

If you're asked to move an entire paragraph or choose a paragraph to move a sentence to, clue words (like pronouns) may not be helpful. You will have to consider the main ideas of the paragraphs, something you've hopefully been thinking about anyway. Focus on your keywords.

To identify Organization questions for paragraphs, the answer choices will give placement options within the passage for a given paragraph or for a sentence given in the question.

You'll also notice that *paragraphs* in the passage are labeled —1—, —2—, etc.

■

30- and 40-hour programs: Now is a good time to go back to Test 9 and correct all Grammar and Sentence Structure questions. See page 222 for details. You'll correct Main Ideas and Organization questions later.

4. ANSWER THE QUESTION

This lesson may sound obvious, but make sure you carefully read Main Ideas and Organization questions. Sometimes, if you read a question too quickly, more than one answer choice seems to work. The SAT sometimes asks very *specific* questions—we call them Answer-the-Question questions. You must read them carefully and answer *exactly* what the question is asking.

 These questions often seem to have multiple correct answers. When more than one answer choice appears to work, go back and carefully reread the question. These questions sometimes begin "Given that all the following statements are true . . ."

Let's go back to Paragraph 3 from the sample essay at the beginning of the chapter to look at an example.

—3—

Of the many great Snooker players, Stephen Hendry stands out. Born on January 13, 1969 in Scotland, Hendry became the youngest player to become a Snooker World Champion—at the age of 21. He went on to win six more World Championships, and he was Snooker's number one player for eight consecutive years, between 1990 and 1998. Hendry's skill as a player lead to amazing riches and fame for him, and helped popularize the sport of Snooker around the world. It's hard to imagine that Snooker, a sport with such humble beginnings, **1** <u>could become what it is today.</u>

1. Which choice would conclude the essay by giving credit to Snooker players for the popularity of Snooker?

   A) NO CHANGE
   B) could become the international phenomenon it is today.
   C) could become, thanks to competitors like Hendry, what it is today.
   D) could provide such wealth to its champions.

First of all, notice that every answer choice is true. According to the essay, Snooker *is* an "international phenomenon" (B) and *does* "provide such wealth" to its players (D). But look carefully at the question. It asks you to find an answer that credits *Snooker players* for Snooker's popularity. Which one does that?

Answer Question 1 now.

Here's something interesting about these types of questions:

> ⟋ **Answer-the-Question questions can sometimes be answered without even looking back to the essay!**

Just make sure you read the question carefully. If you read the question too quickly, choosing the correct answer can be difficult, if not impossible. But if you "answer the question," the problem becomes straightforward. Here's one more Answer-the-Question question. Try answering it without looking at the passage.

(EX)

2. Given that all of the choices are true, which one provides the most specific information about a break in Snooker?

A) Unlike pool breaks, Snooker breaks are entirely defensive.

B) The break in Snooker—also called "breaking off"—can set the tone for an entire game.

C) When breaking, most players try to hit the "end red" of the triangle just hard enough for the cue ball to hit three cushions and come to rest near what's called the "baulk cushion."

D) When hitting the cue ball, a player can achieve different spins— including top spin, back spin, and side spin—depending on what part of the ball is struck.

5. STYLE

Style questions ask you to consider *consistency* of style. For example, if an essay is written as a formal essay, as most are, then make sure the answers to questions reflect this formality. But the answer shouldn't be *too* formal.

 Look for questions with answer choices that contain overly formal or informal language. If you see a word or phrase that would sound right at home on the "schoolyard" (for example, *awesome*), it's probably too *informal*. If you see a word or phrase that would absolutely never show up in a student's essay (for example, *whilst*), it's probably too *formal*.

Here's an example:

Besides the World Championship, there are a number of other Snooker tournaments held throughout the world. The UK Championship is right behind the World Championship in importance, and The Masters is also **1** deemed to be a prestigious tournament.

1. A) NO CHANGE
   B) definitely a lot of fun
   C) high on the list of renowned tournaments.
   D) hailed as nonpareil.

The paragraph above is formally written (as is the entire essay on Snooker). Do any of the answer choices sound informal? Do any sound *too* formal?

Answer the question now. Find the answer that isn't too informal or too formal.

6. *MAIN IDEAS AND ORGANIZATION: SUMMARY*

The following summarizes the techniques that will help you tackle Main Ideas and Organization questions:

1. Main Ideas

    - Look for keywords in the essay that capture main ideas.

    - Answer Yes or No questions before looking (in detail) at the answer choices.

    - When adding or deleting information, watch out for answer choices that are off topic or redundant.

    - Watch out for, and eliminate, false answer choices.

    - Make sure a topic sentence reflects the main idea of its paragraph.

    - Make sure a transition sentence leads clearly from the main idea of one paragraph or sentence to that of the next one.

    - Make sure the answers to Passage questions aren't too broad or too narrow, and remember to check the essay's title.

2. Transitions

    - Learn the three types of transitions.

    - Consider main ideas.

    - Ignore the underlined transition word (it's probably wrong).

    - Watch out for illogical conjunctions.

    - Sometimes, no transition is best.

    - Make sure the transition word works in context (special support transitions).

3. Organization

    - Look for clue words.

    - Consider main ideas and transitions.

4. Answer the question.

5. Keep style consistent.

7. MAIN IDEAS & ORGANIZATION: PRACTICE & CORRECTIONS

PRACTICE PROBLEMS

After covering the lessons in this chapter, tackle the lesson and homework passages on the following pages. Note that, unlike the passages on the SAT, these passages only test material taught in the Main Ideas and Organization chapter.

- ☐ Lesson Passage: "The Cat Who Lived and Died"
- ☐ Homework Passage: "A Prickly Subject"

For extra practice (beyond the passages in this tutorial), complete passages from Test 1 of the *The Official SAT Study Guide*. For these passages, complete all questions (including Grammar and Sentence Structure ones). Make sure you time yourself on each passage:

- **11-questions**: 8 minutes, 30 seconds (8:30)

Here are the passages for Test 1:

- ☐ Passage I
- ☐ Passage II
- ☐ Passage III
- ☐ Passage IV

See the Tutoring Schedules section in the Introduction for more on when to tackle these passages for different programs.

TEST CORRECTIONS

After completing and grading each practice test, you should correct Main Ideas and Organization questions that you missed or guessed on. Below are the three steps to correcting practice tests:

1. Turn to the Techniques section at the end of this tutorial and circle the Main Ideas and Organization questions that you missed or guessed on for each test.
2. Correct the problems in *The Official SAT Study Guide*. As you correct the problems, go back to the tutorial and review the techniques. The idea is to (1) identify techniques that have given you trouble, (2) go back to the tutorial so you can review and strengthen these techniques, and (3) apply these techniques to the specific problems on which you struggled.

3. If you have trouble identifying the best technique to use on a problem, refer to the Techniques chapter. This is an important part of correcting the tests.

LESSON PRACTICE PASSAGE

The following lesson passage only tests material taught in the Main Ideas and Organization chapter. Do not time yourself on this passage.

Questions 1–11 are based on the following passage.

The Cat Who Lived and Died

[1] In 1935, three famous physicists (one of them Einstein), published an article that **1** highlighted the nature of something called quantum superposition. [2] The idea was that a quantum system exists as a combination of multiple states, each state corresponding to a different possible outcome. [3] Einstein even called it "spooky." [4] The system would stay in this state until someone or something outside of the system observed it, at which point the system would "collapse" into one of the possible outcomes. [5] Most would agree that it's a strange idea for something to be in more than one state at once. **2**

Continued →

1. Which choice provides the most appropriate introduction to the passage?

   A) NO CHANGE
   B) explained the differences between quantum mechanics and general relativity.
   C) discussed the importance of physicists in helping people understand the world.
   D) brought fame and notoriety to its writers.

2. To make this paragraph most logical, sentence 3 should be placed

   A) where it is now.
   B) after sentence 1.
   C) after sentence 4.
   D) after sentence 5.

Which leads us to Schrödinger's cat. Erwin Schrödinger was a Viennese physicist who won the Nobel Prize in Physics in 1933. **3** Schrödinger's cat was not actually a real one. **4** It was part of his famous thought experiment. The experiment involved putting the following items inside a sealed box: a glass container of poison; a hammer; radioactive material; a Geiger counter, a device used to detect radiation; and, of course, his imaginary cat. To put it simply, the amount of radioactive material was small enough so that there was only a 50/50 chance that the Geiger counter would detect it. If the radiation was detected, the hammer would drop on the glass container, releasing the poison, and killing the cat. **5** Likewise, the cat would live.

Continued →

3. At this point, the writer is considering adding the following sentence.

> Despite being raised in a religious household—his father was Catholic and his mother was Lutheran—Schrodinger was an atheist.

Should the writer make this addition?

A) Yes, because it supports the fact that Schrödinger was a great physicist.
B) Yes, because it serves as a transition from a description of Schrödinger to a discussion of his experiment.
C) No, because it weakens the focus of the paragraph by discussing a subject unrelated to physics.
D) No, because it interrupts the flow of the sentences by supplying information about Schrödinger rather than his experiment.

4. Which choice best supports the statement made in the previous sentence?

A) NO CHANGE
B) Schrödinger had a real cat, named Milton, that was not part of his experiment.
C) Schrödinger would need more than just a cat for his experiment.
D) Schrödinger's experiment could have used any living creature.

5. A) NO CHANGE
   B) On the other hand,
   C) Otherwise,
   D) However,

Schrödinger stressed that until someone opened the box, it would be impossible to predict the experiment's outcome. **6** In other words, the system would be in an un-collapsed state: the cat would exist in a superposition of being both alive and dead. Of course, to most people, the idea is ridiculous, and this was exactly Schrödinger's point. While quantum superposition could work on a small scale, for example with tiny particles such as electrons, on a larger scare the theory was inherently flawed. **7** A cat cannot be both alive and dead at the same time.

Continued →

6. A) NO CHANGE
   B) Nevertheless,
   C) Finally,
   D) In addition,

7. The writer is considering deleting the previous sentence. Should the writer make this change?

   A) Yes, because it introduces information that is irrelevant at this point in the passage.
   B) Yes, because it contradicts the sentence that follows.
   C) No, because it provides an example of why superposition is flawed on a larger scale.
   D) No, because it develops Schrödinger's point, as mentioned in the previous sentence.

[1] An interesting solution to this apparent paradox is the many-worlds interpretation. [2] Schrödinger wasn't around to comment on this new theory—unless, of course, he did so from some other reality. [3] First formulated in 1957, the theory **8** propounds that even after the box is opened, both a living cat and a dead cat exist, but in two different realities. [4] That is, reality is split into one world where the observer is looking into a box with a live cat, and another world where the observer is looking into a box with a dead cat. [5] **9** For example, it goes without saying that these different outcomes cannot interact with each other. [6] In any case, Schrödinger's thought experiment is still discussed in physics classes around the world. [7] **10** In that sense at least, one could say that the cat definitely lived. **11**

8. A) NO CHANGE
   B) shouts out
   C) states
   D) disseminates

9. A) NO CHANGE
   B) Finally,
   C) However,
   D) DELETE the underlined portion and capitalize the first word of the sentence.

10. The writer wants a conclusion that emphasizes the continued popularity of Schrödinger's experiment. Which choice best accomplishes this goal?

   A) NO CHANGE
   B) Many people erroneously assume that Schrödinger agreed with the idea of large-scale superposition.
   C) The ideas of quantum mechanics continue to evolve today.
   D) Whether anyone actually understands his experiment is another question.

11. To make this paragraph most logical, sentence 2 should be placed

   A) before sentence 1.
   B) after sentence 3.
   C) after sentence 4.
   D) after sentence 5.

The following HW passage only tests material taught in the Main Ideas and Organization chapter. Do not time yourself on this passage.

The passage begins on the next page.

Questions 1–11 are based on the following passage.

A Prickly Subject

Bad news travels quickly. In 1998 British medical researcher Dr. Andrew Wakefield **1** studied tissue rejection problems using animal models. Wakefield's study focused on a possible—and unexpected—connection between the vaccination of children and the sharp rise in autism diagnoses over the past 20 years. **2** Research suggests that some combination of genetics and environmental factors leads to the disorder, but the recent rise in cases cannot be attributed to genetics alone. Something else must be going on, **3** and Wakefield wanted to get to the bottom of it.

1. Which choice most effectively sets up the information that follows?
   A) NO CHANGE
   B) performed a study that would later be discredited.
   C) conducted a study that shocked the world.
   D) became widely known as an expert of autism.

2. At this point, the writer is considering adding the following sentence.

   > Autism is a disorder that impairs brain development.

   Should the writer make this addition here?
   A) Yes, because it briefly introduces a disorder that is discussed throughout passage.
   B) Yes, because it confirms the need to find an effective vaccine for a serious disorder.
   C) No, because the autism was not a part of Wakefield's study.
   D) No, because it unnecessarily repeats information from earlier in the passage.

3. The writer wants to link the first paragraph with the information that follows. Which choice best accomplishes this goal?
   A) NO CHANGE
   B) and the world would hear about soon enough.
   C) and Wakefield's study held the key.
   D) and Wakefield thought he found the explanation: vaccinations.

258 • MAIN IDEAS AND ORGANIZATION

[1] Edward Jenner is considered the first to introduce vaccinology in the West, when, in 1796, he developed the first smallpox vaccine. [2] Louis Pasteur's work in the 1800s ushered in vaccines for cholera and anthrax. [3] Perhaps the best known vaccine was Jonas Salk's polio vaccine, which, after the vaccine's introduction in the 1950s, helped nearly eradicate the disease. [4] Vaccinations have been around since seventeenth-century Buddhist monks drank snake venom to become immune to snake bites. [5] Vaccines have also helped nearly eliminate measles, mumps, and rubella. **4** [6] **5** Moreover, over the past several years, thanks largely to Wakefield's study, vaccination rates have plummeted, and, unsurprisingly, infection rates of preventable diseases have skyrocketed. **6**

Continued →

4. At this point, the writer is considering adding the following sentence.

   > Measles is the most serious of the three diseases, sometimes leading to pneumonia, inflammation of the brain, and even death.

   Should the writer make this addition here?

   A) Yes, because it provides a link between the effectiveness of vaccines and the decline in their acceptance.
   B) Yes, because it clarifies the differences in the types of diseases that vaccines are used against.
   C) No, because it fails to explain how vaccines helped eliminate measles, mumps, and rubella.
   D) No, because it provides information that blurs the focus of the paragraph.

5. A) NO CHANGE
   B) However,
   C) Also,
   D) Likewise,

6. To make this paragraph most logical, sentence 4 should be placed

   A) where it is now.
   B) before sentence 1.
   C) after sentence 1.
   D) after sentence 2.

In his study, Wakefield reported on the onset of autism-like symptoms in several children soon after they received the popular MMR, or Measles, Mumps, and Rubella, vaccine. The paper made no claim of causal connection, but Wakefield, in a press conference before his paper was published, expressed concern about the MMR vaccine. One doesn't need a degree in sociology to know that even the slightest hint that something might harm the health of children will instill fear in the hearts of parents. **7** Some parents, however, were skeptical of Wakefield's findings.

But was the vaccination–autism link real? After the paper was published, researchers scrambled to confirm its claims. After numerous studies of more than 25 million children, researchers concluded that there was no causal relationship between vaccines and autism. Wakefield's findings simply could not be reproduced. The publisher of the original paper fully retracted Wakefield's article in 2010, noting that parts had been falsified. **8** Nevertheless, Wakefield was taken off the UK medical register and was barred from practicing medicine.

Continued →

7. Which choice best provides a likely consequence of the point made in the previous sentence?
   A) NO CHANGE
   B) Wakefield's ideas spread like wildfire around the world, leaving millions of children unvaccinated.
   C) Immunologists immediately went to work on a new MMR vaccine that would not harm children.
   D) Wakefield's paper brought him considerable acclaim.

8. A) NO CHANGE
   B) Likewise,
   C) Conversely,
   D) Consequently,

9 People love a good controversy. After the article was published, Vaccination rates in Britain dropped from 92 percent to 73 percent. In the United States, an estimated 125,000 children did not receive the MMR vaccine. Childhood diseases that had been nearly eradicated had reemerged. One 2011 journal article described the vaccine–autism connection as the most damaging medical hoax of the past 100 years. And yet, many **10** apprehensive parents still choose not to vaccinate their children. The safety of vaccinations has been confirmed by scientists, **11** but parents recognize that scientists are not infallible.

9. Which sentence best introduces the main topic of this paragraph and connects this paragraph with the previous paragraph?
   A) NO CHANGE
   B) Wakefield's study isn't the only thing people should be worried about.
   C) The fear that Wakefield helped cause will dissipate over time as new information is released.
   D) Wakefield's claims, however, have suffered a slow death.

10. The writer wants to convey parents' concerns and avoid the appearance of disparagement. Which choice best accomplishes this goal?
    A) NO CHANGE
    B) gullible
    C) naïve
    D) ignorant

11. Which choice most effectively concludes the sentence and paragraph?
    A) NO CHANGE
    B) and soon enough parents will get the message.
    C) but only time will tell if the benefits of vaccinations outweigh their potential side effects.
    D) but good news, it seems, travels much slower than bad.

■

30- and 40-hour programs: Now is a good time to go back to Tests 2 and 3 and correct all Main Ideas and Organization questions. See page 252 for details.

 30- and 40-hour programs: After completing all relevant assignments and reviewing the tutorial, take Practice Test 8 in *The Official SAT Study Guide*.

PART 3

MATH

I
MATH INTRODUCTION AND BASIC CONCEPTS

This chapter will introduce the SAT Math Test, including test layout and timing strategy. It will also cover the use of your calculator and other basic mathematical concepts and terminologies.

1. INTRODUCTION

The Math section is divided into eight chapters:

    I.   Introduction and Basic Concepts

    II.   Arithmetic

    III.   Functions

    IV.   Algebra

    V.   Advanced Algebra

    VI.   Graphs of Functions

    VII.   Geometry

    VIII.   Math Odds & Ends

The primary purpose of this part of the tutorial is to teach you *how* to use mathematical techniques. However, while knowing *how* to apply these techniques is obviously important, knowing *when* to use the techniques is perhaps just as important. You may be an expert at a particular technique, but if you come across a problem on the SAT and do not *use* this technique, then your mastery of the technique may not help you. For this reason, the tutorial also focuses on *identifying* the correct technique to use on a particular problem. Throughout the tutorial, look for the magnifying glass for information about identifying techniques:

TEST LAYOUT

The Math Test covers two sections (Sections 3 and 4 on the SAT): Section 3 is a *no-calculator* section, and Section 4 is a *calculator* section. Each section includes two subsections: a *multiple-choice* part followed by a *student-produced-response* (grid-in) part:

- Section 3: No-Calculator section (20 questions): <u>25 minutes</u>
  - 15 multiple-choice questions and 5 grid-in questions
- Section 4: Calculator section (38 questions): <u>55 minutes</u>
  - 30 multiple-choice questions and 8 grid-in questions

ORDER OF DIFFICULTY AND TIMING STRATEGY

Generally, for each multiple-choice section and each grid-in section, the SAT Math section gets harder as you go. However, many students will likely find several relatively easy questions near the end of the test and several relatively difficult questions near the beginning. Use the following strategy:

STEP 1

As you work your way through each math section, plan to leave some questions blank—even if some of these questions occur early in the test. (Don't forget to leave the answer choice bubbles blank as well!) Don't get bogged down on problems that you find especially difficult. Just skip them and keep moving. Stay aggressive and try to get to the last question of the section, even if you have to skip several questions to get there. Because the questions *generally* get harder as you go, the further into the test you get, the more questions you'll likely have to skip.

STEP 2

After you get to the end of a section, with whatever time you have left, go back to the questions you left blank, starting from the beginning. If, for a particular question, you have no idea how to tackle it, take a guess and move on to the next one. (Remember, you don't lose points on the SAT, so you should answer every question, even if you have to guess.)

STEP 3

Make sure you leave yourself about 30 seconds at the end of each section to guess on any remaining questions.

As you learn the techniques in this tutorial and get better at identifying problems that use these techniques, you'll get better at choosing which problems to tackle your first time through. Taking real practice tests will definitely help you develop a timing strategy that works for *you*. If you have trouble finishing the test in time, review Timing in the Introduction of this tutorial for a detailed timing strategy.

QUESTIONS THAT LOOK HARD ARE OFTEN <u>NOT</u> HARD

Don't assume that just because a question looks hard you should skip it. Some of the hardest-looking questions are often the easiest. There are two types of questions that typically scare away students:

1. Questions with lots of words
2. Questions with long formulas

Stay aggressive on these problems. They may not be too difficult, and getting them correct will certainly give you an edge over other students who will likely skip them or guess. It's worth noting, however, that questions with lots of words often take longer to complete than shorter questions, so as you get into the later (and potentially harder) parts of the sections, these long, wordy questions may be good ones to skip and come back to if you have time.

STUDENT-PRODUCED-RESPONSE QUESTIONS

These questions, also called "grid-in" questions, make up about 20% of the test. Simply put, they don't have answer choices, so you must come up with (and *grid in*) your own answers. Make sure you are comfortable with the grid-in instructions (see the beginning of any grid-in section in *The Official SAT Study Guide*). Remember, you *must* bubble in your answers. Your written answers will not be read.

The problems for each grid-in section generally start relatively easy and get harder. Be aggressive on the first several questions, but watch out for traps as you tackle the higher-numbered questions.

2. CALCULATORS

You should indeed plan to use a calculator on the calculator portion of the SAT. Since functions and their graphs are part of the test, a graphing calculator is highly recommended. Most graphing calculators are fine; however, you might check the list of acceptable calculators at the College Board website (https://sat.collegeboard.org/register/calculator-policy).

Many students make careless mistakes because they try to solve difficult computations in their heads. Other students, on the other hand, tend to use calculators for all computations, even the easy ones, costing them valuable seconds on the test. **Keep in mind that the SAT does not require the use of a calculator.** If you find that you're using one on every problem, you might be slowing yourself down. Find a good balance. Don't use your calculator for 2 × 1, but if you have a tendency to make careless mistakes, *do* use it for 20 × 100.

Make sure you are comfortable with your calculator. Bring it to all of your tutoring lessons and use it on your homework assignments and practice tests.

 Your calculator can be used to solve problems involving *fractions*, *radicals*, *scientific notation*, and the π symbol.

If you are not comfortable with any of the above numerical forms, just use your calculator to simplify the problem into one of *decimal numbers*. Of course, you will likely have to convert the answer choices to decimals so you can compare them to the answer you found with your calculator.

FRACTIONS AND YOUR CALCULATOR

It will be very helpful to learn how to use the **fraction key** that is found on most calculators. This will allow you to maintain perfect accuracy and check answer choices more quickly (when they are in fraction form). Check your calculator's manual to see how to enter fractions or convert decimals into fractions, or ask a tutor for assistance.

MIXED FRACTIONS

Mixed fractions include a whole number and a fraction, for example:

$$2\frac{3}{4}$$

To enter a mixed fraction into your calculator, think about how you *say* the number:

$$2\frac{3}{4} \equiv \text{"two \textbf{and} three-fourths"}$$

You probably know that the word "and" is used to describe addition ("1 *and* 1 is 2"). So to enter a mixed number into your calculator, use addition:

$$2\frac{3}{4} \rightarrow 2 + \frac{3}{4}$$

ORDER OF OPERATION

Most calculators follow the standard *order of operation* rules. You should be familiar with these rules for tackling more difficult algebra problems. Remember *PEMDAS*: (1) parentheses, (2) exponents, (3) multiplication/division (in order from left to right), and (4) addition/subtraction (in order from left to right).

CALCULATOR LESSON PROBLEMS

Try the following problems using your calculator. The point of these problems is to become comfortable with your calculator.

1. $-2^2 =$

2. $(-2)^2 =$

3. $\dfrac{317 + 257}{2} =$

4. $254 - 550 \div 25 =$

5. $2 \times (16 - 3)^2 =$

6. $2\frac{3}{4} + 3\frac{3}{8} =$

7. $\frac{3}{4} \times \frac{2}{3} =$

8. $\frac{3}{4} \div \frac{2}{3} =$
    - A) $\frac{1}{2}$
    - B) $\frac{7}{8}$
    - C) 1
    - D) $1\frac{1}{8}$

9. $\dfrac{\frac{1}{2} + \frac{2}{3}}{\frac{3}{4} + \frac{4}{5}} =$
    - A) $\frac{70}{93}$
    - B) $1\frac{1}{2}$
    - C) $2\frac{17}{90}$
    - D) $2\frac{16}{45}$

10. $125,000 \times 200,000 =$
    - A) 250,000
    - B) 2.5×10^8
    - C) 2.5×10^{10}
    - D) 2.5×10^{12}

11. $\sqrt{108} + \sqrt{48} =$
    - A) $6\sqrt{3}$
    - B) $2\sqrt{39}$
    - C) $\sqrt{156}$
    - D) $10\sqrt{3}$

3. NO-CALCULATOR SECTION

Of course, you will not be allowed to use your calculator on the no-calculator section (Section 3). Thus, you should be comfortable doing some basic math by hand. It's beyond the scope of this tutorial to completely review these topics—we'll just give a quick overview of what you should know. If you have trouble with any of the following examples, consider reviewing some of these basic operations in a good Algebra 1 book. If you're already comfortable with the following material, feel free to skim through it quickly and move on to the next section.

FRACTIONS

ADDING OR SUBTRACTING FRACTIONS

You must find a *common denominator* (the *denominator* is the bottom number in a fraction) before adding or subtracting fractions. A *common denominator* is simply a *common multiple* of all the denominators. We'll discuss finding common multiples in more detail in the next section.

$$\frac{1}{3}+\frac{3}{4}=\frac{1\cdot4}{3\cdot4}+\frac{3\cdot3}{4\cdot3}=\frac{4}{12}+\frac{9}{12}=\frac{13}{12}$$

MULTIPLYING FRACTIONS

When you multiply fractions, simply multiply the numerators and multiply the denominators.

$$\frac{1}{3}\times\frac{3}{4}=\frac{1\times3}{3\times4}=\frac{3}{12}=\frac{1}{4}$$

DIVIDING FRACTIONS

Dividing one fraction by another is the same as multiplying the top fraction by the *reciprocal* of the bottom fraction. The reciprocal of a fraction is simply that fraction with its numerator and denominator swapped.

$$\frac{\frac{1}{3}}{\frac{3}{4}}=\frac{1}{3}\times\frac{4}{3}=\frac{4}{9}$$

SIMPLIFYING FRACTIONS

You should be comfortable *reducing* fractions:

$$\frac{25}{75} = \frac{25 \cdot 1}{25 \cdot 3} = \frac{1}{3}$$

You should also be able to turn an improper fraction into a mixed fraction, and vice versa:

$$\frac{70}{20} = 3\frac{10}{20} = 3\frac{1}{2} \quad \leftarrow \text{ 20 divides evenly into 70 } 3 \text{ times, with a remainder of 10.}$$

$$3\frac{1}{2} = \frac{3 \times 2 + 1}{2} = \frac{7}{2} \quad \leftarrow \text{ Note that the denominator does not change.}$$

CONVERTING DECIMALS TO FRACTIONS

Sometimes it's easier to work with fractions than decimals. You need to understand the names of the places to the left of a decimal point: they are, starting next to the decimal point, tenth, hundredth, thousandth, and so on. So, for example, the decimal 0.7 is equivalent to "7 tenths":

$$0.7 = \frac{7}{10}$$

The decimal 0.361 is equivalent to "361 thousandths":

$$0.361 = \frac{361}{1000}$$

LONG MULTIPLICATION

You should be prepared to do some long multiplication on the no-calculator section. Again, we're not going to get into the details, but hopefully the example below rings a bell.

```
  2
  25
 ×14
 100    ← 4 × 5 = 20 (write 0 and "carry" the 2); 4 × 2 + 2 = 10 (write 10 next to 0)
  25    ← move one one space to the left: 1 × 5 = 5; 1 × 2 = 2
 350    ← add the columns
```

4. BASIC CONCEPTS

TERMINOLOGY

The following are some commonly misunderstood terms that show up on the SAT:

- **Integer**: positive or negative whole number or zero: …–3, –2, –1, 0, 1, 2, 3…

- **Zero**: remember, zero is an integer. Zero is also an *even* number, but it is not a *positive* or a *negative* number—think of it as *neutral*.

- **Real Number**: Any number that is not *imaginary*. If you don't know what imaginary numbers are (yet), don't worry about it; we'll cover imaginary numbers in Chapter VIII. At this point, assume *all* numbers are real numbers.

- **Rational Number**: Any number that can be written as an integer or a *fraction* of integers. Examples: -4, $21/93$, $\frac{\sqrt{16}}{\sqrt{25}}$ (because it equals $4/5$)

- **Irrational Number**: Any number that can *not* be written as an integer or a fraction of integers. Examples: π, $\sqrt{2}$, $\sqrt{22}$ (any radical that cannot be simplified to a whole number)

- **Factor** (or **divisor**): any of the numbers multiplied together to form a *product*. For example: $2 \times 3 = 6$ ← 2 and 3 are *factors* (or *divisors*) of the *product* 6.

- **Multiples**: the multiples of a number are simply the products of that number and integers. For example: the multiples of 3 are 3, 6, 9, 12, 15, …

- **Prime number**: number *greater than one* whose only integer factors are one and itself. For example: The number 11 is only divisible by 11 and 1; it is therefore a *prime number*.

ABSOLUTE VALUE

The SAT may test absolute value. Simply put, the absolute value of a number is the positive form of that number. Just get rid of the negative sign, if there is one.

$$|-20| = 20$$
$$|3 - 6| = |-3| = 3$$

Sometimes you'll have to solve for a variable in an absolute value equation. We'll cover this in the Algebra chapter (Basic Algebra).

BASIC OPERATIONS

It may be helpful to memorize the rules below. If you ever forget one of these rules, just make up some numbers and use your calculator:

- even + even or even − even = even
- odd + odd or odd − odd = even
- odd + even or odd − even = odd

- even × even = even
- odd × odd = odd
- odd × even = even

- positive × positive or positive ÷ positive = positive
- negative × negative or negative ÷ negative = positive
- positive × negative or positive ÷ negative = negative

- (positive or negative real number)^2 = positive
- (positive real number)^3 = positive
- (negative real number)^3 = negative

FACTOR TABLE

When you are asked to find the *positive integer factors* (sometimes simply called the *positive factors*) of a number, use a *factor table*.

 Look for the words *positive integer factors (or divisors)* or *positive factors (or divisors)*.

1. Start with 1 in the first column and the original number in the second column of a table.
2. If the original number is even, mentally increase the number in the first column by 1. If the original number is odd, mentally increase the number in the first column by 2 (only odd numbers are divisors of odd numbers).
3. Is the new number a factor of the original number? Hint: you may want to use your calculator. If it is, place it in a new row in column one, and write the quotient (the number displayed on your calculator) in column 2.
4. Repeat steps 2 and 3 until the number in column one exceeds the number in column 2. When done, the numbers in the table will be the positive factors of the original number.

(EX) What are the positive integer factors of 66?

FACTOR TREE

When you are asked to find the *prime factors* of a number, use a *factor tree*. This is different from a factor table, so make sure you read carefully for the mention of *prime* factors.

 Look for the words *prime factors (or prime divisors)*.

1. Write the original number in your work space.
2. Think of a prime number that divides evenly into the original number. Write this prime number and its quotient as *branches* below the original number. Circle or underline the prime number.
3. Repeat step 2 with the quotient branch.

4. When all branches end with prime numbers, those prime numbers are the prime factors of the original number.

(EX) What are the prime factors of 66?

GREATEST COMMON FACTORS

Remember, a *factor* is part of a product of another number. For example, previously we learned that 2 and 3 are factors of 6. Sometimes you may be asked to find the *greatest common factor* (GCF) of two or more numbers. For example, the GCF of 6 and 21 is 3 (the greatest number that is a factor of both 6 and 21). **Usually you can simply check the answer choices (starting with the greatest number) and use your calculator.**

Optional [40-hour program only]: On rare occasions (for example, on grid-in problems) the above approach won't work. Here's the official method (but skip this if you're short on time):
1. Find the prime factors of all numbers in question.
2. Look for any prime factors that are common to <u>all</u> of the original numbers.
3. Multiply these prime factors together to find the GCF.

(EX) What is the greatest common factor of 52 and 78?

LEAST COMMON MULTIPLES

The *least common multiple* (LCM) is the *smallest* number that is a multiple of a given set of other numbers. For example, the LCM of 6 and 9 is 18 (18 is the smallest multiple of 6 and 9). One trick to finding LCMs is to use trial and error. **Just check multiples of the <u>largest</u> number in the set until you find one that is also a multiple of the other number(s).** The concept is best explained with an example:

(EX) What is the least common multiple of 10 and 14?

You can also often just check the answer choices. Make sure to start with the *smallest* number, as more than one answer will often be a multiple of the numbers in question, but only one will be the *least* common multiple.

Optional [40-hour program only]: For harder LCM problems, or if on a particular problem the methods above are taking too long, use the following method (again, skip this if you're short on time):

1. Find the prime factors of all numbers in question.
2. For each prime factor, count the greatest number of times this factor shows up for any one of the original numbers.
3. *Raise* each prime factor to the power of the greatest number of times the factor shows up, and multiply these values. This might sound confusing, so follow along with the example below.

(EX) What is the least common multiple of 52 and 78?

BASIC CONCEPTS LESSON PROBLEMS

1. Circle all integers: 203   2.03 π 0   –2 $\frac{2}{3}$ 4.0

2. Circle all rational numbers: $\sqrt{18}$ $\sqrt{9}$ π $\frac{7}{8}$ 1.2 $\frac{1}{3}$

Continued →

3. What are the prime numbers between 1 and 10?

4. $\left| 4-5 \right| - \left| 5-4 \right| =$

5. $\left| 2(-3) - (-2)(-3) \right| =$

6. If $\left| x \right| = 4$, what are all possible values of x?

7. What are the positive integer factors of 42?

8. What are the prime factors of 42?

9. What is the least common denominator of $\dfrac{1}{3}$ and $\dfrac{1}{7}$?

10. What is the least common multiple of 3, 21, and 45?

5. BASIC CONCEPTS: PRACTICE & CORRECTIONS

PRACTICE PROBLEMS

The following worksheet tests techniques taught in this chapter. It is very important to look back to the lessons in this chapter and review the techniques while completing these problems. Try to determine which technique relates to each problem and apply the methods taught in the tutorial. Do not time yourself on these problems. The problems are provided to give you an opportunity to practice, and hopefully master, the techniques in this tutorial before you apply them on real SATs in a timed setting.

   ☐   Basic Concepts Worksheet

TEST CORRECTIONS

The SAT rarely tests the techniques in this chapter *on their own*—the techniques usually show up with those taught in later chapters. If a question *does* show up that only tests a technique from this chapter, we'll include it as part of the Arithmetic chapter's correction assignments. But that doesn't mean this chapter isn't important. Many of the topics covered help create the mathematical foundation for everything to come, so make sure you are comfortable with this material.

BASIC CONCEPTS WORKSHEET

For all worksheets, problem numbers represent the *approximate* level of difficulty for each problem. For more on order of difficulty, review page 267.

[CALCULATOR SECTION: 1–30 MULTIPLE-CHOICE / 31-38 GRID-IN]:

1. $|-2-4| =$
    A) −6
    B) −2
    C) 2
    D) 6

3. What is the least common denominator for adding the fractions $\frac{2}{3}$, $\frac{6}{7}$, and $\frac{11}{12}$?

    A) 36
    B) 84
    C) 126
    D) 168

5. What is the largest prime number that is a factor of both 35 and 77?

    A) 7
    B) 11
    C) 35
    D) 385

11. What is the least common multiple of 9, 105, and 210?

    A) 210
    B) 630
    C) 945
    D) 22,050

Continued →

16. Which of the following is equal to $-\left(\dfrac{\dfrac{2}{5}-\dfrac{2}{3}}{\dfrac{2}{5}+\dfrac{2}{3}}\right)$?

A) $-\dfrac{1}{2}$

B) $-\dfrac{1}{4}$

C) $\dfrac{1}{4}$

D) $\dfrac{1}{2}$

19. What is the correct ordering of $\dfrac{5}{6}$, $\dfrac{6}{7}$, and $\dfrac{7}{9}$ from least to greatest?

A) $\dfrac{5}{6} < \dfrac{6}{7} < \dfrac{7}{9}$

B) $\dfrac{6}{7} < \dfrac{5}{6} < \dfrac{7}{9}$

C) $\dfrac{7}{9} < \dfrac{5}{6} < \dfrac{6}{7}$

D) $\dfrac{7}{9} < \dfrac{6}{7} < \dfrac{5}{6}$

21. If $\dfrac{a}{10} - \dfrac{b}{55} = \dfrac{11a - 2b}{x}$ and a, b, and x are all integers greater than 1, then $x = $?

A) 55
B) 100
C) 110
D) 550

23. Which of the following is a rational number?

A) $\sqrt{\dfrac{1}{4}}$

B) $\sqrt{\dfrac{1}{2}}$

C) $\sqrt{2}$

D) $\sqrt{8}$

Continued →

24. $\dfrac{1}{\sqrt{2}} + \dfrac{1}{\sqrt{3}} = ?$

   A) $\dfrac{2}{\sqrt{5}}$

   B) $\dfrac{2}{\sqrt{2} + \sqrt{3}}$

   C) $\dfrac{\sqrt{2} + \sqrt{3}}{\sqrt{5}}$

   D) $\dfrac{\sqrt{2} + \sqrt{3}}{\sqrt{6}}$

25. For real numbers p and q, when is the equation $|p + q| = |-p - q|$ true?

   A) Always
   B) Only when $p = q$
   C) Only when $p = q = 0$
   D) Never

27. If $x = ab$, $y = bc$, and $z = ac$, where a, b, and c are prime numbers, which of the following is the least common multiple of x, y and z? **[40-hour program only]**

   A) $a + b + c$
   B) abc
   C) $(abc)^2$
   D) Cannot be determined
      from the information given

II
ARITHMETIC

The Arithmetic chapter covers topics such as percent, proportions, ratios, and exponents. In this chapter, you may have to use some simple algebra, such as solving for a single variable in a simple equation, but more complex algebra will be covered later (in the Algebra chapter).

1. PERCENT

PERCENT ↔ DECIMAL

You must be able to quickly convert a number in percent form to a number in decimal form, and vice versa. This will always involve moving the decimal point *two places* to the right or to the left. An easy way to see which way to move the decimal point is to use 50%. You probably already know that 50% is equivalent to one half, or .50, so when you are working on a percent problem and can't remember which way to move the decimal point, just write:

$$50\% \leftrightarrow 0.50$$

You can easily see which way to move the decimal point:

50% → 0.50 for *percent to decimal* - move decimal point two places to the <u>left</u>.

0.50 → 50% for *decimal to percent* - move decimal point two places to the <u>right</u>.

When using your calculator on percent problems, remember that the calculator only "understands" *decimals* and will only give answers as *decimals*. You must convert percent to decimal before entering data into your calculator, and remember to convert decimal answers back to percent, if necessary.

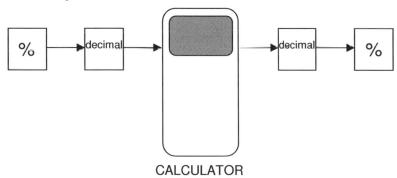

CALCULATOR

1. 4.25 equals what percent?

2. 25% is equivalent to what fraction?

3. 220% is equivalent to what decimal?

4. $\frac{7}{8}$ equals what percent?

5. 0.0013 equals what percent?

OF/IS PERCENT PROBLEMS

Of/is problems require you to turn percent word problems into mathematical equations. Use the information in the following table.

word	operation
of *as big as, as old as, as fast as*, etc.	$\times$
is *are, was, has, will be, equals*, etc.	$=$
what, what percent *what number, how much*, etc.	variable (a, x, etc.)

 Of/is problems are percent problems that do not involve *change*. In other words, no time passes and no values or variables change in the problem. **These problems are usually identifiable by the words *of* and *is* in the question.** For harder problems where the *of* or the *is* is not written, try creating an of/is sentence in your head.

(EX) 20% of 50 =

(EX) 15% of what number is 60?

(EX) 18 is what percent of 20?

(EX) Bill is 20. Fred is $\frac{3}{5}$ as old as Bill. How old is Fred?

Throughout this tutorial, you will notice nonconsecutive question numbers. **Unless stated otherwise, assume these problems are from the *calculator* section—Section 4—of the SAT** (1–30 multiple-choice / 31–38 grid-in). The number will indicate the *approximate* level of difficulty for that problem. See note about problem difficulty on page 267.

1. 25% of 25% of 32 is ?

   A) $\frac{1}{4}$
   B) $\frac{1}{2}$
   C) 1
   D) 2

3. During a 10%-Off sale at a store, if a shopper buys an item originally priced at $5.50, by how much is the item discounted?

   A) $0.50
   B) $0.55
   C) $4.95
   D) $5.40

12. If 40% of a number is 32, what is 50% of that number?

    A) 16
    B) 40
    C) 50
    D) 80

22. The volume of a cube with edge of length 1 inch is what percent of the volume of a cube with edge of length 2 inches?

    A) $12\frac{1}{2}\%$
    B) 20%
    C) 25%
    D) 50%

PART-OVER-WHOLE PERCENT PROBLEMS

Part-over-whole percent problems deal with finding a percent *of completeness* by comparing *part* of something to its *whole*.

> Like of/is problems, part-over-whole percent problems do not involve change (no time passes, and no values or variables change in the problem). **Look for part of something, and look for its whole.**

 If you have traveled 200 miles of a 1000 mile trip, what percent of the trip have you completed?

Try the following lesson problems:

2. If a 12-ounce can of soda currently contains 8 ounces of soda, how full is the can?

    A) $33^1/_3$%
    B) 50%
    C) $66^2/_3$%
    D) 75%

12. Before starting a trip from City A to City B, George sets his odometer to 0 miles. After driving for 3 hours, he passes a sign that says that City B is 800 miles away. If his odometer shows 200 miles at this point, what percent of the trip remains?

    A) 20%
    B) 25%
    C) 60%
    D) 80%

PERCENT INCREASE/DECREASE

These problems deal with increasing or decreasing a value by a given percent. This involves finding a "percent of" something (see the of/is technique), and then adding or subtracting this value to the original value. Here's an example:

(EX) If a scarf normally costs $18, how much will it cost if the price is reduced 25%?

A SHORTCUT: MULTIPLIERS

Some students prefer to tackle these types of problems using what we call a *multiplier*. This method is faster than the standard approach:

1. For a percent *increase*, *add* the percent change to 100%: 100% + percent increase. For a percent *decrease*, *subtract* the percent change from 100%: 100% – percent decrease.
2. Convert the percent to a decimal; this is called the *multiplier*.
3. To find the new (final) value, multiply the original value by the multiplier.

(EX) If a scarf normally costs $18, how much will it cost if the price is reduced 25%?

To summarize:

- Multiplier for percent *increase* = **100% + percent increase**
- Multiplier for percent *decrease* = **100% − percent decrease**

Note that in decimal form, the multiplier for a given percent change *r* is simply **1 ± r**.

❗ NEVER COMBINE PERCENT CHANGES

You must never combine percent changes. For example, you might assume that increasing a number by 20% and then increasing the result by 30% would be the same as increasing the original number by 50%, but this is not the case:

(EX) If the number 10 is increased by 20%, and then the result is increased by 30%, what is the final number?

 Percent increase/decrease problems involve *change*, which obviously means a value or values in the problem change, sometimes over a period of time. The easiest way to identify these problems is to look for a **given percent change**— either a percent increase or a percent decrease.

PERCENT INCREASE/DECREASE LESSON PROBLEMS

3. A store marks up all items 10% of their wholesale cost. In dollars, how much would a radio sell for if its wholesale cost is $200?

   A) 180
   B) 190
   C) 210
   D) 220

16. A book sold for $4.80 after a 20% discount was taken off the list price. What was the list price of the book?

   A) $3.84
   B) $5.00
   C) $5.76
   D) $6.00

DIFFERENCE-OVER-ORIGINAL PERCENT PROBLEMS

Difference-over-original percent problems ask for the percent that a value or values have changed. These problems compare some new value to an older or *original* value. The *difference* is simply the new number subtracted from the original number.

 As with percent increase/decrease problems, these percent problems involve change. The easiest way to identify difference-over-original problems is to see if the question is asking you to find the percent by which something has increased or decreased; in other words, **the question is asking you to find a percent change**.

(EX) A school had 1000 students in 1980. It now has 1200 students. What percent did the school's population change since 1980?

Try the following lesson problem:

17. When Bob started his job, he earned $7 per hour. At the end of 3 years, he earned $28 per hour. By what percent did his hourly rate increase?

   A) 3%
   B) 25%
   C) 300%
   D) 400%

Let's summarize the ways to identify each of the four percent techniques:

 Of/is: Look for the words "of" and "is."
Part-Over-Whole: Look for *part* of something and look for the *whole*.
Percent Increase/Decrease: The question *gives* you a percent change.
Difference-Over-Original: The question *asks you to find* a percent change.

PICK 100

Often, difficult percent problems will involve several percent changes. If no original number is given, it becomes easier to tackle these types of problems by *picking 100* as the original number. Pick 100, and after you've gone through the steps of the problem, compare your final answer to 100. (You can also pick 100 on other types of problems that do not have original numbers given. This will give you a number to work with and a place to start.)

Look for percent problems that have no original number given. Harder problems may have several percent changes.

Try the following lesson problem. Remember to pick 100 for your starting number (the number of workers in 1990):

27. The number of workers at a company increased 30 percent between 1990 and 2000. Employment increased 40 percent between 2000 and 2009. The employment in 2009 was what percent greater than in 1990?

    A) 30%
    B) 70%
    C) 80%
    D) 82%

[CALCULATOR SECTION: 1–30 MULTIPLE-CHOICE / 31–38 GRID-IN]:

3. If $300 is deposited into a savings account that pays 4% interest per year, how much money will be in the account after one year?

    A) $304
    B) $312
    C) $340
    D) $420

4. If it rained 12 days in November and was clear the other 18 days, what percent of the days in November did it rain?

    A) 40%
    B) 50%
    C) $66^2/_3$%
    D) 75%

9. John scored 80 points on test 1 and 92 points on test 2. What was the percent increase?

    A) 8%
    B) 12%
    C) 13%
    D) 15%

Continued →

14. At a company, 60 percent of the employees are women. If one-third of the women and one-half of the men drive to work, what percent of the employees do NOT drive to work?

A) 20%
B) 40%
C) 60%
D) 75%

27. A positive number p is reduced by 25 percent to produce q. If q is increased by 50 percent to produce r, then r is:

A) p decreased by 12.5 percent
B) p increased by 12.5 percent
C) p increased by 25 percent
D) p increased by 75 percent

30. A machine takes m hours to close 50 boxes. After the machine is upgraded to a new design, it can close 90 boxes in $0.6m$ hours. By what percent did the machine's per-hour production rate increase after the upgrade?

A) 40%
B) 80%
C) 200%
D) 300%

2. PROPORTIONS

A *proportion* is two equal *ratios*, or fractions, for example:

$$\frac{2}{3} = \frac{34}{51}$$

In proportion problems, solve unknown values by cross multiplying:

 If $\frac{2}{3} = \frac{62}{x}$, what is the value of x?

> Proportion problems have at least one *known relationship* between two items. Here are a few examples of *known relationships*. Note that each known relationship includes *two* numbers (no unknowns):
>
> - 12 socks cost 4 dollars
> - 2 ounces of vanilla are needed to make 3 cakes
> - 20 miles per gallon
>
> You might also see the words "directly proportional" on some proportion problems.

Proportion problems are fairly straightforward to set up. Just use the following method:

1. Identify and underline the known relationship.
2. Write the **units** as a ratio (no numbers yet!). Leave space to the right of the units for the eventual numbers. You can think of this step as similar to setting up a table, with the "headings" (the units) to the left of each row.
3. Now, add the numbers, starting with the known relationship. The units on the top of each ratio must be the same, and the units on the bottom of each ratio must be the same (that's why we only write the units *once*, to the left of the proportion). Of course, use a variable (such as x) for the unknown.
4. Solve by cross multiplying.

(EX) 1. If 5 dozen flowers cost $25, how much do 24 flowers cost?

MORE THAN ONE KNOWN RELATIONSHIP

More difficult problems may involve two or more known relationships. Set up a proportion for *each* known relationship. See the following example:

(EX) 28. A florist must purchase 72 flowers to make 6 bouquets. If 8 flowers cost $20, how much would the florist spend to make 8 bouquets?

THE "SCIENCE" APPROACH

Optional [40-hour program only] Often in physics and chemistry classes, students are taught a different method for solving proportions. When you're given multiple known relationships, this "science" approach is typically faster. Here's the method:

1. Start with the number that is *not* part of a known relationship. This number should be part of the simple question. <u>Make sure to write the units</u>.
2. Multiply this value by the known relationships, making sure that units cancel (you may have to flip the known relationships).
3. Confirm that your final answer has the correct units.

Here's an example (same question as above):

(EX) 28. A florist must purchase 72 flowers to make 6 bouquets. If 8 flowers cost $20, how much would the florist spend to make 8 bouquets?

If you're already comfortable with this approach, go ahead and use it. If you haven't covered it yet in school, we recommend you stick with the first approach.

RATE PROBLEMS

Problems involving rates (speeds) can also be solved using proportions. A rate is typically a measure of *distance* over *time*:

$$r = \frac{d}{t}$$

Make sure to watch your units. Here's an example:

(EX) 15. A car is traveling x feet per second. Which of the following is equivalent to how far, in feet, the car will travel in 10 minutes?

A) $10x$
B) $60x$
C) $600x$
D) $1,000x$

INVERSE VARIATION

Not all relationships are proportional, where one value increases (or decreases) as another value also increases (or decreases). Some relationships are *inversely* related, where one value increases as another value *decreases* (or vice versa). For example, the volume of a gas varies *inversely* as its pressure. Think of a balloon: If the balloon gets bigger (volume increases), the pressure *decreases*.

Instead of setting up equal *ratios*, as with proportion problems, you'll set up equal *products*. For example, using pressure (P) and volume (V), we would have $P_1 \cdot V_1 = P_2 \cdot V_2$. Inverse variation problems are not common on the SAT, but if one shows up, just think *products*, not ratios, of two variables.

LESSON PROBLEMS

[CALCULATOR SECTION: 1–30 MULTIPLE-CHOICE / 31–38 GRID-IN]:

6. If Bryan takes 6 minutes to light 15 candles, how many minutes would it take him working at the same rate to light 35 candles?

A) 8
B) 10
C) 12
D) 14

13. A bullet train takes 45 minutes to travel 300 kilometers. If it continues at the same rate, how many hours will it take the train to travel 1600 kilometers?

    A) 3
    B) 4
    C) 5
    D) 6

27. A 7-pound bag of apples costs 10 dollars and 5 pounds of apples are needed to make 2 apple pies. What is the dollar cost of apples needed to make 14 apple pies?

    A) 40
    B) 50
    C) 60
    D) 70

[CALCULATOR SECTION: 1–30 MULTIPLE-CHOICE / 31–38 GRID-IN]:

2. If cans of soda sell at the rate of 25 every 4 hours, how many cans of soda will be sold in 20 hours?

    A) 125
    B) 100
    C) 80
    D) 50

5. Lowell takes 40 minutes to drive 30 miles. If he continues at this rate, how many hours will it take him to drive 135 miles?

    A) 1
    B) 2
    C) 3
    D) 4

10. A tree casts a shadow 140 feet long. To determine the height of the tree, Craig stands next to the tree and has someone measure the length of his shadow. If Craig is 6 feet tall and casts a 14-foot shadow, what is the height of the tree?

    A) 36
    B) 60
    C) 132
    D) 140

21. Robot A can assemble 30 computer chips per hour and robot B can assemble 39 computer chips per hour. How many more minutes will it take robot A than robot B to assemble 26 computer chips?

A) 12
B) 15
C) 20
D) 52

3. RATIOS

BASIC RATIO PROBLEMS

 Basic ratio problems can be recognized by numbers or variables separated by the word *to* or a colon (:), such as 2:3, 2 to 3, *x:y*, or *x* to *y*.

Each ratio symbol—the word "to" or a colon (":")—is equivalent to a *divided-by line*, so ratios can be rewritten as standard fractions. Use the following method for ratio problems:

1. First, get rid of all ratio signs by rewriting the ratios as fractions.
2. Use your calculator and your knowledge of proportions or algebra to solve.

The following examples illustrate basic ratio techniques:

(EX) What fraction is equivalent to the ratio 3:5 (or 3 to 5)?

(EX) If the ratio of blue marbles to yellow marbles in a jar is 3:5, and there are 39 blue marbles in the jar, how many yellow marbles are in the jar?

PART-OVER-WHOLE (REVISITED)

Sometimes, the techniques taught in the Percent section come in handy on Ratio problems. Here's an example of the *part-over-whole* technique:

(EX) What fraction of the marbles in the jar described above are blue?

OF/IS (REVISITED)

Here's an example that tests the *of/is* technique:

 Bob has $200. If he gives $\frac{1}{5}$ of his money to charity, how much does he have left?

RATIO SHARE PROBLEMS

Ratio share problems are different from basic ratio problems, even though their identification is similar.

> Ratio share problems are also recognized by numbers or variables separated by the word *to* or a colon (:), but **they involve splitting some *whole* value or quantity into different *shares*.** Any problem with a ratio containing more than two terms, for example 2:3:4, is *definitely* a ratio share problem.

The method is straightforward and is best explained using the examples below:
1. Add up all the numbers in the ratio.
2. Remember, these problems typically involve some *whole* value (of dollars, eggs, students, etc.) that will be divided into shares. Divide this given whole value by the sum of the ratio numbers (from Step 1). This will give you the value of each "part."
3. To find each share, multiply the value from Step 2 (the "part") by the appropriate number in the original ratio.

 If two friends split $700 dollars in a ratio of 3:4, how much does each friend get?

 If three friends split $700 dollars in a ratio of 3:4:7, how much does each friend get?

(EX) A high school play is made up entirely of sophomores, juniors, and seniors. If the ratio of sophomores, juniors, and seniors in the play is 1:3:2, respectively, each of the following could be the number of students in the play EXCEPT

A) 12
B) 15
C) 18
D) 24

RATIOS LESSON PROBLEMS

[CALCULATOR SECTION: 1–30 MULTIPLE-CHOICE / 31–38 GRID-IN]:

7. If the ratio of x to y is 1 to 6, then the ratio of $15x$ to y is

A) $\dfrac{5}{18}$

B) $\dfrac{5}{6}$

C) $\dfrac{5}{2}$

D) 3

12. Prize money for the top three finishers in a golf tournament is divided up in a ratio of 10:4:1. If the total prize money for the three top golfers is $75,000, how much does the first place golfer receive?

A) $5,000
B) $20,000
C) $50,000
D) $67,500

4. The ratio of n to 9 is equal to the ratio of 33 to 198. What is the value of n?

A) $\dfrac{2}{3}$

B) 1

C) $1\dfrac{1}{2}$

D) 3

18. Apple juice, grape juice, and orange juice are mixed by volume in the ratio of 5:4:1, respectively, to produce fruit punch. In order to make 10 gallons of punch, how many gallons of orange juice are needed?

A) $\dfrac{1}{2}$

B) 1

C) 4

D) 5

23. A basket contains only red and green apples. If there are 20 apples in the basket, which of the following could NOT be the ratio of red to green apples?

A) $\dfrac{1}{2}$

B) $\dfrac{1}{3}$

C) $\dfrac{2}{3}$

D) $\dfrac{1}{9}$

4. EXPONENTS

RULES FOR EXPONENTS

 These problems involve an *exponent* (raised number) or a *root* ($\sqrt{}$).

Memorize the following exponential rules:

MULTIPLYING WHEN BASES ARE THE SAME

Remember, the bases must be the same.

$$a^m \times a^n = a^{m+n}$$ (EX) $p^2 \times p^3 =$

DIVIDING WHEN BASES ARE THE SAME

$$a^m \div a^n = a^{m-n}$$ (EX) $\dfrac{p^3}{p^2} =$

RAISING POWERS TO POWERS

Don't confuse this rule with the first rule above.

$$(a^m)^n = a^{mn}$$ (EX) $(p^2)^3 =$

DISTRIBUTING EXPONENTS

Don't forget to distribute the outside exponent to *number* terms within the parentheses.

$$(ab)^m = a^m \times b^m$$ (EX) $(2p^2q^3)^2 =$

NEGATIVE EXPONENTS

Write answers with positive exponents:

$$a^{-m} = \frac{1}{a^m}$$

(EX) $\dfrac{p^2}{p^3} =$

(EX) $\dfrac{p^{22}}{p^{30}} =$

THE ZERO EXPONENT

$$a^0 = 1$$

(EX) $(2x^2y^3)^0 =$

ROOTS AND FRACTIONAL EXPONENTS

Make sure you can convert all roots to fractional exponents. Get comfortable plugging these into your calculator (use parentheses carefully), or use the rules above.

$$\sqrt{a} = a^{\frac{1}{2}}$$

$$\sqrt[n]{a} = a^{\frac{1}{n}}$$

$$\sqrt[n]{a^m} = a^{\frac{m}{n}}$$

(EX) $\sqrt[3]{64} =$

(EX) If $\sqrt[3]{p^2} = p^x$, $x =$

(EX) $\sqrt[7]{2{,}187} =$

COMPARE APPLES TO APPLES

Sometimes, you will be asked to compare the exponents of expressions with different bases, but that's like comparing apples and oranges. **The trick is to make the bases the same so you can easily compare the exponents** (compare apples to apples).

(EX) Which real number for x satisfies $2^x = 4^4$?

A) 2
B) 4
C) 6
D) 8

COMMON MISTAKES

Watch out for these common mistakes. For practice, see if you can correctly simplify each one, or put an ✗ if the expression cannot be simplified:

	simplify?			simplify?
(EX) $(2pq)^2 \neq 2p^2q^2$		4. $\sqrt{p^2+q^2} \neq p+q$		
1. $p^2+p^3 \neq p^5$		5. $p^2p^3 \neq p^6$		
2. $(p+q)^2 \neq p^2+q^2$		6. $\dfrac{p^2}{p^3} \neq p^{\frac{2}{3}}$		
3. $p^{-2} \neq -p^2$		7. $2p^{-2} \neq \dfrac{1}{2p^2}$		

EXPONENTS LESSON PROBLEMS

1. $x^2x^7 =$

2. $\dfrac{x^5}{x^2} =$

3. $(x^4)^5 =$

4. $(5xy)^2 =$

5. $4^{\frac{3}{2}} =$

6. $\dfrac{(3x^2y)^3}{3x^5y^4} =$

[CALCULATOR SECTION: 1–30 MULTIPLE-CHOICE / 31–38 GRID-IN]:

14. If $(2^t)^t = 2^{20}$ and $t > 0$, what is the value of t?

    A) $\sqrt{10}$
    B) $2\sqrt{5}$
    C) 10
    D) $4\sqrt{5}$

Continued →

16. $(-2xy^3)^2(3x^3y) = ?$

    A) $-12x^5y^6$
    B) $-6x^5y^7$
    C) $12x^6y^6$
    D) $12x^5y^7$

18. For all real numbers x and y, which of the following expressions is equivalent to $x^{\frac{1}{2}}y^{\frac{2}{3}}$?

    A) $\sqrt{xy^3}$

    B) $\sqrt{x^2y^3}$

    C) $\sqrt[6]{x^3y^4}$

    D) $\sqrt[6]{x^2y^3}$

21. $3^{n+1} \cdot 3^2 = ?$

    A) 3^{2n+2}
    B) 3^{n+3}
    C) 9^{2n+2}
    D) 9^{n+3}

26. If $9^x = \sqrt[3]{81}$, then what is the value of x?

    A) $\dfrac{1}{3}$

    B) $\dfrac{1}{2}$

    C) $\dfrac{2}{3}$

    D) 3

5. TABLES & GRAPHS

GENERAL APPROACH

Tables and graphs can have many different forms. There are two general steps to tackling these kinds of problems:

1. Carefully study and understand the table or graph *before* trying to answer the question.
2. Watch the problem number. A higher-numbered question may contain a trap, so be careful.

Try the following lesson problems:

8. According to the graph below, Company X showed the greatest change in net income between which two consecutive years?

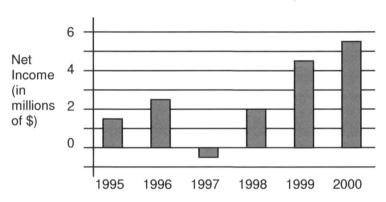

NET INCOME FOR COMPANY X, 1995-2000

A) 1995 and 1996
B) 1996 and 1997
C) 1997 and 1998
D) 1998 and 1999

21. How many <u>hours</u> will it take to clean all 40 streets in City A listed in the table below?

STREET CLEANING IN CITY A	
Number of Streets	Cleaning Time per Street
7	20 minutes
8	40 minutes
10	80 minutes
15	100 minutes

A) 4
B) 46
C) 240
D) 2,760

LINE GRAPHS

Many of the graphs that show up on the SAT are *line* graphs, where a line displays the relationship between two variables. The *steepness* of the line is important:

- **The *steeper* the line, the *faster* the rate of change (that is, the faster that one variable changes relative to the other variable).**
- **The *flatter* the line, the *slower* the rate of change.**
- **A flat, or horizontal, line has a rate of change of 0.**

You'll see this tested on question 3 below:

Note: The following problems are part of a *multi-question set*. Typically, for these multi-question sets, **regardless of the number, the first one will often be relatively easy, but the last one will often be relatively difficult**. Watch out for these problems on the SAT.

▼

Questions 2 and 3 refer to the following information.

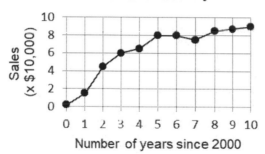

2. According to the line graph above, which of the following is the closest to the annual sales at Sina's Stationery in 2006?

   A) $3,000
   B) $8,000
   C) $30,000
   D) $80,000

3. According to the line graph above, between which two consecutive years did Sina's Stationery store have the greatest change in sales?

   A) 2000–2001
   B) 2001–2002
   C) 2004–2005
   D) 2005–2006

▲

SCATTERPLOTS

A graph of *points* is called a *scatterplot*. Below is a scatterplot that displays the relationship of the height and weight of 11 dogs at a kennel show. (Each point represents a dog.)

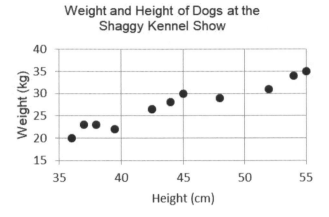

Scatterplots usually give hints about the *shape* of the relationship of the two variables. When the relationship is assumed linear, scatterplots will often provide a "line of best fit." We'll cover linear equations in Chapter IV, but you still might be able to answer most of these scatterplots problems. Try the one below:

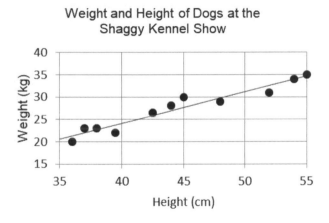

20. The scatterplot above displays the relationship between the heights and weights of 11 dogs randomly chosen from the Shaggy Kennel Show. According to the line of best fit, which of the following is closest to the weight of a dog, in kilograms, if its height is 45 centimeters?

A) 27.5
B) 30.0
C) 32.5
D) 35.0

[CALCULATOR SECTION: 1–30 MULTIPLE-CHOICE / 31–38 GRID-IN]:

7.

Number of Registered Voters by Political Party in Vollmann City in 2000

Political Party	Age (years)				Total
	18–24	25–44	45–64	65 and older	
Democrat	1,234	4,268	6,843	4,854	17,199
Republican	578	3,258	7,288	5,505	16,629
Independent	998	800	667	207	2,672
Total	2,810	8,326	14,798	10,566	36,500

The table above shows the number of registered voters for each political party in 2000 for Vollmann City. What proportion of the voters are registered as Democrat or Independent *and* are 18–44 years of age?

A) $\dfrac{1}{8}$

B) $\dfrac{1}{6}$

C) $\dfrac{1}{5}$

D) $\dfrac{1}{4}$

Continued →

9. The circle graph below represents all income for a sports stadium in 1999. If the stadium made $15,000 in beverage sales, what was the total dollar income of the stadium in 1999?

INCOME FOR STADIUM *A* IN 1999

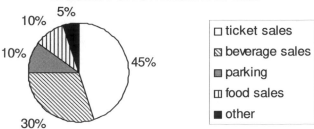

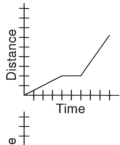

☐ ticket sales
▨ beverage sales
▦ parking
▥ food sales
■ other

A) 19,500
B) 45,000
C) 50,000
D) 55,000

14. Chris lives 6 miles from school. On a particular day, he walked for 2 miles, stopped for 5 minutes to talk with some friends, and then ran the rest of the way to school. Which of the following graphs could correctly represent his journey to school on this day?

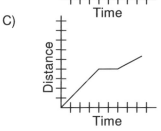

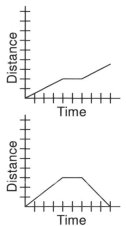

Continued →

Questions 17 and 18 refer to the following information.

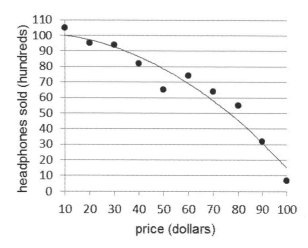

An audio company test-marketed its headphones at different prices. The scatterplot above shows the prices of the headphones and the number of headphones sold at each price. A quadratic model that best fits the data is also shown.

17. According to the figure, of the 10 different prices tested by the audio company, how many of these prices corresponded with sales amounts that were less than those predicted by the quadratic model of best fit.

   A) 2
   B) 3
   C) 4
   D) 6

18. For a price of $50, which of the following best approximates the percent increase from the number of headphones sold during the market test to the number of headphones predicted by the quadratic model?

   A) 15%
   B) 17%
   C) 19%
   D) 23%

Continued →

Wallace's Brick Company sells three different styles of bricks. The sale prices and number of bricks per pallet are given in the table below. The sale price is the amount a customer pays for one pallet of the indicated style.

Style of brick	Number of bricks per pallet	Sale price per pallet
A	75	$75.00
B	50	$80.00
C	30	$90.00

19. Which of the following is the sale price per brick for a Style B brick?

A) $1.00
B) $1.50
C) $1.60
D) $2.00

20. For a special sale, Wallace's Brick Company offers customers a 5% discount off the total sale price for any style of brick when at least 5 pallets are purchased. If a customer buys 8 pallets of Style C bricks, what is the sale price per pallet of these bricks?

A) $85.00
B) $85.50
C) $95.00
D) $684.00

21. If Conrad bought an equal number of Style A, B and C bricks, what is the minimum number of bricks of each style that he could have bought? (Note: customers may not purchase individual bricks at Wallace's Brick Company.)

A) 5
B) 75
C) 150
D) 300

Continued →

25. Volts Electric Car Company manufactures only compact and family cars, both of which are available as either all-electric or hybrid. On the basis of the information in the table below, how many family, all-electric cars will the company produce in 2011?

VOLTS ELECTRIC CAR COMPANY'S
SALES FOR 2011

	All-electric	Hybrid	Total
Compact	a	b	
Family		c	
Total			d

A) $d - (a + b)$
B) $d - (a - b - c)$
C) $d + (a - b - c)$
D) $d - a - b - c$

6. PROBABILITY

BASIC PROBABILITY

Probability is a way of describing the mathematical likelihood of a particular event occurring. It is usually written as a fraction and is always a number between 0 and 1 ($0 \leq P \leq 1$). Memorize the following equation:

$$\text{Probability} = \frac{\text{Outcomes giving a desired result}}{\text{Total possible outcomes}}$$

 Probability problems will include one of the following words: *probability, likelihood, chance,* or *odds.*

(EX) If a fair die is rolled one time, what is the probability of rolling a 6?

(EX) If a fair die is rolled one time, what is the probability of rolling an even number?

(EX) If a fair die is rolled one time, what is the probability of rolling a prime number?

Try the following lesson problem:

3. A box contains 30 marbles. If the chance of drawing a red marble from the bag is ⅔, how many marbles in the bag are <u>not</u> red?

   A) 5
   B) 10
   C) 15
   D) 20

PROBABILITY AND TABLES

The SAT loves to test probability with tables of data. The main challenge with these questions is blocking out all the information that you won't use in your calculations. You usually need to focus on selected members of a subgroup. Here are the steps:

1. First, identify the *subgroup* that is being asked about. Look for clues such as "of the students who play at least one sport" or "if a person with at least 5 years' experience is chosen at random." This information will give you your <u>denominator</u>.

2. Next, identify the *target group*, that is, the group you're asked to find the probability of. Remember, the target group will only include members that are *also* in the subgroup. The number of members in the target group will be your <u>numerator</u>.

3. Finally, the ratio of the target group to the subgroup is your answer. You may have to reduce your ratio on some problems.

Results of an Entrance Exam

	Passed the entrance exam	Did not pass the entrance exam
Used Smarty Pants Tutoring Company	20	5
Used Easy Does It Tutoring Company	22	28

The table above shows the results of 75 students who took an entrance exam for a private school. If one of the students who passed the exam is chosen at random, what is the probability that the student used Easy Does It Tutoring Company?

A) $\dfrac{20}{42}$

B) $\dfrac{22}{42}$

C) $\dfrac{22}{75}$

D) $\dfrac{22}{50}$

Try the following lesson problem:

16.

Results of Adults in Weight Loss Programs

	Lost Weight	Gained Weight	Total
Diet program	187	13	200
Exercise program	102	98	200
Total	289	111	400

The table above shows the results of a research study designed to investigate the weight loss effectiveness of dieting and exercise. A random sample of 400 adults participated in either the diet program or the exercise program for a month. At the end of the month, each adult's weight was compared to his or her weight at the beginning of the program. If an adult gained weight, what is the probability that the adult was in the exercise program?

A) $\dfrac{1}{2}$

B) $\dfrac{98}{111}$

C) $\dfrac{13}{98}$

D) $\dfrac{111}{400}$

[CALCULATOR SECTION: 1–30 MULTIPLE-CHOICE / 31–38 GRID-IN]:

1. A bag contains 5 green marbles, 6 blue marbles, and 7 yellow marbles. If a marble is selected at random from the bag, what is the probability that the marble selected will be blue?

A) $\frac{5}{18}$

B) $\frac{1}{3}$

C) $\frac{7}{18}$

D) $\frac{1}{2}$

Continued →

3.

Gender	Movie Grade		Total
	Thumbs up	Thumbs down	
Male	22	5	27
Female	7	11	18
Total	29	16	45

The table above shows the opinions given by 45 audience members for a recent movie. If a member is selected at random, what is the probability that the member will be either a male who liked the movie ("Thumbs up") or a female who did <u>not</u> like the movie ("Thumbs down")?

A) $\dfrac{11}{45}$

B) $\dfrac{11}{15}$

C) $\dfrac{22}{29}$

D) $\dfrac{4}{5}$

20.

Number of Sports Played per Student

	None	1 to 2	3 or more	Total
School A	86	110	4	200
School B	166	409	125	700
Total	252	519	129	900

The table above displays the number of sports played by students at two schools. School A is a rural school with an enrollment of 200 students. School B is an urban school with an enrollment of 700 students. If a student is chosen at random who plays at least one sport, what is the probability that the student attends School B?

A) $\dfrac{534}{700}$

B) $\dfrac{534}{900}$

C) $\dfrac{115}{648}$

D) $\dfrac{534}{648}$

Continued →

23. In a game, 100 cards are labeled 1–100. A player draws 2 cards at random, without returning the first card. If both cards have the same tens digit, the player is a winner. If the first card Grant draws is a 12, what is the probability that he will be a winner on the next draw?

A) $\dfrac{1}{9}$

B) $\dfrac{1}{10}$

C) $\dfrac{1}{11}$

D) $\dfrac{1}{99}$

7. ARITHMETIC: PRACTICE & CORRECTIONS

PRACTICE PROBLEMS

The following worksheets test techniques taught in this chapter. In addition, we'll use Practice Test 1 from *The Official SAT Study Guide* for more practice questions. It is very important to look back to the lessons in this chapter and review the techniques while completing these problems. Try to determine which technique relates to each problem and apply the methods taught in the tutorial. Do not time yourself. The problems are provided to give you an opportunity to practice, and hopefully master, the techniques in this tutorial before you apply them on real SATs in a timed setting.

- ☐ Arithmetic Worksheet 1
- ☐ Arithmetic Worksheet 2
- ☐ Test 1 (practice problems): See the Techniques chapter at the end of this tutorial.

You might choose to space the above assignments out over the course of your studies. See the "Schedules" section in the introduction for more details about programs.

TEST CORRECTIONS

After completing and grading each practice test, you should correct Arithmetic questions that you missed or guessed on. Below are the three steps to correcting practice tests:

1. Turn to the Techniques section at the end of this tutorial and circle the Arithmetic questions that you missed or guessed on for each test.

2. Correct the problems in *The Official SAT Study Guide*. As you correct the problems, go back to the tutorial and review the techniques. The idea is to (1) identify techniques that have given you trouble, (2) go back to the tutorial so you can review and strengthen these techniques, and (3) apply these techniques to the specific problems on which you struggled.

3. If you have trouble identifying the best technique to use on a problem, refer to the Techniques chapter. This is an important part of correcting the tests.

ARITHMETIC WORKSHEET 1

[CALCULATOR SECTION: 1–30 MULTIPLE CHOICE / 31-38 GRID-IN]:

3. In a table, Luther recorded the number of minutes he watched television over the course of a week during his summer vacation, as shown below. For a day chosen at random, which of the following is the closest to the probability that Luther did *not* watch at least 2 hours of television?

Day	Mon.	Tues.	Wed.	Thurs.	Fri.	Sat.	Sun.
Minutes	20	120	100	0	140	220	360

A) 29%
B) 43%
C) 57%
D) 71%

4. The ratio of two numbers is 4:5. If one of the numbers is 80, what is a possible value of the other number?

A) 64
B) 74
C) 84
D) 94

6. If 20% of x equals 1, what is 50% of x?

A) 0.5
B) 1
C) 1.5
D) 2.5

Continued →

Questions 7 and 8 refer to the following information.

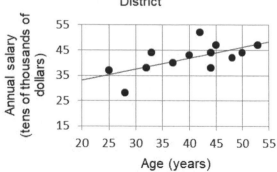

The scatterplot above shows the annual salaries, in tens of thousands of dollars, for 13 teachers in the Omaha School District with respect to their ages, in years. The line of best fit is also shown.

7. According to the line of best fit in the scatterplot above, which of the following best approximates the number of years it would take for a teacher to raise his or her annual salary by $10,000?

    A) 18
    B) 22
    C) 26
    D) 30

8. Elvin is a 50-year-old teacher at the Omaha School District. If his current annual salary is $55,000 per year, which of the following is closest to the difference, in dollars, between Elvin's annual salary and the annual salary predicted by the line of best fit shown above?

    A) 4,000
    B) 9,000
    C) 11,000
    D) 21,000

Continued →

12. If, for all x, $\left(x^{3a-1}\right)^2 = \left(x^4\right)^{\frac{1}{2}}$, then $a =$?

A) $\dfrac{1}{3}$

B) $\dfrac{1}{2}$

C) $\dfrac{2}{3}$

D) $\dfrac{3}{4}$

13. A new car loses 20% of its value after a year of ownership. Which of the following gives the cost, after one year, of a car that cost $20,000 new?

A) $20,000 - 20$
B) $20,000(0.20)$
C) $20,000 - 20,000(0.02)$
D) $20,000 - 20,000(0.20)$

22. The distance the earth travels around the sun in a year is about 5.80×10^8 miles. Assuming 365 days in one year, approximately how many miles does the earth travel in d days?

A) $(365)(5.80 \times 10^8)d$

B) $\dfrac{(5.80 \times 10^8)d}{365}$

C) $\dfrac{(365)(5.80 \times 10^8)}{d}$

D) $\dfrac{5.80 \times 10^8}{365 d}$

26. At Wright High School, 80% of the students of the graduating class plan to go to four-year universities. Of the remaining graduating class members, 90% plan to go to community colleges. What percent of the graduating class do NOT plan to go to a four-year university or a community college?

A) 1%
B) 2%
C) 20%
D) 98%

ARITHMETIC WORKSHEET 2

3. If a player plays one game on a slot machine, the probability that she will win is 0.01. What is the probability that she will NOT win if she plays one game?

    A) 0.09
    B) 0.19
    C) 0.90
    D) 0.99

4. The product of $(3x^2y^3)(4x^5y^4)$ is equivalent to:

    A) $7x^7y^7$
    B) $12x^7y^7$
    C) $7x^{10}y^{12}$
    D) $12x^{10}y^{12}$

7. The distance from Town A to Town B is 20 miles, the distance from Town B to Town C is 15 miles, and the distance from Town C to Town D is 5 miles. An automobile starts at Town A, travels through Towns B and C, and stops at Town D. If the total time for the trip is 1 hour, what is the automobile's average speed, in miles per hour?

    A) 20
    B) 30
    C) 40
    D) 50

11. Pedro copied a map of the world onto a square sheet of paper with a side of 11 inches. He measures the distance from Los Angeles to the Panama Canal as 2 inches. If he enlarges the map so it fits on a square poster board that has a side of 40 inches, what is the new distance, to the nearest inch, between Los Angeles and the Panama Canal?

    A) 7
    B) 8
    C) 9
    D) 10

Continued →

12. The recipe for rice pilaf calls for 2 parts vegetable broth to 3 parts rice to 4 parts water. If you want to make 8 cups of rice pilaf, how many cups of vegetable broth will you need?

A) $\dfrac{8}{9}$

B) $1\dfrac{7}{9}$

C) $2\dfrac{2}{3}$

D) 16

14. The number 0.2 is 1,000 times as large as what number?

A) 0.0002
B) 0.002
C) 20
D) 200

19.

Number of Cats or Dogs per Household in Two Regions

	None	1	2 or more	Total
Households in Region A	52	35	13	100
Households in Region B	17	38	45	100
Total	69	73	58	200

The table above displays the number of cats or dogs in each of 200 households. Region A is an urban area, and Region B is a rural area. If a household is chosen at random from those that have at least one cat or dog, what is the probability that the household is in an urban area?

A) $\dfrac{13}{58}$

B) $\dfrac{48}{131}$

C) $\dfrac{83}{131}$

D) $\dfrac{48}{200}$

24. In the real numbers, what is the solution of the equation $8^a = 4^{2a+1}$?

A) −8
B) −6
C) −4
D) −2

Continued →

26. Marc is trying to increase his weight for an upcoming wrestling match. After each training session, Marc's weight increases 2%. If Marc has two training sessions, by what percent does his weight increase?

    A) 2.02%
    B) 4%
    C) 4.04%
    D) 8%

III
FUNCTIONS

Before we tackle algebra in the next chapter, we'll quickly introduce functions and cover a few specific types of functions that frequently show up on the test. We'll cover graphs of functions, and associated topics, in a later chapter.

1. BASIC FUNCTIONS

It is important to be familiar with basic function notation. A function is typically notated with a letter (often f) and parentheses containing a variable, number, or expression. The letter is the "name" of the function. Whatever is inside the parentheses is the *input* of the function. It may be helpful to think of a function as a *rule* that tells you how to find an *output* for any given input. For example:

$$f(x) = 2x + 3$$

The function above is called "the function f." The variable inside the parentheses, x, represents the input. The rule for this function is: "multiply the input by 2 and then add 3." Several examples are below.

 Look for the function notation, such as $f(x)$, $g(a)$, $P(2)$, etc. When functions are represented graphically, they may only contain the letter of the function without the parentheses (f, g, P, etc). Not surprisingly, the word "function" will also help you identify these problems.

We'll use $f(x) = 2x + 3$ for the following examples:

EX $f(2) =$

EX $f(\frac{a-3}{2}) =$

EX $f(2 + 3) =$

EX $f(g(x)) -$

EX $f(a) =$

EX If $f(x) = -1$, what is the value of x?

Use the following general method for function problems. The steps are illustrated in the example following the method.

1. **Identify the function rule.** It will usually be represented as an equation (as above), but functions can also be represented by graphs or tables. In all cases, the function will give you a *rule* that will allow you to find outputs for given inputs.
2. **Find another expression or equation that contains the function found in step 1.**
3. **Write the problem without the function notation by following the rule of the function.** The trick is to get rid of the function notation so you can solve using basic algebra.
4. Use basic math or algebra to answer the question.

(EX) Let the function g be defined by $g(x) = x + 3$. If $g(m) = 2m$, what is the value of m?

 A) 6
 B) 5
 C) 4
 D) 3

LESSON PROBLEMS

[CALCULATOR SECTION: 1–30 MULTIPLE-CHOICE / 31–38 GRID-IN]:

▼

Questions 12–14 refer to the following information.

$$f(n) = n^2$$

$$g(n) = n^2 - n$$

12. $f(6) - f(-6) =$

 A) −6
 B) 0
 C) 36
 D) 72

13. Which of the following is equivalent to $g(m + 1)$?

 A) $f(m) + 1$
 B) $f(m) + 3$
 C) $f(m) + m$
 D) $g(m) + m$

14. Which of the following is an expression for $f(g(x))$?

 A) $x^2 - x$
 B) $(x^2 - x)^2$
 C) $x^4 - x^2$
 D) $(x^4 - x^2)^2$

▲

7. A function f satisfies $f(7) = 9$, a function g satisfies $g(5) = 7$, and a function h satisfies $h(3) = 5$. What is the value of $f(g(h(3)))$?

    A) 3
    B) 5
    C) 7
    D) 9

9. For the function $f(x) = -2x^3 - 3x^2 + 4$, what is the value of $f(-2)$?

    A) 8
    B) 4
    C) 0
    D) –12

10. A function h of the variables p and q is defined as $h(p,q) = p^p - q^q$. What is the value of $h(5,4)$?

    A) 1
    B) 9
    C) 399
    D) 2,869

27. According to the table below, if $a = g(3)$, what is the value of $h(a)$?

x	$g(x)$	$h(x)$
0	3	4
1	1	3
2	2	2
3	0	1

    A) 0
    B) 2
    C) 3
    D) 4

2. GROWTH & DECAY FUNCTIONS

This section introduces growth and decay functions. These functions show up frequently on the test. Often, the equations will be given, but occasionally you'll be expected to know them (hence, the flashcard symbols).

COMPOUND INTEREST EQUATION

When money is invested, it earns interest over time. *Compound interest* means that interest is paid both on a *principal* (initial investment) *and* on any interest that has accrued. The growth will be *exponential*. Compound interest may be "compounded" multiple times per year. Here's the equation for *A*, the final amount of money after *t* years:

$$\boxed{\begin{array}{c} FLASH \\ CARDS \end{array}} \quad A = P\left(1 + \frac{r}{n}\right)^{nt}$$

In the equation above, *P* is the principal, *r* is the annual interest rate (<u>as a decimal</u>), *t* is the length the deposit is held (typically in years), and *n* is the number of times the interest is compounded per year. Note that if interest is paid once per year, $n = 1$, and the equation simplifies to $A = P(1 + r)^t$.

r AS A PERCENT

Sometimes the equation will be given with *r* in *percent*, rather than *decimal*, form. In this case, you'll use $\frac{r}{100}$ in the equation above. For example, if $r = 20\%$, we have $\frac{20}{100}$ (which of course equals 0.20). Here's the equation:

$$\boxed{\begin{array}{c} FLASH \\ CARDS \end{array}} \quad A = P\left(1 + \frac{r}{100n}\right)^{nt}$$

Try the following lesson problem:

22. Alberto invests \$1,000 in an account that earns 2.5% interest compounded annually. To determine how much he will have in the account after 10 years, he uses the expression \$1,000$(a)^t$, where *t* is the number of years after he made his investment. What is the value of *a* in the expression?

    A) 0.025
    B) 1.025
    C) 2.5
    D) 10

SIMPLE INTEREST EQUATION (JUST IN CASE)

Simple interest problems are rare, but they may show up. *Simple interest* means that the interest is payable only on the the initial amount. In other words, the interest never changes (because the principal never changes): the interest each year is always $P \times r$. The growth is *linear*, not exponential. The equation for the final amount is $\boldsymbol{A} = \boldsymbol{P}(\textbf{1} + \boldsymbol{rt})$. Again, P is the principal, r is the annual interest rate (<u>as a decimal</u>), and t is the length the deposit is held (typically in years). As an exercise, you might try to derive this equation. Again, these problems are rare, so it's probably not worth memorizing the equation (but if you can derive it, you're safe).

EXPONENTIAL GROWTH/DECAY

Functions grow or decay *exponentially* when the rate of change also grows or decays. In other words, as an exponential growth function gets bigger, it gets bigger *faster*. As an exponential decay function gets smaller, it gets smaller *slower*.

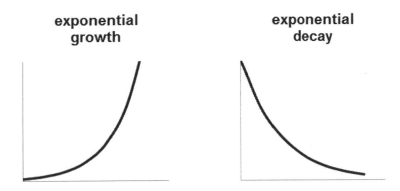

exponential growth **exponential decay**

Below is the general equation for exponential growth and decay functions.

$$\boxed{\textit{FLASH CARDS}} \quad \boldsymbol{A} = \boldsymbol{P}\left(\textbf{1} \pm \boldsymbol{r}\right)^{\frac{t}{n}}$$

P is the starting value, r is the rate of change (as a decimal), t is the total time, and n is how often the change occurs. The units for t and n must be the same (days, years, etc.). (Note that $1 \pm r$ is the same as the "multiplier" discussed in the percent increase/decrease section.)

Some exponential growth/decay problems will give you as equation similar to the one above, either in the question or in the answer choices. Some questions will simply mention "exponential growth" or "exponential decay." For others (like the one below), you'll just have to have a sense of the exponential nature of the growth.

(EX) The population of a colony of penguins doubles every 8 years. At this rate, if a colony of this type starts with 5 penguins, how many penguins will be in the colony after 56 years?

A) 640
B) 760
C) 870
D) 980

Try the following lesson problem:

36. Luke increased the number of stamps in his stamp collection by 50% each year. On January 1, 2009, he had 405 stamps in his collection. If he started his collection on January 1, 2005, how many stamps did he start with?

[CALCULATOR SECTION: 1–30 MULTIPLE-CHOICE / 31–38 GRID-IN]:

26. A house increases in value by 10% each year. If the house was purchased for $500,000, which of the following functions f models the value of the house, in dollars, t years after the date of purchase?

A) $f(t) = 500{,}000(1.10)^t$
B) $f(t) = 500{,}000(0.10)^t$
C) $f(t) = 1.10(500{,}000)^t$
D) $f(t) = 0.10(500{,}000)^t$

Continued →

27. Madeleine deposits $1,000 into a bank account that earns 4% interest compounded monthly. If she uses the expression $A = \$1{,}000\left(1 + \dfrac{0.04}{n}\right)^{5n}$ to find the value of the account after 5 years, what is the value of n?

A) 1
B) 12
C) 60
D) 100

28. The bacteria in a large petri dish increases by 25% every 15 minutes. Currently, there are 20,000 bacteria in the dish. Which of the following expressions represents the number of bacteria in the dish 4 hours from now?

A) $20{,}000(0.25)^4$
B) $20{,}000(1.25)^4$
C) $20{,}000(0.25)^{16}$
D) $20{,}000(1.25)^{16}$

Below is a high-level grid-in question from the no-calculator section:

[NO-CALCULATOR SECTION: 1-15 MULTIPLE-CHOICE / 16-20 GRID-IN]:

20. The cells of a certain type of bacteria increase in number by splitting into two every 10 minutes. At this rate, if a colony starts with a single cell, how many <u>hours</u> will elapse before the colony contains 2^{12} cells?

3. FUNCTIONS: PRACTICE & CORRECTIONS

PRACTICE PROBLEMS

The following worksheet tests techniques taught in this chapter. In addition, we'll use Practice Test 1 from *The Official SAT Study Guide* for more practice questions. It is very important to look back to the lessons in this chapter and review the techniques while completing these problems. Try to determine which technique relates to each problem and apply the methods taught in the tutorial. Do not time yourself. The problems are provided to give you an opportunity to practice, and hopefully master, the techniques in this tutorial before you apply them on real SATs in a timed setting.

- ☐ Functions Worksheet
- ☐ Test 1 (practice problems): See the Techniques chapter at the end of this tutorial.

You might choose to space the above assignments out over the course of your studies. See the "Schedules" section in the introduction for more details about programs.

TEST CORRECTIONS

After completing and grading each practice test, you should correct Functions questions that you missed or guessed on. Below are the three steps to correcting practice tests:

1. Turn to the Techniques section at the end of this tutorial and circle the Functions questions that you missed or guessed on for each test.
2. Correct the problems in *The Official SAT Study Guide*. As you correct the problems, go back to the tutorial and review the techniques. The idea is to (1) identify techniques that have given you trouble, (2) go back to the tutorial so you can review and strengthen these techniques, and (3) apply these techniques to the specific problems on which you struggled.
3. If you have trouble identifying the best technique to use on a problem, refer to the Techniques chapter. This is an important part of correcting the tests.

FUNCTIONS WORKSHEET

[NO-CALCULATOR SECTION: **1-15** MULTIPLE-CHOICE / **16-20** GRID-IN]:

7. If $f(x) = x^2$, which of following is equal to $f(x^3)$?

    A) x^3
    B) x^4
    C) x^5
    D) x^6

[CALCULATOR SECTION: **1–30** MULTIPLE CHOICE / **31-38** GRID-IN]:

4. If $f(x) = 2x^2 + x$ and $g(x) = 5x$, what is the value of $f(2) \times g(2)$?

    A) 1
    B) 10
    C) 20
    D) 100

16. If $f(x) = 2x + 5$ and $g(x) = x^2$, what is the value of $g[f(x)]$?

    A) $4x^2 + 25$
    B) $4x^2 + 20x + 25$
    C) $2x^2 + 20x + 25$
    D) $2x^2 + 5$

17. To study population growth, a biologist released 70 frogs on an island. The population, p, of

    frogs on the island is given by the function $p(t) = 300t^{\frac{3}{4}} + 70$, where t is the number of days

    after the frogs were released. According to this function, how many frogs will be on the

    island after 1 year (1 year = 365 days)?

    A) $300(1)^{\frac{3}{4}} + 70$

    B) $300^{\frac{3}{4}} + 70$

    C) $300(365)^{\frac{3}{4}} + 70$

    D) $365^{\frac{3}{4}} + 70$

Continued →

25. If $f(x) = 2x^2$, then what is the value of $\dfrac{f(x+h) - f(x)}{h}$?

A) $4x + 2h$
B) $2x + 4h$
C) $4x^2 + 2h$
D) $2x^2 + 4h$

26. Which of the following, to the nearest dollar, is the value after 10 years of a $5,000 investment at a 6% annual interest compounded yearly?

A) $\$\dfrac{5,000}{(1.06)^{10}}$

B) $\$\dfrac{5,000}{(1.06)(10)}$

C) $\$5,000(1.06)^{10}$

D) $\$5,000(1.6)^{10}$

27. Let the function g be defined by $g(x) = x + 4$. If $\frac{1}{2}g(\sqrt{a}) = 4$, what is the value of a?

A) 4
B) 6
C) 16
D) 36

Continued →

28. When Jessie adds an antibacterial solution to a sample of polluted water, he finds that the bacterial population decreases at a rate of 11% per hour. If the initial population of the bacteria in the water was 5×10^5, which of the following functions b models the population 1 day after Jessie adds the solution?

A) $b(t) = 5 \times 10^5 (0.11)^{24}$
B) $b(t) = 5 \times 10^5 (0.89)^{24}$
C) $b(t) = 5 \times 10^5 (1.11)^{24}$
D) $b(t) = 0.11(5 \times 10^5)^{24}$

29. Larry wants to save up for a new bike that costs $1,000, including tax. He deposits $900 in a savings account that pays 2% interest per year, compounded semiannually (twice a year). Which of the following inequalities could Larry use to determine the minimum time, in years, after he makes his deposit until he will have enough to purchase the bike?

A) $900(1.01)^{2t} > \$1,000$
B) $900(1.02)^{t} > \$1,000$
C) $900(1.01)^{t} > \$1,000$
D) $900(1.02)^{2t} > \$1,000$

▼

Questions 37 and 38 refer to the following information.

Nils deposits $1,000 into a savings account that offers an annual interest rate of 4%, compounded quarterly. He uses the equation $A = \$1,000(1 + a)^{4t}$ to determine how much money he will have in the account after t years.

37. What is the value of a in the equation above?

38. To the nearest dollar, how much will Nils have in the savings account after 10 years? (Note: Disregard the $ sign when gridding your answer.)

▲

IV

ALGEBRA

Algebra is an important part of the SAT. In this chapter, we'll cover basic algebra, algebraic word problems, and linear equations. We'll also cover special techniques called *Pick Tricks*, which may help you on some of the more difficult SAT problems.

1. BASIC ALGEBRA

EQUALITIES

If you've come this far, you probably already have a grasp of the basic algebraic operations that allow you to solve simple equalities. If not, the Working with Variables lesson on page 341 might help you get started, or find a good Algebra 1 book and review. For problems 1-10, solve for a.

1. $3a = -54$

2. $10a - 4 = 6$

3. $4 - 5a = 14$

4. $3a + 6 = 4\frac{1}{2}a$

5. $3a - 4 = 2a + 2$

6. $2(a - 6) = -4$

7. $\frac{2}{3}(9 - a) = \frac{1}{2}a - 8$

8. $\dfrac{1}{a+2} = \dfrac{3}{5}$

9. $\dfrac{1}{2a+2} = \dfrac{3}{a+11}$

10. $a = b - 2$ and $b = 2a$, $a = ?$

If necessary:
Hint for #8 and #9: *cross multiply*; this gets variables out of denominators.
Hint for #10: use *substitution*; since we're solving for a, substitute $b = 2a$ into the first equation.

SOLVING INEQUALITIES

If you can solve equalities like the ones on the previous page, then solving *inequalities* shouldn't be a problem. Just treat the inequality sign ($<, >, \leq, \geq$) as if it were an equal sign, but you must remember one important rule:

When multiplying or dividing both sides of an inequality by a negative number, the inequality sign changes direction. For example:

$$-2a \geq 14 \rightarrow \frac{-2a}{-2} \leq \frac{14}{-2} \rightarrow a \leq -7$$

inequality sign changes direction

Solve for *a*:

1. $4a < 120$

2. $-\frac{1}{2}a + 6 \leq 8$

SOLVING EXPONENTIAL EQUATIONS

To solve for a squared variable (such as x^2), use the method below. Look at the following example as you read each step:

1. Get the squared variable alone on one side of the equal sign.
2. Take the square root of each side of the equation.
3. **Add a plus or minus sign (±).** This is the most common mistake on these problems. You should generally expect *two* answers when you solve a squared variable.

(EX) If $x^2 = 121$, what is a possible value of $x + 11$?

A) 0
B) 11
C) 21
D) 133

SOLVING EQUATIONS WITH RADICALS

Radicals were introduced in the Exponents lesson. To solve radical equations:

1. Isolate the radical expression so it is alone on one side of the equal sign.
2. Square both sides.
3. Always check your answers when working with radicals. Sometimes you will get an "extraneous solution," one that is actually *not* a solution to the equation. (Hint: This may occur when you have variables inside *and* outside the radical sign.)

(EX) If $2\sqrt{a} = 12$, then $a =$

Solve for *a*:

1. $2\sqrt{a} - 5 = 11$

2. $2\sqrt{a-5} = 8$

SOLVING ABSOLUTE VALUE EQUATIONS

There are two steps to solving absolute value equations:

1. Isolate the absolute value expression on one side of the equal sign.
2. Set whatever is inside the absolute value bars equal to ± whatever is outside the bars. This should give you two new equations.
3. Solve each equation separately. As with radicals, check your answers. Sometimes you will get an extraneous solution.

(EX) If $|x + 5| - 3 = 0$, then $x =$

WORKING WITH VARIABLES

Some SAT problems will ask you to perform operations on variables. You should be comfortable with the following three rules:

- **Distributive property**: $a(b + c) = ab + ac$
- **Combine like terms**, for example: $2x^2 + 5x^2 = 7x^2$
- **Canceling terms**, for example: $\dfrac{8ab}{4b} = \dfrac{2 \cdot 4ab}{4b} = 2a$

Caution: You can only cancel terms that are *factors* of the whole top and the whole bottom of a fraction. In other words, if a term is part of an addition or subtraction expression, you can *not* cancel it. This is a very common mistake. For example:

$$\frac{8 + ab}{4b} \neq \frac{2 \cdot 4 + ab}{4b}$$

Try the following lesson problem:

2. $m^2 - 22m + 11 - 12m^2 + 11m$ is equivalent to:

   A) $-22m^6 + 11$
   B) $-22m^2 + 11$
   C) $-11m^2 - 11m + 11$
   D) $-11m^2 + 11m + 11$

LOOK FOR SHORTCUTS

The SAT loves to put shortcuts into algebra problems. Always look for ways to solve problems quickly. Do you see the shortcut in the following question?

10. If $x(3x^3 + 2x^2 - x) = 2(3x^3 + 2x^2 - x)$ and $x \neq 0$, what is the value of x? **[NO CALCULATOR]**

    A) 2
    B) 4
    C) 6
    D) 8

BASIC ALGEBRA HOMEWORK

[CALCULATOR SECTION: 1–30 MULTIPLE-CHOICE / 31–38 GRID-IN]:

1. What is the value of the expression $a \cdot \sqrt{a} \cdot \sqrt{a+3}$ for $a = 1$?

   A) 5
   B) 4
   C) 3
   D) 2

Continued →

4. If $50(4x) = 200$, then what is the value of $4x$?

A) $\dfrac{1}{4}$

B) 1

C) 2

D) 4

7. For what value of x is $p = 2$ a solution to the equation $x - 3 = px - 1$?

A) -3
B) -2
C) 0
D) 3

10. If $a = x + y$ and $b = x - y$, which of the following equals $(a + b) - (a - b)$?

A) $2x$
B) $2y$
C) $2x - 2y$
D) $2y - 2x$

15. What is the solution to the equation below?

$$\frac{11}{x+3} = \frac{7}{x+1}$$

A) $\dfrac{2}{5}$

B) $\dfrac{5}{2}$

C) $\dfrac{7}{2}$

D) $\dfrac{11}{2}$

25. What is the solution set of the equation below?

$$|x+2| = 2x + 13$$

A) $\{-11\}$
B) $\{-5\}$
C) $\{-11, -5\}$
D) $\{-11, -5, 0\}$

2. ALGEBRAIC WORD PROBLEMS

Algebraic word problems require one of the following:

1. Plugging numbers into a given equation.
2. Coming up with your own equation or equations.

 As the name suggests, these problems can get *wordy*. Some may have variable equations or expressions given, either in the questions or in the answer choices. Others will have variables within the words (for example: *x* hats or *t* minutes). Harder ones may ask you to come up with your own variables and equations.

Of course, you will likely have to use some of the algebra techniques from the previous lesson while answering these types of questions.

GIVEN EQUATIONS

Sometimes the equation you need is conveniently given in the problem. You will usually simply plug numbers into the equation. These problems may look difficult (because they are wordy or have difficult-looking equations), but they tend to be easier than they look. Try the following problem:

15. The surface area, *S*, of a sphere is determined by the formula $S = 4\pi r^2$, where *r* is the radius of the sphere. What is the surface area, in square inches, of a sphere with diameter 6 inches long?

    A) 24π
    B) 36π
    C) 48π
    D) 60π

If you thought the problem above was fairly straightforward, great! Notice that it's a number 30 (out of 30). Stay aggressive on these problems, especially the wordier ones, and you'll gain valuable points on problems that other students tend to skip or guess on.

CREATE YOUR OWN EQUATION(S)

Some questions *do* require you to make up your own equations and sometimes your own variables for these equations. The following table will help:

Word	Operation
product, of, multiplied, times	$\times$
sum of, more than, older than, farther than, greater than, added	$+$
difference, less than, younger than, fewer, subtracted	$-$
quotient, per, for, divided	$\div$
square	x^2
cube	x^3

Let's try a lesson problem:

16. When the square of the product of x and 4 is subtracted from the square of the difference of x and 4, the result is 0. Which of the following equations will allow you to solve for x?

    A) $(x-4)^2 - (4x)^2 = 0$
    B) $(x-4)^2 - 4x^2 = 0$
    C) $(4x)^2 - (x-4)^2 = 0$
    D) $4x^2 - (x-4)^2 = 0$

A COMMON EXPRESSION

Perhaps the most common operation found in algebraic word problems is a simple product of two variables. We'll explain with an easy example:

If each javelin weighs p pounds, we could write the total weight of j javelins using the expression **jp**. In other words, the number of javelins times the weight of each javelin will give you the total weight of all javelins. Easy enough, right?

As you can see, it's just a simple product, but it's something the SAT tests again and again. Try the following lesson problem:

2. To rent scuba gear, a customer must pay a flat fee of $25 plus d dollars for each hour h that the gear is rented. Which of the following expressions correctly models the amount a customer would pay for renting scuba gear for h hours?

    A) $25 + dh$
    B) $25d + h$
    C) $25 + d + h$
    D) $25dh$

A COMMON ALGEBRAIC WORD PROBLEM

You will likely come across a two-unknown/two-equation algebraic word problem similar to the one below. The example below covers the steps:

 Look for questions that have two unknowns, and two "situations" involving these unknowns. Often, these will include one for the total number of items, and one for a total cost or income.

(EX) 20. The Bakerville Library held a charity event. Tickets for library members cost $5, and tickets for nonmembers cost $15. If an amount of $2,500 was collected from the 200 guests who paid admission, how many guests were members?
A) 15
B) 25
C) 50
D) 75

A COUPLE TRICKY EQUATIONS

Students frequently make mistakes on the following two types of word problems. We'll use examples to teach them:

(EX) In a parking lot, let c be the number of cars and t be the number of trucks. If there are 50 more cars than trucks, which of the following displays the relationship between c and t?
A) $c = 50 - t$
B) $50 - c = t$
C) $c = t + 50$
D) $c + 50 = t$

(EX) In a parking lot, let c be the number of cars and t be the number of trucks. If there are three times as many cars as trucks, which of the following displays the relationship between c and t?

A) $3c = t$

B) $c = 3t$

C) $ct = 3$

D) $ct = \dfrac{1}{3}$

INEQUALITY WORD PROBLEMS

Not all word problems deal with *equations*. Some will include *inequalities*. Look for the keywords below to recognize these problems.

Most of these problems will have *less than* or *greater than* signs in the answer choices ($<$, $>$, $\leq$, $\geq$). You can also look for words such as these:
- maximum or greatest possible
- minimum or least possible
- at least
- at most
- up to
- greater than
- less than

(EX) 14. Joseph set a goal to save at least 1,000 pounds of newspapers for a school recycling drive. Starting Monday morning, he had 50 pounds of newspapers, and he collected 20 pounds of newspapers per day. If d represents the number of days that Joseph collected newspapers, which of the following inequalities could be used to determine how many days Joseph must collect newspapers before he has met his original goal?

A) $20 + 50d \geq 1,000$
B) $20 + 50d \leq 1,000$
C) $50 + 20d \geq 1,000$
D) $50 + 20d \leq 1,000$

12. Hugh, Rupert, and Benedict each order a milkshake that costs x dollars. Rupert leaves early without paying, so Hugh and Benedict must split the bill. If they add a 20% tip to the bill, which of following expressions represents the amount, in dollars, each of them paid. (Assume there is no sales tax.)

   A) $1.20x$
   B) $1.40x$
   C) $1.60x$
   D) $1.80x$

14. Norman can use a computer terminal at the local library for free for the first hour, and then must pay 5 cents per minute for each minute after an hour. The cost c, in dollars, for using the computer for t minutes can be modeled using the following equation $c = 0.05(t - 60)$, where $t > 60$. What does the expression $t - 60$ represent in the equation?

   A) It represents the cost to use the computer for one hour.

   B) It represents the cost to use the computer for each minute after one hour.

   C) It represents the time that Norman uses the computer.

   D) It represents the time that Norman will be charged to use the computer.

Continued →

8. Four times a number is four more than two times the number. What is the number?

   A) −2
   B) 0
   C) 2
   D) 4

15. You have been hired to make sales calls for a small company. For each day of calling, you make $50 plus a fixed amount for each call you make. Currently you earn $140 per day for making 60 calls. If you increase the number of calls per day by 20, what would be your new daily earnings?

   A) $170
   B) $165
   C) $160
   D) $155

28. Nick purchased a box that contained red, blue, and yellow straws. There were ⅓ as many red straws as there were blue straws. If ⅓ of the straws were blue and 20 of the straws were yellow, how many straws were in the box?

   A) 12
   B) 24
   C) 36
   D) 48

3. THE PICK TRICKS

Some problems can be solved using what we call the *Pick Tricks*. These techniques can make problems easier, often by eliminating difficult algebra. In addition, the Pick Tricks may allow you to solve a problem that would otherwise require a specific mathematical approach that you may not be familiar with. In other words, the Pick Tricks are tools that can often get you out of jams. The next several pages will ensure that you are comfortable using these tools.

There are two types of Pick Tricks: *Pick Numbers* and *Pick Answers*.

PICK NUMBERS

The Pick Numbers technique allows variables (or unknowns) to be replaced with actual numbers that you pick. There are four types of Pick Numbers problems:

- Type 1: Variables in the answer choices
- Type 2: Variables in the question only
- Type 3: No variables
- Type 4: Guess and check

PICK NUMBERS TYPE 1: VARIABLES IN THE ANSWER CHOICES

 The first type of Pick Trick is the easiest to identify and the most straightforward and systematic to solve. Simply look for problems with **variable *expressions* in the answer choices**, for example:
A) $x - 3$
B) $x - 2$
C) $x - 1$
D) x

Note: For most problems with equal signs (=) or inequalities (<,>...) in the answer choices, this technique will not work. Make sure the answer choices are variable *expressions* (not equations or inequalities).

The following is a step-by-step method for solving these types of problems:

1. **Pick numbers for variables found in the answer choices.** The numbers 0 and 1 are usually not good choices (but see the note at the end of this lesson). If there is more than one variable, pick *different* numbers for each variable. Write your picked numbers somewhere close to the answer choices—you will have to plug them in later. Draw a *box* around the numbers so they are easy to keep track of.

2. **Answer the question using an appropriate technique.** Remember, the variables should now be read as the numbers you picked in step 1, thereby simplifying the problem. Once you've solved the problem, *circle* or *underline* the answer.

3. **Plug your picked numbers into *each* of the answer choices.** You must plug in the number values that you picked in step 1. Cross out any answer choices that don't match your circled or underlined answer from step 2. **YOU MUST CHECK EVERY ANSWER CHOICE!** If only one answer equals your circled answer from step 2, you're done. Occasionally, more than one answer choice works, and you will have to go back to step 1 and pick new numbers to complete the elimination process. Once an answer choice has been eliminated, you do not have to check it again.

(EX) If a pen costs p cents, how many pens can be purchased for \$4.00?

A) $4p$

B) $400p$

C) $4/p$

D) $400/p$

Try the following lesson problems:

17. The expression $(a + b + 1)(a - b)$ is equivalent to: ?

A) $a^2 - b^2 - b$
B) $a^2 - b^2 + b$
C) $a^2 + a - b^2 - b$
D) $a^2 + a - b^2 + b$

21. If m and n are consecutive even integers and $m > n > 0$, how many integers are greater than $m + n$ and less than $m \times n$?

A) 1
B) 2
C) $m - n$
D) $n^2 - 3$

A NOTE ON PICK NUMBERS (TYPE 1) IDENTIFICATION

 As mentioned on the previous page, you should look for variable *expressions* in the answer choices (no equations or inequalities), but if every answer choice begins with the same variable and an equal sign (see example below), then you can still probably use Pick Numbers (type 1):

A) $y = x - 3$
B) $y = x - 2$
C) $y = x - 1$
D) $y = x$

Since the "$y =$" could have been the last words in the question, we can look at the answer choices as just variable expressions ($x - 3$, $x - 2$, etc.). In other words, pick a number for x, and follow the steps described above.

PICKING NUMBERS ON THE NO-CALCULATOR SECTION

We said earlier that when you pick your numbers, "0 and 1 are usually not good choices." Sometimes on the no-calculator section, however, you might test one of these numbers first. Yes, there's a greater chance of finding two or more "correct" answers, but if you're dealing with difficult expressions—especially ones containing exponents—you might get lucky with 0 or 1, and your calculations will be much easier. Just remember to check every answer choice.

PICK NUMBERS TYPE 2: VARIABLES IN THE QUESTION ONLY

 These problems have **variables in the question** and **no variables in the answer choices**. This means the answer choices are actual numbers.

Picking numbers for some or all of the variables in the question may lead you to the correct answer. You must read the question carefully to avoid picking numbers that break the specific rules of the problem. **You will usually <u>not</u> pick numbers for *every* variable.** Use the following method (follow along with the example):

1. Start with the easiest equation or expression in the problem and pick a number for *one* of the variables.
2. Solve for as many other variables as possible.
3. If necessary, pick numbers for additional variables (that could not be solved in step 2) until you have enough information to solve the problem.

Remember to read the problem carefully. To avoid picking numbers for too many variables, make sure all of the specific rules for the problem are being followed.

(EX) If $a(b - c) = 6$ and $ab = 12$, what is the value of ac?

    A) −6
    B) 2
    C) 3
    D) 6

Try the following lesson problem:

24. If $\dfrac{a}{b} = \dfrac{2}{3}$ and $\dfrac{b}{c} = \dfrac{2}{5}$, then $\dfrac{a}{c} = ?$

    A) $\frac{4}{15}$
    B) $\frac{3}{10}$
    C) $\frac{2}{5}$
    D) $\frac{2}{3}$

PICK NUMBERS TYPE 3: NO VARIABLES

Picking numbers when there are no variables allows you to create an example problem with your own numbers. This will give you a place to start and something to work with. The number 100 is sometimes a convenient number to pick, as we've already seen in some of the percent problems in Chapter II.

 These problems feel "open ended" because they usually do not give the actual values or quantities of the main subject of the question, such as a population, the size of a square (see below), etc. Usually these problems do not include variables.

On the following lesson problem, pick a length for the side of the initial square. This will be your starting point. Make sure to read the question carefully. You may have to brush up on your percent techniques for this one.

16. When the perimeter of a square doubles, then the square's area increases by what percent?

    A) 100%
    B) 200%
    C) 300%
    D) 400%

PICK NUMBERS TYPE 4: GUESS AND CHECK

Sometimes you may run into trouble when you Pick Numbers (type 2). For example, if you pick a number and end up with 2 = 3, you know something's wrong. Or perhaps you know the answer is supposed to be an integer and you keep getting fractions. You may have to *guess* numbers and *check* to see if you're getting closer to the correct answer. Use the following general method (as always, follow along with the example):

1. Pick a number or numbers for variables, as with the Pick Numbers (type 2) technique. You will usually *not* pick numbers for every variable. This is your *guess*.

2. *Check* to see if your picked number or numbers lead you to the correct answer. **Always keep track of your results. You need to make sure that, when you pick new numbers, you're getting closer to the correct answer. You will often want to use a table to keep track of your picked numbers and their results.**

3. Continue picking numbers until you find the correct answer. Sometimes you might have to pick decimals, fractions, or negative numbers (not all problems on the SAT deal only with positive integers).

 This technique works on many types of difficult, high-numbered problems, often ones that involve one or more equations that you cannot easily solve.

(EX) If $xy = 91$ and $x + y = 20$, then $x^2y + xy^2 = ?$

A) 111
B) 1,820
C) 1,919
D) 2,000

25. If $7x + 3y = 29$, where x and y are positive integers, what is the value of $x + y$?

A) 3
B) 7
C) 8
D) 10

PICK ANSWERS

If the answer choices are actual numbers, you may be able to *pick answers* to make the problem easier to solve. Essentially, this technique allows you to solve a problem by picking answers and *working backwards*.

Before picking answers, you must identify the *barebones question*. This is the question in its simplest form and describes exactly what the problem is asking. Barebones questions are usually very simple, such as: "...what is the value of *x*?" or "...what was the price of the book?"

 These problems generally have **numbers as answer choices** (no variables). **Usually, the barebones question is very simple and involves at most one variable**. If you are ever stuck on a high-numbered problem, consider picking answers.

Here's the method:

1. **Identify and underline the barebones question**, as described above.
2. **Answer this question by picking one of the answer choices.** Since the answers are often in ascending order, you should usually start with one of the middle answer choices (B or C). This may allow you to eliminate answers more quickly. If some answer choices appear easier to check than others, however, you can check these first.
3. **Look at the rest of the question to see if the answer you picked makes sense.** Essentially, you are creating an *if-then* question: *If* the answer to the barebones question is C (for example), *then* are the parameters of the problem possible? **Once you find the answer that works, stop—you do *not* have to check all the answers for picking answer problems.**

(EX) If Ed and Lorena divide a deck of 52 cards so that Lorena has 8 fewer cards than Ed, how many cards does Lorena receive?

A) 18
B) 22
C) 26
D) 34

Try the following lesson problem:

21. Raymond has 8 buckets and 22 rocks. Each bucket can hold at most 5 rocks. What is the greatest possible number of buckets that can contain 5 rocks if NONE of the buckets are empty?

    A) 1
    B) 2
    C) 3
    D) 4

PICK NUMBERS: ADVANCED

You can often pick numbers on problems that have *ranges* of possible values—either in the question or in the answer choices—such as inequalities, tables, or graphs (especially graphs with shaded regions).

 As described above, these questions usually have *ranges* of values, such as inequalities, either in the question or in the answer choices.

WHERE TO START?

There are two possible starting places when using this technique:

1. **The question**: When it's easier to pick a number or numbers that satisfy the information given in the *question*, start with the question, and then check your picked number(s) in the answer choices.

2. **The answer choices**: Sometimes you'll find that it's easier to pick numbers for the *answer choices* and then check your picked number(s) in the question.

STARTING WITH THE QUESTION

When you can easily pick a number that satisfies the *question*, use the following technique (follow along with the example):

1. Pick a number or numbers that satisfy the question.
2. Eliminate answer choices that do NOT include this number.
3. Continue picking numbers until you have eliminated all three incorrect answers. (Note: If necessary, you may have to pick a number that does NOT satisfy the question, in which case you will eliminate answer choices that DO include the number.)

! As with Pick Numbers (type 1), which also have variables in the answer choices, the key is to <u>eliminate answer choices</u>. If a number you check (in the question) *works*, eliminate answer choices that do *not* contain that number. If a number you check *fails*, eliminate answer choices that *do* contain that number.

(EX) On a roller coaster ride at an amusement park, riders must be greater than 4 feet tall but less than 6 feet tall. If x represents the allowable height of a rider, in feet, which of the following represents all of the possible values of x?

A) $|x+6| < 4$

B) $|x-6| = 4$

C) $|x-5| < 1$

D) $|x-5| > 1$

Try the following problem using this technique:

20. Which of the following equations gives the relationship between t and d in the table below?

t	1	2	3	4
d	1	3	6	10

A) $d = t + (t-1)$

B) $d = \dfrac{t(t+1)}{2}$

C) $d = \dfrac{t+1}{2}$

D) $d = 2t$

STARTING WITH THE ANSWER CHOICES

When picking numbers that satisfy the question is difficult, start with the *answer choices*. Here's the technique (follow along with the example):

1. Pick a number that works for at least one answer choice. But be careful: the number you pick should not work for *all* of the choices:

/ **The number you pick should be true for *at least one* of the choices, but *not all* of them.**

2. Check your picked number in the question and eliminate answer choices. Once again, eliminating answer choices is the key. If the number you picked *works* in the question, eliminate answer choices that do *not* contain that number. If the number you picked *fails* in the question, eliminate answer choices that *do* contain that number.

3. Repeat the steps until you have eliminated three of the answer choices.

(EX) If $\dfrac{x-5}{2}$ is an integer, then x must be: ?

A) a negative integer
B) a multiple of 5
C) an even integer
D) an odd integer

Try the following lesson problem:

28. If $x \geq 0$, which of the following is the solution set of $\left| x^2 - 10 \right| \leq 6$?

A) $0 \leq x \leq 4$

B) $1 \leq x \leq 4$

C) $2 \leq x \leq 4$

D) $2 \leq x \leq 8$

PICK TRICK HOMEWORK

Use at least one of the Pick Tricks on each of the following problems. Yes, you may know how to solve some of these problems using more "traditional" techniques, but remember that the goal of this section is to get comfortable with the *Pick Tricks*, so you can use them, when you choose to, on the SAT.

[CALCULATOR SECTION: **1–30** MULTIPLE-CHOICE / **31–38** GRID-IN]:

10. Six people visit Anna's blog every x seconds. At this rate, how many people will visit her blog in y minutes?

    A) $10x/y$

    B) $10y/x$

    C) $360x/y$

    D) $360y/x$

11. If $a = b$, $c = d$, and $e = f$, which of the following equations must be true?

    A) $a + b = e + f$
    B) $a + c = d + e$
    C) $a + d = a + f$
    D) $a + d = b + c$

17. If $3^x = 8$, then $3^{2x} = $?

    A) 16
    B) 24
    C) 40
    D) 64

Continued →

18. Anna, Tanya, and Stephanie decide to split the buried treasure that they find so that Anna receives $\frac{3}{5}$ of the treasure, Tanya receives $\frac{1}{3}$ of the treasure, and Stephanie receives the rest. What is the ratio of Anna's share to Tanya's share to Stephanie's share?

    A) 15:5:3
    B) 9:5:1
    C) 9:3:1
    D) 5:3:1

19. Max can sweep his patio in x minutes. What fraction of the task remains if he sweeps his patio steadily for y minutes, where $y < x$?

    A) $\dfrac{x+y}{y}$

    B) $\dfrac{x+y}{x}$

    C) $\dfrac{x-y}{x}$

    D) $\dfrac{x-y}{y}$

20. Which of the following is the solution set for the inequality below?

$$|x+2| > 6$$

    A) $x < -6$ or $x > 6$
    B) $x < -8$ or $x > 4$
    C) $x < 4$ or $x > 8$
    D) $x < -8$ or $x > 6$

21. Joshua is ½ as old as Keith and ¼ as old as Sean. If the average of all three ages is 21, how old is Keith now?

    A) 9
    B) 12
    C) 18
    D) 36

26. Jody played a video game three times and improved his score by the same percent each time. If he scored 600 points the first time and 864 points the third time, what was the percent change after each game?

    A) 13.2%
    B) 20%
    C) 22%
    D) 44%

4. LINEAR EQUATIONS

A *linear equation* has the form $ax + by = c$, where a, b, and c are numbers, called *coefficients*. As the name says, linear equations represent *lines*. A useful form of a linear equation is the "point-slope" equation ($y = mx + b$). We'll discuss this in detail soon.

COORDINATE PLANE

Before getting into lines, you should be comfortable with the *xy-coordinate plane* (skip ahead if you're familiar with this already). This plane consists of two perpendicular axes called the *x*-axis and the *y*-axis. The *x*-axis is horizontal and the *y*-axis is vertical. A *point* (x,y) on the coordinate plane is simply a pair of coordinates, an *x*-coordinate and a *y*-coordinate (in that order). For example, below is the point (3,5):

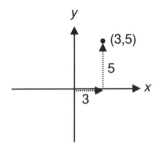

SLOPE OF A LINE

The *slope* of a line describes its angle, or slant. Memorize the formula below:

$$\boxed{\begin{array}{c} FLASH \\ CARDS \end{array}} \quad m = \frac{y_1 - y_2}{x_1 - x_2} \begin{array}{l} \leftarrow (rise) \\ \leftarrow (run) \end{array}$$

Make sure the difference of the *y*-coordinates (the "rise") is in the *numerator* and the difference of the *x*-coordinates (the "run") is in the *denominator*. The order of the points does not matter as long as the order in the numerator is the same as that in the denominator.

POSITIVE AND NEGATIVE SLOPE

Lines with a *positive* slope angle up to the right, and lines with a *negative* slope angle up to the left:

VERTICAL AND HORIZONTAL SLOPE

Vertical lines have an *undefined* slope, and horizontal lines have a slope of *zero*:

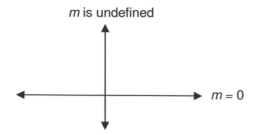

SLOPE OF PARALLEL AND PERPENDICULAR LINES

For the following examples, the slope of line *a* is m_a, and the slope of line *b* is m_b.

When two lines are parallel, their slopes are *equal*:

Line *a* is parallel to line *b*.

$$m_a = m_b$$

When two lines are perpendicular, use the following formula:

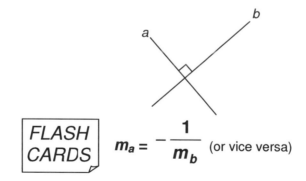

FLASH CARDS

$$m_a = -\frac{1}{m_b} \quad \text{(or vice versa)}$$

Try the following lesson problem:

3.

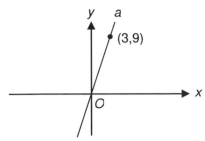

Line *a* in the *xy*-plane above passes through point (3, 9) and the origin. If line *b* (not shown) is perpendicular to line *a*, what is the slope of line *b*?

A) −3

B) $-\frac{1}{3}$

C) $\frac{1}{3}$

D) $\frac{2}{3}$

THE SLOPE-INTERCEPT EQUATION

An equation of a line defines all of the points that form that line. The *slope-intercept equation* is convenient because, at a glance, it gives you the *slope* of the line and the place where the line crosses the *y-axis* of the coordinate plane (called the *y-intercept*).

$$y = mx + b$$

Slope-intercept equation of a line

In the equation above, *m* is the slope, *b* is the *y*-intercept, and *x* and *y* are the variables. The variables *x* and *y* are the coordinates of points on the line—for example, if you know an *x*-coordinate of a point, you could use the equation to find the *y*-coordinate.

OTHER LINEAR EQUATIONS → THE SLOPE-INTERCEPT FORM

If the equation for a line is not in the slope-intercept form, use basic number operations to rearrange the equation so that y is alone on the left side of the equal sign. See the following example:

(EX) What is the y-intercept of the line defined by the equation $(y + 2) = 2(x - 1)$?

FINDING THE SLOPE-INTERCEPT EQUATION

When you are given the y-intercept and the slope of a line, finding the slope-intercept equation is straightforward. Just plug values for m and b into the slope-intercept equation above.

You can also find the slope-intercept equation when you are given:

1. **A point on the line and the slope of the line**

    OR

2. **Two points on the line**

Use the following method:

1. Identify or calculate the slope of the line (m).
2. Plug the x and y values of a given point and the slope (m) from step 1 into the slope-intercept equation.
3. Solve for b.
4. Rewrite the equation with x and y as variables: $y = mx + b$.

(EX) What is the slope-intercept equation of the line that goes through the point (2,0) and has a slope of 3?

WHERE'S THE *x*? WHERE'S THE *y*?

Equations that involve only the *x* variable are vertical lines. Equations that involve only the *y* variable are horizontal lines. Write the equations for the following lines:

 Line *A*:

1. Line *B*:

2. Line *C*:

3. Line *D*:

4. Line *E*:

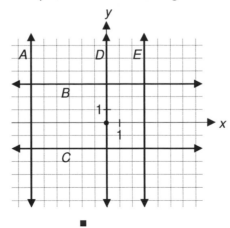

Try the following line equation lesson problems:

5. The point (2, *p*) lies on the line with equation $y - 3 = 2(x - 4)$. What is the value of *p*?

   A) −1
   B) 0
   C) 1
   D) 2

18. In the figure below, if line *l* has a slope of $\frac{3}{2}$, what is the *y*-intercept of *l*?

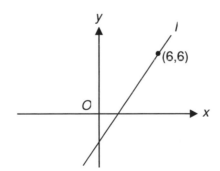

   A) −1
   B) $-\frac{3}{2}$
   C) −2
   D) −3

APPLICATIONS

The SAT will test the *application* of linear equations in real-life situations, which typically means describing what the slope or *y*-intercept of an equation means. Keep in mind that these application questions will typically involve variables other than *x* and *y*, but you should still recognize the basic $y = mx + b$ form, even if the variables are different.

SLOPE

Most of these linear equation application questions have to do with slope. Remember, slope is the measure of "rise over run," or, to put it another way, the "change in *y* for each unit change in *x*": slope $= \dfrac{\text{change in } y}{\text{change in } x}$. Here's an example:

$$h = 4t + 136$$

(EX) The equation above models the height *h* of a tree, in inches, over time *t*, in years. What does the number 4 mean in this equation?

A) The tree's height increases 4 inches each year.

B) The tree's height increases 1 inch every 4 years.

C) The tree's height is 4 inches after 1 year.

D) The tree's height is 1 inch after 4 years.

There are actually several ways that the slope can be interpreted. When in doubt, you can always create a proportion, using the given slope as a "known relationship" (see the Proportions lesson if necessary).

$$h = 4t + 136$$

(EX) The equation above models the height *h* of a tree, in inches, over time *t*, in years. Based on the equation, which of the following must be true?

    I.   The tree's height increases 4 inches each year.

    II. The tree's height increases 1 inch every 3 months.

    III. The tree's height increases 136 inches every 4 years.

A) I only
B) II only
C) I and II only
D) I, II, and III

When the slope is given as a fraction, you may see more interesting possibilities:

$$h = \frac{4}{3}t + 136$$

(EX) The equation above models the height h of a tree, in inches, over time t, in years. Based on the equation, which of the following must be true?

    I.   The tree's height increases 4 inches every 3 years.

    II. The tree's height increases $1\frac{1}{3}$ inches every year.

    III. The tree's height increases 1 inch every 9 months.

A) I only
B) II only
C) I and II only
D) I, II, and III

Here's a lesson problem:

26. The profit, p, in dollars, that a company made selling calculator X from 1990 to 2000 can be modeled by the equation $p = 5c - 500$, where c is the number of calculators sold. Which of the following best describes the meaning of the number 5 in the equation?

A) The profit increased 5 dollars for each additional calculator sold.

B) The profit increased 1 dollar for every additional 5 calculators sold.

C) The profit increased 5 dollars each year between 1990 and 2000.

D) The company sold 5 calculators in 1990.

y-INTERCEPT

The *y*-intercept (b in the $y = mx + b$ equation) is the value of y when $x = 0$. Make sure to note the variables. You should be able to say something like "when x equals 0, y equals b." Here's a lesson problem:

15. An amusement park charges a certain flat fee for a customer to use the batting cages plus a cost per pitch. The park models the total cost y, in cents, using the equation $y = 75 + 50x$, where x is the number of pitches. When the equation is graphed in the xy-plane, what does the y-intercept of the graph represent in terms of the model?

A) A flat fee of 50 cents
B) A flat fee of 75 cents
C) The total cost for 75 pitches
D) A cost of 50 cents per pitch

POINTS

Finally, a question may ask about the meaning of a point, or *solution*, of a linear equation. Once again, pay attention to the units. Here's a lesson problem:

$$y + 50x = 1250$$

14. To keep track of a company's inventory of a certain type of hat for the month of January, the company uses the equation above, where y is the number of hats in inventory and x is the day of the month. What does it mean to say that (25, 0) is a solution to the equation?

A) In 25 days the inventory decreases by 50 hats.

B) The inventory decreases by 25 hats per day during January.

C) There are 25 hats in inventory at the beginning of January.

D) On January 25 there are 0 hats left in inventory.

LINEAR EQUATIONS HOMEWORK

[CALCULATOR SECTION: 1–30 MULTIPLE-CHOICE / 31–38 GRID-IN]:

9. The *xy*-plane has four quadrants, as labeled below. If a line has one point in quadrant II and another point in quadrant IV, which of the following gives the possible values of the slope of the line? (Note: the points do not lie on the *x*-axis or *y*-axis.)

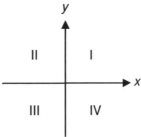

A) Any negative real number
B) 0
C) Any positive real number
D) Cannot be determined from the information given

11. In the figure below, line *l* passes through the origin. What is the value of $\dfrac{b}{a}$?

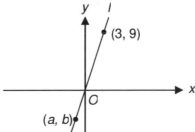

A) −3
B) $-\frac{1}{3}$
C) $\frac{1}{3}$
D) 3

Continued →

Questions 12 and 13 refer to the following information.

A wind turbine is a machine that uses wind to rotate a turbine and thus create electrical power. For a given wind turbine, a scientist measures electrical power, in kW, for various wind speeds, in meters per second. The data is shown below. The line of best fit for the data is also shown.

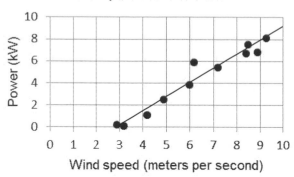

Wind speed versus Power

12. During a second experiment, the scientist measures a 10 kW power output for a wind speed of 9 meters per second. This value is how much greater, in kW, than the power output predicted by the line of best fit?

    A) 0
    B) 1
    C) 2
    D) 4

13. The equation for the line of best fit in the scatter plot above is $y = \frac{4}{3}x - 4$. Which of the following is the best interpretation of the meaning of the y-intercept, −4, in the equation?

    A) When the power output is 0 kW, the wind speed will likely be close to −4 meters per second.

    B) When the wind speed is 0 meters per second, the power output will likely be close to −4 kW.

    C) When the wind speed is 0 meters per second, the power output will be exactly −4 kW.

    D) The y-intercept does not represent a realistic scenario in this context.

▲

Continued →

14.
$$P(t) = 5{,}000t + 25{,}000$$

The function P above models the profit, in dollars, of a flower shop t years since 2010.

Which of the following best describes the meaning of the number 5,000 in the function?

A) The increase in profit each year since 2010

B) The increase in profit t years since 2010

C) The company's profit in 2010

D) The company's profit each year since 2010

26. In the xy-plane below, line b is perpendicular to line a. Which of the following is the equation for line a?

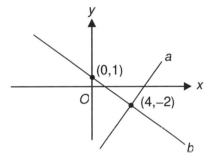

A) $y = -\frac{3}{4}x + 1$

B) $y = -\frac{3}{4}x - \frac{22}{3}$

C) $y = \frac{4}{3}x - \frac{10}{3}$

D) $y = \frac{4}{3}x - \frac{22}{3}$

Continued →

28.

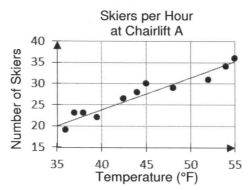

Skiers per Hour
at Chairlift A

The scatterplot above shows the average number of skiers *s* riding Chairlift A per hour and the temperature *t*, in degrees Fahrenheit (°F), at a small ski area on 11 different spring days. A line of best fit for the data is also shown. Which of the following could be an equation of the line of best fit?

A) $y = 1.33x - 26.7$
B) $y = 1.33x + 20$
C) $y = 0.75x - 6.25$
D) $y = 0.75x + 20$

5. SYSTEMS OF EQUATIONS & INEQUALITIES

SYSTEMS OF EQUATIONS

When you have two equations, the "solution" is the point (or points) where the graphs of these equations intersect. Rather than finding this point geometrically, you should typically find it algebraically, either using the *elimination* method or *substitution* method (both described below).

> To identify systems of equations problems, look for *two* equations with *two* unknowns.

SOLVING BY ELIMINATION

You'll often use the elimination method with *linear equations*, which have the form $ax + by = c$, where a, b, and c are numbers, called *coefficients*:

Coefficient – a number or constant that multiplies a variable (for example, in the expression $2x$, the coefficient is 2).

Use the following method:

1. Stack the equations (one above the other)—make sure that the variables line up vertically.
2. If necessary, multiply one or both of the equations by a constant (or constants) so that one of the variables has the same coefficient in each equation.
3. Add or subtract the equations to eliminate this variable.
4. Solve for the remaining variable using algebra.
5. Plug this value into one of the original equations to find the other variable.

Solve for x and y:

 $x + 2y = 8$ and $x - 2y = -4$

1. $2x + 2y = 8$ and $3x - 2y = 2$

2. $100x + y = 25$ and $200x + y = 45$ 3. $5x - 5y = -10$ and $2x + 3y = 16$

SOLVING BY SUBSTITUTION

Usually, solving systems of equations by *substitution* is faster than the *elimination* approach above, especially when one of the variables is already by itself on one side of an equation (as with *y* in the example below). Here's the method:

1. Solve for a variable in one of the equations. Often this is already done for you, as in the example below. Note: This variable is usually *not* the variable you are being asked to find.

2. Substitute your result from step 1 into the other equation. You should now have one equation and one unknown.

3. Solve for the unknown.

(EX) 10. **[NO CALCULATOR]**

$$y = x^2 - \frac{1}{2}x$$
$$2y + x = 32$$

If (x, y) is a solution of the system of equations above and $x > 0$, what is the value of x?

A) 4
B) 8
C) 12
D) 16

INTERSECTING LINES

ONE SOLUTION

As mentioned before, when two lines intersect at a point, this point is the "solution" of the system of equations. But, again, you usually want to solve these algebraically (not geometrically). Try the following lesson problem:

10. When graphed in the xy-plane, the lines $y = 5$ and $y = 5x - 5$ intersect at what point?

    A) (0, 5)
    B) (1, 5)
    C) (2, –5)
    D) (2, 5)

INFINITE SOLUTIONS

When would two lines have an infinite number of solutions? When the two lines are in fact *the same line*. In other words, if the equations of both lines are simplified to point-intercept forms ($y = mx + b$), the slopes will be the same and the y-intercepts will be the same.

- Infinite solutions: **Same slopes, same y-intercepts**

NO SOLUTIONS

When would two lines have no solutions? When the two lines are *parallel*. The lines never cross. In other words, if both equations are simplified to point-intercept forms, the slopes will be the same but the y-intercepts will be *different*.

- No solutions: **Same slopes, different y-intercepts**

Try the following lesson problem:

21. For which of the following values of k will the system of equations below have no solutions?

$$y = 2x + 20$$
$$y = kx + 40$$

    A) –2
    B) 0
    C) 2
    D) 4

SYSTEMS OF LINEAR INEQUALITIES

We covered inequalities in the Algebra chapter (see Basic Algebra and Algebraic Word Problems). Now we'll discuss systems of linear inequalities. Here's the ID:

 Look for systems of inequalities ($<$, $>$, $\leq$, $\geq$), either in the question or, more likely, in the answer choices. You can also look for words such as maximum or greatest possible, minimum or least possible, at least, at most, etc.

Here's an example. Note that you don't have to solve the system—just identify it:

(EX) 20. Donna sells two types of computers, one that sells for $200 and one that sells for $300. Let x be the number of $200 computers and y be the number of $300 computers. To earn a promotion, she must sell at least $6,000 worth of computers in a month. If the computer shop can sell at most 40 computers in a month, which of the following systems of inequalities represents Donna getting a promotion?

A) $200x + 300y \geq \$6,000$
$x + y \geq 40$

B) $200x + 300y \geq \$6,000$
$x + y \leq 40$

C) $x + y \leq \$6,000$
$200x + 300y \geq 40$

D) $x + y \geq \$6,000$
$200x + 300y \leq 40$

Try the following lesson problem

20. Rutherford's Sofas sells sofas of two sizes: small and large. Each small sofa sells for $250 and weighs 100 pounds. Each large sofa sells for $500 and weighs 160 pounds. The company would like to sell at least $15,000 worth of sofas in January, but the company cannot sell more than 5,000 pounds of sofas. If x is the number of small sofas sold in a month and y is the number of large sofas sold in a month, which of the following systems of inequalities represents the company's goal for January?

A) $100x + 160y \leq 15,000$
$250x + 500y \geq 5,000$

B) $100x + 160y \geq 15,000$
$250x + 500y \leq 5,000$

C) $250x + 500y \geq 15,000$
$100x + 160y \geq 5,000$

D) $250x + 500y \geq 15,000$
$100x + 160y \leq 5,000$

Optional [40-hour program only]: Very rarely will the SAT actually ask you to *solve* a system of inequalities. Most students should skip this part of the lesson, but if you're looking for a perfect score, here's the method, just in case one of these questions shows up:

1. Graph the lines as if they were equations (ignore the inequality signs).
2. You will *lightly* shade the side of each line that satisfies the inequality. To determine which side to shade, test a simple coordinate. When possible, (0, 0) is usually the easiest to test. If the point works, shade that side of the line. If not, shade the other side.
3. The region of the graph where the shades overlap is the solution to the system of inequalities.

(EX) 30.

$$y \leq x + 2$$
$$y \geq 2x - 2$$

In the *xy*-plane, if a point with coordinates (*a*, *b*) lies in the solution set of the system of inequalities above, what is the maximum possible value of *a* + *b*?

A) 4
B) 6
C) 8
D) 10

Important note: Points of intersection are often important on these problems. These points may be either the intersection of two lines or functions (as above) or the intersection of a function and the *x*- or *y*-axis. Pay close attention to these points.

6.

$$2x - 2y = 12$$
$$x + 3y = -6$$

If (x, y) is a solution of the system of equations above, what is the value of y?

A) -3
B) -1
C) 1
D) 3

13.

$$y = 3x$$
$$\frac{2}{3}(y + 2x) = -\frac{20}{3}$$

If (x, y) is a solution of the system of equations above, what is the value of x?

A) -6
B) -4
C) -2
D) 0

Continued →

14. The nth term of an arithmetic sequence is given by the linear equation $a_n = a_1 + (n - 1)d$, where a_1 is the first term of the sequence and d is the constant difference between adjacent terms. If the 5th term of an arithmetic sequence is 6 and the 9th term is 13, what is the 17th term of the sequence?

A) 20
B) 27
C) 29
D) 34

17.

$$y = ax + b$$
$$y = bx + 10$$

In the system of equations above, a and b are constants, and $b \neq 10$. If the system has no solutions, what is the value of $a - b$?

6. ALGEBRA: PRACTICE & CORRECTIONS

PRACTICE PROBLEMS

The following worksheets test techniques taught in this chapter. In addition, we'll use Practice Test 1 from *The Official SAT Study Guide* for more practice questions. Don't forget to look back to the lessons in this chapter and review the techniques while completing these problems. And do not time yourself.

- ☐ Algebra Worksheet 1
- ☐ Algebra Worksheet 2
- ☐ Algebra Worksheet 3
- ☐ Test 1 (practice problems): See the Techniques chapter at the end of this tutorial.

Once again, see the "Schedules" section in the introduction for more details about when to tackle these assignments.

TEST CORRECTIONS

After completing and grading each practice test, you should correct Algebra questions that you missed or guessed on. Below are the three steps to correcting practice tests:

1. Turn to the Techniques section at the end of this tutorial and circle the Algebra questions that you missed or guessed on for each test.

2. Correct the problems in *The Official SAT Study Guide*. As you correct the problems, go back to the tutorial and review the techniques. The idea is to (1) identify techniques that have given you trouble, (2) go back to the tutorial so you can review and strengthen these techniques, and (3) apply these techniques to the specific problems on which you struggled.

3. If you have trouble identifying the best technique to use on a problem, refer to the Techniques chapter. This is an important part of correcting the tests.

ALGEBRA WORKSHEET 1

[NO-CALCULATOR SECTION: **1-15** MULTIPLE-CHOICE / **16-20** GRID-IN]:

3. If x is a positive real number and $\dfrac{3}{x} \leq \dfrac{1}{3}$, what is the smallest possible value of x ?

A) $\dfrac{1}{9}$

B) $\dfrac{1}{3}$

C) 3

D) 9

5. If $2mn = 3$, what is the value of $3mn$?

A) $\dfrac{3}{2}$

B) $\dfrac{9}{2}$

C) 6

D) 9

11. For all $x > 4$, $\dfrac{x^2 - 4x}{x^2 + 4x - 32} = ?$

A) $\dfrac{-x}{x + 8}$

B) $\dfrac{x}{x + 8}$

C) $\dfrac{-1}{x + 8}$

D) $\dfrac{-1}{32}$

Continued →

11.

$$h = \frac{1}{8}t + \frac{3}{4}.$$

Rachel grows 20 bamboo plants in her backyard and measures the heights of the plants every day for 2 months. From her data, she models the average height h, in inches, of a bamboo plant t days from the start of her experiment using the equation above. Which of the following statements is the best interpretation of the number $\frac{1}{8}$ in this context?

A) The bamboo plants grow on average 1 inch every 8 days.

B) The bamboo plants grow on average 8 inches every day.

C) The average starting height of the bamboo plants was $\frac{1}{8}$ inch.

D) The average height of the bamboo plants after 2 months was $\frac{1}{8}$ inch.

13.

$$P = 45m - 20n$$

Alex sells indestructible cellphone cases at his internet store. The equation above shows Alex's profit, in dollars, where m is the number of cases that he sells, and n is the number of cases that he buys from his supplier. Which of the following is the best interpretation of the number 20 in the equation?

A) Alex must sell 20 cases to make a profit.

B) Alex buys 20 cases from his supplier.

C) Alex sells each case for $20.

D) Alex pays his supplier $20 per case.

[CALCULATOR SECTION: 1–30 MULTIPLE CHOICE / 31-38 GRID-IN]:

2. For what value of x is the equation $3(2x - 4) = 2x - 16$ true?

A) 0
B) −1
C) −3
D) −4

Continued →

5. If a, b, and c are all nonzero real numbers and $a + b = c$, which of the following equations is always true?

A) $a = b - c$
B) $a = -(c - b)$
C) $-a = c - b$
D) $-a = b - c$

7. When graphed in the xy-plane, the lines $2x - 2y = 30$ and $x - 5y = 7$ intersect at what point?

A) $(16, 2)$
B) $(2, 16)$
C) $(17, 2)$
D) $(2, 17)$

18. Which of the following is equivalent to the identity $-3x + 6 < -6x$?

A) $x < -\frac{2}{3}$
B) $x < 2$
C) $x < -2$
D) $x > -2$

28. In the xy-plane, lines a and b intersect at point $(-2, 3)$ and lines a and c intersect at point $(-2, -2)$. Which of the following is an equation for line a?

A) $y = -2x - 1$
B) $y = -2x + 3$
C) $x = -2$
D) Cannot be
determined from the
information given

Continued →

33. Wallace is taking a test for a new job. The test has two types of problems, one type worth 2 points each and one type worth 3 points each. To be eligible for the job, Wallace must score at least 100 points. If x is the number of 2-point questions he answers correctly and y is the number of 3-point questions he answers correctly, and if $y = 22$, what is the least possible value for x such that Wallace will be eligible for the job?

ALGEBRA WORKSHEET 2

[NO-CALCULATOR SECTION: 1-15 MULTIPLE-CHOICE / 16-20 GRID-IN]:

6.

$$T = 2\pi\sqrt{\frac{m}{k}}$$

The formula above gives the period, T, of a spring in motion, where m is the mass of the spring and k is the force constant. Which of the following gives k in terms of T and m?

A) $k = \dfrac{4\pi m}{T^2}$

B) $k = \dfrac{4\pi^2 m}{T^2}$

C) $k = \dfrac{T^2}{4\pi m}$

D) $k = \dfrac{T^2}{4\pi^2 m}$

14. At a fair, red tickets are good for rides and blue tickets are good for carnival games. Red tickets cost r dollars and blue tickets cost b dollars. The difference between the cost of 5 red tickets and 10 blue tickets is \$15. Which of the following equations could be used to find possible costs for the two types of tickets?

A) $r - b = 15$

B) $\dfrac{5r}{10b} = 15$

C) $|5r - 10b| = 15$

D) $|10r - 5b| = 15$

Continued →

15.

$$T = 20t - 10$$

The equation above gives the temperature T, in °C, of a convection oven over time t, in minutes. If the relationship between temperature and time is graphed on a coordinate plane where T is the vertical axis and t is the horizontal axis, what does the slope of the line represent?

A) The increase in temperature per minute

B) The total increase in temperature after 20 minutes

C) The number of minutes it takes the oven to increase 20°C

D) The temperature of the oven when $t = 0$

18. A used book store sells softcover books for $2 each and hardcover books for $5 each. If on Monday the store sold 150 books and made $420 on the book sales, how many softcover books did the store sell on Monday?

[CALCULATOR SECTION: 1–30 MULTIPLE CHOICE / 31-38 GRID-IN]:

4. If $q = -10$, then $-q^2 + q - 100 = ?$

A) −210
B) −200
C) −190
D) 110

7. Which of the following is equivalent to $\dfrac{x + x}{x}$?

A) 2
B) x
C) $2x$
D) $2x^2$

Continued →

16. Which of the following lines has the largest slope?

    A) $y = 2x + 4$
    B) $y = 4x + 2$
    C) $2y = 4x + 4$
    D) $2y = 6x + 2$

17. A boat sits in still water off the coast of an island with two lighthouses. The light from the first lighthouse is visible every 21 seconds and the light from the second lighthouse is visible every 60 seconds. If the captain of the boat sees the lights from both lighthouses at the same time, how many seconds will pass before he again sees the lights at the same time?

    A) 120
    B) 210
    C) 420
    D) 840

18. If $\sqrt{x-3} - 3 = 3$, then $x = $?

    A) 3
    B) 7
    C) 36
    D) 39

27. Which of the following inequalities is represented by the graph below?

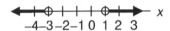

    A) $|x+1| < 3$
    B) $|x+1| > 3$
    C) $|x+1| > 2$
    D) $|x+1| < 2$

29. Let x be a positive 2-digit number with a tens digit a and units digit b. If y is the 2-digit number formed by reversing the digits of x, which of the following is equal to $x + y$?

    A) $11|a-b|$
    B) $11|b-a|$
    C) $a + b$
    D) $11(a + b)$

Continued →

30. For all real numbers x and y, if the sum of 10 and x is y, which of the following expressions represents the product of 10 and x in terms of y?

A) $10y + 100$
B) $10y - 100$
C) $y + 100$
D) $y - 100$

ALGEBRA WORKSHEET 3

7.

$$2\sqrt{y} = 12$$
$$x - 2\sqrt{y} = 12$$

If (x, y) is a solution of the system of equations above, what is the value of x?

A) 0
B) 12
C) 24
D) 36

12. If $x - y = -8$, then $\sqrt{2y - 2x} = ?$

A) $2\sqrt{2}$

B) $4\sqrt{2}$

C) 4

D) 8

17. A ring-toss game at an arcade calculates each player's score in points, y, based on the number of successful "ringers," x. If $y = x + 5$, how many additional ringers are needed for each extra point in the game?

Continued →

18. Lorenzo completes the same puzzle two times. He completes the puzzle 20 minutes faster the second time than the first time. If the total time he spent completing the two puzzles was 3 hours, how long, in <u>minutes</u>, did he spend completing the second puzzle?

| | | | | | |

[CALCULATOR SECTION: 1–30 MULTIPLE CHOICE / 31-38 GRID-IN]:

2. The total cost to hire a web service company is $50.00 for each day plus 75¢ for each customer click on a keyword. What is the total cost, in dollars, to hire this company for 30 days if a total of 2,500 keywords are clicked?

A) (50)(30) + (0.75)(2,500)
B) (50)(30) + (75)(2,500)
C) (50)(2,500) + (0.75)(30)
D) (50)(2,500) + (75)(2,500)

4. The five consecutive integers below add up to 115.

$$x - 3, x - 2, x - 1, x, x + 1$$

What is the value of x?

A) 21
B) 22
C) 23
D) 24

12. Which of the following is equivalent to $a(a + a) - a(a + a - 1)$?

A) $-a$
B) $-4a^2 - a$
C) $-2a^2 - a$
D) a

Continued →

13. A car rental company charges $25.00 per day to rent a car plus 25¢ per mile driven. Which of the following expressions represents the cost, in dollars, to drive a rented car m miles per day for d days?

A) $25.00(d + m)$
B) $25.00d(1 + m)$
C) $25.00d + 0.25m$
D) $25.00d + 0.25md$

17. Which of the following could be the equation for the graph of the line shown in the xy-plane below?

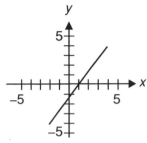

A) $y = -\frac{4}{3}$
B) $y = -\frac{4}{3}x + \frac{4}{3}$
C) $y = -\frac{4}{3}x - \frac{4}{3}$
D) $y = \frac{4}{3}x - \frac{4}{3}$

24.

$$d + 0.66t = 20$$

Charlotte is driving from Boston to Concord, Massachusetts. She uses the equation above to approximate the distance d, in miles, remaining in her trip t minutes after she has left Boston. Which of the following is the best interpretation of the number 20 in this context?

A) The initial speed, in miles per minute.
B) The distance, in miles, between Boston and Concord.
C) The speed, in miles per minute, t minutes after leaving Boston.
D) The decrease in distance remaining in the trip, in miles, for each minute after leaving Boston.

Continued →

27. A company wants to buy phones for its employees. Employee executives will get smart phones at a cost of $250 each and regular employees will get flip phones at a cost of $50 each. If the company spends $4,000 on a total 40 phones, and every employee gets a phone, how many more regular employees than executives work at the company?

A) 20
B) 25
C) 30
D) 35

28. Patrick's basketball team has won 8 of its first 16 games. What is the minimum number of additional games his team must play to raise its win percentage to 80%?

A) 4
B) 8
C) 16
D) 24

Continued →

30. Art plays a quiz game with two types of questions: easy questions and hard questions. Easy questions score 2.5 points each, and hard questions score 4.5 points each. Art's goal is to score at least 160 points and correctly answer at least twice as many hard questions as easy questions. If a is the number of easy questions Art answers correctly and b is the number of hard questions Art answers correctly, which of the following systems of inequalities could be used to determine the minimum number of hard questions Art would need to answer correctly to meet his goal?

A) $2.5a + 4.5b \geq 160$
$2b \geq a$

B) $2.5a + 4.5b \geq 160$
$b \geq 2a$

C) $2.5a + 9b \geq 160$
$b \geq 2a$

D) $2.5a + 9b \geq 160$
$2b \geq a$

V

ADVANCED ALGEBRA

The topics covered in this chapter include factoring and working with polynomials. Many of these problems can be solved using the Pick Tricks (see Chapter IV), but often the algebraic approaches taught in this chapter are faster. You will learn techniques that will help on some of the SAT's harder algebra questions.

SKIP THIS CHAPTER?

Many of the problems in this chapter are quite difficult. In fact, some students might choose to skip this chapter altogether. If you're comfortable with the material in the Algebra chapter, you'll be in good shape for most algebra-based questions on the test. And, as stated above, the Pick Tricks will often allow you to solve Advanced Algebra questions. But for students looking for high scores, the material in this chapter is important.

1. FACTORING

There are only four types of *factoring* you need to be familiar with for the SAT:

1. Common factors
2. Factoring quadratics
3. Difference of two squares
4. Grouping method

COMMON FACTORS

First, some terminology:

- **Term:** a product of numbers and/or variables, such as $4x$ or $\frac{1}{2}x^2$

- **Coefficient:** a number multiplied by the variable component of a term, such as 4 in $4x$

- **Expression:** one or more terms added or subtracted together, such as $4x + \frac{1}{2}x^2$

If you are solving a difficult equation, always check to see if you can pull a common factor out of every term of an expression. This may sound complicated, but the method is fairly straightforward and is best displayed with examples:

Factor the following expressions:

$$\text{(EX)} \quad \frac{1}{2}x^2 + 4x =$$

1. $20q^2 - 40q =$

$$\text{(EX)} \quad 12a^3b - 6a^2b^2 =$$

2. $2x^2y + 3xy^2 =$

 Look for difficult equations that have common factors in every term on one side of the equal sign.

SOLVING EQUATIONS BY FACTORING

Factoring will often help you solve an otherwise difficult equation. First, remember that whenever the product of two expressions equals zero, either the first expression equals zero or the second expression equals zero (or they both do). This is called the *Zero Product Theorem*:

If $a \cdot b = 0$, then $a = 0$ or $b = 0$

For example, if $x(\frac{1}{2}x + 4) = 0$, then $x = 0$ or $(\frac{1}{2}x + 4) = 0$. If you solve the second equation for x, you'll get $x = -8$. So the solutions are: $x = 0$ or $x = -8$.

The following method is useful on many *common factor* problems:

1. For most of these problems, add or subtract terms so that one expression equals zero (all terms on one side of the equal sign).
2. Factor out common factors.
3. Set each new expression equal to zero and solve (as explained by the Zero Product Theorem). These solutions are sometimes called "zeros" because the original expression equals zero when any of the solutions are plugged in.

(EX) If $x^2 + 9x = 0$, then what is the <u>sum</u> of the possible values of x?

A) −9
B) −3
C) 3
D) 9

Try the following lesson problem:

14. If $x^2 = 4x$, which of the following is a possible value of $x - 4$?

A) −4
B) −2
C) 2
D) 4

FACTORING QUADRATICS

INTEGER SOLUTIONS / $a = 1$

Quadratics usually take the form $ax^2 + bx + c = 0$, where a, b, and c are coefficients. When the leading coefficient is $a = 1$, you can usually solve the quadratic "by hand," using the method below. If you are unfamiliar with factoring quadratics, read over the following method carefully (follow along with the example):

1. Set the quadratic equal to zero with the *x-squared term* (x^2) first and the *number term* (no x) last.
2. Find two numbers that *multiply* to the number term. If necessary, use a *factor table* to find the pairs of factors (see Basic Mathematical Concepts), but don't forget about negative numbers, as well.
3. The factor pair from step 2 that *adds* to the coefficient of the *x-term* is the correct pair.
4. Write the quadratic in a factored form (see example).
5. Solve for x using the Zero Product Theorem.

(EX) Factor $x^2 - 7x + 10 = 0$ and solve for x.

 Look for quadratics ($ax^2 + bx + c = 0$) where $a = 1$. Most of the time these quadratics can be solved "by hand," without using the quadratic formula.

Factor the following quadratics and solve for x.

1. $x^2 + 5x = -6$

3. $x^2 + 4x = 21$

2. $x^2 - 12x + 12 = -8$

4. $x^2 + 22x - 23 = 0$

THE QUADRATIC FORMULA ($a \neq 1$ OR NON-INTEGER SOLUTIONS)

When $a \neq 1$, or if the quadratic cannot be factored using the method above (usually because the solutions aren't integers), you might have to use the *quadratic formula*. Here's the formula for a quadratic equation of the form $ax^2 + bx + c = 0$:

$$\boxed{\text{FLASH CARDS}} \quad x = \frac{-b \pm \sqrt{b^2 - 4ac}}{2a}$$

The expression within the square root ($b^2 - 4ac$, called the *discriminant*) offers some useful information:

- If $b^2 > 4ac$, then the quadratic equation has 2 *real* solutions (since you'll be taking the square root of a positive number).
- If $b^2 = 4ac$, then the quadratic equation has 1 real solution ($b^2 - 4ac = 0$).
- If $b^2 < 4ac$, then the quadratic equation has 2 *imaginary* solutions (since you'll be taking the square root of a negative number—we'll cover imaginary numbers in the Odds & Ends chapter).

 Look for quadratics ($ax^2 + bx + c = 0$) where $a \neq 1$ or the solutions are not integers (often you can check the answer choices for non-integer solutions).

DIFFERENCE OF TWO SQUARES

A *square* is just a number or variable (or term) that has been squared. Some examples of squares are: 16 (square of 4), x^2 (square of x), and $36y^4$ (square of $6y^2$). Expressions that are a *difference* (subtraction) of two squares can be factored using the following formula:

$$a^2 - b^2 = (a + b)(a - b)$$

 To identify these problems, look for an expression that is a difference of squared items. Note that these squared items can be numbers, variables, terms, or expressions.

(EX) If $(x - 4)^2 - (4x)^2 = 0$, what is the <u>product</u> of the possible values for x? **[NO CALCULATOR]**

A) $-\dfrac{7}{15}$

B) $-\dfrac{8}{15}$

C) $-\dfrac{11}{15}$

D) $-\dfrac{16}{15}$

GROUPING METHOD

If you're comfortable with identifying common factors, the grouping method is straightforward. You'll use this method when you have <u>four</u> terms to factor. Here's the method (as always, follow along with the example):

1. Add parentheses around the first two terms and the last two terms. Caution: If the middle operation is subtraction, you'll have to change the sign of the last term after adding the parentheses.
2. Factor each parenthetical expression by finding a common factor.
3. After factoring, you should have a common expression. Factor this expression (as you would if it were a common term).

$$ax - 2a + bx - 2b = 0$$

If a and b are positive integers, for what value of x is the equation above true? **[NO CALCULATOR]**

A) 0
B) 2
C) 4
D) 6

If you have to factor an expression with four terms, such as: ax – 2a + bx – 2b, the grouping method is usually the way to go.

FACTORS AND ROOTS

As discussed earlier (Zero Product Theorem), when an equation is factored, each part can be used to find a zero, or *root*, of the equation. For example, the polynomial $f(x) = x^3 + 6x^2 - x - 30$ factors as follows (trust us):

$$f(x) = (x - 2)(x + 3)(x + 5).$$

If we set the function equal to zero and use the Zero Product Theorem, we find the roots 2, –3, and –5. In the Graphs of Functions chapter, we'll learn that these values are the actual points where a function crosses the *x*-axis (see below):

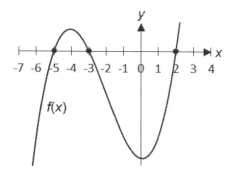

Here's a lesson problem that tests factors and roots:

11. If the polynomial $ax^3 + bx^2 + cx + d$, where *a*, *b*, *c*, and *d* are constants, has roots –1, 0, and 2, which of the following could be the factored form of the polynomial?

    A) $x(x + 1)(x - 2)$
    B) $x(x - 1)(x + 2)$
    C) $(x + 1)(x - 2)$
    D) $(x - 1)(x + 2)$

[NO-CALCULATOR SECTION: 1-15 MULTIPLE-CHOICE / 16-20 GRID-IN]:

8. Which of the following gives all the solutions of $x^2 - 2x = 35$?

    A) –5 and 7
    B) –7 and 5
    C) –2 and 0
    D) 0 and 2

Continued →

10. If $x^3 + x^2 = 0$, which of the following is the <u>sum</u> of the possible values of x?

    A) -3
    B) -2
    C) -1
    D) 0

14. If $\dfrac{x^{3a^3}}{x^{3a^2 b}} = 1$ and $a - b = 2$, what is the value of b?

    A) -4
    B) -2
    C) 0
    D) 2

15. Which of the following is a quadratic equation that has $\dfrac{1}{3}$ as its only solution?

    A) $9x^2 - 6x + 1 = 0$
    B) $9x^2 + 6x + 1 = 0$
    C) $9x^2 + 6x - 3 = 0$
    D) $9x^2 - 1 = 0$

Continued →

7. Which of the following equations has both $x = 3$ and $x = -4$ as solutions?

    A) $(x - 3)(x + 4) = 0$
    B) $(x + 3)(x - 4) = 0$
    C) $x + 3 = x - 4$
    D) $x - 3 = x + 4$

17. What is the solution set of the equation below?

$$\sqrt{a+7} = a+5$$

    A) $\{-6, -3, -2\}$
    B) $\{-6, -4\}$
    C) $\{-6, -3\}$
    D) $\{-3\}$

23. If $a^2 - ka + 6 = (a - 3)(a - 2)$, then $k = ?$

    A) 1
    B) 3
    C) 5
    D) 6

2. WORKING WITH POLYNOMIALS

A *polynomial* is the sum of a one or more terms of the form ax^n, where a is a coefficient and n is a whole number. Here are some examples of polynomials:

- -5
- $-5x$
- $-5x^2 + 4x - 3$

 This section covers problems that involve adding, subtracting or multiplying polynomials, as described above.

DEGREE OF A POLYNOMIAL

The *degree* of a polynomial is the greatest power (exponent) of any term of the polynomial:

- The degree of $-5x$ is 1.
- The degree of $-5x^2 + 4x - 3$ is 2.

COMPARING POLYNOMIALS

When two polynomials are equal, the coefficients of variables raised to the same power will also be equal. For example, in the following equation $a = d$, $b = e$, and $c = f$:

$$ax^2 + bx + c = dx^2 + ex + f$$

This is best explained with an example. Follow the steps below:

1. First simplify both sides of the equation so that the polynomials are arranged in decreasing powers for x.

2. Now, compare coefficients. To put it algebraically, if $ax^n = bx^n$, then $a = b$.

(EX) If $x(2x^2 + 3x) = ax^3 + bx^2 + cx + d$, where a, b, c, and d are constants, what is the value of b? [NO CALCULATOR]

A) 6
B) 3
C) 2
D) 0

Of course, these questions can get more difficult. Try the following lesson problem:

15. If $(x + 4)(x - a) = x^2 + bx + b + 2$, what is a? **[NO CALCULATOR]**

   A) -2

   B) $-\dfrac{1}{2}$

   C) 0

   D) 2

OPERATIONS WITH POLYNOMIALS

ADDITION/SUBTRACTION

Adding and subtracting polynomials is just a matter of combining like terms. For example, $2x^2 + 3x^2 = 5x^2$. Go back to the Basic Algebra section if you need to review this topic.

MULTIPLICATION

You're probably already comfortable using *FOIL*. It's an important part of working with quadratics (see the last section). To *FOIL*, multiple *F*irst terms, *O*uter terms, *I*nner terms, and *L*ast terms, and then add these products. For example:

$$(x + y)^2 = (x + y)(x + y) = x^2 + xy + xy + y^2 = x^2 + 2xy + y^2$$

You won't always multiply two *binomials*, as above, but the process is similar:

1. Multiply the first term of the first polynomial by every term of the second polynomial.

2. Multiply the second term of the first polynomial by every term of the second polynomial. And so on . . .

3. Add up the resulting products (combine like terms).

Try the lesson problem below:

9. Which of the following is equivalent to $(2x - 1)(x^2 + 2x - 3)$? **[NO CALCULATOR]**

    A) $x^2 + 4x - 4$
    B) $2x^2 + 4x + 3$
    C) $2x^3 + 4x^2 - 6x + 3$
    D) $2x^3 + 3x^2 - 8x + 3$

DIVISION

Some of the most difficult problems on the SAT will involve polynomial *division*. We'll cover this topic in the the next section.

[NO-CALCULATOR SECTION: 1-15 MULTIPLE-CHOICE / 16-20 GRID-IN]:

2.

$$(x^2y + 3x) - (2x^2y - 3y)$$

Which of the following is equivalent to the expression above?

A) $-x^2y + 3x + 3y$
B) $-x^2y + 6x$
C) $-3x^2y + 3xy$
D) $-3x^2y + 3x + 3y$

11. If $a^2 - ka + 6 = (a - 3)(a - 2)$, then $k = $?

    A) 1
    B) 3
    C) 5
    D) 6

Continued →

12. What binomial must be subtracted from $2x^2 + 7x - 14$ so that the difference is $x^2 - 14$?

A) $x^2 + 7$
B) $x^2 - 7$
C) $x^2 + 7x$
D) $x^2 - 7x$

15. If $2x^2 + a^2x - b^2x = 2(x^2 + 5x)$ and $a + b = 5$, what is the value of $a - b$?

A) -2
B) 0
C) 2
D) 4

3. POLYNOMIAL DIVISION

In this section, we'll cover polynomial long division and the related topic of *synthetic* division.

LONG DIVISION

Before covering polynomial division, let's review basic long division. First, some terminology:

- **divisor**: a number or quantity to be divided into another number or quantity (in the example below, the divisor is 2).
- **dividend**: the number or quantity divided by the divisor (in the example below, the dividend is 7).
- **quotient**: the integer part of the result of a division problem (in the example below, the quotient is 3).
- **remainder**: the portion of the dividend that is not evenly divisible by the divisor.

(EX)
$$2\overline{)7}^{\;3}$$
$-\underline{6} \quad \leftarrow\ 3 \times 2$
$\quad 1 \quad \leftarrow\ \text{remainder } (7 - 6)$

So, $7 \div 2 =$ **3 with a remainder of 1**

REMAINDER AS A FRACTION

The remainder will usually be expressed as a fraction, more specifically as "the fraction of the divisor that did not go evenly into the dividend." This sounds harder than it is. Just remember this equation:

$$\text{fraction} = \frac{\text{remainder}}{\text{divisor}}$$

The solution to a long division problem will be the quotient plus this fraction. In the example above, the fraction is ½ (remainder = 1; divisor = 2). So, $7 \div 2 = 3 + \tfrac{1}{2} = $ **3½**.

POLYNOMIAL LONG DIVISION

The steps for polynomial long division follow those of basic long division. Make sure to follow along with the example that follows the method:

1. First, set up the problem as long division. Make sure both polynomials are written with decreasing powers from left to right (standard form), including any terms with coefficients of 0. The denominator (bottom polynomial) is the divisor. The numerator (top polynomial) is the dividend.
2. Focus on the *first terms* of both the divisor and the dividend. Divide the dividend's first term by the divisor's first term. Write the quotient above the "divided by" line.

3. Multiply the quotient and the divisor, and write the product beneath the dividend. **Make sure to keep like terms lined up vertically.**

4. Subtract, as you would with numerical long division. The resulting difference is the new "dividend."

5. Repeat steps 2–4 until you have a remainder (or zero).

(EX) The expression $\dfrac{x^2 + 5x + 5}{x + 1}$ is equivalent to which of the following? [**NO CALCULATOR**]

A) $x + 4 + \dfrac{1}{x + 1}$

B) $x + 4 + \dfrac{5}{x + 1}$

C) $x^2 + 4x + \dfrac{1}{x + 1}$

D) $x^2 + 10$

THE PICK TRICKS (A REMINDER)

Could you use the Pick Numbers (type 1) technique on the example above? Absolutely! The Pick Tricks can be used on many, if not most, of these Advanced Algebra problems. Use whatever technique you're most comfortable with.

REPRESENTATION WITH FUNCTIONS

Make sure you're comfortable with how polynomial division, in this case $f(x) \div g(x)$, is represented with functions, where $q(x)$ is the quotient polynomial:

$$\frac{f(x)}{g(x)} = q(x) + \frac{\text{remainder}}{g(x)}$$

Note that when the divisor $g(x)$ divides evenly into the dividend $f(x)$, the remainder will be 0. In other words, $g(x)$ is a *factor* of $f(x)$.

When dividing polynomials, use the technique above, with two exceptions: (1) always check to see if the polynomials can be factored, which may allow you to cancel expressions, and (2) when the divisor is of the form $x - a$, you may choose to use synthetic division (see below).

SYNTHETIC DIVISION

In the special case when the divisor is a polynomial of the form **x – a**, where *a* is a real number, you can use a technique called *synthetic division*. Most students find this approach easier than polynomial division.

 You can use synthetic division when the divisor is of the form **x – a**.

Here are the steps:

1. First, make sure the coefficients of the dividend are in descending order, as usual, and include 0 if any degrees of *x* are missing. Write these coefficients on row 1 of a table. To the left of this row, write *a* (from the divisor: *x* – *a*). See the example below.

    Caution: make sure you write *a*, not –*a*. This is a common error. For example, if the divisor is *x* – 2, then *a* = 2. If the divisor is *x* + 2, then *a* = –2. You might just remember that the sign of *a* is the opposite of the sign in the divisor.

2. Drop the first coefficient to the "total row." Multiply this value by *a*, and record the product under the second coefficient, in row 2.

3. Add the second coefficient and the product from step 2. Write the result in the total row. (Make sure you're following along with the example below.)

4. Repeat steps 2 and 3 for all coefficients. The last result in the total row, under the last coefficient of the dividend, is the <u>remainder</u>. The next number to the left is the *number* term of the quotient polynomial. The next number is the coefficient of the *x*-term of the quotient polynomial. The next is the coefficient of the x^2-term. And so on.

(EX) In the polynomial $x^3 + 10x^2 + 29x + c$, *c* is a constant. If the polynomial is divisible by *x* + 4, what is the value of *c*? **[NO CALCULATOR]**

A) 10
B) 16
C) 20
D) 24

REMAINDER AND FACTOR THEOREMS

While synthetic (or long) division gives you the entire quotient and remainder of a polynomial division problem, sometimes you only need to worry about finding the *remainder*. Use the following theorem:

Remainder Theorem: When a polynomial $f(x)$ is divided by a binomial $x - a$, the remainder will equal $f(a)$, that is, $f(a) = $ **remainder**.

This theorem is convenient because you can find the remainder (and *only* the remainder!) of a polynomial division problem without going through all the steps of polynomial or synthetic division. For example, suppose a question asks you to find the remainder of the following division problem: $\dfrac{x^2 + 5x + 5}{x + 1}$. Note that the denominator is a binomial in $x - a$ form ($a = -1$), so we *could* find the remainder using synthetic division:

$$\begin{array}{r|rrr} -1| & 1 & 5 & 5 \leftarrow x^2 + 5x + 5 \\ & & -1 & -4 \\ \hline & 1 & 4 & 1 \leftarrow \text{The remainder is 1.} \end{array}$$

But the faster approach is to use the Remainder Theorem:

(EX) If $f(x) = x^2 + 5x + 5$ and $g(x) = x + 1$, what is the remainder when $f(x)$ is divided by $g(x)$?

A) −1
B) 0
C) 1
D) 5

The Remainder Theorem leads to another theorem, the Factor Theorem:

Factor Theorem: When a binomial $x - a$ is a factor of a polynomial $f(x)$, then $f(a) = 0$. In other words, when $f(x)$ is divided by a factor in the form $x - a$, the remainder will be 0.

We'll test the Factor Theorem in the following homework assignment.

POLYNOMIAL DIVISION LESSON PROBLEMS

[NO-CALCULATOR SECTION: **1-15 MULTIPLE-CHOICE / 16-20 GRID-IN**]:

15. The expression $\dfrac{x^2 + 3}{x^2 + 2}$ is equivalent to which of the following?

A) $\dfrac{1}{2}$

B) $\dfrac{3}{2}$

C) $\dfrac{x^2}{x^2 - 1}$

D) $1 + \dfrac{1}{x^2 + 2}$

[CALCULATOR SECTION: **1–30 MULTIPLE-CHOICE / 31–38 GRID-IN**]:

28. If a polynomial $p(x)$ has a remainder of 5 when divided by the expression $x + 1$, which of the following must be true?

A) $\dfrac{p(x)}{x+1} = 5$

B) $p(x) = x + 6$

C) $p(1) = 5$

D) $p(-1) = 5$

[NO-CALCULATOR SECTION: **1-15 MULTIPLE-CHOICE / 16-20 GRID-IN**]:

5. The function f is defined as a polynomial. If $f(0) = 2$, $f(1) = 1$ and $f(3) = 0$, which of the following must be a factor of $f(x)$?

A) $x - 3$
B) $x - 2$
C) $x - 1$
D) $x + 3$

Continued →

14. If $p(x) = 8x^3 + 125$ and $q(x) = 2x + 5$, which of the following is equivalent to $\dfrac{p(x)}{q(x)}$?

A) $4x^2 + 25$
B) $4x^2 - 10x + 25$
C) $4x^2 + 20x + 100$
D) $4x^3 - 10x^2 + 25$

[CALCULATOR SECTION: 1–30 MULTIPLE-CHOICE / 31–38 GRID-IN]:

15.

$$x^3 - x^2 + ax + b = 0$$

In the equation above, a and b are constants. If the equation is true when $x = 2, 3,$ or -4, which of the following is a factor of $x^3 - x^2 + ax + b$?

A) $x + 2$
B) $x + 3$
C) $x - 4$
D) $x + 4$

30.

$$x^2 - bx + 2$$

In the polynomial above, b is a constant. When the polynomial is divided by $x + 1$, the remainder is 5. What is the value of b?

A) -1
B) 0
C) 2
D) 3

4. COMMON DENOMINATORS

The SAT likes to test your ability to add or subtract fractions with variable expressions in the denominators. As with numerical fractions, you'll have to find the *common denominator* (see Chapter I). These questions also typically test your factoring skills, so review the Factoring section in this chapter if necessary.

 Common Denominator questions involve adding or subtracting fractions with variable expressions in the denominators.

The method below is usually the fastest way to solve these kinds of problems. Follow along with the example below:

1. Make sure any variable expressions in the denominators are completely factored.
2. Find the maximum number of times each factor shows up in any one denominator. Multiply these factors to find the least common denominator (LCD). (If there are any separate integers in the denominators, include the *least common multiple* of these numbers. See Chapter I if you need a refresher on LCMs.)
3. Multiply each fraction (or expression) in the equation by the LCD. This should allow you to cancel all denominators.
4. Finally, combine like terms, and solve using algebra or the Zero Product Theorem.

(EX) What is the solution to the equation $\dfrac{2}{x-1} - \dfrac{3}{x+1} = \dfrac{1}{x^2-1}$, where $x > 1$? **[NO CALCULATOR]**

ADDING/SUBTRACTING FRACTIONS

For some problems you might have to simply add or subtract the fractions after finding the common denominator, as you would with numerical fractions:

$$\frac{A}{C} \pm \frac{B}{C} = \frac{A \pm B}{C}$$

Here's the method:

1. Find the common denominator of the fractions, as described above.
2. For each fraction, multiply the numerator and denominator by whatever value will give you the common denominator.
3. Add or subtract the fractions.

(EX) Which of the following is equivalent to the expression $\dfrac{x^2+6}{3x^2}$, where $x \neq 0$? [NO CALCULATOR]

A) 2

B) $2\dfrac{1}{3}$

C) $\dfrac{1}{3x}+\dfrac{2}{x^2}$

D) $\dfrac{1}{3}+\dfrac{2}{x^2}$

COMMON DENOMINATOR LESSON PROBLEM

[NO-CALCULATOR SECTION: 1-15 MULTIPLE-CHOICE / 16-20 GRID-IN]:

12. If $x \neq 0$, what is the sum of the possible solutions to the equation $\dfrac{1}{x}-\dfrac{1}{x^2}-\dfrac{1}{x^3}=-1$

A) −3
B) −2
C) −1
D) 0

14. If the equation $\dfrac{x^2 - x + 1}{x + 3} = x + a - \dfrac{2x - 7}{x + 3}$ is true for all values of $x \neq -3$, where a is a constant, what is the value of a?

A) −2
B) −1
C) 0
D) 1

19.

$$\frac{3}{t^2 - 7t + 10} - \frac{1}{2} = \frac{4}{t - 5}$$

In the equation above, t is an odd number and $t \neq 5$. If t is the solution to the equation, what is the value of t?

5. ADVANCED ALGEBRA: PRACTICE & CORRECTIONS

PRACTICE PROBLEMS

The following worksheet tests techniques taught in this chapter. In addition, we'll use Practice Test 1 from *The Official SAT Study Guide* for more practice questions. Don't forget to look back to the lessons in this chapter and review the techniques while completing these problems.

- ☐ Advanced Algebra Worksheet
- ☐ Test 1 (practice problems): See the Techniques chapter at the end of this tutorial.

TEST CORRECTIONS

After completing and grading each practice test, you should correct Advanced Algebra questions that you missed or guessed on. Below are the three steps to correcting practice tests:

1. Turn to the Techniques section at the end of this tutorial and circle the Advanced Algebra questions that you missed or guessed on for each test.

2. Correct the problems in *The Official SAT Study Guide*. As you correct the problems, go back to the tutorial and review the techniques. The idea is to (1) identify techniques that have given you trouble, (2) go back to the tutorial so you can review and strengthen these techniques, and (3) apply these techniques to the specific problems on which you struggled.

3. If you have trouble identifying the best technique to use on a problem, refer to the Techniques chapter. This is an important part of correcting the tests.

ADVANCED ALGEBRA WORKSHEET

8.

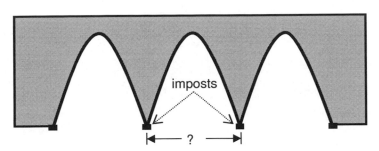

imposts

?

The bridge above is made up of three arches. The height y, in meters, of each arch can be defined by the equation $y = -\dfrac{2}{5}x^2 + 4x$, where x is the distance, in meters, measured from the left impost to the right impost at the base of the arch. If $y = 0$ represents the elevation at the base of the arches, what is the width of each arch, in meters, at its base?

A) 4
B) 10
C) 20
D) 40

13. If $x(5x^2 + 10x - 20) = 0$, which of the following could be true?

    I. $x = 0$
    II. $x = -1 \pm \sqrt{5}$
    III. $x = -5 \pm \sqrt{10}$

A) I only
B) I and II only
C) I and III only
D) II and III only

Continued →

14. If $x \neq 0$ and $y \neq 0$, which of the following is equivalent to $\dfrac{1}{x^2} + \dfrac{1}{y^2} + \dfrac{2}{xy}$?

A) $\dfrac{4}{(x+y)^2}$

B) $\dfrac{4}{x^2 + y^2 + xy}$

C) $\dfrac{x+y}{xy}$

D) $\left(\dfrac{x+y}{xy}\right)^2$

18.

$$x^4 - 25x^2 = -144$$

If $x > 0$, what is one possible solution to the equation above?

19.

$$y = x^2 + x$$
$$y - 12x = -30$$

If (x, y) is a solution of the system of equations above, what is the product of the possible values of x?

20. If $(3x - 3)(ax + 1) + 2x^2 = bx + c$, what is $b + c$?

Continued →

11. For all $x > 4$, $\dfrac{x^2 - 4x}{x^2 + 4x - 32} = ?$

   A) $\dfrac{-x}{x + 8}$

   B) $\dfrac{x}{x + 8}$

   C) $\dfrac{-1}{x + 8}$

   D) $\dfrac{-1}{32}$

27.

$$x^3 + 2x^2 - 16x - 32 = 0$$

If $x > 0$, for what value of x is the equation above true?

   A) 4
   B) 8
   C) 16
   D) 32

29. If $p(x) = -5x^3 + 2x^2 + 7x$, and $\dfrac{p(x)}{q(x)} = -5x^2 + 7x$, then $q(x)$ is equivalent to which of the

following expressions?

   A) $x - 1$
   B) $x + 1$
   C) $x - 2$
   D) $x + 2$

Continued →

37. For polynomials $f(x)$ and $g(x)$, $\dfrac{f(x)}{x-2} = g(x) + \dfrac{R}{x-2}$, where R is a constant. If $f(2) = 5$, what is the value of R?

VI
GRAPHS OF FUNCTIONS

We introduced functions in Chapter III. This chapter discusses topics relating to the *graphs* of functions.

1. GRAPHS OF FUNCTIONS

GRAPHING BASICS

The function $f(x)$ can be represented graphically on an xy-plane. The x-axis represents the values of x (the inputs of the function) and the y-axis represents the values of $f(x)$ (the outputs of the function). There are several characteristics of these graphs that you should be comfortable with. They will be taught using the following graph of $f(x)$:

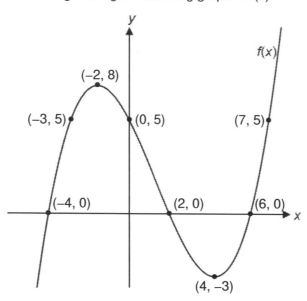

POINTS

Each point on the graph of a function has an x-coordinate and a y-coordinate. Remember, the x-coordinates are the function's *inputs*, and the y-coordinates are the function's *outputs*:

$$(x, y) \Leftrightarrow (x, f(x))$$

(EX) 1. $f(-2) =$

(EX) 2. $f(7) =$

(EX) 3. If $f(x) = 5$, what are the possible values of x?

AXIS INTERCEPTS

The points at which a function crosses (or touches) the x- and y-axes are called *axis intercepts*. The x-intercepts are often called *zeros* or *roots* of the function (see "Factors and Roots" in the Factoring lesson [Advanced Algebra chapter]). There may be more than one x-intercept. A function, however, will never have more than one y-intercept. (You might remember that functions must pass the "vertical-line test"—there can be no more than one intercept for any vertical line; the y-axis, of course, is a vertical line.)

(EX) 4.   What are the roots of $f(x)$?

(EX) 5.   If $x < 0$ and $f(x) = 0$, what is the value of x?

(EX) 6. $f(0) =$

Note: When a function is given, you can find axis intercepts using algebra:
1.   To find the y-intercept, let $x = 0$. Solve for y.
2.   To find the x-intercept(s), let $y = 0$. Solve for x.

POSITIVE/NEGATIVE

A function is positive when $f(x)$ is greater than zero, and negative when $f(x)$ is less than zero. Remember, when we say "$f(x)$," we're talking about the *outputs* of $f(x)$ (the y values).

(EX) 7.   What are the values of x for which $f(x)$ is positive?

(EX) 8.   What are the values of x for which $f(x)$ is negative?

INCREASING/DECREASING

When $f(x)$ slopes up as x increases (in other words, as we move left to right), we say the function is *increasing*. When $f(x)$ slopes down as x increases (again, as we move left to right), we say the function is *decreasing*.

(EX) 9.   What are the values of x for which $f(x)$ is increasing?

(EX) 10. What are the values of x for which $f(x)$ is decreasing?

MAXIMA/MINIMA

Here are some terms you should be comfortable with:
- **maximum**: the value of a function at a certain point that is greater that the values at all other points in the immediate vicinity (also called the **relative maximum**).
- **minimum**: the value of a function at a certain point that is less that the values at all other points in the immediate vicinity (also called the **relative minimum**).
- **absolute maximum**: the largest value for a given function.

- **absolute minimum**: the smallest value for a given function.

Note that the function at the beginning of this lesson does not have an absolute maximum or an absolute minimum, but the relative maxima (one maximum and one minimum) should be easy to spot.

(EX) 11. At which point does $f(x)$ have a relative maximum?

(EX) 12. At which point does $f(x)$ have a relative minimum?

■

Try the following lesson problems:

[NO-CALCULATOR SECTION: **1-15** MULTIPLE-CHOICE / **16-20** GRID-IN]:

10.

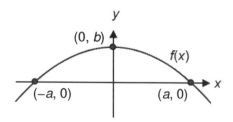

The function f shown above is defined as $f(x) = \dfrac{(x-4)(x+4)}{-8}$. What is the value of b?

A) 2
B) 3
C) 4
D) 8

12. What is the y-intercept of the quadratic function f given by $f(x) = ax^2 + bx + c$ where a, b, and c are different positive integers?

A) a

B) a/c

C) b/c

D) c

Continued →

17. Based on the graph of the function f below, what are the values of x for which $f(x)$ is negative?

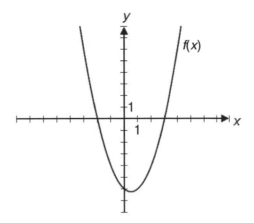

A) $-6 < x < 0$

B) $-\frac{7}{2} \leq x < -2$

C) $-2 < x < 3$

D) $-2 < x < 0$

HW

8. In the xy-plane, the graph of f has x-intercepts only at 2 and -2. Which of the following could define f?

A) $f(x) = x^4 + 16$
B) $f(x) = x^4 - 16$
C) $f(x) = x^4 - 6x^2 + 8$
D) $f(x) = x^4 + 6x^2 + 8$

Continued →

14. In the *xy*-plane, if a function *f* has roots at $x = 5$, -5, and 1, which of the following could define $f(x)$?

A) $f(x) = (x^2 - 5)(x^2 + 5)(x - 1)$
B) $f(x) = (x^2 - 25)(x + 1)$
C) $f(x) = (x^2 + 25)(x - 1)$
D) $f(x) = (x^2 - 25)(x - 1)$

[CALCULATOR SECTION: 1–30 MULTIPLE-CHOICE / 31–38 GRID-IN]:

10. The graph of the piecewise function $f(x)$ in the *xy*-plane is shown below. If $f(x) = -1$, what is the value of x ?

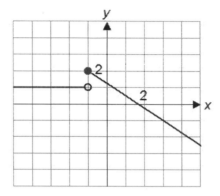

A) −1
B) 1
C) 2
D) 3

Continued →

14.

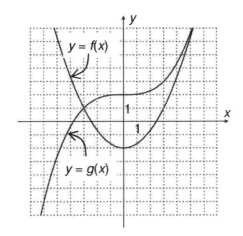

Graphs of functions *f* and *g* are shown in the *xy*-plane above. For which of the following values of *x* does $f(x) - g(x) = 0$

A) −4
B) −3
C) 0
D) 3

27. *ABCD* is a rectangle with one side on the *x*-axis and point *A* on the graph of $f(x)$, as shown in the figure below. If $f(x) = \sqrt{x} + 2$, what is the area of *ABCD*?

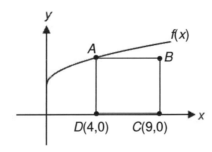

A) 18
B) $6\sqrt{10}$
C) 20
D) $10\sqrt{6}$

Continued →

29. The graph of $f(x)$ is shown below. Which of the following is the graph of $|f(x)|$?

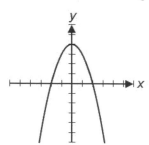

A)

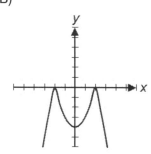

C)

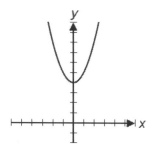

B)

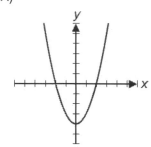

D)

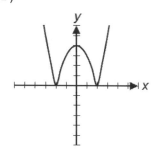

■

All Programs: After correcting all relevant questions from Practice Test 10 and reviewing the tutorial, take Practice Test 9 in *The Official SAT Study Guide*.

2. MORE GRAPHS OF FUNCTIONS

Here are a few more graphs-of-functions topics that may show up on the test.

END BEHAVIOR

End behavior of a polynomial function refers to the behavior of a function as x approaches positive and negative infinity ($\pm\infty$). Of course, we can look at the graph and easily see the end behavior, but you might have to consider end behavior based on a polynomial (without the benefit of a graph). Here are a few rules you should know:

When the degree of a polynomial is *even* and the leading coefficient is *positive*:
   • $x \to \infty,\ f(x) \to \infty$
   • $x \to -\infty,\ f(x) \to \infty$
$f(x) = x^2$

When the degree of a polynomial is *even* and the leading coefficient is *negative*:
   • $x \to \infty,\ f(x) \to -\infty$
   • $x \to -\infty,\ f(x) \to -\infty$
$f(x) = -x^2$	

When the degree of a polynomial is *odd* and the leading coefficient is *positive*:
   • $x \to \infty,\ f(x) \to \infty$
   • $x \to -\infty,\ f(x) \to -\infty$
$f(x) = x^3$
	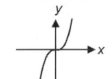

When the degree of a polynomial is *odd* and the leading coefficient is *negative*:
   • $x \to \infty,\ f(x) \to -\infty$
   • $x \to -\infty,\ f(x) \to \infty$
$f(x) = -x^3$	

Try the following lesson problem:

21.

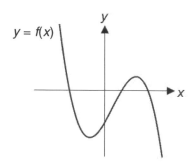

The graph of the function f is shown in the xy-plane above. If a, b, c, and d are positive integers, $f(x)$ could equal which of the following polynomials?

A) $ax^2 + bx - c$
B) $-ax^2 + bx - c$
C) $-ax^3 + bx^2 + cx - d$
D) $ax^3 + bx^2 + cx - d$

DOMAIN AND RANGE

DOMAIN

The *domain* of a function $f(x)$ is the set of allowable *inputs* for a function.

 These problems may mention the word *domain*. They may also ask for the values of x for which $f(x)$ is a real number, or, alternatively, they may ask for the values of x for which $f(x)$ is "undefined."

There are two rules used for finding the domain of a function:

1. **The denominator of a fraction cannot equal zero.**

2. **It is impossible to take the square root (or any *even* root) of a negative number.**

The following rules are used to find the domain of a function:

1. **If there is a variable in the denominator of a fraction, set the entire denominator *not-equal* ($\neq$) to zero.** Solve for the variable. Any values of the variable that make the denominator zero are *not* part of the function's domain.

(EX) What is the domain of $f(x) = \dfrac{25}{x - 25}$?

2. **If there is a variable under an <u>even</u> root ($\sqrt{}$, $\sqrt[4]{}$, $\sqrt[6]{}$ etc.), set the entire expression under the root *greater than or equal* ($\geq$) to zero.** Solve for the variable. These values are the domain of the function. (Note: if the root is *odd*, then negative numbers are allowed.)

(EX) What is the domain of $f(x) = \sqrt{x - 25}$?

3. **If there is a variable under an even root that is in the denominator of a fraction, set the entire expression under the root *greater than* (>) zero.** Solve for the variable. These values are the domain of the function.

(EX) What is the domain of $f(x) = \dfrac{25}{\sqrt{x - 25}}$?

RANGE

The *range* of a function $f(x)$ is the set of all *outputs* of a function. These outputs are the *y* values in the *xy*-plane. Range questions are not very common on the SAT, and the method for finding range is not as straightforward as that for domain. You should, however, be able to recognize the range of a function by looking at the function's graph. Don't forget, you may use your graphing calculator if the function is given. Try the following lesson problem:

10. The graph of the function $f(x) = \dfrac{-1}{x-1} + 2$ is shown below. Which of the following could be the range of the function *f*?

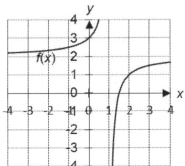

A) $\{y \mid y \neq 1\}$
B) $\{y \mid y \neq 2\}$
C) $\{x \mid x \neq 1\}$
D) $\{x \mid x \neq 2\}$

ASYMPTOTES

An asymptote is a straight line that is approached by a function. The function will never reach the line (in any finite distance). Asymptotes show up when we have *rational expressions*, which are expressions of the form $p(x)/q(x)$, where p and q are polynomial functions. There are two kinds of asymptotes:

VERTICAL ASYMPTOTES

Vertical asymptotes are usually found at the zeros of the denominator, $q(x)$, of a *simplified* rational expression (in other words, at the places where the function $p(x)/q(x)$ is undefined).

Note: Make sure you factor and simplify the rational expression *before* finding vertical asymptotes. Sometimes factors can be canceled, in which case any corresponding zeros will *not* be vertical asymptotes (they are called "holes").

HORIZONTAL ASYMPTOTES

A function approaches a *horizontal asymptote* (when there is one) as x approaches $\pm\infty$. Here are the rules (review *degrees* in the Working with Polynomials section, if necessary):

- If the degree of $p(x)$ is less than the degree of $q(x)$, then the horizontal asymptote is $y = 0$.

  For example: $\dfrac{p(x)}{q(x)} = \dfrac{5x^2 - 6x + 7}{4x^3 - 6x + 7}$ → $(2 < 3)$ → horizontal asymptote: $y = 0$

- If If the degree of $p(x)$ is equal to the degree of $q(x)$, then the horizontal asymptote is the leading coefficient of $p(x)$ divided by the leading coefficient of $q(x)$.

  For example: $\dfrac{p(x)}{q(x)} = \dfrac{5x^2 - 6x + 7}{4x^2 - 6x + 7}$ → $(2 = 2)$ → horizontal asymptote: $y = \dfrac{5}{4}$

- If the degree of $p(x)$ is greater than the degree of $q(x)$, then there is no horizontal asymptote.

  For example: $\dfrac{p(x)}{q(x)} = \dfrac{5x^3 - 6x + 7}{4x^2 - 6x + 7}$ → $(3 > 2)$ → no horizontal asymptote

EVEN AND ODD FUNCTIONS

An *even function* is one where $f(x) = f(-x)$. Below are examples of even functions. Notice that the right and left sides of each function (on either side of the *y*-axis) are mirror images of each other; in other words, the part of the graph to the right of the *y*-axis is *reflected* across the *y*-axis:

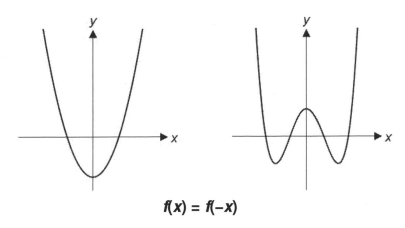

$$f(x) = f(-x)$$

An *odd function* is one where $f(x) = -f(-x)$. Below are examples of odd functions. Notice that the right and left sides of each function (on either side of the y-axis) are *upside-down* mirror images of each other:

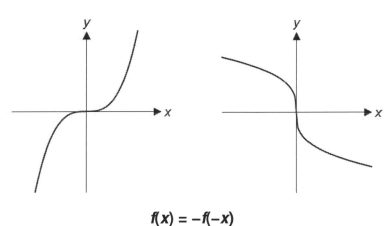

$$f(x) = -f(-x)$$

SYMMETRY

When a function is symmetrical across an axis or a line, it appears to have a mirror image reflected across that axis or line. The quadratic function is a common function that is symmetrical across some vertical line. In the figure below, the line of symmetry is $x = 2$.

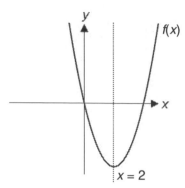

13. The figure above shows a quadratic function f. The vertex of f is (2, −4). If two points (not shown) on f are (−2, 12) and (a, 12) and $a > 0$, what is the value for a?

A) 12
B) 6
C) 4
D) 2

GRAPHING CALCULATOR

If you have a graphing calculator, make sure you are comfortable using its graphing features. If you don't have a graphing calculator, don't worry: no problems on the SAT *require* you to graph functions. But if a function is given, don't be shy. (Note: Make sure to review the calculator guidelines on the SAT website. See the Calculators section in Chapter I.)

TRANSFORMATIONS

Some questions may ask you to identify the effects of a *transformation* on the graph of a function. There are several types of transformations, including movements (translations), reflections, stretches, contractions, and rotations.

REFLECTIONS

As mentioned above, a *reflection* creates a mirror image of a shape across a line (called the *line of reflection*). For example, $\triangle A'B'C'$ is the reflection of $\triangle ABC$ across line l below:

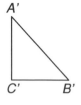 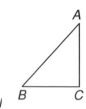

ROTATIONS

A *rotation* spins a shape around some given point. Rotation problems tend to use degrees to tell you how much to spin the shape. For example, point A' below is a 90° clockwise rotation of point A around the point (0,0):

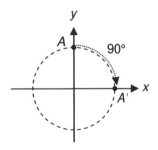

ALGEBRAIC TRANSFORMATIONS

Sometimes, instead of *visually* transforming a graph, as in the examples above, you may have to transform a graph by making changes to the function's *algebraic expression*. If you've covered this in school, the following offers a good review of the material. If you have not yet covered this, you might want to skip this part of the lesson. These algebraic transformations are not common on the SAT.

TRANSFORMATION RULES FOR MOVING (OR TRANSLATING) A FUNCTION

- $f(x) + a$ → moves graph UP *a* units
- $f(x) - a$ → moves graph DOWN *a* units
- $f(x + a)$ → moves graph to the LEFT *a* units
- $f(x - a)$ → moves graph to the RIGHT *a* units

TRANSFORMATION RULES FOR REFLECTING A FUNCTION

- $-f(x)$ → reflects graph across *x*-axis
- $f(-x)$ → reflects graph across *y*-axis

TRANSFORMATION RULES FOR STRETCHING/CONTRACTING A FUNCTION

- $af(x)$, where $a > 1$ → STRETCHES the graph vertically
- $af(x)$, where $0 < a < 1$ → CONTRACTS the graph vertically
- $f(ax)$, where $a > 1$ → CONTRACTS the graph horizontally
- $f(ax)$, where $0 < a < 1$ → STRETCHES the graph horizontally

Transformation questions involve the *movement* (or *translation*), *reflection*, *rotation*, *stretch*, or *contraction* of a graph of a function. *Algebraic* transformations ask about the change in the graph of a function when that function is algebraically changed in some way.

Try the following lesson problem:

28. The graph of $f(x)$ is shown below. Which of the following could be the graph of $-f(x-1)$?

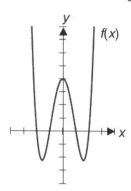

A)

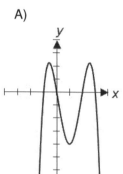

C)

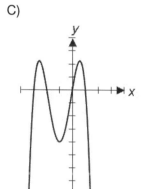

B)

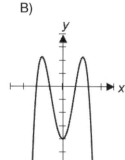

D)

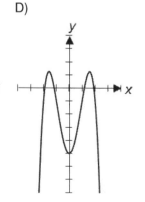

7. In the *xy*-plane, $\triangle ABC$ has vertices $(-2, -2)$, $(-1, 4)$, and $(2, 3)$. Suppose $\triangle ABC$ is transposed 1 unit to the right and 2 units up to form $\triangle A'B'C'$. Which of the following shows the coordinates for the vertices of $\triangle A'B'C'$?

   A) $(0, -1)$, $(0, 6)$, $(4, 5)$
   B) $(0, -1)$, $(1, 5)$, $(4, 5)$
   C) $(-1, 0)$, $(1, 6)$, $(3, 1)$
   D) $(-1, 0)$, $(0, 6)$, $(3, 5)$

12. Which of the following could be the graph of $f(x) = ax^6 + bx^3 + cx + 2$, where a, b, and c are negative integers?

   A)

   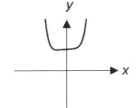

   C)

   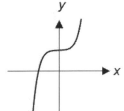

   B)

   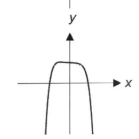

   D)

   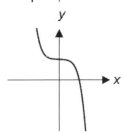

Continued →

18.

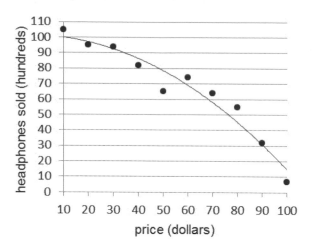

An audio company test-marketed its headphones at different prices. The scatterplot above shows the prices of the headphones and the number of headphones sold at each price. A quadratic model that best fits the data is also shown. In the following equations, y represents hundreds of headphones and x represents dollars. Which equation best models the data in the scatterplot?

A) $y = -0.008x^2 - 0.043x + 101.3$
B) $y = 0.008x^2 - 0.043x + 101.3$
C) $y = -0.008x^2 + 0.043x - 101.3$
D) $y = 0.008x^2 - 0.043x - 101.3$

21. What is the domain of the function f, defined below?

$$f(x) = (x + 2)^{\frac{1}{4}}$$

A) All real numbers
B) $x \geq -2$
C) $x \geq 0$
D) $x \geq \frac{1}{4}$

Continued →

25. The graph of $f(x) = 4\sin(0.5x)$ on the xy-plane is shown below. Which of the following is true?

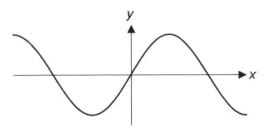

A) $f(x)$ is an even function
B) $f(x)$ is an odd function
C) $f(x)$ is neither even nor odd
D) $f(x)$ is symmetrical about the x-axis

30. The figures below show the graphs of f and g. The function f is defined by $f(x) = x^2 + 2x + 3$. The function g is defined by $g(x) = f(x + h) + k$, where h and k are constants. What is the value of $h - k$?

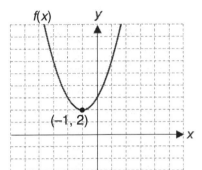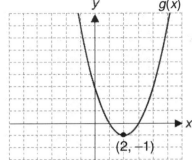

A) -6
B) -3
C) 0
D) 3

3. GRAPHS OF FUNCTIONS: PRACTICE & CORRECTIONS

PRACTICE PROBLEMS

The following worksheet tests techniques taught in this chapter. In addition, we'll use Practice Test 1 from *The Official SAT Study Guide* for more practice questions. Don't forget to review the lessons in this chapter while completing these problems:

- ☐ Graphs of Functions Worksheet
- ☐ Test 1 (practice problems): See the Techniques chapter at the end of this tutorial.

TEST CORRECTIONS

After completing and grading each practice test, you should correct Graphs of Functions questions that you missed or guessed on. Below are the three steps to correcting practice tests:

1. Turn to the Techniques section at the end of this tutorial and circle the Graphs of Functions questions that you missed or guessed on for each test.

2. Correct the problems in *The Official SAT Study Guide*. As you correct the problems, go back to the tutorial and review the techniques. The idea is to (1) identify techniques that have given you trouble, (2) go back to the tutorial so you can review and strengthen these techniques, and (3) apply these techniques to the specific problems on which you struggled.

3. If you have trouble identifying the best technique to use on a problem, refer to the Techniques chapter. This is an important part of correcting the tests.

GRAPHS OF FUNCTIONS WORKSHEET

14. For the function *f*, defined below, what are the values of *x* for which *f*(*x*) is a real number?

$$f(x) = \frac{5}{\sqrt{x+4}}$$

A) $x = -4$
B) $x = 0$
C) $x \geq -4$
D) $x > -4$

6. Point *P* lies in the *xy*-plane and has coordinates (2, 2). Suppose point *P* is translated 4 units to the left, then translated 4 units down, and then reflected across the *y*-axis, forming point *P'*. What are the coordinates of *P'*?

A) (2, 2)
B) (2, –2)
C) (–2, 2)
D) (–2, –2)

8. The graph of *f*(*x*) in the *xy*-plane is shown below. For what value or values of *x*, if any, is *f*(*x*) = 4?

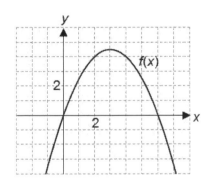

A) 0 and 6 only
B) 2 only
C) 4 only
D) 2 and 4 only

Continued →

9. For which value or values of x is the expression $\dfrac{(x-4)}{(x+3)(x-2)}$ undefined?

   A) 4 only
   B) −3 and 2 only
   C) 3 and −2 only
   D) −3, 2, and 4

10. The graph of $f(x)$ is shown in the xy-plane below. Which of the following is NOT a zero of $f(x)$?

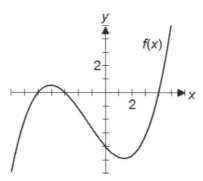

   A) −5
   B) −4
   C) −3
   D) 4

21. The graph of $f(x)$ in the xy-plane, shown below, has roots at −5 and 5, and has a y-intercept at −5. For what real values of x, if any, is $f(x) < 0$?

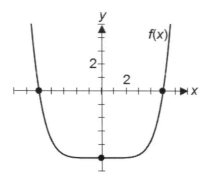

   A) $-5 < x < 5$
   B) $x > -5$
   C) $x < 0$
   D) $x < -5$ or $x > 5$

Continued →

22. The graphs of $f(x)$ and $nf(x)$ are shown in the xy-plane below, where n is a constant. What is a possible value of n?

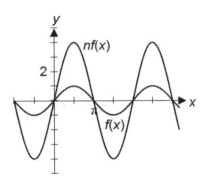

A) −4

B) −1

C) $\dfrac{1}{4}$

D) 4

26. In the standard (x,y) coordinate-plane, the equation of line l is $y = -3x - 4$. If line m is the reflection of line l across the y-axis, what is the equation of line m?

A) $y = 3x + 4$
B) $y = 3x - 4$
C) $y = \frac{3}{4}x - 4$
D) $y = \frac{3}{4}x + 4$

27. If $f(x) = ax^{\frac{1}{3}}$ and point A lies on the graph of $f(x)$ below, what is the value of a?

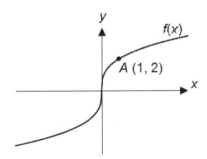

A) $\dfrac{1}{3}$

B) $\dfrac{1}{2}$

C) 2

D) 4

Continued →

28. Which of the following functions in the xy-plane is an even function?

A)

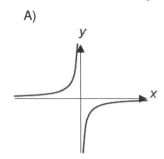

C)

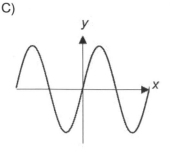

B)

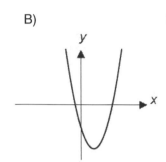

D)

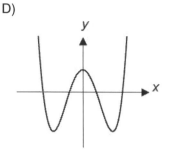

32. In the figure below, $ABCD$ is a square centered on the y-axis. If points B and C lie on the graph of $f(x) = ax^4$, where a is a constant, what is the value of a?

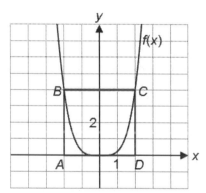

35. In the xy-plane, the point $(2, 0)$ lies on the graph of the function $f(x) = -2x^2 - bx + b^2$. If $b > 0$, what is the value of b?

VII

GEOMETRY

This chapter will cover all relevant geometry topics. Preparing for geometry problems is a matter of familiarizing yourself with the geometry formulas and rules that are tested on the SAT and completing practice problems.

REFERENCE INFORMATION

The SAT (unlike the ACT) provides geometry reference information on the first page of both math sections. You do not need to memorize any of this information (although much of it you probably already know).

! **Note: If a formula in this chapter is <u>not</u> found on the SAT's reference page, you will see a flashcard symbol; memorize these formulas.**

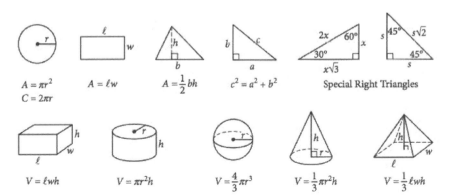

$A = \pi r^2$
$C = 2\pi r$

$A = \ell w$

$A = \frac{1}{2}bh$

$c^2 = a^2 + b^2$

Special Right Triangles

$V = \ell wh$

$V = \pi r^2 h$

$V = \frac{4}{3}\pi r^3$

$V = \frac{1}{3}\pi r^2 h$

$V = \frac{1}{3}\ell wh$

The number of degrees of arc in a circle is 360.
The number of radians of arc in a circle is 2π.
The sum of the measures in degrees of the angles of a triangle is 180.

FIGURES

All figures on the SAT are drawn to scale unless indicated otherwise (in which case they are almost certainly NOT drawn to scale). Feel free to use the scaled figures to help find, or just check, your answers.

1. AREA & PERIMETER

AREA OF A TRIANGLE

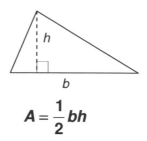

$$A = \frac{1}{2}bh$$

Finding the area of a triangle can be difficult. The base, *b*, can be *any* side of the triangle, not just the lowest and, oftentimes, horizontal side. The height is defined as the *perpendicular distance* from the corner *opposite the base* to the *line containing the base.* The following method will help you find the height of a triangle relative to a given base:

1. **Identify the base.** Note that the base is a *line segment*.

2. **Identify the corner opposite this base.** This is the corner that is *not* an endpoint of the base's line segment.

3. **With your pencil starting on this corner, draw a perpendicular line to the line containing the base.** Sometimes, the height line will intersect the actual base, as in the first example below. Other times, you may have to extend the base's line segment because the height falls *outside* the triangle, as in the second example below. Note that this does not change the length of the base, which is bound by the endpoints of the triangle.

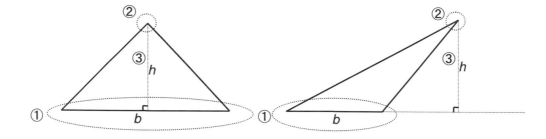

In each drawing below, sketch the height relative to the given base. Note that the bases are different from above.

1. 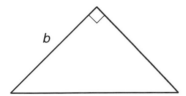   2.

AREA & CIRCUMFERENCE OF A CIRCLE

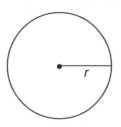

$$A = \pi r^2$$
$$\text{Circumference} = 2\pi r$$

We call the "perimeter" of a circle its *circumference*. If you're worried about remembering which formula is which above, it might help to know that measures of area have "square" units (for example, the size of a house is measured in *square* feet). Thus, the formula for area is the one with the r^2.

AREA OF A PARALLELOGRAM

A *parallelogram* is a four-sided shape (a *quadrilateral*) that has *parallel* and *congruent* (equal-length) opposite sides.

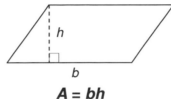

$$A = bh$$

AREA OF A TRAPEZOID

A *trapezoid* is a quadrilateral that has *two* parallel sides.

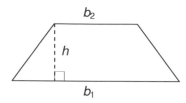

$$A = \left(\frac{b_1 + b_2}{2} \right) h$$

SHADED REGION PROBLEMS

There are two ways to solve shaded region area problems:

1. **Area Cutting**: Cut the shaded region into simpler shapes whose areas you can find, and add up these areas:

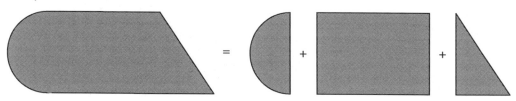

2. **Area Subtracting:** Subtract the areas of known shapes from the total area of the entire figure so that you're left with the shaded area.

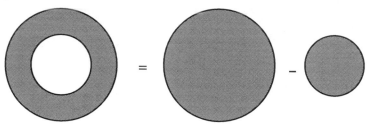

AREA FITTING PROBLEMS

You may be asked to find the the number of small two-dimensional shapes (such as tiles) that can fit onto a larger shape (such as a floor).

 Area fitting problems will ask how many shapes can fit onto or within a larger shape.

The method for area fitting problems is straightforward:

1. Find the areas of the large shape and the small shape.
2. Divide the large area by the small area.

Number of *small areas* that will fit into the *larger area* = $\dfrac{\textbf{Large Area}}{\textbf{Small Area}}$

(EX) How many 24 inch × 24 inch square tiles are needed to cover the 20 foot × 30 foot floor shown below?

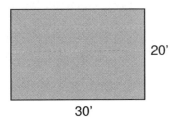

20'

30'

A) 50
B) 100
C) 150
D) 600

PERIMETER

The *perimeter* of a shape is simply the sum of the lengths of each side. We'll see several perimeter problems on the following pages.

AREA & PERIMETER LESSON PROBLEMS

2. The figure below is composed of square *ACDF* and equilateral triangles △*ABC* and △*DEF*. The length of *AF* is 5 inches. What is the perimeter, in inches, of *ABCDEF*?

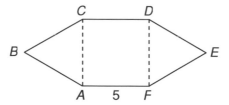

   A) 20
   B) 30
   C) 35
   D) 40

4. If the rectangle below has a perimeter of 20, what is the area of the rectangle?

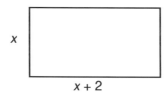

   A) 16
   B) 24
   C) 36
   D) 40

12. A parallelogram, with dimensions in inches, is shown in the diagram below. What is the area, in square inches, of the parallelogram?

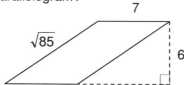

   A) $42\sqrt{85}$
   B) $7\sqrt{85}$
   C) $6\sqrt{85}$
   D) 42

Continued →

20. The figure below is made up of a square with side of length 8 and two semicircles with diameters of length 3. What is the area of the shaded region?

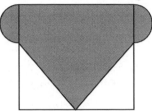

A) $24 + \frac{9}{4}\pi$
B) $24 + \frac{9}{2}\pi$
C) $44 + \frac{9}{4}\pi$
D) $44 + 9\pi$

24. The eight equal semicircles below are placed so that they exactly cover the sides of the square. If the perimeter of the square is 32, what is the area of one of the semicircles?

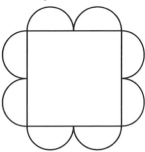

A) 2π
B) 4π
C) 8π
D) 16π

5. In the figure below, the large square is divided into two smaller squares and two rectangles (shaded). If the perimeters of the two smaller squares are 8 and 24, respectively, what is the sum of the perimeters of the two shaded rectangles?

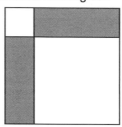

A) 12
B) 16
C) 24
D) 32

14. The equilateral triangle below is formed by connecting the centers of three tangent circles. If the perimeter of the triangle is 12, what is the sum of the circumferences of the three circles?

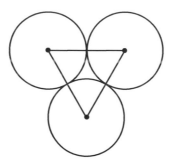

A) 4π
B) 8π
C) 12π
D) 18π

Note: the problem above used the word "**tangent**," which means *touching at exactly one point.* Each circle above touches each of the other circles at exactly one point.

Continued →

21. Square *ABCD* has side of length 8. The width of the border between squares *ABCD* and *EFGH* is 2. What is the area of the shaded region?

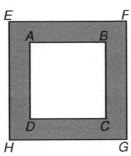

A) 36
B) 40
C) 48
D) 80

23. In the figure below, O is the center of the circle of diameter 12. What is the area of △*AOB* ?

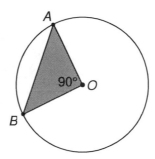

A) 36
B) 18
C) 15
D) 12

Continued →

26. In the figure below, points *A, B, C, D, E, and F* are equally spaced on line segment *AF*. If the sum of the areas of the three circles is 18π, what is the radius of the smaller circle?

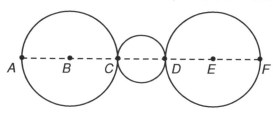

A) 1
B) $\sqrt{2}$
C) 2
D) $2\sqrt{2}$

27. The area of circle *O* is *x* square inches, and the circumference of circle *O* is *y* inches. If *x* = *y*, what is the radius of the circle?

A) 1
B) 2
C) 3
D) 4

29. In the figure below, *ABCD* is a rectangle inscribed in the semicircle with center *O*. If *AD* = 5 and the semicircle has an area of 84.5π, what is the length of segment *AB*?

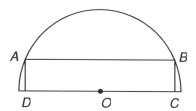

A) 12
B) 13
C) 24
D) 26

2. TRIANGLES

In addition to finding the area of a triangle, as discussed in the previous section, a number of other topics relate to triangles.

TYPES OF TRIANGLES

Isosceles triangles have two equal sides (and two equal angles).

Equilateral triangles have three equal sides (and three equal angles, each measuring **60°**).

RIGHT TRIANGLES

PYTHAGOREAN THEOREM

When you use the *Pythagorean Theorem*, make sure the *c* side is the *hypotenuse*, which is the longest side and always opposite the right angle.

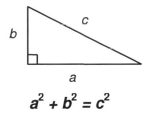

$$a^2 + b^2 = c^2$$

 You can use the Pythagorean Theorem with *right* triangles when you know *two* of the three sides.

SPECIAL RIGHT TRIANGLES

30-60-90 AND 45-45-90 TRIANGLES

Make sure you are comfortable with the 30-60-90 triangle and the 45-45-90 triangle (also called the *isosceles-right* triangle). You do not have to memorize these relationships: they are found on the reference page of each math section on the SAT:

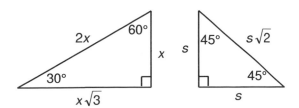

Never assume a triangle is a special right triangle. You must confirm that the angles are 30-60-90 or 45-45-90 triangles. Remember that all isosceles-right triangles are 45-45-90 triangles.

PYTHAGOREAN TRIPLES: 3-4-5 AND 5-12-13 TRIANGLES

These right triangles with integer sides, called *Pythagorean triples*, show up frequently. You can save time if you have them memorized. You might also see multiples of these sides, such as 6-8-10.

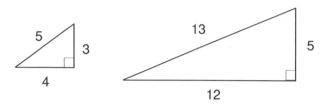

SIMILAR TRIANGLES

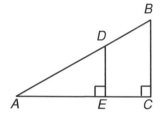

$\triangle ABC$ is similar to $\triangle ADE$

The SAT loves *similar triangles*—triangles with equal angles. There are two ways to consider side relationships with similar triangles:

1. **The ratio of any two sides of one triangle is equal to that of any two *related* sides of a similar triangle.** For example, in the triangle above:

$$\frac{AB}{AC} = \frac{AD}{AE}$$

2. **The ratio of *equivalent* sides of similar triangles remains constant.**

$$\frac{AD}{AB} = \frac{AE}{AC} = \frac{DE}{BC} = k \text{ , where } k \text{ is some constant.}$$

 To identify similar triangle problems, look for triangles that have equal angles. Usually, on the SAT, triangles that *appear* similar are indeed similar, but if you can, try to identify angles. Similar triangle problems often also test parallel lines (next section).

ANGLE-SIDE RELATIONSHIPS

In any triangle, the largest angle is opposite the longest side; the smallest angle is opposite the shortest side; and so on. Similarly, if two angles are equal, then their opposite sides are equal.

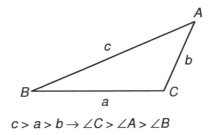

$$c > a > b \rightarrow \angle C > \angle A > \angle B$$

THIRD SIDE RULE

In any triangle, the sum of the two shortest sides must be greater than the longest side.

If a, b, and c are the lengths of sides of a triangle and $a \leq b \leq c$, then:

> FLASH
> CARDS

$$a + b > c$$

CONGRUENT TRIANGLES

Occasionally, a problem may require you to recognize *congruent triangles*. Two congruent triangles have the exact same size and shape. If you've covered congruent triangles in school, then the following rules should be a review. If you haven't covered congruent triangles, you might skip the following rules—rest assured that these types of problems are not common on the SAT.

RULES FOR CONGRUENT TRIANGLES

- **Side-Side-Side (SSS):** If all sides of one triangle are congruent to those of another triangle, then the triangles are congruent.
- **Side-Angle-Side (SAS):** If two sides and the included angle of one triangle are congruent to those of another triangle, then the triangles are congruent.
- **Angle-Side-Angle (ASA):** If two angles and the included side of one triangle are congruent to those of another triangle, then the triangles are congruent.
- **Angle-Angle-Side (AAS):** If two angles and the adjacent side of one triangle are congruent to those of another triangle, then the triangles are congruent.
- **Hypotenuse-Leg (HL):** For right triangles, if the hypotenuse and one leg of one right triangle are congruent to those of another right triangle, then the triangles are congruent.

TRIANGLE PROBLEMS WITH NO TRIANGLES

Many geometry problems on the SAT are triangle problems even though there is no triangle given. Remember that drawing a triangle, usually a right triangle, can often help you solve a problem. The last homework question in the previous section is a good example of this. We will see many more of these types of problems.

TRIANGLE LESSON PROBLEMS

In the following triangles, find the lengths of all sides. You do *not* need to simplify you answers:

1.

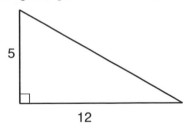

5.

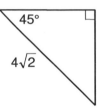

2.

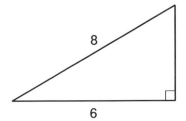

6.

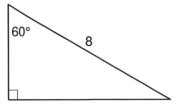

3.

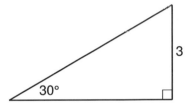

7.

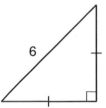

4.

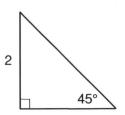

8.

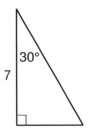

[NO-CALCULATOR SECTION: 1-15 MULTIPLE-CHOICE / 16-20 GRID-IN]:

1. In the right triangle shown below, which of the following statements is true about side *AB*?

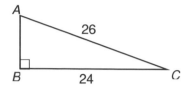

A) $AB = 26 - 24$
B) $AB = 26^2 - 24^2$
C) $AB^2 = 24^2 + 26^2$
D) $AB^2 = 26^2 - 24^2$

5. If the area of the triangle below is 54, what is the length of the hypotenuse?

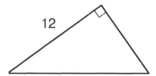

A) 9
B) 13
C) 15
D) 18

6. The lengths of corresponding sides of two similar right triangles are in the ratio 3 to 4. If the hypotenuse of the larger triangle is 10 centimeters, then how long, in centimeters, is the length of the hypotenuse of the smaller triangle?

A) 5

B) $\dfrac{20}{3}$

C) $\dfrac{15}{2}$

D) $\dfrac{40}{3}$

Continued →

20. If an equilateral triangle with a perimeter of 6 is inscribed in a rectangle, as shown in the figure below, what is the area of the rectangle?

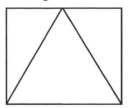

A) $\sqrt{3}$
B) $2\sqrt{3}$
C) 4
D) $3\sqrt{3}$

7. If the area of a square is 50, how long is the longest straight line that can be drawn between any two points of the square?

A) $5\sqrt{2}$
B) 10
C) 25
D) $25\sqrt{2}$

Continued →

12. A triangle has sides of lengths 4 and 5. If the third side is an integer, what is the shortest possible length for this side?

A) 1
B) 2
C) 3
D) 5

[CALCULATOR SECTION: 1–30 MULTIPLE-CHOICE / 31–38 GRID-IN]:

9. Given the equilateral triangle below, what is the value of x?

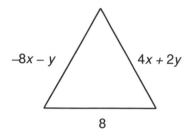

A) –2
B) –1
C) 0
D) 1

Continued →

20. In the figure below, *AB* and *DE* are each perpendicular to *AE*. If *AB* = 2, *DE* = 4, and *CD* = 10, what is the length of *AE*?

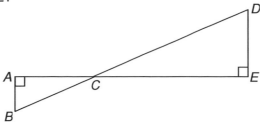

A) $\sqrt{21}$
B) $2\sqrt{21}$
C) 5
D) $3\sqrt{21}$

22. What is the <u>perimeter</u> of the figure shown below?

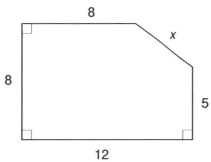

A) 33
B) 36
C) 38
D) 40

Continued →

23. In △ABC below, AB > AC. Which of the following must be true?

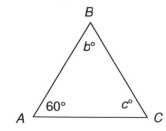

Note: Figure not drawn to scale.

A) BC > AB
B) b = c
C) c = 70
D) b < 60

3. ANGLES

Let's see what you know. Fill in the missing information below.

LINE

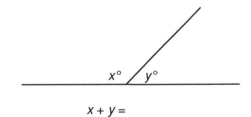

$x + y =$

TRIANGLE

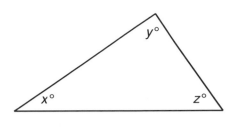

$x + y + z =$

CIRCLE

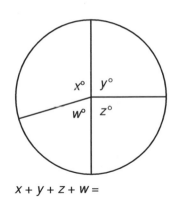

$x + y + z + w =$

RIGHT ANGLE

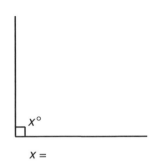

$x =$

VERTICAL ANGLES

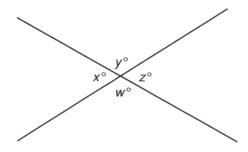

If $x = 50°$, then:

$z =$

$y =$

$w =$

PARALLEL LINES

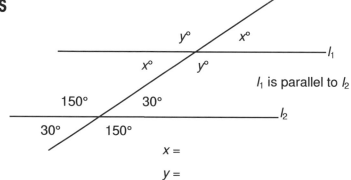

l_1 is parallel to l_2

$x =$

$y =$

ANGLE INSCRIBED IN A CIRCLE

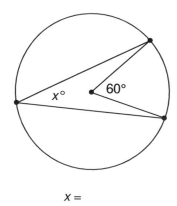

$x =$

Note that there are many (infinite) ways to draw inscribed angles, each intersecting the same arc (in this case, arc AB):

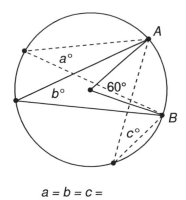

$$a = b = c =$$

LINE TANGENT TO A CIRCLE

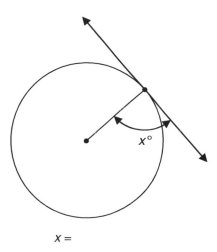

$$x =$$

SUM OF INTERIOR ANGLES

Here is a simple method for finding the sum of the interior angles for any polygon of four or more sides:

1. Start at one vertex (corner) of the polygon.
2. From this one vertex, draw straight lines to all other (non-adjacent) vertices.
3. Count the number of triangles and multiply by 180°.

QUADRILATERAL

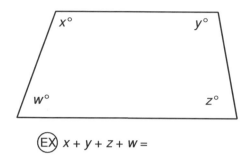

(EX) $x + y + z + w =$

OTHER POLYGONS

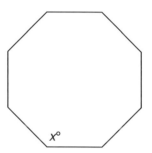

1. What is the sum of the interior angles of the polygon above?

2. If the above polygon is a *regular polygon* (all sides and angles are equal), what is the value of x?

COMPLEMENTARY/SUPPLEMENTARY ANGLES

Memorize these terms:

- If two angles add up to 90°, they are called *complementary* angles.
- If two angles add up to 180°, they are called *supplementary* angles.

ANGLE BISECTOR

As the name implies, an *angle bisector* is a line that divides an angle into two equal angles.

Segment *BD* is the angle bisector of $\angle ABC$, below:

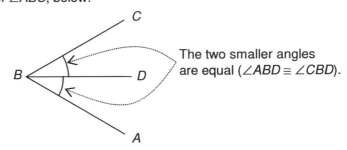

The two smaller angles are equal ($\angle ABD \cong \angle CBD$).

ANGLES LESSON PROBLEMS

[NO-CALCULATOR SECTION: 1-15 MULTIPLE-CHOICE / 16-20 GRID-IN]:

2. In the figure below, what is the value of *x*?

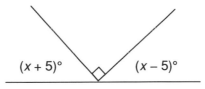

$(x + 5)°$ $(x - 5)°$

A) 30
B) 45
C) 60
D) 90

10. In the figure below, lines *m* and *n* are parallel, segment *BC* = 4, and segment *CD* = 2. What is the length of segment *AE*?

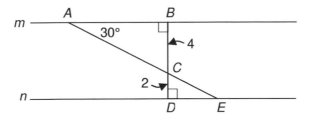

A) 8
B) $6\sqrt{3}$
C) 12
D) $12\sqrt{3}$

Continued →

14. In the figure below, points *A*, *B*, *C*, and *D* are on circle *O*. Which of the following statements must be true?

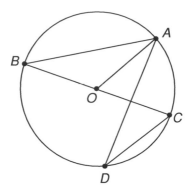

    I.   *m∠ABC* = *m∠ADC*
    II. *m∠ABC* + *m∠ADC* = *m∠AOC*
    III. *m∠ADC* = *m∠DAO*

A) I only
B) II only
C) I and II only
D) I, II, and III

24. In triangle *PQR* below, what is the value of *y* in terms of *x*?

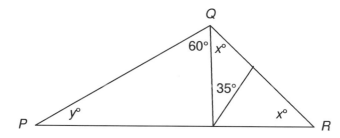

A) *x*
B) 2*x*
C) 100 − 2*x*
D) 120 − 2*x*

2. In the right triangle below, what is the value of x?

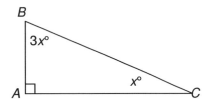

A) $22\frac{1}{2}$

B) 30

C) 45

D) $67\frac{1}{2}$

7. In the figure below, lines m and n are parallel, segment $AB = 15$, segment $BC = 7$, segment $CD = 4$. What is the length of segment DE?

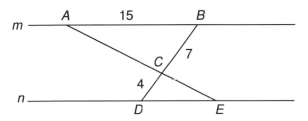

A) $\dfrac{60}{7}$

B) $\dfrac{15}{4}$

C) $\dfrac{28}{15}$

D) $\dfrac{15}{28}$

Continued →

4. In the figure below, $l_1 \parallel l_2$ and $l_3 \parallel l_4$. What is the measure, in degrees, of angle x?

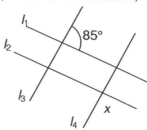

A) 85
B) 95
C) 100
D) Cannot be
    determined
    from the given
    information

13. In hexagon *ABCDEF* below, $\angle A$ is given. What is the measure of angles $B + C + D + E + F$?

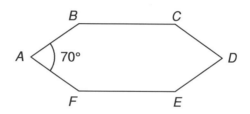

A) 630°
B) 650°
C) 670°
D) 700°

Continued →

14. In the figure below, what is the value of *y*?

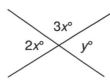

A) 36
B) 45
C) 60
D) 72

25. In the figure below, lines *l* and *m* are parallel. What is *y* in terms of *x*?

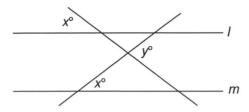

A) *x*
B) ¾ *x*
C) 2*x*
D) 180 − 2*x*

26. Pentagon *ABCDE* below has equal angles and equal sides. If *O* is the center of the pentagon, what is the degree measure of ∠*AOB* (not drawn)?

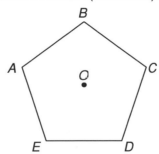

A) 45°
B) 60°
C) 72°
D) 108°

4. MORE CIRCLES

We have already discussed the area and circumference of a circle. We have also looked at the sum of the degrees in a circle (360°). There are a few more topics that have to do with circles.

EQUATION OF A CIRCLE

The equation of a circle in the *xy*-plane is shown below:

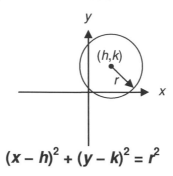

FLASH CARDS

$$(x - h)^2 + (y - k)^2 = r^2$$

> To identify circle equation problems, make sure you can identify the equation of a circle in its standard form. You'll either see the equation in the question or in the answer choices.

(EX) In the *xy*-plane, what is the radius of the circle defined by the equation:

$(x + 2)^2 + (y + 2)^2 = 25$?

A) 2
B) 5
C) 10
D) 25

COMPLETING THE SQUARE

Some problems may ask you to find the standard form of a circle's equation (see above) from an equation of the form: $ax^2 + by^2 + cx + dy + f = 0$. The method involves "completing the square." The steps may sound confusing, so make sure to follow along with the example:

1. If necessary, group the x^2 and x terms together, group the y^2 and y terms together, and move the numerical term (*f*, above) to the right side of the equation. Leave room to the right of the x and y terms, and add parentheses, as shown in the example.

2. If necessary, divide each term by the coefficient of the x^2 and y^2 terms (for a circle, these coefficients will always equal). Usually, on the SAT, the coefficient will already be 1, as in the example below.

3. To both sides of the equation, add the **square of ½ the x term** and the **square of ½ the y term**. Again, see the example for where to put these numbers (in bold).

4. Finally, "complete the square" by factoring. Review factoring quadratics if necessary (Chapter V). Your equation should now be in standard form.

(EX) The equation of a circle in xy-plane is shown below. What is the radius of the circle?

$$x^2 + 4x + y^2 - 6y = -4$$

A) 2
B) 3
C) 4
D) 9

SECTORS OF CIRCLES

A *sector* of a circle is like a piece of pizza. Below are the three most common measurements we can use to evaluate the size of a sector:

1. **Angle** – this is the measure of $\angle AOB$ in the figure below. It is sometimes called the "**measure of arc AB**" or the "**central angle**" to arc AB.

2. **Arc length** – this is the actual curved distance from point A to point B along the circle.

3. **Area** – this is the area between line segments AO and BO and arc AB (shaded below).

We can write each of these measurements as a *part over whole* ratio, where the *part* is relating to the sector of the circle and the *whole* is relating to the entire circle. The trick to sector problems is to realize that each of these ratios is *equal*:

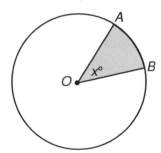

$$\frac{\text{part (sector)}}{\text{whole (circle)}} \rightarrow \frac{x}{360} = \frac{\text{length of arc } AB}{\text{circumference of circle}} = \frac{\text{area of sector } AOB}{\text{area of circle}}$$

Look for circles with sectors, but don't confuse these problems with circle-graphs (pie-graphs), which also have sectors drawn.

The method below should be used for circle sector problems. An example follows.

1. **Identify which *two* of the three measurements of the sector are mentioned in the problem.** Remember, the three measurements are *degrees*, *arc length*, and *area*. Usually, only *two* of them will be tested in a problem.

2. **Set up a proportion problem with the two appropriate ratios above, and solve for the missing information.** Keep in mind that if the radius (or diameter) of the circle is given, then you can calculate the circumference or area of the circle.

(EX) If the area of circle *O* below is 240 in^2 and the area of sector *AOB* is 20 in^2, what is the value of *x*?

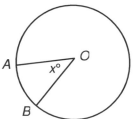

A) 25
B) 30
C) 35
D) 40

SECTORS OF CIRCLES: OTHER MEASUREMENTS

We've looked at the *areas*, *arc lengths*, and *angles* of sectors, but there are other ways sectors can be measured, including:

- Minutes (or hours) on a clock (think of the sector formed by the sweep of a hand)
- Volume or weight of a disk
- Any quantity (population, dollars, etc.) on a pie graph

Just remember that the part-over-whole ratios of any two measurements will always equal.

MORE CIRCLES LESSON PROBLEMS

16. If the length of arc AB in the circle below with center O is 5 and angle AOB is 120°, what is the circumference of the circle?

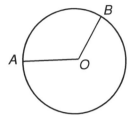

   A) 10
   B) 15
   C) 5π
   D) 10π

20. Which of the following equations represents a circle in the xy-plane that has center (3, 5) and radius $\sqrt{5}$ units?

   A) $(x-3)^2 + (y-5)^2 = 5$
   B) $(x+3)^2 + (y+5)^2 = 5$
   C) $(x-3)^2 + (y-5)^2 = \sqrt{5}$
   D) $(x+3)^2 + (y+5)^2 = \sqrt{5}$

25. The equation of a circle in xy-plane is shown below. Which of the following are the coordinates of the center of the circle?

$$x^2 + y^2 - 2x - 4y - 95 = 0$$

   A) (1, 0)
   B) (2, 0)
   C) (1, 2)
   D) (2, 10)

[CALCULATOR SECTION: 1–30 MULTIPLE-CHOICE / 31–38 GRID-IN]:

9. Each of the 200 students at George Washington High School voted for his or her favorite American president. The results of the poll are given in the table below.

President	Number of Voters
George Washington	60
Abraham Lincoln	58
Thomas Jefferson	35
Franklin D. Roosevelt	17
Other	30

If the information in the table were converted into a circle graph (pie chart), then the central angle of the sector that voted for George Washington would measure how many degrees?

A) 60°
B) 100°
C) 108°
D) 110°

17. In circle O below, $x = 36$. What is the area of sector AOB?

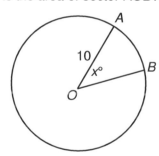

A) 2π
B) 10
C) 20
D) 10π

Continued →

20. A circle in the *xy*-plane has center (0, 2) and radius 2 units. Which of the following equations represents the circle?

A) $x^2 + (y-2)^2 = 2$
B) $x^2 + (y+2)^2 = 2$
C) $x^2 + (y-2)^2 = 4$
D) $x^2 + (y+2)^2 = 4$

21. Which of the following is an equation of the circle in the *xy*-plane shown below?

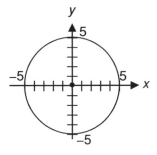

A) $x^2 + y^2 = 5$
B) $x^2 + y^2 = 10$
C) $x^2 + y^2 = 25$
D) $(x+y)^2 = 5$

30. In the figure below, segments *AB* and *AC* are tangent to circle *O*. If the radius of circle *O* is 3, and *m∠BOC* is 120°, what is the area of the shaded region?

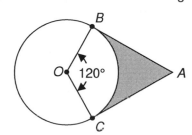

A) $9\sqrt{3} - \pi$

B) $9\sqrt{3} - 3\pi$

C) $12\sqrt{3} - \pi$

D) $12\sqrt{3} - 3\pi$

5. SOLIDS & VOLUME

Solids are shapes that occupy three dimensions, such as cubes, cylinders, or rectangular boxes. Most solids problems are *volume* problems. The following solids have formulas given in the SAT reference section of each test:

- rectangular box
- cylinder
- sphere
- cone
- square pyramid

Volume – the amount of space occupied by a solid or a substance.

Surface area – the sum of the areas of all the faces of a solid.

RECTANGULAR SOLIDS

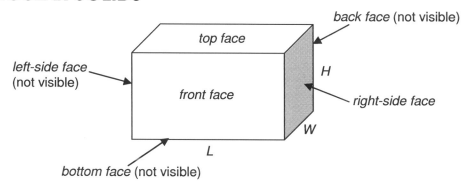

$$V = L \cdot W \cdot H$$

To find surface area, notice that there are 3 different rectangular faces (the 3 faces you can see above), and each one has an opposite rectangular face of the exact same size. For example, the front face (visible above) is the exact same size as the back face (*not* visible above). This can help you find the formula for surface area. Don't memorize this. Just make sure you understand how we found it:

$$SA = 2LH + 2LW + 2WH$$

Try the following lesson problems, based on the rectangular solid below:

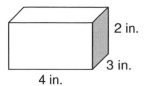

2 in.

3 in.

4 in.

1. What is the area of the front face?

2. What is the area of the top face?

3. What is the area of the right-side face?

4. What is the total surface area of the box?

5. What is the volume of the box?

CUBES

Since all sides of a cube are the same length, the formulas for volume and surface area are simplified:

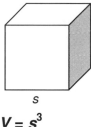

s

$$V = s^3$$
$$SA = 6s^2$$

SURFACE AREA → VOLUME

You might need to find the *volume* of a cube when the *surface area* is given. Consider a cube with a surface area of 600 in^2:

1. What is the area of one face?

2. What is the length of an edge?

3. What is the volume of the cube?

The above example illustrates the following method for finding the volume of a cube when the surface area is given. If you understand the steps above, you shouldn't have to memorize:

1. *Divide* the surface area by 6 to find the area of one face.

2. Take the *square root* of this area to find the length of a side.

3. *Cube* this length to find the volume of the cube.

VOLUME OF PRISMS

A *prism* is a three-dimensional shape that has the same cross section along its entire length. Prisms have two *bases*, one at each end. Below is a prism with a triangular cross section:

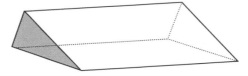

Below is a prism with a circular cross section (a cylinder):

The volume of any prism is:

V = Area of base × Length of prism

The most common prism tested on the SAT is the cylinder: **V = $\pi r^2 h$.**

Try the following lesson problem:

23. The figure below shows the elliptical cross section of a 20 foot long storage tank. If the area of the cross section is found to be 18π square feet, what is the volume, in cubic feet, of the tank?

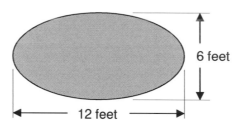

    A. 1440
    B. 360π
    C. 180π
    D. 72π

VOLUME FITTING PROBLEMS

Some volume problems will ask you to find the volume or number of small solids that can fit into a larger volume or solid. These problems are similar to *area fitting* problems (see the Area & Perimeter section).

 Volume fitting problems will ask you to find the volume or number of small solids that can fit into a larger volume or solid.

Here's the method:

1. Find the volumes of the large solid and the small solid.
2. Divide the large volume by the small volume.

Number of *small volumes* that will fit into the *larger volume* = $\dfrac{\textbf{Large Volume}}{\textbf{Small Volume}}$

Try the following lesson problem:

24. A cylindrical cup has a radius of 2 inches and a height of 6 inches. A cylindrical water jug has a radius of 10 inches and a height of 12 inches. If the jug is full of water, how many cups of water can be filled before the jug is empty?

   A) 5
   B) 20
   C) 35
   D) 50

[CALCULATOR SECTION: 1–30 MULTIPLE-CHOICE / 31–38 GRID-IN]:

5. Elisa has two boxes, each with lengths 10 inches, widths 8 inches, and heights 6 inches. If she wants to ship these boxes in a third, larger box with length 20 inches, width 10 inches, and height 8 inches, how much additional space, in cubic inches, will be left in the larger box?

   A) 640
   B) 680
   C) 720
   D) 1120

14. If cube A has an edge of length 2 centimeters and cube B has an edge of length 3 centimeters, what is the ratio of the volume of cube A to the volume of cube B?

    A) 2:3
    B) 8:27
    C) 5:9
    D) 4:9

16. A steel worker is going to pour 300 cubic inches of molten steel into the rectangular mold shown below. If the molten steel is spread evenly over the entire base of the mold, what will be the approximate height, in inches, of the molten steel?

6 inches

5 inches

30 inches

    A) 0.5
    B) 1
    C) 2
    D) 4

27. Soap cubes, each with a total surface area of 54 square centimeters, are stacked in a cube box. If the box has a volume of 729 cubic centimeters, what is the maximum number of soap cubes that can fit in the box?

    A) 13
    B) 27
    C) 100
    D) 192

6. COORDINATES

We briefly covered coordinates in the Linear Equation section (Chapter IV). What follows is a more thorough overview, but if you're already comfortable with the coordinate plane, you might skip to the lesson and homework questions.

The *xy*-coordinate plane (often called the *xy*-plane on the SAT) consists of two perpendicular axes called the *x*-axis and the *y*-axis. The *x*-axis is horizontal and the *y*-axis is vertical.

POINTS

The most common mistake on simple coordinate problems is to confuse the *x*- and *y*-coordinates of *points*. **Remember, the *x*-coordinate is always the *first* coordinate of a point, and the *y*-coordinate is always the *second* coordinate of a point.** Identify the coordinates of the following points:

1. $A =$
2. $B =$
3. $C =$
4. $D =$
5. $E =$

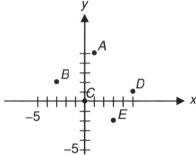

HORIZONTAL AND VERTICAL DISTANCES

The coordinate plane allows you to easily find horizontal and vertical distances between points, just by knowing the points' *x*- and *y*-coordinates.

1. **To find the *horizontal* distance between two points, find the *positive difference* between the points' *x*-coordinates.** In other words, *subtract* the *x*-coordinates and take the *absolute value* of the result.
2. **To find the *vertical* distance between two points, find the *positive difference* between the points' *y*-coordinates.** In other words, *subtract* the *y*-coordinates and take the *absolute value* of the result.

Try the following lesson problem:

3. On the *xy*-plane shown below, Matt wants to draw a rectangle (not shown) that has two of its vertices at points (3, 9) and (−1, −3). If two sides of the rectangle are parallel to the *x*-axis, what is the perimeter of the rectangle?

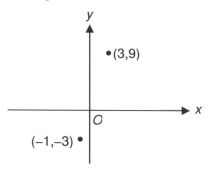

A) $4\sqrt{10}$
B) 16
C) 32
D) 48

SLANTED DISTANCES BETWEEN POINTS

If you need to find the straight-line distance between two points that do *not* lie on a vertical or horizontal line, you have two options:

1. THE PYTHAGOREAN THEOREM REVISITED

If you draw a right triangle, with the hypotenuse connecting the two points in question, you can use the Pythagorean Theorem to find the distance between the points, as shown below:

(EX) In the *xy*-plane, what is the distance between the points (−1,−1) and (2,3)?

A) $\sqrt{7}$
B) 4
C) 5
D) 25

2. THE DISTANCE FORMULA

The other option is the *distance formula*. The distance between two points with coordinates (x_1, y_1) and (x_2, y_2) is:

$$\boxed{\text{FLASH CARDS}} \quad d = \sqrt{(x_1 - x_2)^2 + (y_1 - y_2)^2}$$

For the example above, $d = \sqrt{(-1-2)^2 + (-1-3)^2} = \sqrt{9+16} = \sqrt{25} = 5$, which agrees with our answer using the Pythagorean Theorem approach. (You might be interested to know that the distance formula actually derives from the Pythagorean Theorem. The calculations are the same. It's not surprising that you'll get the same answer using either approach.)

■

For finding slanted distances between points, we recommend the first approach (using the Pythagorean Theorem) because you don't have to memorize a new formula and there are fewer chances of careless calculator mistakes. However, both approaches work.

MIDPOINT

You may have to find the coordinates of the *midpoint* between two points. The formula is straightforward. The x-coordinate of the midpoint is the average of the x-coordinates of the two endpoints. Similarly, the y-coordinate of the midpoint is the average of the y-coordinates of the two endpoints:

$$\boxed{\text{FLASH CARDS}} \quad \text{Midpoint} = \left(\frac{x_1 + x_2}{2}, \frac{y_1 + y_2}{2} \right)$$

COORDINATE PLANE MODELING

Some problems will require you to set up a two-dimensional problem using a coordinate plane. Once you have the problem drawn onto a coordinate plane, you should be able to use the previous rules to answer the question. For example:

(EX) An architect places an overlay of the *xy*-plane on the blueprint of a house to find the length of a diagonal pathway. If one end of the pathway lies at (0,0) and the other end lies at (6,2), what is the unit length of the pathway?

A) $\sqrt{8}$
B) 6
C) $\sqrt{40}$
D) 8

COORDINATES LESSON PROBLEMS

[CALCULATOR SECTION: 1–30 MULTIPLE-CHOICE / 31–38 GRID-IN]:

2. In the *xy*-plane below, both circles are centered at point *O* and *OA = AB*. If the coordinates of *A* are (0,–6), what are the coordinates of *C*?

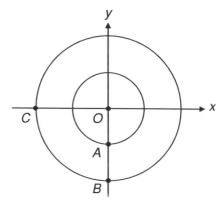

A) (–6,0)
B) (–12,0)
C) (0,–12)
D) (0,–6)

8. In the *xy*-plane, what are the coordinates of the midpoint of a line segment with endpoints at (–2,–6) and (2,5)?

A) (0,–11)
B) (0,–5.5)
C) (0,–0.5)
D) (0,–1)

Continued →

26. What is the equation of a circle if the two endpoints of a diameter of the circle are (–5,0) and (5,12)?

A) $x^2 + (y - 6)^2 = 61$
B) $x^2 + (y - 6)^2 = 244$
C) $x^2 + (y + 6)^2 = 61$
D) $x^2 + (y + 6)^2 = 244$

[CALCULATOR SECTION: 1–30 MULTIPLE-CHOICE / 31–38 GRID-IN]:

5. In the *xy*-plane below, $\triangle ABC$ is an isosceles right triangle. Which of the following are the coordinates of point *A*?

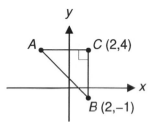

A) (4,–3.5)
B) (–2,4)
C) (–2.5,4)
D) (–3,4)

Continued →

20. In the *xy*-plane, what is the area of the triangle shown below?

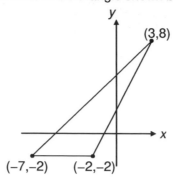

A) 15
B) 25
C) 50
D) 100

7. ONE-DIMENSIONAL LINES

We already covered slope and linear equations in Chapter IV. Two other topics having to do with lines might show up on the SAT: number lines and line segments. We call these *one-dimensional* line problems because you won't have to worry about vertical distances or slanted lines with these problems—the lines will generally be *horizontal*, like the *x*-axis of a standard coordinate plane.

 One-dimensional line problems tend to test horizontal lines (no vertical or slanted lines).

NUMBER LINES

Number line problems usually have tick marks. The tick marks may *not* always be a distance of *1* apart, but the marks will be equally spaced. Number lines generally increase to the right. As taught in the Coordinates section, to find the distance between two points, find the *positive difference* between them. In other words, *subtract* the endpoints and find the *absolute value* of the result. Try the following lesson problem:

3. The marks on the number line below are equally spaced. What is the distance between points *A* and *B*?

A) $\dfrac{1}{5}$

B) 1

C) $\dfrac{6}{5}$

D) 6

LINE SEGMENTS

Some number line problems won't have tick marks. These problems tend to deal with *line segments*. The Pick Tricks often prove useful on these types of problems.

 On line segment AB, if point C lies one third of the distance from A to B and point D is the midpoint of AC, what is $\dfrac{DB}{AB}$?

A) $\dfrac{1}{3}$

B) $\dfrac{1}{2}$

C) $\dfrac{2}{3}$

D) $\dfrac{5}{6}$

LINES HOMEWORK

![calculator icon]

[CALCULATOR SECTION: 1–30 MULTIPLE-CHOICE / 31–38 GRID-IN]:

2. If R is the midpoint of segment QS below, then $x = $?

$$\overset{\displaystyle x+3 \qquad\quad y-1}{\underset{\displaystyle Q \qquad\qquad R \qquad\qquad S}{\vdash\!-\!\!\!-\!\!\!-\!\!\!+\!\!\!-\!\!\!-\!\!\!-\!\dashv}}$$

A) $y - 4$
B) $y - 3$
C) $y - 2$
D) $y - 1$

Continued →

5. If point *C* is the midpoint of segment *AB* and point *D* is the midpoint of segment *CB*, which of the following is NOT true?

   A) $AC - CD = DB$
   B) $CB < AD$
   C) $AB - CD = AD$
   D) $CB < AC$

37. The marks on the number line below are equally spaced. What is the value of *A*?

8. GEOMETRY: PRACTICE & CORRECTIONS

PRACTICE PROBLEMS

The following worksheets test techniques taught in this chapter. In addition, we'll use Practice Test 1 from *The Official SAT Study Guide* for more practice questions. Don't forget to review the lessons in this chapter while completing these problems:

- ☐ Geometry Worksheet 1
- ☐ Geometry Worksheet 2
- ☐ Test 1 (practice problems): See the Techniques chapter at the end of this tutorial.

TEST CORRECTIONS

After completing and grading each practice test, you should correct Geometry questions that you missed or guessed on. Below are the three steps to correcting practice tests:

1. Turn to the Techniques section at the end of this tutorial and circle the Geometry questions that you missed or guessed on for each test.

2. Correct the problems in *The Official SAT Study Guide*. As you correct the problems, go back to the tutorial and review the techniques. The idea is to (1) identify techniques that have given you trouble, (2) go back to the tutorial so you can review and strengthen these techniques, and (3) apply these techniques to the specific problems on which you struggled.

3. If you have trouble identifying the best technique to use on a problem, refer to the Techniques chapter. This is an important part of correcting the tests.

GEOMETRY WORKSHEET 1

6. In the figure below, Z is on line AB and $AB \parallel XY$. Which of the following is NOT true?

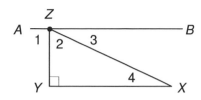

 A) $m\angle 3 = m\angle 4$
 B) $m\angle 3 + m\angle 4 = 90°$
 C) $m\angle 1 = 90°$
 D) $m\angle 2 + m\angle 3 = 90°$

7. A rectangular water tank 4 ft wide, 8 ft long, and 10 ft high is filled to 20% of capacity. How many additional cubic feet of water must be added to the tank so that it is 30% full?

 A) 32
 B) 64
 C) 96
 D) 160

12. You want to build a square garden that will be fenced on all four sides. If you have enough material to build 30 feet of fence, what can be the maximum area, to the nearest square foot, of your garden?

 A) 128
 B) 64
 C) 60
 D) 56

Continued →

14. A rope is stretched straight from the top of a 50 foot vertical tower to a point on the ground 120 feet from the base of the tower. Assuming level ground, how long, in feet, is the rope?

    A) 125
    B) 130
    C) 135
    D) 140

22. In right triangle *ABC* below, points *A*, *D*, and *C* are collinear and line segment *BD* bisects ∠*ABC*. If the measure of ∠*ACB* is 35°, as shown, what is the measure of ∠*BDC*?

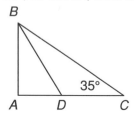

    A) 110°
    B) 112.5°
    C) 115°
    D) 117.5°

23. In △*ABC* shown below, $\overline{DE}$ is parallel to $\overline{AC}$. The length of $\overline{AB}$ is 8 inches, the length of $\overline{BC}$ is 9 inches, and the length of $\overline{DE}$ is 4 inches. If points *D* and *E* are the midpoints of $\overline{AB}$ and $\overline{BC}$, respectively, which of the following is the length, in inches, of $\overline{AC}$?

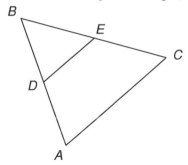

    A) 8
    B) 8½
    C) 9
    D) 9½

Continued →

24. The target below is made up of three circles with the same center. The radius of the small circle is one-third of the radius of the middle circle and one-fifth of the radius of the large circle. If the radius of the small circle is 2, what is the area of the shaded region?

- A) 36π
- B) 64π
- C) 68π
- D) 72π

25. The equation of a circle in xy-plane is shown below. Which of the following is the length of the radius of the circle?

$$x^2 + 40x + y^2 - 40y = -400$$

- A) 4
- B) 10
- C) 16
- D) 20

27. The area of trapezoid $ABCD$, shown below, is 108 square inches. If the lengths of the bases are 14 and 22, what is the height, h, in inches, of the trapezoid?

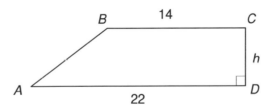

- A) $4\frac{10}{11}$
- B) 6
- C) $7\frac{5}{7}$
- D) 8

Continued →

28. Which of the following is an equation of the circle in the *xy*-plane shown below?

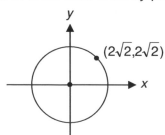

A) $x^2 + y^2 = 16$

B) $x^2 + y^2 = 8$

C) $x^2 + y^2 = 4\sqrt{2}$

D) $x^2 + y^2 = 4$

29. In the figure below, points *A*, *B*, and *C* lie on circle *O*. If the radius of the circle is 6, what is the length of arc *AB* ?

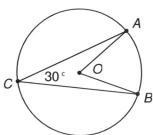

A) π

B) $\dfrac{3}{2}\pi$

C) 2π

D) 3π

Continued →

31. Bill completely fills a 5-inch tall cylindrical container, as shown below, with 20π cubic inches of liquid. What is the radius of the cylinder, in inches?

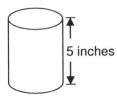

5 inches

36. In circle O below, the length of arc AB is π and the $m\angle AOB$ is 45°. What is the length of the diameter of the circle?

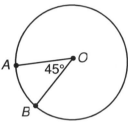

A 45° O

B

GEOMETRY WORKSHEET 2

[CALCULATOR SECTION: 1–30 MULTIPLE-CHOICE / 31–38 GRID-IN]:

1. Chuck wants to determine the height of a wall. He props a 10-foot long ladder against the wall, so that the top of the ladder meets the top of the wall and the base of the ladder is 2 feet from the base of the wall, as shown below. What is the height, in feet, of the wall?

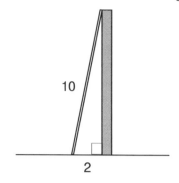

A) 8

B) 9

C) $\sqrt{96}$

D) $\sqrt{104}$

6. In the triangle shown below, what is the sum of a, b, and c?

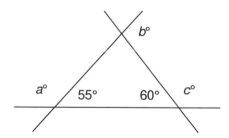

A) 360
B) 245
C) 180
D) Cannot be determined from the given information

Continued →

9. The mayoral election results for the 54,000 voting residents of Vonnegut City are shown below. If the information in the table were converted into a circle (or pie) graph, then what would be the measure of the central angle of the sector for the candidate named Pilgrim?

Candidate	Number of voters
Pilgrim	20,400
Rumfoord	17,100
Trout	10,500
Hoover	5,280
Hoenikker	720

A) 130°
B) 132°
C) 134°
D) 136°

12. In the figure below, Δ*I* is similar to Δ*II*, with lengths given in inches. What is the perimeter of Δ*II*?

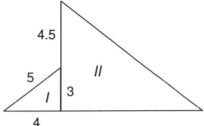

A) 23.5
B) 26
C) 28.5
D) 30

Continued →

13. In the circle with center O shown below, which of following statements is NOT true?

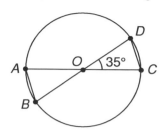

- A) AO = DO
- B) AB = DC
- C) measure of arc ABD = 215°
- D) ∠ABO = 70°

16. The figure below shows square XYZO, with vertices X and Z lying on circle O. If the area of the square is 25 square centimeters, what is the area, in square centimeters, of the circle?

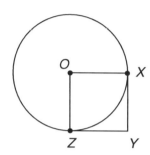

- A) 25π
- B) 50π
- C) 100π
- D) 250π

20. What is the distance in the xy-plane between the points (−12,−5) and (12,5)?

- A) √13
- B) √26
- C) 13
- D) 26

Continued →

22. In the figure below, segment *AB* is tangent to circle *C* and has a length of 12. If circle *C* has a radius of 4, what is the area of △*ABC*?

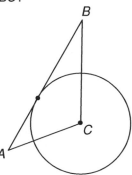

A) 12
B) 18
C) 24
D) 30

23. In the circle below, *O* is the center. Chord $\overline{AB}$ is 8 inches long and line segment $\overline{OC}$ is 3 inches long. What is the circumference of the circle?

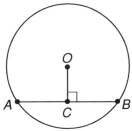

A) 5π
B) 8π
C) 9π
D) 10π

Continued →

24. Tom models an ice cream cone using a cone and a hemisphere, with internal measurements represented by the figure below. What is the volume, in cubic inches, of Tom's model? [Note: the volumes of a sphere ($V = \frac{4}{3}\pi r^3$) and a cone ($V = \frac{1}{3}\pi r^2 h$) are given on the SAT's reference page.]

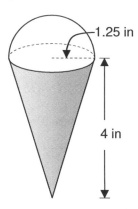

                                1.25 in

                                4 in

A) $\dfrac{125}{96}\pi$

B) $\dfrac{75}{32}\pi$

C) $\dfrac{325}{96}\pi$

D) $\dfrac{75}{16}\pi$

25. A 5-inch tall cylindrical can is shown below. If the area of the can's label, as shown, is 30π square inches, what is the <u>volume</u> of the can in cubic inches?

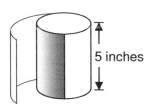

                                5 inches

A) 45π
B) 90π
C) 150π
D) 180π

Continued →

26. The circle below is inscribed in a square with sides of length 4 units. What is the perimeter, in units, of the shaded region shown below?

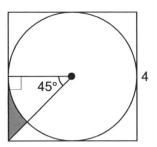

A) $2\sqrt{2} + \dfrac{\pi}{2}$

B) $2\sqrt{3} + \dfrac{\pi}{2}$

C) $4\sqrt{2} + 2\pi$

D) $4\sqrt{3} + 2\pi$

29. In $\triangle ABC$ below, the measure of $\angle A$ is 45° and the measure $\angle C$ is 30°. What is the perimeter of the triangle?

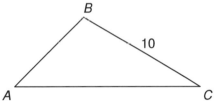

A) $10 + 5\sqrt{2} + 5\sqrt{3}$

B) $15 + 5\sqrt{5}$

C) $10 + 10\sqrt{3}$

D) $15 + 5\sqrt{2} + 5\sqrt{3}$

Continued →

30. The cross section of a 10 foot long trough used for watering cattle is an equilateral triangle. If the trough is filled with water to a depth of 6 inches, as shown below, what is the volume, in cubic inches, of water in the trough?

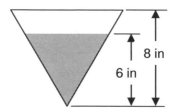

    6 in   8 in

A) $360\sqrt{3}$

B) $640\sqrt{3}$

C) $720\sqrt{3}$

D) $1{,}440\sqrt{3}$

VIII
MATH ODDS & ENDS

This chapter covers a number of topics that occasionally show up on the SAT, including statistics, trigonometry, and parabolas.

1. MEANS, MEDIANS, & MODES

TERMINOLOGY

Mean, or what we usually just call **average** (*A*) – the sum (*S*) of a set of values divided by the number (*N*) of values in the set:

$$A = \frac{S}{N}$$

Note that on the SAT, the average is usually called the *mean* or the *arithmetic mean*.

Median – the middle number in a set of increasing values. If the set has an even number of values, average the two middle numbers. **Don't forget the values must be in order before you can find the median.**

Mode – the value or values in a set of numbers that occur(s) the most frequently.

 Means, Medians, & Modes problems are easy to identify because you only need to look for the words *mean* (or *average*), *median*, or *mode*.

1. What is the median of {2, 6, 0, 10, –5} ?

2. What is the median and mode of {2, 6, 0, 10, –5, 10} ?

The table below shows the hourly wages for 11 workers at a small company.

Hourly wage (in $)	# of workers
9	2
10	2
12	1
13	2
14	4

3. What is the mean of the <u>5 wages</u>?

4. What is the median of the <u>5 wages</u>?

5. What is the mean hourly wage of the <u>11 workers</u>?

6. What is the median hourly wage of the <u>11 workers</u>?

7. What is the mode of the workers' wages?

Make sure you can find medians from a table of many values without writing the values out in order. Here's an example:

Number of Top-Four Finishes in the
World Cup for 25 Countries

Number of Top Four Finishes	Frequency
13	1
11	1
8	1
5	4
4	2
2	8
1	8

In 2014, there were 25 countries that had finished in the top-four at least once in the history of World Cup soccer competition, as shown in the table above. Based on the table, what was the median number of top-four finishes for the 25 countries?

A) 5
B) 4
C) 3
D) 2

Try the following lesson problems:

4. If the mean of five numbers is −10, what is the sum of these numbers?

A) −50
B) −25
C) −10
D) 0

15. Spencer measures the noon temperature once a day for a week and records the following values: 62°, 70°, 80°, 72°, 72°, 65°, x°. If the median temperature for the seven days is 70°, then x could be any of the following EXCEPT

A) 59
B) 66
C) 70
D) 73

18.

Number of Ski Areas Visited in 2011 by
21 Residents of a Colorado Town

Number of Ski Areas	Frequency
10	1
6	3
5	5
4	2
3	6
2	2
1	1
0	1

A reporter for the newspaper of a town in Colorado asked 21 residents of the town how many ski areas they visited in 2011. The results are shown in the table above. Which of the following gives the correct order of the mean, median, and mode of the number of ski areas visited by the residents?

A) median = mean < mode
B) mode < median = mean
C) mode < mean < median
D) mode = median < mean

HARDER AVERAGE PROBLEMS

Harder average (or mean) problems typically deal with two groups of numbers, each group with its own average. With these problems, you'll usually need to consider the sum of all of the numbers, or the "sum of both of the sums." Here's the method:

1. Using the equation for average (mean) and the information given in the question, find any missing information (usually the sum) for each group separately.

2. The average of both groups combined will be the sum of both sums, divided by the sum of all of the numbers.

Note: The most common error involves averaging the averages of both groups. This is generally a trap.

(EX) If the average age of 500 students at school A is 14 and the average age of 300 students at school B is 18, what is the average age of all the students at the two schools?

A) 14.5
B) 15
C) 15.5
D) 16

MEANS, MEDIANS, & MODES LESSON PROBLEMS

[CALCULATOR SECTION: 1–30 MULTIPLE-CHOICE / 31–38 GRID-IN]:

5. If the mean of x, y, and z is 20 and the mean of p and q is 25, then $x + y + z + p + q = ?$

A) 22.5
B) 45
C) 60
D) 110

11. An average of 14 people use a park's tennis courts each weekday and an average of 42 people use the courts each weekend day. What is the average daily use of the courts over the entire week?

A) 20
B) 22
C) 25
D) 26

Continued →

25. If the mean of six numbers is –2 and the mean of four of the numbers is 2, what is the mean of the other two numbers?

A) –10

B) –2

C) $-\dfrac{2}{5}$

D) 0

[CALCULATOR SECTION: 1–30 MULTIPLE-CHOICE / 31–38 GRID-IN]:

4. The average (arithmetic mean) of 24 numbers is –2. If each of the numbers is increased by 2, what is the average of the 24 new numbers?

A) –2

B) 0

C) 24

D) 48

12. Samara takes a logic test five times and scores 12, 10, x, 20, and 27 points. If the mean of her five scores is 18, what is the median of the five scores?

A) 10

B) 12

C) 20

D) 21

Continued →

16. A 20-year-old bank gave away an average of 152 toasters a year for the first 15 years of its existence. For the past five years, the bank did not give away any toasters. What was the average number of toasters given away per year over the bank's entire 20 years?

   A) 76
   B) 98
   C) 114
   D) 120

24. The table below shows the number of three point shots made by Team A in each of its 25 games during a tournament. What is the mean and median number of three-point shots made by Team A per game?

Total number of 3-point shots in a game	Number of games with this total
0	1
1	0
2	2
3	4
4	8
5	2
6	5
7	2
8	1

   A) Mean = 4.0, Median = 2.0
   B) Mean = 4.4, Median = 4.0
   C) Mean = 4.0, Median = 4.0
   D) Mean = 4.4, Median = 2.0

2. STATISTICS

This section will cover the most important topics having to so with statistics. The questions in this section often also test topics found in the Arithmetic chapter (Chapter II). You should also be comfortable with the Linear Equations section (Chapter IV). Feel to review these topics, as indicated in the solutions, as you work your way through the section.

We've already seen how data can be displayed in tables and graphs (Chapter II). Now we'll get into some more specific ways that data can be presented. We'll use the following information, from a class of ten typing students, for some of these examples:

Student	Typing speed (words/minute)	Student	Typing speed (words/minute)
Leopold	42	Blazes	43
Stephen	24	Patrick	37
Molly	45	Simon	98
Buck	38	Mina	20
Gerty	60	Milly	40

HISTOGRAM

A histogram is a bar graph in which the horizontal axis represents *classes*—in this case, ranges of typing speeds—and the vertical axis represents *frequencies*, or the number of members in each class. Here's a histogram for the data above:

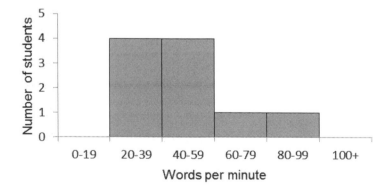

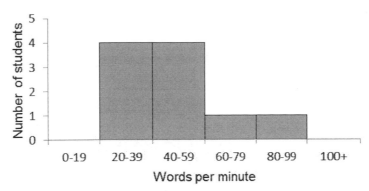

(EX) Based on the histogram above, what is the least possible value of the mean of the 10 students?

A) 24
B) 38
C) 48
D) 58

STEM-AND-LEAF PLOT

A *stem-and-leaf plot* displays data by separating each value into two parts: the stem to the left (for example the tens digit) and the leaves to the right (for example the units, or ones, digit). Here's a stem-and-leaf plot for the example above. Remember, the data are (in order): {20, 24, 37, 38, 40, 42, 43, 45, 60, 98}.

Stem	Leaves
2	04
3	78
4	0235
5	
6	0
7	
8	
9	8

So the first row (2|04) means that the numbers 20 and 24 are in the data set. The second row (3|78) means that the numbers 37 and 38 are in the data set. And so on. Try answering the following question without looking back to the original data (just use the stem-and-leaf plot below):

10. The stem-and-leaf plot below displays the typing speeds, in words per minute, for ten students. What is the median, in words per minute, of the students' speeds?

Stem	Leaves
2	04
3	78
4	0235
5	
6	0
7	
8	
9	8

A) 41
B) 42
C) 42.5
D) 60

DOT PLOT

A *dot plot* displays each data value as a point (or dot). Dot plots are similar to histograms in that they display how data is distributed. Dot plots are most useful, or at least most visually interesting, when some data values are repeated, so let's use the data from above, but round to the nearest 10: {20, 20, 40, 40, 40, 40, 40, 50, 60, 100}.

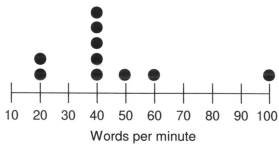

11. For a class of 10 students, the dot plot above summarizes the typing speeds (in words per minute) rounded to the nearest 10. If two new students take a typing test and type 60 and 100 words per minute, what is the difference between the median of the original 10 students and the new median of the 12 students?

A) 0
B) 10
C) 20
D) 30

BOX PLOT (BOX-AND-WHISKER DIAGRAM)

A *box plot*, sometimes called a *box-and-whisker diagram*, displays the data in four regions. At a glance, you can see the spread of the data, from the minimum value to the maximum value. You can also see what are called *quartiles*, which are really, in a way, just *medians*. Let's go back to our original data, in order from least to greatest: {20, 24, 37, 38, 40, 42, 43, 45, 60, 98}. We can divide these data evenly into two subgroups: {20, 24, 37, 38, 40} and {42, 43, 45, 60, 98}. Note the five *vertical* lines in the box plot below as we cover the following:

- The first line, starting from the left, is the smallest value in the data set (20).
- The second line, which begins the box, is called the first quartile (Q_1). It is the median of the first subgroup. The median of {20, 24, 37, 38, 40} is 37, so $Q_1 = 37$.
- The third line, the middle of the box, is called the second quartile (Q_2). It is simply the median of all the values, the average of 40 and 42: $Q_2 = 41$.
- The fourth line, which ends the box (again, from left to right), is called the third quartile (Q_3). It is the median of the values in the second subgroup. The median of {42, 43, 45, 60, 98} is 45, so $Q_3 = 45$.
- Finally, the last line at the far right is the largest value in the data set (98).

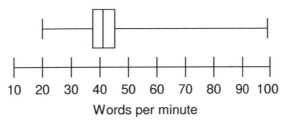

22. The box plot above displays the typing speeds, in words per minute, of 10 students. The center of the box corresponds to a speed of 41 words per minute. If x is the number of students who type slower than 41 words per minute and y is the number of students who type faster than 41 words per minute, which of the following must be true about x and y?

A) $x < y$
B) $x > y$
C) $x = y$
D) $x = 0.25y$

TERMINOLOGY

Below are a few terms that may come up on a Statistics problem (in addition to some of the terms you already know, such as *mean*, *median*, and *mode*):

- **Standard deviation**: a measure of the spread of a data set. Standard deviation measures how far away, on average, the values in a data set are from the average of the data.

- **Outlier**: a value that is well outside of the expected range of a data set's values, and which is often discarded from the data set. Note that outliers affect mean, but not medians.

- **Range**: the difference between the largest and smallest values in a statistical distribution.

19.

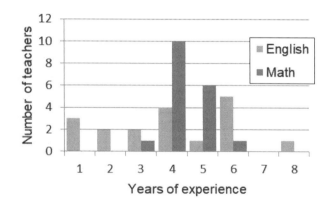

The histogram above displays the years of experience for 36 English and Math teachers at a school. Which of the following is true about the standard deviations of the English and Math teachers' years of experience?

A) The standard deviation of the English teachers' years of experience is greater.

B) The standard deviation of the Math teachers' years of experience is greater.

C) The standard deviation of the English teachers' years of experience is the same as that of the Math teachers.

D) The standard deviation of the teachers' years of experience cannot be calculated

11. The histogram below summarizes the number of siblings of 40 students at school X. Which of the following is the median and mean number of siblings for the 40 students?

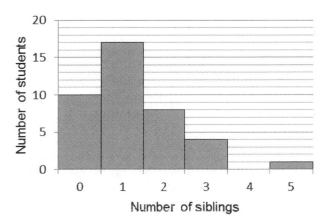

A) Median = 1, Mean = 3
B) Median = 2.5, Mean = 1.25
C) Median = 1, Mean = 1.25
D) Median = 2.5, Mean = 3

Continued →

26.

March		August	
Stem	Leaves	Stem	Leaves
5	244	5	
5	577	5	99
6	004	6	1344555
6	59	6	6666779
7	2334	7	0001
7	67999	7	

A robotics company makes small robots that can be used to find survivors in collapsed or unstable buildings. The stem-and-leaf plots above summarize the lengths, to the nearest millimeter, of random samples of 20 robot legs during March and August of a given year. Which of the following correctly compares the standard deviation of each of the two sets of data?

A) The standard deviation of leg lengths in March is smaller.
B) The standard deviation of leg lengths in August is smaller.
C) The standard deviation of leg lengths in March and August is the same.
D) The relationship cannot be determined from the information given.

3. STUDIES

The SAT may ask you about the results of a *study*. The most common mistake that students make on these problems is *jumping to a conclusion*. You need to recognize the information presented and understand the conclusions that you can appropriately draw from this information.

WHERE? WHO? HOW MANY?

To avoid jumping to conclusions, ask yourself the following questions:

- *Where* **was the study conducted?** For example, a survey conducted at a bowling alley about how often people bowl will not give a clear picture of the bowling habits of the *entire population*.

- *Who* **took part in the study?** Asking college graduates with advanced degrees a question about politics is not a great way to determine the opinions of the *nation as a whole*.

- *How many* **people took part in the study?** All studies focus on a *sample* of some population, and the size of this sample matters. Asking 2 people at a school about their interests in school sports doesn't tell us much. Asking 100 people might.

ACCURACY

Students sometimes jump to incorrect conclusions about *accuracy*. Remember that any results from a study are associated with the *sample* that was surveyed. We may be able to draw a conclusion from the results, but we don't know exact numbers *for sure*. For example, if 27% of the respondents of a well-designed survey with a large sample size prefer Candidate A, we might say that *about* 27% of the associated population prefers Candidate A, but we probably cannot say for certain that *exactly* 27% of the population will vote for him.

 Look for words like *survey*, *study*, or *research study*. Additionally, these questions, and their answer choices, tend to be wordy. You probably won't see any equations or variables, and any numbers will be minimal.

Here's a method for solving Study questions:

1. Underline the *purpose* of the study, if available. The question will often make this clear in the first sentence ("A study was done to . . .").

2. Underline the *location* of the study, if available, and the *group* that was surveyed. Remember, you need to ask the *Where?* and *Who?* questions described above.

3. Finally, from the information given, DON'T JUMP TO CONCLUSIONS!

Try the following lesson problem:

7. A city wanted to know peoples' opinions on the quality of the city's sidewalks, so volunteers selected at random 1,000 residents walking on the sidewalks at several locations around the city. Each person was asked if he or she was satisfied with the quality of the sidewalks. Of those surveyed, 65% responded that they were satisfied with the quality of the sidewalks. Which of the following is likely true?

A) Of all residents of the city, approximately 65% of them are satisfied with the quality of the sidewalks.

B) Of all residents of the city, exactly 65% of them are satisfied with the quality of the sidewalks.

C) Of those residents of the city who use the sidewalks, approximately 65% of them are satisfied with the quality of the sidewalks.

D) For most cities, of the residents who use the sidewalks, approximately 65% of them are satisfied with the quality of the sidewalks.

Not jumping to conclusions, as described above, is enough to get you most of these Studies questions, but some students might want to look over the terminology below. While unlikely, these terms might show up on the SAT. **[40-hour program only]**

TERMINOLOGY

- **Population parameter**: a numerical value that describes a characteristic of a population (such as age or income).

- **Random sample:** Since it is usually time consuming to ask an entire population a particular question, statisticians usually ask members of a *random sample*. The more random the sample, the better the data will reflect the entire population.

- **Margin of error**: a measure of the accuracy of an estimate. You won't have to calculate a margin of error on the SAT, but you should understand how factors such as randomization and the number of test subjects might affect the error. Note that the larger the standard deviation, the larger the margin of error. The larger the size of the random sample, the smaller the margin of error.

- **Confidence interval**: a range, or interval, of values used to estimate the true value of a population parameter. The SAT always uses a 95% confidence interval. This means that some given confidence interval will include the true population parameter 95% of the time. Put another way, we are 95% confident that the confidence interval contains the true population parameter.

Skip the following question unless you covered the terminology above:

28. A student measures the typing speed of 100 students at random from School X in Hamilton County and finds that the average typing speed has a 95% confidence interval of 41 to 49 words per minute. Which of the following conclusions is the most reasonable based on the confidence interval?

A) 95% of all students in Hamilton County have an average typing speed of between 41 and 49 words per minute.

B) 95% of all students at School X have an average typing speed of between 41 and 49 words per minute.

C) There is a 95% chance that the average typing speed of all students in Hamilton County is between 41 and 49 words per minute.

D) There is a 95% chance that the average typing speed of students at School X is between 41 and 49 words per minute.

4. A market researcher selected a random sample of 200 people shopping at various bookstores in Chicago to determine how often people read literary journals. Of those surveyed, 59% said they read at least one literary journal a year. Which of the following inferences can appropriately be drawn from this survey result?

   A) Most people who shop at bookstores read at least one literary journal a year.

   B) Most people who shop at bookstores in Chicago read at least one literary journal a year.

   C) Most people who read literary journals also shop in bookstores in Chicago.

   D) Most people in Chicago read at least one literary journal a year.

24. To determine how many times per month people in a community purchase groceries online, Stephanie surveyed 500 adults at an online community website. For those surveyed, the mean number of times per month that groceries were purchased online was 1.2. Which of the following statements must be true?

   A) The mean number of times per month that people in the community purchased groceries online was 1.2.

   B) The sample size is too small to make any conclusions about the mean number of times per month that people in the community purchased groceries online.

   C) The sampling method was flawed and may overestimate the mean number of times per month that people in the community purchased groceries online.

   D) The sampling method was flawed and may underestimate the mean number of times per month that people in the community purchased groceries online.

■

30- and 40-hour programs: After correcting all relevant questions from Practice Tests 2 and 3 and reviewing the tutorial, take Practice Test 8 in *The Official SAT Study Guide*.

4. BASIC TRIGONOMETRY

Basic trigonometry, or *trig*, is the study of the relations between the angles and the sides of *right triangles*. Look at the triangle below:

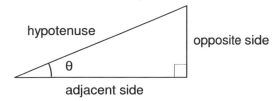

In a right triangle, each trig function of an angle is a ratio of 2 of the sides of the triangle. Notice that relative to each angle (such as the angle θ—pronounced "THEY-tuh"—in the figure above), there is an *opposite* side, an *adjacent* side, and the *hypotenuse*. Note that the hypotenuse is always the longest side of the triangle and is always opposite the right angle. **Don't confuse the hypotenuse with one of the other sides.** Let's get started with an important word:

SOH·CAH·TOA

Memorize this acronym. It will help you remember the basic trig functions:

SOH: The **Sine** (*sin* for short) of an angle is the ratio of the **Opposite** side to the **Hypotenuse**:

$$\sin\theta = \frac{\text{opposite}}{\text{hypotenuse}} = \frac{O}{H}$$

CAH: The **Cosine** (*cos* for short) of an angle is the ratio of the **Adjacent** side to the **Hypotenuse**:

$$\cos\theta = \frac{\text{adjacent}}{\text{hypotenuse}} = \frac{A}{H}$$

TOA: The **Tangent** (*tan* for short) of an angle is the ratio of the **Opposite** side to the **Adjacent** side:

$$\tan\theta = \frac{\text{opposite}}{\text{adjacent}} = \frac{O}{A}$$

(EX) In the right triangle below, what is the value of cos θ?

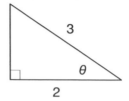

A) $\dfrac{2}{3}$

B) $\dfrac{3}{2}$

C) $\dfrac{\sqrt{5}}{3}$

D) $\dfrac{\sqrt{5}}{2}$

FINDING MISSING INFORMATION

The power of trig is that it allows us to find the missing sides of any right triangle when we know just *one* of the sides. In the past, we could only do this with the two special right triangles (30-60-90 and 45-45-90). So trig is an important tool. Let's put it to work:

(EX) Side *BC* of △*ABC* below is 10 inches long. If the sin of ∠*A* is $\frac{5}{13}$, how long, in inches, is the hypotenuse of the triangle?

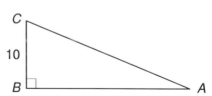

A) 12
B) 13
C) 24
D) 26

THE SPECIAL RIGHT TRIANGLES, REVISITED

Remember these? The 30-60-90 and 45-45-90 triangles are found on the reference section of each math test:

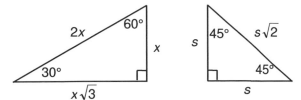

Sometimes, you will be asked for the trig functions of the special angles: 30°, 45°, and 60°. Using the triangles above, you can quickly find these trig values. First, let $x = s = 1$, above, so you have the following triangles:

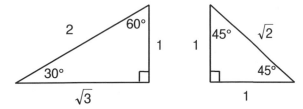

Now, just by looking at these triangles, you can find the trig functions of important angles. Try filling in the information in the following table:

	30°	45°	60°
sin			
cos			
tan			

Note: The fractions above have been simplified by "rationalizing the denominator." Below is an example:

$$\sin 45° = \frac{O}{A} = \frac{1}{\sqrt{2}} = \frac{1}{\sqrt{2}} \frac{\sqrt{2}}{\sqrt{2}} = \frac{\sqrt{2}}{2}$$

As you can see, it can get a little tricky. You can either memorize the values, or if you're on the calculator section, convert the fractions to decimals.

BASIC TRIGONOMETRY LESSON PROBLEMS

21. What is the value of tan θ in the triangle shown below?

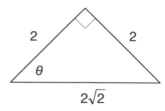

    A) $2+2\sqrt{2}$
    B) 2
    C) $\sqrt{2}$
    D) 1

28. Henry wants to measure the length of the pond shown below. If the length of leg YZ of $\triangle XYZ$ is 50 feet and the measure of $\angle X$ is 20°, which of following expresses the length of the pond?

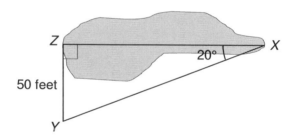

    A) $\dfrac{50}{\cos 20°}$

    B) $\dfrac{50}{\tan 20°}$

    C) 50 sin 20°
    D) 50 tan 20°

[CALCULATOR SECTION: 1–30 MULTIPLE-CHOICE / 31–38 GRID-IN]:

15. In the right triangle pictured below, x, y, and z are the lengths of its sides, as shown. What is the value of cos θ?

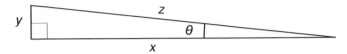

A) $\dfrac{x}{y}$

B) $\dfrac{y}{x}$

C) $\dfrac{x}{z}$

D) $\dfrac{y}{z}$

18. Right triangle ABC is shown below. Which of the following is equal to sin α – cos β?

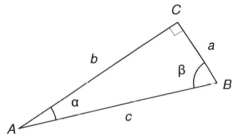

A) 0

B) 1

C) $\dfrac{a-b}{c}$

D) $\dfrac{a-c}{b}$

5. *MORE TRIGONOMETRY*

THE UNIT CIRCLE

We can analyze trig functions for the angles of right triangles, but what if we're dealing with angles that wouldn't fit into a right triangle? For example, what's the cosine of 120°? This angle could not be part of a right triangle—it's too big—but it *does* have a cosine. That's where the unit circle comes in.

THE FOUR QUADRANTS

The unit circle has a radius equal to 1 and is centered at the origin of the *xy*-plane. The *x* and *y* axes divide the circle into four quadrants, labeled I, II, III, and IV below. **Notice that the top right quadrant is I, and the subsequent quadrants are numbered *counterclockwise*.**

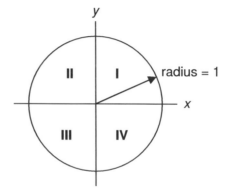

ANGLES

The circle is used to display the measures of angles. Like the quadrants, the angles are measured *counterclockwise* from the positive side of the *x*-axis. The example below shows the angle 120°. The line where the angle ends is called the *terminal side* of the angle:

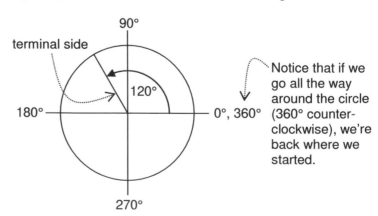

REFERENCE TRIANGLE

If you draw a *vertical* line to the *x*-axis from the end of the angle's terminal side, you create what is called a *reference triangle*. This is a right triangle. Remember, the unit circle has a radius of 1, so the hypotenuse of this right triangle is 1. **Make sure you always draw a *vertical* line to the *x*-axis.**

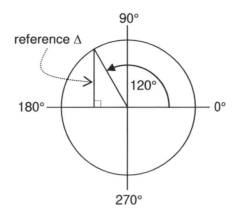

REFERENCE ANGLE

Let's enlarge the triangle. Can you calculate the measure of the angle between the *x*-axis and the terminal side? This is an important angle. It's called the *reference angle*.

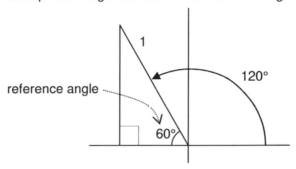

The reason for looking at these reference triangles and reference angles is that they allow us to find trig functions of larger angles. Remember our original question? What's the cosine of 120°? We couldn't figure that out because 120° isn't part of a right triangle, but the reference angle for 120°, which we found to be 60°, *is* part of a right triangle. So:

$$\cos 120° \overset{?}{=} \cos 60°$$

Not quite. We have to think about one more thing:

THE QUADRANTS AND THE TRIG FUNCTIONS

Reference angles and triangles will give us the *absolute value* of a trig function, but we need to know whether the trig function is positive or negative. That's where the four quadrants and the acronym *ASTC* come in to play:

Starting in Quadrant I and moving counterclockwise (as usual), we write *ASTC*. There are several ways to memorize this acronym. The most popular is "All Students Take Calculus." Feel free to think of your own. Just remember to move in a *counterclockwise* direction from Quadrant I.

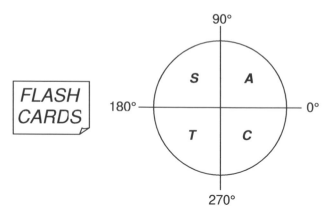

Each letter tells us something important about the trig functions in that letter's quadrant:

- *A*: All trig functions are positive in Quadrant I.
- *S*: Sine only is positive in Quadrant II.
- *T*: Tangent only is positive in Quadrant III.
- *C*: Cosine only is positive in Quadrant IV.

USING THE UNIT CIRCLE TO FIND TRIG FUNCTIONS: SUMMARY

Finally, we can answer the original question. What is the cosine of 120°? The reference angle tells us that the absolute value of cos 120° is equal to cos 60°. But we're in Quadrant II, so cosine must be *negative*. So we have:

$$\cos 120° = -\cos 60°$$

If you remember the special right triangles, you can find that $\cos 60° = \dfrac{1}{2}$, so:

$$\cos 120° = -\cos 60° = -\dfrac{1}{2}, \text{ and we're done!}$$

Here's a summary of the method:

1. Draw the angle in question on a unit circle.
2. Draw the reference triangle and identify the reference angle.
3. Consider the sign of the trig function (positive or negative) by using the *ASTC* acronym.
4. Find the trig function of the reference angle, and apply the correct sign from step 3.

There are a few ways you can identify these trig problems. Some problems will have a drawing of a unit circle. Otherwise, look for a reference to one of the quadrants—such as the degree inequality shown in the example below—or look for large angles (> 90°) that wouldn't fit into a right triangle.

$\widehat{EX}$ If $180° \leq x \leq 270°$ and $\sin x = -\dfrac{4}{5}$, then $\cos x =$? **[NO-CALCULATOR]**

A) $-\dfrac{3}{5}$

B) $-\dfrac{3}{4}$

C) $\dfrac{3}{5}$

D) $\dfrac{3}{4}$

COORDINATES

An interesting thing about the points along the unit circle is that they can tell you the sine and cosine of an angle. **Each *x*-coordinate is the *cosine* of the related angle, and each *y*-coordinate is the *sine* of the related angle.**

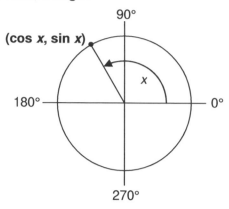

FOUR IMPORTANT POINTS

The most useful reason for memorizing the relationship above (cos *x*, sin *x*) is that you can find the trig functions for angles that don't have reference triangles, namely (0°, 90°, 180°, and 270°):

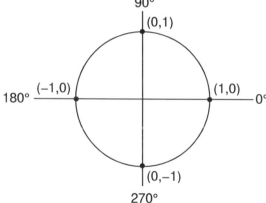

$$\cos 0° = 1, \sin 0° = 0$$
$$\cos 90° = 0, \sin 90° = 1$$
$$\cos 180° = -1, \sin 180° = 0$$
$$\cos 270° = 0, \sin 270° = -1$$

You shouldn't have to memorize these values. Just use the unit circle, and remember that cos *x* is the *x*-coordinate and sin *x* is the *y*-coordinate.

DEGREES AND RADIANS

Up until now, we've only worked with *degrees* when measuring an angle. Sometimes, the SAT will use alternate units of angle measurement called *radians*. Radians may look and sound complicated, but if you memorize the known relationship 180° = π radians and use the proportion below, the calculation is straightforward:

$$\boxed{\begin{array}{c} FLASH \\ CARDS \end{array}} \quad \frac{\text{degrees}}{\text{radians}} \frac{180°}{\pi} = \frac{?}{?}$$

Let's use this proportion to find a few important radian measures: **[NO-CALCULATOR]**

(EX) What is the radian measure of 90°?

1. What is the radian measure of 180°?

2. What is the radian measure of 270°?

3. What is the radian measure of 360°?

THE UNIT CIRCLE, WITH RADIANS

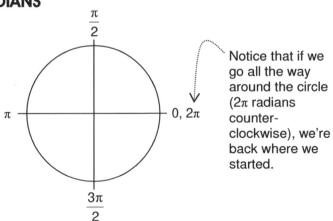

Notice that if we go all the way around the circle (2π radians counter-clockwise), we're back where we started.

TRIG AND YOUR CALCULATOR

While you won't likely be asked for values of trig functions that require a calculator, that doesn't mean you won't be able to use your calculator to help on trig questions (assuming, of course, that you're on the calculator section). Here are a couple things to watch out for:

DEGREES/RADIANS

Calculators have separate modes for *radians* and *degrees*. Make sure you have your calculator set correctly. If you're in radian mode and you type in degrees, your answer will be incorrect. (And vice versa.)

POWERS OF TRIG FUNCTIONS

You have to be careful when you raise a trig function to a power. For example, how do we square the sin x? Math books will usually notate $(\sin x)^2$ as $\sin^2 x$. This makes clear that the entire function is squared, not just the variable (x). For most calculators, you can type either: $(\sin (x))^2$ or $\sin (x)^2$. Just make sure you don't type $\sin (x^2)$; this will not give the correct answer (unless of course you're looking for the sine of x^2).

TRIG PROPERTIES

There are a couple trig properties that you should memorize for the SAT:

$$\boxed{\textit{FLASH CARDS}} \quad \tan x = \frac{\sin x}{\cos x}$$

$$\sin^2 x + \cos^2 x = 1$$

> These trig properties questions tend to look more *algebraic* and less *geometric* than other kinds of trig questions. Notice that there is no triangle in the example below.

 Which of the following is equivalent to $(\tan x)(\cos x)$? **[NO-CALCULATOR]**

A) $\cos^2 x$
B) $\sin^2 x$
C) $\cos x$
D) $\sin x$

SINE/COSINE COMPLEMENTARY ANGLE RULES

The SAT often tests the following relationships between sine and cosine. They're worth memorizing:

$$\boxed{\begin{array}{l} FLASH \\ CARDS \end{array}} \quad \begin{array}{l} \textbf{sin } \boldsymbol{\theta} = \textbf{cos } (\textbf{90}° - \boldsymbol{\theta}) \\ \textbf{cos } \boldsymbol{\theta} = \textbf{sin } (\textbf{90}° - \boldsymbol{\theta}) \end{array}$$

MORE TRIGONOMETRY LESSON PROBLEMS

[NO-CALCULATOR SECTION: 1-15 MULTIPLE-CHOICE / 16-20 GRID-IN]:

12. If $\sin \theta = -\dfrac{5}{13}$, and $\dfrac{3\pi}{2} \le \theta \le 2\pi$, then $\tan \theta = ?$

    A) $-\dfrac{13}{12}$

    B) $-\dfrac{12}{5}$

    C) $-\dfrac{12}{13}$

    D) $-\dfrac{5}{12}$

13. If $\tan x = \sqrt{3}$, which of the following could be true about x?

    A) $90° \le x \le 135°$
    B) $135° \le x \le 180°$
    C) $180° \le x \le 225°$
    D) $225° \le x \le 270°$

12. If $\cos x = a$, where $\dfrac{\pi}{2} \le x \le \pi$, then what is $\sin x$?

A) $-\dfrac{1}{a}$

B) $-a$

C) $\dfrac{1}{\sqrt{1-a^2}}$

D) $\sqrt{1-a^2}$

13. Which of the following is equivalent to the expression $(1 - \sin x)(1 + \sin x)$?

A) $\cos^2 x$
B) $\sin^2 x$
C) 1
D) $\cos x$

14. If $\cos 30° = \dfrac{\sqrt{3}}{2}$, what is $\cos 330°$?

A) $\dfrac{\sqrt{3}}{2}$

B) $\dfrac{1}{2}$

C) $-\dfrac{1}{2}$

D) $-\dfrac{\sqrt{3}}{2}$

Continued →

15. Which of the following is equivalent to $\sin^2 x + \sin^2(90° - x)$?

    A) 0
    B) 1
    C) $2\sin^2 x$
    D) $\sin^2 2x$

6. COMPLEX NUMBERS

IMAGINARY NUMBERS (*i*)

Try finding $\sqrt{-25}$ using your calculator. You'll get an error message (unless your calculator is smarter than most). There is no *real number* solution to $\sqrt{-25}$, but there *is* what is called an *imaginary* solution, which uses the variable *i* to refer to $\sqrt{-1}$. First, make sure you are comfortable with the following property of radicals:

$$\sqrt{ab} = \sqrt{a}\sqrt{b}$$

Using this property, we can write:

$$\sqrt{-25} = \sqrt{25(-1)} = \sqrt{25}\sqrt{-1} = 5i$$

That's all *i* is—just a way for us to refer to the square roots of negative numbers.

WORKING WITH *i*

Notice what happens when we take some simple powers of *i*:

$i^1 = i$

$i^2 = \left(\sqrt{-1}\right)^2 = -1$

$i^3 = i^2 \cdot i = (-1)(i) = -i$

$i^4 = i^2 \cdot i^2 = (-1)(-1) = 1$

If we go on to find i^5, you'll see that the pattern begins to repeat:

$i^5 = i \cdot i^4 = i \cdot 1 = i$

This is an important pattern to memorize: $\{i, -1, -i, 1, i, -1, -i, 1...\}$. It allows us to find *i* to the power of large numbers, using the following rules:

1. If the power is divisible by 4, *i* to that power is 1.
2. If the power is NOT divisible by 4, find the nearest power that IS divisible by 4, and count up or down to the power in question.

Look at the following example:

(EX) What is the value of i^{45}? (Note: $i = \sqrt{-1}$)

   A) −1
   B) 1
   C) −*i*
   D) *i*

ALGEBRA WITH *i*

Nearly all of the SAT problems that involve *i* have to do with basic algebraic operations. When you're solving equations with *i*, you can pretend that *i* is just like any other variable, but with one exception: **You must remember the power rules for *i*.** For example, if you get an i^2, you have to remember to turn it into −1. Simplify the following expressions:

1. $3i + 7i =$
2. $(3i)(7i) =$
3. $\dfrac{24i^5}{12i} =$
4. $(2 + i)(3 - i) =$
5. $(x - i)(2x + 2i) =$

 These problems will obviously include the letter *i*. The SAT tends to be nice enough to tell you that $i^2 = -1$, so look for that, too.

14. What is the value of $2i^4 + 2i^2$? (Note: $i = \sqrt{-1}$)
    A) 4
    B) 2
    C) 1
    D) 0

COMPLEX NUMBERS

A complex number is the sum (or difference) of a real number and an imaginary number. If *a* and *b* are real numbers, a complex number takes the form:

$$a + bi$$

An example of a complex number is 3 + 5*i*. The real number part is 3; the imaginary part is 5*i*.

You should be able to convert an expression into a complex number, which, remember, has the form *a* + *bi*. You can use the algebra rules, as described before.

(EX) Which of the following is equivalent to $\dfrac{6+9i}{3}$? (Note: $i = \sqrt{-1}$)
    A) −1
    B) 2 + 3*i*
    C) 2 + 9*i*
    D) 9 + 12*i*

i IN THE DENOMINATOR

Problems that require you to simplify a fraction with *i* in the denominator are rarely found on the SAT, but in case one shows up, there are two tricks:

1. If *i* (or a term including *i, such as 3i*) is alone in the denominator, multiply the numerator and denominator by *i*. This will give you an i^2 in the denominator (and thus, because i^2 = –1, the *i* goes away). Now you can put the number in complex form, as in the example above.

2. If the denominator is a complex number, multiply the numerator and denominator by the *complex conjugate* of the complex number. The complex conjugate of a complex number is simply the complex number with the *i* term multiplied by –1. For example: 2 – 3*i* is the conjugate of 2 + 3*i*. Multiplying by a complex conjugate gets rid of the imaginary number when you FOIL the two expressions. Look at the example below:

(EX) Which of following is equivalent to $\dfrac{20}{6+2i}$? (Note: $i = \sqrt{-1}$)

A) 1 – *i*
B) 2 – *i*
C) 3 – *i*
D) 4 – *i*

[NO-CALCULATOR SECTION: 1-15 MULTIPLE-CHOICE / 16-20 GRID-IN]:

12. Which of the following is equivalent to $(3 - 5i)^2$? (Note: $i = \sqrt{-1}$)

A) –16 – 30*i*
B) –16
C) 9 + 25*i*
D) 9 – 25*i*

14. Which of the following is equivalent to $\dfrac{5}{2+i}$? (Note: $i = \sqrt{-1}$)

A) 10 – *i*
B) 5 – *i*
C) 3 – *i*
D) 2 – *i*

7. PARABOLAS

We discussed quadratic equations in the Factoring section of Chapter V. These equations take the form form $y = ax^2 + bx + c$, where a, b, and c are coefficients. When graphed, a quadratic equation is called a *parabola*. Below is the graph of $y = x^2 - 6x + 5$:

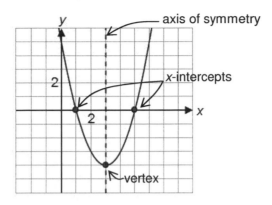

EQUATIONS FOR PARABOLAS

QUADRATIC FORM

We discussed the quadratic form above:

$$y = ax^2 + bx + c$$

This form can, at a glance, tell us the direction that the parabola opens:

- If $a > 0$, the parabola opens *up*—see the example above.
- If $a < 0$, the parabola opens *down*.

The quadratic form allows for easy input into the quadratic formula (see Factoring in Chapter V). We can also determine the number of x-intercepts (0, 1, or 2) by calculating the *discriminant* ($b^2 - 4ac$), as discussed in the Factoring section. Here's a review:

- If $b^2 > 4ac$, then the quadratic equation has 2 *real* solutions (since you'll be taking the square root of a positive number). These solutions are represented graphically as x-intercepts.
- If $b^2 = 4ac$ ($b^2 - 4ac = 0$), then the quadratic equation has 1 real solution/x-intercept.
- If $b^2 < 4ac$, then the quadratic equation has 2 *imaginary* solutions (since you'll be taking the square root of a negative number). There are no x-intercepts. The parabola either opens up above the x-axis or opens down below the x-axis.

Finally, the quadratic form can tell us the x-coordinate of the vertex:

$$\boxed{\begin{array}{c} FLASH \\ CARDS \end{array}} \quad x_v = -\frac{b}{2a}$$

To find the y-intercept of the vertex, plug x_v into the original equation and solve for y. Here's a lesson problem:

26. The equation $y = -x^2 - 2x + 3$ represents a parabola in the xy-plane. Which of the following are the coordinates of the maximum value of the parabola?

   A) $(-1, 3)$
   B) $(-1, 4)$
   C) $(-1, 6)$
   D) $(1, 0)$

x-INTERCEPT FORM

When a quadratic equation is factored, it takes the following form:

$$y = a(x - p)(x - q)$$

In the equation, a, p, and q are real numbers (often integers). This is called the *x-intercept* form because, at a glance, you can see the x-intercepts. They are $x = p$ and $x = q$.

7. The equation $y = x^2 - 6x + 5$ represents a parabola in the xy-plane. Which of the following equations correctly displays the x-intercepts of the parabola as constants or coefficients?

   A) $y - 5 = x^2 - 6x$
   B) $y = (x - 3)^2 - 4$
   C) $y = (x + 5)(x + 1)$
   D) $y = (x - 5)(x - 1)$

VERTEX FORM

The *vertex* of a parabola is the minimum point for an upward opening parabola, or the maximum point for a downward opening parabola. The vertex form is:

$$y = a(x - h)^2 + k$$

In the equation, a, h, and k are real numbers (again, often integers). When an equation is in this form, the vertex is at the point (h, k), and the *line of symmetry* will be the vertical line $x = h$.

20. The equation $y = x^2 - 6x + 5$ represents a parabola in the xy-plane. Which of the following equivalent equations correctly displays the x- and y-coordinates of the vertex of the parabola as constants or coefficients?

A) $y = (x - 3)^2 - 4$
B) $y - 5 = x^2 - 6x$
C) $y = x(x - 6) + 5$
D) $y = (x - 5)(x - 1)$

A more difficult question on the vertex form might require you to *complete the square*. This technique was covered in the More Circles section (Chapter VII). You might want to review it before completing the homework.

[CALCULATOR SECTION: 1–30 MULTIPLE-CHOICE / 31–38 GRID-IN]:

6. The equation $y = x^2 - 36$ represents a parabola in the xy-plane. Which of the following equivalent forms of the equation displays the x-intercepts of the parabola as constants or coefficients?

A) $y + 36 = x^2$

B) $y = (x - 6)(x + 6)$

C) $y = (x - 18)^2 - 324$

D) $y = x\left(x - \dfrac{36}{x}\right)$

28. The height h, in feet, of a model rocket over time t, in seconds, can be modeled by the function $h(t) = -14t^2 + 224t$. Which of the following is an equivalent form of the function h in which the maximum height appears as a constant or coefficient?

A) $y = 14(t - 8)^2 + 896$
B) $y = -14(t - 8)^2 + 896$
C) $y = 14t(t - 16)$
D) $y = -14t(t - 16)$

8. MIXTURES

The SAT may test *mixtures*. In these problems, different solutions are mixed together to create a final solution. For example, a 20% salt solution is mixed with a 50% salt solution to create a 40% salt solution. These problems use the following equation, where x is the amount of the first solution and y is the amount of the second solution:

$$a\% \cdot x + b\% \cdot y = c\% \cdot (x + y)$$

You can use this equation to solve for whatever the question may ask. Just plug in what you know and solve for the unknown. Here's an example:

(EX) If 80 grams of a 20% saline solution is mixed with 40 grams of a 50% saline solution, what percent saline is the final solution?

    A) 25%
    B) 30%
    C) 35%
    D) 70%

Did you notice that Mixture problems test the percent *of/is* technique? Here's the question in word form: 20% of 80 plus 50% of 40 equals what percent of 120? Another way of thinking about it is that the amount of saline in the first solution plus the amount of saline in the second solution will equal the amount of saline in the final solution. Seeing the connection to the *of/is* technique might help you memorize the formula above. Here's a lesson problem:

21. Stan needs 10 liters of a 15% sugar solution. If he adds x liters of 10% sugar solution and y liters of 30% sugar solution to create the desired mixture, which of the following systems of equations could be used to find the values of x and y?

    A) $0.10x + 0.30y = 0.15(x + y)$
         $x + y = 10$

    B) $0.10x + 0.30y = 0.15$
         $x + y = 10$

    C) $0.10x + 0.30y = 10(x + y)$
         $x + y = 0.15$

    D) $0.10x + 0.30y = 10$
         $x + y = 0.15$

21. Hillary wants to make 100 milliliters of 5% alcohol solution. If she has 40 milliliters of 2% alcohol solution, the remaining 60 milliliters of solution should be what percent alcohol?

    A) 7%
    B) 8%
    C) 9%
    D) 10%

30. The octane number of a mixture of gasoline gives the percent of isooctane in the gasoline. If x liters of 89 octane gasoline is mixed with 5 liters of 92 octane gasoline, in terms of x, which of the following gives the octane number of the final mixture?

    A) $89 + \dfrac{15}{x+5}$

    B) $89 + \dfrac{460}{x+5}$

    C) $0.89 + \dfrac{15}{x+5}$

    D) $0.89 + \dfrac{4.6}{x+5}$

9. MATH ODDS & ENDS: PRACTICE & CORRECTIONS

PRACTICE PROBLEMS

The following worksheets tests techniques taught in this chapter. In addition, we'll use Practice Test 1 from *The Official SAT Study Guide* for more practice questions. Don't forget to review the lessons in this chapter while completing these problems:

- ☐ Math Odds & Ends Worksheet 1
- ☐ Math Odds & Ends Worksheet 2
- ☐ Test 1 (practice problems): See the Techniques chapter at the end of this tutorial.

TEST CORRECTIONS

After completing and grading each practice test, you should correct Odds & Ends questions that you missed or guessed on. Below are the three steps to correcting practice tests:

1. Turn to the Techniques section at the end of this tutorial and circle the Odds & Ends questions that you missed or guessed on for each test.

2. Correct the problems in *The Official SAT Study Guide*. As you correct the problems, go back to the tutorial and review the techniques. The idea is to (1) identify techniques that have given you trouble, (2) go back to the tutorial so you can review and strengthen these techniques, and (3) apply these techniques to the specific problems on which you struggled.

3. If you have trouble identifying the best technique to use on a problem, refer to the Techniques chapter. This is an important part of correcting the tests.

MATH ODDS & ENDS WORKSHEET 1

[NO-CALCULATOR SECTION: 1-15 MULTIPLE-CHOICE / 16-20 GRID-IN]:

12. Which of the following is equivalent to $\dfrac{5+6i}{6-5i}$? (Note: $i = \sqrt{-1}$)

    A) $\dfrac{5}{6} + \dfrac{6i}{5}$

    B) $\dfrac{5}{6} - \dfrac{6i}{5}$

    C) $-i$

    D) i

14. If $\pi \le \alpha \le \dfrac{3\pi}{2}$ and $\sin \alpha = -\dfrac{\sqrt{3}}{2}$, then $\tan \alpha = ?$

    A) $\sqrt{3}$

    B) $\dfrac{\sqrt{3}}{2}$

    C) $-\dfrac{\sqrt{3}}{2}$

    D) $-\sqrt{3}$

15. If $\cos(x°) = \sin[(10x - 9)°]$, what is a possible value of x ?

    A) 1
    B) 4
    C) 5
    D) 9

[CALCULATOR SECTION: 1–30 MULTIPLE-CHOICE / 31–38 GRID-IN]:

5. The graph of $y = 4x^2 - 32x + 60$ is a parabola in the xy-plane. In which of the following equivalent equations do the x-intercepts of the parabola appear as constants or coefficients?

    A) $y = 4(x - 4)^2 - 4$
    B) $y = 4(x^2 - 8x + 15)$
    C) $y = (4x - 20)(x - 3)$
    D) $y = 4(x - 5)(x - 3)$

Continued →

13. A researcher surveyed 500 adults who were selected at random from the 10 most-populated cities in America and asked each adult, "How concerned are you about the air quality in your city?" Of those surveyed, 82% indicated that they were "very concerned" about the air quality in their city. Based on the results of the survey, which of the following is probably true?

    A) If 500 additional adults were selected at random from the 10 most-populated cities in America, 82% would be very concerned about air quality.

    B) Most adults in American cities are very concerned about air quality.

    C) Of adults who live in the 10 most-populated cities in America, 82% are very concerned about air quality.

    D) Most adults who live in the 10 most-populated cities in America are concerned about air quality.

14. In right triangle $\triangle ABC$ below, which of the following is equal to sin A?

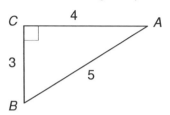

    A) sin B
    B) cos B
    C) tan B
    D) cos A

22. Rachel needs to average 80.0 points on 5 equally weighted gymnastics tests if she hopes to be invited to an upcoming tournament. If she has taken 4 of the tests, and her average score is 75.5, how many points must she score on the 5th test to get invited to the tournament?

    A) 92
    B) 94
    C) 96
    D) 98

Continued →

23. In △ABC, shown below, the length of side BC is 5 units, the length of side AC is 10 units, and sin x = 0.8. What is the area, in square units, of △ABC?

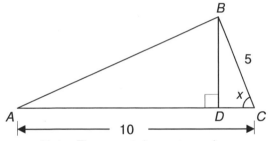

Note: Figure not drawn to scale.

A) 20

B) $\dfrac{25\sqrt{3}}{2}$

C) 25

D) $25\sqrt{3}$

29. Which of the following is an equivalent form of the parabolic function $f(x) = (x - 5)(x + 1)$ in which the coordinates of the vertex can be identified as constants in the equation?

A) $y = x^2 - 5$
B) $y = x^2 - 4x - 5$
C) $y = (x - 2)^2 - 9$
D) $y = (x - 2)^2 - 5$

MATH ODDS & ENDS WORKSHEET 2

[NO-CALCULATOR SECTION: 1-15 MULTIPLE-CHOICE / 16-20 GRID-IN]:

9. What is the value of $(4 + i)(-3 - i)$? (Note: $i = \sqrt{-1}$)

   A) $-7 - 7i$
   B) $-11 - 7i$
   C) $-11 - i$
   D) $-12 - 7i$

10. If c is a nonzero constant, which of the following equations could define a parabola in the xy-plane with vertex (a, b)?

   A) $y = c(x - a)^2 + b$
   B) $y = c(x - a)^2 - b$
   C) $y = c(x + a)^2 + b$
   D) $y = ax^2 + bx + c$

13. If $0° \le \theta \le 90°$ and $\tan \theta = 2$, then $\sin \theta = $?

   A) $\dfrac{1}{2}$

   B) $\dfrac{\sqrt{5}}{2}$

   C) $\sqrt{5}$

   D) $\dfrac{2}{\sqrt{5}}$

Continued →

▼

Questions 15 and 16 refer to the following information.

A linguist wants to determine the average number of words per sentence in written English in books published in the last 25 years. From a large local library, the linguist chooses 10 books at random that were published in the last 25 years, and from each book she chooses one sentence at random. She finds that the mean number of words per sentence is 20.1, with a 95% confidence interval of 13.0 to 27.2 words.

15. Which of the following would most likely result in a smaller confidence interval in the study above?

    A) Choose one book from each of ten libraries.

    B) Increase the number of books in the study.

    C) Decrease the number of books in the study.

    D) Increase the range of years in the study.

16. Based on the design and results of the study above, which of the following is an appropriate conclusion?

    A) There are between 13.0 and 27.2 words in 95% of all sentences in English books published in the last 25 years.

    B) There are between 13.0 and 27.2 words in 95% of all sentences in all published English books.

    C) There is a 95% chance that the true mean number of words per sentence for English books published in the last 25 years is between 13.0 and 27.2.

    D) There is a 95% chance that the true mean number of words per sentence for all published English books is between 13.0 and 27.2.

▲

Continued →

19. For right triangle $\triangle ABC$ below, what is the cos $\angle B$?

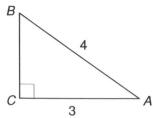

A) $\dfrac{3}{4}$

B) $\dfrac{4}{\sqrt{7}}$

C) $\dfrac{\sqrt{7}}{4}$

D) $\dfrac{\sqrt{7}}{3}$

24. A vertical structure casts a shadow at an angle of 40° from the ground, as shown below. If the shadow ends 30 feet from the edge of the structure, how high, in feet, is the structure?

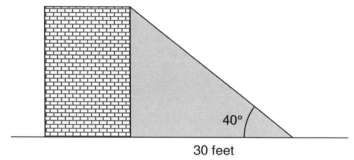

30 feet

A) $30 \tan 40°$

B) $30 \cos 40°$

C) $\dfrac{30}{\sin 40°}$

D) $\dfrac{30}{\tan 40°}$

Continued →

28. A scientist measures the lengths of the back legs of lizards from two different islands. She measures 200 lizards from Island A and 250 lizards from Island B. If the mean back-leg length of the lizards from Island A is 5 centimeters and the mean back-leg length of the lizards from Island B is 4 centimeters, to the nearest tenth of a centimeter, what is the mean back-leg length of all 450 lizards?

A) 4.3
B) 4.4
C) 4.5
D) 4.6

36. Alex has an empty 5 liter container and an unlimited supply of pure water and 30% saline solution. If Alex wants a final solution of at least 10% saline, what is the greatest volume of water, in liters, that Alex can mix with the 30% saline solution in the 5 liter container?

REVIEW WORKSHEET (CHAPTERS I–VII)

[NO-CALCULATOR SECTION: 1-15 MULTIPLE-CHOICE / 16-20 GRID-IN]:

2.

$$\frac{2}{5}x - 4 = -\frac{3}{10}x - \frac{1}{2}$$

What is the value of x in the equation above?

A) $\dfrac{1}{5}$

B) 5

C) 10

D) 25

5. Which of the following is equivalent to the expression $2x^2 - 2xy + 3x - 3y$?

A) $(2x + 3)(x + y)$
B) $(2x - 3)(x + y)$
C) $(2x + 3)(x - y)$
D) $2x(x - y) + 3x(x - y)$

7.

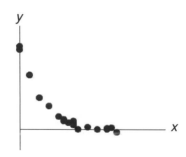

The scatterplot above is graphed on an xy-plane. If a and b are positive integers, which of the following equations could be used to describe the curve of best fit (not shown) for the scatterplot?

A) $y = a\left(\dfrac{1}{b}\right)^x$

B) $y = a(b)^x$

C) $y = a\left(\dfrac{1}{x}\right)^b$

D) $y = a(x)^b$

Continued →

8.

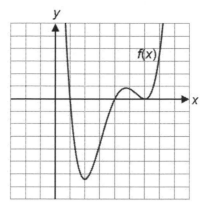

Which of the following could be an equation for the graph of the function f shown in the xy-plane above?

A) $f(x) = 0.2(x + 1)(x + 4)(x + 6)$
B) $f(x) = 0.2(x - 1)(x - 4)(x - 6)$
C) $f(x) = 0.2(x + 1)(x + 4)(x + 6)^2$
D) $f(x) = 0.2(x - 1)(x - 4)(x - 6)^2$

11. The function f is defined by $f(x) = x^2 + x - 12$. If $f(a) = f(3)$ and $a < 0$, what is the value of a?

A) 3
B) -3
C) -4
D) -12

Continued →

13. For x > 0, which of the following is equivalent to $\dfrac{4x+5}{\dfrac{1}{4x}+\dfrac{1}{5}}$?

    A) 1
    B) 2
    C) 20x
    D) 16x^2 + 25

14. Which of the following is equivalent to $\dfrac{2x^2+3x}{2x+1}$?

    A) $x + 3$

    B) $4x$

    C) $x - \dfrac{1}{2x+1}$

    D) $x + 1 - \dfrac{1}{2x+1}$

Continued →

15.

$$c = 250 + 22n$$

The equation above estimates the number of cookies, c, sold by Marla's Cookie Company on the nth day of December for a given year. The number 22 in the equation above gives which of the following estimates?

A) Marla's Cookie Company sold 22 cookies on the first day of December.

B) Marla's Cookie Company sold 22 more cookies in December than in November.

C) Each day of December, Marla's Cookie Company sold 22 cookies.

D) Each day of December, Marla's Cookie Company sold 22 more cookies than the previous day.

19.

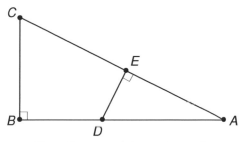

Note: figure not drawn to scale.

In the right triangle ABC above, $AD = 6$ and $AC = 10$. If the length of side BC is one less than twice the length of side DE, what is the length of side DE?

Continued →

20.

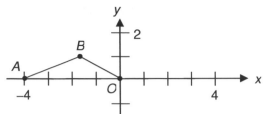

In the figure above, the coordinates of points *A* and *B* are (−4, 0) and (−$\sqrt{3}$,1) respectively.

What is the measure, in degrees, of angle *AOB*?

[CALCULATOR SECTION: 1–30 MULTIPLE-CHOICE / 31–38 GRID-IN]:

1. Which expression is equivalent to $(3x^2 + 4x) - (-4x^2 - 3x + 2)$?

   A) $7x^2 + 7x + 2$
   B) $7x^2 + 7x - 2$
   C) $-x^2 - x + 2$
   D) $-x^2 - x - 2$

3. One postal machine can sort 20 envelopes in 30 minutes. How long, in <u>hours</u>, will it take 10

   postal machines, each working at the same rate, to sort 10,000 envelopes?

   A) 20
   B) 25
   C) 200
   D) 250

Continued →

10. Last year, a small bicycle company sold ten-speeds for $250 each and cruisers for $125 each. If the company sold 820 bikes and earned $167,500 in sales, how many ten-speeds did the company sell?

    A) 300
    B) 420
    C) 480
    D) 520

11. Bradley paid $40.88 for a tank of gas. This price included a tax of $4.38. Which of the following is closest to the tax percent for the gas?

    A) 9%
    B) 10%
    C) 11%
    D) 12%

15. Paula takes 2 minutes to read each page of *Slaughterhouse-Five* and 5 minutes to read each page of *Ulysses*. She has no more than 20 hours per week to read, but she wants to read at least 500 pages per week. Which of the following systems of inequalities represents this situation in terms of x and y, where x is the number of pages she reads from *Slaughterhouse-Five* and y is the number of pages she reads from *Ulysses*?

    A) $2x + 3y \leq 20$
       $x + y \geq 500$

    B) $2x + 3y \geq 1{,}200$
       $x + y \leq 500$

    C) $2x + 3y \leq 500$
       $x + y \geq 1{,}200$

    D) $2x + 3y \leq 1{,}200$
       $x + y \geq 500$

Continued →

16.

	Number of visitors			
Age (years)	Emerald City Rides	Poppy Field Games	Yellow Brick Road Stores	Total
4 to 12	40	132	35	207
13 to 18	161	20	32	213
19 or older	87	156	119	362
Total	288	308	186	782

The manager of the Land of Oz amusement park analyzed attendance at each of the three parts of the park at noon on a single day. The data is shown above. Based on the table, what is the approximate probability that one of the park's visitors was at the Emerald City Rides at this time, if the visitor was age 13 or older?

A) 0.32
B) 0.37
C) 0.43
D) 0.76

18.

$$x + y = 20$$
$$3x + 3y = \frac{20}{3}$$

Which of the following is true about the system of linear equations above?

A) The lines intersect at $(0, 20)$.

B) The lines intersect at $(20, 0)$.

C) The lines intersect at an infinite number of points.

D) The lines never intersect.

20. A department store sells socks for x dollars per pair. After the first pair, the store gives customers 5 percent off the price of the <u>previous</u> pair, for up to a total of 3 pairs of socks. The store also charges 12.5 percent sales tax on the entire order. In terms of x, which of the following expressions gives the total cost, in dollars, for 3 pairs of socks?

A) $1.125(0.95x)^4$
B) $1.125(x + 2\cdot0.95x)$
C) $1.125x + 0.95x + 0.95\cdot0.95x$
D) $1.125(x + 0.95x + 0.95\cdot0.95x)$

26.

$$1{,}000\left(1+\frac{r}{100n}\right)^{nt}$$

The expression above gives the amount of money, in dollars, generated by a $1,000 deposit in t years, compounded n times per year, with an interest rate of r percent. In terms of r, which of the following expressions shows how much money will be <u>added</u> to the original deposit after 5 years if the deposit is compounded monthly?

A) $1{,}000\left(1+\frac{r}{100}\right)5$

B) $1{,}000\left(1+\frac{r}{1{,}200}\right)^{60}$

C) $1{,}000\left(1-\left(1+\frac{r}{1{,}200}\right)^{60}\right)$

D) $1{,}000\left(\left(1+\frac{r}{1{,}200}\right)^{60}-1\right)$

27. In the xy-plane, the graph $x^2-6x+y^2+6y=-15$ is a circle. What is the radius of the circle?

A) 3

B) $\sqrt{3}$

C) $\sqrt{15}$

D) $3\sqrt{2}$

28. For all values of x, if $\sqrt[3]{x^4}\cdot\sqrt[5]{x^6}=\dfrac{x^m}{x^n}$ and $m=38$, what is the value of n?

A) 15

B) $\dfrac{532}{15}$

C) $\dfrac{182}{5}$

D) $\dfrac{437}{12}$

Continued →

29.

$$\frac{3}{(x+3)} - \frac{4}{(x+4)} = \frac{ax-b}{(x+3)(x+4)}$$

If the equation above is true for all $x > 0$, where a and b are positive constants, what is the value of $a + b$?

A) 7
B) 1
C) 0
D) −1

33. A right cylinder has a height equal to the diameter of the cylinder's base. If the volume of the cylinder is 686π cubic inches, what is the radius of the cylinder?

| | | | | |

36.

$$p = 1.20(a - b)$$

A lake charges fishermen a fee for each fish caught according to the equation above, where p is the fee, in dollars, a is the weight of the fish, in pounds, b is the minimum allowable weight for a fish, in pounds, and $a > b$. The units of the constant 1.20 are dollars divided by pounds. The state also charges a 10% tax, based on the lake's fee, for each fish. If a fisherman paid a total of $1.98, including the state's tax, for a fish that weighed 3 pounds, what was the minimum allowable weight for a fish?

| | | | | |

PART  4

TECHNIQUES

TECHNIQUES

One of the keys to improving your SAT scores is learning from your mistakes. As stated throughout this tutorial, you should go back to practice tests and correct questions that relate to chapters, as these chapters are completed. The specific questions to (potentially) correct for each test are found on the following pages, at the beginning of the relevant test.

As you correct questions, you need to make sure that you're using the correct techniques, as taught in this tutorial. The following pages list the techniques, as taught in this tutorial, for every question in *The Official SAT Study Guide* (2020 edition).

Note that on the following pages, the actual answers are <u>not</u> given. The point of this section is to give you direction, by listing techniques and, often, hints. This will help you tackle problems using the techniques you've learned and give you an idea of what lessons to review in the tutorial.

Each subtest (Reading, Writing & Language, and Math) presents techniques differently, as described below.

READING

The Reading techniques typically provided two pieces of information: question types and line numbers (context).

QUESTION TYPES

Knowing what type of question you're answering is an important part of the Reading test. If you have trouble identifying any of these questions types, make sure to review the magnifying glass information in the Reading part of this tutorial. Of course, pay attention to the types of questions that you frequently miss, and review these sections in the tutorial.

LINE NUMBERS (CONTEXT)

The most important technique for Reading questions is the use of *context*. The answers must be clearly stated or supported by *the text*. If you miss a Reading question, you must find the part of the passage that contains the information or evidence that will lead you to the correct answer. The following pages display the pertinent line numbers for each question. When necessary, clarifying words or phrases are sometimes included.

Of course, finding the context is only part of it. You have to *understand* the context, not to mention the language in the questions and the answer choices. If you still have trouble with a question even after you have found the appropriate context in the passage, check the solutions in the SAT book.

Note that on the following pages we generally only refer to context related to *correct* answers. Of course, you may often choose to use context to *eliminate* answer choices. This is encouraged, especially when you are not sure of the correct answer. Again, the solutions in the SAT book may be helpful.

WRITING & LANGUAGE

Eliminating answer choices is an important part of tackling the SAT Writing & Language questions. Recognizing errors in the answer choices also gives you a good idea of what technique or techniques are being tested on a particular question. **For each question on the following pages, the given technique or techniques apply to *all incorrect answer choices*, unless labeled otherwise.** For example, look at the following question:

1. Run-ons / + Pronoun Agreement (B)

Here's what this means: <u>All three</u> incorrect answer choices have Run-on errors. *In addition*, answer choice B (and <u>only B</u>) has a Pronoun Agreement error.

Here's a similar example:

2. Run-ons (A, C) / Pronoun Agreement (B)

Now, <u>only A and C</u> have Run-on errors, and <u>only B</u> has a Pronoun Agreement error.

As you correct missed questions, look at your answer sheet, and make sure to focus on the technique or techniques associated with *your* incorrect answer.

MATH

You may be able to solve some math questions with more than one technique. Which technique is best is often a personal decision, based on your own strengths and weaknesses. Sometimes you may want to review *all* given techniques for a missed problem. Often, the more ways you can tackle a problem, the better.

THE PICK TRICKS

You will notice that the Pick Tricks (Pick Numbers or Pick Answers) show up frequently, either as preferred methods, or as optional ones. For most students, we recommend using a Pick Trick when one is given. It's good practice. These techniques are designed to get you out of jams, so make sure you're comfortable with them.

ALGEBRAIC WORD PROBLEMS

We'll often give you the equations on Algebraic Word problems. We recommend you first try to find them on your own, before looking at our solution. If you do need to peak, make sure you understand how we found them. Being able to convert word problems into equations (or inequalities) is one of the most important parts of the test.

ABBREVIATIONS

We use the following abbreviations on the following pages:

- CTE: Citing-Textual-Reference (Reading)
- WIC: Words-in-Context (Reading)
- IG: Informational Graphics (Reading and Writing & Language)
- POE: Process of Elimination (all sections)

1. PRACTICE TEST 1

QUESTIONS BY SECTIONS/CHAPTERS

The following information lists every question on the test according to its relevant chapter or section in this tutorial. If you're correcting a test, circle the question numbers below that you missed or guessed on. Make sure to follow the Tutoring Schedule in the Introduction to know when to correct or tackle various types of questions.

READING
BY PASSAGE
- [1, 2, 3, 4, 5, 6, 7, 8, 9, 10] [11, 12, 13, 14, 15, 16, 17 ,18 19, 20, 21] [22, 23, 24, 25, 26, 27, 28, 29, 30, 31] [32, 33, 34, 35, 36, 37, 38, 39, 40, 41] [42, 43, 44, 45, 46, 47, 48, 49, 50, 51, 52]

BY QUESTION TYPE
- Direct & CTE (stand-alone): 9, 10, 13, 14, 16, 17, 23, 24, 36, 37, 43, 44
- Extended Reasoning & Purpose: 4, 5, 7, 11, 19, 22, 25, 26, 27, 32, 34, 35, 40, 41, 42
- WIC & Main Idea: 1, 3, 8, 12, 18, 33, 45, 47, 48
- Comparison & IG: 20, 21, 28, 29, 30, 31, 49, 50, 51, 52
- Tone, Structure, & Relationship: 2, 6, 15, 38, 39, 46
  Note: Most Citing-Textual-Evidence (CTE) questions are grouped with their relevant preceding questions.

WRITING & LANGUAGE
- Grammar & Sentence Structure: [1, 3, 4, 7, 8, 10, 11] [13, 15, 16, 17, 18, 19, 21] [23, 24, 25, 26, 30, 32, 33] [35, 36, 39, 40, 41, 43, 44]
- Main Ideas & Organization: [2, 5, 6, 9, 12*] [14, 20, 22] [27, 28, 29*, 31] [34, 37, 38, 42]
  Note: Brackets display separate passages.
  * Informational Graphics

MATH
- Arithmetic: §3 (14); §4 (1, 5, 6, 7, 13, 21, 23, 27, 31, 33, 34)
- Functions: §4 (37, 38)
- Algebra: §3 (1, 3, 4, 6, 7, 8, 9, 10, 11, 12, 16, 18); §4 (2, 4, 8, 9, 10, 11, 15, 16, 18, 19, 20, 26, 28, 32)
- Advanced Algebra: §3 (5, 13, 15); §4 (25, 29)
- Graphs of Functions: §4 (17, 36)
- Geometry: §3 (17); §4 (3, 24, 35)
- Odds & Ends: §3 (2, 19); §4 (12, 14, 22, 30)
  §3 = Section 3; §4 = Section 4

TECHNIQUES AND HINTS

READING

PASSAGE I

1. Main Idea: 46–47, 60

2. Structure: 31–32, etc. You might try POE (process of elimination) on this one. Choice A is false: the meeting is not a traditional one. Choice C is false: there is no resolution given. Choice D violates tone ("cheerful").

3. Words-in-Context (WIC): 65 (without a "go-between"). Remember, try to define the word in question *before* looking at the answer choices.

4. Extended Reasoning: 39–41, 63–64

5. Citing-Textual-Evidence (CTE): See above.

6. Tone: 31–32 (respect), 69–70 (lack of deference), 71–73 (lack of deference followed by respect), 77–78 (respect, followed by implied lack of deference)

7. Purpose: 1–4 (". . . would Chie have been more receptive?"): Try POE if the answer is not apparent.

8. WIC: 2–4. The passage suggests that Akira did not follow standard practice (see 63–66).

9. Direct: 39–42. Remember, if you're not sure where to look for context, always check to see if the next question is a Citing-Textual-Reference (CTE) one. This will help you narrow down your search to one of four places—better than skimming the whole passage.

10. CTE: See above.

PASSAGE II

11. Purpose: 1–3

12. WIC: 10–16. People "relish" (a good thing) and, at the same time, "dread" (a bad thing) buying gifts.

13. Direct: 10–13 ("build stronger bonds")

14. CTE: See above.

15. Tone: 30 ("not surprising")

16. Direct: 44–47 ("unfounded")

17. CTE: The answer will question or discredit the "link between gift price and feelings of appreciation" (45). Note that sometimes the contextual support you find for an answer does not coincide with the lines given in the subsequent CTE question. That's fine. Sometimes more than one part of a passage may support an answer choice.

18. WIC: 57 ("signal"). Gift givers are trying to "signal their positive attitudes" by buying expensive gifts. If you have trouble with this one, plug in the answer choices and trust your ear.

19. Purpose: 51–52. The work by Camerer and others likely tries to answer the question at the beginning of the paragraph.

20. Informational Graphics (IG) (extended reasoning): Focus on the gift-giver data. What do gift-givers think drives gift appreciation?

21. IG (make connections): 31–32, 66–68

PASSAGE III

22. Purpose: 4 ("regular alteration of sugar and phosphate groups"—the keyword is *regular*)

23. CTE (stand-alone): This is one of those CTE questions that doesn't refer to a previous question. Check the answer choices and use POE. One challenge to this problem is that "nitrogenous bases" is not mentioned near the correct answer. You might need to review lines 5–8 to make the connection.

24. Direct: 12–14. This is an example of a direct hit. The context is easy to find and very clear. All students need to search out these easier questions, even if they choose to skip some of the harder ones.

25. Purpose: 18–19. This problem required you to skim for context on "X-ray evidence," but luckily the word "X-ray" is fairly easy to find, and the context is clear.

26. Extended Reasoning: You can actually answer this one without looking at the passage. What does the statement in the question imply?

27. Purpose: 48–51 (especially "duplicate itself")

28. IG (make connections): See line 7 for the make-up of purine.

29. IG (make connections): 34–35

30. IG: This is similar to a CTE question. If you found the correct answer for the previous question, this one is straightforward.

31. IG (make connections) / CTE (stand-alone): Answer in parts; the first part should be the easiest (the percentage of adenine clearly varies from organism to organism); then use POE for the remaining two choices.

PASSAGE IV

32. Purpose: 7–8 ("we are pressed for time"), 48–51 (". . . so important")

33. Main Idea: 25–34, 53–57. It's important to recognize that Woolf is referring throughout the passage to educated women: see line 24 ("we go ourselves")—educated women are joining the procession of educated men.

34. Purpose / Extended Reasoning: The answer to this one is not found directly in the passage, but consider how the word "we" affects the tone of the author's message. Imagine, as an educated woman, how you might feel about the author if she had instead used "they."

35. Purpose: 1–3. The answer almost feels too easy (D is tempting), but remember, don't extend your reasoning if you don't have to. In this case, you don't have to extend reasoning at all— the answer is explicitly supported by the text.

36. Direct: 19–24 ("But now . . . we go ourselves")

37. CTE: See above. Note that D is tempting, but C provides better context specifically for "the procession" mentioned in the prior question.

38. Tone: 48–49 ("very important," "very little time"), 49–53

39. CTE: See above.

40. Extended Reasoning: 30–34. Also see the questions in lines 53–57 and 77–

83. The challenge here is that the best context (30–34) is not especially close to the line numbers given in the question.

41. Purpose: See question 38. We know the questions are "momentous and pressing." Which answer best supports these ideas? Note that choice A is tempting—the challenge does seem novel (new) (see lines 19–24)—but this novelty is not discussed in lines 72–76.

PASSAGE V

42. Purpose: 5–8 (especially "all working to make space mining a reality")

43. Direct: 18–22

44. CTE: See above.

45. WIC: 18–22. Note that precious metals are already in "demand[ ]," and the rare earth metals are "vital." Which word captures these sentiments?

46. Structure or Purpose: 29–30. The answer choices mention the "previous paragraph," so this is similar to a Structure question.

47. Main Idea: 53–54, 57–59, 85–88. Not surprisingly, the main ideas are found following contrast signals and at the end of the passage.

48. WIC: 67–69. If you understand the second clause of this sentence (". . . it may be difficult . . .), the context becomes clear. The ideas in the preceding paragraphs will be difficult to keep up or preserve.

49. Comparison: See question 47 (and lines 53–54, 57–59, and 85–88).

50. Comparison: 53–54, 57–59, 85–88. Again, this question reflects the main idea of the passage.

51. CTE / Comparison: See above.

52. Comparison: 29–30, 74–76

WRITING & LANGUAGE

PASSAGE I

1. Vocabulary

2. Main Ideas: Note the previous sentence ("To address the problem of disposal . . .")

3. Apostrophes & Confused Words (B, D) / Verb Tense (C). Not surprisingly, the correct verb tense is the shortest (see Avoid Wordy Answer choices in the Grammar & Sentence Structure Guidelines chapter).

4. Punctuation: Make sure you understand how to use commas (or sometimes semicolons) in lists.

5. Organization: The clue word is "it," referring to acid whey, but every answer choice places the sentence after the introduction of acid whey in sentence 1. So we must find another clue. Consider the negative tone of the sentence. Sentence 2 introduces the idea that acid whey is "difficult to dispose of" (negative tone). Sentence 3 transitions to a positive tone ("To address the problem . . ."). Where should we put sentence 5?

6. Main Idea (topic sentence): Note the main idea of the paragraph, as made clear in its second half: "health benefits," "nutritional benefits."

7. Idioms

8. Verb Tense (B, D) / Parallelism (A)

9. Transitions: The information in this sentence is *related* to the previous sentence (benefits of Greek yogurt), but it is not a restating (B), a consequence (C), or an example (D) of the information in the previous sentence.

10. Vocabulary

11. Redundancies (A, C): The word "Because" already makes the cause-and-effect relationship clear. / Punctuation (D): Colons should generally only follow complete sentences.

PASSAGE II

12. Informational Graphics (IG): If you have trouble with IG questions, review the Reading part of the tutorial.

13. Combining Sentences: When combining sentences, correct answers are often shorter than incorrect ones.

14. Transitions: Compare "late summer" in the first sentence of the paragraph with "mid-July" in this sentence. Is mid-July late summer?

15. Punctuation

16. Punctuation: Review the correct use of semicolons and colons. Here are the specific techniques or guidelines that apply to each incorrect answer choice: Fragment (A), Wordy (B), -*ING* (D).

17. Run-ons: Only one choice does not create a run-on sentence. Note that there is no FANBOYS conjunction after the comma, so what follows the comma can*not* be a complete sentence.

18. Verb Tense

19. Apostrophes & Confused Words (A, C) / Pronoun Agreement (B)

20. See the Answer the Question section in the Reading part of the tutorial. Note that the cycle begins with ice melting ("As the ice melts . . ."). So how would the cycle complete? The key word is *cycle*, which suggests a return to a starting point.

21. Redundancies: Every wrong answer is redundant to something in the passage, but to different words: "repeat" (A), "harmful effects" (C), "may" (D).

22. Organization: clue words = "this crucial information"

PASSAGE III

23. Redundancies: Note the word "quickly."

24. Misplaced Words (improper modifier): Who does the modifying phrase "Having become frustrated . . ." modify? Only one choice works.

25. Idioms

26. Punctuation: Review the rules for colons if necessary.

27. Transitions

28. Main Ideas (deletions): The main idea of the paragraph has to do with the physical "coworking spaces." Does the sentence in question stay on topic?

29. IG: Just use POE on this one. Again, if you have trouble with Informational Graphics questions on the Writing & Language test, review the relevant chapter in the Reading section.

30. Pronoun Case (A, B) / Subject-Verb Agreement (B, C)

31. Organization: clue words = "the facility"

32. Punctuation

33. Style: This first-person passage is written with simple, straightforward prose.

PASSAGE IV

34. Transitions: The sentence is supportive (so you can eliminate C and D). Is the sentence providing an example of relevant skills in the modern workplace?

35. Concision: Note that one choice is considerably shorter than the others.

36. Verb Tense: See "offers" later in the sentence. / + -*ING* (A, D)

37. Transitions: Note the change in tone from the first sentence to the one that follows (in the passage).

38. Transitions

39. Combining Sentences: Once again, shorter choices are usually correct.

40. Subject-Verb Agreement: The subject is "students."

41. Apostrophes & Confused Words: "majoring in philosophy" describes the students, but it does not *belong* to them. (Remember, -*ing* words are *usually* wrong, but not always.)

42. Main Ideas (additions): The main idea of this paragraph is philosophy's applications to "other disciplines."

43. Fragments: The subject of this sentence is actually the whole first phrase: "That these skills are transferable across professions." Consider a simpler example of one of these "that subjects": *That I am here* is obvious. Once you recognize the subject, you'll hopefully find the one choice that does not create a fragment.

44. Pronoun Agreement

MATH (no calculator)

1. Basic Algebra

2. Complex Numbers

3. Algebraic Word or Pick Numbers (type 1)

4. Linear Equations: Review "Applications" in the Linear Equations lesson.

5. Working with Polynomials or Pick Numbers (type 1): If you Pick Numbers, be prepared to move quickly. We recommend you pick small numbers, whose squares you can calculate easily in your head.

6. Linear Equations: Review "Applications" in the Linear Equations lesson.

7. Basic Algebra: Look for a shortcut on this one: consider the numerator as one easily moved "chunk," and the denominator as another one.

8. Basic Algebra or Pick Numbers (type 2): For Pick Numbers (type 2), you'll pick a number for only *one* of the variables, and solve for the other.

9. Systems of Equations or Pick Answers: Interestingly, if you plug the answer choices into the second (easier) equation, only one works.

10. Basic Functions / Basic Algebra: Use the first equation (and the given "function rule") to solve for *a*. Then find $g(-4)$.

11. Basic Algebra

12. Linear Equations: Once you have the equation, check the points.

13. Common Denominators or Pick Numbers (type 1): Unless you struggle with mental math on non-calculator problems, you'll probably want to use the Pick Trick on this one. Don't forget, $x > 3$.

14. Exponents or Pick Numbers (type 2): Hint: $8^x = (2^3)^x = 2^{3x}$.

15. Working with Polynomials / (Pick Numbers (type 4) or Basic Algebra / Factoring): This is not an easy problem. The first step is to FOIL the left side of the equation. After simplifying, you should end up with $(ab)x^2 + (7a + 2b)x + 14$. Comparing coefficients on both sides of the equation, you'll have $ab = 15$ and $7a + 2b = c$. And the question gives $a + b = 8$. Now what? You have two options. You can Pick Numbers (type 4); in other words, guess and check *a*'s and *b*'s until you find ones

that satisfy the two equations ($ab = 15$ and $a + b = 8$); then find c. Or solve for a and b algebraically, using substitution and factoring: $b = 8 - a \rightarrow$ (substitution) $a(8 - a) = 15 \rightarrow$ (after simplifying) $a^2 - 8a - 15 = 0 \ldots$

16. Basic Algebra (solving exponential equations)

17. Triangles (similar)

18. Systems of Equations

19. More Trigonometry (sine/cosine complementary angle rules): If you forgot the complementary angle rules, you could also draw a right triangle that satisfies the given sine equation. Note that you're trying to find the cosine of the angle *opposite* the one in the sine equation.

20. Basic Algebra (solving equations with radicals)

MATH (calculator)

1. Tables & Graphs

2. Basic Algebra

3. Angles (parallel lines)

4. Algebraic Word: Here's the equation (always try to find these equations on your own *before* looking at our solution): $16 + 4x = 10 + 14$

5. Tables & Graphs (scatterplot)

6. Proportions: You're given two known relationships, so you should set up two proportions.

7. Tables & Graphs

8. Basic Algebra (solving absolute value equations): There's a shortcut on this one: Can $|n - 1|$ ever equal -1? In other words, can the absolute value of something ever be negative?

9. Basic Algebra

10. Basic Algebra: Of course, this question relies on answering the previous question correctly, although you could Pick Answers.

11. Basic Algebra (inequalities) or Pick Answers

12. Statistics (histograms)

13. Tables & Graphs / Percent (of/is)

14. Means, Medians, & Modes / Statistics: We briefly discuss "range" in the Statistics lesson: it is simply the difference between the smallest and largest measurements. This value will change significantly when the error is removed (since the error value is considerably larger than the next-largest value). Removing the error will not change the mean significantly, since there are so many other values, and it will not change the median at all. Note: You will NOT have time to calculate any values for this problem.

15. Linear Equations (applications)

16. Linear Equations

17. Graphs of Functions

18. Systems of Inequalities: Since (0, 0) is a solution to the inequalities, we have $0 < a$ and $0 > b$. If the correct answer is not apparent, plug in numbers (Pick Numbers (advanced)).

19. Algebraic Word: Review "A Common Algebraic Word Problem." These two-equation/two-unknown problems show up frequently.

20. Percent (increase/decrease) / Algebraic Word: Here's the algebra: We'll use "multipliers," so 20% discount means $\times$ 0.80 and 8% increase means $\times$ 1.08 (review the Increase/Decrease lesson if necessary). Let x be the original price: $x(0.80)(1.08) = p \rightarrow$ solve for x. Note that this problem is inconvenient to use Pick Numbers (type 1) because it is difficult to work backward from p, the amount Alma paid. It's probably easier to use algebra.

21. Probability: Make sure you read these probability questions carefully. You're choosing someone from among those "who recalled at least 1 dream." So the denominator will be the number of people who meet this criterion. The numerator will be the number of people *in Group Y* who meet this criterion. The tables on these probability questions often have considerable superfluous (unneeded) information.

22. Tables & Graphs / Means: The question is simply asking you to find the average of the 2008–2009 change and

the 2009–2010 change (both found by subtracting). Or, you could find the total (2008–2010) change (again by subtracting) and divide by 2.

23. Tables & Graphs / Ratios: There's a shortcut to this one: If we round the human resources budgets for 2007 and 2010 to the nearest million, our ratio becomes 4,000,000:6,000,000 = 4:6 = 2:3. Only one choice has a ratio, when similarly rounded and reduced, close to 2:3. No need for your calculator.

24. More Circles (equation of) / Coordinates (slanted distances): To find the radius, either use the Pythagorean Theorem approach (recommended) or the distance formula. Both are discussed in the Coordinates lesson.

25. Factoring: Note the word "approximately" in the question. Also note that the given velocity (25 m/s) is not needed to answer the question.

26. Percent (increase/decrease) / Basic Algebra or Pick Answers

27. Tables & Graphs / Proportions: There's a lot of information given here, and the known relationship is not explicit. The units of the proportion are meters squared (m^2) and number of earthworms. The table shows the number of earthworms in each square-meter area. A reasonable guess for the average number of earthworms per square-meter is 150 (take a glance at the answer choices). The area for the entire field is $10 \times 10 = 100\ m^2$. Here's the proportion (solve for x):

$$\frac{m^2}{earthworms} \quad \frac{1}{150} = \frac{100}{x}$$

28. Systems of Inequalities: The first step is to graph the two lines (ignore the inequalities). Then, to determine which side of each line to shade, check a point or two. Review the lesson if necessary.

    Pick Numbers (advanced): Another approach is to pick a point in one of the answer-choice quadrants, check the inequalities, and eliminate choices.

29. Polynomial Division (remainder theorem)

30. Parabolas (equations: vertex form)

31. Proportions: Pick a number between 12 and 18 ears of corn for the numerator of your known relationship. The denominator = 1 hr.

32. Algebraic Word: $4{,}500 + 14x < 6{,}000$

33. Tables & Graphs / Ratios (of/is)

34. Proportions: Make sure to write your units before plugging numbers into your proportion. Hint: The known relationship is 2 slots every 1 hour (or 1 slot every 0.5 hours).

35. Solids & Volume / Basic Algebra

36. More Graphs of Functions (domain) / Factoring: Set the denominator equal to 0 and, by factoring, solve for x.

37. Growth & Decay Functions: A common error is to guess that $x = 0.02$ (2%). Review the lesson, if necessary.

38. Growth & Decay Functions: See the previous question.

2. PRACTICE TEST 2*

QUESTIONS BY SECTIONS/CHAPTERS

The following information lists every question on the test according to its relevant chapter or section in this tutorial. If you're correcting a test, circle the question numbers below that you missed or guessed on. Make sure to follow the Tutoring Schedule in the Introduction to know when to correct or tackle various types of questions.

READING
BY PASSAGE
- [1, 2, 3, 4, 5, 6, 7, 8, 9, 10] [11, 12, 13, 14, 15, 16, 17 ,18 19, 20, 21] [22, 23, 24, 25, 26, 27, 28, 29, 30, 31, 32] [33, 34, 35, 36, 37, 38, 39, 40, 41, 42] [43, 44, 45, 46, 47, 48, 49, 50, 51, 52]

BY QUESTION TYPE
- Direct & CTE (stand-alone): 12, 13, 17, 22, 23, 24, 27, 35, 36, 40, 41, 45, 46
- Extended Reasoning & Purpose: 2, 11, 15, 26, 28, 29, 34, 38, 43, 48, 49
- WIC & Main Idea: 1, 14, 16, 18, 25, 33, 37, 39, 44, 47
- Comparison & IG: 19, 20, 21, 30, 31, 32, 50, 51, 52
- Tone, Structure, & Relationship: 3, 4, 5, 6, 7, 8, 9, 10, 42
  Note: Most Citing-Textual-Evidence (CTE) questions are grouped with their relevant preceding questions.

WRITING & LANGUAGE
- Grammar & Sentence Structure: [1, 3, 5, 6, 7, 8, 10] [13, 14, 16, 18, 19, 20, 21] [23, 27, 28, 29, 30, 32, 33] [34, 35, 36, 38, 39, 41, 44]
- Main Ideas & Organization: [2, 4, 9, 11] [12, 15, 17, 22] [24†, 25, 26, 31] [37, 40, 42, 43]
  Note: Brackets display separate passages.
  † Informational Graphics

MATH
- Arithmetic: §4 (2, 4, 5, 11, 14, 15, 16, 17, 20, 27, 31, 32)
- Functions: §3 (14); §4 (10)
- Algebra: §3 (1, 2, 3, 5, 8, 9, 10, 12, 16, 20); §4 (1, 3, 6, 8, 9, 12, 21, 22, 23, 25, 28, 29, 34, 35, 37, 38)
- Advanced Algebra: §3 (4, 7, 13, 15, 17)
- Graphs of Functions: §4 (26, 33)
- Geometry: §3 (6, 18); §4 (24, 30, 36)
- Odds & Ends: §3 (11, 19); §4 (7, 13, 18, 19)
  §3 = Section 3; §4 = Section 4

* Test 2 is no longer found in *The Official SAT Study Guide* (2020), but it is currently available at the CollegeBoard website.

TECHNIQUES AND HINTS

READING

PASSAGE I

1. Main Idea: 6–7 ("irksome" = annoying, bothersome), 27–33 (following "But"), 34–35 ("Antipathy")

2. Purpose: 6–10. The narrator states that a man will stick with a job ("row long against wind and tide"), even if he finds the work unpleasant. So the job must be extremely unpleasant indeed for a man to jump ship (so to speak) and leave a job. The first sentence gives us context about how miserable the narrator must be. If in doubt on this one, try POE.

3. Structure: 1–6 (first part of answer choice), 6–33 (second part of answer choice). Hint: Try eliminating answer choices just using the second part of each choice.

4. Tone: 28 ("antipathy"), 31 ("sunshine of life"), 34–35 ("Antipathy"). The words "shade" and "darkness" are used metaphorically, referring to the narrator's general unhappiness.

5. Direct / Tone: 39–45

6. Extended Reasoning / Tone: 61–62. The narrator uses the word "brother" not literally but figuratively (a close associate, a fellow man).

7. Citing-Textual-Evidence (CTE): See above.

8. Relationship: 50–56. The narrator refers to himself as lynx-like ("Caution, Tact, Observation") and to Edward as snake-like ("prowling and prying"), thus describing the nature of their relationship.

9. Tone: 72–74 ("no cheering red gleam"). Remember, if you're not sure where to look for context on these questions that lack line numbers, always check the next question to see if it's a CTE one. This narrows down possible places to look in the passage.

10. CTE: See above.

PASSAGE II

11. Purpose: 11–12, etc.

12. Direct: 4–5. Note the words "Some argue." The statement that follows is one the author anticipates. (Because the author separates himself from this group, he may likely disagree with or question the statement.)

13. CTE: See above.

14. Words-in-Context (WIC): 6 ("accepted")

15. Purpose: 45. If you're counting approaches, this is the third. See also 57–58 ("three versions").

16. WIC: 57–59. The author is referring to different versions, or views, of ethical economics. Only one choice makes sense in this context.

17. CTE (stand-alone) / Direct: 58–59. Note what follows the contrast signal in line 58: ". . . but clashes are not inevitable." In other words, common ground is possible.

18. Main Idea: The paragraph claims that behavioral economists are "trying to understand our psychology" to "anticipate our decisions in the marketplace" (79–83). Furthermore, psychology may help scientists understand how we react to "economic injustice" (which has to do with economic ethics) (83–86).

19. Informational Graphics (IG) (direct)

20. IG (direct)

21. IG (make connection): 59–66, especially 64–66. The definition of "fair trade" is given in lines 59–61.

PASSAGE III

22. Direct: 1–2, etc.

23. CTE: Note the change in tone at line 23 ("But . . ."). The passage is positive about computers and Web browsing up to this point, but not after it.

24. Direct: 34–36 ("those gains" refers to using "the Net and other screen-based technologies" (lines 31–32)), 47–50

25. WIC: 40 ("change"). Sometimes the answer to a WIC question is a word found nearby in the passage.

26. Purpose: 60–65. Note the contrast signal "but" in line 63. Clearly, speed reading did not help Allen understand the novel.

27. Direct: 77–79

28. Purpose: 81–84. The author is criticizing those—such as "Media critics"—who think that "consuming electronic media" will have significant impact. See also the first paragraph.

29. Purpose: 23–25, 81–82. The main ideas (and purposes) of the passages can be found in the lines above. As you read these passages, make sure to look for main ideas, and indicate them accordingly (we recommend an asterisk). If you spot these main ideas ahead of time, questions that test them become much easier.

30. Comparison: 23–25, 81–82

31. Comparison: 29–38, 70–74

32. Comparison / CTE (stand-alone): The key words in lines 41–43 are "a different brain," meaning the brain changes.

PASSAGE IV

33. Main Idea: The first two paragraphs especially discuss the problems of a society controlled by "man." Note the language: "social disorganization" (3), "destructive" (4), "discord, disorder, disease, death" (6–7), and so on. In the third paragraph, Stanton stresses that a movement of femininity (namely, the right to vote) would create a positive influence on society that has been lacking: 57–60 (". . . but a new evangel of womanhood . . ."). You might also use POE on this one: There is no mention of "equal educational opportunities" (A) or women "serving as legislators" (D). Watch out for C: this choice mentions voting, a central idea of the passage, but the passage does not mention "poor candidates" or "important elections."

34. Purpose: 16–17

35. Direct: 20–22 ("until within the last century"). The incorrect choices are all, most likely, long-established social realities. Hint: If you didn't know where to find the answer to this one, look at the next question.

36. CTE: See above.

37. WIC: 17 ("overpowering")

38. Purpose: 31–34 ("object," "suffrage"). Hopefully you're familiar with the terms "suffrage" (the right to vote) and "disfranchised" (deprived of the right to vote, line 35).

39. WIC: 36–40. The women are mere "reflections, varieties, and dilutions of the masculine gender." They are not *real* women.

40. Direct: 53–55

41. CTE: See above.

42. Relationship: 67–73. The author distinguishes between "all men" (line 68) and "the masculine element" (line 67), or "those characteristics . . . that distinguish what is called the stronger sex" (lines 71–73). The distinction is between men and their characteristics. If necessary, try POE for this one.

PASSAGE V

43. Purpose: 4–6 (description), 7–9 (importance: "fundamental")

44. WIC: 16–17 ("take . . . into account").

45. Direct: 13–14

46. CTE: As we've seen in the past, sometimes the lines referred to in a CTE question do not exactly match the lines we used for context on the previous question. In this case, the lines are close by.

47. WIC: 65–70

48. Extended Reasoning: 53–55 ("distinct double-ridge shape"), 67–70 ("in other places")

49. CTE: See above.

50. IG (direct)

51. IG (make connection): 1–5. The internal waves, as, we can assume, represented by the lines in the graph, are always below the ocean's surface. If necessary, try POE (again, this means *process of elimination*) for this one, just focusing on the graph. The graph says nothing about *salinity* (A) or *density* (B). And, according to the graph, choice C appears false; cold

water might move up, but not *above* warmer water.

52. IG (make connection): 8–9. Before going to the passage, eliminate choices that are not supported by the graph. In this case, you can get rid of all three incorrect answers. The graph does not provide information on "density" (B), "surface temperature" (C), or "normal tides" (D).

WRITING & LANGUAGE

PASSAGE I

1. Vocabulary / + -*ING* (A, C): There's nothing inherently wrong with an -*ing* word here, but unless you have a good reason to choose an -*ing* answer choice, it's usually a good idea to guess another choice (review Grammar & Sentence Structure Guidelines).

2. Transitions: Always ignore the underlined transition word when you tackle these. Don't let it influence your choice (it's wrong 75% of the time).

3. Subject-Verb Agreement (B) / Fragments (C, D)

4. Main Ideas (additions): The main idea of the paragraph is "nonprint formats."

5. Concision / + -*ING* (C)

6. Parallelism: See "compiling" and "updating." Remember, parallelism is one of the important reasons why an -*ing* word may be correct.

7. Combining Sentences: Watch out for sentences or parts of sentences that are in the passive voice (A and D). Consider the previous sentence and consider flow as you choose your answer.

8. Run-ons: The first clause ("While these . . .") is a dependent clause, so the next clause must be independent.

9. Main Ideas (transition sentences) / Answer the Question: The examples that follow have to do with "job searches," and other economic concerns ("taxes," "law troubles" [sic], etc.).

10. Parallelism: Mirror the construction of "income taxes" and "retirement

programs." Note that "law troubles" (B) sounds stylistically a little too casual (see Style in the Main Ideas chapter).

11. Main Ideas (passage): Note the title of the passage.

PASSAGE II

12. Transitions

13. Punctuation

14. Apostrophes & Confused Words / Punctuation: Make sure you are comfortable with the correct use of a colon.

15. Main Ideas (additions): keywords = "intricate details of the . . . rooms"

16. Run-ons: The construction might be tricky. There is one subject ("couch and chairs") and two actions ("are characterized by . . ." and "are covered in . . ."). All three incorrect choices are run-ons.

17. Answer the Question: Describe the size of something.

18. Combining Sentences: Try POE if necessary. Here's a simplification of the two sentences: Even though some rooms are plain, or sparse, they are still "true to the periods they represent." It's subtle, but there is a contrast ("Even though," above).

19. Parallelism

20. Apostrophes & Confused Words (A) / Noun Agreement/-*ING* (B): Note the "a" before "visitors'" [sic]. Also, how many visitors are quoted? / Verb Tense (C)

21. Misplaced Words: The phrase "dotted with pin-sized knobs" should not modify "another visitor" (a disquieting possibility indeed).

22. Organization: Consider main ideas. ¶1: "the Thorne Miniature Rooms"; ¶2: "a replica of a solon"; ¶3: "sixty-eight miniature rooms"; ¶4: "plainer rooms"; ¶5: "exquisite craftsmanship and level of detail." ¶3 describes the rooms generally, and ¶2 describes a specific room, so what order seems best.

PASSAGE III

23. Fragments: All three incorrect choices lack a verb for the subject of the *that*

clause ("sea otters"). Review "*That Clauses*" in the Fragments lesson.

24. IG

25. Transitions

26. Main Ideas (additions): The real reason we need to make this addition is that the phrase "has increased 40 percent" is indefinite without some mention of when the increase started. In any case, since this paragraph discusses "global warming" and "carbon dioxide in the atmosphere," the "Industrial Revolution" is fair game.

27. Punctuation: Remember that sometimes, no comma or other punctuation mark is the best choice. Use the pause rule: if you don't need to pause, keep the comma out.

28. Vocabulary

29. Pronoun Case (A, B): Is "kelp" singular or plural? Note the correct subject-verb agreement: "kelp removes." It must be singular. / Apostrophes & Confused Words (B, D)

30. Pronoun Ambiguity

31. Organization: Note that sentence 6 expresses a surprise: "Far from making no difference" (which was expected), "the presence of otters" made a *big* difference.

32. *-ING* (A, D): "having" is usually wrong, even when other *-ing* words are present. / Choice C is more difficult to eliminate, but choice B better captures the scientists' active role in increasing the otter's population.

33. Punctuation: An *or*-phrase is a common way to define a term. E.g.: He is the imam, or leader, of the mosque. Make sure you are comfortable with this construction. You could also try removing comma-bound phrases and see if the sentence still makes sense (E.g.: He is the imam of the mosque).

PASSAGE IV

34. Idioms: Use POE. It is not *at* or *from* the "practice" that the products are designed (eliminate A and B). Nor does the practice *cause* the products to be designed; the practice *is* the designing of the products (eliminate C—"so that" is a cause and effect transition).

35. Punctuation

36. Vocabulary: The correct answer is a bit of an idiomatic set phrase (two words often placed together). If your ear "hears" the correct answer, great. If not, just take a guess.

37. Answer the Question: Find the answer that supports the claim that "it is easier to replace goods than to mend them."

38. Apostrophes & Confused Words: Hopefully you eliminated the answer choices that include "then." As discussed in the tutorial, comparisons use *than*, not *then*. From there, it's a question of spelling.

39. *-ING* (A) / Pronoun Case (B) / Run-ons (D)

40. Transitions: Remember to eliminate synonyms (A and C).

41. Style (A, B) / Verb Tense (C)

42. Organization: This one is tricky. The clue word is in the passage. Sentence 4 begins with the word "Participants," but the previous sentence discussed "Her goals." To make the flow more logical, the passage should return to the subject of the "Repair Café," or others like it (sentence 5), before sentence 4.

43. Main Ideas (additions): The main idea of this paragraph has to do with fixing items that are otherwise considered junk. Does the added sentence stay on-topic?

44. Concision & Redundancies

MATH (no calculator)

1. Basic Algebra

2. Systems of Equations

3. Algebraic Word: The trick to this one is to recognize that *nh* equals the total number of *worker hours* for the job. For example, if $n = 2$ (2 workers) and $h = 3$ (a 3-hour job), then $2 \times 3 = 6$ hours (the total number of worker hours for the job). Since *nh* is multiplied by 12 (and since the whole expression gives the

price, in dollars, of the job), 12 must be the cost for each worker hour.

4. Factoring (quadratics) or Pick Answers: If you recognize that the expression factors similarly to a typical quadratic, factor away. Otherwise, Pick Answers, starting with A (the easiest to FOIL). Choices B and D will likely take too long to expand, so cross your fingers that A or C works.

   You can also Pick Numbers (type 1), but you must pick very easy numbers (since you can't use a calculator). If we pick $a = b = 1$, we luckily (and easily) will find only one correct answer choice. This is worth keeping in mind if you're unsure how else to tackle a non-calculator problem with otherwise tricky calculations.

5. Basic Algebra (solving equations with radicals)

6. Triangles (similar) / Coordinates

7. Exponents / Factoring (difference of squares): Your first step should be to simplify the left side of the equal sign:

$$\frac{x^{a^2}}{x^{b^2}} = x^{a^2 - b^2}$$

   Now, as taught in the Exponents lesson, you can "compare apples to apples" (both bases are x's).

8. Algebraic Word: On Algebraic Word problems, don't forget to try to come up with these equations or inequalities on your own first, before you check the solution. Here's the inequality:

$$A = \frac{360}{n} > 50 .$$ You can Pick Answers if

   you have trouble calculating n.

9. Linear Equations / Systems of Equations: First find the equations of the lines. Then solve for the point of intersection.

10. Pick Numbers (advanced): Start with the question. Hint: Conveniently, picking $x = 0$ will allow you to eliminate all three incorrect answer choices. Just because 0 and 1 are usually not great choices for Pick Numbers (type 1), for most of the other Pick Tricks they are often good choices.

11. Complex Numbers: When simplifying a fraction with a complex number in the denominator, multiply numerator and denominator by the "complex conjugate" of the denominator (see the lesson). Be forewarned: the math is a bit of a pain. If you're not comfortable working with complex numbers, you might skip this one.

12. Basic Algebra (working with variables) or Pick Numbers (type 1): Since "$F =$" is part of each answer choice, you can pretend it's the last part of the question, and pick numbers for R and N (solve for F).

13. Factoring (quadratic formula)

14. Growth & Decay Functions: What is the multiplier for a 13 percent decrease? Review Percent (increase/decrease) if necessary.

15. Polynomial Division or Pick Numbers (type 1): This is an easy one to use the Pick Trick on. Otherwise, either use long division or synthetic division.

16. Algebraic Word / Pick Numbers (type 4): If x is the number of $250 bonuses and y is the number of $750 bonuses, the equation is $250x + 750y = 3,000$. To make things easier, divide both sides by 250: $x + 3y = 12$. Now guess and check (Pick Numbers (type 4)).

17. Working with Polynomials: Simplify the left side and compare polynomials (as described in the lesson).

18. Angles (parallel lines) / Triangles (similar)

19. More Trigonometry (the unit circle) / : Triangles (special right): Create a right triangle by drawing a vertical line from A to the x-axis. Since the lengths of the legs of the triangle are 1 and $\sqrt{3}$ (review the Coordinates lesson if necessary), the hypotenuse is 2, and we have a 30-60-90 triangle: $m\angle AOB = 30°$. Convert to radians, as described in the More Trigonometry lesson.

20. Systems of Equations: The two equations are linear. Put them into standard form ($y = mx + b$). If there are infinitely many solutions, what do you know about their slopes?

MATH (calculator)

1. Algebraic Word

2. Proportions: Remember to write your units before plugging your numbers into the proportion. Review the lesson if necessary.

3. Algebraic Word (equation given)

4. Proportions: The known relationship is $120 for 8 people.

5. Percent (of/is)

6. Algebraic Word: Here's the equation (solve for x): $4x + 12 = 8$. Read the question carefully; there is a trap answer choice.

7. Parabolas

8. Algebraic Word or Pick Answers: The equation is $k - 2t = p$, where t is an uncompleted task and p is points. If you have trouble solving the equation with the given values, Pick Answers.

9. Systems of Inequalities

10. Basic Functions: Start on the inside ($g(3)$), and work out. Note that the question gives you more information than needed.

11. Tables & Graphs / Proportions: The table gives more information than needed (as you may have noticed, this is not uncommon on the SAT). Since we're only given Tony's *word* rate (the fourth row), the number of *parts*, *chapters*, and *pages* of the novel are irrelevant. You will use two proportions, one for *words* and *minutes*, and one for *minutes* and *days*.

12. Algebraic Word: Here are some hints: The landfill starts with 175,000 tons. In y years, we add $7,500y$ tons. When the total amount is greater than (or equal to) 325,000 tons, the landfill is above capacity. Can you put the pieces together?

13. Studies: review Terminology in the lesson.

14. Tables & Graphs (scatterplots)

15. Proportions: The trick to this one is figuring out how many hours are in a year. You could use two proportions (hours to days → days to years), or, as a shortcut, just multiply 24 hours by 365

days. The rest is for your calculator ($580,000,000 \div (24)(365)$). (You're looking for the "closest" answer choice.)

16. Probability: Once again, these probability tables typically give you more information than you need. You should only focus on those graduates who passed the bar exam (the first column).

17. Percent (increase/decrease)

18. Means, Medians, & Modes

19. Means, Medians, & Modes: Often, when finding medians, you can just write out all the values, and count to the middle number. But this problem has 600 values (300 from each of two schools). The first step is to figure out how many students belong to each row (for example, 260 students (120 +140) have 0 siblings). Write these numbers to the right of the table. The middle number (really the average of the 300th and 301st student) should be apparent.

20. Proportions: This may not sound like a Proportion problem, but we're given a known relationship for each school (10 4-sibling students for every 300 students), and a total number of students at each school (2,400 and 3,300). Set up two proportions, one for each school. Shortcut: You might recognize that $300 \times 8 = 2,400$ and $300 \times 11 = 3,300$. So multiplying by 8 for Lincoln school and 11 for Washington School will give you the expected total for any result in the table.

21. Algebraic Word or Pick Numbers (advanced): Unless you're very comfortable with difficult algebra, use the Pick Trick. For example, you might say $x = 110$ hours ($x > 100$), and $y = 105$ hours (within 10 hours of the estimate). Check the answers. Only one works!

22. Basic Algebra (working with variables) or Pick Numbers (type 1): If you use the Pick Trick, pick numbers for I and P (see Section 3, #12).

23. Pick Numbers (type 3): Pick appropriate numbers for the two measures of l. We recommend $l_A = 16$

and $I_B = 1$. Use the answer to #22 to find $\dfrac{r_A}{r_B}$.

Some students might choose to solve this one algebraically. We'll call the intensity for Observer B I and the intensity for Observer A $16I$. Again, we'll use the answer to #22:

$$\frac{r_A}{r_B} = \frac{\sqrt{\dfrac{P}{4\pi(16I)}}}{\sqrt{\dfrac{P}{4\pi I}}} = \sqrt{\frac{P}{4\pi(16I)}}\sqrt{\frac{4\pi I}{P}}$$

$$= \sqrt{\frac{\cancel{P}}{4\pi(16\cancel{I})} \cdot \frac{4\pi\cancel{I}}{\cancel{P}}} = \sqrt{\frac{1}{16}} = \frac{1}{4}$$

24. More Circles (completing the square)

25. Linear Equations / Pick Numbers (type 2): Make sure your picked numbers for a and b satisfy the constraints of the problem.

26. Graphs of Functions

27. Tables & Graphs: With line graphs, always remember that the steeper the line, the greater the rate of change.

28. Linear Equations (finding the slope-intercept equation): The endpoints of the line in question are apparent. Find the equation.

29. Basic Algebra / Pick Answers: First, solve for x in terms of a and b (substitute $y = 3$ into the second equation). You should get

    $x = \pm\sqrt{\dfrac{3-b}{a}}$. So, to get two real

    solutions, $\dfrac{3-b}{a} > 0$. Check the answer choices.

30. Area & Perimeter / Triangles: This problem is not easy. First, note that the hexagon can be divided into 6 equilateral triangles (review the Angles lesson if necessary to see why these triangles are equilateral). Each triangle will have an area 1/6 the area of the hexagon:

Next, note that each triangle can be divided into two 30-60-90 triangles. This will allow you to find the height of each equilateral triangle (we'll call the base the side with length a):

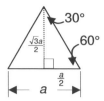

Finally, you can solve for a, which will lead you to the correct answer:

$$\frac{1}{2}bh = \frac{1}{2}(a)\left(\frac{\sqrt{3}a}{2}\right) = \frac{384\sqrt{3}}{6}$$

31. Proportions

32. Proportions: The known relationship is 1 hour equals 60 minutes. Here's a shortcut: If h hours and 30 minutes equals 450 minutes, then h hours equals 420 minutes (450 − 30). Just divide 420 by 60.

33. Graphs of Functions

34. Algebraic Word or Pick Numbers (type 4): Let d be the number of hours Doug spent in the lab and l be the number of hours Laura spent in the lab. Here are the two equations: $d + l = 250$ and $d = l + 40$. Solve for l. You could also Pick Numbers (type 4): Just guess and check numbers until you find the answer. A good first guess is $d = 150$ and $l = 100$.

35. Linear Equations (applications)

36. More Circles (sectors) / Angles (line tangent to a circle / sum of interior angles): A line tangent to a circle creates a right angle to the radius of the circle at that point (see the Angles lesson). So we know three of the four angles in quadrilateral *LMNO*. We also know the sum of the angles in any quadrilateral (again, see the Angles lesson, if necessary). Once we have the central angle, it becomes a More Circles problem. One ratio will be for *degrees*, and one will be for *arc length*. Remember, each ratio should be "part over whole," where the *part* refers to the sector, and the *whole* refers to the entire circle.

37. Algebraic Word: This problem is easier than it looks (the equation is given), but it does involve some busy work. Note that $N_{this\ year}$ is given in the pre-question text (3000 plants). Use your calculator carefully, and don't forget to apply the formula twice—once for one year from now, and again for two years from now.

38. Algebraic Word: You must make a connection between the question and the pre-question text. The question asks "how many plants must the modified environment support." This is K! Plug your numbers for $N_{this\ year}$ (3000) and $N_{next\ year}$ (3360) into the given equation and solve for K.

3. PRACTICE TEST 3

QUESTIONS BY SECTIONS/CHAPTERS

The following information lists every question on the test according to its relevant chapter or section in this tutorial. If you're correcting a test, circle the question numbers below that you missed or guessed on. Make sure to follow the Tutoring Schedule in the Introduction to know when to correct or tackle various types of questions.

READING
BY PASSAGE
- [1, 2, 3, 4, 5, 6, 7, 8, 9, 10] [11, 12, 13, 14, 15, 16, 17 ,18 19, 20] [21, 22, 23, 24, 25, 26, 27, 28, 29, 30] [31, 32, 33, 34, 35, 36, 37, 38, 39, 40, 41] [42, 43, 44, 45, 46, 47, 48, 49, 50, 51, 52]

BY QUESTION TYPE
- Direct & CTE (stand-alone): 12, 13, 18, 26, 27, 34, 36, 37, 43, 44, 45, 46
- Extended Reasoning & Purpose: 5, 7, 8, 11, 23, 24, 25, 29, 30, 32, 33, 48, 49
- WIC & Main Idea: 1, 2, 6, 14, 15, 16, 17, 22, 28, 31, 35, 47
- Comparison & IG: 19, 20, 38, 39, 40, 41, 50, 51, 52
- Tone, Structure, & Relationship: 3, 4, 9, 10, 21, 42
  Note: Most Citing-Textual-Evidence (CTE) questions are grouped with their relevant preceding questions.

WRITING & LANGUAGE
- Grammar & Sentence Structure: [1, 4, 5, 8, 10, 11] [12, 14, 15, 16, 18, 19, 21] [23, 24, 25, 26, 27, 28, 29] [34, 35, 36, 38, 40, 41]
- Main Ideas & Organization: [2, 3, 6, 7, 9] [13, 17, 20, 22] [30, 31*, 32*, 33] [37, 39, 42, 43, 44]
  Note: Brackets display separate passages.
  * Informational Graphics

MATH
- Arithmetic: §3 (3); §4 (1, 2, 3, 5, 9, 19, 20)
- Functions: §4 (21, 28)
- Algebra: §3 (1, 2, 4, 5, 6, 8, 9, 15, 17, 19); §4 (4, 7, 8, 10, 11, 13, 14, 17, 18, 22, 24, 26, 29, 30, 31, 36, 37, 38)
- Advanced Algebra: §3 (7, 13, 14, 16); §4 (6, 33)
- Graphs of Functions: §4 (12, 16)
- Geometry: §3 (10, 11, 18); §4 (25, 27, 34)
- Odds & Ends: §3 (12, 20); §4 (15, 23, 32, 35)
  §3 = Section 3; §4 = Section 4

TECHNIQUES AND HINTS

READING

PASSAGE I

1. Main Ideas: 36–40

2. Words-in-Context (WIC): 2–3

3. Extended Reasoning / Tone: 10–14: The language is clear at the end of the sentence ("'none of her business'"). Apparently, Lady Carlotta has a tendency of "interfering" in others' business. What answer choice comes closest? Use process of elimination (POE) if necessary. Be careful of D. Lady Carlotta may have been *unfriendly*, especially in the case of the boar-pig, but the question focuses on how "other people" felt about her. The context does not explicitly support unfriendliness.

4. Citing-Textual-Reference (CTE): See above.

5. Purpose: 14–23. This story, arguably humorous, definitely gives us insight into Lady Carlotta's character. If you don't spot the correct answer, try POE. You can eliminate A (she is not being deceptive in the story), B ("cruelty" is too strong), and D (there is no mention that the story reveals change; note the words "Only once").

6. WIC: 54–55, 62. What had been "thrust upon her"? Children. Line 62 makes clear that she is to teach them.

7. Extended Reasoning: 58–61 ("equally commonplace"). The phrase implies that all four children have characteristics common to "children of that class and type in the twentieth century." Don't be fooled by the language prior to this point. The narrator is likely being sarcastic.

8. Extended Reasoning: 62–69, especially 68–69.

9. Direct / Tone: 34, 37–38 (imposing: "imposingly," "a tone that admitted of very little argument"); 76–82: (defied: "knocked off her perch," "cowed [intimidated] and apologetic"): As usual, try eliminating double answers one part at a time.

10. CTE: See above. Note that lines 76–82 make clear that any resistance is "unexpected," which supports the idea that Mrs. Quabarl is outwardly imposing; the earlier lines are unnecessary.

PASSAGE II

11. Purpose: 20–25 ("opposite of glamour," "squalid," "depressing"). Note the contrast signal "yet" at the beginning of the paragraph.

12. Direct: 32–34

13. CTE: See above.

14. Main Idea: 35–37

15. CTE: See above.

16. WIC: 59–63. Note: Saying that something "has legs" means that it is viable or possible—it may continue for a while.

17. WIC: 62–63. The word "over" makes clear that Millennials prefer cities to suburbs. You might also connect "buses and subways" to the city.

18. CTE (stand-alone): 62–67. The implication is clear. Millennials ride buses and subways at least in part because of their "ease with iPads, [etc.]."

19. Information Graphics (IG) (direct): Remember, when we label IG questions as "direct," you should only use the graphic (table or graph); you should *not* worry about the text of the actual passage.

20. IG (direct)

PASSAGE III

21. Structure: 41–43 ("the 'aha' moment"), 45–46 ("came up with a series of ingenious experiments"), 49–50 ("they angled their wings differently from birds in flight")

22. WIC: 7. There's not much context to help you on this one; knowledge of the word in question is helpful. Don't extend your reasoning any more than necessary. You can always try plugging

in the answer choices and trusting your ear on these WIC questions.

23. Extended Reasoning: 6–11, 69–70. Make sure to read the introduction so you understand the two theories. You're looking for Dial's *central* assumption. The fact that he uses "baby game birds" in his experiments is important in answering the question.

24. CTE: See above.

25. Purpose: 23–32. What follows the contrast signal ("But") in line 24 is important.

26. Direct: 45–48

27. Direct: 50–52

28. WIC: 46. What is Ken doing with the birds? He is "filming" them. The author may not be saying that Ken literally filmed other species (*document* could simply mean *to support with evidence*), but thinking in this way will lead you to the correct answer.

29. Extended Reasoning: 70–74. This is an Extended Reasoning question because there is no mention that the gliding animals do not use a flapping stroke *in climbing slopes*, but it's a fair inference, since climbing slopes is a main focus of the passage (lines 44–68).

30. CTE: See above.

PASSAGE IV

31. WIC: 10–11 ("happiness of the greatest number"), 40 ("good of all"). The happiness described in line 22 should be experienced by all people.

32. Extended Reasoning: 25–30. The language is clear ("delicate constitutions," "peaceful inclinations," "strenuous habits," etc.), making this more of a Direct question, even though it is worded like an Extended Reasoning one ("inferred").

33. CTE: See above.

34. Direct: 42–45, 57–58

35. WIC: 42–50. This paragraph is primarily about *education*. Note some of the key words: "knowledge" (45), "know" (48), "comprehend" (50).

36. Direct: 72–76 ("subjugate women"). The word *subjugate* means *to bring

under control. Make sure you find the part of the passage that discusses "freedom granted by society's leaders" (or " legislator[s]"). Hint: the next question is a CTE one.

37. CTE: See above.

38. Comparison: 61–71. The argument made by the author of Passage 1 is "impossible to explain," that is, to justify.

39. Comparison: Compare 13–17 with 78–85. Talleyrand claims that women should be excluded from "public employments." Wollstonecraft believes that this line of thinking is tyrannical (81) and "crush[es] reason" (83).

40. Comparison: 1–8, 85–88

41. Comparison: 24–36. See #32.

PASSAGE V

42. Tone: 19–21 ("suspect"), 21–22 ("postulate" – assert without proof)

43. Direct: 24–28. The "hypothesis" (line 42) refers to the claims made in the third paragraph (lines 19–41), one of which is found in lines 24–28.

44. CTE: See above.

45. Direct: 31–35. The context is clear but may be hard to find. You could skim for the words "commercially produced insecticides," or note that the next question is a Citing-Textual-Evidence one, which narrows down the possible location of relevant context.

46. CTE: See above.

47. WIC: 19–21 ("suspect"). See #42. As usual, go with the answer choice that requires the least amount of extended of reasoning. The authors may be doing many things, but there is no question that they are making a claim (lines 19–21).

48. Purpose: 42. You don't have to read past this first line; it's clear the authors are proposing a "trial," or experiment.

49. Extended Reasoning: 44–46. The words "as well as" distinguishes what follows from what came before. Apparently, clover is not a pyrethrum producing plant.

50. IG (direct): As mentioned before, if you have trouble on Informational Graphics questions, you might want to review the Tables & Graphs and Statistics sections in the Math part of this tutorial.

51. IG (direct)

52. IG (direct): This question sounds like you must make a connection with the text, but the connection is made in the question itself. Simply note that the data in the table do not contain any information on "mites."

WRITING & LANGUAGE

PASSAGE I

1. Parallelism: The word "healthier" sets the form for the words that follow. Note that "more productive" is the correct comparative form of the word productive (*productiver* is not a word). / + -*ING* (D)

2. Main Ideas (passage): Note the title of the essay.

3. Main Ideas (additions): While the sentence in question does tie into "employees' health" (the main idea of the paragraph), it does not tie into the main idea of this *part* of the paragraph ("circadian rhythms"); note the last words of the previous sentence and the first words of the next sentence.

4. Apostrophes & Confused Words

5. Subject-Verb Agreement: The subject is "absenteeism." (B, D) / -*ING* (C)

6. Answer the Question: Focus on "productivity."

7. Main Ideas (topic/transition sentences): This appears to be a mere Combining Sentences question, but it is really testing the role of a topic and transition sentences. The previous paragraph ended with a discussion of worker "productivity." This paragraph discusses the cost of artificial light sources. Which choice provides the best transition from the previous paragraph to this one?

8. Redundancies: Note the word "annual" in the passage.

9. Transitions

10. Run-ons (A, B): Remember, independent clauses cannot be separated with a comma only. / -*ING* (D)

11. Idioms: You will often either "hear" idioms or you won't.

PASSAGE II

12. Pronoun Agreement (B, D) / Idioms: Choice C is not specifically covered in the tutorial, but the phrase "their selves" is unidiomatic; hopefully you "hear" the awkwardness.

13. Main Ideas (transition sentences): The travelers were "in need of refreshment," but the food was "terrible." Which choice transitions from these ideas?

14. Punctuation

15. Subject-Verb Agreement (A, C) / Pronoun Agreement (A, D)

16. Vocabulary (A, B) / Style (D)

17. Main Ideas (topic sentences): The main idea of the paragraph is unconventional business practices, especially the hiring of women in restaurants.

18. Concision & Redundancies

19. Fragments / + Paired Conjunctions (C) / + -*ING* (B, C)

20. Answer the Question: Similar to an Organization question, look for clue words in the answer choices. Which one logically follows a discussion of the workers' compensation?

21. Punctuation (A, B) / Fragments (C)

22. Main Ideas (changes): Consider the main idea of the sentence: the Harvey Girls became a "transformative force."

PASSAGE III

23. Combining Sentences: Review "Clauses and Phrases" in this lesson. Watch out for choices with excess punctuation, and ones that awkwardly break up cohesive phrases. Let's focus on what's wrong with the incorrect choices. You might stay away from B because it has the most punctuation. Choice C awkwardly breaks up the phrase "lengthens storage life . . . by three to four times." Choice D awkwardly breaks up the phrase "have been harvested . . . in the off-season."

24. Run-ons (A, C) / -*ING* (B): Always be on the lookout for the two most commonly incorrect -*ing* words: *being* and *having*.

25. Vocabulary

26. Apostrophes & Confused Words (B, D) / Pronoun Agreement (C, D)

27. Pronoun Case (A, C) / Run-ons (B)

28. Verb Tense: See "do" earlier in the sentence.

29. Punctuation: A comma is needed after the independent clause ("Take Bartlett pears")—yes, this is an independent clause; the subject *you* is implied. The colon correctly follows a complete sentence and leads the reader to what follows. Note that D is grammatically correct (as far as punctuation goes), but changes the meaning of the sentence: the "Bartlett pears" are the example (the "instance").

30. Organization: Sentence 2 is already negative: the independent clause—the most important part of a sentence—discusses "limits" to the positive effects of 1-MCP. What is the tone of sentence 4? Note the word "But."

31. Informational Graphics (IG)

32. IG

33. Answer the Question: Only one answer choice mentions both "shortcomings" of 1-MCP *and* "people in the fruit industry."

PASSAGE IV

34. Fragments

35. Punctuation: These long dashes often come in pairs.

36. Subject-Verb Agreement (A, D): The subject is "works." / Fragments (B) / -*ING* (B)

37. Main Ideas (transition sentences): Read the first sentence of the next paragraph. (You might note that this sentence cannot be moved—see the answer choices for #39.) The focus is on a specific museum.

38. Verb Tense / + -*ING* (B)

39. Organization: Clue words = "continuing the tradition" and "Peter's daughter."

40. Vocabulary

41. Punctuation: The words "digital artist" function as an adjective for "Eldar Zakirov," so do not place a comma between the words (as in A and B); see "Nouns as Adjectives" in the Punctuation lesson.

42. Main Ideas (transition sentences): Note some of the important words that follow: "aristocratic tilt," "stately," "royal court dress," etc.

43. Main Ideas (additions): The focus of the paragraph is the paintings of the cats.

44. Main Ideas (passage): This may not look like a Main Ideas question, but note that it is the last sentence of the passage, a common place to test main ideas. Only one answer mentions "the productive partnership" (¶2) between cats and humans. Choice A may be tempting, but it emphasizes the "killing" of mice and rats, something the passage never explicitly mentions (the closest it gets is with the words "ridding" (¶2), which could simply mean scaring off).

MATH (no calculator)

1. Algebraic Word: This problem is long and, thus, harder looking than it is. (Also note that it's the first question of the test.) Only one variable has anything to do with money. Obviously, the number of walls, or the walls' length and height, will not change when a more expensive paint is used.

2. Basic Algebra

3. Exponents: If you have a calculator that allows you to input roots other than square roots ($\sqrt{\ }$), you could Pick Numbers (type 1). But, in any case, you should be comfortable converting fractional exponents to roots (and vice versa). Review the lesson if you need a refresher.

4. Algebraic Word: Let y be the number of states that joined the U.S. between 1776 and 1849 and x be the number of states that joined between 1850 and 1900 (as specified in the question). Here's the equation: $y = 2x$. (Remember to try to find equations for

Algebraic Word problems on your own before checking these solutions.)

5. Basic Algebra: Hint: When dealing with variables in denominators, you'll usually want to cross multiply.

6. Systems of Equations

7. Polynomial Division (Factor Theorem)

8. Linear Equations: Do you see the slope in the original equation? It's in the form $y = mx + b$. So $k = m$. Plug in the given point (c, d)—you should get $d = kc + 4$—and solve for k (the slope).

9. Systems of Equations (intersecting lines): The equations are linear. Convert them into $y = mx + b$ form. For what slopes do two lines have no solutions?

10. Basic Algebra (solving exponential equations) / Coordinates: You don't need to know anything about parabolas on this one. Just plug $y = 25$ into the equation, and solve for x. Review the Coordinates lesson if you need help finding horizontal distances.

11. Angles (vertical angles): Vertical angles are congruent, so $y = u$, $x = t$, and $w = z$. Using substitution, we can simplify the given equation: $x + y = u + w \rightarrow x = w$ (since $y = u$, we canceled them). So now we know that $x = w = t = z$ (see the vertical angle equalities above). Finally, check the answer choices.

    You could also Pick Numbers (type 4): You must find angles that satisfy both the given equation ($x + y = u + w$) and the straight line angle measure (for example, $x + y + z = 180°$). But be careful: picking 60° for every angle—which works in the equations—will give you a "false positive" (the figure is not drawn to scale).

12. Parabolas: You could FOIL the equation and complete the square (see More Circles) to put the equation in vertex form. The faster approach, however, is to recognize that the equation is in x-intercept form, and the x-coordinate of the vertex will be half way between the x-intercepts.

13. Common Denominators: Hint: Multiply both sides of the equation (every expression) by $ax - 2$, and then, after

simplifying, compare coefficients (see Working with Polynomials).

14. Factoring (quadratic formula): To make things easier, divide the equation by 3 (this will not change the solutions). Note: Do *not* try to factor this "by hand"; the answer choices make clear that the solutions will not be integers.

15. Linear Equations (applications): The equation is not in $y = mx + b$ form, but it's close enough to see the slope. The y-intercept (b) is not needed.

16. Factoring (common factors / factoring quadratics / difference of squares) or Pick Numbers (type 4): Here are the first four factoring steps: $x^5 - 5x^3 = -4x$ $\rightarrow x^5 - 5x^3 + 4x = 0 \rightarrow x(x^4 - 5x^2 + 4) = 0 \rightarrow x(x^2 - 4)(x^2 - 1) = 0 \ldots$ If you're not comfortable trying to factor this one, try guessing some numbers (Pick Numbers (type 4))—you might get lucky.

17. Basic Algebra: If you're not comfortable working with fractions (don't forget, this is the no-calculator section), try multiplying both sides (every term) by the least common multiple of 4, 9, and 12 (36). But be careful: the multiplication isn't a snap.

18. Angles (triangles / straight lines) / Basic Algebra: The first step is algebra: plug the given value of y into the equation and solve for z. Once you find z, calculate the base angles, we'll call them each b, of the isosceles triangle ($b + b + z = 180$). Finally, find x.

19. Algebraic Word: Let h be the number of calories in a hamburger and f be the number of calories in an order of fries. Here are the equations: $h = f + 50$ (students sometimes get this one backwards—quickly test some easy numbers if in doubt) and $2h + 3f = 1700$. You can solve using substitution.

20. Trigonometry: This problem is easier than it looks. Since the two triangles are similar, $\sin F = \sin C$. Focus on the larger triangle ($\triangle ABC$)—the numbers are easier. Another shortcut: the triangles are both 3-4-5 right triangles.

MATH (calculator)

1. Tables & Graphs

2. Probability / Tables & Graphs

3. Tables & Graphs: The biggest challenge to this problem is interpreting the x-axis: 0 corresponds with 1997, 1 corresponds with 1998, and so on.

4. Basic Functions / Pick Numbers (advanced): Hint: The first column—in this case, (1, –2)—often gives multiple correct answers. It's sometimes faster to start with another column. When you "pick" the numbers in the second column—(2, 1)—and plug into the answer choices, all three incorrect choices can be eliminated.

5. Percent (of/is)

6. Working with Polynomials (addition)

7. Basic Algebra: If you struggle with fractions, use your calculator, but make sure to use parentheses; this is correct: $w = (4/3)/(3/5)$; but this is incorrect: $w = 4/3/3/5$.

8. Linear Equations (applications): Remember slope is rise (y) over run (x); in other words, it's the increase (or decrease, if the slope is negative) in y for each unit of increase in x. In this problem, y represents the average number of students per classroom and x represents years.

9. Proportions: On the SAT, we use proportions for rate problems. Here's the setup: $\dfrac{m}{\sec} \dfrac{25}{13.7} = \dfrac{x}{4 \times 60}$

10. Algebraic Word: The equation is given ($W = mg$).

11. Algebraic Word: Use the equation above to find m. Then guess and check until you find the planet that gives an approximate weight of 170 newtons.

12. Graphs of Functions (zeros)

13. Basic Algebra (working with variables): If you find yourself stuck, you could Pick Numbers (type 1) for h, k, and t (solve for v).

14. Algebraic Word / Proportions: Here's the proportion: $\dfrac{\$\ 0.20}{\min\ 1} = \dfrac{c}{60h}$; ($60h$ is the number of minutes in h hours).

You could also Pick Numbers (type 1): pick a number for h and solve for c.

15. Studies: Be careful of D: The only people treated were those with poor eyesight, so D is unsubstantiated (compare with A).

16. Graphs of Functions

17. Linear Equations (applications) or Pick Numbers (type 3) / Basic Functions: Most students should simply test some numbers (Pick Numbers (type 3)). For example, Find S when $P = \$0$. Then find S when P is increased by \$10 ($P = \$10$).

18. Basic Algebra: The question is asking for the value of P when $S(P) = D(P)$—make sure to go back to the introductory information if you didn't make this connection. Once you set the equations equal, the problem tests basic algebra.

19. Proportions: There are two known relationships (1 ounce = 7 fields and 1 field = $1\frac{1}{3}$ acres), so you should set up two proportions.

20. Tables & Graphs (scatterplots)

21. Growth & Decay Functions: Exponential growth will occur when interest is paid on both the initial amount (principal) *and* on the accrued interest. Review compound interest in the lesson if necessary. The three incorrect answer choices are all *linear*, not exponential.

22. Pick Answers or Algebraic Word / Percent (increase/decrease): We recommend using the Pick Trick, but if you want to use algebra, here are the two equations: $x + y + z = 855$ and $x = 1.5(y + z)$ (we used 1.5 as the multiplier for a 50% increase). Solve either equation for $y + z$ (in terms of x) and substitute into the other equation to solve for x.

23. More Trigonometry (sine/cosine complementary angles rules) or Pick Answers: Since $\sin \theta = \cos (90 - \theta)$ (see the lesson), we can write $\sin (a) = \cos (90 - a)$. So $90 - a = b$. Substitute the given expressions for a and b and solve for k.

Pick Answers: If you're quick with your calculator, using the Pick Trick is probably the better approach. Pick answers, solve for a and b, and see if $\sin a = \sin b$.

24. Pick Answers or Algebraic Word / Systems of Equations: We recommend using the Pick Trick. For example, here's how you would check choice B: 21 students → Each student gets 3 milliliters (mL) and Mr. Kohl has 5 mL left over, so the total solution is 21×3 mL + 5 mL = 68 mL. If each student gets 4 mL: 21×4 mL = 84 mL. This is NOT 21 mL more than 68 mL (as specified in the question), so try another answer choice.

    If you use algebra, here are the equations, where s is the number of students and n is milliliters of solution: $3s + 5 = n$ and $4s = n + 21$.

25. Solids & Volume: Formulas for the volumes for these shapes (two cones and and a cylinder) are given in the reference section at the beginning of each Math test.

26. Linear Equations / Basic Algebra or Pick Answers: Using algebra is probably the faster approach. Since the line passes through the origin, it will be of the form $y = mx$ ($b = 0$). So, plugging in the two points, we get two equations: $k = 2m$ and $32 = mk$. Use substitution to solve for k.

    If the algebra is challenging for you, Pick Answers until you find two points that give $b = 0$ in the $y = mx + b$ equation.

27. Area / Percent (increase/decrease and difference/original) / Pick Numbers (type 3) → Pick Answers or Algebraic Word: We'll display the Pick Trick approach: Make sure you're comfortable working with multipliers (10% increase → $\times$ 1.10; 12% decrease → $\times$ 0.88). Pick Numbers for the sides of the original rectangle. Let's say $l = 2$ and $w = 3$. So the initial area is $2 \times 3 = 6$. Now, Pick Answers. Let's check B (width decreases 15%, so the multiplier is 0.85): The new rectangle has sides $(1.1)(2) = 2.2$ and $(0.85)(3) = 2.55$ → area = $(2.2)(2.55) = 5.61$. Using difference/original, the percent change

in the area was 6.5% (not enough). So check a larger number (C).

Algebraic Word: If you'd rather use algebra, here are the equations (using multipliers, as described above): $A_1 = lw$. $A_2 = (1.1l)\left(1 - \dfrac{p}{100}\right)w = 0.88A_1$. So $(1.1l)\left(1 - \dfrac{p}{100}\right)w = 0.88lw$. The lw will cancel from both sides, and you can solve for p.

28. Growth & Decay Functions (exponential)

29. Probability / Tables & Graphs / Algebraic Word / Systems of Equations: Let x be the number of left-handed female students and y be the number of left-handed male students. So, according the problem, $5x$ and $9y$ are the number of female and male right-handed students, respectively. Using the table, we can write the two equations: $x + y = 18$ and $5x + 9y = 122$. Solve for x. Make sure to ignore extraneous information in the table while finding the probability (read the last part of the question carefully).

30. Algebraic Word / Systems of Equations / Pick Numbers (type 2): The first step is combining like terms for each equation: $-2x + b = -7$ and $-2y + c = -7$. Since the right sides of both equations are equal ($-7 = -7$), we can write: $-2x + b = -2y + c$. Now, Pick Numbers (type 2), using the given relationship for b and c—for example, if $c = 2$, then $b = 2 - \dfrac{1}{2} = \dfrac{3}{2}$. Plug these numbers into the equation above and solve for x (see the answer choices).

31. Algebraic Word or Pick Numbers (type 4): Let x be the number of student tickets Chris buys. Here's the inequality: $11 \le 2x + 3 \le 14$. If you have trouble either finding this inequality, or solving it, use the Pick Trick (guess and check).

32. Means, Medians, & Modes: There's no trick to this question. Just use your calculator carefully.

33. Working with Variables (subtraction)

34. More Circles (sectors): As taught in this lesson, the ratio of the area of the sector to the area of the circle will equal the ratio of the angle of the sector (the central angle) to the angle of the circle (360°). Since the angle of the sector is given in radians, the angle for the whole circle should also be in radians (2π); review "Degrees and Radians" in the More Trigonometry lesson if necessary.

35. Means, Medians, & Modes: Using the equation for average (mean), $A = \dfrac{S}{N}$, find the sum of the first 10 ratings and the sum of all 20 ratings. You can subtract to find the sum of the last 10 ratings. Since you're looking for the *least* value for the 11th rating, assume the other 9 ratings (the 12th rating through the 20th rating) are each 100.

36. Systems of Inequalities: As discussed in the lesson, graph the lines as if they were equations and find the shaded regions by plugging in easy points (the solution will be where the shaded regions overlap). The answer to the question is found at the lines' point of intersection (use substitution).

37. Algebraic Word / Proportions: There's a lot of information thrown at you on this one, but just remember: r is the shoppers per minute, T is the average time in the store (or wherever) per shopper, and N is the number of shoppers in the store (or wherever). The equation that relates these variables is given: $N = rt$. Now to the question. Use a proportion to find r in shoppers per minute (the given known relationship is 84 shoppers per <u>hour</u>): $\dfrac{\text{shoppers}}{\text{min}} \dfrac{84}{60} = \dfrac{r}{1}$. T is given as 5 minutes. Find N using the formula above.

38. Algebraic Word / Proportions / Percent (difference-over-original): Follow the same steps as on the previous problem to find N for the new store, and compare this value with N of the original store (given as 45)—review "Difference-Over-Original" in the Percent lesson, if necessary. Note: Do *not* use N from the previous question.

4. PRACTICE TEST 4*

QUESTIONS BY SECTIONS/CHAPTERS

The following information lists every question on the test according to its relevant chapter or section in this tutorial. If you're correcting a test, circle the question numbers below that you missed or guessed on. Make sure to follow the Tutoring Schedule in the Introduction to know when to correct or tackle various types of questions.

READING
BY PASSAGE
- [1, 2, 3, 4, 5, 6, 7, 8, 9, 10] [11, 12, 13, 14, 15, 16, 17 ,18 19, 20, 21] [22, 23, 24, 25, 26, 27, 28, 29, 30, 31] [32, 33, 34, 35, 36, 37, 38, 39, 40, 41] [42, 43, 44, 45, 46, 47, 48, 49, 50, 51, 52]

BY QUESTION TYPE
- Direct & CTE (stand-alone): 5, 6, 12, 14, 15, 16, 17, 27, 28, 29, 46, 47, 49
- Extended Reasoning & Purpose: 4, 8, 22, 25, 26, 30, 31, 35, 41, 42, 45, 48
- WIC & Main Idea: 3, 9, 10, 11, 13, 18, 24, 33, 34
- Comparison & IG: 19, 20, 21, 36, 37, 38, 39, 40, 50, 51, 52
- Tone, Structure, & Relationship: 1, 2, 7, 23, 32, 43, 44
  Note: Most Citing-Textual-Evidence (CTE) questions are grouped with their relevant preceding questions.

WRITING & LANGUAGE
- Grammar & Sentence Structure: [1, 3, 5, 6, 7, 8, 9] [12, 13, 14, 16, 19, 21, 22] [24, 26, 28, 29, 30, 32] [34, 35, 36, 40, 41, 42, 43]
- Main Ideas & Organization: [2, 4, 10, 11] [15, 17, 18, 20] [23, 25, 27, 31†, 33] [37, 38, 39, 44]
  Note: Brackets display separate passages.
  † Informational Graphics

MATH
- Arithmetic: §4 (1 (Basic Concepts), 3, 4, 7, 9, 10, 11, 22, 31, 33)
- Functions: §4 (13, 14, 20, 37, 38)
- Algebra: §3 (2, 3, 4, 6, 7, 8, 9, 10, 12, 19, 20); §4 (1, 2, 5, 6, 8, 16, 17, 19, 26, 27, 32, 34, 35)
- Advanced Algebra: §3 (5, 11, 15, 18); §4 (25)
- Graphs of Functions: §3 (13); §4 (12, 15, 30)
- Geometry: §3 (16); §4 (18, 24, 36)
- Odds & Ends: §3 (11 (use the Parabola approach), 14, 17); §4 (21, 23, 28, 29)
  §3 = Section 3; §4 = Section 4

* Test 4 is no longer found in *The Official SAT Study Guide* (2020), but it is currently available at the CollegeBoard website.

TECHNIQUES AND HINTS

READING

PASSAGE I

1. Tone / Structure: 9–10 (uncertainty: "my motives . . . are not entirely clear"), 53–57 (recognition: "of my own volition," "What I am on the brink of knowing . . .").

2. Citing-Textual-Evidence (CTE): See above. The words "now see" (56) suggest that prior to this point the narrator did not recognize his motives, thus supporting the first part of the correct answer to #1.

3. Words-in-Context (WIC): Notice the keywords in the passage: "complicated" (1), "I don't know" (4–5), "not entirely clear" (9–10). These all suggest a lack of understanding or comprehension. Interestingly, if you take the phrase in question out of context, the incorrect choices all sound better than the correct one. As usual, using context is essential.

4. Purpose: 10–13 ("my destiny has worked in secret")

5. Direct: 16–17, 20–21, 54–55

6. CTE: Any of the lines above support the answer.

7. Tone: first part of answer: 27–29, 44, 48–49; second part of answer: 35–41

8. Extended Reasoning: 27–30, 42–47. The author's tone makes clear that he sees no rational reason for going to the North Pole; his reasons for going are beyond utility or human benefit (see lines 35–41).

9. WIC: 48–49. The author, a Swede (see the introduction), feels he is the only one who might take interest in the North Pole's "completely featureless wasteland." Don't forget to try plugging answer choices into the passage on WIC questions. Your ear will often hear the right answer.

10. WIC: 49–51. Remember, the narrator is in a balloon (see the introduction).

PASSAGE II

11. Main Idea (paragraph): 11–13: "Population growth" in the correct answer refers to the "raw census numbers" in the passage—the answer is camouflaged. 13–22: These lines describe "demographic inversion" (see the introduction); 31–33: These lines imply (and confirm) the existence of demographic inversion. Watch out for B. It's true, but it doesn't reflect the main idea of the paragraph. Focus on the last half of the paragraph.

12. Direct: 14–16

13. WIC: 33–35. Consider what a line graph looks like when whatever is being measured is not changing—this is the likely source of the term "flat."

14. Direct: 36–39. The correct answer is camouflaged: "Economic hardship" = "fiscal problems" (36–37), and "promises made in past years" = "obligations they incurred in the more prosperous years" (38–39).

15. CTE: See above.

16. Direct: 66–71. Even though this question sounds like an Extended Reasoning question ("implies"), the context is clear and about as close to direct as we can hope for; just count the zones. If you had trouble finding the context, note that numbers are often easy to find ("1974"), or note that the next question is a Citing-Textual-Reasoning question, which narrows down the possible locations in the passage.

17. CTE: See above.

18. WIC: 66–68. You probably know that "commercial life," that is, the activities of commerce (business and trade), *takes place* in a downtown. Choices B and C are probably true but require more extended reasoning than necessary.

19. Informational Graphics (IG) (make connections): 11–13. The chart merely gives the percent of the population in three regions; this is just basic census information, something the author

claims is "an ineffective blunt instrument."

20. IG (direct): Make sure you focus on the correct bars (for 2000–2010). See the key at the top right of the graph.

21. IG (extended reasoning): Note the labels beneath the chart: large metro, small metro, and non-metro. These are the same as those on the pie graph, which includes 100% of the U.S. population.

PASSAGE III

22. Purpose: 9–11, 35–38 (etc.). Consider what the author is trying to do in the passage. He introduces "pharming," gives some background, and then discusses a pharming success story (ATryn). But be careful: His primary purpose is not just to discuss ATryn. Too much of the first part of the passage discusses "pharming" in general. You might try POE: In choice B, there is no specific "scientific discovery" discussed (see lines 54–56). Choice C focusses too much on ATryn (assuming that this is the "long-term research project"); in addition, there is no mention that the project was "long-term." Choice D doesn't focus on Atryn *enough*.

23. Tone: 5–11 ("saved human lives"), 29–30 ("medicine by the bucketful"), 70 ("human medicine!")

24. WIC: 16–21. It's "difficult and expensive to make these compounds," referring to proteins (see line 12), but dairy animals are *very good* at making protein, "their udders swollen with milk." Note that the passage is discussing *animals*, so B and arguably A are ridiculous answers.

25. Extended Reasoning: 35–36. Even if you're not comfortable with the language ("gee-whiz, scientific geekery, lab-bound thought experiments come true"), the fact that ATryn *did* prove particularly useful to humans means that what came before was *not* particularly useful, at least not in a practical sense. See also #22.

26. CTE: See above.

27. Direct: 38–44

28. CTE: See above.

29. Direct: 60–62. The "human gene" (61) refers to the "gene for human antithrombin" (57). Since some of the kids were born with the gene, it's a small extension of reasoning (so small, in fact, that we categorize this question as Direct) to say that some of the kids were *not* born with the gene.

30. Purpose: 63–64. Note that the parenthetical information follows an unfamiliar term ("promoter").

31. Extended Reasoning: 70–76. The passage shifts to a discussion of economics ("the market"), and the tone is positive (we can assume that "a kilogram of medicine from a single animal" is impressive). Even without context, you might have a sense of what "liquid gold" likely means. Hint: cha-ching!

PASSAGE IV

32. Relationship: 17–29. Consider first focusing on the second word of each answer choice. The contract with society is different from "Subordinate contracts" because it is not "temporary" (23), it should not be "dissolved by the fancy [whim] of the parties" (23–24), and it is not "of a temporary and perishable nature" (27). The emphasis is on the contract's *permanence*. Check the answer choices.

33. WIC: The context isn't a great help here, but look at a couple of the key words: "country" (11) and "constitution" (15). The next paragraph discusses a contract with "Society" (17). These words all reflect government and politics. If you had trouble with this one, you might come back to it after reading the next passage, in which the references to "government" are clear; these double passages typically discuss the same topic (albeit in different ways). See also #41.

34. WIC: 17 ("Subordinate contracts"), 19–25. You're looking for the opposite of "reverence." Also, your answer on this question should directly contrast your answer on #32.

35. Extended Reasoning: 41–45, 48–54, etc. The context is quite explicit, requiring little to no extended reasoning.

36. Comparison: 64–72.

37. Comparison / CTE: The challenge to this CTE question is that all the choices sound pretty good, so we need to be picky. Look for the lines that best argue against the idea of a "partnership . . . between those who are living, those who are dead, and those who are to be born" (31–34). The line numbers given for #36 best question this "partnership" between the dead ("out of existence") and the unborn ("not in [existence]"). Note that the lines refer to a rhetorical question, one with an implied negative answer.

38. Comparison / Tone: 24–27, 34–40. Burke disagrees with Paine's idea of a "continually changing" government and argues against the idea of a group (the living) having the right "to separate and tear asunder" (37–38) that "universal kingdom" (the government) (35). See also #32.

39. Comparison / CTE: See above.

40. Comparison: 4–9 & 34–40 vs. 41–43 & 73–76. Not surprisingly, the main ideas for both passages can be found at their beginnings and ends.

41. Purpose: 4–9, 73–76

PASSAGE V

42. Purpose: 3–4, 33–35

43. Structure: 1–3, 33–35. This one can be tricky. Try POE. First, focus on just the second parts of the answer choices. This should help you narrow it down to A and B (don't be fooled by Eye Catchers). Finally, the first part of A ("criticism") is not mentioned in the passage.

44. CTE: The correct answer gives context especially for the *second* part of the previous answer choice (that is, the *cause* of the Little Ice Age). It is at this point in the passage that the shift occurs.

45. Purpose: The information given in the passage ("layers of sulfate deposits and tiny shards of volcanic glass") is *evidence* of a powerful volcano. This is similar to a WIC question—you must use context.

46. Direct: 33–35, 61–64. As usual, if you can't quickly find the relevant information in the passage, see if the next question is a CTE one.

47. CTE: See above.

48. Extended Reasoning: 68–71. This is a strange question. First, the context is crystal clear. Of course, "Another possible candidate" means that scientists knew of . . . well . . . *another possible candidate* for a volcanic eruption that may have caused the Little Ice Age. In that sense, the question is straightforward (review lines 61–62 if necessary). However, there's no evidence that scientists knew of *more than one* other eruption (as the correct answer suggests). Thus, we think the correct answer may be flawed.

49. CTE (stand-alone): Focus on what follows the contrast signal "But" in line 71. Quilotoa is another possible candidate (see the previous question), *but . . .*

50. IG (direct): Read the question carefully. You're looking for the greatest *below-average* temperature variation—in other words, the number that is *most negative*. Some students look for when the *greatest* temperature variation occurred, but the fact that 2000 CE is not an available answer choice is a clear sign that this reading of the question is incorrect.

51. IG (make connections): 23–24. You can see from the graph where the temperature variations begin to fall (the question asks for the "onset" of the Little Ice Age). Confirm your answer with the passage at the line numbers given above.

52. IG (direct): Make sure you stay focused with these direct IG questions; they make no mention of the passage (only the data presented in the figure). Eliminate answers that are not directly supported by the figure.

WRITING & LANGUAGE

PASSAGE I

1. Run-ons: All three incorrect choices create an independent clause following

the comma (and, thus, a comma splice).

2. Transitions: Compare "during the day" with "at night."

3. Punctuation: Note the comma after "mural." This comma opens a brief descriptive phrase.

4. Main Ideas (topic/transition sentences): Read the question carefully. Since you must make a connection with the previous paragraph, focus on what is at the end of this paragraph: "to avoid scrutiny, Siqueiros painted . . . at night."

5. Vocabulary: The correct answer is a verb commonly used in reference to works of art. If your ear "hears" the correct answer, great. If not, take a guess and move on.

6. Verb Tense / + -ING (A): The verb in question should be parallel to "dominated," not to "being." The sentence contains one subject with two verbs: "The centerpiece . . . was dominated by . . . and ????? an eagle . . ."

7. Pronoun Ambiguity: Recall that Pronoun Ambiguity questions typically have relatively long correct answers (review Avoid Wordy Answer Choices in the Grammar & Sentence Structure Guidelines chapter). Usually, when the SAT includes several pronouns in the answer choices, and one answer that includes the noun being referred to, the correct answer is the latter, the one choice that removes any potential ambiguity.

8. Combining Sentences: Eliminating incorrect choices is often the key to Combining Sentences questions (review the lesson, if necessary). A: Note the extra punctuation and the awkward break in the phrase "explosion . . . of mural paintings." C: This choice feels especially passive; the focus should be the "result" or the "Chicago mural movement"; also note the -ing word ("resulting"). D: This is actually a run-on (two independent clauses—no comma before the "and"); additionally, the extra independent clause (following the semicolon) creates a needlessly choppy feel to the sentence.

9. Parallelism: Stay parallel to "in abandoned lots" and "on unused buildings." / Redundancies (A, B): That the murals were painted is understood.

10. Main Ideas (transition sentences): The "powerful work is now a tourist attraction"; use POE. / Redundancies (B): See the previous sentence ("clean, restore"). You could also probably eliminate this choice because of the word "being" (watch out for all -ing words—they're usually wrong).

11. Main Ideas (additions): Additions are usually incorrect for one of two reasons: either the addition is off topic, or it is redundant. In this case, we already know that the mural is "powerful" and successful. We also learned that it "did not please" everyone when it was painted (¶2).

PASSAGE II

12. Illogical Comparisons: Compare apples to apples. The first item of comparison is "organically grown crops."

13. Fragments / + -ING (A, C): On questions that test Fragments, it's not unusual to have -ing words show up in incorrect answer choices.

14. Concision & Redundancies: Choice B is notably redundant (see "pesticides and synthetic fertilizers" in the previous sentence).

15. Transitions: Remember to read these questions without looking at the underlined transition words. Focus on context: (1) consumers spend a lot of extra money on organic food; (2) they do not reap significant health benefits from organic food. The transition should be clear.

16. Vocabulary

17. Transitions: You hopefully recognize the need for a support signal (A, C, or D). Make sure you understand the different uses of these support transitions (review "Special Support Transitions," if necessary). The sentence provides an example of science not supporting organic foodies' claims.

18. Main Ideas (additions): The focus of the paragraph is the lack of scientific evidence for the benefits of organic

food (see the independent clause of the topic sentence).

19. Subject-Verb Agreement: The subject is "amounts." / + -*ING* (B)

20. Answer the Question: You often don't need to go back to the passage to answer these types of questions. Only one choice answers the question.

21. Apostrophes & Confused Words (A, D) / Subject-Verb Agreement (C, D): The subject, which comes after the verb, is "reasons."

22. Punctuation: Try using the pause rule on this one. If you selected B, review the use of colons.

PASSAGE III

23. Answer the Question: Some students may be tempted by choice A, but would how people refer to carbonated beverages ever be considered "life-altering"? Probably not. Choice A is mocking a possible interest in this topic.

24. Paired Conjunctions: Note the "not only" earlier in the sentence. / + Run-ons (A): The "it" creates an independent clause, but the previous independent clause was not completed with appropriate punctuation (or with a comma and a FANBOYS conjunction). / + -*ING* (D)

25. Main Ideas / Answer the Question: Try this one using POE. The first paragraph mentions "traditional, human-intensive" data collection. The next paragraph discusses an example of this "traditional methodology," describing it as a "signal achievement in linguistics" (sentence 6)—in other words, still useful. So you can eliminate A and D. But, apparently, "social media" is another means of data collection ("explosion of social media")—eliminate C.

26. Concision

27. Organization: The data collection took place over six years (see sentence 3), but the dictionary itself took much longer to complete (see sentences 2 and 5). The added sentence serves as a transition between these two ideas.

28. Subject-Verb Agreement / + -*ING* (B)

29. Punctuation: If a colon comes after an independent clause, and logically continues or completes the thought of what came before, it's probably correct. / + Fragments (C): Review the use of a semicolon, if necessary—both sides must be complete sentences.

30. Apostrophes & Confused Words: This one is clearly testing the correct use of *cite/site/sight*. If you know which of the following words is spelled correctly—*webcite*, *website*, or *websight*—you'll probably see the correct answer. / + Idioms (C, D): You might be searching *for* something, but you are in search *of* something.

31. Informational Graphics (IG): Your first thought might be to consider *geography* in ordering the words, maybe west to east (the way we read), but the answer is actually easier than that. Just look at the map's key.

32. Apostrophes & Confused Words: Review *there/their/they're*.

33. Main Ideas (passage): The question refers to the "sentence and paragraph." What is the main idea of this paragraph? Consider the second sentence: social media is used as a source of information. Choice B may be a tempting, but the passage has moved past soft drinks ("their true value . . .").

PASSAGE IV

34. Verb Tense: Note the "is" (present tense) later in the sentence. / Subject-Verb Agreement (B, D): The phrase "*a* number of [plural things]" is usually considered *plural*, while "*the* number of [plural things]" is always considered *singular* (see the example in the Subject-Verb Agreement lesson). In any case, Verb Tense led us to the correct answer without worrying about Subject-Verb Agreement.

35. Punctuation: There are some fragments among the answer choices, but the important thing to recognize here is that the words "the settings . . . unique" is a modifying phrase, describing the "fundamental elements." It should be separated from the rest of the sentence with identical punctuation (either commas or long dashes). Try removing the phrase to hear the

barebones sentence: "The designer envisions the game's fundamental elements and is thus . . ."

36. Run-ons: First, eliminate A and D, which are clear run-ons. Next, you'll have to answer the following question: Does contrast word ("however") belong with the first clause ("Conceptualizing a game . . ."), thus transitioning from the previous paragraph (B), or with the second clause ("no matter . . ."), thus transitioning from the first clause (C)? Here's the answer: The contrast is between designers conceptualizing the game (previous paragraph) and the *communication* of this conceptualizing (the main idea of the current paragraph); thus, the contrast should be part of the first clause.

37. Main Ideas (additions): The previous sentence makes clear that concepts must be "communicated effectively."

38. Main Ideas (changes) / Answer the Question: The topic is *effective communication*. See the previous question.

39. Transitions: Because good communication is important, being a good writer and speaker is also important. Be careful of choice A: Good writing and speaking is not *like* good communication—it *is* good communication.

40. Noun Agreement: To identify these problems, remember to look for common nouns (*writer*, *speaker*) in both plural and singular forms (*writer/writers*, *speaker/speakers*).

41. Redundancies

42. Vocabulary / Style: When in doubt, use simple vocabulary. Most of these passages are written in straightforward prose.

43. Misplaced Words (improper modifier): What is "demanding and deadline driven"? Hint: Just focus on the first word or two of each answer choice.

44. Organization: Sentence 5 broadly mentions "educational preparation." Note the other topics: programming (sentences 1–3), psychology (sentence 4), and business (sentence 6). Topics

of discussion frequently move from the general to the specific.

MATH (no calculator)

1. Basic Concepts (absolute value): You must recognize that the absolute value of any expression must always be ≥ 0.

2. Basic Functions / Basic Algebra

3. Systems of Equations: Solve for x in the first equation. Then use substitution.

4. Basic Functions / Pick Numbers (type 1) (optional)

5. Working with Polynomials (multiplying) or Pick Numbers (type 1): Review FOIL if necessary. If you choose to use the Pick Trick, pick a small number for x, such as 2 (no calculator allowed).

6. Pick Numbers (type 2) or Common Denominators: Most students should probably use the Pick Trick. Hint: Pick 7 for b, and solve for a. Then check the answer choices.

   If you choose to solve this one algebraically, you must consider Common Denominators in reverse for the left side of the equation:
   $\frac{a-b}{b} = \frac{a}{b} - \frac{b}{b} = \frac{a}{b} - 1$. Set this equal to the right side, and solve for $\frac{a}{b}$.

7. Linear Equations or Proportions: Since Amelia's run increased by a "constant amount" each week, the relationship is linear. The answer choices are asking for the change in distance to the change in time, so let y be distance, in miles, and x be time, in weeks. The given points are (4 weeks, 8 miles) and (16 weeks, 26 miles). Find the slope. Remember, the slope is the change in y (distance) per change in x (time):
   $\frac{26-8}{16-4} = \frac{18}{12} = 1.5$ miles/week.

   Proportions: To solve this problem using a proportion, you must recognize that Amelia increases her distance by 18 miles (26 miles – 8 miles) over 12 weeks (16 weeks – 4 weeks). Use these numbers as your known relationship, and find the increased distance for one week:

$$\frac{\text{increased distance (miles)}}{\text{weeks}} \quad \frac{18}{12} = \frac{x}{1}$$

8. Linear Equations

9. Basic Algebra (radicals) or Pick Answers

10. Basic Algebra or Pick Answers: Because this is the no-calculator section, solving this one using algebra is probably easier (hint: cross multiply). But if you find yourself stuck, and you're comfortable working with fractions, use the Pick Trick.

11. Systems of Equations / Factoring (quadratic formula): This is a difficult question. We cannot solve the system of equations without a calculator, but we can take the first few steps, and then apply what we know about the quadratic formula. First, substitute the expression for y into the first equation: $x = 2y + 5 \rightarrow x = 2[(2x - 3)(x + 9)] + 5$. Next, simplify this equation into a standard quadratic ($ax^2 + bx + c = 0$): $x = 2(2x^2 + 18x - 3x - 27) + 5 = 2(2x^2 + 15x - 27) + 5 = 4x^2 + 30x - 54 + 5 = 4x^2 + 30x - 49$. So we have $x = 4x^2 + 30x - 49$, or, subtracting x from both sides: $4x^2 + 29x - 49 = 0$. Finally, recall that in the quadratic formula, when $b^2 > 4ac$, the quadratic will have *two* real solutions (review the lesson if necessary): $29^2 > 4(4)(-49)$.

Alternate (easier) approach: Parabolas / Linear Equations: If you've covered the Parabolas lesson, you might have noticed that the second equation, which defines a parabola, can fairly easily be converted into the x-intercept form:

$$y = 2\left(x - \frac{3}{2}\right)(x + 9).$$ You should

probably find the y-intercept as well (plug in $x = 0$). Finally, quickly sketch the graph of the parabola and the line (convert the first equation to $y = mx + b$ form). The number of solutions (i.e. intersections) should be apparent. This approach is probably faster than the algebraic approach.

12. Algebraic Word / Percent (increase/decrease): A 20% increase is equivalent to multiplying by 1.20 (review

"multipliers" in the Percent lesson). So the total price for the two sandwiches, including the tips, is $x(1.2) + (x + 1)(1.2)$. The solution will be half this (since they split the cost evenly). If you have trouble working with the variable, you could try Pick Numbers (type 1).

13. Graphs of Functions or Pick Answers: Find the x-intercepts of either function by solving for x when $y = 0$.

If you'd rather Pick Answers, just plug the answer choices into either function for k (the x-coordinate), and make sure the y-coordinate is 0.

14. Complex Numbers (i in the denominator)

15. Factoring (quadratic formula) / Pick Numbers (type 1): This one can be tricky (as the problem number suggests). The first step is putting the equation in $ax^2 + bx + c = 0$ form. You should find that $a = 1$, $b = -\dfrac{k}{2}$ and $c = -2p$. Next, plug these values into the quadratic formula. You should get the

following: $$\dfrac{\dfrac{k}{2} \pm \sqrt{\left(-\dfrac{k}{2}\right)^2 - 4(-2p)}}{2} =$$

$$\dfrac{k}{4} \pm \dfrac{\sqrt{\dfrac{k^2}{4} + 8p}}{2}.$$ From the first part of

the expression, we know that the answer is A or B. Now use the Pick Trick. Pick a couple easy numbers for k and p (2 is an easy one for k) and check the answers to determine the correct answer.

16. Triangles (similar): Let's call the height of the shampoo h. There's more than one way to tackle this one, but the fastest approach involves creating two similar triangles by drawing vertical lines:

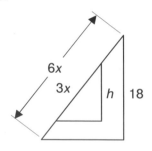

Since the triangles are similar, you can find h: $\dfrac{h}{3x} = \dfrac{18}{6x}$. (Note that, after cross multiplying, the x's cancel.)

17. Basic Trigonometry

18. Factoring (grouping method)

19. Systems of Equations

20. Linear Equations or Proportions: As given, for every 10 km of distance, the temperature decreases $k°$ C—thus, the relationship is linear. You are given two points (we'll call the x-values distance and the y-values temperature): (50 km, –5°C) and (80 km, –80°C). Find the slope, which will give you the change in temperature for each unit change in distance (1 km). Use this to find k, the temperature change in 10 km. You could also set this up as a proportion: $\dfrac{\text{decrease in decrees (C)}}{\text{increased distance (miles)}} \dfrac{75}{30} = \dfrac{k}{10}$. See #7 for a similar problem.

MATH (calculator)

1. Algebraic Word or Pick Answers: Here's the equation (don't forget to try to find these equations on your own before checking the solution): $\$9.80 + \$1.50x - \$12.80$.

2. Algebraic Word or Pick Numbers (type 1): If you have trouble finding the correct equation, use the Pick Trick. You might note that the given goal of typing 225 wpm is superfluous information. By now, you're hopefully used to this little SAT trick.

3. Ratios (of/is) / Proportions: First, you must find the weight of each slice, in pounds: $3 \times \dfrac{1}{2} \times \dfrac{1}{3}$. If you had trouble with this step, consider the of/is rule from the Percent lesson: "one half of 3 is what?" → "one third of that answer is what?" Then set up a proportion, if necessary.

4. Percent (of/is): Note the word "about" in the question. You can assume that the given percent can apply to all 225 people.

5. Algebraic Word: First find the equation. Then plug in the given numbers.

6. Algebraic Word: Here are the two equations (let r = the number of hours Raul worked and a = the number of hours Angelica worked): $r = a + 11$ and $r + a = 59$. Solve using substitution. Note: Some students have trouble with the first equation. If in doubt, just plug in a number for a, and make sure r is 11 greater (for example, if $a = 2$, we calculate that $r = 13$ ✓). If your numbers don't work, swap a and r.

7. Tables & Graphs / (Probability): This is similar to a typical Probability problem, and solved in the same way. As usual with these, there's far more information given in the table than you need. Focus on what's relevant to the problem (in this case, the total number of movies and the number of movies that are comedies *and* PG-13).

8. Linear Equations: While this question primarily tests your knowledge of slope, you must know how the quadrants of the xy-plane are labeled. The quadrants were discussed briefly in the Linear Equations section (see the homework questions). For more on the quadrants, see the More Trigonometry lesson.

9. Tables & Graphs / Probability

10. Tables & Graphs (scatterplots)

11. Tables & Graphs (scatterplots) / Ratios

12. Graphs of Functions (axis intercepts)

13. Growth & Decay Functions (exponential): You could probably just solve this one using Process of Elimination: The population is clearly growing (eliminate B and D). Is the relationship linear? That is, does each 5-week change in time correspond to a constant change in population?

14. Growth & Decay Functions (compound interest equation): Note that since r is defined here as a percent, not a decimal, it must be written as $\dfrac{r}{100}$. Since the rate is compounded *monthly*, we have $\dfrac{r}{(100)(12)} = \dfrac{r}{1,200}$. This equation is discussed in more detail in the lesson.

15. Graphs of Functions / Pick Numbers (type 3): Pick appropriate numbers for *a* and *b*, and graph the equation (either with a graphing calculator or by hand); you should be able to see the general shape of the graph.

16. Tables & Graphs / Algebraic Word: The equation for total cost is given in the intro to the problem. Here's the inequality for comparing the two stores (Store B is to the left of the inequality, and Store A is to the right): $600 + 105x \leq 750 + 80x$. Review solving inequalities (Basic Algebra), if necessary.

17. Linear Equations (applications): Remember, slope is change in *y* (in this case, *cost*) over change in *x* (in this case, *days*). Make sure you are comfortable with these application questions—the SAT likes them.

18. Solids & Volume / Proportions: First find the volume of the glass (relevant formulas are found at the front of each math section)—you should get about 42.4 cubic inches. Once you find the volume, use the following proportion:
$$\frac{\text{glasses}}{\text{volume (cubic inches)}} \quad \frac{1}{42.4} = \frac{x}{231}.$$

19. Basic Algebra (inequalities): Solve for *p* in the first inequality. What is the smallest possible value for *p*? Plug this value into the given expression.

20. Growth & Decay Functions: The current biomass doubles each year. In other words, the value added each year is *not* constant (which would be a linear relationship). Rather, the value added increases as the biomass increases. As the biomass gets bigger, it gets bigger *faster*. Review "Exponential Growth/Decay" if necessary.

21. Statistics (bar graphs) / Tables & Graphs (scatterplots): To give you an idea of how to graph the five points, the first point (for "biofuels") is (0.25, 1.80). Remember, the first number is for 2000 (*x*-value) and the second number is for 2010 (*y*-value).

    Shortcut: You don't really have to graph these points. The points that will be above the line $y = x$ will have a *y*-value greater than the *x*-value. Just look at the bar graph.

22. Tables & Graphs / Percent (increase/decrease)

23. Statistics (terminology: standard deviation): You won't be expected to calculate standard deviation, but you should understand what it measures, that is, the *spread* of a data set.

24. More Circles (sectors) / Area & Perimeter (circumference): You don't actually have to use a proportion on this one (as you would with most problems testing sectors of circles). Just note that

    since *AB* is a diameter, arc *AB* , no matter how it is measured, is half the circumference of the circle. So the circumference is $8\pi \times 2 = 16\pi$. Now find *r* by working backwards, using the equation for circumference; or, if necessary, Pick Answers.

25. Pick Numbers (advanced): You can pick a number for *x*, and check the answer choices. For example, if you pick $x = 2$, you have $f(2) = 48$ and $g(2) = 12$. Eliminate answer choices that are not divisible by 7 ($2x + 3 = 7$). Note: Picking $x = 2$ only eliminates two choices, so you'll have to pick a new number. In this case, $x = 1$ will eliminate the remaining incorrect answer choice.

    Alternate approach (Factoring): There's a (difficult) shortcut to this one. By factoring, we can write $f(x) = 2x^3 + 6x^2 + 4x = 2x(x^2 + 3x + 2)$. Since $g(x) = x^2 + 3x + 2$, we know that $f(x) = 2x \cdot g(x)$. Now check the answer choices, substituting $2x \cdot g(x)$ for $f(x)$. After factoring out the $g(x)$, one choice will have a factored expression of $2x + 3$ (which means that it is divisible by $2x + 3$). See the College Board solution for more details.

26. Pick Numbers (advanced): This one is not easy. Before we pick any numbers, let's start by looking at the inequality in the question: $-y < x < y$. It's a small step to recognize that $-y < y$ (we can ignore the *x* part of the inequality). And finally, you can try picking numbers for *y* to learn that *y* must be greater than 0 ($y > 0$). So III must be true (eliminate A and B).

    Now we can check the other two Roman numerals, starting with I. Let's pick a number for y, such as $y = 3$ (remember, $y > 0$). So we have (from the question) $-3 < x < 3$. Now, start picking xs that fall in this range, such as $x = -2$, 0, and 2. You should quickly see that I is always true.

Since negative values for x worked above, II is *not* always true.

27. Linear Equations (applications) / Tables & Graphs (scatterplots): Hopefully you recognize that 61 in the equation is the y-intercept. But what does it mean? If this were a simple line problem, it would mean that when the population density of a city is exactly 0 (yes, an odd thought), the relative housing cost is 61%. But since this is a line of best fit (and a real-life application), it means that as a city's population density gets very small, relative housing cost for that city will *probably* get close to 61%.

28. Parabolas: You're looking for the vertex form. The answer must be C or D. Only one, when expanded, is equivalent to the given equation.

29. Means, Medians & Modes / Pick Numbers (type 1): Of course, you could solve this algebraically, but we recommend using the Pick Trick. Just pick a number for m (the variable found in the answer choices), and find x, y, and z. Then find the average (mean) of x, y, and z.

30. Graphs of Functions: It may help to imagine a horizontal line at the y-value where $f(x)$ has 3 solutions—this line will intersect the graph at 3 places (hence the 3 solutions).

31. Proportions: The known relationship is 8 gallons = 1 minute. Note that the given 600 gallons is superfluous.

32. Linear Equations (applications) or Pick Numbers (type 3): First, convert the equation into $y = mx + b$ form:

$P = \dfrac{1}{2}x + 110$. The y-variable is P

(blood pressure), and the x-variable is time, in years. The slope will be the change in blood pressure per year.

The Pick Trick is straightforward. For example, if we pick $x = 10$ (years), $P = 115$. When we increase x by 1 year ($x =$

11), $P = 115.5$. The increase in P was 0.5.

33. Proportions: You have two known relationships, so plan to use two proportions. Don't forget to label your units carefully (write them to the left of each proportion).

34. Algebraic Word / Ratios (part-over-whole): The first part of this question is needlessly wordy. Simply put, we're starting with 240 male bats and 260 female bats. How many additional male bats will yield the ratio given in the question? Here's the equation, where m is the number of added male bats:

$$\frac{\text{part}}{\text{whole}} = \frac{3}{5} = \frac{240 + m}{(240 + 260) + m}.$$

35. Ratios / Basic Algebra or Pick Numbers (type 3): We recommend using the Pick Trick. Pick a number for the slower velocity (v_1), and calculate the faster velocity ($v_2 = 1.5v_1$). Calculate q_1 and q_2, and find the ratio (make sure you put q_2, the pressure for the faster fluid, on top). Note that the constant n will cancel in your ratio.

36. More Circles (sectors): Using the proportion given in the lesson, find x (central angle, in degrees) when the length of arc AB is 5, and again when the length of arc AB is 6. Note: You will have to calculate the circumference (the radius is given). There are several correct answers.

37. Growth & Decay Functions: This problem tests your knowledge of "multipliers"—review the Percent (increase/decrease) lesson, if necessary.

38. Growth & Decay Functions: If you got the previous question correct, this one's a gimme.

5. PRACTICE TEST 5

QUESTIONS BY SECTIONS/CHAPTERS

The following information lists every question on the test according to its relevant chapter or section in this tutorial. If you're correcting a test, circle the question numbers below that you missed or guessed on. Make sure to follow the Tutoring Schedule in the Introduction to know when to correct or tackle various types of questions.

READING
BY PASSAGE
- [1, 2, 3, 4, 5, 6, 7, 8, 9, 10] [11, 12, 13, 14, 15, 16, 17 ,18 19, 20, 21] [22, 23, 24, 25, 26, 27, 28, 29, 30, 31] [32, 33, 34, 35, 36, 37, 38, 39, 40, 41] [42, 43, 44, 45, 46, 47, 48, 49, 50, 51, 52]

BY QUESTION TYPE
- Direct & CTE (stand-alone): 4, 5, 6, 9, 11, 12, 17, 18, 23, 28, 33, 34, 35, 42, 43, 45, 46, 49
- Extended Reasoning & Purpose: 2, 3, 13, 36, 48, 50, 51, 52
- WIC & Main Idea: 8, 10, 14, 15, 16, 22, 29, 37, 38, 44, 47
- Comparison & IG: 19, 20, 21, 30, 31, 39, 40, 41
- Tone, Structure, & Relationship: 1, 7, 24, 25, 26, 27, 32
Note: Most Citing-Textual-Evidence (CTE) questions are grouped with their relevant preceding questions.

WRITING & LANGUAGE
- Grammar & Sentence Structure: [2, 4, 5, 6, 9, 10, 11] [13, 14, 15, 17, 18, 20, 21, 22] [23, 24, 26, 29, 30, 31] [35, 36, 37, 39, 42, 44]
- Main Ideas & Organization: [1, 3, 7, 8] [12, 16, 19] [25, 27, 28, 32, 33*] [34, 38, 40, 41, 43]
Note: Brackets display separate passages.
* Informational Graphics

MATH
- Arithmetic: §3 (12, 15); §4 (1, 3, 5, 9, 14, 16, 17, 18, 22, 24, 25, 31, 32, 37, 38)
- Functions: §4 (34)
- Algebra: §3 (1, 5, 7, 8, 9, 10, 13, 16, 17, 18); §4 (2, 4, 6, 7, 10, 11, 12, 13, 21, 23, 28)
- Advanced Algebra: §3 (3, 6, 19); §4 (8)
- Graphs of Functions: §3 (4, 14); §4 (20)
- Geometry: §3 (2, 11, 20); §4 (19, 26, 29, 33, 35, 36)
- Odds & Ends: §4 (15, 27, 30)
§3 = Section 3; §4 = Section 4

TECHNIQUES AND HINTS

READING

PASSAGE I

1. Structure: 8–10. etc., 41–44, etc.

2. Purpose: 1–2 (place), 8–18 (object)

3. Extended Reasoning: 34

4. Direct: 43 ("all talking at once"), 52–53 ("They laughed more than there seemed any occasion for"), 55–59 ("too loud," "terrible not quite sober pitch . . .")

5. Citing-Textual-Evidence (CTE): See above.

6. Direct: 66–70. The context is fairly clear (clear enough for us to label this question Direct). Because his father's coat was hung up, and the narrator started speaking to him, the narrator's father very likely joined him at the table.

7. Tone: 74–78 ("physical decay," "hair was turning gray and his scalp showed through on top," etc.)

8. Main Idea: 85–93. The "young man" refers to Mr. Peters when he was younger. This aspect of Mr. Peters "ma[de] him do things that were not becoming in a man of forty-five."

9. CTE (stand-alone): The context is clear (". . . so that the two women at the next table would notice . . .").

10. Words-in-Context (WIC): 90–93. Don't forget to define the word in question using context (before you look at the answer choices). You may have come up with something like *appropriate* or *correct*. Eliminate answer choices accordingly.

PASSAGE II

11. Direct: 6–12. Women hold a "subordinate" (lesser) relation to men, but their influence is not "any the less important."

12. CTE: See above.

13. Extended Reasoning: 25–27 ("domestic and social circle"), 34–37 ("then, the fathers, the husbands . . ."): To summarize, women must influence men at home, and then men will expand that influence to society (see also 13–18).

14. WIC: 1–2. The passage describes the relative *positions* or *statuses* of men and women.

15. WIC: 12. You're looking for a word similar to "distinct." As always, be wary of the most common definitions of the word in question (probably A or B).

16. Main Idea: 65–68, 77–81

17. Direct: 61–65. You might have trouble with the word "alienated," but the contrast signal "but" makes clear that while rights may be taken from the slave, these rights are, none the less, "stamped on his moral being"; they are "imperishable."

18. CTE: See above.

19. Comparison: Of course, you must consider main ideas on this one. The first passage says that women should avoid "conflict" and "coercive influences" (44–45); the second passage says that women should "oppose slavery publicly" (see the introduction). The passages disagree—the second takes issue with the first.

20. Comparison: 8–10, 83–87

21. Comparison: 1–2, 6–12

PASSAGE III

22. WIC: The author refers simply to the amount of food that can come from some area of land. Later in the passage, this "simple" ratio is complicated with other issues (health, taste, pesticides, etc.). Which choice best captures the idea of "simple" in this context?

23. Direct: 40–42, 51–53. Remember, you're looking for the best answer choice. Choice A is probably true, but another choice is directly supported by the passage.

24. Tone: 27–31

25. CTE: See above.

26. Relationship: 61–65

27. CTE: See above.

28. Direct: 81–82 ("the best from both systems"), 92–93 ("different kinds of practices")

29. WIC: 84–91. You must consider the first sentence of the paragraph, which emphasizes "nutrition." The second sentence, following the contrast signal "But," focuses on calories alone.

30. Informational Graphics (IG) (direct): According to the graph, the crop types "all crops" and "cereals" each yield a little over 70% (organic yield as a percentage of conventional yield). The other choices can be eliminated.

31. IG (direct): All species are below 100%; that is, when they are organically grown, their yields are less than when they are conventionally grown.

PASSAGE IV

32. Structure: 73–75 ("But one question . . ."), 82 ("What explains the difference?), 85–86 ("Will companies be able to boost their products . . . ?). You might have an easier time using POE on this one. Choices C and D are too negative, and practical applications (A) are not emphasized.

33. Direct: 9–17. Arriving at a "true number" (14) is a *quantitative* situation; judging "something less tangible, such as . . . quality or worth," is *qualitative*. The answer is camouflaged.

34. CTE: See above.

35. CTE (stand-alone): This question is a little harder than the typical Citing-Textual-Evidence question. First, you must understand the view of the "skeptics," which is made clear in lines 20–21: "people's opinions are easily swayed by those of others." Next, find supportive evidence, as with a typical CTE question.

36. Extended Reasoning: 74–75

37. WIC: 85. What would a company want to do with their products by manipulating online ratings? Be careful of choice A. A company might want to increase *sales*, but saying that it wants to increase a *product* is unidiomatic. When an answer choice sounds awkward when plugged into the passage, it's probably wrong.

38. WIC: 85–86. Define the word in question using context. You hopefully came up with something like *size* or *extent.*

39. IG (direct): Make sure you focus on the "artificially up-voted" data (see the key in the top right of the figure).

40. IG (direct)

41. IG (make connection): Even though this question asks you to consider the passage (which is why we labeled it a "make connection" IG question), you can actually avoid the passage and just use POE. The figure makes no mention of "artificially down-voted comments" (A), "negative social influence" (B), or "human behavior in other contexts" (C).

PASSAGE V

42. Direct: 20–26. The passage is fairly clear. Maguire's research was "groundbreaking" (27) because it proved that "old inherited wisdom was simply not true."

43. CTE: See above.

44. WIC: 20–25. While the brain does change in some ways ("synapses . . . rearrange themselves" and "new links between brain cells . . . form"), the *main* or *general* structure of the brain does not change ("is more or less static"). Which choice is closest to *main* or *general*?

45. Direct: 33–37

46. CTE: See above.

47. WIC: 38–39. There's not much in the way of context for this one. You must have some idea of experimental method. When scientists conduct an experiment, they strive to test a variable (in this case, *memorizing ability*), while keeping other factors constant (such as age, socioeconomics, education, etc.). Thus, the subjects would be *similar*, with the exception of their memorizing abilities (the variable). (Students are often tempted by choice B, but the subjects would certainly not be *identical*, especially in terms of memorizing capabilities.) If you're not sure about

this one, take a guess and move on. It's not really testing information given in the passage.

48. Purpose: 57–62

49. Direct: 59–65. The answer is slightly camouflaged. You might be looking for some mention of "different circuitry" or different "regions of the brain." The correct answer puts it more generally.

50. Extended Reasoning: 66–70 ("Surprisingly"). See also lines 72–73, which reinforce the idea that these "regions of the brain" (68) are not normally used in memorization.

51. CTE: See above.

52. Purpose: 66–73. This paragraph focuses on the "Surprising[ ]" nature of the results.

WRITING & LANGUAGE

PASSAGE I

1. Main Ideas (additions): The main idea of the paragraph has to do with "understanding . . . the distant past," or, more specifically, "knowledge of ancient species." The "age of rock," while obviously related, is off topic.

2. Vocabulary: Sometimes, you just have to trust your ear on these Vocabulary questions. The incorrect choices are all actions that *people* might take, but not "models."

3. Main Ideas (deletions): There's actually a clue word here. The next sentence begins with "The plastic." The underlined sentence must introduce this plastic (so it should not be deleted).

4. Run-ons: Only one choice does not erroneously create an independent clause following the comma.

5. -*ING* (B, C) / Idioms (D): While short, this phrase is unidiomatic.

6. Apostrophes & Confused Words: The possessive pronoun refers to "fossils" (plural).

7. Organization: You might be tempted by choice C, but sentence 5 continues the idea of sentence 4, the "limit[s]" of the research. Sentence 2 contrasts ("But now . . .") sentences 4 and 5.

8. Transitions: Remember to ignore the underlined word on Transitions questions (it's wrong 75% of the time). What follows is clearly an example of "reproduce[ing] fossils that scientists cannot observe firsthand."

9. Subject-Verb Agreement (A, D) / Verb Tense (C)

10. Combining Sentences: Focus on the shortest choice, usually the correct answer on Combining Sentences questions.

11. Pronoun Agreement: The pronoun refers to "the researchers."

PASSAGE II

12. Transitions: Remember, sometimes the best choice is the one with no transition.

13. Combining Sentences: As is often the case, the shortest combination is the best one.

14. -*ING* (B) / Run-ons (C) / Wordy (D): Note that the correct answer is the shortest choice. Some students are uncomfortable putting modifying phrases at the ends of sentences, but it's a perfectly acceptable usage.

15. Punctuation

16. Main Ideas (deletions): The topic of this part of the paragraph is Boss Tweed's stealing, power, and corruption (all key words). Does the sentence in question have anything to do with these ideas?

17. Punctuation: The comma before the quote is necessary, but the others are unneeded. Try using the pause rule.

18. Redundancies

19. Main Ideas (additions): The focus is on Nast's depiction of Tweed's "power." He is depicted as a "big bloated thief." Which choice supports this idea?

20. Vocabulary: If you know the difference between *persecuted* and *prosecuted*, this one's straightforward.

21. Verb Tense: See "escaped" and "fled."

22. Vocabulary

PASSAGE III

23. Apostrophes & Confused Words (A, C) / Pronoun Agreement (D): The word in

question is referring to "the system" (singular).

24. Combining Sentences: Once again, focus on the shortest choice, and make sure you are comfortable with the correct use of colons (see the Punctuation section, if necessary).

25. Transitions: Note the flow. The previous sentence used the word "vital." The next sentence states that the group "may not be large enough."

26. Punctuation

27. Main Ideas: Does this added sentence maintain the focus of the "problems" (key word) of crowdfunding?

28. Transitions: The list of problems continues.

29. Run-ons (A) / -*ING* (B) / Idioms (D)

30. Passive Voice (A, C) / Pronoun Agreement (C, D)

31. Pronoun Agreement

32. Organization: Note the clue word in sentence 2: "the price." Not until sentence 5 is the price of the tickets discussed.

33. Informational Graphics (IG)

PASSAGE IV

34. Organization: Sentence 3 introduces "Newspapers," so any sentence that also mentions newspapers must come after it. You might also note the flow of ideas, from the general ("print journalism") to the specific ("newspapers"). This construction is typical in these essays.

35. Apostrophes & Confused Words (A, D) / Run-ons (C)

36. Idioms: This question requires you to have a sense of what the author is trying to say: investigative journalists seek to serve the the public interest. The correct choice captures this idea.

37. Redundancies: Read carefully: "street crime," "corporate wrongdoing," etc. are examples of "illegal activities."

38. Main Ideas (additions): The easiest way to get this one is to note the words "More recently" in the previous sentence. We don't want to jump from

1974 to 2004 and back to 1954. Moreover, a television show is not "print journalism."

39. Vocabulary (A): The word "blockade" is oddly used in this context. / Idioms (B): The word "interference" should use the preposition *in*, not *to*. The usage is questionable in any case. / Style (C): The phrase "drag on" is too casual for this context.

40. Answer the Question: Only one choice answers the question. Note that A, C, and D all sound as though the end of investigative journalism is *not* a real possibility.

41. Main Ideas: The passage's main idea is moving away from print journalism.

42. Punctuation: Usually, the comma before "such as" is fine, because it opens a phrase (e.g., *Leafy greens, such as kale, are good for you*), but in this case, the phrase is not closed (after "Project"), so any punctuation opening the phrase would be incorrect.

43. Transitions: How does the Help Me Investigate project relate to "a public conversation about key issues" (previous sentence)?

44. Misplaced Words: This one looks tricky, but if you realize that the opening phrase must modify the subject of the independent clause ("the advent of the digital age"), you won't have to read every word of the answer choices (review "Improper Modifiers").

MATH (no calculator)

1. Linear Equations

2. More Circles (sectors): Note that the central angle for arc AC is given (90°). So you can write the following proportion, where x is our unknown arc length (the first ratio is for degrees, and the second ratio is for arc length): $\dfrac{\text{part}}{\text{whole}} \dfrac{90}{360} = \dfrac{x}{36}$. You might also simply recognize that the central angle of the arc in question is ¼ of the circle's degrees (that is, ¼ of 360°), so the arc length will be ¼ of the circle's circumference.

3. Factoring: First, factor out the common monomial (4). Then factor what remains: $x^2 - 2x - 3 = (x - ?)(x + ?)$. Finally, apply the zero-product theorem.

4. Graphs of Functions: Remember, "zeros" are x-intercepts (also called *roots*).

5. Basic Algebra (radicals)

6. Working with Polynomials (addition) or Pick Numbers (type 1)

7. Systems of Inequalities

8. Linear Equations (applications)

9. Systems of Equations: First, substitute $y = x^2$ into the second equation. You should get $2x^2 + 6 = 2(x + 3)$ → $2x^2 + 6 = 2x + 6$ → $2x^2 - 2x = 0$ → factor: $2x(x - 1) = 0$. Since $x > 0$ (given), $x = 1$. Solve for y using the first equation, and find xy.

10. Pick Numbers (type 1): While there's an algebraic approach (see below), this one is easier if you use the Pick Trick. Since it's the no-calculator section, pick easy numbers, such as $a = 1$ and $b = 2$.

    Factoring: If you use substitution, you'll see that $4z + 8y = 4(a^2 + b^2) + 8ab$. This can be written as $4a^2 + 8ab + 4b^2 = 4(a^2 + 2ab + b^2) = 4(a + b)^2$. Can you see the correct answer choice?

11. Solids & Volume / Algebraic Word: The volume of a cylinder is found in the reference section. You should get the following equation: $\pi r^2 h = 22$. When you double the radius and halve the height, you have:

$$\pi(2r)^2 \frac{h}{2} = \pi \cdot 4r^2 \cdot \frac{h}{2} = 2\pi r^2 h.$$

Substitution: $2\pi r^2 h = 2(22) = 44$.

12. Exponents: You'll probably have to use the answer choices on this one. First, let's rewrite the given term in radical form: $9^{\frac{3}{4}} = \sqrt[4]{9^3}$. At this point, you can probably guess that A and B are incorrect. Now, let's rewrite the given term in terms of 3:

$9^{\frac{3}{4}} = \left(3^2\right)^{\frac{3}{4}} = 3^{\frac{6}{4}} = 3^{\frac{3}{2}}$. Check the

answer choices: C: $\sqrt{3} = 3^{\frac{1}{2}}$ (nope); D:

$3\sqrt{3} = 3^1 \cdot 3^{\frac{1}{2}} = 3^{\left(1 + \frac{1}{2}\right)} = 3^{\frac{3}{2}}$ (done).

13. Linear Equations (applications): Note the linear equation. The slope is 1. This means that for each additional tea bag, the restaurant can make one additional cup.

    You could also simply try out some numbers, using the given equation ($t = n + 2$, where t is tea bags and n is cups). If you have 2 cups, you need $2 + 2 = 4$ tea bags. To make an additional cup (3 cups total), you need $3 + 2 = 5$ tea bags (<u>one</u> more tea bag).

    Note: This question, at first glance, may look like a Proportions question, but cups and tea bags are *not* proportional, and there is no "known relationship" given. (The variables in linear equations are not necessarily proportional.)

14. More Graphs of Functions (transformations): If you're comfortable with the shape of the graph 2^x, then just apply the transformation rules (move up one, and then reflect across the x-axis). Otherwise . . .

    Pick Numbers (advanced): Find a point on $y = -f(x)$, and eliminate answer choices. For example, $-f(0) = -(2^0 + 1) = -(1 + 1) = -2$. Eliminate choices that do NOT contain $(0, -2)$.

15. Proportions: This is a tricky problem (remember, it's the last question of the multiple-choice section, so we expect it to be difficult). It's a good one to skip and come back to if you have time. The College Board solution uses an approach that we think most students wouldn't know to use, so we'll use proportions. First, let's find how much Alan spends on gas when he drives 100 miles: 100 miles = 4 gallons (25 miles per gallon) and 4 gallons = $16 ($4 per gallon). Alan wants to spend $5 less ($16 − $5 = $11). You could create multiple proportions, but if you recognize that he spends $4 every 25 miles, you can tackle the question with one proportion, where m is how many *fewer* miles (than 100) he must drive:

$\dfrac{\$}{\text{miles}}\ \dfrac{4}{25}=\dfrac{11}{100-m}$. You'll have to simplify the answer choices to find the correct one.

16. Algebraic Word: Here's the inequality: $10 + 60h \le 280$. Solve for h (review solving inequalities in the Basic Algebra section, if necessary).

17. Basic Algebra: Distribute and combine like terms carefully.

18. Systems of Equations: Substitute $y = 2x$ into the first equation, and solve for x.

19. Common Denominators: The common denominator is $(x + 2)^2$, so you must multiple the top and bottom of the fraction on the right by $(x + 2)$. This will give you:
$$\dfrac{2x+6}{(x+2)^2} - \dfrac{2(x+2)}{(x+2)^2} = \dfrac{2x+6-2(x+2)}{(x+2)^2}.$$
To find a (see the question), simplify the numerator.

20. Angles (straight line, triangle): This math section included some difficult questions, but if you're comfortable with angles, this last question is straightforward. This is why it's important to skip harder questions (such as #15) so you can get your eyeballs on questions at the end.

MATH (calculator)

1. Tables & Graphs: The greatest change will occur where the line is steepest.

2. Functions / Pick Numbers (advanced): Don't forget to check every answer choice with your picked numbers. Not surprisingly, all four choices work when you check (1, 5). Hint: Start with the bigger numbers in the table.

3. Proportions: Read carefully. The answer should be in <u>pounds</u>, not ounces.

4. Basic Algebra (working with variables): If you have any trouble with this one, Pick Numbers (type 2): pick a number for c and solve for d.

5. Ratios (of/is): Remember, "of" means multiplication.

6. Algebraic Word: Make sure you are comfortable with this type of Algebraic

Word question. Here are the two equations (where m is the number of magazines and n is the number of novels): $m + n = 11$ and $m + 4n = 20$. Solve using elimination or substitution (see Systems of Equations).

7. Linear Equations (applications): This is a typical linear application. We're starting with b businesses (the y-intercept) and increasing the business by n per year (nx).

   Pick Numbers (type 1): Feel free to use a Pick Trick on this one. For example, if we start with 4 business ($b = 4$), and add 3 businesses per year ($n = 3$), then how many businesses will we have in 2 years ($x = 2$)? $(4 + 3 + 3 = 10.)$ Plug in your numbers and look for $y = 10$.

8. Working with Polynomials: FOIL the first expression (in parentheses), and then combine like terms. Shortcut: Just worry about the x^2 terms (eliminate 2 choices) and the number terms (eliminate the remaining choice).

9. Proportions

10. Basic Algebra (working with variables) / Algebraic Word

11. Linear Equations: Convert the equation into $y = mx + b$ form. You should find $m = \dfrac{2}{3}$. The slope of a line perpendicular to this line will have a slope of $-\dfrac{1}{\frac{2}{3}} = -\dfrac{3}{2}$. Check the answer choices (convert to $y = mx + b$ form).

12. Systems of Equations: These systems are often set up for easy substitution. Just plug $\dfrac{1}{2}y = 4$ into the second equation, and solve for x: $x - \dfrac{1}{2}y = 2$ $\rightarrow$ $x - 4 = 2$ ...

13. Pick Answers: The easiest approach to this one is to simply plug the answer choices into the system of inequalities until you find one that works for both inequalities.

14. Probability

15. Studies: Remember not to jump to conclusions on these. The agency surveyed 1,000 adults from a large city.

All we know is that 78% of these adults were satisfied with air quality. If all adults in the city were surveyed, or if another 1,000 adults were surveyed, or if adults were surveyed in another city, we might expect a *similar* percent to be satisfied with air quality (especially for the first two scenarios), but we don't know if the percent would be *exactly* the same (it probably would not).

16. Tables & Graphs: Read the introductory text: approx. age = diameter × growth factor.

17. Tables & Graphs (scatterplots): Usually these scatterplots questions give you the best fit line, but this one requires you to draw one. Just eyeball a line that runs through the points. Then check a point or two (use the equation from #16).

18. Tables & Graphs: Once again, we'll use the equation from #16. First, use it to find the age of both trees (based on a 12 inch diameter). Then add 10 years to both ages, and calculate the new diameters. Here's the math: Pin oak (now): 12 inches × 3.0 (growth factor) = 36 years. White birch (now): 12 inches × 5.0 (growth factor) = 60 years. → Pin oak (in 10 years): 46 years = d × 3.0. White birch (in 10 years): 70 years = d × 5.0. Solve for both ds and subtract.

19. Triangles: First, fill in the missing angles. Since the base angles ($\angle A$ and $\angle C$) are equal, $\triangle ABC$ is isosceles: side $AB \cong$ side BC. The two smaller triangles are congruent (by hypotenuse-leg or SAS). By the 30-60-90 side relationships, side $DC = 6$. Thus, side $AD = 6$. Note that the drawing is drawn to scale, so the correct answer is evident.

20. Graphs of Functions: This is an unusual question. Hopefully you can see that the graph $y = d(t)$ displays the distance of the mark from the ground, as the wheel rolls. If you saw this, great. If not, try POE; the three incorrect choices can be fairly easily eliminated.

21. Pick Numbers (type 3): Simply pick numbers for a and b (read carefully), solve for c, and check the answer choices.

22. Percent (of/is): A common error for this one is to use 34.6 percent, but the question is asking for students who have <u>fewer</u> than two siblings, so use 100% − 34.6% = 65.4%. The total number of students is 1,800 × 26.

23. Tables & Graphs / Linear Equations / Pick Numbers (advanced): Note that the purchase price (p) should be in *thousands* of dollars. Pick one of the points from the table (such as $p = 128$ ($128,000) and $r = 950$), plug into the answer choices, and use POE.

24. Tables & Graphs / Percent (increase/decrease): First, review "multipliers": 40% discount means × 0.60 and 20% discount means × 0.80. To find the original price x, use the following equation: $(x \cdot 0.60)(0.80) = 140,000$.

25. Percent (part-over-whole): The problem is wordy, but what we really have is 36 + p people, out of 300, who chose the first picture. So, using part-over-whole, the percent of all participants who chose the first picture is: $\dfrac{\text{part}}{\text{whole}} \dfrac{36 + p}{300}$. The question states that this percent is greater than 20%, so create an inequality and simplify until you see the correct choice.

26. Solids & Volume: You should know that the surface area of a cube of side s is $6s^2$ (review the lesson, if necessary). Since $6s^2 = 6\left(\dfrac{a}{4}\right)^2$ (given), it's clear that $s = \dfrac{a}{4}$. Use this to find the perimeter of one face (a square).

27. Means: First, use $A = \dfrac{S}{N}$ to find the sum (S) of the scores of the 8 players (N). Then, find the sum of the scores of the 7 remaining players. The difference in these sums must be the score of the highest-scoring player (removed).

28. Linear Equations: The slope of the line defined by the linear function f is $m = \dfrac{1}{2}$ (calculate using two points on the graph), so the slope of the linear

function g is $4 \times \dfrac{1}{2} = 2$. Since we know a point on line g, we can find the $y = mx + b$ equation (review the lesson, if necessary). Finally, plug in $x = 9$ to find $g(9)$.

29. More Circles: To find the standard equation of the circle, review completing the square.

30. Parabolas / Pick Numbers (type 1): You could pick numbers for x and a, find y in the given equation, and check the answer choices. Hint: Pick a perfect square for a (such as 4) since choice B includes the square root of a.

    Note: If you're comfortable working with variables, use FOIL for each answer choice. Only one is equivalent to the given equation.

31. Proportions

32. Ratios: Just apply the *of/is* rule: $\dfrac{1}{3}$ "of"
    $29 = \dfrac{1}{3} \times 29$.

33. One-Dimensional Lines / Basic Algebra: Since $PQ = RS$, $x - 1 = 3x - 7$. Solve for x, and find PS.

34. Basic Functions: If the point $(2, 5)$ lies on the graph of f, then $f(2) - 5$ (remember, $f(x) = y$). The function "rule" is given: $f(x) = k - x^2$, so $f(2) = k - 2^2 = k - 4$. Putting the two pieces together, we have $5 = k - 4$. Solve for k.

35. Area & Perimeter / Algebraic Word / Factoring or Pick Numbers (type 4): Let x be the width of the rectangle. The length is $x + 5$, and the area is $x(x + 5) = 104$ (given). This can be written as a quadratic: $x^2 + 5x - 104$. Factor, or use the quadratic formula to solve for x. Don't forget, you're looking for the *length* $(x + 5)$.

    Shortcut (Pick Numbers (type 4)): Most students could probably guess and check for x in the equation $x(x + 5) = 104$. Just pick some values for x, and keep track of your results so you know you're getting closer to the correct answer. This is probably faster than factoring.

36. Angles (interior angles, inscribed angles, circle): Focus on quadrilateral *ABPC*. In the Angles lesson, we found that the sum of the interior angles of a quadrilateral is 360°. Two angles are given (both 20°). Since $\angle A$ is an inscribed angle, we know that m$\angle A$ is ½ the measure of the central angle (x) of the intercepted arc. We also know that the measure of the obtuse $\angle P = 360° - x$ (sum of the angles in a circle is 360°). Set the four angles of the quadrilateral equal to 360°: $20 + 20 + \frac{1}{2}x + (360 - x) = 360$. Solve for x.

37. Proportions / Tables & Graphs: We covered rates in the Proportions lesson. Use the equation $r = \dfrac{d}{t}$. Make sure to convert the time to hours, so your final answer is in miles per hour. Use your calculator carefully:
    $$r = \frac{(0.6 + 15.4 + 1.4)}{\left(\dfrac{24}{60}\right)}.$$

38. Proportions / Percent (increase/decrease) / Tables & Graphs: Once again, we'll use the equation for rate, as introduced in the Proportions lesson: $r = \dfrac{d}{t}$. From this, we know that $t = \dfrac{d}{r}$ (review "Working with Variables" in the Basic Algebra lesson). Since only the middle time (freeway entrance to freeway exit) varies, just focus on this segment.

    If she leaves at 6:30 a.m., the time for this middle section is $\dfrac{15.4}{50} = 0.308$ hours = 18.48 minutes.

    If she leaves at 7:00 a.m., we must increase the middle time by 33% (multiply by 1.33): $18.48 \cdot 1.33 = 24.58$ minutes. Subtract these times.

    Note: You could have found the total time, but since the first and last segments of Ms. Simon's drive didn't change, they will simply cancel out. The shortcut above is recommended.

6. PRACTICE TEST 6

QUESTIONS BY SECTIONS/CHAPTERS

The following information lists every question on the test according to its relevant chapter or section in this tutorial. If you're correcting a test, circle the question numbers below that you missed or guessed on. Make sure to follow the Tutoring Schedule in the Introduction to know when to correct or tackle various types of questions.

READING
BY PASSAGE
- [1, 2, 3, 4, 5, 6, 7, 8, 9, 10] [11, 12, 13, 14, 15, 16, 17 ,18 19, 20, 21] [22, 23, 24, 25, 26, 27, 28, 29, 30, 31, 32] [33, 34, 35, 36, 37, 38, 39, 40, 41, 42] [43, 44, 45, 46, 47, 48, 49, 50, 51, 52]

BY QUESTION TYPE
- Direct & CTE (stand-alone): 10, 12, 13, 16, 17, 23, 25, 31, 32, 38, 39, 47, 48
- Extended Reasoning & Purpose: 1, 3, 4, 5, 6, 7, 8, 11, 15, 22, 24, 27, 28, 29, 30, 33, 34, 36, 37, 45, 46, 50
- WIC & Main Idea: 2, 14, 18, 26, 35, 43, 44, 49
- Comparison & IG: 19, 20, 21, 40, 41, 42, 51, 52
- Tone, Structure, & Relationship: 9
  Note: Most Citing-Textual-Evidence (CTE) questions are grouped with their relevant preceding questions.

WRITING & LANGUAGE
- Grammar & Sentence Structure: [1, 2, 3, 4, 6, 7] [12, 14, 15, 17, 19, 20, 21] [24, 25, 27, 28, 29, 30, 33] [34, 35, 36, 39, 41, 42, 44]
- Main Ideas & Organization: [5, 8, 9, 10, 11] [13, 16, 18, 22] [23, 26, 31, 32*] [37, 38, 40, 43]
  Note: Brackets display separate passages.
  * Informational Graphics

MATH
- Arithmetic: §4 (3, 6, 8, 9, 12, 23, 24, 26, 29, 38)
- Functions: §3 (8); §4 (37)
- Algebra: §3 (1, 5, 6, 7, 9, 14, 16, 17); §4 (2, 4, 5, 10, 11, 13, 14, 15, 17, 18, 19, 25, 28, 31, 32)
- Advanced Algebra: §3 (4, 12, 13, 15); §4 (1, 20, 34)
- Graphs of Functions: §4 (35)
- Geometry: §3 (18, 20); §4 (16, 27, 33)
- Odds & Ends: §3 (2, 3, 10, 11, 19); §4 (7, 21, 22, 30, 36)
  §3 = Section 3; §4 = Section 4

TECHNIQUES AND HINTS

READING

PASSAGE I

1. Purpose: 6–7, etc. ("his sources of revenue")

2. Words-in-Context (WIC): 14–17

3. Purpose: 26–28. The idea of a "foundering steamer in an Atlantic gale" should give you some idea of the challenge of Nawab's work. The phrase "superhuman efforts" (28) might also help.

4. Citing-Textual-Evidence (CTE): See above.

5. Purpose: 45–47. Try Process of Elimination (POE) with this one. Choice A does not reflect the main idea of the paragraph (though the size of the lands is mentioned in the first sentence, making this a bit of an Eye Catcher). Choice B is apparently false ("I cannot fulfil my duties"). There is no mention that Nawab will "quit" his job (choice D); he merely asks to be released.

6. Purpose: 58–63. The best clue is the phrase "with my old legs."

7. Extended Reasoning: 66–68. These lines reveal Harouni's attitude: his own "comfort" is "a matter of great interest to him." If you don't spot the correct answer, POE will probably lead you to the correct answer with this one; for example, as stated in question 5, there is no mention that Nawab threatens to quit the job (choice D).

8. CTE: See above.

9. Tone: 73–74. Assuming you find the correct context ("disgust" in line 74), it doesn't get much easier than this one.

10. Direct: 81–82. These last two questions were perhaps the easiest of the passage. Make sure you get to the last questions of a passage—perhaps by skipping harder questions along the way. You never know where the easier questions are hiding.

PASSAGE II

11. Purpose: 33–40, 70–73: In 33–40, the passages discusses "the general process of the transformation of authority," and how "Centres of news production . . . have not been exempt from this process." In 70–73, the passage discusses a "growing feeling" that the news media should be "'informative rather than authoritative.'"

12. Direct: 33–38. The correct answer is somewhat camouflaged, but if you understand the idea of making "explicit the frames of value which determine their decisions"—that is, in simpler words, making clear how and why they say what they say—the correct answer should be clear.

13. CTE: See above.

14. WIC: 22. The idea of something being "generally accepted" (22)—or in this context a *lack* of general acceptance—should lead you to the correct answer.

15. Purpose: 40–42. Remember to always minimize extending reasoning when possible. We know the quotes display how "some news journalists feel uneasy." Don't read more into it.

16. Direct: 70–77: These lines are perhaps the most important in the passage. The news media should be "informative," not "authoritative"; journalists should give "raw" news without "slant"; people should be able to form "opinions of [their] own."

17. CTE: See above.

18. WIC: See question 16. Which choice describes information given without "slant," or opinion?

19. Informational Graphics (IG) (direct): The table doesn't have a category for "trust," but if people think that news organizations "Get the facts straight," "Are pretty independent," and "Deal fairly with all sides," it's safe to say the organizations are trusted.

20. IG (direct): Make sure to focus on the the columns for 2003 and 2007. *Accuracy* is covered by the first bullet,

independence by the fourth bullet, and *fairness* by the seventh bullet.

21. IG (make connection): You probably understand that the table supports the central ideas of the passage (see lines 70–77). The main challenge to this question is the potential complexity of the correct answer. Try using POE. Spoiler: We could rewrite the correct answer as: "skepticism toward the authority of experts"—just skip the big words.

PASSAGE III

22. Purpose: 17–20 ("In one recent study" and "how to attract enough pollinators but not too many beetles"), 33–57 ("To find out . . ."), 65–74 ("What they saw . . .").

23. Direct: 61–64. This is a relatively uncommon Direct question that provides no line numbers but is *not* followed by a CTE question. Hopefully you can skim and find the answer (or use POE).

24. Extended Reasoning: 2–12. We can assume that the "mild, squashy aroma" (3–4), or whatever compound creates this scent, attracts both squash bees (specifically introduced in lines 21–22) and the striped cucumber beetles.

25. Direct: 26–29

26. WIC: 35–38. If swabs are tucked "deep inside" the flowers, the flowers are [plug in answer choices here].

27. Extended Reasoning: 41–50. We think this is one of the hardest questions on the test, mainly because of the wording of the question itself (including the given line numbers, which might head you in the wrong direction). The researchers wanted to know if the bees were repelled by the beetles (and not just the fragrance), so they made sure that there were some fragrance-enhanced flowers available that were free of beetles (as described especially in lines 45–50). If you get it, great. If not, move on. Allowing yourself to let some questions go, especially if time is an issue, is an important part of your strategy.

28. CTE: See above.

29. Purpose: 65–70 ("What they saw . . ."), 76–79 ("Gourds . . . weighed . . .")

30. Extended Reasoning: 67–72. If you know what "indifferent" means (*without interest or concern*; *uncaring*), you'll probably have no trouble with this one. If you don't, then you'll have to use context (and, perhaps, POE). It was "surprising" that the bees did not prefer fragrance-enhanced blossoms, but only the honey bees visited these flowers "less often" than normal ones. Thus, the squash bees must have visited the enhanced flowers neither more nor less often. Check the answer choices. Note: There is no mention that the bees could not distinguish between enhanced and normal flowers (A).

31. Direct: 85–89

32. CTE: See above.

PASSAGE IV

33. Extended Reasoning: 9–12. While this question reads like a Direct one, the answer requires some extended reasoning. The passage states that to break the law is to "trample on the blood of his father . . . to tear the character of his own . . . and his children's liberty." The passage also uses the words "*religion*" (19) and "*religiously*" (32) in expressing the importance of following the law. Try using POE. The correct answer broadly reflects the context of the passage.

34. CTE: See above.

35. WIC: Lincoln's viewpoint is made clear in the first paragraph (lines 1–4, for example)—he argues that people should not "violate . . . the laws." If you have a sense of what "urge" means (to recommend something strongly), you'll be able to decide between the two best choices (C and D). As stated in the tutorial, sometimes your familiarity with the word in question will help you find the answer.

36. Purpose: 24–28. Lincoln's argument, that people should follow all laws, might suggest that Lincoln believes all laws are good. In this paragraph, Lincoln corrects this possible misconception of his viewpoint. Choices A and B may be tempting, but Lincoln does not refute the notion that some laws are bad (see

28–30) (A), and he would not likely consider his belief in the (possible) existence of bad laws to be a "crucial shortcoming" of his argument (C).

37. WIC: 1–5, etc. Hopefully you're clear about the basic idea of the passage. Lincoln believes that laws must not be *violated* (3, 9). In other words, laws should be [plug answer choices here]?

38. Direct: 58–61. The context is direct, but not necessarily easy. What does Thoreau mean by "let it go" (59)? What does he mean when he says "perchance it will wear smooth"? Perhaps the easiest part of the context is at the beginning: "injustice is . . . necessary . . ." One answer choice reflects this idea.

39. CTE: See above.

40. Comparison / Purpose: 1–5, 45–48, etc.

41. Comparison: 33–35. Lincoln believes that even bad laws must "be borne with," that is, be followed, until they are legally repealed.

42. Comparison: 37–43, 79–82. In the first passage, Lincoln merely states that abolitionism may be right or wrong (he does not take a stand). In the second passage, by referring to "those who call themselves Abolitionists," Thoreau distances himself from these abolitionists.

PASSAGE V

43. Main Idea: The passage gives an overview of the solar panel "industry" (¶1), and then gets into new solar-panel–related technologies, including "crystalline silicon" (¶2), "screen-printing techniques" (¶4), "flexible solar cells" (¶5), "two-sided" solar cells (¶6), and "semiconductors" (¶7). This all adds up to a discussion of advances (or changes) in the field. Now, who is writing the passage? Go with the answer that requires the least amount of extended reasoning. You might also note the passage's source (MIT Technology Review).

44. WIC: 2–3 ("doldrums"). Even if you're not sure what "doldrums" means (*a state of inactivity or stagnation*), the

contrast signals and the word in question should be pretty clear.

45. Extended Reasoning: 27–29

46. CTE: See above.

47. Direct: 58–62

48. CTE: See above.

49. WIC: 69–71. Don't fall for choice B ("gambling" is often synonymous with "betting"). Use the context of this sentence, especially Green's plan to "take advantage of the huge reduction in cost . . ."

50. Purpose: 81 ("challenge")

51. IG (direct): We have to look at both figures. Figure 2 gives the 2009 US average electricity cost ($120 / MWh). Now, which fuel in Figure 1 has the same energy cost?

52. IG (direct)

WRITING & LANGUAGE

PASSAGE I

1. Run-ons: Make sure to read to the end of the sentence (". . . Area.") Three of the choices create run-ons.

2. Punctuation

3. Combining Sentences: As usual with these, focus on the shortest choice.

4. Punctuation: Make sure you are comfortable with the correct use of colons. / + Run-ons (D)

5. Main Ideas (transitions): The previous paragraph was discussing "algal blooms," that is, *algae*. You might also note the clue words "the lake" in the second sentence. Only one choice introduces a lake.

6. Concision & Redundancies: Keep it simple, and watch out for Redundancies.

7. Subject-Verb Agreement (B, C): The subject is "half" (singular) / Verb Tense (C, D): The tense is set as past ("confirmed").

8. Style: The style is (as usual) straightforward, formal prose.

9. Transitions: Remember to read these without reading the underlined word. It's usually wrong (75% of the time).

10. Answer the Question: The question is clear. Find the answer choice that mentions a "policy outcome."

11. Answer the Question: Only one choice answers the question (even if you hadn't read the passage). Note that choice A does not *address* the counterargument (read the question carefully).

PASSAGE II

12. Apostrophes & Confused Words: You can get this one just by focusing on *its/it's/its'*.

13. Transitions: Note that you can eliminate the two contrast synonyms (C and D) (synonyms can never be correct on these). Is the flow one of support (A) or cause and effect (B)?

14. Run-ons (A): This is a typical "comma splice." / Fragment (D). Choice C is difficult to categorize, but hopefully it just sounds awkward to you.

15. Vocabulary: Sometimes, you'll either have a feel for these Vocabulary questions or you won't. They're largely based on what you've heard and read. If you didn't get this one, don't worry. Just move on to easier questions.

16. Main Ideas (additions): Did you note the shift from something positive (the tower became an "icon") to something negative (the tower was closed). A transition sentence is needed.

17. Punctuation: If you chose B or C, review the "one-comma rule" in the lesson. If you chose D, review colons.

18. Main Ideas (topic sentence): The focus is on "attempt[s]" to reduce the tower's tilt.

19. Run-on (A, B): Review "comma splices." / -*ING* (C): You should usually avoid "being." Note: You should by now be comfortable seeing modifying phrases at the ends of sentences (after commas). It's a common, correct, and concise construction.

20. Concision & Redundancies: The process has already been described as "years-long."

21. Idiom: If your ear "hears" the correct answer, great. If not, feel free to move on. In addition to having idiom errors, note that choice C is wordy (see the Grammar & Sentence Structure Guidelines chapter) and choice D is a Fragment.

22. Organization: Logically, Burland would advocate (speak or write in favor of) using "soil extraction" (sentence 5) *before* actually beginning the process (sentence 2).

PASSAGE III

23. Main Ideas (topic sentence): The paragraph is about the "supply of physicians," specifically their "shortage." On a question like this, where the entire topic sentence is underlined, try reading the paragraph without reading the underlined sentence. Remember, the underlined portion is wrong 75% of the time. As with Transitions questions, reading the underlined portion may head you down the wrong path.

24. Vocabulary: As with many of these Vocabulary questions, the correct answer will hopefully simply sound good to your ear.

25. Vocabulary: You might also consider Style on this one: Choices A and D both sound too casual in this context.

26. Main Ideas (topic sentence): The paragraph discusses several reasons why PAs should see an expanded role. Also, note that the sentence in question mentions "such an expanded role." Does the last sentence of the previous paragraph lead logically to this sentence by mentioning the growing role of PAs? (Hint: Yes.)

27. Apostrophes & Confused Words (A, B) / Pronoun Agreement (D): The word in question refers to PAs, or physician assistants (plural).

28. Punctuation: Review lists in the Commas section if necessary.

29. Punctuation: The important thing for this one is identifying the modifying phrase ("earning . . . $90,930"). This phrase must be bound on *both sides* with punctuation (commas,

parenthesis, or long dashes). Of course, only one answer gets it right.

30. Illogical Comparisons (A, D): Make sure to compare "training period[s]" (apples to apples). / Concision & Redundancies (B): The comparison is clear ("shorter than").

31. Transitions: If you got this one wrong, note that "a broader spectrum of such services" is not a consequence of or contrast to the "cost-efficient, widely appreciated" services mentioned in the previous sentence.

32. Informational Graphics: Does the sentence in question reflect the information in the table?

33. Apostrophes & Confused Words: First, you can eliminate choices that incorrectly use "then" as part of a comparison (see the Comparisons lesson). From there, it's a question of spelling, although a good hint is that we're focusing on a plural group of people. Which word looks plural, *patience* or *patients*?

PASSAGE IV

34. Combining Sentences: Use POE if necessary on this one: Choice A has an excessive number of clauses and phrases (count the commas). Choice C focuses more on "popular film franchises" than "Superhero comic books," the focus of the passage (see the title). Choice D is awkward (for example, note the -*ING* word "being").

35. Vocabulary

36. Punctuation: Use the "pause rule" on this one; if you don't need to pause, keep the comma out.

37. Answer the Question: You might also consider this a test of Parallelism (but of *ideas*, not grammatical construction).

38. Main Ideas (topic sentence): The paragraph focuses on how superheroes "had to cope with mundane, real-life problems."

39. Punctuation

40. Main Ideas: Focus on the sentence in question carefully, especially the contrast signal ("Although"). Without worrying about the correct answer, the sentence must go something like this:

"Although sales remained strong for Golden Age stalwarts Superman and . . . Batman, *Silver Age superheroes grew in popularity and importance.* In other words, we know we're looking for something good about these Silver Age superheroes (the focus of the paragraph). Only one choice works. You can also try POE: A: "these characters" are ambiguous (Superman and Batman? Silver Age superheroes?); Choice B does not "complete the discussion of the Silver Age"; D: the words "these characters" seem to be referring to Superman and Batman (off-topic).

41. Verb Tense: Note the time ("in 2011") and the tense set by "has failed" later in the sentence. Don't be tricked by the tense of the previous sentence: "would take place."

42. Apostrophes & Confused Words: The company is "DC Comics," so the possessive is *DC Comics'*. The possessive of superhero is incorrect: The "line" does not belong to the superheroes—rather, the *superhero line* belongs to DC Comics. / + Punctuation (A)

43. Transformations: Use POE if necessary by looking for synonyms; all three incorrect answers are contrast signals (thus, they're all probably wrong).

44. Illogical Comparisons: Compare "transition" to "transition" (apples to apples). (Of course, a pronoun is an acceptable substitute for the second one.) Question 30 is similar to this one.

MATH (no calculator)

1. Linear Equations (applications)

2. Mixtures: These Mixtures questions can be tricky (it's perhaps surprising to see one this early in a section). Review the lesson (in the Odds & Ends chapter) carefully.

3. Complex Numbers

4. Working with Polynomials: FOIL the right side of the equation, and then "compare polynomials," as described in the lesson.

5. Linear Equations

6. Basic Algebra: Just plug in $y = 18$ and simplify.

7. Basic Algebra (working with variables)

8. Basic Functions: You'll have to check the answer choices. For example, for choice A ($x = 1$) we check to see if $w(1) + t(1) = 1$ → from the table: $w(1) = -1$ and $t(1) = -3$ → $w(1) + t(1) = -1 + (-3) = -4 \neq 1$. Stop when you find the answer choice that works.

9. Basic Algebra (equations with radicals): The first step is to simplify the two numerical radicals. (Hint: $3^2 = 9$ and $8^2 = 64$.)

10. Algebraic Word / Means, Medians & Modes: Note: Saying that Jaime wants to average "at least" 280 miles per week means that his average (mean) should be ≥ 280.

11. Parabolas (vertex form)

12. Pick Numbers (type 1) or Polynomial Division: We recommend using the Pick Trick for this one. Pick a small number, such as $x = 1$, since you can't use your calculator. Remember to check every answer choice.

13. Factoring (quadratic formula): When a quadratic in standard form ($2x^2 - 4x - t = 0$) has no real solutions, the *discriminant* of the quadratic formula must be less than 0, or $b^2 < 4ac$: plug in 2 for a, -4 for b, and t for c, and solve for t.

14. Algebraic Word / Systems of Inequalities: Let's first focus on weight. Each container of detergent (d) weighs 7.35 pounds and each container of fabric softener (s) weighs 6.2 pounds, so we have $7.35d + 6.2s$. This must be "no more than" 300 pounds; in other words, the total weight must be less than or equal to 300 pounds. So the answer must be A or B. Now, the second inequality: Since we want "at least twice as many" containers of detergent as containers of fabric softener, $d \geq 2s$ (see "A Couple Tricky Equations" in the Algebraic Word lesson).

15. Working with Variables or Pick Numbers (type 1): If you'd like to solve algebraically, use FOIL. You could also use the Pick Trick (pick easy numbers such as 1 or 2, and don't forget to check every answer choice).

16. Pick Numbers (type 4): Just Pick Numbers for b until you find one that works for some integer a.

17. Basic Algebra: To make this one easier, you might multiply through by 6 (the least common multiple of 3 and 2) to cancel the denominators.

18. Triangles (similar)

19. Mixtures: Here's another Mixtures problem (see question 2). Make sure you understand how we get the following equation: $0.25x + 0.10 \cdot 3 = 0.15(x + 3)$.

20. More Circles (sectors): The circumference of the circle is $2\pi r = 2\pi$. So the part-over-whole ratio is $\dfrac{\frac{\pi}{3}}{2\pi}$. Simplify the ratio. Hint: the πs cancel.

MATH (calculator)

1. Working with Polynomials

2. Tables & Graphs: The head start is the difference in Paul's and Mark's distance (y-axis) at time = 0 (x-axis).

3. Tables & Graphs

4. Algebraic Word: Can you come up with the expression for "d dollars for each month" (let m be the number of months)? (It's md.) Here's the final equation: Charge = \$350 + md. Plug in what is given and solve for d.

5. Basic Algebra (solving inequalities): The trick to this one is to recognize that one of the answer choices is the original inequality divided by an integer.

6. Percent (of/is) / Tables & Graphs: Simply add the appropriate percents and find the "percent of" the 1,200 responses.

7. Studies: Unless all members of the city own dogs (unlikely), the survey is biased. Check the answer choices.

8. Probability / Tables & Graphs: As always with these types of questions, make sure you focus on the correct

sub-group (your denominator), in this case "people who chose vanilla."

9. Ratios: The density is defined for us as the number of people per square mile. Just set up a ratio and use your calculator. Make sure you focus on the "land area."

10. Pick Answers or Algebraic Word: Some students have trouble with the algebra, so we recommend the Pick Trick. For example, if the second voyage lasted 520 days (choice C), then the first voyage lasted 520 + 43 = 563 days. 520 + 563 = 1,083 < 1,003. So check a lower number.

    If you'd like to try the algebra, here are the equations: Let a be the length of the first journey and b be the the length of the second journey. Since a is 43 more than b, our first equation is $a = b + 43$ (plug in $b = 0$ to prove this). Our second equation is $a + b = 1,003$. Use substitution to find b.

11. Systems of Equations: Hint: Use the elimination method: Subtract the bottom equation from the top equation to get rid of the y terms and solve for x.

12. Tables & Graphs: By now you should be getting comfortable with the idea that the steeper a line graph, the faster the rate of change, and the flatter the graph, the slower the rate of change. This is an important idea that comes up often on the SAT.

13. Linear Equations (applications): The variable a represents the slope of the line. Make sure you note the units of the vertical axis (in this case, the h-axis) and the horizontal axis (in this case, the t-axis). The slope is always the change in the vertical axis's units to the change in each unit of the horizontal axis.

14. Linear Equations: Note that the answer choices are linear equations. Find the slope of the line between days 14 and 35 (according to the graph). You don't have to worry about the y-intercept (only one answer choice has the correct slope).

15. Pick Numbers (advanced): As mentioned in the tutorial, the first (and usually easiest) choice (in this case, the first column: $x = 1$ and $y = 11/4$), will

usually *not* eliminate every wrong answer choice. Try starting with the the values in the second or third column.

16. Triangles (similar): Find the two missing angles to see that the triangles are similar. Next, as you set up your proportion, make sure you compare the sides of the two triangles correctly. For example, side BC (opposite the 32° angle of $\triangle ABC$) corresponds with side DF (opposite the 32° angle of $\triangle DEF$).

17. Basic Algebra (working with variables): Even though we're past the half-way point of the multiple-choice section, sometimes the first of these multi-question problems is fairly straightforward. Yes, there are a lot of words, but try this one with confidence.

18. Pick Numbers (advanced) or Algebraic Word: The Pick Trick, starting with the answer choices, is the easiest approach. We can eliminate choice A right off the bat, since h must be "at least 5 inches." Now, check a number that's true for one or two (but not all three!) of the remaining choices. For example, if you pick $h = 6$ (true for choices B and C), and solve for d (using the given equation $2h + d = 25$), you'll get $d = 13$. This works (d must be "at least 9 inches"), so eliminate any choices that do not include $h = 6$ (choice D). Finally pick a number true for C but not B.

    If you want to solve algebraically, here's the inequality: $d = 25 - 2h$ (from the given equation) and $d \geq 9$ (given in the question), so $25 - 2h \geq 9$. Solve for h. Finally, remember $h \geq 5$ (given in the question).

19. Pick Answers or Algebraic Word (with a shortcut): This one is tricky, no matter how you approach it, but once again, we recommend the Pick Trick. Keep in mind that rise height (h) must be between 7 and 8 inches and we must have an *odd* number of stairs (number of stairs = total rise in <u>inches</u> divided by h). The answer choices give values for tread depth (d). For each choice, solve for h, and check the two conditions above. Stop when you find the one that works.

If you'd like to use algebra, you'll probably need to use the following shortcut: Find the number of stairs. If h is a minimum (7 inches), the number of stairs is 15.4 (108 inches ÷ 7 inches). If h is a maximum (8 inches), the number of stairs is 13.5 inches (108 ÷ 8). So the number of stairs is between 13.5 and 15.4, and since the number must be an odd number (see the question), there must be <u>15 stairs</u>. Divide the total height (108 inches) by 15 to find h. Then use the given equation to find d.

20. Factoring (zero product theorem)

21. Studies: Remember not to jump to conclusions with these. The only information we're given is about "largemouth bass."

22. Means, Medians, & Modes: The median will be the number of electoral votes for the 11th state. Count up or down to this state. For example, counting down from the top of the table, there are 10 states with 10, 11, 12, or 13 electoral votes (4 states with 10 votes, 4 states with 11 votes, etc.).

23. Tables & Graphs: Hint: Just draw (or imagine) a horizontal line at a height of 2 feet. How many times does the graph of the ball cross this line?

24. Percent (difference-over-original)

25. Linear Equations / Basic Functions: First, find the $y = mx + b$ equation for the line using any two points. Then plug in $x = 3$ and find y (in other words, find $f(3)$).

26. This can be a tricky problem. It sounds like a regular Proportions problem, but the relationship between the teeth and revolutions of a gear is actually *inversely* related, that is, the more teeth, the *fewer* the revolutions. So instead of using ratios, as with a proportions problem, we'll use *products*: (let r = revolutions at t = teeth): $r_A t_A = r_B t_B$. So to find the revolutions of Gear B (r_B), we'll use the following equation: $r_A t_A = r_B t_B$ → $20 \cdot 100 = 60 \cdot r_B$. Then use a similar equation to find the revolutions of Gear C.

27. More Circles (completing the square)

28. Pick Numbers (advanced): First, find the two points that are "three units from

the point with coordinate –4" (you're not really "picking" numbers here—you're *finding* them). Then plug these numbers into the answer choices and eliminate.

29. Proportions (rates): Remember that rate equals distance (given as s) over time (given as t). Since the problem defines s in terms of t, we can write the rate as $\dfrac{\text{inches}}{\text{seconds}}$ $\dfrac{16t\sqrt{t}}{t}$. Simplifying should be straightforward.

30. Parabolas / Graphs of Functions / Tables & Graphs (scatterplots): First, note that the points appear to be modeled by a parabola that opens down: eliminate A and C, which both represent upward opening parabolas (positive leading coefficients). Next, checking the y-intercept is often pretty easy (just plug in $x = 0$). Since, according to the scatterplot, the parabola would intersect the y-axis at around 740, the last number of the equation must be close to 740 (positive) (eliminate B).

31. Algebraic Word / Common Denominators / Factoring (quadratics) or Pick Numbers (type 4): This is a surprisingly difficult question for the first of the grid-ins. We'll start with finding the equation and then discuss solving it. Let x be the number of friends. Since the friends had planned to divide the $800 equally, each friend would have to spend $\dfrac{800}{x}$ dollars. When two friends decided not to go, each of the remaining friends would spend $\dfrac{800}{x-2}$. Since the new amount is given as $20 more than the original amount, we have $\dfrac{800}{x} + 20 = \dfrac{800}{x-2}$. Now, to solve this, we recommend multiplying through by $x(x-2)$ and solving the resulting quadratic for x. (Review the Common Denominators and Factoring lessons, if necessary.)

Many students will probably have more luck guessing and checking (Pick Numbers, type 4) than trying to tackle the algebra above. As a quick example, let's guess that there were 8 original friends. They would each pay $100 (800/8). Two of them decide not to go on the trip, so now they each pay 800/6 = $133.33. That's not $20 more (but it's not too far off). Guess again. This might be a good one to come back to if you have time.

32. Basic Algebra

33. Solids & Volume: Don't let the idea of "internal" radius or height confuse you. The volume of the cylinder, that is, how much it could hold, is logically measured using internal dimensions. You should probably know the formula by heart (see Prisms), but if necessary, you can check the reference information at the beginning of the section.

34. Systems of Equations / Factoring: We need to find the points of intersection, which involves solving the system of equations. Since $y = x$, we can substitute x for y in the first equation: $x = 3x^2 - 14x$. Solve for x. Hint: Set the equation equal to 0, factor a common monomial, and use the Zero Product Theorem. We know that $x = 0$ is one solution (see the question). The other solution is our answer.

35. Graphs of Functions (axis intercepts): As described in the lesson, let $y = 0$ and solve for x.

36. Means, Medians, & Mode: There's no shortcut to this one. Just calculate the means, or averages, carefully (and use your calculator).

37. Growth & Decay Functions: This is a standard exponential growth question. Use the equation $A = P(1 + r)^t$ (review the lesson if necessary). Doubling each year means that our rate (r) is 100%, or 1.0 (our "multiplier" is 2.0). So, after 4 years, we have: $480 = P(2)^4$. Solve for P, the starting value (defined as x in the question).

38. Percent (of/is): We must find the total number of committee members. The percent for each of three of the four groups—parents (15%), teachers (45%), and administrators (25%)—is given. The 6 students must make up the remaining 15% of the committee (100% − (15% + 45% + 25%)). To find the number of members, we can answer the question: 6 is 15% of how many people?—$6 = 0.15x$. Once you know the number of members, you can answer the question.

Here's another approach. As above, let x be the total number members of the committee. Simply put, the number of parents ($0.15x$) plus the number of teachers ($0.45x$) plus the number of administrators ($0.25x$) plus the number of students (6) will equal the total number of members (x): $0.15x + 0.45x + 0.25x + 6 = x$ → $0.85x + 6 = x$ . . .

7. PRACTICE TEST 7

QUESTIONS BY SECTIONS/CHAPTERS

The following information lists every question on the test according to its relevant chapter or section in this tutorial. If you're correcting a test, circle the question numbers below that you missed or guessed on. Make sure to follow the Tutoring Schedule in the Introduction to know when to correct or tackle various types of questions.

READING
BY PASSAGE
- [1, 2, 3, 4, 5, 6, 7, 8, 9, 10] [11, 12, 13, 14, 15, 16, 17 ,18 19, 20, 21] [22, 23, 24, 25, 26, 27, 28, 29, 30, 31] [32, 33, 34, 35, 36, 37, 38, 39, 40, 41] [42, 43, 44, 45, 46, 47, 48, 49, 50, 51, 52]

BY QUESTION TYPE
- Direct & CTE (stand-alone): 3, 8, 9, 12, 13, 46, 47, 48
- Extended Reasoning & Purpose: 5, 6, 7, 11, 14, 22, 23, 24, 25, 26, 27, 28, 30, 33, 34, 36, 37, 43, 44, 45
- WIC & Main Idea: 1, 2, 10, 15, 18, 29, 31, 32, 35, 49
- Comparison & IG: 19, 20, 21, 38, 39, 40, 41, 50, 51, 52
- Tone, Structure, & Relationship: 4, 16, 17, 42
  Note: Most Citing-Textual-Evidence (CTE) questions are grouped with their relevant preceding questions.

WRITING & LANGUAGE
- Grammar & Sentence Structure: [1, 2, 3, 4, 6, 7, 8] [12, 13, 16, 17, 19, 22] [24, 26, 27, 29, 30, 31, 32**] [34, 36, 37, 39, 41, 43]
- Main Ideas & Organization: [5, 9, 10, 11] [14, 15, 18, 20, 21*] [23, 25, 28, 33] [35, 38, 40, 42, 44]
  Note: Brackets display separate passages.
  * Informational Graphics ** Not specifically covered in the tutorial—see Techniques & Hints.

MATH
- Arithmetic: §3 (6, 11); §4 (1, 3, 7, 8, 10, 12, 13, 15, 18, 30, 31, 38)
- Functions: §3 (5); §4 (24, 27)
- Algebra: §3 (1, 2, 3, 8, 9, 14, 16, 20); §4 (5, 6, 11, 16, 17, 19, 20, 21, 25, 26, 28, 32, 33)
- Advanced Algebra: §3 (10, 13, 15); §4 (2, 9, 35)
- Graphs of Functions: none
- Geometry: §3 (17, 19); §4 (14, 23, 29, 34)
- Odds & Ends: §3 (4, 7, 12, 18); §4 (4, 22, 36, 37)
  §3 = Section 3; §4 = Section 4

TECHNIQUES AND HINTS

READING

PASSAGE I

1. Main Idea: 24–29, 54–57

2. Words-in-Context (WIC): 9–15. Note some of the key words associate with Eppie: "changes and hopes," "onward," and "new things."

3. Direct: 2, 9–11, 20–23. Choice B may be tempting (see "notorious miser" in the introduction), but there is no mention of the gold reproducing on its own (a bold claim, to be sure).

4. Purpose / Tone: Eppie has "trust in new joy," the key word being "new." Be careful of choice A: Eppie may be "stirring the human kindness" (8), but this does not say that Eppie is kind, or "friendly." She may be, but we need contextual support.

5. Extended Reasoning: 11–18 ("forced his thoughts onward"), 25–29 ("reawakening"), 55–57 ("his soul was unfolding . . . into full consciousness")

6. Citing-Textual-Evidence (CTE): See above.

7. Purpose: 34–35 ("strolling out . . . to carry Eppie"), 40 (Eppie "calling 'Dad-dad's' attention"), 42–43 ("Silas learned to please her by making signs of hushed stillness"), etc.

8. Direct: 53–57: "as her life unfolded . . ."

9. CTE: See above.

10. WIC: 66 ("ingenious"), 67 (Eppie's capacity for mischief "found much exercise"): Eppie was obviously very good at being troublesome. Use process of elimination (POE) if you're not comfortable with all the answer choices.

PASSAGE II

11. Purpose: 1–6, etc. Consider POE if necessary. Watch out for choice A: remember, every word counts; the passage focuses on jobs, not "workers' lives."

12. Direct: 38–40

13. CTE: We typically hope that the lines we used for context for the previous question match those of the CTE question, but sometimes this won't be the case. We're looking for lines 38–40. Lines 35–38 are close, but be careful: these lines describe what happened *before* 2000. Additional context to support the previous question must be elsewhere in the passage.

14. Purpose: 25–28. Note that the phrase between the dashes comes immediately after the word "productivity." How does this phrase relate to "productivity"?

15. WIC: 32–34. If the answer is not apparent, try plugging the choices into the passage. Trust your ear.

16. Direct / Tone: 89–92. Be careful of choice A, which is too strong.

17. CTE: See above.

18. WIC: 86–89

19. Informational Graphics (IG) (direct): Remember, with these "direct" IG questions, you shouldn't have to worry about the passage's text. Just focus on the figure.

20. IG (direct)

21. IG (make connection): 60 ("we have fewer jobs"). Choice A, with mention of "median income" (straight from the passage), is tempting at first glance, but we're interested in changes over many years, not "in a single year." Watch out for eye catchers in answer choices, and remember that every word counts.

PASSAGE III

22. Purpose: 3 ("a new study . . ."), 22 ("The study . . ."). We recommend POE for this one.

23. Purpose: 15–17. You might agree that this is a "direct hit." If an answer choice matches context perfectly, choose it and move on.

24. Extended Reasoning: 22–24. The context is fairly clear. Usherwood "took advantage of an existing project."

25. CTE: See above.

26. Purpose: If you have a sense that measuring position "to within 30 cm" is impressively precise, you'll find this one straightforward. If not, use POE.

27. Extended Reasoning: 45–47. Technically this is an Extended Reasoning question ("imply"), but the evidence is clear.

28. CTE: Here's another needlessly tricky CTE question. Lines 45–47 provide the best evidence, but these lines are not among the answer choices. Try eliminating choices that have nothing to do specifically with "pelicans, storks, and geese." The correct answer at least provides an indirect comparison to these "long-winged birds."

29. Main Idea: 62–63 ("Scientists do not know . . ."), 67–68 ("In future studies, . . .")

30. Purpose: 66–67. If you have a sense of what a "sweet spot" is, you'll find this one straightforward. Hint: it has to do with *position*.

31. WIC: 71–73. Once again, try plugging the choices into the passage. Trust your ear.

PASSAGE IV

32. WIC: 10 ("more and more the equal of man")

33. Extended Reasoning: 22–26. Note some of the key words: "degraded," "weak men and disorderly women."

34. CTE: See above.

35. WIC: 49–50 ("one of them . . . superior of the other.")

36. Extended Reasoning: 54–61. Make sure to focus on relations "between men and women" (54).

37. CTE: See above.

38. Comparison: 1–3, 50–53

39. Comparison: 15–24. Note the mention of "people in Europe."

40. Comparison: 29–37, 62–65, etc. You might have an easier time using POE on this one.

41. Comparison: 75–86

PASSAGE V

42. Structure: 28–45 ("peculiar environment . . ."), 46–83 ("The paper was rejected," etc.)

43. Purpose: 36–39, 40 ("For a mental toehold . . .")

44. Extended Reasoning: 49–53 ("invisible something," "overwrought speculation")

45. CTE: See above.

46. Direct: 58–63 ("allowed them to have their cake and eat it too"). If you're not familiar with this expression, you must understand that, thanks to the Higgs paper, scientists could now reconcile two conditions: (1) the "fundamental equations" worked perfectly and (2) the particles did not have to be massless; see the second paragraph, especially after "But" (line 22).

47. CTE: See above.

48. Direct: 70–83: Note the shift to first-person ("I").

49. WIC: 83 ("confirm")

50. IG (make connection): Of course, you must have read the passage, which focuses entirely on the Higgs boson, to get this one. If necessary, use POE. Be careful of choice C: there's no mention that the Higgs boson was "regarded differently," even if, according to the figure, its duration from introduction to confirmation is longer than the other particles.

51. IG (direct): This is a straightforward IG question. Don't be distracted by the passage. Just focus on the graph.

52. IG (make connection): 67–70. Note that physicists "bought into" the Higgs field theory by the mid-1980s, even though it had not yet been established experimentally. Only one choice reflects a similar situation with one of the other particles in the graph.

WRITING & LANGUAGE

PASSAGE I

1. Redundancies: Once you recognize a Redundancies question ("frequently many times"), look to the shortest answer.

2. Apostrophes & Confused Words (B, D): A good rule of thumb is for *effect* to be used as a noun and *affect* to be used as a verb. / Idioms (C): "to" is poor idiom. / Choice D violates plural-singular agreement; something would not have *an affects* (or *an effects*).

3. Parallelism: Note the trend: "serving . . ." and "showing . . ."

4. Punctuation (lists)

5. Main Ideas (transitions): Make sure to read the question carefully. You must read the next sentence or two. The passage goes on to discuss "inventions."

6. Vocabulary

7. Verb Tense / +-*ING* (D)

8. Verb Tense / +-*ING* (A)

9. Organization: Note the clue words in sentence 2: "the contribution." Clearly, the contribution must have been mentioned already.

10. Main Ideas (additions): The addition is clearly off-topic ("expansive vision," "global consciousness," "responsibilities to the planet").

11. Transitions

PASSAGE II

12. Parallelism

13. Punctuation: Note the punctuation that closes the phrase "from social services to manufacturing."

14. Transitions: Note the connection from "not only employees but also their employers" to the next sentence's "shared responsibility."

15. Main Ideas (transitions): The correct answer should focus on employee (not employer) responsibility.

16. Punctuation: As with question 13, if a phrase ("these critics contend") is opened with one type of punctuation, it should be closed with the same type.

17. Concision & Redundancies: Note the different lengths of the answer choices, an clue that the question is testing Concision & Redundancies.

18. Style: Only one answer maintains the formal prose of the passage.

19. Subject-Verb Agreement (A, D): The subject is "forms." / Fragments and -*ING* (C)

20. Transitions: Don't forget, often the answer with no transition is the best one.

21. Informational Graphics: Since, according to the graph, "coaching and consultation" and "foundation and skill-building" fall within the "professional networks" circle, this last item must be the "overarching framework" of professional development.

22. Punctuation: When there is no need to pause, you should usually avoid punctuation.

PASSAGE III

23. Transitions: Make sure you read to the end of the sentence ("feared," "death of a way of life"). Also, remember *not* to read the underlined word when you tackle Transitions questions. The word is wrong most of the time (75%), and reading it can often throw you off course.

24. Punctuation

25. Main Ideas: You might initially answer the question "yes," but (luckily) the second parts of the two "yes" answers are definitely wrong. Don't be afraid to go back to the drawing board on these yes/no questions.

26. Verb Tense: We can assume that the movement still opposes "the standardization of taste," so the past-of-the-past tense (choice A) is incorrect.

27. Punctuation: Always try removing comma-bound phrases to make sure the sentence still makes sense. Also, the pause rule for commas should help on this one (see "Pausing" in the the Punctuation lesson).

28. Main Ideas: Note some of the keywords in the paragraph: the movement "opposed standardization of taste" and "consistency" and celebrates "different" tastes. Which choice reflects these ideas?

29. Pronoun Agreement (A, B): The pronoun must agree with "the movement" (singular). / Apostrophes &

Confused Words (B, D): "it's" is a contraction of *it is*.

30. Concision: There are other issues with some of the answer choices (such as Style with choice A and Vocabulary with choice D), but Concision will lead you to the correct answer.

31. Vocabulary: You're looking for a word similar to *caused* or *lead to*.

32. Misplaced Words (B, D): "adequately and affordably" should be kept next to the word they modify ("feed"). / To choose the correct answer from the remaining two, you must consider the difference between an actual question and merely the mention of a question. For example, note the difference between the following sentences (both correct): (1) Bob asked, "What's for dinner?" (2) Bob asked about what's for dinner. The first includes a question; the second makes a statement.

33. Transition: This one can be tricky. The important point is that the information in the last sentence is not a summary of what came before. It is a logical result or consequence. Can you spot the answer choice that reflects this cause and effect?

PASSAGE IV

34. Punctuation: Try using the pause rule, if necessary. Remember, if the pause is unnecessary, the comma is probably unnecessary as well. You might also review our Essay tutorial, which gets into the correct uses of commas with quotations.

35. Answer the Question: As with many of these "Answer the Question" questions, you probably don't need to read the passage to get this one. Just read the question carefully.

36. Idiom: This one can be tricky. It is poor idiom to say that a broadcast *had people*, but it is acceptable to say that it *had people fearing* something. Here's a simpler example: Does a storm have people(,) who run for their lives? Or does a storm have people running for their lives? It's an "ear thing"—if you heard the awkwardness in the first example, great. If not, that's OK. Idiom problems make up a small part of the

test. / Pronouns (case) (B): Avoid "that" when referring to people.

37. Idiom: Here's another question that tests your ear. Students either get these, or they don't. Hopefully you simply hear the correct answer. If not, focus on the easier questions, ones covered by specific grammar rules.

38. Transitions: The passage goes into a discussion of "an article" (see the second sentence of the paragraph).

39. Combining Sentences: As always with these, focus on shorter answer choices; the shortest choice is usually the correct one.

40. Main Idea (topic): The paragraph questions the number of people who listened to the broadcast and how frightened they really were.

41. More Confused Words: Use "much" and "less" for things that cannot be counted (such as mashed potatoes). Use "many" and "fewer" for things that *can* be counted (such as peas or people).

42. Organization: Sentence 4 refers to people feeling "unsettled" by the broadcast. How people felt about the program is not revealed until sentence 5, so we can eliminate A and B. Sentence 6 must follow sentence 5 (both sentences are referring to the number of listeners). Only one answer choice works.

43. Punctuation: Make sure to read to the end of the sentence. Note the comma after "afterward." / + -*ING* (A)

44. Main Idea: The writer is saying that both the "American public" and people who listened to the broadcast may have a tendency to get "caught up in the excitement." So the two groups are similar. You might also note that one answer is different from the other three—this answer is probably correct.

MATH (no calculator)

1. Algebraic Word

2. Basic Algebra

3. Systems of Equations: Usually, substitution is the easier approach on

these (substitute $y - 3$ for x in the second equation).

4. Complex Numbers

5. Basic Functions

6. Ratios: The trick to this problem is recognizing that after 4 years, the equipment will have lost 1/3 of its value (4 is 1/3 of 12). In other words, the equipment's value will be 2/3 of its starting value: $2/3 \cdot 32{,}400 \ldots$

   Shortcut: Instead of calculating by hand, note that 2/3 of 32,400 should be a little over 20,000 (2/3 of 30,000 is 20,000). Only one answer choice is close.

7. Parabolas or Pick Numbers (type 1): If you use the Parabola approach, you'll have to "complete the square" (review More Circles). The faster approach is to Pick Numbers (type 1). Hint: Pick small numbers, such as 0 or 1, since you have to solve by hand. Don't forget to check every answer choice.

8. Algebraic Word or Pick Answers: This one can be a little tricky. Here's the equation (x is the number of additional hours): $(10 \cdot 8 + 10x)\dfrac{90}{100} \geq 270$. Solve for x.

   The faster approach is to Pick Answers. Since we're looking for the the least number of hours, start with D: $(10 \cdot 8 + 10 \cdot 16)\dfrac{90}{100} = 216 \not\geq 270 \ldots$

9. Systems of Inequalities: This is a scary looking problem, but it's fairly straightforward. Eliminate answer choices as you come up with the inequalities: you don't need to come up with all four of them.

10. Factoring (factors and roots): We know that a polynomial with roots of −1, −3, and 5 must have factors of $(x + 1)$, $(x + 3)$, and $(x - 5)$. (Note that plugging each root into its respective factor will equal zero.)

11. Exponents: Make sure you're comfortable converting fractional exponents into roots. Hint: Don't combine the x terms and y terms; just move negative exponents across the divided-by line.

12. Parabolas (x-intercept form)

13. Polynomial Division or Pick Numbers (type 1): Even if you're comfortable with dividing polynomials (long division or synthetic division), the Pick Trick is probably faster. Hint: Pick $x = 1$ (remember, on the no-calculator section, you can pick 0 and 1).

14. Algebraic Word: Let $x =$ width (as specified in the problem), $l =$ length, and $h =$ height. The perimeter of the box is $2x + 2l$. The inequality is $2x + 2l + h \leq 130$. Since $h = 60$ and $l = 2.5x$, we can write: $2x + 2(2.5x) + 60 \leq 130$. Solve for x. Note: If necessary, review perimeter in the Area & Perimeter section (Geometry chapter).

15. Factoring (difference of squares) or Pick Answers: Note that $\dfrac{1}{3}x^2 - 2 = \dfrac{1}{3}(x^2 - 6)$. Of course, 6 isn't a perfect square, but you can write the equation as follows: $\dfrac{1}{3}(x^2 - 6) = \dfrac{1}{3}\left(x^2 - \sqrt{6}^2\right)$ (now we have a difference of squares). Finally, use the difference-of-squares technique to factor the equation.

   Another approach is to Pick Answers (plug in for k), and FOIL. One choice should lead you to the original expression. This may take a while, depending on how quickly you can FOIL, but you should get the question correct.

16. Basic Algebra: Look for a shortcut on this one (hint: just divide by 2).

17. Angles / Triangles: First, find $m\angle MPR$ ($m\angle MPR + 60° = 180°$). Since $MP = PR$ (given), we know that $\triangle MPR$ is isosceles. You thus have enough information to find the base angles (which include $\angle QMR$).

18. More Trigonometry (degrees and radians)

19. Linear Equations: You might agree that some of these higher numbered grid-in problems are fairly straightforward (assuming you're comfortable with our basic techniques). This is why it's important not to get bogged down on

harder questions at the end of the multiple choice section.

20. Basic Algebra: Just carefully combine like terms. Not a bad problem for a #20 (see note for the previous problem).

MATH (calculator)

1. Tables & Graphs / Ratios (part-over-whole): This one is similar to a Probability questions. Make sure you focus on the relevant part of the table (the row for dogs).

2. Working with Polynomials or Pick Numbers (type 1)

3. Proportions: Watch your units as you set up the proportion (6 meters = 600 centimeters): $\dfrac{\text{packages}}{\text{cm}} \dfrac{1}{3} = \dfrac{x}{600}$

4. Studies: Make sure you don't jump to conclusions on these.

5. Pick Answers: The technique is perhaps obvious. Just plug in the ordered pairs and eliminate accordingly.

6. Basic Algebra (solving exponential equations): Plugging in $x = -3$, we have: $(-3a+3)^2 = 36$. Take the square root of each side—don't forget the ±. So we have $-3a + 3 = 6$ and $-3a + 3 = -6$. One of these equations will lead you to the correct answer.

   Note: Expanding the squared expression (using FOIL) will also lead you to the correct answer, but this approach is slower.

7. Tables & Graphs (scatterplots)

8. Tables & Graphs (scatterplots): At a distance of 1.2 AU (see the x-axis), we expect a density between than 4.5 and 4.75. Check the answer choices.

9. Factoring or Pick Numbers (type 2): If you're comfortable working with variables and factoring, you'll find that $ax + b$ is easy to find: $9ax + 9b = 21 + 7$ → $9(ax + b) = 27 \ldots$ If you found this challenging, use the Pick Trick. For example, pick $a = 1$ and $x = 1$; solve for b.

10. Percent (of-is): Watch your units: How many minutes are in 8 hours?

11. Algebraic Word: While wordy, this problem is very similar to "A Common Algebraic Word Problem" (see the lesson). Try eliminating answer choices as you come up with your equations. Hint: The volume of standard edition games is $20s$ and the volume of collector's edition games is $30c$. This alone is enough to spot the correct answer.

12. Percent (increase/decrease): A 6% tax is equivalent to multiplying by 1.06 (review "multipliers"). So we have $1.06x = 53$, where x is the pre-tax price. Solve for x. If you had trouble coming up with this equation, you can Pick Answers.

13. Tables & Graphs: Hint: Theresa's speed was increasing when the line has a positive slope (increasing to the right) and decreasing when the line has a negative slope (decreasing to the right). (When the line is horizontal, her speed is not changing.)

14. Angles (sum of interior angles)

15. Proportions: Use the "known relationship" 50 coins : $3\dfrac{7}{8}$ inches.

16. Systems of Equations: First solve for b using the second equation. Then solve for a in the first equation.

17. Linear Equations (applications)

18. Tables & Graphs (scatterplots): First, find the point with the greatest percent (it's the highest point on the graph). This percent is approximately 92%. Now, what percent does the line of best fit predict for this company (one with an income of approximately 3,400 millions of dollars)? Find the difference.

19. Basic Algebra

20. Basic Algebra: If the two formulas give the same value for A, we can write: $\dfrac{\sqrt{hw}}{60} = \dfrac{4+w}{30}$. Solve for $\sqrt{hw}$.

21. Linear Equations (slope / applications) / Tables & Graphs (scatterplots): The slope of the line is the change in total fat (y-axis) for every 1 gram increase of total protein (x-axis). That's exactly

what we're looking for! So find the slope (pick two points on the line).

22. Means, Medians, & Modes: Be careful: the values in the table are NOT in order.

23. Solids & Volume: First find the volume of the can (review Volume of Prisms). Since the volume of the syrup is given, you'll have to subtract to find the volume of the fruit (volume of fruit + volume of syrup = volume of can).

24. Basic Functions: This problem is similar to other "application" problems (see Linear Equations). To understand what 72 represents, consider the value for $h(t)$ when $t = 0$. (Hint: It's 72!) What does this height represent?

25. Pick Numbers (advanced): Just pick a pair of numbers (one row) from the table (such as the first row: $x = 4.0$ and $k = 16.7$), and check the answer choices. Only one choice will be close.

26. Algebraic Word Problems: This one can be tricky. First, we're focusing on the "Food Calories" column of the table (the question doesn't mention "Kilojoules"). To set up the equation, you have to understand that p grams of protein will provide $4p$ calories, g grams of fat will provide $9g$ calories, and so on (again, this comes from the "Food Calories" column of the table—each number represents the "energy per gram" of the given macronutrient). So our equation is $180 = 4p + 9f + 4c$. Solve for f.

27. Growth & Decay Functions: This is a standard exponential growth function. You might need to review "multipliers" in the Percent lesson: increasing by 1.9% is the same as multiplying by 1.019.

28. Linear Equations (slope / equation of): Since the line goes through the origin, we have the equation $y = mx$ (the y-intercept is 0). You can find the slope using the given point: $m = 2$. So we have $y = 2x$. Thus, the y to x ratio of any point will be 2 to 1. Shortcut: There's no reason not to let (s, t) be the given point $(3, 6)$: t to $s = 6$ to $3 = 2$ to 1.

29. More Circles (equation of): Find the center and radius of the circle using the given equation. You might try a quick sketch of the circle by marking the four "perpendicular" points of the circle (that is, noon, 3 o'clock, 6 o'clock, and 9 o'clock). One answer choice will obviously not lie in the interior of the circle (be careful of the one that is hard to tell visually—just keep looking until you find the one that's obvious).

30. Percent (difference-over-original / increase/decrease): Follow the instructions carefully. First, use difference-over-original to find the percent change between 2012 and 2013. Then use half of this percent, and the increase/decrease technique, to find the expected value in 2014.

31. Proportions: As always with Proportions problems, keep track of your units.

32. Linear Equations (slope): This problem tests your calculator skills. Make sure you can easily type fractions into your calculator. Watch out for careless mistakes, such as missing parentheses. Here's how we typed it in: $(-2 - (-27/5))/(5/2 - (-6))$.

33. Algebraic Word / Systems of Equations: Let x be the number of correct questions and y be the number of incorrect questions. The first equation is $2x - y = 50$. Since the player answered 40 questions, we have $x + y = 40$. Solve by substitution or elimination.

34. More Circles (sectors) / Ratios (part-over-whole): As described in the More Circles lesson, the ratio of the sector area to the total area of the circle will equal the ratio of the sector degree measure to the total degree measure of the circle (always 360°). Note that you're not asked to find the area of the shaded region (not enough information is provided).

35. Systems of Equations / Factoring: Hint: Plug substitute $x^2 - 4x + 4$ for y in the second equation, combine like terms, and factor.

36. Triangles / Basic Trigonometry: This one's tricky. We know that $\tan B = \dfrac{3}{4}$, but what does this tell us? This is the trick to the problem. Since the two triangles ($\triangle ABC$ and $\triangle DBE$) are right,

knowing that $\tan B = \dfrac{3}{4}$ tells us that the triangles are 3-4-5 ones. We also know that the triangles are similar (they share $\angle B$). Here are the first few steps: Since $\triangle ABC$ is 3-4-5, $AB = 12$ and $AC = 9$ (3:4:5 = 9:12:15). $\rightarrow BD = 12 - 4 = 8 \rightarrow$ similar triangles:

$$\frac{BA}{AC} = \frac{BD}{DE} \rightarrow \frac{12}{9} = \frac{8}{DE} \dots$$

If all else fails, you could try measuring the drawing with the edge of your answer sheet. Use $DA = 4$ to create a ruler. DE appears to be $1.5 \times DA$.

37. Means, Medians, & Modes:
Remember, there are 20 data points: 2 contestants scored 5 points, 3 scored 4 points, etc. So the total points will be $(2 \times 5) + (3 \times 4) + \dots$ Use this total to calculate the average (mean).

38. Probability: This one sounds harder than it is. The first sentence is important; it means that the 7 perfect 5-point scores over the three days were each scored by a unique contestant: 7 contestants scored 5 points. This gives the denominator of the probability ratio ("given that the contestant received a score of 5 on one of the three days"). So how many contestants scored 5 on Day 2 or Day 3? This will be the numerator.

8. PRACTICE TEST 8

QUESTIONS BY SECTIONS/CHAPTERS

The following information lists every question on the test according to its relevant chapter or section in this tutorial. If you're correcting a test, circle the question numbers below that you missed or guessed on. Make sure to follow the Tutoring Schedule in the Introduction to know when to correct or tackle various types of questions.

READING
BY PASSAGE
- [1, 2, 3, 4, 5, 6, 7, 8, 9, 10] [11, 12, 13, 14, 15, 16, 17 ,18 19, 20, 21] [22, 23, 24, 25, 26, 27, 28, 29, 30, 31] [32, 33, 34, 35, 36, 37, 38, 39, 40, 41] [42, 43, 44, 45, 46, 47, 48, 49, 50, 51, 52]

BY QUESTION TYPE
- Direct & CTE (stand-alone): 7, 14, 15, 16 ,17, 24, 26, 43, 44, 47, 48, 52
- Ext. Reasoning & Purpose: 2, 3, 4, 5, 6, 9, 11, 18, 32, 33, 34, 36, 37, 42, 46, 50, 51
- WIC & Main Idea: 8, 12, 13, 22, 25, 27, 35, 38, 49
- Comparison & IG: 19, 20, 21, 30, 31, 39, 40, 41
- Tone, Structure, & Relationship: 1, 10, 23, 28, 29, 45
  Note: Most Citing-Textual-Evidence (CTE) questions are grouped with their relevant preceding questions.

WRITING & LANGUAGE
- Grammar & Sentence Structure: [2, 3, 4, 7, 8, 9, 11] [12, 13, 16, 17, 18, 20, 21, 22] [24, 26, 27, 29, 30, 32] [35, 36, 37, 38, 40, 42, 44]
- Main Ideas & Org.: [1, 5*, 6*, 10] [14, 15, 19] [23, 25, 28, 31, 33] [34, 39, 41, 43]
  Note: Brackets display separate passages.
  * Informational Graphics

MATH
- Arithmetic: §4 (2, 3, 10, 16, 18, 22, 31, 34, 37)
- Functions: §3 (8, 15)
- Algebra: §3 (1, 2, 3, 6, 7, 10, 12, 13, 18, 19); §4 (1, 4, 6, 7, 8, 9, 12, 13, 20, 21, 23, 25, 27, 29, 32, 33, 35, 38)
- Advanced Algebra: §3 (14, 16, 17)
- Graphs of Functions: §3 (11); §4 (14, 19, 30)
- Geometry: §3 (4, 5, 9, 20); §4 (5, 11, 15)
- Odds & Ends: §4 (17, 24, 26, 28, 36)
  §3 = Section 3; §4 = Section 4

TECHNIQUES AND HINTS

READING

PASSAGE I

1. Structure: 5-8. etc., 47–48, etc. Focus on main ideas for this one ("main focus"). Choice B may be tempting, but the passage does not offer an "examination" of the author (Dickens). Remember, every word counts in the answer choices.

2. Purpose: 5–10. Note some of the key words: "fascinated me," "boundless world," "safe haven." Might these ideas explain why the narrator disobeyed his father and spent his money on books?

3. Extended Reasoning: 11, etc.

4. Citing-Textual-Evidence (CTE): Unfortunately, the line given above is not among the answer choices (this happens!), but it shouldn't be too hard to find additional context for the previous answer.

5. Extended Reasoning: 66–68. The context is really quite clear (making this one close to a Direct question). Be careful of D: If you're familiar with the author Charles Dickens, you probably know that he is not really "a lifelong friend" (57) of Sempere. This is irony, a common device on fiction passages. Sempere and Dickens are friends in a *figurative* sense.

6. CTE: See above.

7. Direct: 40–43

8. Words-in-Context (WIC): 43–46. Note that you're looking for a "weight" that is non-literal ("a weight on my soul" as opposed to a weight on a scale).

9. Purpose: 53–54. Use Process of Elimination (POE) on this one. Note that the use of "friend" links Sempere and "Mr. Dickens." The three incorrect answer choices focus on the narrator, not Sempere.

10. : 53–54. The narrator points out the "care with which [Sempere] handled the volume." This suggests that Sempere thinks highly of the book and, by extension, the author. All choices are possible—make sure to choose the one

that requires the least amount of extended reasoning. For choice C, note that "Dicken's biography" is not mentioned in the passage.

PASSAGE II

11. Purpose: 12–15 ("[null results] are rarely published"), 16, etc. ("a recent study")

12. WIC: 21. Try plugging the choices into the passage. Don't make this one harder than it is. For example, "grants" (C) reads more into the passage than necessary.

13. WIC: 45–46. Conveniently, the word in question is defined in line 46.

14. Direct: 59–62

15. CTE: See above.

16. Direct: 62–65. Perhaps you noticed the words "Even more troubling" in the passage. The answer follows. Note that "a smaller sample" (65) means that the scientists excluded some data from their original results. The correct answer is camouflaged.

17. CTE: See above.

18. Purpose: 69–70 ("A registry . . . would address these problems"). This one is not easy, mainly because some of the incorrect choices are tempting. For A, a "registry" is not really a "research project"; as always, every word counts. For D, the paragraph doesn't actually discuss the importance of reexamining data, at least not explicitly. The correct answer requires no extended reasoning and is thus the better choice.

19. Informational Graphics (IG) (direct)

20. IG (direct): If you're comfortable with the graph, stop when you find the correct answer.

21. IG (make connection) / CTE (stand-alone): We won't put line numbers for this one (because it would give away the answer), but note that the "strong results" in the graph are synonymous with the "statistically significant results" described in the passage.

PASSAGE III

22. Main Idea: 17–18 (Note the contrast signal "But," and of course what follows), 50 ("bizarre behavior").

23. Structure: 1–3, etc. ("Inflexible old salt becomes a softy . . ."), 25–26, etc. (". . . discovered salt's stretchiness accidentally"), 58–60, etc. ("suggests new techniques . . .")

24. CTE (stand-alone): With these "stand-alone" CTE questions, just go through the answer choices while focusing on the question. Note the word "surprised" in the question.

25. WIC: 21–24. To help with this one, consider that the "different forces" rule the nanoworld in an analogous way to how "gravity" rules our macroworld. So the word in question ("rule") should work with the word "gravity." Let's look at the choices. Does gravity *mark*, *control*, *declare*, or *restrain* our world? Answering this question should lead you to the correct answer.

26. Direct: 39–42

27. WIC: 42. Try plugging the answer choices into the passage and trusting your ear.

28. Relationship: 1–3, 50–51. You might try POE for this one. All three wrong answers are false: B (17–18), C (53; "Perhaps"), D (50–53; the focus is on the "macroworld" here). Be careful of all the Eye Catchers in the answer choices.

29. CTE: Clearly, the best context is lines 50–51 (as labeled above). We're not sure why these lines are not found in the answer choices, so use POE (eliminate the three "worst" choices).

30. IG (direct): Make sure to focus on the second graph ("moving away").

31. (IG) (make connection): 46–48. You must extend your reasoning with this one. We know that the salt stretches as the tip pulls away (46–48). We can assume this is happening along the smooth curve of the second graph (between 0 and 21 nanometers). Logically, what do you think happens at point T, when the force on the tip goes to 0?

PASSAGE IV

32. Purpose: 7–18

33. Extended Reasoning: 25–27. The question is rhetorical—the author answers in the affirmative: "It can thus exist . . ."

34. CTE: See above.

35. WIC: This one is quite tricky. See line 57, where Lincoln mentions "matters" of discussion. In fact, "matter" would be the perfect answer, but, sadly, it's not among the answer choices. Slavery is clearly an important issue in this discussion. Which choice works best, and is closest to a "matter"?

36. Extended Reasoning: 70–76

37. CTE: See above.

38. WIC: As always with WIC questions, try to define the word in question using context before checking the answer choices. Note some of the tone words: "trouble and convulsion" (77), "agitation and resistance" (83). Consider these words as you come up with your definition and check the answer choices.

39. Comparison: 18–20, 51–66. Douglas criticizes Lincoln's apparent disparagement of the Constitution in lines 18–20. Lincoln clarifies his position in lines 51–66 (it is apparently only *one* aspect of the Constitution with which Lincoln disagrees. i.e. its allowance for the expansion of slavery).

40. Comparison / Relationship: 31–35, 76–78

41. Comparison: Use POE for this one. There is no mention in the passage of "the other's sincerity" (A), ". . . methods" (B), or ". . . actions" (C).

PASSAGE V

42. Purpose: The last three paragraphs discuss studies that deal with the flytrap's closing action. See "Their model" (39), "their studies" (40), and "Subsequent research supports this model" (65).

43. Direct: 3–7. The challenge to this one is that you're probably looking for some mention of the insect's *size*. This may draw you to choice A. But the the

flytrap's ability to identify "the species" is not mentioned in the passage (size and species are only very loosely related—consider how size varies among young insects and mature insects of the same species). If necessary, use POE for his one. Also, if you're not sure where to look for context, don't forget that you can check the line numbers given in the following CTE question.

44. CTE: See above.

45. Tone: The words given in the question are really all we have to go on with this one (lines 6, 27, 28–29). Hopefully they give you a sense of the author's tone. The word "bug," instead of a word like *insect*, is a good clue.

46. Purpose: 11–16. A key word is "analogous" (15). The mechanism behind a flytrap's closing action is being compared with short-term memory. In other words, the idea of short-term memory—something we probably understand—is being used to help explain the flytrap's behavior. Choice C sounds correct, but the word "distinction," signifying *difference*, is exactly wrong. Also, be careful of D: "detailed information" is too strong; the flytrap only learns about the prey's *size*, hardly detailed information, and this retention is short-lived (82–84).

47. Direct: 50–56

48. Direct: 82–84. If you understand the general idea, that the hairs need to be touched within a short time, you'll probably spot the correct answer. Don't forget, this is a "NOT" question.

49. WIC: 69–74

50. Extended Reasoning: 72–74. Volkov's model would have been stronger if he had measured calcium levels.

51. CTE: See above.

52. Direct: 69–77. It's worth mentioning that many students might find these last three questions relatively straightforward. Make sure you have a timing plan in place so you get to the end of the test; easy questions may be lurking.

WRITING & LANGUAGE

PASSAGE I

1. Transitions

2. Vocabulary: The passage is written in straightforward prose. Go with the answer choice that maintains this style. (We categorize this question as a Vocabulary one, but your knowledge of the Style lesson in the Main Ideas & Organization chapter applies as well.)

3. Parallelism: Note the list of three items, especially the third one ("compost . . . helps"). You can imagine a colon after the word compost: compost: (1) *minimizes* water . . ., (2) ?????, and (3) *helps* reduce . . .

4. Punctuation (A, C) / Fragment (D)

5. Informational Graphics (IG): The key word in the question—and indeed the main idea of the passage—is *compost*. Which waste type in the graph is synonymous with compost (read the first couple paragraphs again, if you're not sure).

6. IG: See the previous question to eliminate A and B. To decide between C and D, make sure the answer is correct, according to the graph.

7. Apostrophes & Confused Words (A, C): Use *than*, not *then*, in comparisons (see also the Comparisons lesson). / Punctuation (D)

8. Subject-Verb Agreement: The subject is "material" (singular).

9. Vocabulary: If you don't spot the correct answer, try eliminating answers that sound wrong to your ear.

10. Main Ideas (transitions): Read the question carefully. We must "transition from the previous paragraph," which just discussed a number of unfortunate facts about the current state of composting. Here's some elimination help: A: off topic; composting is only portrayed as *good* in the passage. B: doesn't tie into the previous paragraph. D: ambiguous: *which* setback? The "cities" are responding to several problems, not just the last one mentioned.

11. Paired Conjunctions: Note "either" in the passage.

PASSAGE II

12. Combining Sentences: As usual, the shortest answer is the best answer. As discussed in the Misplaced Words lesson, sometimes modifying phrases ("the traditional . . .") show up at the ends of sentences (see "Improper Modifiers"). Choices B and C both have Transition problems, and choice D has a Redundancy.

13. Punctuation: If you chose A, review Adjectives in the Commas part of the lesson.

14. Answer the Question: Only one choice explains a possible "origin" of the dance.

15. Main Ideas (topic / transition): Find an answer that mentions the paragraph's main idea and begins to transition to other elements of the dance.

16. Pronoun Case (B): Usually you should use *who* or *whom*, not *which* or *that*, when referring to people. / Run-on (C, D)

17. Illogical Comparisons: You're comparing "moves" of the lion dance. Only one choice compares "apples to apples."

18. Parallelism: We might also call this an Answer the Question question, but Parallelism should get you to the correct answer. Just find the answer choice that is most parallel to the parenthetical comment for a "tortoise." If you chose D, which *appears* parallel to "(for longevity)," note that this choice is too general; we want the *specific* symbolism of the phoenix.

19. Organization: The clue words are "Their older counterparts." So the sentence should be placed after younger lions.

20. Apostrophes & Confused Words (A, C) / Pronoun Agreement (C, D): The "dance" is singular.

21. Misplaced Words (improper modifiers): Hint: It is not the lion's *teeth* or the *envelope* that is "Approaching a doorway . . ." It is, of course, the *lion*.

22. Concision & Redundancies

PASSAGE III

23. Style: The style, as usual, is formal and straightforward.

24. Punctuation: If you missed this one, review the correct use of a semicolon.

25. Main Ideas (additions): Does the paragraph discuss, or even mention, *salary*?

26. Idiom: Choice B reverses the intended "direction" of the errors, from the machine to humans. This is a subtle but important distinction. Consider the differences in the following sentences: (1) The donkey is *subject to* laziness. (2) The donkey is *subjected to* abuse. In the first, the donkey is lazy. In the second, someone is mean *to* the donkey. Choices C and D both use incorrect prepositions.

27. Noun Agreement

28. Organization: Did you notice the awkward shift in the passage from "stenography" to "Digital audio recording"? If so, you'll know where to put sentence 6 (note the transition word "However").

29. Combining Sentences: None of the choices is grammatically wrong. When in doubt on these, go with the shortest choice. In this case, a simple long dash (a punctuation mark hard to get wrong) gets the job done fine. (Yes, long dashes need not always show up in pairs.)

30. Fragments

31. Transitions: Note that the previous sentence states that digital devises "cannot discern important parts of the proceedings from other noises in the courtroom." The sentence in question states basically the same thing: digital devices "record everything." There's no cause and effect or contrast.

32. Concision & Redundancies

33. Main Ideas: The main idea is that digital technology leads to errors. Which answer choice most strongly reinforces the possible consequences of these errors?

PASSAGE IV

34. Transitions: Note the shift from "Earth" to "space." You might also note the words "fundamentally different."

35. Misplaced Words: At first glance, this looks like a tricky problem. Should we say that the students *tried*, *strove*, *looked*, or *sought*? All sound fine. But look at the phrase in the parentheses—it describes "biofuels." Thus, the word immediately preceding the parentheses should be "biofuels." Only one choice works.

36. Vocabulary: This is primarily a Vocabulary question, although, of course, you should Answer the Question (see the Main Ideas & Organization chapter). The droplets "lose spherical symmetry," a relatively minor change.

37. Subject-Verb Agreement: The subject is "variations" (plural), not "density"—note that "density" is part of a prepositional phrase.

38. Pronoun Ambiguity / Concision & Redundancies: What is "this" referring to?

39. Main Ideas (transitions): Did you notice "the program" in the next sentence (note the word *the*)? This is a clue word (see Organization questions). The sentence in question must mention this program.

40. Punctuation: Use process of elimination. If you chose A, review the "One-Comma Rule." For the other incorrect answers, try removing comma-bound phrases and trust your ear.

41. Main Ideas (additions): This one is tricky. The added sentence seems somewhat unnecessary. We get it: the students don't have to go to space. But the second parts of the two "No" answer choices are both wrong (choice D is tempting, but the sentence really doesn't say that the students don't have to travel into space). Always be prepared to go "back to the drawing board" when these second parts (after the No/Yes) don't work. So go with the best "Yes" answer choice.

42. Parallelism: This looks like a Verb Tense question (and you might jump to A) until you get to "to perform" later in the sentence. Always read to the ends of sentences.

43. Answer the Question: This is why you should read these passages (and not just skip to the parts being tested). Go back to the second paragraph if necessary.

44. Punctuation: As is often the case, when in doubt, keep the commas out.

MATH (no calculator)

1. Basic Algebra (working with variables)

2. Linear Equations

3. Basic Algebra (working with variables)

4. Angles: There are several ways to get this one, but here's the fastest approach, in three steps: (1) First focus on $\triangle RTU$. This triangle is isosceles ($RT = TU$), so the base angles are equal. You can thus find $m\angle U$: $m\angle U + m\angle R + 114° = 180° \rightarrow m\angle U = m\angle R \rightarrow$ substitution: $m\angle U + m\angle U + 114° = 180°$, etc.). (2) Now focus on $\triangle SUV$. We know two of the angles, so we can find $m\angle SVU$ (sum of angles in $\triangle$ is 180°). (3) Finally, knowing that the angles on one side of a line are supplementary, we can find x.

5. Area & Perimeter / Algebraic Word

6. Basic Algebra (inequalities): Probably the easiest approach is to solve for x using the second inequality: $x > \dfrac{5}{2}$. Then plug this into the first inequality and solve for y.

7. Basic Algebra (equations with radicals) or Pick Answers: Whichever approach you use, it's a good idea to first isolate the radical: $\sqrt{2x+6} = x-1$. We recommend that you Pick Answers (just checking −1 is enough to eliminate the three incorrect answer choices). If you choose to solve algebraically (by squaring both sides, combining like terms, and factoring), you should end up with $(x-5)(x+1) = 0$, giving $x = 5$ and $x = -1$. But be careful! As stated in

the tutorial, you should always check solutions when solving equations with radicals. One of these solutions turns out to be "extraneous."

8. Basic Functions / Factoring or Pick Numbers (type 1): If you're comfortable factoring, go for it. Otherwise, use the Pick Trick. Here are the first few factoring steps: $\dfrac{f(x)}{g(x)} = \dfrac{x^3 - 9x}{x^2 - 2x - 3}$

$= \dfrac{x(x^2 - 9)}{(x-3)(x+1)} = \dfrac{x(x-3)(x+3)}{(x-3)(x+1)} \cdots$

9. More Circles (equation of): Draw a quick sketch of the circle, taking note of its center and radius. You should find that point $(10, -5)$ lies at "3 o'clock" on the circle. Point Q will lie at "9 o'clock."

10. Pick Answers or Algebraic Word: We recommend using the Pick Trick on this one. For example, start with B: 20 2-person tents will sleep 40 people. There must be 40 4-person tents $(60 - 20 = 40)$, which will sleep $40 \cdot 4 = 160$ people. $40 + 160 = 200 \neq 202$. We need more 4-person tents (fewer 2-person tents), so check C.

If you use the algebraic approach, here are the two equations (let x be the number of 2-person tents and y be the number of 4-person tents): $x + y = 60$ and $2x + 4y = 202$. Use substitution or elimination (Systems of Equations lesson) to solve for x.

11. Graphs of Functions / More Graphs of Functions / Factoring (factors and roots): Since we have zeros (or roots) at -3, 0, and 2, we know that $(x + 3)$, x, and $(x - 2)$ are factors of the function. So is the answer A or B? Consider "end behavior" (see More Graphs of Functions). Since the graph increases to the right *and* the left, the degree of the polynomial must be *even*. (Hint: multiplying just the xs in each equation will give you the degree.)

Pick Numbers (advanced): Another option, once you've eliminated C and D, is to pick a point on the graph, and check answer choices. Hint: pick $x = -2$ → $y \approx -15$ (according to the graph). ($x = -3, -1, 0, 1,$ and 2 all give the same answers for A and B).

12. Basic Algebra or Pick Numbers (type 2): The algebra is not bad. First, write the equation as the inverse of both fractions: $\dfrac{b}{2a} = \dfrac{2}{1}$. Then multiple through by 2. If you're uncomfortable with the algebra, use the Pick Trick: Pick a number for a, and cross multiply to solve for b.

13. Linear Equations: This one can be a little tricky. The answer choices display linear equations, where y (or $f(t)$) is gas production and t is years after 2000 (so 2000 is $t = 0$). We need to find the slope of the line. We're given two points: For the year 2000, we have (0, 4), and for 2013 we have (13, 1.9). We can calculate the slope:

$\dfrac{4 - 1.9}{0 - 13} = \dfrac{2.1 \times 10}{-13 \times 10} = -\dfrac{21}{130}$.

(The y-intercept is the same for all equations.)

14. Systems of Equations / Factoring (quadratics): Solve for y in the second equation ($y = 5x - 8$), substitute into the first equation ($5x - 8 = x^2 + 3x - 7$ → $x^2 - 2x + 1 = 0$), and solve for x by factoring the quadratic.

15. Basic Functions: If you're comfortable with functions, this one is straightforward. Here are the first two steps: $h(0) = 1 - g(0)$ (all xs become 0s) → So we must find $g(0)$: $g(0) = 2 \cdot 0 - 1 = -1$. Finally, plug this value into the first equation (for $g(0)$).

16. Factoring (quadratics)

17. Working with Polynomials (addition)

18. Systems of Equations: Usually these are easier to solve using substitution, but in this case just adding the equations will lead you to the correct answers (see the elimination method in the lesson).

19. Linear Equations (applications): The question is asking for b, the y-intercept of the equation. This is the value when $x = 0$, that is, when the company started. So how many employees did the company start with? Since we don't have to worry about slope (a), note how much of the question you can ignore.

20. More Circles (sectors) / Pick Numbers (type 3) (optional): This problem might

be easier if you pick a number for the circumference (an easy number is 1). So, using the proportions given in the sectors lesson, we have the equation $\dfrac{\frac{2}{5}}{1} = \dfrac{x}{360}$. Solve for x (you might have to do some long division).

MATH (calculator)

1. Proportions / Basic Algebra or Pick Numbers (type 1)

2. Tables & Graphs: Remember, the steeper the line going up, the greater the rate of increase, and the steeper the line going down, the greater the rate of decrease.

3. Proportions

4. Linear Equations / Tables & Graphs (scatterplots): Don't be distracted by the scatterplot. Just focus on the given linear equation ($y = 1.67x + 21.1$). Don't forget to freely use your calculator.

5. Angles (parallel lines / triangles): Focus on the small triangle above line l. The unlabeled angle "corresponds" with angle y (parallel lines). So you have two of the three angles of this small triangle. Solve for x.

6. Algebraic Word: This is one of those standard 2 equation–2 unknown problems (see "A Common Algebraic Word Problem" in the lesson). Make sure you are comfortable with these. They tend to look harder than they are.

7. Linear Equations

8. Basic Algebra (exponential equations) or Pick Answers: Cross multiplying gives $(x+1)^2 = 2$. Solve for x. If you're not comfortable with the algebra, Pick Answers and use your calculator.

9. Basic Algebra or Pick Answers: Here's the equation: $\dfrac{7\pi k^3}{48} = 473$. To solve for k, isolate k^3, and take the cube root of both sides. You could also Pick Answer.

10. Tables & Graphs: The trick to this question is to realize that as the diameter of the glass increases, the rate that the glass will fill will decrease. A simple way to imagine this is to compare a long test tube (with a small diameter) to a wide glass jar (with a large diameter). If you pour water into each at the same rate, the test tube will obviously fill much faster than the jar. In other words, the larger the diameter, the slower the height increases. Apply this idea to the glass in question. As the diameter increases (as it fills with water), how does the height—or more importantly the *rate* of the change in height—of the water level change? Note: This question is not directly covered by our techniques. If you struggled on it, that's OK. Just pick an answer and move on.

11. Solids & Volume (volume fitting)

12. Systems of Inequalities: Watch out for the trap on this one: Roberto did *not* meet his goal (so $x + y < 57$), but he *did* sell over $3,000,000 in policies.

13. Exponents / Basic Algebra: The first step is to rewrite the equation using your knowledge of fractional and negative exponents:
$a^{-\frac{1}{2}} = \dfrac{1}{a^{\frac{1}{2}}} = \dfrac{1}{\sqrt{a}} = x$. Now, use algebra to solve for a in terms of x (hint: invert and then square both sides of the equation). Some students might prefer using the Pick Numbers (type 1) technique, but the algebraic approach is recommended.

14. More Graphs of Functions (domain/range) / Factoring (quadratics): A function is undefined when the denominator equals 0, so set the denominator equal to 0, and factor to solve for x (Zero Product Theorem).

15. Solids & Volume / Proportions (optional): First, find the volume of the block. If you're not sure what to do from there, set up a proportion (note the known relationship: 2.8 grams per cubic centimeter).

16. Tables & Graphs / Ratios (part-over-whole): Make sure you focus on the correct row; we must focus on only those adults "who received a sugar pill." Use your calculator to reduce your fraction, if necessary. (Note that this

one is similar to many typical Probability questions, but instead of using the word "probability," the questions asks for a "proportion.")

17. Means, Medians, & Modes: When calculating the mean (average), make sure you consider the frequency of each value (age). For example, we have six 18s, five 19s, and so on: mean $= \dfrac{(18 \cdot 6 + 19 \cdot 5 + ... + 30)}{20}$. A shortcut for finding the median is to just find the 10th and 11th values by looking at the table; we don't recommend writing the numbers out (this takes too long).

18. Tables & Graphs: Don't let the scatterplot confuse you. Just focus on the line of best fit. What is the percent (vertical axis) at –2°C (horizontal axis)? This is an example of a wordy problem, with tons of unneeded information, that is actually fairly straightforward (assuming you're comfortable reading a basic line graph).

19. Graphs of Functions / More Graphs of Functions (domain/range): Knowing the range should allow you to eliminate two answer choices that clearly have y-values greater than 4. To find the correct answer, review *zeros* in the Graphs of Functions lesson.

20. Algebraic Word: Sometimes the trick to these word problems is keeping track of what you're given. The average annual energy cost is $4,334. After installing the heating system, the annual cost will be $2,712. So how much will the homeowner save each year? Hint: just subtract, but don't use your calculator (the answer choices are left unsolved). Then multiply this value by t years (for the savings over t years). Hopefully this will lead you to the correct answer.

    Shortcut: We're looking for the answer that displays when the savings *exceeds* the installation cost ($25,000). Only one answer choices shows anything exceeding $25,000, that is, 25,000 < something. Without finding the expression for savings over t years, we have our answer.

21. Tables & Graphs / Linear Equations (applications): Once again, don't be distracted by all the information given in the problem. In this case, just focus on the line (and its equation).

22. Tables & Graphs / Percent (difference-over-original): Make sure you understand the horizontal axis. Since 2000 is 15 years since 1985, your first x-value is 15. Three years later will be 18. When finding your y-values, you can use the line of best fit (as the CollegeBoard does in its solution) or the data points (the better approach, according to the question); either way should get you close enough to the correct answer.

23. Growth & Decay Functions / Pick Numbers (advanced): This is a hard one. We recommend you use the Pick Trick. The obvious number to pick is $q = 4$. After 4 "quarter years," we would expect the same value as after 1 year ($t = 1$). Only one choice equals $1,800(1.02)^1$ when you plug in $q = 4$.

    If you want to tackle this one algebraically, note that there are 4 quarter years for every 1 year, so $t = \dfrac{q}{4}$ (go ahead and plug $q = 4$ into the equation to see that $t = 1$). This, of course, will lead you to the correct answer.

24. Studies: Don't fall into this rabbit hole. You might be tempted to analyze the actual percent of voters for each contestant (perhaps by Picking 100?). But you don't have to. All we need to know is that Contestant 2 earned 70% of the social media votes and 40% of the text message votes. The answer is obvious. (Review "Don't Jump to Conclusions" in the Studies lesson, if necessary.)

25. Linear Equations: Read the question carefully: t refers to the "years after 2000" (so, for example, 2000 is $t = 0$). So our two data points are (0, 862) and (10, 846). Find the slope. (The y-intercept will be the population in 2000, that is, at $t = 0$.)

26. Studies: You might be tempted by choice B (20 is arguably too small a sample size to get accurate results), but the bigger issue is *where* the survey was conducted. Clearly, families at a

playground are more likely to have children than other families (note the purpose of the survey, as stated in the first sentence of the question). Also, remember not to jump to conclusions, as described in the lesson.

27. Linear Equations / Systems of Equations: Plugging the given points into the linear equations should give you the following equations: $r = p + b$ and $5r = 4p + b$. If you subtract the first equation from the second (the elimination method), the bs cancel, and you'll have $4r = 3p$. Divide both sides by $4p$ to find the ratio in question.

28. Statistics (terminology): The *range* is just the difference between the highest and lowest values of data. You can quickly calculate to see that $r_1 = r_2$. Next, review *standard deviation* if necessary: It is a measure of the "spread" of data. Clearly, just from looking at the dot plots, the standard deviations will not equal ($s_2 > s_1$).

29. Proportions (rates) / Algebraic Word or Pick Numbers (type 1): We must find the rate that the machine copies (see Proportions). If x is pages and t is time, in minutes, we have:

$$r = \frac{x}{t} = \frac{0.30 \cdot 5,000}{20} = 75 \text{ pages per}$$

minute. So, in m minutes, the machine will copy $75m$ pages. If you're comfortable with Algebraic Word problems, you should be able to find the equation that gives the number of *remaining* sheets of paper (p).

You could also Pick Numbers (type 1). For example, using the rate proportion (75 sheets/minute), if $m = 2$ minutes, the number of sheets used is 150, so the remaining sheets p is $5,000 - 150 = 4850$. Check the answer choices (plug in $m = 2$).

30. Basic Functions / Graphs of Functions: If you understand these lessons on functions, this is relatively straightforward problem for a #30. Hint: the "maximum value" is referring to the maximum y-value on the graph.

31. Proportions: The known relationship is 2 hydrogen atoms to 1 molecule of water.

32. Basic Algebra

33. Linear Equations: You could put both equations in $y = mx + b$ form and set the bs equal, but the faster approach is to multiply the first equation by 3: $3(x + 2y) = 3(10)$. Hopefully you'll see the shortcut. (Hint: $3(x + 2y) = 3x + 6y$.)

34. Proportions (rates): The question is asking for miles per <u>hour</u>, so convert 26 minutes to hours (hint: divide by 60) before plugging into the proportion.

35. Linear Equations or Graphs of Functions / Factoring: You could set the two functions equal, and solve for x by factoring, but the faster approach is to simply graph $g(x)$ (a line) and find a point of intersection with $f(x)$—but be careful: Watch the scale of the x-axis.

36. More Trigonometry / Pick Numbers (type 3) (optional): This one tests the sine/cosine complementary angle rules: for example, $\sin \theta = \cos (90° - \theta)$. Since the two angles in question are complementary (they add up to $\angle S$, a right angle), we know that the sine of one will equal the cosine of the other. Thus, the difference must be 0.

If you don't see this rule right away, the Pick Trick is a snap: pick numbers for $\angle RSW$, and calculate $\angle WST$ (of course, the two angles must add to 90°). Use your calculator.

37. Tables & Graphs / Proportions: First, note that the table and the graph provide the same basic information. We'll use the table. Remember, proportions need *known relationships*. Each value in the second column is a known relationship (the number of micrograms per milliliter). The known relationship for 5 minutes after injection is 152 micrograms per milliliter. The known relationship for 10 minutes after injection is 118 micrograms per milliliter. Set up a proportion for each known relationship (review the lesson if necessary), solve for the given values (10 milliliters and 8 milliliters, respectively), and subtract to find the difference.

38. Pick Numbers (type 3) / Basic Algebra (solving exponential equations): Pick any pair of points from the table, plug into the given equation, and solve for b. For example, if we use $t = 5$ and $P =$

152 (the second row of the table), we
have: $152 = 200b^{\frac{5}{5}}$ → $152 = 200b$ . . .
Don't forget to find b to the "nearest
tenth," that is, round the number to the
right of the decimal point.

9. PRACTICE TEST 9

QUESTIONS BY SECTIONS/CHAPTERS

The following information lists every question on the test according to its relevant chapter or section in this tutorial. If you're correcting a test, circle the question numbers below that you missed or guessed on. Make sure to follow the Tutoring Schedule in the Introduction to know when to correct or tackle various types of questions.

READING
BY PASSAGE
- [1, 2, 3, 4, 5, 6, 7, 8, 9, 10] [11, 12, 13, 14, 15, 16, 17 ,18 19, 20] [21, 22, 23, 24, 25, 26, 27, 28, 29, 30, 31] [32, 33, 34, 35, 36, 37, 38, 39, 40, 41, 42] [43, 44, 45, 46, 47, 48, 49, 50, 51, 52]

BY QUESTION TYPE
- Direct & CTE (stand-alone): 6, 12, 16, 17, 22, 23, 33, 38, 41, 42, 44, 45
- Ext. Reasoning & Purpose: 4, 5, 7, 8, 13, 14, 21, 24, 26, 27, 28, 32, 36, 37, 39, 43, 46, 48
- WIC & Main Idea: 1, 2, 9, 10, 15, 18, 25, 35, 40, 47
- Comparison & IG: 19, 20, 29, 30, 31, 49, 50, 51, 52
- Tone, Structure, & Relationship: 3, 11, 34
  Note: Most Citing-Textual-Evidence (CTE) questions are grouped with their relevant preceding questions.

WRITING & LANGUAGE
- Grammar & Sentence Structure: [1, 4, 5, 6, 8, 9, 10] [12, 13, 14, 15, 17, 21] [23, 26, 30, 31, 32] [35, 36, 38, 39, 40, 43]
- Main Ideas & Org.: [2, 3, 7, 11] [16, 18, 19*, 20*, 22] [24, 25, 27, 28, 29, 33] [34, 37, 41, 42, 44]
  Note: Brackets display separate passages.
  * Informational Graphics

MATH
- Arithmetic: §4 (2, 5, 6, 9, 11, 12, 18, 20, 33, 35, 38)
- Functions: none (all function questions are combined with other techniques)
- Algebra: §3 (1, 3, 4, 5, 7, 8, 9, 14, 15, 17, 20); §4 (1, 3, 4, 8, 10, 13, 14, 15, 17, 19, 29, 30, 32, 36)
- Advanced Algebra: §3 (2, 10, 11, 12); §4 (16)
- Graphs of Functions: §3 (18); §4 (20, 21, 24, 27)
- Geometry: §3 (6, 16); §4 (7, 31)
- Odds & Ends: §3 (13, 19); §4 (22, 25, 26, 28, 34, 37)
  §3 = Section 3; §4 = Section 4

TECHNIQUES AND HINTS

READING

PASSAGE I

1. Main Idea: 1–2, 76–77. Unsurprisingly, the first lines and last lines of a passage help with a Main Idea question.

2. Main Idea: 50–51. If you had trouble finding context, use POE (process of elimination).

3. Tone: 22–23, etc.

4. Extended Reasoning: 18. The key word is "weak." Old Widow Lau is not really trying to leave; it seems she would like to stay for tea.

5. CTE: See above.

6. Direct: 30–32

7. Extended Reasoning: 51–55. Precious Auntie believes art must require effort and thought.

8. CTE: See above.

9. WIC: 56–59. The text claims that "mind" and "heart" should both be cleansed, apparently in similar ways. For the word in question, you might come up with words such as *harmonizes with* or *relates favorably with*. Don't forget to plug answer choices into the text and avoid awkwardness.

10. WIC: 68–69. There's not much context for this one, but you're probably looking for a word similar to "pure," and one that could describe the sound of a silver bell. Use POE.

PASSAGE II

11. Purpose / Tone: 8–14. Note that the "study" (8) includes the "four experiments" discussed in the fifth paragraph. There is indeed *one* study, not several. You can use tone to eliminate all three incorrect choices; see the last two paragraphs, following "But" (68).

12. CTE (stand-alone): 68–77. See the question above, regarding tone. As is often the case, the author's tone is made clear following a contrast signal ("But" in line 68).

13. Purpose: 16–21. Always try to answer questions *before* looking at the answer choices. Most students will get this one using context, but a choice such as A may be tempting if you're reading the choices before having an answer in mind.

14. Extended Reasoning: 17–24. A "transactive memory source" is simply a way for us to *not* have to remember something (someone or something else is doing the remembering for us). Which choice captures this idea? Note: The answer is not C because the library's database is not taking the place of one's memory (it's unlikely that anyone would attempt to memorize the locations of a library's books).

15. WIC: 22–26. This "network of memory" (22) is a virtual *extension of* our actual memory. Some possible words that may work: *enlargement of*, *enhancement of*, etc.

16. Direct: 42–45. The "specific information sources" mentioned in the question refer to "Yahoo" and "Google" (44). Note that the correct answer is camouflaged ("difficult trivia questions" is rewritten in the correct answer).

17. CTE: See above.

18. WIC: 66-69. You may have come up with a word such as *use* or *make use of*.

19. IG (direct): Focus on the bar that includes both "statements" *and* "folder locations."

20. IG (make connections): 53–61. The fourth experiment is discussed in the lines indicated. There is no mention (in the passage) that any of the participants "remember nothing" (the largest group in the graph).

PASSAGE III

21. Purpose: 3–5

22. Direct: 14–16

23. CTE (stand-alone): The information is explicit: "Although small predatory killifish occurred in these new sites . . ." (57–58).

24. Extended Reasoning: 40–46. Focus on the quote in the question ("giant test tubes").

25. WIC: Hopefully you have a feel for the word in question and the tone of this part of the passage. Saying that "experimental evolution" is becoming increasingly *popular* means that scientists are increasingly *using* this method of experimentation. A possible synonym for *popular* in this context is *accepted*, *prevalent*, or *widely used*. If you don't spot the correct answer right away, try plugging answer choices into the passage and listen for awkwardness.

26. Extended Reasoning: 57–59. Look for an answer that directly contradicts a statement made in the passage about Reznick's experiment. Note: Choice A may be tempting, but Reznick never claims that his results should be identical to those found elsewhere.

27. Extended Reasoning: 67–72

28. CTE: See above.

29. IG (direct): Remember, with these "direct" IG questions (those that do not mention the passage), focus only on the figure(s).

30. IG (extended reasoning): Note that the mean embryo mass (the height of the bars) is much higher for the two "low-predation" environments than for the two "high-predation" environments (regardless of "slope" location), suggesting that predation is the more important factor in the experiment.

31. IG (direct): You don't have to worry about the passage for this question, but if you're comfortable with the main ideas of the third and fifth paragraphs (especially lines 21–29 and 63–65), the answer is clear.

PASSAGE IV

32. Purpose: 76–77, etc.

33. (Direct): Hopefully you noticed that much of the passage—especially the second, third, and fourth paragraphs— is filled with rhetorical questions. We labeled this question "Direct," but it's a rare question that's really testing *rhetoric*, or authorial method.

34. Structure: 4–11, 58–59 . . . : The contrast signal "But" at the beginning of the last paragraph is important. After spending most of the passage arguing that abolitionism is *not* (exclusively) a political question, Smith, in this last paragraph, changes course and imagines that it *is* a political question.

35. Main Idea: 4–7 ("It is not true that [slavery] is *merely* a political question . . ."): The rest of the paragraph, most clearly in lines 6–11, explains why Smith takes the stance quoted above.

36. Extended Reasoning: 22–33. You might try POE for this one, using the "not mentioned" elimination technique ("politically neutral," "financial security," and "[r]esisting calls for war"). The challenge to this question is that the support is in the form of a rhetorical question (one with an implied negative answer). We cover this idea in greater detail in our SAT Essay curriculum.

37. CTE: See above. Again, the challenge here is that the support is in the form of a question, but a rhetorical question with a strongly implied negative answer is indeed tantamount to a positive statement of support.

38. Direct: 34–42. Note that "domestic insurrections" (36) refers to slave rebellions. The "tyrant" (40) is, of course, the slave owner. (Not surprisingly, Smith considers the potential Northern support of these slave owners "unholy" (44).)

39. Extended Reasoning: 44. The best context is the mention of "unholy warfare." The tone is clear. But using POE, and having a basic understanding of the author's main points, should leave you with one answer choice. Choice A is a common choice, but there is no mention of a "specific individual"—the word "tyrant" is used to represent *all* slave owners.

40. WIC: 52. You're looking for a word such as *hidden* or *not yet apparent*. Try POE. Some of the choices don't make sense when describing "energies."

41. Direct: 68–73. The context is clear but may have been difficult to find. Don't forget to look ahead at the next question when you have trouble quickly finding context; if it's a CTE question, you can at least narrow down the location to one of four places in the passage.

42. CTE: See above.

PASSAGE V

43. Purpose: 1–3. In this first paragraph, we have both a "claim" (A) and a "problem" (C). Lines 5–10 (and the rest of the passage) answer the question as to whether the passage is *developing* this claim/problem (A) or *addressing* it (by offering a solution) (C).

44. Direct: 17–21. Note that there is no mention of "artificial soil" (A). Choice C is filled with eye catchers (44–50).

45. CTE: See above.

46. Extended Reasoning: 53–56 ("it has long been suspected . . . that we might find new natural antibiotics")

47. WIC: To get the tone of *caveats*, see line 71 ("is less exciting") and lines 79–94 (this paragraph lists *concerns* or *doubts*—both words are good synonyms for *caveats*—about teixobactin).

48. Purpose: 85–87. The author is emphasizing the "long haul of clinical trials."

49. Comparison: 79–94. You'll probably want to use POE on this one. Here are reasons for elimination (if you're correcting, try answering the question before reading ahead): (B) Passage 2 does *not* suggest any methodology modifications; (D) "dismissive stance" is too strong. In deciding between A and C, consider the end of Passage 2 (line numbers above).

50. Comparison: 7–10, 72–78

51. Comparison: 80–82. You'll have to extend your reasoning a bit here. If teixobactin works against Gram-positive bacteria (72–73) but *not* Gram-negative (80–81), and if it *worked* for the mice in both passages, then what can you say about the mice's infections?

52. CTE: See above. Make sure to focus on Gram-negative bacteria (as mentioned in the correct answer above).

WRITING & LANGUAGE

PASSAGE I

1. Concision & Redundancies

2. Organization: Clue words: "at that depth." Always look for pronouns, such as *that*. Only one sentence mentions a specific depth.

3. Transitions: NW Rota-1 is far below the ocean's photic zone, so we wouldn't expect bacteria to survive there. But bacteria "have adapted."

4. Pronoun Agreement: Note "their" earlier in the sentence.

5. Concision & Redundancies: Note "remove" earlier in the sentence.

6. Punctuation

7. Main Ideas (transitions): Which choice best sets up the information in the following sentence about how this "previously unknown" species of shrimp goes from eating "bacterial filaments as juveniles" to eating "Loihi shrimp and other organisms"?

8. Combining Sentences: Always start by looking at the shortest choice. Watch out for choices with -*ing* words (usually wrong).

9. Illogical Comparisons (A, B): The passage means to compare *water* (near NW Rota-1) with *acid* in the stomach. Choice B would also violate Pronoun Agreement. / Concision & Redundancies (C): "the acid from stomach acid" is clearly redundant.

10. Apostrophes & Confused Words

11. Main Ideas (additions/changes): Without the addition, the connection between carbon dioxide and acidity would be unclear.

PASSAGE II

12. Fragments

13. Passive Voice (A, D) / Wordy (C): As you can see, this question primarily

tests the Grammar & Sentence Structure Guidelines chapter.

14. Punctuation / + Fragments (A, D) / + Run-ons (C)

15. Pronoun Ambiguity

16. Main Ideas (topic sentence): The main idea of this paragraph has to do with the economic *challenges* of free public transportation.

17. Run-ons (A, B) / Transitions (D): Choice D also begins an independent clause with a FANBOYS conjunction ("but"); this construction is not *always* incorrect, but it is unusual on the SAT and should usually be avoided.

18. Style: Hopefully your ear hears the informal answer choices.

19. IG: Only one choice is true, according to the table.

20. IG / Main Idea: See Question 16 for the main idea of the paragraph.

21. Verb Tense: Note the tense earlier in the sentence: "embrace" and "can go."

22. Main Idea (passage): Review the first paragraph, if necessary.

PASSAGE III

23. Pronoun Agreement: The pronoun refers to "digital camera."

24. Organization: This one's a little tricky. You have to sense that the added question is rhetorical. Here's an example of a similar use: *I brought an umbrella to Seattle. **Why wouldn't I?** It's one of the rainiest cities in America.* (If this still sounds strange, try emphasizing the word *wouldn't* while you read it.) So, in other words, the question functions somewhat like a cause & effect transition (such as *because*).

25. Main Ideas (addition): If you're thinking in terms of keywords, we have the following words: *wet plate photography* (of course), *film creation (challenges and process)*. Clearly, the added sentence is on-topic.

26. Pronoun Agreement (A, B) / Apostrophes & Confused Words (A, C): The pronoun is referring to "photographers."

27. Transitions: Make sure to read to the end of the sentence (see Grammar & Sentence Structure Guidelines).

28. Answer the Question: Some students are tempted by choices B and C, but neither of these is the best answer. B would be better if it read *just* (or *only*) *a few*, and C would be better if it read *just* (or *only*) *a matter of*. Without these qualifiers, another of the answer choices better captures the *quickness* of the process.

29. Transitions: Hopefully you noticed that the paragraph provides the *steps* of the wet plate process. Which choice is best for the last step of this process?

30. Punctuation: Remember the rhyme, when in doubt, keep the comma (or other punctuation) out.

31. Verb Tense: Note the words "appear" (previous sentence) and "emerge" (next sentence).

32. Concision & Redundancies

33. Answer the Question: Sternbach's techniques are *old*, but her subjects are *contemporary*. Only one choice has anything to do with time.

PASSAGE IV

34. Main Idea (addition): The revision provides clarifying information about an "urban archaeologist." Even if you thought it was unneeded, you hopefully read the second parts of C and D carefully and decided to "go back to the drawing board"; always let the second parts of yes/no questions potentially persuade you to change your original yes/no answer.

35. Subject-Verb Agreement: The subject is not "funds"; it's the whole phrase: "Any New York City construction project"—or just think of it as "Any project."

36. Concision & Redundancies

37. Transitions: See "rich history" in the previous paragraph (positive tone) and "obstacles" in this paragraph (negative tone).

38. Punctuation

39. Concision & Redundancies / Parallelism: The "noise" applies to all

three items. Mentioning it again for "pedestrians," explicitly or as a pronoun, is redundant and non-parallel (see "car horns").

40. Fragments (A, D) / Run-on (B)

41. Main Idea (transitions): Only one choice relates to the work of bringing in fresh water, as discussed in the passage. You can use POE: there is no mention of "various kinds of construction materials" (A), "hospitality" (B), or financing (D).

42. Style: Note that *hassle* (C) is too negative for this context.

43. Pronoun Agreement: Check the first paragraph to recall Loorya's occupation (she is quoted in the next sentence).

44. Answer the Question / Main Idea (passage): As usual, checking the title can help with these Main Idea questions for the whole passage.

MATH (no calculator)

1. Systems of Equations

2. Working with Polynomials or Pick Numbers (type 1)

3. Linear Equations: Make sure to convert the equation into the slope-intercept form ($y = mx + b$).

4. Linear Equations (applications) or Pick Numbers (type 1): Note that the answer choices are linear equations. If you recognize that the starting height (15 feet) is the y-intercept and 8 feet/second is the slope, the answer is clear. If not, pick a number for s, solve for h, and check all answer choices. For example, if $s = 2$ seconds, then the roller-coaster will climb $8 \cdot 2 = 16$ feet. Since it started at 15 feet, the height after 2 seconds is $15 + 16 = 31$ feet. Don't forget to check all answer choices.

5. Linear Equations (applications) or Pick Numbers (type 3): If you're comfortable with these applications questions, you should note that the slope is 75 dollars/hour. So 2 additional hours is easy to calculate. Otherwise, just pick two easy numbers for h, such as $h = 2$ and $h = 4$, and compare C for each.

6. More Circles (segments): The first ratio is for degrees and the second is for arc length: $\dfrac{part}{whole} \dfrac{100}{360} = \dfrac{5\pi}{x}$. Hint: since you can't use a calculator, reduce the first ratio before cross multiplying.

7. Basic Algebra

8. Basic Algebra: Solve for x (in terms of a). What value of a make x undefined? If necessary, review (or cover) domain in the More Graphs of Functions section.

9. Systems of Equations: Each equation is represented by a curve or line on the graph. The solution (or solutions) of all three equations must be a point (or points) common to all three equations. Be careful: several of the points are common to only *one* or *two* of the equations.

10. Working with Polynomials: Simplify the polynomial on the left-hand side (LHS) into standard quadratic form ($Ax^3 + Bx^2 + Cx + D$); the capital letters can be variables, numbers, or expressions (make sure you combine like terms). In this case, the LHS polynomial simplifies to $5ax^3 + (15 - ab)x^2 + (4a - 3b)x + 12$. Finally, compare coefficients on both sides (see "Comparing Polynomials" in the Working with Polynomials lesson). Since the question asks for ab, set the x^2 coefficients of both sides equal: $15 - ab = -9$. . . .

11. Basic Algebra / Factoring or Pick Answers: If you're comfortable working with variables, just cross multiply, move all terms to one side of the equal sign, factor, and use the Zero Product Theorem. Otherwise, Pick Answers.

12. Common Denominators or Pick Numbers (type 1): The Pick Trick is straightforward (hint: pick $x = 1$). The "official" approach is to find the common denominator and simplify: $\dfrac{1}{2x+1} + 5 = \dfrac{1}{2x+1} + \dfrac{5(2x+1)}{2x+1}$ . . .

13. Parabolas / Graphs of Functions / Pick Numbers (advanced): The vertex is (3, 1), so eliminate the two choices that show a vertex of (−3, 1) (B and D) (review "Vertex Form" in the Parabolas

lesson if necessary). Then, pick a point from the graph—(2, 5) or (4, 5)—and plug it into the remaining choices.

14. Systems of Inequalities or Pick Numbers (advanced): If you use the Pick Trick, pick a point that is true for one of the answer choices and test it in the given system of inequalities. Since there is no overlap among the shaded regions, when you find a point that works, you're done (eliminate all choices that do *not* include this point).

15. Basic Algebra ("Solving Equations with Radicals") or Pick Answers: The lesson reminds you to always check for "extraneous solutions." Since this is a #15 (supposedly difficult), you can be pretty sure there will be an extraneous solution. Using the Pick Trick on this one is easier and safer.

16. Solids & Volume: A "right rectangular prism" is just a fancy way of saying *box*.

17. Basic Algebra: Always look for shortcuts. In this case, simply dividing by 2 leads you to the expression in question.

18. More Graphs of Functions (transformations): The maximum point of $f(x)$ (2) simply moves up 6 units.

19. Basic Trigonometry

20. Linear Equations: Find the slope of the linear function f, calculate the slope of the linear function g (perpendicular to f), and, using the given point, find the equation for $g(x)$. Then, find $g(0)$ (the y-intercept of $g(x)$).

MATH (calculator)

1. Basic Algebra

2. Proportions

3. Basic Algebra

4. Pick Answers: You might also simply note that the square root of a real number will never be negative.

5. Tables & Graphs

6. Tables & Graphs: Review "Line Graphs" in this lesson, where we discuss the relationship between the steepness of a line and the relative "rate of change."

7. Angles (triangles / vertical angles)

8. Linear Equations (applications) or Pick Numbers (type 3): The question is simply asking for the slope of the line (change in cost (y) per additional mile traveled (x)). Students who don't see this right away can pick a couple of points (one mile apart) and compare the costs.

9. Probability: The subgroup (denominator) is made up of all customers ("a gas station customer"). The target group (numerator) is made up of those customers who "did not purchase gasoline."

10. Algebraic Word: We labeled this an Algebraic Word question, and it doesn't look like an easy one, but your clue that it's probably not as difficult as it looks is the problem number: only 10 out of 30 (multiple choice). The question is in fact relatively straightforward if you're comfortable with ratios (see the Ratios lesson) and using your calculator:

    336 students took the survey. 1/4 were freshman (1/4·336 = 84) and 1/3 were sophomores (1/3·336 = 112). This leaves 140 students (336 − 84 − 112 = 140). 1/2 of these were juniors (1/2·140 = 70). How many were left (these will be seniors)?

11. Proportions: The known relationship between the heights of Plant A and Plant B (20 cm to 12 cm) is the same as that between Plant C and Plant D. Use this ratio for your proportion.

12. Proportions: Another relatively straightforward proportions question. Make sure you are comfortable identifying questions that test this technique (look for "known relationships").

13. Systems of Inequalities / Pick Answers: Try to come up with the system of inequalities on your own before looking ahead. . . . If x is the number of 100-pound packages and y is the number of 120-pound packages, the system is:

    $100x + 120y \leq 1{,}100$ (pounds)
    $x + y \geq 10$ (packages)

    You could Pick Answers, starting with the "maximum" value for y. For example, if $y = 6$ (D), according to the second inequality above, the least possible value for x is 4. Plug these values into the first inequality above: 1,120 is *not* ≤ 1,100. Move on to C. . . .

To solve algebraically, multiply the second inequality by −100 (don't forget to change the direction of the sign). Now that the signs are both ≤, you can use the elimination method to solve for y.

14. Algebraic Word or Pick Numbers (type 1): We like the Pick Trick on this one. Just pick $t = 10$ years. Which choice gives $v = \$30,000$? That's all there is to it. You see how the Pick Tricks make some problems almost too easy!

15. Linear Equations: Calculate the slope using the given points. Note that the second point is the y-intercept.

16. Working with Polynomials (comparing polynomials): There are a few variations to this solution, depending on how many terms you move to the right-hand side (RHS) of the equation. We recommend the following approach: $(4x + 4)(ax − 1) = x^2 + bx − 4$ → FOIL LHS: $4ax^2 − 4x + 4ax − 4 = $ RHS → combine like terms of x on LHS: $4ax^2 + (4a − 4)x − 4 = x^2 + bx − 4$ → compare coefficients on both sides: $4a = 1$ and $4a − 4 = b$. Solve for a, and then solve for b.

17. Systems of Equations: There's a shortcut to this one: If you simply stack the two equations and add them together, you'll get $6w + 9t = 39$. In one step, can you turn $6w + 9t$ into $2w + 3t$? (Whatever you do to the LHS you must do to the RHS.) If you didn't see the shortcut, simply solve for w and t using the "elimination" method.

18. Proportions / Percent (of/is): Since the question provides so much unneeded information, we consider this a tricky one. Here's the solution:

First, use the of/is percent technique to find the daily allowance of potassium: 180 mg is 5% of the daily allowance → $108 = 0.05 \cdot$ daily allowance → daily allowance = $108/0.05 = 3600$ mg.

Next, set up a proportion. The question mentions servings and amount of potassium (mg), so look for a given known relationship with those units: 1 serving = 180 mg. Since p is a percent, we must write it as $p/100$ in the proportion:

$$\frac{\text{servings}}{\text{mg}} \quad \frac{1}{180} = \frac{x}{(p/100)3600}$$

Finally, solve for p in terms of x.

Note: You could Pick Numbers (type 1) for x, which will make the algebra easier.

19. Proportions / Algebra Word or Pick Answers: This one is also tricky. Here's the fastest approach: First, use a proportion to find the calories per cup for Crunchy Grain:

$$\frac{\text{calories}}{\text{cups}} \quad \frac{210}{3/4} = \frac{x}{1} \rightarrow x = 280 \text{ cals/cup}$$

Then set up an equation for the total calories of the 1 cup mixture; the first expression below is for Super and the second is for Crunchy (let c be cups of Super, which means $1 − c$ is cups of Crunchy): $240c + 280(1 − c) = 270$ → $240c + 280 − 280c = 270$ → $−40c = −10$ . . .

Picking answers is probably easier. For example, if you pick C, you have 1/3 cup of Super (and, thus, 2/3 cup of Crunchy). Since Crunchy has 280 calories per cup (see above), we have: $1/3 \cdot 240 + 2/3 \cdot 280 = 266.67 < 270$. Check B. . . .

20. Tables & Graphs: The relationship is fairly clear: the greater the number of servings, the greater the number of calories of fat (and 0 servings logically provides 0 grams of fat). Usually the last question on these multi-question sets is the hardest one, but in this case, it's probably the easiest.

21. More Graphs of Functions (axis intercepts): Just check answers (plug in $x = 0$, and look for a solution of d).

22. Means, Medians, and Modes / Statistics (terminology)

23. Studies: As always with these Studies questions, consider the *where* and *who*. Clearly, viewers of a particular news show will not represent the population as a whole.

24. Basic Functions / Working with Polynomials (comparing polynomials):

Follow the steps given in the lesson. First, find $f(x + a)$ using the definition of $f(x)$ (the question's first equation). Then set your answer equal to the given expression for $f(x + a)$ (the RHS of the question's second equation) and "compare polynomials." You should get the following equation:
$5x^2 + 10ax + (a^2 - 3) = 5x^2 + 30x + 42$
→ Comparing the x terms, we have:
$10a = 30$. . . .

25. More Trigonometry or Pick Numbers (type 2): You should have the following relationship memorized:
$\sin x = \cos(90 - x)$. You could also pick a number for x, solve for a, and check the answer choices.

26. Basic Functions / Parabolas: This function is a parabola opening down. When the parabola crosses the x-axis, h equals 0. Since the x-intercept is positive (given), this must be the time when the projectile hits the ground. The figure below, while not necessary for answering the question, should make this clear:

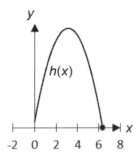

27. Graphs of Functions (axis intercepts)

28. Parabolas / Graphs of Functions (axis intercepts): As discussed in the Graphs of Functions lesson, to find the y-intercept, set $x = 0$. You can quickly see that the y-intercept is 2, which is the third "constant or coefficient" in the given equation. While you could find the other coordinates mentioned in the answer choices (see the Parabolas lesson), this is time-consuming and luckily unnecessary.

29. Linear Equations (applications): Hint: Ignore the graph; the slope and y-intercept are given in the question. Make sure to review the lesson if you have trouble on this one; these "applications" questions show up frequently.

30. Linear Equations: Be careful! The bottom left corner of the graph is not (0, 0). Just pick two convenient points and calculate the slope, and then use one of the points to approximate the equation. Review the lesson if necessary.

31. More Circles / (Triangles (special right)): This one is more difficult than we usually see for the first grid-in question. There are two ways to tackle it: algebraic and geometric. Both require you to recognize that h equals the x-coordinate of the midpoint of the line with endpoints (4, 0) and (20, 0); since the line is $20 - 4 = 16$ units long, h will be $4 + 16/2 = 12$.

Algebra: Use the equation of a circle to solve for k: $(x - h)^2 + (y - k)^2 = r^2$
→ plug in a given point on the circle, such as (4, 0), and our known value for h: $(4 - 12)^2 + (0 - k)^2 = 10^2$
→ $64 + k^2 = 100$ . . .

Geometry: Draw two radii from the center of the circle to the two given points, (4, 0) and (20, 0), and draw a vertical line from the center to the x-axis. We now have two right triangles. The hypotenuse of each is the radius (10 units) and the base of each is $16/2 = 8$ units long. These are two sides of a (special) right triangle. The third side will give you k.

32. Linear Equations: Remember, when two lines are perpendicular, the slope of one is the *negative reciprocal* of the slope of the other.

33. Probability: The *subgroup* includes all people who are rhesus negative (−), that is, the bottom row: $7 + 2 + 1 + x$. The *target group* includes only those people in the subgroup who have blood type B (2 people). Use the equation for probability to solve for x.

34. Means, Medians, & Modes: Make sure you can use the shortcut for finding medians. There are 29 games (given); it's helpful to think of 29 as the sum $14 + 1 + 14$: the median number of goals will occur at that 15th game (in the middle). Counting from the left bar of the graph, there were 8 games with 1 goal and 9 games with 2 goals, so the 15th game must be in this second group: 2 goals. Now answer the

question: In how many games did the team score 2 goals?

35. Percent (difference-over-original): Make sure you can identify which technique to use on these percent problems (review the magnifying glass information if necessary). Since the question is asking you to *find* a percent change, use the difference-over-original technique (both the difference and original are given).

36. Linear Equations: Write the equations in slope-intercept form ($y = mx + b$) and set the slopes equal (parallel lines, that is those with equal slopes, have no solutions, assuming the y-intercepts are different). Shortcut: If you're comfortable with finding the slope of a linear equation in "standard form" ($Ax + By = C$), you can solve this problem without converting the equations into the slope-intercept form, which saves some time.

37. Means, Medians & Modes

38. Percent (increase/decrease): Using the "multiplier" for a 13.5% increase, we have 24.7 (million) = $1.135x$, where x is the number of tourists in Russia for 2011 (in millions). Find x and subtract. Don't forget to round to the nearest integer.

10. PRACTICE TEST 10

QUESTIONS BY SECTIONS/CHAPTERS

The following information lists every question on the test according to its relevant chapter or section in this tutorial. If you're correcting a test, circle the question numbers below that you missed or guessed on. Make sure to follow the Tutoring Schedule in the Introduction to know when to correct or tackle various types of questions.

READING

BY PASSAGE

- [1, 2, 3, 4, 5, 6, 7, 8, 9, 10] [11, 12, 13, 14, 15, 16, 17 ,18 19, 20, 21] [22, 23, 24, 25, 26, 27, 28, 29, 30, 31, 32] [33, 34, 35, 36, 37, 38, 39, 40, 41, 42] [43, 44, 45, 46, 47, 48, 49, 50, 51, 52]

BY QUESTION TYPE

- Direct & CTE (stand-alone): 2, 8, 12, 14, 17, 22, 23, 31, 32, 33, 43, 46
- Ext. Reasoning & Purpose: 5, 6, 7, 9, 10, 11, 26, 27, 28, 29, 30, 34, 36, 37, 44, 47, 48
- WIC & Main Idea: 1, 13, 18, 24, 25, 35, 38, 45, 49
- Comparison & IG: 19, 20, 21, 39, 40, 41, 42, 50, 51, 52
- Tone, Structure, & Relationship: 3, 4, 15, 16
  Note: Most Citing-Textual-Evidence (CTE) questions are grouped with their relevant preceding questions.

WRITING & LANGUAGE

- Grammar & Sentence Structure: [1, 3, 4, 7, 8, 9, 10] [12, 14, 15, 17, 18, 19, 20] [23, 24, 25, 26, 28, 32] [36, 37, 38, 39, 40, 41, 42, 43]
- Main Ideas & Org.: [2, 5, 6, 11] [13, 16, 21, 22] [27*, 29*, 30, 31, 33] [34, 35, 44]
  Note: Brackets display separate passages.
  * Informational Graphics

MATH

- Arithmetic: §4 (2, 3, 8, 12, 13, 14, 16, 18, 37, 38)
- Functions: §3 (18); §4 (5, 9, 22, 26)
- Algebra: §3 (1, 2, 3, 4, 5, 6, 9, 14, 15, 16, 17, 19); §4 (1, 4, 6, 17, 23, 24, 25, 27, 29, 31, 34)
- Advanced Algebra: §3 (20)
- Graphs of Functions: §3 (7, 10); §4 (25)
- Geometry: §3 (8, 11); §4 (15, 30, 32)
- Odds & Ends: §3 (12, 13); §4 (7, 10, 11, 19, 20, 21, 28, 33, 36)
  §3 = Section 3; §4 = Section 4

TECHNIQUES AND HINTS

READING

PASSAGE I

1. Main Idea: 58–60 ("all twenty-six of us"). The correct answer is also apparent in the introduction (the narrator is "eleven years old").

2. Direct: 52–55 ("most remote and forgotten corner of America"). Again, the introduction also leads to the correct answer ("small Georgia town").

3. Tone / Extended Reasoning: 10–14

4. CTE: See above.

5. Purpose: 26–30. There's not much context for this one, so, if necessary, use process of elimination (POE): B: no specific mention that her travels encouraged her to attend medical school; C: the "fruitful intermission" occurred *after* boarding school (an eye-catcher); and D: no mention that her time off "lasted several years."

6. Purpose: 33–38. As with Question 5, the context is not particularly clear. Miss Spivey expected the students to have heard of Columbia University (see 37–38). The reader might get the impression from the rest of the passage that the students had in fact probably *not* heard of the school. Only one answer choice is supported by this context. You could also use POE.

7. Extended Reasoning: 39–41 ("she wandered"), 47–50 ("all aflame")

8. Direct: 50–54

9. Extended Reasoning: 82–86. Miss Spivey waited for the students to be "amazed and delighted," but instead they "hung there for a minute, thinking hard," implying silence and stillness (and thus, indeed, something less than amazement or delight). Note: Choice D is too strong.

10. CTE: See above.

PASSAGE II

11. Purpose: 5–8, 15–18, 51–52, 73–75. The main purpose is made clear in several places (as indicated): We must

"replace and eliminate driving" (6–7) to improve the environment, and to do so, we must make driving more "inconvenient" (74).

12. CTE (stand-alone): 1–5

13. WIC: 8–15. You might come up with a word such as *supported* or *reinforced*.

14. Direct: 14–15 ("not popular")

15. Tone: 39–40 ("we actually make the sprawl problem worse")

16. CTE: See above.

17. Direct: 45–48. Remember, always make sure you know what type of question you're answering. This one sounds like a Direct question, and indeed the answer is found explicitly in the text, as we would expect.

18. WIC: 71–73. Hopefully you have a feel for the word in question. You might come up with a word such as *advocates* or *pushes for*. (Yes, sometimes one of our picked words actually shows up as an answer choice—this will hopefully happen for you as well.)

19. IG (direct): The answer is found in Figure 1, in the "Before alteration" column and "Southhampton city center" row.

20. IG (make connections): 8–12. This one's a little tricky. If you understand the main argument of the passage (see Question 11), then what you're looking for is support for the idea that making driving less convenient will reduce traffic (and, thus, improve the environment). Figure 1 seems to suggest that making driving less efficient (see data on "altered roads") leads to less traffic (see last column). It's not a slam-dunk, so hopefully you can get to the correct answer through POE.

21. IG (direct): Focus on the black ("no") bars in the figure. Two categories have clearly larger black bars than the others (and luckily only one is an available answer choice).

PASSAGE III

22. Direct: 4–6. This question is worded like an Extended Reasoning one ("most likely"), but the context directly answers the question.

23. CTE: See above.

24. WIC: 15–19. As always with WIC questions, remember to come up with words before looking at the answer choices. Possible words for this one: *found, functioning, working.* Don't forget to try plugging answer choices into the text, if necessary. Incorrect answers often sound awkward.

25. WIC: 25. Sometimes a word in the text ("measure") is a perfect picked word. Another good word: *detect.*

26. Extended Reasoning: 26–28. Note how camouflaged the answer is: "soft stroking" becomes "[g]entile pressure," "immediate" becomes "fast," and "delayed" becomes "slow." This is a typical way that the CollegeBoard can make relatively easy problems difficult.

27. CTE: See above.

28. Purpose: 43–45. This one is tricky. You're contextual answer (before looking at the answer choices) was probably something along the lines of: "to identify something *unexpected* in the results." But none of the choices really match this idea. So use POE: A: no mention of "factors" that the team "failed to consider"; B: no mention of a "solution" (in the given lines); C: "criticism" is probably too strong.

29. Extended Reasoning: 37–38

30. Purpose: 73–75. As always, focus on information following contrast signals (such as "But").

31. Direct: 84–90. You'll have to skim for some mention of "other test subjects" in relation to G.L. (in the passage, these test subjects are called "normal subjects").

32. Direct: 90–94. If you found the mention of "emotion" at the end of the passage, this one is straightforward.

PASSAGE IV

33. Direct: 1–5

34. Purpose: 28–29 ("justice and safety!"), 31 ("order and equity"), etc.

35. WIC: 71–73. You might come up with something like *taken back.*

36. Extended Reasoning: 77–81. "God himself . . . placed in every human heart the love for liberty." In other words, this "love for liberty" (or, as it's worded in the question, "preference for national sovereignty") is innate.

37. CTE: See above.

38. WIC: 82–85. Possible picked word: *measure.* See also line 83: "consider."

39. Comparison: 1–25 (Passage 1), 50–70 (Passage 2). POE: B: no mention of "diversity"; C: no mention of "worldwide history" in Passage 1.

40. Comparison: 26–41 (Passage 1), 82–87 (Passage 2). If you don't see the correct answer right away, try POE: A: no mention of "direct inheritance of European colonization" in Passage 1; C: Beveridge (Passage 1) claims that the land was given to Americans already "noble" (1) and that the people, already "mighty," were "planted on this soil" (6–7), so the word "matured" in the answer choice is false; D: Bryan (Passage 2) believes the concept of liberty indeed could work elsewhere, just not as ministered by the United States as a colonial power.

41. Comparison (Extended Reasoning / Tone): 46–48, 79–81

42. CTE: See above.

PASSAGE V

43. Direct: 26–30, 33–36

44. Purpose: 18–19, etc.

45. WIC: 10–17. Read the lines indicated to get a feel for the context surrounding the word in question. You might pick a word such as *activated* or *brought about.* You might also note the word "stimulates" in line 29; the context is similar.

46. CTE (stand-alone): 38–47. Starting at line 38 makes clear that "these conditions" (43–44) refer to plowing "during the night" (40).

47. Extended Reasoning: 60–62. Read these lines carefully. We can infer from context that if crops (such as wheat or corn) had been planted, the weeds would have probably experienced "competition" (61), and thus would have logically been *less* abundant than if no crops were planted.

48. CTE: See above.

49. WIC: 63–66. The context should be clear: 80% is significantly more than 2%.

50. IG (direct)

51. IG (direct): Note that this question and the previous two were arguably the easiest questions on the entire Reading section. This is why it's important to find a timing plan that ensures that you'll get your eyeballs on every question, even if you have to skip harder questions along the way. Easy points are often lurking near the ends of sections (especially for Reading and Writing & Language).

52. IG (make connection) / CTE: You should probably have some idea of what you're looking for in the passage (based on the table): more seedlings emerge in soil disturbed in light than in darkness (a central idea of the passage).

WRITING & LANGUAGE

PASSAGE I

1. Concision & Redundancies

2. Main Ideas: You might gather from the first several sentences, and the title of the passage, that the main idea of the passage has to do with making reading more enjoyable for children. Also, note the beginning of the next paragraph.

3. Punctuation: Note the comma after "Mifflin."

4. Combining Sentences: Typically with these types of questions we do *not* expect the correct answer to maintain the two independent clauses—one will usually be altered in some way to become a phrase or dependent clause, or they'll be combined in other ways. In this case, however, the two

independent clauses are maintained in all four choices, so go with the shortest and simplest choice.

5. Main Ideas (transitions): Read the question carefully. Which choice *best* supports the idea that Geisel was an "experienced writer and illustrator."

6. Transitions: The contrast should be clear ("obstacle"). Be careful of D: "At any rate" can be used as a contrast transition, but it's somewhat weak for this use (it's usually used to get back on track in a conversation); there's certainly a more common contrast signal among the answer choices.

7. Misplaced Words (Improper Modifiers): Who was "[o]n the verge of giving up"? The first word following a modifying phrase at the beginning of a sentence should be whatever is being modified.

8. Concisions & Redundancies

9. Subject-Verb Agreement: The subject is "Children," and the verb "were" is used for two actions: The children "were entertained" and "captivated." Here's a shorter example that illustrates this construction (read it aloud if necessary): *They were entertained by the story and captivated by the pictures*. The words *entertained* and *captivated* both share the "to be" verb *were*.

10. Punctuation / + Fragment (B)

11. Main Ideas (passage): Remember, a main them is making children's books "more interesting" (end of first paragraph). Also, note the title.

PASSAGE II

12. Parallelism: Choices with *-ing* words are *usually* incorrect, but parallelism is one of the most common exceptions to this guideline.

13. Main Idea (transitions) / Answer the Question: This one is a little tricky. Read the question carefully. None of the choices *clearly* criticize "compulsory volunteering," but one choice at least does so subtly, by highlighting the very meaning of the word "volunteer."

14. Apostrophes & Confused Words: Is there one student or several? You

could probably guess, but note the word "their" later in the sentence.

15. Concision & Redundancies: A *proponent* (opposite of *opponent*) of something is by definition in favor of it.

16. Answer the Question: The tone of compulsory volunteering in this paragraph (and *only* in this paragraph!) is positive. Find the choice that reflects this tone.

17. Apostrophes & Confused Words / + -*ING* (C) / Subject-Verb Agreement (D): This one is primarily testing confused words. It's good to know that *affect* is usually used as a verb, and *effect* is usually used as a noun. For example: *The* effects *of the storm will* affect *the town for a long time.*

18. Vocabulary: Some of the choices are too strong for this context (see the Reading section for more on eliminating answer choices that are "too strong").

19. Run-on (A) / Punctuation (B, C): A is a clear run-on. If you went with B or C, remember: "When in doubt, keep the comma out."

20. Illogical Comparison (A, C): Make sure to compare students to students, not students to "service hours" (A) or "hours" (C). Comparisons (D): In this lesson we discussed using the word *than* for comparisons. *Mel is happier* than *Amy*. Not: *Mel is happier* compared to *Amy*.

21. Main Ideas (topic sentence): The most important part of the next sentence is the idea that students volunteer "of their own free will."

22. Main Ideas (passage): As usual with these passage questions, check the title. The last sentence of the first paragraph also states the passage's main idea.

PASSAGE III

23. Verb Tense / + -*ING* (A, B): Note that choice D is awkward: the correct verb phrase is *long believed*; the word *long* implies a past tense.

24. Concision & Redundancies

25. Punctuation: Once again, don't forget the punctuation guideline: *When in doubt, keep the comma out.*

26. Idiom: If you're not familiar with the word *correlates*, here's a hint: Since we're looking for a positive connection between "a trait" and "handedness," consider which preposition (*as*, *with*, *from*, or *on*) best reflects making a connection.

27. IG: Just read the graph carefully; this one is fairly straightforward.

28. Punctuation: Note that the "red kangaroo" is the third item in a list.

29. IG: Another fairly straightforward IG question. Just make sure to read the graph carefully.

30. Main Idea (topic sentence): The previous paragraph focused on "bipedal marsupials" (see last word of the first paragraph, third sentence of the second paragraph, and the title of the figure). This third paragraph focuses on "*quadru*pedal marsupials" (italics added).

31. Main Idea: Consider the last sentence of the first paragraph and the results of the experiment presented in the figure.

32. Pronouns (case): The word in question is referring to "tasks." The grammatical construction allows the author to avoid ending the sentence with a preposition ("in").

33. Main Idea (passage) / Answer the Question: You might try POE on this one: B: this choice does not answer the question; C: "certain neurological disorders" is off topic; D: standing "upright only some of the time" is not mentioned in the first paragraph.

PASSAGE IV

34. Transitions / Main Ideas (transitions): You hopefully sense the need for a contrast transition: yes, some companies help employees, but "*more* companies should consider" doing so (italics added). So the answer must be A or C. Which one makes a connection to "the previous sentence" (see the question)?

35. Main Idea: The passage focuses on *employees* and how companies should

assist in their continued education (note the title and read the first sentence of each paragraph). You could always come back to this one after completing the passage.

36. Apostrophes & Confused Words

37. Fragments / + -*ING* (C)

38. Combining Sentences / + -*ING* (B): Choices C and D are the shortest. Go with the one that removes one of the independent clauses (review "Independent Clauses" in the Combining Sentences lesson if necessary).

39. Fragments (A, D) / Punctuation (B): As with the "when in doubt, keep the comma out" rule, resist the urge to add punctuation when none is needed.

40. Punctuation: Make sure to go back in the sentence to determine which type of punctuation mark opens the modifying phrase ("an employee . . .").

41. Vocabulary: The correct choice creates a typical word pair. If you hear this, great. If not, guess and move on.

42. Concision & Redundancies: Remember the guideline: Get to the end of a sentence before making a choice.

43. Idiom / + -*ING* (C)

44. Organization / Main Ideas (passage): Since the passage is primarily in *support* of reimbursement programs for employees, it's unlikely the author would end the passage on a negative note ("reimbursement may not be appropriate in all cases"). Also consider that the word "Still" is a contrast transition, suggesting that what comes before the added sentence would describe reimbursements somewhat negatively (once again leading us to the end of the passage).

MATH (no calculator)

1. Basic Algebra

2. Algebraic Word

3. Linear Equations: At first glance, because the numbers in the right column ("Shipping charges") are not integers, this problem looks like it might be difficult. But we can get to the correct answer by rounding these numbers. Use the first two rows: (5, 17) and (10, 22), find the slope, and then plug one of the points and the slope into the slope-intercept equation to find the y-intercept. (This method is covered in the lesson.)

4. Linear Equations: To be safe, you might label the graph yourself: the x-axis is for diameter (in feet) and the y-axis is for height (also in feet). Then, find the heights for the two given diameters and subtract.

5. Basic Algebra or Pick Numbers (type 1): Most students should be comfortable solving this one algebraically, but if you use the Pick Trick, pick an easy number, such as $x = 2$ (caution: picking $x = 1$ will lead to multiple "correct" answers).

6. Pick Answers: You could factor the numerator (see "Difference of Squares" in the Factoring lesson), cancel the $(x - 1)$ expressions, and solve the simplified equation for x, but the easiest approach is to simply Pick Answers.

7. Graphs of Functions

8. Angles (right angle): Make sure you read the question carefully: it is *not* asking for the value of x.

9. Linear Equations: Find the slope-intercept form (which should be a snap: both the slope and the y-intercept are apparent), and then move the x term to the right hand side to match the answer choices.

10. Graphs of Functions: The point $(0, k)$ simply means that when $x = 0$, $y = k$. So plug $x = 0$ into the given equation, and solve for y.

11. More Circles (equation of)

12. Basic Trigonometry: Since the triangles are similar, we know that $m\angle B = m\angle E$. So if we can find the $\cos(B)$, which should be straightforward, we'll have the $\cos(E)$. (Trig functions are determined by the sizes of *angles*, not the sizes of triangles.)

13. Parabolas / Factoring: Factoring the quadratic will put the equation in x-intercept form.

14. Basic Algebra or Pick Answers: We recommend that you simply Pick Answers on this one. If you solve algebraically (by squaring both sides and solving for x), remember to check your answers for "extraneous solutions" (see the lesson). Since this is a #14 (out of 15), it's no surprise that one of the (apparent) solutions will be extraneous.

15. Systems of Equations: Put the two equations in slope-intercept form. Remember, when there are no solutions, the slopes of the two lines will equal (and the y-intercepts will not).

16. Algebraic Word: Plugging in the given numbers, you should get: $47{,}000 = 5c + 12 \cdot 3000$. The rest is a test of your non-calculator math skills.

17. Basic Algebra (absolute value)

18. Growth & Decay Functions: You should use the equation for interest growth (compounded once per year): $A = P(1 + r)^t$. So we have $A = 200(1 + 0.10)^2 = 200(1.10)^2 = 200a$ (given). Thus, $a = 1.10^2$. (Review long multiplication with decimals if you have trouble with the calculation.)

19. Systems of Equations: Always look for shortcuts: For this one, simply adding the equations (as given) leads directly to the expression in question!

20. Factoring (difference of squares): Write the expression in question in factored form: $(u - t)(u + t)(u - t)$ (review "difference of squares"). The value of each of these expressions is given in the question, so simply substitute and multiply.

MATH (calculator)

1. Algebraic Word or Linear Equations (applications)

2. Tables & Graphs: A "flat fee" means a constant rate for any number of text messages up to 100. This is graphed as a horizontal line (eliminate C and D). The cost increases for each additional text message greater than 100 (a line slanting up).

   Alternate approach: Pick Numbers (advanced): Just pick a few numbers of text messages, and check the answer choices. For example, if you send 50 text messages, the cost is $5 (eliminate C and D). Next, pick a number greater than 100. . . .

3. Tables & Graphs

4. Basic Algebra: Make sure you read the question carefully: it is *not* asking for the value of x.

5. Basic Functions

6. Basic Algebra (working with variables) or Pick Numbers (type 1): You may have been tempted to factor the expression $x^2 - 3x$, but a quick glance at the answer choices tells you to simply distribute the $2x$. If you have trouble with the algebra, use the Pick Trick.

7. Studies: As always with these Studies questions, selecting test subjects "at random" is important. (Of course, only surveying employees at *one* store, as in A, would not be appropriate for a study investigating "all employees" of the company.)

8. Tables & Graphs: Just check a couple of weeks. For example, looking at weeks 0 and 1, Ian deposited $100 (his total went from $100 to $200) and Jeremy deposited $50 (his total went from $300 to $350). . . .

9. Basic Functions: If you're not 100% comfortable with exponents, use your calculator. Some students think that $2^5 - 2^3 = 2^{(5-3)} = 2^2$. This is not correct!

10. Studies: Review "margin of error" and "confidence interval" in the Studies lesson (you may have skipped these topics if you're not following the 40-hour program).

11. Means, Medians, & Modes / Statistics (standard deviation): After calculating the means and eliminating two choices, you have to consider standard deviation, which is a measure of the "spread" of the data. If the values of one list *deviate* further (from the mean) than the values of the other list, then the standard deviations will be different (the first list will have a greater standard deviation).

12. Percent (increase/decrease): The "multiplier" for "40% off" is 0.60. Since

we're given the final (discounted) price, the equation is $0.60x = 18$. If you chose B, then you misread the problem ($18 is *not* the original price). Another possible error is increasing $18 by 40% (18·1.40), which violates the "never combine percent changes" rule (although this answer choice is luckily not an option).

13. Tables & Graphs

14. Tables & Graphs / Ratios

15. Solids & Volume: The formula for the volume of a right circular cone is found on the reference page of each math section. Make sure you know what's found on this page (and, importantly, what is *not* found there).

16. Percent (increase/decrease): Let's first review "multipliers": a 20% increase means multiply by 1.20 (100% + 20%), and a 10% decrease means multiply by 0.90 (100% – 10%). Now, to the problem. . . . City X's population in 2010 was 120,000, and it increased by 20%, so in 2015, City X's population was 120,000·1.20 = 144,000. Now, set up an equation for the population (y) of City Y in 2010 (we know the final population (144,000) and the multiplier (0.90)): $144,000 = 0.90y$. . . .

17. Basic Algebra: First, multiple/divide to get r^3 alone. We know from the Basic Algebra lesson that to solve for a *squared* variable we take the *square root* of each side of an equation. Similarly, to solve for a *cubed* variable (such as r^3), we take the *cube root* ($\sqrt[3]{}$, or raise to the power of 1/3) of each side.

18. Probability: First identify the *subgroup*, which will be the denominator ("given that the tablet user did not answer 'Never'"), and then identify the *target group*, which will be the numerator ("a tablet user answered 'Always'").

19. Parabolas: The given equation is in vertex form: $y = a(x – h)^2 + k$. The answer should be apparent. If you were stuck on this one, and if you have a graphing calculator, you could also pick a number for a, graph the equation, and check the answer choices. But, preferably, you should be comfortable with the equations given in the lesson.

20. Statistics (terminology)

21. Mixtures: The equation is conveniently given. Just plug in $y = 100$ and solve for x.

22. Growth & Decay Functions: If necessary, jot down a few numbers to see that the function is *not* linear: 30, 60, 120 . . . (a linear function would add 30 each time: 30, 60, 90 . . .).

23. Linear Equations: First, calculate the slope in terms of a (you can use the points $(a, 0)$ and $(3a, -a)$). Next, find the y-intercept by solving for b in the slope-intercept equation (using the slope from the first step, and one of the given points). Finally, rewrite the equation to mirror the answer choices.

You could also Pick Numbers (type 1) for a, which would make the math above easier.

24. Linear Equations: Just pick a couple of points where the line of best fit crosses the intersections of grid lines (make sure to focus on the *line*, not the points of the scatter plot). Remember, anytime you know two points on a line, you can calculate its equation.

25. Systems of Equations (elimination): The "elimination" method is probably faster than "substitution." Hint: Multiply the second equation by 3, and add the equations to eliminate the y terms.

26. Growth & Decay Functions: This is a straightforward application of these exponential equations. Make sure you have them memorized and understand how to use them.

27. Basic Algebra

28. Parabolas: Review the "x-intercept form" of a parabola.

29. Linear Equations (applications): If you missed this one, review the lesson carefully. We covered how to interpret the slope of a linear equation in detail.

30. Triangles (special right): Create a right triangle by drawing a vertical line down from point B. Let's label point E as the point of intersection on line AD. Since the length of the hypotenuse of this right triangle (AB) is twice that of the short leg (BE), the triangle must be a 30-60-90 one.

If you didn't see this, here's another approach. We know that the figure is drawn to scale (since the question does not say otherwise). Look at the angles formed around point B (after the vertical line is drawn): $\angle EBC$ is clearly a right angle and $\angle ABE$ appears greater than 45°. Only one answer choice works.

3600 seconds: 1 hour × 60 minutes × 60 seconds): $\dfrac{\text{miles}}{\text{seconds}} \dfrac{200}{3600} = \dfrac{0.5}{x}$

31. Algebraic Word: First, find the cost of the 5 apples. Subtract this from Lynne's total ($8). Then divide the remaining money by the cost per orange. Don't forget to round *down*, since Lynne is looking to buy whole oranges.

32. Angles (of a triangle)

33. Means, Medians & Modes

34. Basic Algebra: First, solve for m in terms of a (using the given point (a, 17)). You should now have the equation $y = (17/a)x$. Finally, plug in $x = 2a$ and solve for y (luckily, the a variables cancel).

35. Working with Polynomials (comparing coefficients): Make sure to rewrite the left hand side (by distributing the a) so that you have a polynomial with decreasing powers of x (i.e. $Ax + B$). Then, "compare coefficients" on each side.

36. Parabolas: The trick to this one is recognizing that the line $y = c$ (a horizontal line) must intersect the parabola at its *vertex*. All other lines will either intersect the parabola at two points (if below the vertex) or zero points (if above the vertex). A quick sketch should make this clear:

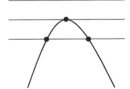

So, find the y-coordinate of the vertex (review the "quadratic form" in the lesson).

37. Proportions: Convert 200 miles to feet and 1 hour to seconds.

38. Proportions (rates): Here's the proportion (we converted 1 hour to

Made in the USA
Las Vegas, NV
09 February 2021